THE CULLISTER COLLECTION

In memory of

MARY MOUAT

Elizabeth Mouat
Malcolm P. & Gertrude McP. Mouat
Malcolm M. Mouat, Lucia Mouat

Digging into the Past

DIGGING INTO THE PAST

An Autobiography by Edwin H. Colbert

DEMBNER BOOKS • New York

DEMBNER BOOKS
Published by Red Dembner Enterprises Corp.,
80 Eighth Avenue, New York, N.Y. 10011
Distributed by W. W. Norton & Company, Inc.,
500 Fifth Avenue, New York, N.Y. 10110

Library of Congress Cataloging-in-Publication Data

Colbert, Edwin Harris, 1905–
    Digging into the past : an autobiography / Edwin H. Colbert.
      p.   cm.
    Includes index.
    ISBN 0-942637-08-9 : $25.00
    1. Colbert, Edwin Harris, 1905–   . 2. Paleontologists—
United States—Biography. I. Title.
QE707.C57A3 1989
560.9—dc 19   88-6883
[B]   CIP

Design by Antler & Baldwin, Inc.

To Margaret and our family

Contents

1

The House

*T*here is a house up in the northwest corner of Missouri, where the rolling hills of the till prairie and the loess bluffs of the Missouri Valley border the high plains to the west, a house like many others of that region yet a house that is very special to me. For it is the house in which I grew up, and in which perhaps the ghosts of many memories remain. It is a square, neat-looking house of two stories, today painted a very deep blue with white trim, with black shutters framing the windows, and with a four-sided pitched red roof. It is placed far back from the street with a deep lawn to serve as its frontispiece, while back behind there is an even deeper expanse of grass and gardens.

A half century and more ago it was a white house and the roof was covered with natural wood shingles, and in the large front lawn there were seven graceful elm trees. Alas! The elms are gone, the victims years ago of Dutch elm disease. It is the house of decades past, with its shady lawn and its considerable back gardens and fruit trees, that time and time again comes to my mind in an elm-bordered vista of years long ago.

This was the house built by my father, not so long after the turn of the century and not so long after the time of my coming into the world. It was the only house I knew until the day when, almost at my majority, I left its familiar and comfortable haven to make my way in a world suddenly become large and occasionally even terrifying.

1

But let us go back to the beginning. I was born in the little town of Clarinda, Iowa, on September 28, 1905, in another house that my father had built. In those distant days it was not felt necessary except in an emergency to go to a hospital for the process of birthing. Things were simpler and more easygoing and certainly much less expensive than they are today. So I was born in a house, not a hospital, and the doctor was paid twenty-five dollars to officiate at the affair, and soon after my birth my eldest brother took one look at me and walked out of the room in disgust. Herschel, his name was, and he was within a few weeks of being fourteen years old when I was born. I had another brother, Philip, nine years my senior.

That was the family—father and mother and three boys, the boys spaced out over a span of fourteen years. It was a closely knit family, in spite of the distance in years between the three sons, and I should add in spite of Herschel's initial disapproval of his new sibling. He soon became very fond of me, as in time I became devoted to him, and in many ways he became a surrogate father to me, giving me gifts and much personal attention. (My father was forty-four years older than I, so that by the time I grew into a little independent being he was a middle-aged person—very loving, but just a bit distant, too.) Phil was always good to me, but since the chronological distance between us was less than that between the oldest and youngest, he did not quite have what might be called the avuncular interest in me that was evinced by Herschel. Of course my mother was always a good companion.

My father had been the county superintendent of schools in Page County, Iowa, for several years before I was born. Then, in 1905, there was established by the state of Missouri a normal school, as it was then called—a teacher-training institute—in Maryville, across the state line and about thirty miles south of Clarinda. My father was appointed as a professor of mathematics in the new institution, and so the family made the short move south in the summer of 1906.

The day of the move was a stressful and discouraging one for my mother. It was midsummer, hot and humid as only it can be hot and humid in the Missouri Valley, and when she arrived with me, a puling babe in arms, at what passed for the Wabash station in Maryville, she had to wait for an inordinate amount of time before there was transportation into town. The wait was almost insufferable, because what passed for the station was a boxcar by the side of the tracks; perhaps the station had not as yet been completed or perhaps some reconstruction was under way.

But such trials come to an end, and in the course of time the family was established in a house on Third Street, where we lived for two or three years, until the new house on East Seventh Street was ready to be occupied. So here we are at the house where this story has its beginning, and where for me my life comes into focus. This home was to be the center of my private universe for a dozen and a half years, and a very nice place it was.

As has been said, it was a square house set in a deep lot. As might further be said, this house had a flat-roofed porch across its front or south side, which continued as an open porch around a part of the east side of the house. That porch was a pleasant place during the summertime and during the warmer months before and after the summer; ivy had been trained up along each pillar, along the railing, and along the top of the porch between the pillars, to form a cool, green screen. There we would spend many spare hours if the weather wasn't too hot, and in the late afternoons and evenings we would move around to the side porch. There were various porch chairs, some of them rockers, and set across the west end of the porch was a swing of the type that is now completely extinct. This swing was a steel spring with a canvas-covered mattress over it, with canvas ends and a canvas side or back, with a series of short ropes attached at intervals to each end and converging up to a large ring. Chains from the porch ceiling came down to the ring at each end of the swing. It was a comfortable swing to sit on or to sleep in, and for several years when I was older, I spent my summer nights in it. I rigged a bamboo pole longitudinally between the centers of each end of the swing, thus making a sort of a ridgepole about thirty inches above the mattress, and over that I draped a mosquito net, pushing it tight against the canvas ends of the swing and tucking it in along the sides. In this airy tent I was much cooler than the folks in the house, and in truth I felt almost as if I were camping out. The nights were sometimes exciting, especially during those summers when three dogs, Mike, Buster, and Blackie, slept with me on the porch. Buster, a collie, and Blackie, obviously a black dog, would sleep on the floor behind the swing, and Mike, a cairn terrier, would make himself comfortable squarely beneath my bed. Several times each night they would leap up with a great hurrah to protect the house from all sorts of dire dangers, the big dogs tearing around the ends of the swing and setting it in violent motion back and forth, Mike jumping up and banging the bottom of the bed. It usually half woke me up. But I was immediately back asleep, and soon the dogs would return, to continue their vigilant slumbers.

So the summer nights would pass on that open porch, for one boy and three dogs. Then with the coming of daylight it was time for me to slip into a bathrobe, cross the porch, and go into the house, where my parents more likely than not had spent a stifling night, so typical of the midsummer nights in the Missouri Valley.

Inside, I entered the long living room, set transversely across the front part of the house, with at one end a raised landing immediately opposite the front door, a landing from which the stairs ascended to a small intermediate landing, and then by way of a right-angle turn to the second floor. Behind the living room was the usual dining room and kitchen. Upstairs were four rooms, three bedrooms and a study. From the study a stair led up to the large attic, and from the kitchen a stair led down to the basement. The basement was divided into three rooms that repeated the pattern of the rooms on the first floor. The front basement room was a dark storage cellar for potatoes and apples and wood (and during several years was a rifle range), and the other two rooms were furnace room and laundry respectively.

Does this give any sort of a picture of the house? Perhaps, and if the impression of this house were to be summarized by a word, that word would be *plain*. Most of the houses of that town in those days were plain. Certainly they didn't appear to have had much benefit of an architect's advice, although I suppose someone must have drawn up plans for them, at least as working guides for the carpenters. And though they may have been plain, those turn-of-the-century houses were no worse esthetically, and perhaps on the whole somewhat better, than the modified boxes that repeat themselves block after dreary block and mile after mile in our modern suburbias.

The point in those days was to have a house with a downstairs and an upstairs, and below the former a basement and above the latter an attic. There was always a front porch, and almost always a back porch. In the basement was a large bin for furnace coal, in the attic was ample space for the storage of worn-out domestic articles and bric-a-brac, and on the back porch was an icebox, visited each day by an iceman who brought in a square chunk of ice from his horse-drawn wagon and deposited it with a loud crash in the compartment in the top of the box.

In our town most of the houses had metal combings (if that is the right word) along the ridge of the roof. These were favorite perches for red-headed woodpeckers; they used the metal ridges for their sounding drums. A woodpecker would fly to the top of the house next door with a flash of jet-black and snow-white wings, and taking a stance on the peak of the roof would with his strong beak drum out a loud tattoo on the metal ridge comb. Then he would stop, look around and let out a few raucous notes, and follow this with another round of drumming. The performance would go on for many minutes before he would fly away in display of black and white and red.

Almost all of the houses had lightning rods on the roofs; ours did not, and I felt left out. Evidently some persuasive salesman had long ago convinced the townspeople that a house was not properly protected without its quota of lightning rods—five-foot-long pointed rods, projecting up at a half-dozen or more places on the roof. Each rod had a heavy copper cable running from it down the roof, and on down the side of the house to the ground. Each rod was decorated with a colored glass ball, skewered by the rod halfway along its length. Perhaps our house escaped Jovian thunderbolts by reason of the lightning-rod-equipped houses around us; perhaps the lightning rods were more decorative than efficacious. This is a problem I've often wondered about in the long span of years that separates me from those days of my midwestern boyhood.

Behind our very ample backyard was a big field, and on the far edge of the field was the line of the Wabash Railroad. So we could look out and watch the trains which were just pleasantly distant. It is said that when the family first moved into the house, and I was about four years old, they sometimes would haul me out of bed to watch the express train go through from Omaha on its way to St. Louis. It was a wonderful sight then, and it would be a wonderful sight even today, if it could be recreated. Down the grade would come the train, with the headlight piercing the black night, and with the red glow from the open door of the boiler (the fireman was always stoking up at that stage of the run) casting its light up on the smoke streaming back overhead from the stack. Then there was a dark part of the train—the baggage and mail cars. Then there were rows of bright windows, which were the chair cars, and at the back of the train irregularly spaced squares of light in the Pullman cars, the lights of travelers who had not as yet gone to sleep.

Away went the train out of sight, and we could hear the long moaning whistle for the grade crossing east of our house. It was a magic sound. The old steam whistle had a melodious note, and in the middle of the night one would wake up just a little bit, to hear through a delicious drowsiness the call of the train whistle across the dark distance. Our modern world is poorer for the disappearance of this haunting sound.

It was a haven, that house on Seventh Street, with its spacious front yard and the more than ample grounds in the back with garden plots and fruit trees and the barn, back of which was our big potato and corn patch. Home is traditionally a haven for all small children; I think our home was especially dear to me because it was the only home I knew until I reached my majority. I did not have the divided loyalties that must be the lot of children whose families move frequently.

It was a haven where on an early morning in summertime, while still in bed and only half awake, I would hear the clear call of a cardinal in the parklike yards that stretched in front of ours and the several adjacent houses to the east of us. Or perhaps it might be the resident wren that woke me up, or a woodpecker, drumming. And never can I forget the plaintive three-toned note of the pewee, repeated over and over again through the quiet somnolence of a hot afternoon.

There were the winter sounds, too, sounds that came from within a house locked against the cold and the chill winds whistling around its corners. In the early morning came the clanking and thumping and scraping as my father shook down the furnace grate and shoveled fresh coal on the fire. And after that there was more clunking as he shook down the ashes in the kitchen stove and started a new fire there.

We had a Majestic range in the kitchen, a big black stove with nickel trim, with round stove lids on top, with a big oven down below, and with small warming ovens on each side of the stovepipe as it ascended to its egress through the back wall of the kitchen. Once the fire was going the stove quickly made of the kitchen a very cozy place, and no spot was cozier than the space between the back of the stove and wall. Here was the favorite resting place for any dog or cat that might be sharing the house with the family. At one stage in my early life we enjoyed the simultaneous company of a dog and a cat: Mike, the cairn terrier, and Timothy, a big Maltese. Theirs was a constant contest for the choice spot behind the stove. If Mike was there first, he would rumble in very positive dog tones, should Timothy attempt to enter his private haven. And if Timothy had preempted the spot, he would flatten his ears back and hiss at Mike when Mike stuck his nose into the reserved space, letting the dog know that an inch farther would bring a swipe from a hostile paw armed with very sharp claws. It was always a marvel to me how these animals, especially Mike, could cook and roast behind the stove, and then dash out with complete aplomb into the frigid snow.

But to get back to early morning in the kitchen—my father would put on a little pan of milk to warm for the cat, and almost invariably he would stand dreaming in front of the stove and allow the milk to get too hot. Then he would put it down and Timothy would go through a lengthy ritual of trying to sip the hot milk and jerking his head back from the pan. Eventually, of course, the milk would get sufficiently cool so that Timothy could enjoy his breakfast.

It must not be thought that just because he let Timothy's morning milk get too hot my father was the dreamy type. Being a mathematician he was truly a very precise and neat man, and ours was a well-ordered household. Things were in their proper places. So it was that our house, which he designed, had certain innovative aspects—in some instances rather crude forerunners of devices that were to become established in future years. For example, we had a comparatively compact and organized kitchen, in days when kitchens frequently were rather sprawling affairs.

Even though there were some innovations in our house, we did not have the plethora of electric motors and other labor-saving devices that are part of modern living. Therefore we had occasional household help, usually furnished by students from the normal school, and for some years we had a young woman one day a week, usually a Saturday I think, to help with the housecleaning.

Audrey Van Buren was certainly one of the more memorable of our helpers. She was a big strapping girl right off the farm and thus was well equipped for doing some of the heavier work that was difficult for my mother. Audrey was an original character; she would set to and work away like a whirlwind, and then during her rest periods she would go into the living room, sit down at the piano, and accompany herself as she sang "Oh, happy day, when Jesus washed my sins away." There was nothing reticent about her singing, which usually was on key, or her playing, which was generally reasonably accurate. It did resound through the house; whether it ascended to heaven I don't know, and I don't think it mattered much. I suppose Audrey had about as many sins as a June bug.

She was a good-natured and hearty soul. One time she took it on herself to teach my mother how to stand on her head. Audrey began with a demonstration, which ended with her falling over with a house-rattling thump that jarred every joint in her body and made the floor vibrate. The demonstration was enough for my mother; anyway she had passed the age for standing on her head.

Following Audrey was her cousin, Amy Van Buren. Amy was a jolly little person, rather plump, and certainly not built along the heroic lines that characterized Audrey. When not attending the normal school she lived on a farm a dozen miles or so from town, and once she invited us out to the farm for a Sunday dinner. It was quite an expedition. We were just into the First World War and my brother Herschel was home on furlough, after having been commissioned a captain in the army. Phil was home that summer, working at a local bank. He had access to the bank car which was used by officers of the institution to visit farms, to appraise them for loans. So on that Sunday he was able to borrow the idle car and drive us out to Amy's farm. The car was a Model T Ford and the five of us made a full load. Consequently we had a labored trip, the car grinding up the steep dirt hills in low, and chugging down the counterpart hills in a careful high. We got there, and had a hearty fried-chicken dinner and a drowsy afternoon, resting and casting surfeited glances at the livestock. Then back home.

My parents wanted to be as independent as possible, and so even with part-time help they were quick to acquire labor-saving appliances. It was our fate that my father usually bought the first and most primitive piece of machinery to come on the market, and then we held on to it for years, long after improved models had been designed. We made things last. So it was that we had an old Thor washing machine with a rotating wooden drum that made a marvelous lot of noise. And I suppose we had one of the original vacuum cleaners for the floors.

Yet with these early ventures into powered appliances our house would today be regarded as very much underpowered. The furnace was hand-fired, the kitchen stove burned coal, there were no exhaust fans in the house, there was no gas, naturally no air-conditioning to alleviate the awful, humid summer days and nights of the Missouri Valley, no dishwasher, and except for the washing machine and the vacuum cleaner, no calls on the electrical power supply except for lighting the carbon-filament bulbs that were sparsely distributed throughout the house.

Since I was at the tail end of a widely spaced family, my first remembrances of my father bring to mind a man in his early middle age, short, compact, indeed rather chubby, with a full head of graying hair, a clipped moustache beneath a rather ample nose, and with blue eyes. In those days of my early childhood he wore pince-nez spectacles of a kind that I have not seen for many years, for the lenses were crescent-shaped, something like segments from an orange, thus enabling him to look out over their tops with unobstructed far-sighted vision.

One of the very characteristic traits of my father was his neat grooming: his clothes were always clean and fresh-looking, his collars were always white (in those days men wore collars separate from their shirts), and his shoes were shiny and free from clinging dirt. His dress was not formal but it was scrupulously well arranged. I recall that in the unbearably hot and humid days of summer he generally wore light, mohair suits—are suits of this kind available today? He never went out in his shirtsleeves, although of course his dress at home was informal enough. In short, he was a product of his age, an age more formal by far than the unbuttoned and sometimes sloppy times in which we now live.

The name *Colbert* is of French origin and although I have not pursued the matter in depth I have a suspicion that our ancestors were Huguenots who had fled to Scotland, perhaps in the seventeenth century. For one thing, I remember my father making some vague remarks about our forebears coming from Scotland; for another, the family was Presbyterian as far back as it can be traced. That is not very far; the earliest Colbert in our family records was one John, who died in New York City in 1795.

He had a son named John William Colbert, who among other things was a member of an artillery company in the city of New York. I suppose such a company was organized for the defense of the city—the War of 1812 was just around the corner, and New York was fully expecting to be besieged by British warships. At any rate there is a document extant, signed by Captain John W. Forbes, Major Charles Snowden, and Brigadier General James Morton, confirming the membership of John William in the company. On October 23, 1806, he was married to Eleanora Jacoby, and in just twenty-three years they had managed to bring twelve children into the world. Of whom David Thorp Colbert, born in 1829, was my paternal grandfather.

In their early New York years John and Eleanora were obviously fairly prosperous folks; I have a sword-cane with an ivory handle that he carried on the streets of New York, which evidently were dangerous, although probably not as terrifying as is the case today. On the blade of the sword is engraved "Newyork"—all one word. And I have also a miniature of Eleanora, painted on ivory and depicting a very elegant lady, with blue eyes, a most fashionable coiffure displaying on each side a demure curl in front of the ear, golden earrings, and a deep-red, off-the-shoulder, narrow-waisted velvet dress. That must have been before the twelve children came along.

Before the fourth child was born, in 1812, the family had moved to Cincinnati, and before the seventh child was born they had settled in Lebanon, Ohio. Perhaps the family fortune, such as it was, had gone downhill by the time my grandfather was born; I often heard my father tell how his father had as a child been a "bound boy," that is, had been contracted by his parents to someone outside the family, to be raised as a sort of apprentice. But such lowly beginnings were no deterrent to my grandfather; he became a very prosperous farmer living outside of Lebanon, and by the time my father was entering his teens the family moved into town, to occupy a large brick house. (A few years ago I was in that part of Ohio and I visited Lebanon and located the house; it is indeed a handsome structure.)

My father, George Harris Colbert, born in 1861, was the last of five children. He grew up on the farm and in Lebanon, and enjoyed a pleasant, comfortable childhood. Perhaps for this reason, as well as because he was the youngest in the family, he was a mild, placid type. Or perhaps he was born that way. Certainly he was born into an orderly household, seemingly free from crises and strife.

One of his early teenage activities was the establishment of a summer ice-cream "parlor" in the ample side yard of their Lebanon home. Actually it was a sort of outdoor refreshment garden, and for several summers it evidently proved to be very popular among the young folks of Lebanon. Well might be the case, because every morning my father made fresh ice cream out of real cream, ready to be served up during the afternoons and evenings. Those were the days before synthetics and substitutes.

They say that mathematics and music go together, and my father was a musician of sorts. In his younger years he had been quite a chorister and had sung tenor in various musical groups. In later years he still had a nice tenor voice, and in church he would always sing the tenor lines, rather than going along on the main melody with the rest of the congregation. What I particularly remember was his flute, an old-fashioned black wooden flute with all sorts of nickel keys arranged along its length in addition to the regular holes. He would frequently get the flute out in the evening for a bit of practicing. The memory of one such evening is still with me. I was quite small, and I sat quietly and listened to his playing, and the pure notes of the flute brought tears to my eyes, young and musically inexperienced though I was.

A rather unexpected aspect of my father's early manhood that he would recount to me now and then was his experience as a baseball player. Of course he was an amateur, or at best a sort of semipro, but he had functioned as a shortstop way back in the days before players wore gloves. As a result he had a permanently crooked finger on one hand, the result of a hot drive caroming off the end of that digit. I could hardly imagine such activities on the part of what seemed to me a sedentary person.

As for my mother, she was anything but sedentary. Hers was a mercurial temperament, so that she often felt somewhat out of place, living the life of a housewife in a small town. She would have loved to have been an actress (and indeed she did perform in amateur dramatics), or an author, or a world traveler. My father's idea of a summer vacation was to sit reading in a rocking chair at home, or something else equally restful; my mother's idea would be to go to the ends of the earth. But she never got the chance. Trips in those provincial days generally were restricted to journeys of a few hundred miles—to Colorado or to Chicago or as far east as Ohio.

My mother came by her lively nature honestly, she being the daughter of Dr. Valentine Valencia Adamson, a somewhat unconventional individual with an unconventional name. He was one of eleven children born to Thomas Adamson and Elizabeth Stockton, Elizabeth being descended from the Stocktons and Nicholsons, who were Quakers, George Nicholson coming from England to Pennsylvania in the sixteen-seventies. A later George Nicholson, the third of that name, was disowned by the Friends for "disorders"—whatever they may have been. Alas, that George was killed during the Revolution. He had a blacksmith shop at Bordentown, New Jersey, and there he was assisting to handcuff a British soldier. As recorded: "George had fastened an iron band on the wrist and as he stooped to pick up the other the soldier struck him on the head with his bound wrist and broke his skull." The soldier took to the woods.

Grandfather Adamson grew up on the western border when that border was the Missouri River. He knew Kansas City when it was merely Westport Landing, and he watched the forty-niners leave St. Joseph, or Roubidoux Landing, as they embarked on their long trek along the Oregon Trail. Eventually Grandfather attended medical school, in the days when a medical education was a rough-and-ready experience. More than once he went graverobbing; that was an illegal but commonly practiced method for medical students to obtain bodies needed in the anatomical laboratories. He told me once about how the relatives of a girl who had died, and whose body was now in the medical school, besieged the students with sticks and stones, while the students counterattacked with odd pieces of anatomy hurled out of the windows of the building. A grisly story indeed.

In 1859, after he had become a doctor, he decided to join the gold rush to Colorado. With three or four companions he set out on his great adventure—to garner riches in the Rocky Mountains. They crossed the plains, encountering buffalo and Indians, and they reached Denver when the settlement consisted, as Grandfather put it, of "a blacksmith shop, a saloon, and a lot of tents." He didn't encounter any gold, so shortly he joined a cavalry troop that was returning eastwardly across the plains. The commander thought it would be nice to have a medical man along.

One day they saw a lone prairie schooner ahead of them, also going toward the east. It was unusual for a wagon to be crossing the plains alone; seemingly this represented some people who also were disillusioned with the riches of Colorado. Suddenly from behind some scattered buttes a band of horse Indians appeared and started to circle the wagon, firing from their galloping ponies at the trapped travelers. And from the wagon there came an intermittent fire from a single rifle.

Of course the cavalry men applied spurs to horses and rode pell-mell to the rescue, just as we have seen them do it in the motion pictures. The Indians broke off their attack and fled across the plain as the cavalry troop rode up to the besieged wagon. When the soldiers arrived they found a man and his wife, she with an arrow through her body, he with a knuckle that had been split by a stray bullet. Grandfather went to work. He cut the feathers off the end of the arrow which was protruding from one side of the wife's body, and pulled the arrow on through from the other side. After treating her he treated the husband's injured hand.

The couple then joined the cavalry detachment and traveled with them. And before long the wife was up and around, helping with the cooking, for the arrow luckily had not touched any truly vital areas, while the man was still nursing a very sore hand. What a span of time and change is represented by this story, told to me in person by one of the participants of the event; here I am in the ninth decade of the twentieth century, having heard at first hand this account of something that took place in the sixth decade of the preceding century!

After his Colorado venture Grandfather settled in the little town of Holton, Kansas, to become a country doctor. Then the Civil War engulfed the nation, and in due course Grandfather was in the Union army, serving as an assistant surgeon in the western theater of the conflict. I heard more grisly stories from him about his experiences—patching up wounded men and dodging bullets in-between times. He survived the war unharmed, and went back to Holton, there to spend the rest of his life. It was there, in an old brick Victorian house, that I delighted to sit and visit with him and to hear his tales of war and of frontier life. He was then a very elderly man, well up in his eighties and for many years married to his second wife, whom I called Grandma although of course she had no blood relationship to me. My own grandmother, Mary Myers, was married to my Grandfather Adamson in 1862; she died of what was then called the bloody flux (almost certainly amoebic dysentery) in 1874, when my mother, also named Mary, was five years old.

My mother and her younger brother, Samuel, were taken over by their Myers grandparents, to live in Indiana for several years until Grandfather Adamson brought his second wife to the Holton house. In Indiana my mother shared a house not only with her grandparents but also with some lively aunts, the younger sisters of her mother. Some cousins lived nearby.

One of those aunts was Kate Myers, another was her younger sister, Jessie Frémont Myers, who married Will Croan, to be mentioned on a later page. Kate was at the time receiving the ardent attention of James Whitcomb Riley, then a young man, subsequently destined to become one of America's minor literary figures, who in the words of Van Wyck Brooks "continued, in point of fact, the line of the popular New England poets" during the later years of the nineteenth century. So for several years, when my mother was a very little girl, Riley more or less haunted the Myers domicile.

One of my mother's young cousins persuaded her that it would be a grand idea if she would pull the chair out from under Mr. Riley just as he was sitting down, and she, being the little girl that she was, concurred in this plan of action. But she thought it might be a good idea to practice the maneuver first, and she chose her dear old grandmother as the guinea pig. So one day just as Grandmother Myers was lowering herself into her chair at the dinner table, my mother yanked it away, and the lady of the house came down on the floor with a resounding crash. That was the end of the conspiracy; Mr. Riley never realized that an awful fate had almost befallen him.

Another time my mother and one of her cousins were having a dispute concerning the ownership of a doll, which culminated in one of them pulling on the doll's head, the other on the legs, with the inevitable result that the doll came apart. My mother was heartbroken, and was crying bitterly when Mr. Riley came along for one of his visits. He consoled her, and later wrote a poem, in its day very popular, about a little girl and her broken doll.

Footnote. Riley never married Aunt Kate—rather she never married him, because she thought he was a bit too fond of alcoholic beverages. She did remain very much in his thoughts for the rest of his life.

After my Grandfather Adamson returned to Holton with his second wife, my mother and her little brother were sent back from Indiana by their grandparents, to live in Kansas. It was there that my mother grew into a teenager, and a very lively one, too. As an example of one of her adolescent escapades, there might be mentioned the day that she and another girl broke into the chemistry room at the high school in their little town and decided to mix together every chemical they could find on the shelves. It was a successful experiment in that they weren't blown sky high, an unsuccessful venture in that it did not produce flames and explosions as I suppose they had hoped would be the case. Or the time that she and some of her girl friends, belonging to a group self-christened "the wicked nine," decided to pretend they would hang one of their number from a railroad trestle outside of town. They fastened a stout rope around the unfortunate girl's neck (incidentally she was a willing participant in this frontier drama), fastened the other end to the beams of the bridge, and leaving sufficient rope so that there would be slack when the girl jumped, commanded her to leap to the ground three or four feet down from the place where she stood. She did—but there was *not* enough slack in the rope and the poor young lady almost came to an unexpected end. Fortunately the horrified members of the wicked nine rescued her before any real damage was done.

As for later lively times, there might be mentioned the day that my parents, then engaged, went with a group of young folks on a picnic out in the middle-western countryside. The young men thought it would be a great idea to raid a neighboring farm and steal some watermelons. My father, who could not brook such unlawful behavior, stayed behind and built a campfire. Before long the fellows returned with some choice watermelons and then, soon after, an irate farmer appeared with blood in his eye. What did my mother do but tell the indignant landowner that my father had stolen the melons, much to the astonishment of her betrothed and the merriment of the assembled crowd. The engagement survived.

Thus I remember her, asking the proprietor of a side show at a street fair to let her hold a very large snake he was displaying; taking me, as a little boy, on a terrifying high ride on a Ferris wheel—perhaps at this same street fair; chasing Mr. Gillam, our neighbor and one of the supposedly dignified town bankers, across our lawn at a neighborhood party and being chased in turn, with the result that Mr. Gillam dropped a big pinching beetle down her neck. Sometimes I wondered what to think of my mother.

Grandfather lived on into the late twenties of this century, and then one day he collapsed on the street in Holton. He was immediately taken to his home and carefully placed on a couch in the living room. A physician was called, while relatives and friends gathered around. It was evident that Grandfather had reached the end of his long road, and the people in the room leaned forward to hear the last words of this respected man—then only a few years from his hundredth anniversary. The attending doctor got a thermometer from his bag, and remarked that perhaps he had better wash it. At which moment Grandfather regained consciousness and faintly uttered his final historic statement.

"Yes," he said, "especially if you have just had it up someone's rectum."

My two brothers were young men with some definite ideas as to what should be done with the property when we moved into the new house on Seventh Street. Herschel was going through an esthetic phase, and he was determined that there was to be a very ornamental and attractive goldfish pool in the backyard. He was sure that a large hole, once excavated and filled with water, would soon establish a natural balance, with clear limpid water providing a suitable environment for trailing aquatic plants and gracefully swimming fish. For some reason concrete didn't come into his calculations, perhaps because it would have been rather expensive. So without a by-your-leave he dug the hole and ran the hose out to it. Alas, it was a mudhole and no more. My father was certainly a tolerant man, because years later, during the First World War, I excavated a dugout and a trench system where the incipient fish pond had been.

Herschel, or perhaps it was Phil, had ideas of a tennis court in the front yard, but that was firmly vetoed. Instead the deep yard became a lawn, and the seven elms, set out when we moved into the place, had, by the time I was a teenager, attained the stature of moderately large, graceful trees.

As things turned out there were to be no fish ponds and tennis courts on our property, but the front lawn with its graceful elm trees provided us with pleasant shade and a certain distance from the traffic on the sidewalk and street, although goodness knows there was little enough of public comings and goings in our quiet neighborhood.

When I had grown up to high school status, or even a little before, I became very much interested in birds, as will be told later, and I conceived the idea of a bird bath in our front yard. It was not to be a shallow dish on a pedestal—rather I thought of it as a sort of rocky retreat. With my father's guidance I cast a large, shallow basin in concrete, intended to be set into the top of a pile of rocks. Which was all very fine, except that in our part of the Midwest, rocks were almost as scarce as hen's teeth—this being a region of deep black soil. Any rocks that might be around were glacial erratics, sandstone and quartzite boulders randomly distributed around the country-side. Consequently my parents and I spent several months driving around in our old Dodge, scanning the roadside for rocks, and by dint of much driving and looking we eventually got together enough rocks to make a proper foundation for the bird bath. It occupied a place on the side of the yard next to a hedge of japonica that marked the boundary between our lot and our neighbors to the west—an ideal place for the birds. Indeed, they were so avid to bathe that several times a day some member of the family would have to go out with a pailful of water to replenish the supply. The bird bath was quite a feature of our yard and provided much opportunity for bird-watching.

The amount of land behind our house exceeded considerably the size of the front yard, and here there was a small back lawn, behind which were various garden plots, fruit trees, a grape arbor, a strawberry patch, other berry bushes, and at the very back the potato and corn patches. (These were too small to be called fields, but quite adequate to supply the family needs for corn in the summer and potatoes all through the winter.) As I have mentioned, in the front room of our cellar, which was partitioned off from the rest of the basement by a brick wall and therefore cool, there were potato and apple bins for the winter storage of these commodities.

That backyard was another grand place for small children to play in.

My father was something less than prophetic of times to come when he built the place, and so behind the house, a hundred feet or more back, he built a barn. For years this barn housed a buggy, but there was never a horse to pull it. Inevitably the buggy room, or whatever one calls such a place, became a garage, but that was quite a number of years later. There was a stall room occupying the rest of the barn, and above a mow for hay, a mow which I think never held any hay. It was our gymnasium, and it had a trapeze and rings suspended from its gambrel roof. Also it was a basketball court, albeit a very restricted one. Eventually the stall room was converted into a carpenter shop.

It should be said that when the family first moved into the place a neat but temperamental Jersey cow occupied the stall in the barn, and also a little fenced-in lot, behind the barn. Her residence was brief. She proved to be so fractious that it was a daily adventure to get in there and milk her. So she was sold to Mr. Trueblood, a retired farmer who lived just a couple of blocks east of us, almost on the edge of the town. Soon after she had left our place my father met Mr. Trueblood and asked about her. "Oh," he said, "she is a grand little cow; she follows me all over the lot." And that same day my mother met Mrs. Trueblood and asked about the cow. "She's a terrible cow," said Mrs. Trueblood, "why she chases my husband all around the lot."

Our house and our family were part of a friendly neighborhood. To our left were several other houses, all set back from the street, so that the combined front yards, with many elms and oaks, made a sizable park, a nice place for birds and squirrels, for dogs and children. The next house on our left belonged to a man with the slightly improbable name of Beal Roseberry, who lived there with his wife and two daughters. Esther, the elder of the two, was just a year my junior, and we were playmates for many years. Laura Phoebe, who turned out to be a very original character, was born some years after we had moved into our house. Beyond the Roseberry's place when we first moved in was a large vacant lot, and beyond that the Frank house, Mr. and Mrs. Walton Frank, an elderly couple, being the parents of Mrs. Roseberry. It was an old Victorian-type house, with gingerbread ornamentations outside, and high, narrow windows downstairs—windows that went down almost to the floor.

A few years after we moved into our Seventh Street house Arch Frank and his wife, Maude, built a home on the lot that was vacant between the Roseberry and Walton Frank houses. Arch was the son of the elder Franks and of course the brother of Mrs. Roseberry; thus with the coming of his family into our neighborhood there was established a closely knit clan on one side of us. His family consisted, beside himself and his wife, of one daughter, Eva Margaret, a year younger than her cousin Esther, and two years my junior. Naturally the three of us became playmates when we were all very young.

Finally, beyond the Walton Frank house was the home of Dr. Wilson, his wife, and his grown-up daughter. I think he must have been retired; at any rate he and his family were ensconced in another Victorian house of considerable size, with long windows going to the floor and fretwork around the eaves.

The long front yards of these several houses—ours, the Roseberrys, the two Frank houses and the Wilson house—were in no way separated each from the other by hedges or fences, and their contiguity thus created the parklike nature of our neighborhood. Furthermore our conjoined yards emphasized the rather communal manner in which all of us lived. We crossed each other's properties with no second thoughts on the part of any of us, and there was a constant mingling of families back and forth.

To the immediate west was the Glass home, set considerably closer to the street than was our house, so that our front was somewhat behind the rear of the Glass home. Furthermore, the Glass house was on a terrace a bit higher than our land, all in all setting that property somewhat apart from the communal Colbert-to-Wilson sequence of houses and lawns. But this physical difference between our properties in no way separated the Glass family from ours in life style and neighborliness. In fact, one of the early projects of my father, after we had moved in to our place, was to build a set of rustic stairs up the terrace between us and the Glass establishment, so that we could walk across their yard at will. This arrangement, which met with the full approval of the Glass family, enabled us to walk through the large back yard of the Glass property to the Gillam house on the other side.

Mr. Glass was a retired farmer, and his youngest son, Claude, was Phil's age. (The other Glass children were older and had left the parental nest.) On summer mornings we would hear Mr. Glass calling for Claude to get up.

"Oh, Claude . . . Claudie . . . Claudie!" Claude and Phil did many things together, including the installation of a telegraph line between their bedrooms. Each of them had a standard railroad telegraph key, of the type then in use which went clickety click, and with these instruments they would talk to each other in halting Morse code signals. When the going got rough they would open their windows and yell back and forth, thus ensuring the accuracy of their communications system.

The Gillam house, set on the corner of the block, was almost a mansion, solidly built in an early Edwardian style. Mr. and Mrs. Gillam lived there with their son Forrest, an only child, who was another of Phil's cronies. Mr. Gillam, as mentioned one of the town bankers, was to me a rather forbidding and aloof figure, but Mrs. Gillam and Forrest were very close friends, Mrs. Gillam taking the role of a kindly aunt, Forrest being to me something like a big brother.

The Gillams always had a Cadillac, except for one brief interlude when they tried some other car of a make long since extinct, and even then far from satisfactory. Forrest could drive the Gillam car even when he was quite young and small (he was a small boy for his age) and I can remember climbing up into the high, padded leather front seat to sit beside him while he drove out into the country to deliver a package at the home of some relatives. And all the time we were at the Tebow house the car stood in front with the engine idling, because Forrest was too little to crank it, and all of the Tebow men were out in the fields and unavailable for such heavy and really rather risky work. In those days before self-starters there was an art to cranking a car engine. The bigger the car the heavier the engine, and the harder it was to "turn over." So one had to know just how to set the gas and the spark, and how to hold the crank, and what was the most effective way to give it a turn. Half a turn or a single turn was usually enough, except when the engine was cold and stiff. But it had to be a good, strong, masterful turn, with the thumb held parallel to the other fingers, *not* wrapped around the crank handle. Many a strong man in those ancient days of the automobile had his arm broken by the crank "kicking back" because of compression in the cylinders, and such broken arms were usually the result of a too firm grip on the crank handle. With the thumb held alongside the other fingers, the crank would kick out of the cranker's hand, and thus no harm would come to him.

The Roseberrys, next to us, had a chain-drive Buick, and that was a noisy car, and Mr. Todd, around the corner, had some kind of a car that cranked up on the side instead of in front. At that time those were about the only cars in the immediate neighborhood. This is not meant to imply that cars were rare, but they certainly weren't numerous. People who could afford them had cars for driving around town and for short trips out into the country on the dirt roads—roads which were narrow and rough in dry weather and completely impassable after any sizable rain. Automobiles were a means for getting about after a fashion, but horses were still the old reliables. They pulled the farmers' plows and other implements and they brought the farmers into town, where horse-drawn cabs were still to be hired and where the volunteer fire company played it safe by having a horse-drawn fire engine. Of course everybody went from one town to another on the train.

Such is a picture of our house and of the intimate world that surrounded it, of the people within it, the people who went in and out of it, and the people who walked past. It was my safe haven, a place of security to which I could retreat, and in which I could feel the tangible love and protection of my parents. Is it any wonder that the house loomed large in my young life; that it had a strong, magnetic force reaching out to hold me even during those first two or three years after I had cut the connections with the house, with the neighborhood, and with the town where I had had grown up? Today I think back to it as the embodiment of an age that now seems incredibly distant, far removed in time and environment and cultural practices from the frenetic world in which I now live.

II

A Little Tiny Boy

"When that I was and a little tiny boy" (to quote from the song of Shakespeare's clown that brings *Twelfth Night* to a close), small things loomed large, and large things often seemed so huge as to be almost overwhelming. How great were the rooms, how high the ceilings, how long and steep the stairs. How distant was the railroad behind our house, and how far it was to the street out in front. How imposing did my elders tower above me: black skirts at my eye level, and above the skirts full-bodied white shirtwaists with long sleeves, from which kindly hands reached down helpfully. Or black trousers and waistcoats, the latter enclosing white shirts with stiff collars and sedate neckties. My horizons were leveled at the lower portions of adult anatomy, always well clothed, but on high were the familiar faces that gave me confidence. The face of my mother and the face of my father—to me kindly and reassuring faces. It was good to know that these faces were never far away.

Among the neighborhood faces a face that was not habitually above but rather at my own level was that of Petty Grandma, Mrs. Cavanaugh. She was Esther's maternal great-grandmother, a very old lady who in her waking moments was confined to a chair and therefore down to our level. She would entertain us with stories, and when a train would go chugging past behind the house, she would tell us that the train was saying "don't tell father—don't tell father," and that seemed quite logical. Then, one day in the early spring or perhaps it was in the late fall, at any rate at a time when the weather was raw and the trees were bare, she passed on.

On the day of the funeral there was a vicious cold rain, and I stood at the big east window of the living room, looking out at the line of carriages drawn up on the long drive to the Walton Frank house. The horses stood disconsolately, with their heads down, enduring the lashing rain. The drivers sat bundled up on their seats, certainly miserable and undoubtedly getting wet, in spite of their wrappings. The carriages were of a closed sort (I suppose they might be called broughams) which was comfortable for the passengers, but the driver, who sat forward on a high seat, was fully exposed to the elements. Horses and drivers made a dismal picture, seen somewhat intermittently through the sheets of rain—a picture of the sort that might have been engraved in earlier times by Thomas Bewick. Certainly it was a picture that has remained etched in my memory.

Esther Roseberry, who lived next door, already has been mentioned two or three times, and more will be said of her, because during my very early years she was a constant playmate. There were no little boys of my age in the neighborhood at the time, so we quite naturally were thrown together pretty much as infant siblings, to spend hours together each day, playing as small children will play. Since she was just a year younger than I was, we had similar interests during those innocent years before boys go their particular ways and girls diverge to follow their own feminine inclinations. Thus we shared our toys and our activities; she liked to play with me and with my iron trains, and I was not above sharing her dolls with her. At the time we were the only two little children in the neighborhood (this was before the Franks built their house beyond us, on the other side of the Roseberry establishment). Under these circumstances we enjoyed what I suppose were rather idyllic hours and days—in and out of our house, of the Roseberry house, of the Walton Frank house (where Petty Grandma sat through the hours in her chair) and back and forth across the spacious yards. We had our small adventures.

One of them involved a little rocking-horse chair that occupied the middle of the floor of her playroom, a little padded seat with a back and with sides, each of which was shaped like a spotted pony with its hooves planted on a rocker. The small occupant of this piece of furniture sat nicely enclosed with a horse on each side, and was able to rock safely for untold minutes (or hours) on the two rockers. No chance of falling over or falling out. Esther and I decided we would both try to sit together in this contraption, but alas, once we were settled side by side we felt ourselves tightly wedged in between the right and left horses, and that made us realize that we were very much constrained. How did we know that we wouldn't have to spend the rest of the day—the rest of our lives—jammed into uncomfortable proximity? So we both began to cry, and as the minutes passed we cried and yowled with ever-increasing stridency. It seemed like an age—undoubtedly it was only two or three minutes—until Mrs. Roseberry came smiling into the room and released us from our self-imposed stocks. Her comforting assistance made the world seem safe again.

Another early vignette. When I was very small I was often taken from place to place in the winter, if there was snow on the ground, in a little sled baby-carriage. It was a wooden sled, on which was mounted a wooden body, nicely shaped and painted red, to the back of which was attached at an angle two long pieces of wood, one on each side, joined by a cross bar, thus making a handle or device by which the sled could be pushed and steered. In this practical conveyance I enjoyed many a ride over the snowy sidewalks and streets, propelled by one of my parents.

In the course of such rides I frequently saw my brother Phil and his companions sliding down the hills on their sleds. So one winter day I had the brilliant idea of hauling my little baby-carriage sled to the top of the Seventh Street hill in front of our house, to a point opposite the Gillam house, to have a nice ride down the snow-covered sidewalk. Accordingly I managed to get the sled up to the starting point, and then I climbed in. Down we went, the sled with me sitting upright in the little box, as trusting a passenger, completely innocent of the laws of physics or anything else, as ever went out on a winter's day. The ride was delightful for a time—and then, there being no method of steering the sled, we collided with a tree on the parkway between the sidewalk and the street in front of our house. The collision was total; not only did the front of the sled crash into the tree, but also my face fetched up against the rough bark as I was thrown forward by the impact. The experience was a painful one, and I let the neighborhood know about it in a loud voice. Further independent sledding was reserved for later years.

Of course tears come easily and quickly to small folk, and I had my share of them, mostly forgotten. But perhaps another tearful incident may here be added, not so much remembered by me as by my elders. My mother had taken me to Chicago to visit some friends. At the friends' house there was a little cup and saucer that caught my eye; I coveted them beyond the telling of it. The cup was decorated with a red hen on the outside, and the saucer had two or three little chicks around its periphery. How I did long for those two pieces of china, and I suppose that, being small and without much tact, I made my wishes known.

Somehow or other, my mother's hostess had learned that I could sing the verses and chorus of "Casey Jones," a ballad of railroading that was then in vogue and since has become famous. So I was told that if I would sing "Casey Jones," I could have the cup and saucer. Which set up conflicting emotions within my small chest; I wanted the china pieces, but for some reason I rebelled at singing for them. Finally, however, desires overcame scruples and I started my song. But at every second or third line I would break off the singing to bawl at the top of my voice, and so it went through the moving ballad of Mr. Jones and his ultimate death in the train wreck. And as my performance continued to its end, the folks in the room became increasingly convulsed with laughter—with the result that by the time the song was over my mother's hostess was streaming tears as liberally as I was, but for a different reason. It was a story often repeated in our family, and one that, as I have said, I can dimly remember through a mist of bygone tears.

The visit to Chicago, just mentioned, points up an aspect of my young life that has been, as a result of our so-called progress, largely denied to children of today, and this was journeying across the land by train. Of course children during these last two or three decades have done their traveling by car and by plane, but such methods of transportation truly cannot be considered as being on a par with train travel as once it existed. There was a romance in riding on a train, especially a train pulled by a steam engine, that has long since vanished and is known only to those of us in the category of the very elderly. Perhaps this cannot be explained to the present generation, yet it is real. Witness the dedication of confirmed railroad buffs in this day and age.

There was a sense of anticipation when setting out on a long train trip, of looking forward to many hours watching the passing scene, without the strain of driving or without the boredom of being strapped in a plane seat, so far above the landscape or above the clouds that the only diversions are reading, watching stale movies, or eating mediocre food. There was real freedom on the train, the freedom to get up and walk around, to go to the dining car, or to mingle, if one so desired, with people other than the occupant of the next seat. And there was the luxury, if one were on a sleeper, of getting into a bed to be lulled by the clicking of the wheels on the rails and the mournful sound of the steam whistle, far ahead.

My train trips go back as far as my memory—to the trip back to Ohio at the time of my Grandmother Colbert's funeral, to a vacation trip to Colorado when I was barely four years old, and to shorter trips such as the ones to Holton to visit my Adamson grandparents.

As for the Ohio trip, my memories center on an enforced sojourn in an upstairs bedroom of the Lebanon home in which my father had lived. My aged grandmother had been laid to rest and my parents were all ready to take the train back to Missouri, when one fine morning I did not look or feel well. A doctor was summoned and he immediately informed the family that I had scarlet fever.

In those days this disease evidently was far more serious than is the case today. My father took off for home; I was quarantined in the Lebanon house, and my mother was confined with me, to spend several weeks taking care of me in my bedroom. It was an ordeal for her, but not much of one for me, because mine was a light case of the affliction. And every day when the doctor came in to look me over he brought me a delicious piece of candy. My final remembrance of that trip is of standing on a balcony or perhaps some sort of an overpass in the St. Louis station and looking down on the tracks with the trains drawn up in parallel rows, some having just arrived, some just ready to leave. Fortunately the station has been saved and today has become one of the choice dining and gathering places in St. Louis.

In Colorado the family settled in a rustic cabin in a canyon, to enjoy a summer vacation. That was in 1909, when I was not quite four years old. The cabin had a large porch, where we could relax and enjoy the mountain air; before us was a roaring mountain stream, behind us rose a sheer cliff, several hundred feet high.

I recall vividly having to go in for my afternoon nap, and enviously watching my brother Phil and some of his friends playing at the edge of the stream. Actually, they were sitting on a little wooden footbridge that crossed the stream to our cabin, and they were lowering into the water little paddle wheels they had made—watching the stream make the wheels go around and around at a furious rate. It was the most lovely pastime I could imagine, and I bitterly resented being excluded from it. Perhaps I expressed myself on this subject in vociferous terms; I suspect so.

That was the cabin that my father and my uncle Charlie Bagnall set afire. Uncle Charlie and Aunt Eva and my cousin Charles (who was a babe in arms) had come up from Denver for the weekend. Uncle Charlie was bit hoity-toity about the fires that my father was building each evening in the fireplace; my uncle was going to show father how to make a real fire.

So Uncle Charlie went up on top of the cliff behind the cabin and secured a pine root full of pitch, which he rolled over the edge so that it came crashing down just behind our domicile. Here, said Uncle Charlie, was a "lallapaloozer" of a log. That evening the fire was lit, and the pine stem, full of pitch, burned merrily, and ever brighter. It grew hot and then hotter, and soon an ominous odor filled the cabin. The throat of the fireplace was made of metal, which was covered with log slabs, to make it look sufficiently rustic. The hot metal ignited the slabs, and smoke and flame began to erupt. My father grabbed a pail with a long rope attached to the handle, and he ran out to the brook, lowered the pail by the rope into the tumbling water, and then came running back into the cabin with a full pail, expecting to dash its contents on the burning log slabs. Alas! The rope attached to the pail was trailing behind him, and just as he reached the center of the room the screen door slammed on the end of the rope, so that the pail and the *pater familias* went end over end across the floor. My mother and Aunt Eva thought it was very funny and it must have been—a regular Laurel and Hardy act in person. But their peals of laughter were not appreciated by father and Uncle Charlie.

In spite of all they got the fire out. The next day the owner of the cabin came around to survey the damage, which was slight. Nevertheless he was highly indignant—not because of the charred logs, but because Pop and Uncle Charlie had not allowed the cabin to burn to the ground. Then he could have gotten a nice chunk of insurance money.

Another early train trip took me to Indiana, where big doings were under way. A cousin of my mother's, Katherine Croan, was to be married—to Walter Greenough, a journalist and writer—and our Indiana relatives who were very close to our family wanted my mother to be there. Naturally I went along, and there I had some little adventures, still remembered.

Since I have had something to say about the pleasure of riding on trains, when there were real trains, perhaps I should mention that this trip to Indiana—it was in 1912—introduced me to the interurban, the Marion Flyer from Indianapolis to Anderson, where the Croans lived, and it was a ride that I still remember with a sense of excitement. Those interurbans were usually large, solidly built trolley cars, and they took you from the middle of one town to the middle of another, or more usually to the middle of several other towns. They ran on the regular streetcar tracks in town, but once at the edge of the city they took off across country, more often than not with breathtaking speed. They were truly rapid transit. Through the fields, through the woods, no slowing down for traffic jams, no smoke and not much noise, no billboards or other forms of visual pollution, always zooming along with the countryside intimately at hand on either side of the rocketing trolley. This latter was owing to the fact that frequently the interurban was a single-track line with a narrow right of way, so that one felt in tune with the landscape. There was none of the isolation from the passing scene that one experiences on modern freeways as they cut excessively broad swaths through the land.

My mother's elder sister, Maggie Tousey, long a widow, lived with the Croans in Anderson. But Aunt Maggie was not a housebound lady, because she operated, of all things, a gravel pit and a cement-block works. Through an inheritance, she had come into the ownership of some land out at the edge of Anderson, on which there were some excellent deposits of glacial gravel, so she went into business. I used to go out there with her, on a tiny little trolley car, and there, alongside the track, was her tiny little office housed in a diminutive structure—out there all by itself. I loved it because it was so small, for little people love little things. Inside was her desk and a few files and a telephone over which she took orders and handled other aspects of her business, while out in front of the door of this little house were several trees making a small shady grove, and under them a lawn swing. Aunt Maggie could sit out there on hot summer days and still hear her telephone jangle.

She had a foreman who ran the operation at the pit, where several men shoveled sand and gravel into horse-drawn wagons to haul to their appointed destinations. One destination was right beside the pit—a long shed where the cement building blocks were made. I use to watch the men pouring wet cement into the forms for casting, and I watched also the men digging in the pit. This latter spectator sport was always enjoyed by me at some distance, because I was under strict injunctions not to go down into the pit where—who knows?—I might be engulfed by slumping gravel.

The foreman had a little boy of my age and we used to play together. His name was Cyril, which I managed to translate into "cereal," thinking that it was strange to name a boy after corn flakes. I remember Cyril telling me about a big boat called the *Titanic* sinking out in the ocean. This was hard for an inlander like me to comprehend; I had visions of a sort of king-size rowboat vanishing beneath the waves.

Only such boats were within the limits of my experience. One hot day my mother took me down to a little river that flowed not far from Aunt Maggie's gravel pit to enjoy the cool air beneath the trees, and while we sat there two men came along, their pants rolled up to their knees, wading down the middle of this stream, pushing between them a small skiff or something like that, with a little cabin amidships. That was the sort of boat I understood.

The day of the wedding approached, the lawn in front of the house was decorated with Japanese lanterns strung among the trees, and an outdoor altar was set up. I was to be a sort of "policeman," so my mother told me, dressed in white and carrying the end of a white ribbon that trailed behind me as I walked along the side of an elongated carpet spread on the grass from the house to the altar. Another little boy was to walk on a parallel course on the other side of the bride's pathway. Everything was set, the people put on their finery, the guests gathered, the lights were turned on (this was an evening affair), and then the rains came. It was a regular middle-western downpour, with celestial fireworks adding frequent flashes and booms to the loud drumming of the rain on the leaves of the trees and on the roof. Of course everybody fled indoors, to be crowded into a hot living room, and there I performed my policeman's duty on a much restricted scale. I remember seeing my cousin Katherine, upstairs, crying bitterly, and I wondered why she should be so upset by an ordinary garden-variety thunderstorm.

The wedding took place, and afterward I was taken up to shake hands with Mr. Marshall, one of guests. This was Thomas Marshall, destined to be for eight years Woodrow Wilson's affable and efficient vice-president.

An aside. Katherine Croan Greenough's father, my uncle Will Croan, the husband of my Aunt Jessie who was the sister of my maternal grandmother, spent the nineties of the last century in the establishment of colleges, and my father was his junior partner in these activities. First there was the Northwestern College in Shenandoah, Iowa, of which Uncle Will was the president and in which my father taught mathematics. The single building housing this institution burned down in 1891, so Uncle Will and my father moved to Lincoln, Nebraska, to found the Western Normal College, again serving respectively as president and faculty member. Three successive years of poor corn crops spelled the end of that school, so they moved back to Anderson, Indiana, to try again with the Anderson Normal College. The records show that this school had a faculty of seventeen, including the president, and a beginning student body of three hundred hopeful scholars. Tuition was "$1 a term of 10 weeks." Room and board was an additional "$2 per week of seven days and 21 square meals." That was in August, 1896.

These figures illustrate money values in those distant days. Even so one wonders how a private college could survive on such slender resources. One wonders even more at the casual manner in which colleges sometimes got under way in the post–Civil War Midwest.

My present story is concerned, however, with a time somewhat more than a decade later than the last of those little colleges. It is, among other things, the story of a small boy who did not enjoy very good health. From the beginning my digestive system was not all that it should have been, so that I had a great deal of trouble in assimilating my food, even in keeping it down, and of course in being properly nourished. In fact, I remember my father saying that he and my mother often were in despair at what seemed to them the remote possibility of my staying alive and growing up. Perhaps with modern medical knowledge the problem might have been quickly solved, but as things were I spent many days in bed, suffering especially from nausea. I was plagued with this condition through my grade school years but about the time I entered high school, or soon after, I grew out of it.

But when I was "a little tiny boy" I was truly little, so that for several years I was smaller than my peers, and suffered accordingly. Boys live in a harsh and competitive world, as I learned at an early age. Consequently I managed to survive by using my wits, which in turn fostered an ornery streak in my nature. I don't think I was really bad, but I certainly made life interesting for my parents with some of my original ideas and actions.

During these years, especially when I was quite small, my eldest brother, Herschel, gave me strong support. On many occasions he would take me along with him when he went places, and was my good companion at such times. One of my early memories is of going to high school with him, and sitting next to him while the teacher up front kept talking about a wolf. (It turned out that the subject was North American history, and that day the topic was Wolfe of Quebec.) I remember too, when I was a little older, and my parents let me walk to the Burlington station to meet Herschel, who was coming in on an early morning train. It was a bright summer morning, the grass shone with morning dew, the flowers were out, and I was in a transport of joy at the prospect of greeting my big brother. We walked home together, Herschel carrying his small suitcase and I scampering alongside, rather like a little dog that is overjoyed to see once again a member of the family who has been absent for all too long a time.

This was but one of many times that I greeted my eldest brother as he returned home for a visit, for it must be remembered that because of our age difference he was already away at the University of Missouri when I was still very small. His trips back to join the family, even though brief, were exciting events in my young life.

It must not be thought, however, that I failed to appreciate attentions from my parents; I suppose that perhaps because I was with them every day their presence was taken for granted and regarded by me in a rather prosaic light. My mother, as I have said, was a good companion, and my father, although a little too old to really play with me as a younger father would, nevertheless spent time with me and helped to make the world around me more or less comprehensible.

One day he took me by the hand and we walked the two or three blocks downtown, where we happened to go past the town blacksmith establishment—a species of business activity that is now very rare indeed. The place fascinated me, and my father, being a product of the horse and buggy age, could explain most satisfactorily the activities taking place in the dark interior, lit largely by the fire of the forge back in one corner. Out near the big open door that fronted the sidewalk a horse was receiving the attentions of the smith, who had one hoof of the horse securely held between his (the smith's) leather-aproned legs, and was nailing a shoe in place. I wonderingly asked my father why this did not hurt the horse, because I knew that I would not like to have nails driven into my foot. He then explained that the nails were driven only through the edge of the hoof, just as one might drill a tiny hole through the free end of my fingernail, and then I understood why the nails did not hurt the horse, and why the horse stood still and let himself be treated in this manner.

Outside the shop were two or three horses hitched to wagons, waiting to be shod. These horses stood still because each of them had a long leather trace, attached to the bit in the horse's mouth and fastened at its other end to an iron weight about the size of a small teakettle. Why did not the horse walk away, pulling the weight with him? And my father explained how the bit pressed down on the horse's tongue and how, if the horse tried to pull the weight, it would hurt him to do so. So I understood how such a big animal could be controlled by such a seemingly small device. It was one item added to my early education.

One of the more memorable events in my early life was when Buffalo Bill's Wild West Show came to town. My mother took me to see it, and bought a rubber balloon for me as we entered the grandstand. Right at the beginning of things the balloon exploded, which made me very unhappy, but the balloon was soon forgotten when I saw people come riding out on horses, and shoot down glass balls thrown into the air by accompanying horsemen. There was other trick shooting and trick riding. (I wonder if I saw Annie Oakley.) The climax of the show occurred when William F. Cody rode to the center of the field, resplendent in white buckskins and seated on a white horse, all complemented by his long, flowing white hair and his neatly trimmed white beard. He took off his broad-brimmed hat and saluted the cheering crowd, sending all of us greetings, in a sense, from a vanished era.

My mother also took me to see my first movie, and this initial encounter with the cinema was not entirely successful. It was of course a show filmed during the very primitive days of movie making, and it included a comedy in which one character in a sculptor's studio whacked another character on the head with a large wooden mallet. I was so terrified by this unseemly behavior that I howled and wailed and had to be removed from the auditorium.

The horses that I saw at the blacksmith shop and at the Buffalo Bill show were all part of my young life, because automobiles were still primitive and not very numerous. Horses were all around us; they delivered goods to our house, they pulled the cabs that were soon to be replaced by taxis, they pulled the plows and corn-planters and harrows and rakes of the farmers, and on Saturdays, hitched to wagons or buggies, they brought the farm families into town to do the weekly shopping. All of the roads were dirt, and after heavy rains, or in the winter and spring, were negotiable only by horse-drawn vehicles or by people on foot or on horseback. The mud of those middle-western roads was of a depth and stickiness that is rarely experienced or even believed by people of our automotive generation.

The courthouse square in those days was lined on three sides by long files of heavy posts, connected each to the next by a stout chain to which horses could be hitched. So on a Saturday afternoon when all of the farmers were in town the red-brick courthouse had the appearance of an equine shrine, with horses of all colors hitched to buggies and wagons facing the courthouse from three of the four cardinal points of the compass. The fourth side of the square on Main Street was kept unimpeded.

It was on that side of the square when one day I saw a man in a very early Model T Ford mount the sidewalk with his right wheels to go bowling along at an angle—two wheels on the sidewalk, two wheels in the street. The driver obviously was thoroughly frightened and didn't know what to do. His predicament did not last long, because at the corner he collided with a lamp post, giving it such a jolt that the five globes surmounting it came down all together, just at the moment when one of our town worthies was driving past in his beautifully appointed open carriage, drawn by a well-groomed, shiny horse. The lamp globes crashed down on and around the horse, and immediately there was an urban runaway, the horse galloping down Main Street wild-eyed and terrified, and the driver sawing at the reins with all his might. There were no serious consequences; it was a rather comical example of the impact of the automobile on an earlier form of transportation.

The age of air travel was still some distance in the offing, even though we had seen our first plane, a primitive Wright biplane that had come to town for an exhibition flight, I suppose in about 1910 or thereabouts. In 1909 Louis Bleriot crossed the English Channel from France to Dover in his little monoplane, and this inspired my brother Phil, who at the time was intensely interested in the infant technology of aviation, to build a model Bleriot plane. It was a beautiful model, but was never much on flying. It was powered by long rubber bands hooked to the propeller, and evidently it was underpowered. So for most of its life it hung suspended from the ceiling in "our" room—the room occupied by Phil and myself—where I admired it through a number of my boyhood years.

Phil was just beginning his high school education at the time of which I am writing, so we were together at home. Most of the time he went his way and I went mine, and when I went his way it was generally to follow him around. Which may or may not always have been to his liking, and sometimes was to my sorrow. Phil was never mean to me, but once in a while I felt abandoned. Such as the time when the Boy Scouts (a very new organization) gathered in our big front yard, where they played "woolly-woolly wolf," a sort of dare-base game, before setting off on a hike. I thought the game was great fun, but I was devastated that I couldn't go along with them on their hike. It was hard for me to comprehend that four-year-olds cannot always participate in the things that thirteen-year-olds do.

I did participate, as a trailing spectator, when Phil and Forrest Gillam and Claude Glass had a running tomato fight through our back yards. The tomatoes were ripening on the vines, and they made very satisfactory ammunition. And the battle was gory (at least it was red) and fine to see. What the elders thought about this I never learned.

For as far back as I can remember I was, or thought I was, beset by problems—problems that formed a background for every day, making that day, no matter how perfect it otherwise might be, not quite perfect. To a considerable extent the problems were of my own making, for I was a worrywart, and I still am. To a large degree the problems were hardly of earth-shaking significance, yet they were none the less real to me. They were for the most part the kinds of problems that every boy faces: how to avoid the aggressive boy three blocks down the street, how to achieve a fair deal during the daily contacts with one's peers, how to keep from being too conspicuous, especially when forced to wear some particular article of clothing by a well-meaning but uninformed parent, how to abide by all of the rules, the dos and the don'ts, prescribed by an adult world, and so on. Naturally such problems loomed large in my own little world, giving the lie to those philosophers who depict childhood as a carefree time of life, a golden age of Arcadian pleasures. Yet in spite of the problems of childhood and their accompanying worries I survived. And at times during those years I caught glimpses of some problems that were part of the larger world in which I lived.

The first time I was brought face to face with an alien and a sometimes bitter world, far removed in spirit if not in distance from the protection of our family home, took place when I was still a little tiny boy. That was when my mother and a neighbor of ours, Mrs. Gillam, made a visit to the county poor farm and I was taken along, perhaps as a matter of expediency. We were driven there over dusty county roads in the Gillams' car by a friend who had been impressed for the day to act as chauffeur, and in due time we arrived at the institution, consisting of a number of brick buildings set in the midst of cornfields, with of course some trees to soften the scene.

The car was parked beneath a large tree, for it was a hot summer day, and we went up some steps into the main building, there to be met by the superintendent, or at least some person of authority. He conducted us around the place, and for me it was a most depressing tour. Such an institution in those days was planned to accommodate for the most part destitute elderly people, and those were the people we saw. It was not the fact that they were poor that affected me; rather it was their generally miserable and often helpless condition but particularly their evident unhappiness that made a sad and lasting impression on my mind, young as I was. The sight of one old lady sitting forlornly in a rocking chair and staring vacantly at a wall had a truly traumatic effect upon me. I don't think my mother realized at the moment how horrified (if that is not too strong a term) I was by what I saw.

When we got back home I asked my mother about it and she tried to explain to me the quite unexpected and somewhat frightening experience I had gone through. It *was* frightening; I had glimpsed an unkind world, the existence of which had been beyond my small experience. It introduced me to the fact that out there past the boundaries of our familiar neighborhood were hopeless people living a barren kind of life. Although I was very small I none the less had some understanding of what I had seen, and what I had seen depressed me in such a way that it was not readily forgotten. I suppose that if I had been a city child I would have been used to seeing unhappiness, perhaps even hardened to it after a fashion, but for me, living in a bucolic environment, this introduction to imposed poverty and unhappiness was almost too much for my small and unprepared psyche.

The inclusion of this little event of my young life in the present story is of consequence mainly because it illustrates in its own way the sort of environment in which I spent my formative years. It was a protected environment, not because it was meant to be that way but because it *was* that way, and it was that way because the setting I was born into and grew up in during the early years of the present century was rural and unsophisticated. In the Middle West of my boyhood many of the tensions and disruptions that pervade life to such a degree today just were not around. Foreign problems were indeed foreign—so far removed as to be rarely thought about (not that a five-year-old would ever think about such things even today)—and therefore did not create any kind of a sociological climate that could be sensed by the young and innocent. Domestic problems, such as they were, involved for the most part local conditions, and although they may have impinged upon my consciousness they were vague. That was why the poor-farm visit made such an impact on me; it brought certain things into focus and thus visible to a small citizen.

In our town there were only limited differences of wealth and social status. There were no people living in grinding poverty although of course some members of our society were almost poor. There were no ostentatiously wealthy people although a few families in town were obviously well-to-do. In general it was a middle-class society, and it was in such a milieu that I first learned about life. So it was that I lived in comfortable circumstances when I was small, a fact about which I make no apologies. In no way can I tell a tale of overcoming the obstacles of little money, few clothes, and insufficient food, although my parents did have to be very careful of how they spent their limited income. Ours was a comfortable life, in some ways perhaps better than the life I live today. As I look back it seems to me that our food, although not so varied as today's menu, was often more wholesome. Vegetables and fruits in season were fresher, meat was more natural (fowls for example were of the free-ranging kind, not raised in chicken factories; cattle were off the pastures, not stuffed with treated grain in feed lots), and little of what we ate was shipped in from halfway across the continent.

The big problem in my hometown was that of race, specifically of black and white, as was the case throughout the nation. There were not many Negroes in town, but most of them were segregated to the east end of town, where they worshipped in their own churches and where the children attended a separate school. Furthermore, the black children were not included in organized activities such as the Boy Scouts. This segregation was accepted by all, unthinkingly by the whites and undoubtedly with inward rage by the blacks. We had a race problem but we didn't seem to know it. (Some years after I had left home it did explode in a horrible lynching.)

But as for me, I was one with the rest of the white population in giving little thought to the situation, neither in my earliest years not later on when I was old enough to think about such things. I accepted segregation and did not become truly aware of its heinous nature until I had grown up and left home. I was one with my fellow Missourian Mark Twain, who stated in his autobiography, "In my schoolboy days I had no aversion to slavery. I was not aware that there was anything wrong about it." Mark Twain saw the wrong in it as he matured to immortalize his views in the undying prose of *Huckleberry Finn*.

Moreover we had no so-called ethnic problems, because almost all of our citizens were of northern European ancestry, several generations removed. Indeed, I seldom heard a foreign language spoken until after I had left home.

These meanderings have led me beyond the story of a little tiny boy, so perhaps it is best to bring this chapter to a close in anticipation of the next phase of my story: the account of growing up in a small town.

III

Small Town

*T*hose unfettered years slipped by, and then it was time to enter school. Kindergarten was an unknown experience for me; I do not recall whether or not there was a kindergarten in the curriculum at that time, in that place; the first twelve years of school were encompassed in eight grades, followed by a four-year high school. In our town the first three grades were endured in three identical little ward school buildings placed within the community so that small children would not have very far to walk. (School buses were not even in the dreams of the planners at that time.) The ward schools were the Franklin School, only a block from our house, the Jefferson School in the east part of town, and the Garfield School in the south part of town. After the regulation stint in the ward schools, the pupils graduated to the Washington School, more or less in the center of town, for the last five grades. The high school also was in the Washington building.

Of course I started in the Franklin School, which in many ways was the nicest of the three ward schools, because it was situated in a large, tree-filled park, just across a small street from the Gillam house. We had a good playground, no doubt about that. But the school was cramped and ill ventilated, so after two years my parents transferred me to the training school that was housed on the ground floor of the "Normal," out on the west side of town, about a mile from our home.

The Normal (as it was commonly designated) was of course the teachers' training institution where my father was a member of the faculty. Soon after this school had been established work was begun on a large building to house it, and when I transferred to the third grade there the building had been newly completed. It was an ideal place for school children, because the building was new, its facilities were new, and, best of all, it was situated in the middle of a large campus of a hundred acres or more. Here, on extensive lawns and among widespread plantings of trees and shrubbery, were ample areas in which to run and play during recess time. Moreover there was an athletic field behind the building, where we could indulge in football and baseball and track events. So it was here that I spent six pleasant years. And it was here that I entered the world of boys of my own age, separated during school hours from my former neighborhood playmates.

Having entered the world of little boys I found myself somewhat estranged from the world of little girls; I had become a member of that phratry, aged six to twelve or thereabouts, characterized by a certain amount of aloofness or even disdain for members of the opposite sex. It was the usual first coming-of-age phase in life, following those infant years when children play together as quite sexless little beings and preceding the electric years when boys and girls become very much interested in each other. So although I still associated with Esther, next door, such association was within the neighborhood and not to be seen by my schoolmates.

It so happened that there was another little girl with whom I spent much time in those early childhood years: Dorothy Eaton, a truly beautiful little doll-like girl, whose parents lived in a house on the corner just opposite the Gillam house. But then Dorothy's parents moved across to the other side of town, so that I had to walk a few blocks, traversing on the way the business district, whenever I went to their place.

One day I was at the Eaton home and it came time for me to go to our house, and for some reason Dorothy was to go with me. The prospect of walking along Main Street with a *girl*, where some of my raucous male associates might see us together, was a prospect that filled me with dread. What to do? Suddenly I had a bright idea, an idea about on a par with many other inspirations that marked this stage of my young life: in short, I would walk down the street and Dorothy would follow me at a distance of about half a block. That would get us across town without the probability of jeers directed toward us, and once at the Colbert house we could go ahead with our customary relationship. I proposed this plan of action to Dorothy, she meekly acquiesced, and the journey was accordingly completed.

Which was fine, until Dorothy's mother found out what had happened. *Then* did Dorothy get a round scolding for having participated in such a degrading spectacle, and did I get a similar scolding for having thought up and put into practice such a chauvinistic exercise! In the end, after a little time had passed by, this incident became one of the comical events in the annals of the two families, to be recounted with much merriment. Even Dorothy and I finally became inured to it, so that when the story was recounted we could manage to endure the telling of the tale—even smiling after a fashion.

One of my new-found friends at school was Dean Dorman, who lived on a farm outside of town. Every day he rode his pony, Buster, to school. Buster was a very fat little piebald steed, with a rocking-horse gait, and it was a familiar sight to see Dean cantering up the long drive to the Normal building as I more prosaically made my way to classes on foot. Once arrived, Dean would ride Buster to a little stable, located in a pine grove just to the west of the building, where the pony would be unsaddled, tied in a stall, and provided with some hay. It should be explained that the Normal grounds had formerly been a large tree nursery, and the stable was part of the original establishment, still standing.

This pine grove was the scene of a pageant, staged at the end of my first or second year at the training school. The affair was supposed to represent the coming of early white settlers to northwestern Missouri, and their meeting with the original Indian inhabitants. I was one of the Indians. Some of the older boys, in the seventh and eighth grades, were to represent the pioneers, and for this purpose they came through the woods on a wide front, presumably peering into the trees for game and shooting down the wherewithal for the evening meal. These boys had .22 rifles and were supplied with blank cartridges, which of course afforded an opportunity not to be missed. During our rehearsal their progress through the woods sounded like the Battle of the Wilderness in the Civil War. So the teachers decreed that for the actual pageant each boy would have just one cartridge, and that made a more convincing demonstration, albeit a noisy one just the same.

Among my companions at the training school were the two Landon boys, Truman and Kurt. Truman, the elder of the two brothers, was an especially close friend of mine. Their father was Perry Oliver Landon, who ran a conservatory of music in town. P. O. Landon had gone to Germany to study music and had married a German lady during his sojourn abroad. So Truman and Kurt grew up speaking both English and German, and that impressed me. Also the Landons raised pedigreed dachshunds, which made visits to their house particularly interesting.

A look into the future. Both boys, when they grew up, went to West Point, and became professional soldiers. During the Second World War Truman was a general in the air force, and after the war he became a four-star commander appointed by President Kennedy. For some years in the fifties he was in command of the American air forces in western Europe.

On one bitterly cold Christmas morning Truman and Kurt appeared at our front door, carrying between them a rather large basket containing something that was securely wrapped in a piece of blanket. We welcomed them into the house; they put the basket down on the floor and began to uncover whatever it was that the blanket concealed. In a moment the secret was revealed: a little dachshund puppy, a son of the Landon dogs, Fritz and Marcella. I need not describe the joy that I felt; I can only say that it was for me a Christmas of memorable import. Our little dog soon had a name; he was Schneider. And for some time, I cannot remember how long, Schneider was a beloved member of our household. Alas! One day while crossing the street in front of our house Schneider was struck by a car and thus vanished from my life.

One of my clear memories involving Truman Landon has to do with the day when one of us looked out of the window of our sixth-grade classroom to see a strange object in the sky. Immediately the class was alerted, and as eager faces crowded to the windows and as the object in the sky got closer and larger we could see that it was a free-floating balloon, its wicker basket occupied by two men. This was an unusual event (free-floating balloons are not common sights even today except in certain selected places such as Albuquerque, New Mexico) and so the teacher excused us from class for fifteen minutes, to go outside for a better look. Truman and I ran along beneath the balloon, which was only a few hundred feet above us, waving to the occupants as they waved back. It was a thrilling experience for the future air force general and me—one that we talked about for days afterward. We were later told that this balloon came from the Signal Corps station in Omaha and was out on a practice flight.

The other balloon event of my young life took place one summer day at the county fair. Our county fair was located on some extensive grounds just east of the town, where there were barns for livestock shows, a building in which ladies exhibited their prize cakes and pies, jams and jellies, and needlework, and all along one side was a sort of a fairway flanked by booths and tents for sideshows, games where one threw baseballs at targets to vie for teddy bears and other such prizes, hot dog stands and the like, and beyond all of this clutter a racetrack with a wooden grandstand along the straightaway. For me the horse races were a prime attraction; there were running races, trotting races, and pacing races, all equally thrilling. Then there were races for amateur riders, and I recall the time that my friend Dean Dorman entered a race with his little piebald pony. It was no show so far as Buster was concerned; he was too comfortably rotund to keep up, so he had the distinction of coming in last by a large margin.

Out in the middle of the racetrack there was of course a large, open grassy area, where special events took place. It was always a bit frightening to see the high diver; he would climb a very high ladder to a little platform at the top and from this airy perch would dive into a tank of water that could not have been more than about five feet in depth. I still don't know how it was done.

The instance of which I am now to relate was a balloon ascension that took place from this same area, inside the race track. A roaring fire was built, and then the balloon was held over the fire by willing volunteers, to be inflated by hot air. How in the world this was accomplished without setting fire to the fabric I shall never know, but it was successfully done as it had been done time and again at county fairs all over the Middle West. Then the balloon went up, with the balloonist underneath the inflated bag—not in a basket but on a trapeze. While the assembled crowd looked on he performed various maneuvers on his trapeze, after which he pulled a string and leaped out and away from his balloon, as simultaneously it collapsed and the parachute with which he was equipped opened, to waft him gently to earth.

I noted the line of his descent, as did several of my companions with whom I had been watching the proceedings, and we all ran pell-mell toward the point at which we thought he would land. The quickest way to get there was to exit from the fairgrounds, run a few hundred feet to the tracks of the Burlington Railroad nearby, and then along the railway to where we hoped to find him. All of this took only a few minutes, and we did find him, sitting on a little trestle where the tracks crossed a small stream. Evidently he had landed just a bit harder than had been intended, for he seemed to be in something of a daze. We stood around respectfully until he regained his equanimity, at which point he gathered up the parachute, which had been draped across the track, and started back to the fairgrounds, accompanied by a gaggle of small boys, bombarding him with questions. That was an event long to be remembered.

The county fair was one of the big happenings of the midwestern summer, but it was viewed with a certain amount of mild disdain by the gentler segment of the population, largely because of the rowdy nature of the folks who came to town with the sideshows. So for these townsfolk the truly exciting summer event was the annual Chautauqua.

The original Chautauqua had been established on the shores of Lake Chautauqua in New York State during the latter part of the nineteenth century. For many years spanning several generations people have flocked to Lake Chautauqua, to spend a week or more attending lectures and concerts and other entertainments and activities, designed to improve the mind and elevate the spirits. Naturally a majority of the far-flung population of America could not make it to Lake Chautauqua, so lesser "Chautauquas" came into being across the land. Most of these were not of the fixed variety, but rather were traveling lyceums that went from town to town during the summer.

First a crew would come to town by freight train, carrying with them a huge tent and benches and other paraphernalia. The tent would be erected in an open field or lot, a wooden stage would be set up, and the benches would be arranged in a sort of semicircular plan, facing the stage. Then everything was ready for a week of culture. It all seems crude and clumsy, but in an age before radio, sophisticated moving pictures, and television it was the accepted way to bring music, lectures, and other forms of entertainment to the hinterlands.

It staggers one's imagination to think of the programming that went into a summer's Chautauqua circuit. For it must be remembered that Chautauqua tents were set up all over the land, and that the participants in the programs had to make their way from town to town by train, and perform day after day. These poor folks must have had iron constitutions and a real sense of dedication. Moreover the people involved in the Chautauqua programs were not all lesser luminaries; indeed some outstanding personalities made their way around the Chautauqua circuits. I remember attending a concert in Clarinda, Iowa, the little town about thirty miles from my hometown of Maryville, to hear Madame Schumann-Heink, the famous opera star, sing.

During my younger years the Chautauqua in Maryville was held on the Normal campus, in a pleasant grove of oak trees. On one side of this grove there was a natural declivity having a slight angle and here the big tent was pitched so that the rows of benches facing the stage, at the low side of the tent, rose one row after the other, more or less as in a theater. A dirt road ran along the back side of the tent, allowing access by horse and carriage and by primitive automobiles. And on the far side of the road was the grove, already mentioned, within which were pitched rows of tents, thus making a little tent city where townsfolk could while away the sultry hours between programs. Many families would bring picnic lunches to be enjoyed in their tents, and some hardy souls spent the nights, camping out and sleeping on cots in cultured style.

Of course certain amenities were provided. A couple of wooden structures, set somewhat apart, housed the toilets. Every here and there throughout the Chautauqua grounds were water pipes protruding from the ground, each crowned with a faucet. Attached to the faucet by a chain was a tin cup for communal use. We must have been a community of reasonably healthy people; I don't recall that there were any outbreaks of epidemics resulting from these primitive drinking arrangements.

One summer our family and the Gillams joined forces and had a big square tent, divided by a canvas partition into two "rooms." It was called Camp Tarryabit, a name devised (of course) by my mother, and one that was not always quite clear to passers-by. I remember, too, that a group of original young ladies had a tent nearby which they christened The Humdrum Club, a locale for chafing-dish suppers and jolly times. (Does anyone today know what a chafing dish was?)

Today, on a bulletin board over my desk at home, I have pinned up a ten-cent stamp issued in 1974. Across the top of the stamp are the words "Rural America," below which is depicted a scene so truly reminiscent of my childhood as to evoke strong feelings of nostalgia every time I look at it. There is the Chautauqua tent, and behind it a house, obviously at the edge of town, and the town water tower. People are going into the tent, above the entrance to which is a sign bearing the word "Chautauqua," while in the foreground is a long rail to which are hitched horses and buggies. At the bottom of the stamp is the legend "Chautauqua 1874–1974." But our Chautauqua suffered its demise long before 1974; I think it was sometime in the twenties. By then the cinema and radio had taken over.

Small-town pride and rivalries were part of the picture as well. In my young years I was envious of the fact that the people of Clarinda, the town of my birth, had a much more sophisticated Chautauqua set-up than we did; theirs was a permanent auditorium that was in effect a large roof supported by steel pillars and beams—open on the sides—and rows of little wooden cabins for the people attending. But the natural setting wasn't so nice as was ours, and that was a source of satisfaction. It seemed to me that the Clarindians may have behaved in a way superior to those of us in Maryville, because even though the two towns were only thirty miles apart they were separated by a state line, above which in Iowa freedom always had reigned while below in Missouri there had once been slavery. The days of slavery in Missouri had of course vanished a half-century before the time of which I am writing; even so I remember one very old lady in town who had once been a slave.

Another event that brought some of the townspeople together, although this was a one-time affair and not an annually recurring happening as were the fair and the Chautauqua, was a so-called religious revival that took place when I was about ten years old. For some reason the white Protestant churches, five of them, got together and sponsored a preacher to hold revival services in a large tent on a vacant lot in town, and for a week or two this caused considerable excitement among certain elements of the population. There were two large Catholic churches in town, and two small black churches, and these were not invited to participate in the proceedings—the Catholic churches because the priests certainly would not even have considered such a possibility, and the black churches because in that day and in that ethnic climate they were conveniently ignored.

The revivalist and his wife were established in the Wilson house down at the end of our block, where they lived in moderately high style and made incessant demands on their hosts and neighbors. Our family immediately recognized the visitors for the charlatans they were, but ours being a small community where contacts could not be avoided, we were constrained to tolerate the preacher and his wife as best we could.

I think I went to one of the revival meetings, which was something of a show, and that was enough for me; I remember my father being quite disgusted with the antics of the man up on the rostrum. Those were the days when the famous Billy Sunday was in the twilight of his career, and I suppose the revival minister, if so he might be called, was trying to carry on the Billy Sunday style in his own small way. At any rate, he ripped and howled, and people got religion and went forward to be saved or redeemed or otherwise washed pure of their sins. In our little farming community sins were generally of the minor sort, so all of the exhortations and grandstand displays put on by the preacher were obviously not very sincere or convincing. That is, not to some people in town. Yet a sort of frenzy ran through the crowd at times, so that individuals and groups of people, even bands of high school youngsters, stood up to proclaim themselves as "saved" and furthermore to pledge considerable sums of money (for them) to the minister. Whatever became of the funds so promised, I do not know.

I only know that I was a bit envious of my Catholic friends who did not have to acknowledge themselves as clan members, so to speak, of people behaving in such ways.

Years later, when I had left home and was embarking upon my career, I thought that perhaps the people of America had grown up, that such things as I have described were fading into history. But within recent years it is all being repeated on television, on a scale of colossal proportions. The TV ministers rant and howl and reveal themselves for the charlatans they are, yet millions of citizens pour billions of dollars into the coffers of the TV ministry. These modern practitioners of an art, so uproariously portrayed by Mark Twain in the person of the Duke and the Dauphin in *Huckleberry Finn*, are even courted and encouraged today by people in high political places. It is all very discouraging to an old man.

Maryville had its contingent of Civil War veterans, including "Uncle Joe" Jackson, still an active banker who stumped around on one good leg and one artificial limb that substituted for the leg that had been his when he went to war to save the Union. And old "Daddy Foster," a Confederate veteran, who had one good eye and one deadlight, another war casualty.

Once a year, on the Sunday nearest to Memorial Day, or Decoration

Day as we called it, the Civil War veterans in a body would attend one of the churches, many of the men wearing remnants of their blue uniforms (they were mostly Union men) and their campaign hats. I remember one occasion when they attended the Presbyterian church to which my parents belonged, and I think there must have been thirty or forty of the old men—some bent and infirm, others straight and full of life. That Sunday was perhaps about fifty years after Appomattox, so some of the veterans might have been still in their late sixties or early seventies.

In those days I seemed always to be having bright ideas of an impractical nature. One of them was my ostrich suit. I took a broomstick and wrapped it with cloth, and fashioned an ostrich head of sorts at one end. Then I rigged up a covering for myself out of an old gunny sack, with side feathers and a tail made out of rags. Having donned the outfit, I seemed to think that I bore some resemblance to an ostrich—for what reason it is hard to say.

One evening I thought I would put on my suit and cross the street and entertain the two little Yeoman children, who lived in the house opposite ours. So I did. I walked down our long front walk in stately ostrich style, crossed the street, and then went up the front steps that led to the Yeoman house, where the family was sitting on the front porch. As soon as I got close, the Yeoman kids set up a terrified howl, a reaction that I had not in the least anticipated. I was so disconcerted that I tried to back off, whereupon I tumbled down the concrete steps and landed on the sidewalk, mashing the beak of the ostrich and ruining my dignity no little bit. It was an ignominious retreat back to our house, and I think that was about the end of the ostrich.

For several years, before, during, and after the First World War, I enjoyed the company and the proximity of the McPherron boys, who lived just around the corner from us. The McPherrons constituted a large family, most of them considerably older than I was. But the two youngest boys, Edwin and Ora, particularly Ora, came more or less within my age bracket. (Edwin was as a matter of fact a little too old to be much of a companion, although I did wander about with him now and then.) But it was Ora, the youngest of the McPherron tribe, with whom I spent many boyhood hours. Ora was always known to us as Little Mac to distinguish him from Edwin, who was Big Mac. Little Mac was a solidly built lad, somewhat larger than I, yet all in all we were very compatible.

Little Mac was always full of ideas, and that made him a lot of fun. He was always building little boats. He built a cannon, consisting of a piece of gas pipe nailed to a heavy block of wood. One end of the pipe was solidly plugged up, and near this end he filed a notch so that it communicated with the interior of the pipe. He would partially fill the pipe with gunpowder, ram a piece of wadding in to hold the powder, and then sprinkle a little powder on top of the pipe so that it dribbled down through the notch. Then we would get set to jump back, Little Mac would touch a match to the loose powder, and before we could retreat more than half a step the cannon would detonate with a loud and very satisfying roar, sailing into the air and turning a couple of somersaults as it fired. That furnished a sort of diversion for idle moments.

But Little Mac's masterpiece was his bean thresher. Before moving into the house near us the McPherrons had lived on a farm, so Little Mac was acquainted with farm machinery. He understood the principle of a threshing machine, so he decided that we should build a small-sized version, to take the hulls off beans or peas. It consisted of a frame, within which was arranged the head of a croquet mallet, studded with nails, the heads of which had been filed off, and mounted on a horizontal axle, driven through its long dimension. The idea was that the croquet mallet, when driven by a pulley attached to one end of its axle, would go around and around, the array of rotating nails making a formidable shredding device. Beneath the croquet mallet was a movable screen, operated by an eccentric, so that it shook back and forth. The screen was tilted, and beneath it was a box, while at its end was another box. A large grindstone was set in place, and aligned with the pulley on the croquet mallet. A heavy cord was passed around the grindstone and around the pulley, and made tight. Then the grindstone was turned and things happened: the mallet went around and around at high speed, the screen shook back and forth, and the whole contraption made a wonderful lot of noise. We would feed the beans or peas into a hopper (which I should have mentioned) placed above the croquet mallet, the vegetables would fall down and get shredded, the unencased beans would drop on to the shaking screen and fall through its meshes to the box below, while the shredded hulls would be shaken down the tilted screen to drop into the other box. That was the theory. In practice, bean hulls flew right and left, and many beans would end up in the trash box instead of where they belonged. Then we would have to pick over the dump, as it were, to rescue the errant legumes. Nevertheless we had a lot of fun shelling beans or peas for our mothers, and it probably didn't take more than twice as long as if we had done it by hand.

In such a setting we developed our own sports. There were no formal playgrounds, but there were lots of back-lot baseball and football games, not to mention shinny, which was a form of field hockey, generally played with homemade sticks, and a tin can for the puck. In the winter we played shinny on the ice on Hasting's pond.

Hasting's pond was a small, man-made pond occupying a natural depression in some fields a little to the north of town. It was on the property of one of the town dairies, and during the day it was a place where the cows went to drink. It was also the place where we went to swim, and when I think back I sometimes have the horrors at the recollection of it. The water was very muddy (all ponds and streams in that part of Missouri were muddy) and much of the time in the summer the surface of the pond was largely covered with nasty-looking green algae. But that didn't matter; we would push the algae back out of the way and go right in to swim and cavort in the water, while the cows at the edge of the pond eyed us with bovine placidity. Often the cows, standing belly-deep in the water, would add their excrement and urine to the pond. Evidently the foul water wasn't foul enough to damage us; we all survived. And that was where I learned how to swim. The owners of the dairy were very tolerant about letting us swim there in the summer, and skate there in the winter. So Hasting's pond was quite an institution.

In the winter we enjoyed sliding along the streets on our sleds. There was no such thing as street sweeping or snow plowing, so that in midwinter many of the streets had good coverings of snow, packed down by the traffic, by horses and wagons, by sleighs, and by such cars as were being used at that season of the year. One of our favorite sports was to hook the lead rope of a sled around a back bumper (if the car had a bumper) or, failing that, a back spring, and get towed around town. This was sometimes done with the permission of the driver, and as often as not without permission. Which made it a somewhat risky sport. One could hitch on to a car, and get towed half-way across town, sometimes without the driver ever being aware that his car had some hangers-on in the rear.

One boy in town named Red Sells (believe it or not) had two or three big dogs that he trained to pull his sled. I always envied him for that, and one time I tried to hitch the Gillam collie, Buster, to my sled. I thought, for the purpose of training, it would be a good idea to start Buster on a gentle hill, namely the Seventh Street hill in front of our house. So I devised a harness for Buster and hitched it to my sled, pointed Buster down the hill, and then jumped on the sled for a ride. Buster leisurely started to trot down the hill, but then the sled with me on it caught up with him and banged his heels. That made Buster take a spurt, pulling the sled after him, but soon he slowed down, and was again cracked in the heels by the front of the sled. In this manner we proceeded down the hill, with Buster alternately pulling and getting hit by the sled. It wasn't a very successful experiment; Buster never became a sled dog.

The Price boys in town had a long sled, to which they attached a motor wheel. In those days motor wheels were manufactured to be attached to bicycles, thus converting the bike into a sort of primitive moped. The wheel had a little engine attached to it; it was a self-contained unit. So it worked admirably as a sled propellor, and the Price boys put-putted around town in grand style.

The big gathering place for coasting was the Sixth Street hill, just a block from our house. There one could start at Market Street, and go zooming down past Vine, past Dewey Street, and for a couple of blocks beyond. Needless to say, nobody attempted to drive any kind of a vehicle on that hill when the snow was in good supply. So all day, when things were right, there would be great crowds coasting down Sixth Street, on all kinds of sleds—kids yelling, young ladies shrieking, and the inevitable dogs bounding along and barking at the tops of their lungs. It was a great place for bobsleds. These were homemade affairs—a long, heavy plank mounted on two sleds, fore and aft. The front sled was pivoted beneath the front end of the plank, and it was the duty of one person to steer that sled, either with his or her feet, or by lying face down on the plank and steering with the hands. The other occupants of the sled would sit in close sequence along the length of the plank. Of course with all of its weight the bobsled would develop great and sometimes frightening speed by the time it was half-way down the hill, and then it was the duty of the steersman to keep it on course. Any slight deviation to right or left would frequently tip the sled over, spilling its occupants in noisy disarray along the side of the street. But it was all good fun, and nobody got hurt, at least not badly.

It was not only snow and sledding that at times closed certain streets to traffic. Every now and then a street fair would come along and, with the permission of the city fathers and merchants (for a goodly fee, no doubt), occupy several blocks of the business section of town. In those days the closing of some streets to traffic was not any great matter; there just wasn't that much traffic. Or to put it in another way, we weren't the complete slaves to the automobile that we are today.

So booths and amusement rides, generally a Ferris wheel and a small merry-go-round, would be set up, and for two or three days and evenings the streets became malls, crowded with people on foot. That was when the Popcorn Man did a thriving business.

The Popcorn Man was a regular town fixture. He was a rather corpulent and florid individual, who through the summer operated a popcorn wagon at the corner of Main and Third streets. The wagon was parked there all summer, and the Popcorn Man was parked next to it on a wooden chair. The popcorn wagon was small, moderately resplendent, and efficient. It was enclosed in glass, and within its interior a toaster was constantly at work, heated by a small flame, emanating from a kerosene or perhaps an alcohol burner. The popped corn formed a white mound in one end of the glass enclosure, and when a customer would come to be served the Popcorn Man would scoop the freshly popped kernels into a paper bag, receiving in turn a nickel as his reward. It was a pleasant institution.

I don't suppose the Popcorn Man could be classed as a "character," but there were characters, those individuals who depart somewhat from the norm, as there always have been in any community. In large cities characters go unnoticed for the most part, but in little towns they stand out in strong relief. I don't remember many of the town characters, perhaps because most of them were not very eccentric.

One that I do recall was the manager of the Fern Theater, a little movie house in a converted store on the south side of the Courthouse Square. His principal eccentricity, if so it can be called, was to come out in front of the theater about five minutes before show time and with the aid of a large megaphone shout out the current show bill. Those were the days before electronic loudspeakers, but he had a voice that could be heard all over the center of town. What he was hollering about usually was not very clear, but to the initiated it was evident that the show was about to begin.

The show was in black and white and it was silent, as were all moving pictures in those days. It was projected from a booth up near the ceiling in the back of the long, narrow room, and it was projected by a stolid employee standing by the projector and turning the machine with a hand crank. Since there was only one projector there were short intermissions between reels, when the audience sat patiently, waiting for the continuation of the show. Down in front, on the right side of the room, was a player piano, and there another employee sat, pumping out music to go along with the film. It was all very primitive, but in principle not so very far removed from the great, ornate movie houses in the large cities.

There, also, the pictures were in black and white and they were accompanied by music. But the music was supplied by a well-trained orchestra or by an organist performing on the mighty Wurlitzer. In many of the metropolitan movie theaters the orchestra and the organ alternated, an hour on and an hour off for each, and of course they chose music to fit the mood of the film. Such theaters had several motor-driven projectors in the booth, so there were no pauses between reels.

The Empire Theater in Maryville was not a great, ornate moving picture theater but it was a theater, constructed in the days before movies had appeared on the scene. So it had a stage with all of the back-stage equipment, and it had a properly constructed auditorium, including a balcony at the back. Of course in my young days the fare at the Empire was principally motion pictures, but on occasions there were stage productions by local amateurs, or by a traveling stock company.

At the Empire there was also piano music to accompany the film, but rather than being cranked out in a mechanical way it was furnished by a pianist, who as in the big houses could choose music to suit the mood of the film, more or less.

Often, when I think back to life in a small midwestern town, more than seven decades ago, I hear the sound of bells. There were no factories in our town, with the whistles that go along with factories, and so the bells of the several churches announced the beginning of the day, noontide, and day's end, or rather the hour between work time and evening time. As I recall, the bells rang at seven in the morning, at noon, and at five in the afternoon. They were pleasant sounds.

They didn't come all at once, because all of the bells were rung by hand, and evidently the watches of the church sextons were not exactly coordinated. Since there were five Protestant churches, two Catholic churches, a chapel at the Catholic hospital, and two black churches, the chorus of bells was varied. No church had more than one bell, but the total effect, especially when several of the churches were ringing together, made for music of a kind on the air. And although the bells rang independently, they almost all of them had a pattern. For each bell there were three rings, a pause, three more rings, another pause, again three rings and still another pause, and then the bell would ring continuously, very generally nine times. All except the chapel bell, which from across town generally came in rather faintly after the other bells were through, and rang only the three times three pattern. After which the hours passed silently, except for the clock in the courthouse tower, which announced the time, day and night, with the appropriate number of strokes.

There was one other bell, the fire bell. When it rang it rang frantically, and we knew that something was happening.

The fire house was only about three blocks from our home, so that its alarm came to us loud and clear. It was a volunteer fire force, but there was always a man on duty at the fire station (I suppose he was a regular paid city employee) ready to ring the bell, which was in a little cupola on the roof of the fire house, and harness the horses. There were two horses, Tom and Jerry, housed in separate stalls at the back of the fire house, where they stored up energy on an ample diet of oats and hay. In front of the stalls was the engine, a hose-and-ladder wagon. And in front of the engine, on each side of the wagon tongue, which as I recall was supported in front by an X-shaped fork standing on the floor, were the two sets of harness, suspended from the ceiling. When the fire engine was called, the driver (I suppose after ringing the bell) would lead or direct Tom and Jerry out to their places, and with a tug of a release rope the two sets of harness would drop into place. A few buckles would be snapped, and then out of the door the horses and the engine would come, with a sharp swing into the street, and then down the street at a full run, the steel tires rattling over the brick pavement. It was a grand sight—when I happened to be on hand to see it.

In the meantime the various firemen would have been alerted by electric bells, conveniently installed in their homes and their business establishments, whereupon these dedicated volunteers would rush to their phones to find out the location of the fire. They would then join the dashing wagon, running out and leaping on if it happened to be passing their place of business, or their home, or following it to the fire, by car or by foot. And you may be sure that if it were a Saturday or Sunday or a summer day—anytime that school was out—there would be a raffish train of small boys following in the wake of the fire fighters. Thus the firemen and their accompanying cohorts would arrive, to do their doughty best to control and extinguish the fire.

The fire bell, with its wild clangor, was one means of communication whereby the town was instantly informed of an impending calamity, happily something that usually did not amount to much, although sometimes the fire might become serious. I will never forget the bitterly cold winter night when one side of the town square went up in flames. I heard the commotion just before it was time for me to go to bed, and almost at the same time my parents received a telephone call from a neighbor to tell us that the town was on fire. So I bundled up and ran to the courthouse square where I stood and shivered with hundreds of other spectators and watched the fire leap up and spread, and with horrified fascination saw roofs collapse and walls come down. No one was hurt, but the damage was great for a small town.

The telephone, too, was one of our methods of communication, at least within the town and its immediate vicinity. Long-distance calls in those days were difficult, almost but not quite impossible. Radio communication was still in the future, and television had not even been thought of. Therefore we kept in touch with the outside world (and our local community as well) largely by means of newspapers. Many people in town received the *Kansas City Star* and the *Kansas City Times* every day, as well as the St. Joseph papers, and even for some the St. Louis papers. But the old reliables for the town and the surrounding region were the local newspapers.

Today it would be almost unheard of for a little town of five thousand population to enjoy *two daily* newspapers, but such was the case in Maryville. There was the *Democrat-Forum*, the name of which reveals its political preference, and there was the *Tribune*, the Republican sheet. I was intimately acquainted with the *Forum* for quite a few years, first as a paperboy and later as the reporter of high school news. When I was a paperboy during the First World War, it was my responsibility to show up at the Forum building about four o'clock in the afternoon—after school during the school months and at the tail end of a summer's day during vacation, when it was hard to cut short the delightful pastimes in which I was engaged—to make the rounds of a paper route.

The paperboys would all assemble to wait for papers to be given out, and then they would all disperse to make their deliveries. The boy who had the largest route would get the first allotment of papers; he with the smallest route was last on the list. I was second in the line of rotation.

Sometimes the papers were ready when we assembled in the back room of the building where the press and other machinery were located. But more often than not the process of printing was still under way, so we would have to hang around for a while to await our turns. Waiting there was never boring; indeed, it was a part of our education.

There was a flat-bed press, a far cry from the modern continuous rotary presses. During the earlier part of the day the linotype men, at two machines, would have composed the news items. These would have been edited and corrected, and then, together with advertising copy and half-tones, all in the form of lead type and blocks, would have been locked together in "forms," assembled on heavy composing tables. I used to admire Ursel Crockett, the boss printer, because he could stand at the composing table and read the locked-in type (all backwards, of course) as rapidly as I could read from a book. Then the heavy forms would be placed on the flat bed of the press, each form oriented in its proper position; the pressman would climb up on a high platform from which elevated position he would feed the large sheets of paper into the press. Each sheet would be picked up by a big roller, to be rolled against the type bed that was moving back and forth on its tracks. After the sheets were all printed on one side they would be hoisted upside down to the top of the press, the old forms would be removed from the bed to be replaced by a new set of forms, and the process would be repeated. The result: huge sheets of news stock printed on both sides.

Then these sheets went to the folder, operated by Mr. Jones. He fed them one by one into the machine, which had blades that went up and down, down as each sheet reached a position beneath each particular blade, thus folding and chopping the paper on its route through the machine. The final result was an eight-page newspaper, ready to be sent on its way.

That is where we picked up our papers and started on our individual journeys, all of us traveling by bicycle. I had a route of between seventy and eighty customers out on the west side of town, and I usually covered it in about an hour's time. Some of the paper boys liked to dawdle along, but I always wanted to get it over with as soon as possible.

Then on Saturday mornings I used to go to all of the houses on my route to make the weekly collection; ten cents from each customer, six cents for the paper, four cents for me. It added up to about three dollars or so a week for me, in other words about fifty cents a day for an hour's work (not counting the waiting time). I suppose it wasn't too bad in that day and age.

The First World War came to our town when I was in the final weeks of my sixth-grade year. Of course it had been looming over America with a threatening cloud for a year or two previous to the spring of 1917, but there was a widespread if not universal hope that our country would not be involved in the conflict. I can remember the presidential campaign of 1916, when Woodrow Wilson, basically a man of peace, ran on a platform that stated, among other things, "he kept us out of war." Eventually he did not; the war inevitably overwhelmed us.

The first two years of the war, which I do remember with a good deal of clarity, seemed very far away from our little town in the center of the nation. In fact, the possibility of a war seemed most unreal in those early days of 1914. I can remember some friends of my parents coming to visit at our house shortly before the war, having just returned from a rather extended trip to Europe, and I still recall most vividly how the husband of this couple told my parents in vehement tones that "Europe was a powder keg, ready to explode." Or words to that effect. And my father just laughed at him, the whole premise being too unreal to be believed—at least out in the Middle West.

Then on a bleak February afternoon of 1917 my mother came home from downtown feeling very depressed; she had just heard that the United States had broken off diplomatic relations with Germany. That didn't mean anything to me, and I could not understand why she would feel so low. So she sat down and explained the matter to me, and she told me she felt sad because my two brothers probably would be in the war. That is exactly what happened.

My eldest brother, Herschel, at the time a newspaper reporter in Chicago, had been a four-year ROTC cadet at the University of Missouri. He immediately volunteered for the first officer's training camp, and at the end of the summer came out of his training as a captain in the army. My small bosom was filled with pride.

My other brother, Philip, was at the time an engineering student at the Missouri School of Mines. He tried to volunteer, but was not successful in that effort, and eventually was caught by the draft. He hoped that he could serve in the Corp of Engineers, but the army in its infinite wisdom made him a hospital orderly in the Medical Corps, and there he served usefully but against his will. He had the traumatic experience of watching men die around him, right and left, during the terrible influenza epidemic that swept across the world during the last year of the war.

In the spring of 1918 Herschel wrote to my parents informing them that he was about to receive orders to go to France, and he would like my mother to come to Camp Bowie, in Texas, so they might have a visit before he left. (Father was pinned down at home by his teaching schedule.) She replied that she could not leave me; Herschel answered telling her to bring me along; he would pay my way. And that is how I went to Texas, for a memorable two-week trip.

Herschel was an instructor in the officer's training school at Camp Bowie, on the edge of Fort Worth. He found us a room in a house nearby, in a little suburb that had been engulfed by the huge cantonment, and there I saw at first hand something of the preparations for war. Men were marching and drilling all around us, the air echoed with bugle calls, and one could hear rifle fire in the distance. On several occasions Herschel arranged for my mother and me to eat with him in the officers' mess, which was a very formal affair. But more particularly I enjoyed eating with Herschel's orderly, a young fellow named Scott, at the enlisted men's mess.

One day there was to be a sham battle, at which the officers' candidates would be in charge. Herschel and the other instructors went along as observers, and I accompanied my big brother. We marched through a hot morning along a dusty Texas road, and within an hour or so we were all white, like ghosts, having been covered by the white dust (derived from Cretaceous marine sediments) kicked up by the feet of the marching columns. Suddenly as we were passing through a grove of trees shots rang out and everybody scrambled for cover and began returning the fire. We had been ambushed. The firing went on for a while, and then our "enemies" came running across the grass at us in a spirited charge. After which both sides sat down on the ground, and were given a review by the instructors of the past proceedings and the tactics that had been used, right and wrong. Then the combatants joined forces and marched back to camp. P.S. Herschel never got to France; he was considered too valuable as an instructor of officers ("ninety-day wonders") to be withdrawn from that activity.

When I got back home I was the envy of my young peers, having such tales to recount. Yet even in Maryville there were war-related tasks, and since I was then a Boy Scout I became involved. For example, I went around ringing door bells in a Liberty Bond drive, and subsequently got a bronze medal for my efforts. On one occasion we, the Scouts, roamed through the wood lots around Maryville, measuring black walnut trees. This was part of an inventory of wood suitable for airplane construction in the days when planes were made of wood and canvas.

Finally the war came to an end. There was the "false armistice" on November 8, 1918, when a rumor spread like wildfire across the land that the fighting was over. In our town the bells began ringing at all of the churches, and the citizens rushed to the Courthouse Square, yelling and making noise with all sorts of noisemakers, including shotguns, of which there were many. There had been no time to get blank shells, so as I ran around the courthouse grounds with my friends I could feel the shot pellets falling out of the air, all around us and on us.

Then we learned that it was a false alarm, and the crowd dejectedly dispersed and people went to their homes. The real armistice came three days later and it was something of an anticlimax. There was a sort of impromptu parade downtown and everything was proper and relatively quiet.

That was the year when I was in the eighth grade, and the next autumn, of 1919, I started my high school education. It was at the town high school, a few blocks from our house. The first few days in my new environment were stressful and unhappy; gone were the intimacy and the freedom of the training school out on the spacious Normal campus, here was the pressure felt from many strangers, and particularly from the upper-class students, who took it upon themselves to make the poor "freshies" feel put down. I suffered under the added disadvantage of being the smallest of all the freshmen, indeed the smallest boy in high school. It wasn't much fun at the time, but soon I grew out of this lowly status.

I suppose it was in high school that my teachers began to have a close personal influence upon me, perhaps in part because each teacher taught a single subject so that I, like my fellow pupils, became intimately involved with the subject and the instructor, and perhaps in part because I was old enough to feel and enjoy the give and take with my instructors.

When I was a senior in high school the school year book had the following comment about me. "Ned Colbert, Slang Slinger. When it comes to spoofing the teachers, I'm there." I don't recall that I spoofed the teachers, but I suppose that such must have been the case. Nor am I aware of having been a slang slinger, although even in my young high school years I loved words and I liked colorful language and I did read a lot. Consequently English was always an interesting subject for me, and luckily I was blessed with a most excellent English teacher. Laura Hawkins was a small, very cheerful, rather bouncy middle-aged lady when I spent four years in her English classes, and I think she was a real force in making my predilection for the language an ongoing and permanent part of my life. (To anticipate briefly, I continued with English courses in college and university, the net result being that I wound up my undergraduate studies with English as my major.)

Miss Hawkins made English interesting in many ways. I remember once that she asked us to produce a narrative poem, if possible modeled after "The Diverting History of John Gilpin" by William Cowper, so I came up with a poem about the time the Fannon's cow got loose, and the efforts of Bill Fannon and me and some other boys to round her up and get her back in her pen. It made a diverting story, and certainly was appreciated by an amused Miss Hawkins.

She was the high school teacher who looms largest in my memory. Another interesting teacher was Mr. Burford, who taught a class in sociology, and made me aware of some of the problems in our modern society, about which I had heretofore been unaware. Another teacher always to be remembered was Miss Perry, who conducted us through the difficult, thorny thickets of Latin. Most of the other teachers were of the usual, garden-variety kind, who labored conscientiously to hammer some learning into the thick skulls of their charges.

The sociological problems that Mr. Burford told us about (he had studied at Columbia in New York City) revealed to me various aspects of human society that seemed strange and distressing. I think high school students in those days, some sixty-five years ago, were more innocent than are the students of today, just as that was as compared to modern times an age of innocence. And in a little backwater like northwestern Missouri the innocence was hardly disturbed by the sins of the city, even though Kansas City, throughout its history anything but a town of impeccable morals and practices, was less than a hundred miles away.

One aspect of my high school career that might be mentioned again at this place was my appointment as school reporter for the *Democrat-Forum.* Just how this came about I do not recall; perhaps my assumption of the post was brought about by a recommendation from some member of the high school faculty. However that may be, it was my task during my last high school year to keep my eyes and ears open and to write up my perceptions of newsworthy happenings in the classrooms and corridors, on the playing field, and in the gymnasium. I received a small stipend and some useful experience for my labors.

My friend Townsend Godsey, also a senior, had a similar post on the *Tribune.* So the two of us were for some months engaged in a friendly rivalry in our efforts to write stories about daily and weekly events at the school. Among other things we reported the sports events; I recall our attending the games together and sitting side by side while we kept scores and made notes on which to base our reports.

None of this amounted to much; however it did put me in the front office of the paper where, a few years previously, I had frequented the back of the shop, waiting for my allotment of papers to be delivered to the customers on my route. And it did give me a little practical experience not only in using the language but also in having my use of the language subjected to a critical editorial eye.

During my high school years and after, I became the chief caretaker and gardener at our home. We had a large front yard, as has already been mentioned, and even larger grounds behind the house, so the upkeep of this property was no small task. By that time my father had reached an age at which he no longer felt like putting in long, hard hours behind a lawn mower or at the upper end of a hoe, so I was nominated to take over. To tell the truth I rather enjoyed the work, especially during the long summer holiday; it kept me busy every morning. Mowing the lawn was a half-day's work, especially with the old, motorless hand-pushed mower that was ours, and the other half days of the week were busily spent in the back area, weeding, trimming, and doing the other jobs that go along with a vegetable garden. There was a strawberry patch, and that required picking berries every day in season. Particularly there was the feeling of accomplishment—of planting in the springtime, of nurturing the plants, and of harvesting the small crops as they ripened. My father paid me a small stipend for this work, and such money was doubly appreciated. Potatoes, tomatoes, corn, beans, peas, asparagus—we did enjoy fresh and delicious food.

At this stage of my life I did not spend much time with the girls of my acquaintance; perhaps I was shy or perhaps I was not quite ready for dating and other boy-girl activities. Perhaps I was something of a misanthrope, for I certainly did not like parties. My interests were with other things, particularly with the natural world, as will be told. At any rate, Esther Roseberry next door and I went our own ways as we grew up, although we always remained good friends. Our long association as little children made us feel like siblings, as has been said, and perhaps that was enough.

Among the activities that occupied part of my time, thus diverting my attention from young female society, there was wood-working. I did enjoy working with wood in a rough-and-ready, practical way; I never did go in for fine cabinet work. So I made things to use around the house and in the yard. One of my prize productions during the summer following my graduation from high school was a large and fairly elaborate marten house, to be placed in our back yard. After it was finished I got from the lumber yard what amounted to a telephone pole, smoothed it, painted it, and fastened the marten house to one end. Then with help from several friends the pole, with the house on top, was raised into a vertical position and its lower end was set securely in a deep hole in the ground. Even before the house had attained its final position in the sky some martens appeared and began to inspect it, much to our pleasure. For several years after that, indeed until after I had permanently left my boyhood home, there was a colony of martens in our backyard every summer, filling the air with their sounds and clearing this same air of many flying insects.

To go back just a few years, the marten house reminds me of another aerial domicile. This was an abandoned chicken coop that in my late grade school years I decided to put up on four long poles, to make a sort of tree house, without a tree. So I got some long willow trees of fair size down by a stream outside of town, hauled them home, set them in the ground, built a platform and raised the chicken house to rest upon the platform. How I accomplished this last task I do not remember. At any rate this served as a sort of clubhouse, reached by a rope ladder, until one stormy night several years later the wind took it down with a mighty crash. By then the bases of the supports had become rotten.

Such is the picture of a small boy's life as lived almost three-quarters of a century ago. It was in many ways a simple life, much more simple in terms of external influences than what is experienced by most children growing up today, and being simple it was perhaps a less stressful life than are the lives of today's youngsters. Of particular significance to me was the fact that it was a life dominantly rural, even though my own milieu was that of a small town. The woods and the fields were not far away, and very probably it was this proximity of the natural world that had much to do with the course my life was to take.

IV

Captain

During those years when I lived in the house on Seventh Street there generally were dogs around the place, and part of the time there were cats, too. My first memory is of Dandy, a water spaniel that belonged to my brother Phil, but that memory is vague. Then there was Buljer, a boxer of sorts, that came into my life when I was in bed with one of my frequent bouts of illness. Buljer was with us for a year or two and then disappeared. After that there was Schneider, the dachshund, who lived a happy life in our house until he was prematurely dispatched by that passing car.

After Schneider came Mike, the vagabond cairn terrier who adopted us as his guardians. Mike was a real character who decided to become the mascot of the students out at the Normal. Mike would go to school in the morning, spend his time visiting classes or chasing squirrels out on the campus, and then come home to our house in the evening. He had some original habits of his own. His procedure for bathing in a pail of water was something to behold; he would jump in head first, and if he could manage to back out without tipping over the bucket he would try to get in tail first. Usually this maneuver would tip the bucket on its side; never mind, he had managed to get reasonably wet. I remember once walking to the Normal with Mike accompanying me, and when we got opposite the Mutz house (one of several Mutz households in town) he spied a pail of water in the back yard, placed beneath a line of laundry. He began his ablutions, at which point Mr. Mutz came out of the back door. Mike's antics amused Mr. Mutz so completely that he sat on the back steps and roared with laughter. This brought Mrs. Mutz out, by which time Mike was standing beneath the clean laundry and shaking himself, to spray the clothes with left-over bathwater. Mrs. Mutz was not amused; she took after Mike with a broom.

Mike met his end by drinking lead arsenate spray that was being used on trees on the campus; he thought the white stuff was milk, and drank deeply before anybody could stop him. The students put up a box on campus with a sign "For the love of Mike" on it and collected a sum sufficient to purchase a little tombstone, suitably engraved, and placed it at the head of Mike's grave on the campus. It is still there.

Then there was Buster, a gentle collie that belonged to Forrest Gillam, but who spent much of his time with me after Forrest left home to attend the University of Missouri. Eventually Buster died, and needless to say that depressed me. For a year or so I was without a dog. Then one winter day during my freshman year in high school, Mrs. Robinson, one of my mother's friends, called to say that they had a new litter of puppies at their house and I could have one if I so desired. I was thrilled at the prospect.

On the following Sunday afternoon I put on my good clothes and went to the Robinson house, across town, to choose a puppy. Paul Diss (of whom, more later) went with me, and my friend Townsend Godsey also appeared on the scene. The Robinsons lived in a large, white Federal-style house with tall, two-story pillars across the front (Mr. Robinson was one of the town's leading bankers) so my future dog was born in affluent circumstances. We went to the front door, and after being ushered inside we were taken to the basement by Mr. and Mrs. Robinson. There was the new mother, a white fox terrier, with four puppies. Three of the pups were predominantly black, one was white, a nice Mendelian ratio. I chose one of the black puppies, and Townsend Godsey chose the white one. Paul Diss already had a dog, so he was not in the running.

A few weeks later I went to collect my dog, and I carried him home, warmly wrapped in an old blanket. He was a nicely marked little dog, black with a white chest, brown legs, and white paws. Throughout his life he had a somewhat raffish look by virtue of the fact that his right ear stood up like a banner, while his left ear was folded down. I had decided to name him Captain, after the big brother who had been an officer in the recent war. (I hope Herschel felt honored.) But Captain was a big name for a little dog, so he immediately became Cap. Cap, the last of my dogs, was quite a dog indeed.

The first night at our house he missed his mother, and he did cry a lot. But within a day or so he had accepted his new surroundings, and soon he was a member of the family. He grew into a lively and a remarkably intelligent dog with a very distinctive character all his own. He managed to make life interesting for me.

Terriers are notoriously courageous and scrappy dogs, and Cap must have been outstanding among terriers. When he first came to us we still had our old gray tomcat, Timothy, and Timothy did not take kindly to the new member of the household. There was an armed truce between the old cat and the new puppy, partly imposed by us, but it was a very uneasy truce. Then one day the truce was broken. For some reason Cap and Timothy did not agree; Cap backed Timothy up against the rear foundation of the house and they had a real sanguinary battle. Cap pushed the fight until in the end Timothy gave way and fled. Cap was terribly raked by Timothy's claws, but he had nonetheless won the contest. From that time on there was no question as to who was dominant, and from that time on Cap had a fierce hatred of cats. He would go after them with a will, and never mind the consequences. Most dogs do not like to get clawed, but that made no difference to Cap. (As a footnote I might add that Cap was fearless, except when it came to thunder. The awesome reverberations of a heavy thunderstorm were beyond his understanding. When the thunder began to roll he would scuttle upstairs and hide under a bed.)

I don't know how many battles Cap had with cats, but I was a witness to several interesting ones. One of Cap's accomplishments was climbing trees. If there was a fork within five feet or so of the ground Cap would make a run for it, and carried by the momentum of his rush would scramble up to the fork, to go on from there as best he could. By this technique he chased many a cat up a tree, much to the surprise and annoyance of the cat. One day Cap treed a big tom in a box elder near the Westfall house, the home of Marvin Westfall, one of my close companions during our high school years. It was a big tree with a fork conveniently near the ground, and two large limbs extending up in a sort of wide V from the fork. The cat went up one of these limbs, Cap got into the fork, and went up the limb after the cat. The cat turned around to face him and Cap came on, digging into the slanting limb as best he could with his claws. When he got near, balancing rather precariously, the cat gave Cap a terrible swipe in the face and knocked him out of the tree. Cap hit the ground with a thud, but he was not in the least discouraged. Up the tree he went again, and the cat, no doubt feeling very much outraged by such an arboreal dog, decided to scuttle into the high branches, safely out of reach. By that time I was able to get hold of Cap and escort him home.

There were some neighbors, named Hansen, down the street who had several fruit trees in the backyard. Every now and then Cap would chase a cat into one of the fruit trees, and then he would go up after it. The result usually was a stalemate. Cap would go as high as he could in the tree, from one fork to the next, and the cat would retreat above him. There they would be, Cap treebound and yapping at the cat and the cat high up and glaring down at Cap. I don't suppose such situations were especially conducive to the Hansen peace of mind.

It was not only cats that felt the sharp teeth of Cap; he also battled with other dogs, frequently and fiercely. As for cats, he surely fought them because he hated them, but as for dogs, I think much of his fighting was for the love of battle. If Cap had one dog fight in his life he must have had a thousand. And he was not in the least choosy about the dogs with which he fought; big or little he took on all of them. More often than not he came out the winner, because what he lacked in size he made up in determination and speed. Cap was incredibly fast; he would hit another dog like a small bolt of lightning and this gave him an initial advantage. Even dogs as large as German shepherds and collies commonly retreated from his onslaughts.

For example, there was a time when a large German shepherd and another dog that lived over on Main Street would join the postman as he made his daily rounds, and of course they would turn up at our house. If Cap saw them he would immediately attack, and would drive them away. Of course he was on his own territory, and that might have had something to do with his dominance over these two large rivals. But even without the territorial advantage I think he had them pretty well cowed.

One day, however, Phil was driving along Main Street with Cap in the seat of our open Dodge touring car. As Phil passed the adjoining residences of these two dogs Cap saw them, and out of the car he went, on the attack. But as he landed he rolled over and over in the street and banged his head on the curb, which of course stunned him. His erstwhile enemies saw their chance, so they lit into him and gave him a pretty good working-over before he was able to get to his feet. That didn't deter him in the least; the next time they appeared at our house he put them in their place.

It must not be thought that I stood idly by when Cap became involved in a fight with a cat or with another dog. I would try to jump in and break it up, but as anyone who has tried to stop a dog fight knows, the task is not easy. Dog and dog or dog and cat go around and around with tremendous energy, and one is hard put to try to get into the middle of things and separate the antagonists. It was especially difficult to break up Cap fights because he was so very fast and aggressive.

I remember one time I had the bright idea of making him a blanket to keep him warm during the winter, for he was a short-haired dog. The first day he wore it, he went over to Sixth Street with me, where all of the boys and girls were coasting. Within minutes Cap got entangled with a big collie, and that was the end of the blanket. Marve Westfall finally succeeded in breaking up the fight by whanging the collie on the back with his sled, while I grabbed Cap. I took him home, decorated with several long slashes from the collie's teeth and a very tattered blanket. Those slashes were only a few of the wounds with which Cap was decorated. Indeed, his body was covered with scars even before he had reached middle age, but he didn't mind; every scar was evidence of a rip-roaring fight, and that made him happy. I truly believe that Cap would rather fight than eat.

There was a time, when Cap was still a young dog, during which our *Kansas City Star* and *Times* were delivered every day by a couple of black boys. One day they rang the front door bell, and my mother went to answer it.

"Mrs. Colbert," one of them said, "did you get your dog from Jim Robinson?"

"Yes, that's so," said Mother.

"Well," said the boy, "we own the father of that dog. Could we bring him around tomorrow for a visit?"

Mother agreed. And the next day the two boys appeared, grinning happily and leading a dog that was the spitting image of Cap—or more properly, Cap was the image of that dog. They were brought together, and without further ado they went like furies at each other's throats. We all pitched in and by pulling and prying we finally got them separated.

Whereupon one of the Negro boys cuffed his dog on the head, saying, "Here, you act like that and I won't bring you around to see your little boy any more."

I had the feeling that neither the father nor the little boy was particularly thrilled to see each other.

Cap's fights were too numerous to remember, and they need not be catalogued at this place. I would like to mention, however, one pattern of dog relationships that prevailed in our neighborhood for a year or two, perhaps even longer. Eva Margaret Frank, who lived two houses east of us, had a little female terrier known as Brownie. And on the other side of the Frank house the Wilsons had a sort of nondescript dog with the rather unusual name (for a dog) of John. Every day, it seemed, Brownie would come out in front of her house and start to bark. What she said I do not know, but evidently it was something designed to stir up Cap and John. So in short order they would advance, one from the west, the other from the east, to where Brownie was yapping, and then there would be the very devil of a dog fight. That was exactly what Brownie was after. She would stand aside with a satisfied air, and watch the two victims of her machinations tear into each other. It worked every time.

So it went, week in and week out, and year after year. As long as I was at home I generally could cope with Cap's fights, but when I went away to the university, and for some years after that, as Cap got progressively older, it became increasingly difficult for my long-suffering parents to manage this aspect of Cap's life. Finally in desperation they had a collar made for him, studded with sharp spikes. That protected him, at a time of life when his reflexes had slowed down and his teeth had become blunt.

It was mentioned above that Cap jumped out of the car when he saw the two dogs that were his sworn enemies. That was not the only time that Cap left the car when it was in motion. The habit became almost chronic with him. He would ride standing on the seat, with his front paws on the side of the car seat (remember, it was an open car as most cars were in those days) and leaning out as far as he dared. So if he saw a dog or a cat or a rabbit by the road out he would go, hitting the ground and rolling over and over from the momentum. Why he wasn't killed or seriously injured I don't know; it must be said that Cap was a very tough little dog.

I had seen dogs that rode on the running boards of cars, so I thought I would train Cap to do this. At least it would not be so far to the ground if, to mix metaphors, he decided to abandon ship. So one day I put him on the running board of the car, on the driver's side, with a leash attached to his collar and, at the other end, secured to the stanchion or whatever it was called that helped to support the car top. I climbed in, took the wheel, and off we went. Everything was fine for a few hundred feet, and then Cap parted company with the running board. Of course he was fastened to the car by the leash, so he was dragged by the leash and came bumping along on his back, on his side, sometimes on his feet, before I got the car slowed to a stop. He was none the worse for wear, for as I have said, he was a very tough dog, but that was the end of my attempts to train him to running board riding.

Cap not only was tough, but also was strong and wiry, and very agile. He could run like the wind and jump like a deer. More than once I have seen him overtake a rabbit on the dead run, fling it up in the air as he grabbed it, and then be there to pounce upon it as it hit the ground. On one memorable occasion, however, he flushed a jackrabbit out in the country (jackrabbits were not common in our area) and that time the big hare left him far behind in the course of a hundred yards or so.

As for jumping, Cap was really something of a phenomenon for a dog his size. Many of the fences in our countryside were made of hog-proof wire; that is, they were of a large strong mesh to a level perhaps three feet above the ground. Above that there might be a strand or two of barbed wire. But such fences were no obstacle to Cap; he would sail over them with the greatest of ease. Indeed, it was beautiful to watch him take such a fence, clearing it with airy grace.

One autumn day I was out in the woods with Cap, and we came to such a fence that ran along the very edge of a little pond. The wind had brought down the autumn leaves on the pond so that it was completely covered; no water was visible and it looked like hard ground on the other side. As we came near the fence Cap took a run for it before I could stop him. I really don't know how I could have explained the situation to him in any case so I watched the sequence of events with interest and amused anticipation. Cap sailed over the fence in his usual style and then down he went with a tremendous splash. He came to the surface with a maple leaf draped across his nose, the most surprised dog in northwestern Missouri. I couldn't help laughing at him as he struck out for shore, so he gave me a reproachful look as he climbed out on dry land. He really did not like being laughed at.

But he loved praise, especially after he had done some of his tricks, or had shown off in some fashion. I built three hurdles, each about three feet in height, and it was no problem to train him to jump over them, one after the other. He liked to do that trick, especially if he had an appreciative audience. He would also climb a stepladder to its top, and then jump off through a hoop that I would hold in a strategic position. To add some class to these tricks he loved to wear a little hat that I had made for him, plus a pair of goggles, plus a corncob pipe held in his mouth. All in all he could put on quite a show.

He didn't need the hurdles and the ladder to put on a show. If we had guests in the evening, Cap would pester me to put on his hat and goggles and give him his corncob pipe. Thus attired and furnished, he would prance into the living room, arching his neck and cavorting and snorting. Everybody was supposed to praise him in extravagant terms; then with these accolades ringing in his ears he would retreat to the kitchen where I would divest him of his hat and goggles and pipe. After that he was satisfied; he would retire to a corner to sleep while the party proceeded.

Cap's activities were not confined to running and jumping, because he never hesitated to go underground if an opportunity presented itself. Being a terrier he loved to explore holes or dark places beneath buildings in the hopes of catching some underground creature. He would regularly work his way beneath our barn, where I would hear him yipping and scratching for all he was worth. Presently he would come out into the light of day, covered with dust and dirt, a cobweb across his face, and now and then a rat or a mouse in his jaws. He was what the farmers would call a good "ratter."

That was important to country people, because rats could be very destructive around a farm. One time when I was visiting my Grandfather Adamson in Holton, Kansas, a farmer stopped at the house and asked if Cap was a good rat dog. I assured the farmer that I thought he was. So the farmer proposed that I bring Cap out to his farm the next day, and he would pay me ten cents for every rat that Cap killed.

The next day I put Cap in our old Dodge car and drove out to the farm. The farmer had an outbuilding with a cement floor, in which he had stored a large pile of corncobs. He and I tied strings around the bottoms of our trouser legs to discourage rats from attempting those avenues of escape; then we each took a pitchfork and began to shift the cobs. Presently the rats started boiling out, and Cap was in his element. He dashed here and he dashed there, and he dispatched rats almost quicker than the eye could follow him. In the end I was able to collect something over two dollars for the joint effort. Everybody except the dead rats was happy; the farmer was free of some loathsome pests, Cap had had a wonderful time, and I had collected some money. With some of the proceeds I got Cap a special treat; I think it was some meat from the store.

Although Cap was good at catching rats, I don't think he ever succeeded in getting a squirrel. Not that he didn't try. He used to spend the long summer days stalking squirrels in the big yards of our neighborhood. He would ever so slowly and quietly approach a squirrel on the ground, but he never got quite close enough for success. At a critical point in the proceedings the squirrel would dash for the nearest tree, with Cap right on his tail. Up the tree the squirrel would go, with Cap running up the trunk as far as he could. Then the squirrel would perch on a convenient limb overhead, and proceed to bless Cap in strong squirrel language, while Cap would return the compliments in his own way. Finally, after what often seemed an interminable spell of barking, Cap would give up and slowly walk back to the house, swiftly turning around every few steps to look back, hoping, I suppose, that the squirrel was again back down on the ground.

Every now and then Cap would see a big robin on the ground in the distance, and being a dog with a dog's poor distant vision he would stalk and charge it, thinking it was a squirrel. Of course when he got close enough he would recognize the robin for what it was but he would carry through, in order according to his way of thinking not to look foolish. He would charge up to the nearest tree, bark for a few moments, and then turn around to walk home with a dignified air. He hated to look foolish.

One summer day he looked foolish in a rather painful way. He quite furtively had followed me to the stores on Main Street, which he knew was against the rules. I dodged into the store, thinking that if he lost me, he would soon go home. In a few minutes I came out of the store, and there was Cap running down the middle of the street, looking right and left to see if he could see me. Somewhat to my horror I saw a Model T Ford coming along the street right behind him, not very fast but nonetheless going his way. The old Model T Fords had a high clearance, yet even so not quite high enough to clear Cap. The front axle bumped him on the head, he ducked down and then raised his head just in time to get it clobbered by the rear axle. That was enough for Cap; he took out for home pronto, as the saying goes.

All of those years Cap was my constant companion on hikes and camping trips. He dearly loved to roam the woods and fields with me, and for every mile I walked he must have covered five miles, exploring byways and crannies. I don't know that either of us accomplished much but we did have a lot of fun. On those hikes Marve Westfall usually was my human companion.

Finally I had reached the stage in my life when it was time for me to depart from home. First I went to the University of Nebraska, after that to Columbia University, and after that to a position at the American Museum of Natural History in New York. Cap was destined to remain at home with my parents, giving them his affection, and at times making life difficult for them. He gradually slowed down, and the brown of his face became gray. Yet he remained an interesting and original character.

In the summer of 1932 I joined my brother Herschel at my parents' home, preparatory to making a trip with him to the Southwest in his car. As we were getting ready to leave, with the usual excitement and bustle, Cap decided that he should contribute something. So he went out and caught a big rat and brought it to us, to lay at our feet just as we were getting ready to enter the car. It was his farewell offering.

We had a very good trip, and in the course of a month or six weeks we returned to Maryville. Herschel went on to Grinnell, Iowa, where he was teaching in the college there, and I remained for a few days with my parents. One day, in the middle of a late summer thunderstorm, Cap suddenly collapsed and died. Thus ended life for a very durable and, in dog years, a very old dog.

He had been through a lot during his life: innumerable fights, contests with motor cars, hunts in the woods, hot summers and cold winters, and exciting experiences beyond counting. Finally for this old warrior the end came in a quite natural way. At the sound of thunder his heart stopped beating.

V

Glimpses of Nature

At a fairly early stage in my young life, when I had passed the little-boy phase and was entering that period just prior to the difficult teenage years, I became enamored (at least in theory) with the life of the outdoorsman. To me there was high excitement in the contemplation of life in the wilds, in the idea of tramping through forests or across mountains with a pack on one's back, in the thought of sleeping out beneath the stars. It was, of course, an impossible dream for one of my few years, and for one situated as I was in the cornfields of the Middle West, where the only forests were narrow strips of trees along muddy streams. Perhaps those nights of repose that I have already described on a vine-enshrouded porch were the beginnings of this desire to live beneath the open sky and to learn something of the natural world. Or perhaps in retrospect I am projecting desires and motives into my young life. I do know that those nights, but more particularly the early mornings, were times of unforgettable impressions— times to be awakened by the early daylight bird chorus, to hear the insects in the grass, to hear a cock crowing in the distance. They were times for reading, because I always took a book to bed with me, so that I might have a delightful half-hour of matutinal adventures, out on the high plains, or in the deep Adirondack woods, or in the rural, half-wild landscapes of England during the time of Ivanhoe. Certainly northwestern Missouri was tame enough. Consequently it had to be within the mind's eye and with the help of magic pages that such a world was opened before me, a world far removed from my immediate surroundings, a world of distant mountains and exotic life.

Although the excitement and romance of a life in wild places had to be within the confines of my imagination, I did at this stage of my young life go through the initiation ceremonies of camping out as a member of the Boy Scouts. This organization has been mentioned briefly on some preceding pages; here it should be said that Scouting was an important part of growing up for me, during three or four years of my seventh grade to sophomore high school career. And except for the wartime deeds of the Scouts, already referred to, the principal attraction I found in Scouting was in hikes through the countryside, and especially in the summer camps. Scouting was fairly new in those days and was not so highly organized as is the case today. In our town it was casual and for the boys quite a lot of fun; there was no great pressure to advance through the ranks and to acquire merit badges. If one could make it to the status of First-Class Scout, as I did, that was enough.

Maryville had two scout troops, one made up of Protestant boys, the other of Catholic lads. The single Jewish boy in town belonged to our troop (Troop One, Protestant), while the other troop (Troop Two, Catholic) was, as I recall, hardly contaminated by boys of strange religious persuasion. The few black boys in town were excluded from the Scouts, and that such a racial injustice prevailed never crossed our young minds. We were the children of our time and of our environment, as children have been since the days of our Paleolithic ancestors—and still are.

It should not be thought that the division of Scouting in our town along religious lines caused any hard feelings; everything was friendly and amicable. We had our meetings and other activities together, and we all went together on the summer scout camps.

There were three such camps during my days of Scouting, in the summers of 1918, 1919, and 1920, and for me they were events of prime importance during those summers. We went out into sparse woods of northwestern Missouri, set up tents, and under the watchful eyes of our long-suffering scoutmasters spent a couple of weeks living a more or less primitive life—half military in organization, half woodcraft.

Each troop consisted of four patrols of eight boys, and each patrol had a "trek cart" designed and made by a carpenter hired by some of the public-spirited citizens of the town. The trek cart was built of a wooden wagon bed mounted on an axle that carried a pair of light wagon wheels, in those days readily available. There was a tongue on the front of the cart, while attached to and beyond the tongue there was a rope, and fastened to the rope were two wooden cross-pieces one in front of the other. On the back of the cart was a long loop of rope. Two boys managed the tongue of the cart, four boys pulled on the cross-pieces, one on each side of the rope, and two boys handled the rope loop at the back of the cart. Thus six boys pulled the cart up hills (with the back boys pushing as necessary) and four boys guided the cart down hills. Our personal duffel was piled in the trek cart and that is how we marched to our camp in the woods. The tents, food, camp stove, and the like were taken to the chosen destination on a light truck.

So it was that on the first morning of that scout camp in 1918 the procession of trek carts left the town square, bound for the campsite. But I was not one of the number. My folks had decided that I was too frail for such a hike, and so arrangements were made for me to ride on the truck that was to carry heavy equipment and supplies to the campsite—large tents, groceries, and some heavy sheets of iron with which a stove was to be improvised. I was a bit mortified by my special status, and of course I came in for some not-too-gentle kidding on the part of my fellows, who had toiled up and down the rolling hills of northwestern Missouri, pulling the trek carts. But that's the way it was, and I had to accept the situation.

The truck was driven by Mr. Diss, the father of Paul Diss, one of my close friends, and among the passengers, besides myself, was John Gooden, a good-natured black man, who came along as cook. John worked for my mother on occasion, so we were well acquainted.

It was a pleasant ride along little dirt roads that conformed completely to the topography of the countryside; there were no cuts or fills to make the going more level, and the numerous small streams were crossed on rackety wooden bridges. Along the way we scared up quite a covey of quail, and the memory of those neat little birds scurrying through the undergrowth has always remained with me.

Finally we reached the campsite, and set to at the task of establishing the camp, aided in due course by the boys who arrived with the trek carts. A sort of company street was laid out, with tents on each side. At one end was a larger tent for the scoutmasters. And off to one side a ditch was dug, its sides built up with stones that had been brought in from a nearby creek, while across the top of this structure were placed the heavy sheets of iron that had been brought in on the truck. This was the camp stove. Next to it was the supply tent containing all of the food, as well as John Gooden, who had a cot placed there so that he not only was conveniently situated in his work area but also was at hand to keep pilfering boys away from the supplies.

It was the last summer of the war, and food was rationed. We had sufficient food of course, but I remember that it did not rest very easily on my sensitive stomach.

Certainly my most vivid and terrifying memories had to do with blanket tossing. Since I was the smallest boy in camp, I became the very unwilling object to be tossed in a blanket. The blanket was manned by the largest boys, who were pretty good-sized oafs, so of course I was tossed sky high, or so it seemed to me. I ascended up to the level of the higher branches of the surrounding trees, and quite frankly I was terrified. So it was a blessed relief to me when the scoutmasters decreed that there would henceforth be no more blanket tossing, a decision that was reached after another boy had come down and missed the blanket. He wasn't seriously hurt, but he was shaken up no little bit.

Finally the camp ended, and I remember that last day when things were packed and we were waiting to get started home. To while away the time one of the larger boys, "Shaky" Crossen, marched around with a drum, singing "The King of England," a very earthy ditty that should never reach the ears of proper Boy Scouts. But we were country boys, and not exactly a namby-pamby lot. (Some years later, in high school, I recall my delight when Shaky sat down on a thumbtack that I had placed point up on the seat of his desk in study hall.)

I had grown in physique and experience by the time the next scout camp was scheduled, so that I joined my patrol in pulling the trek cart. The site for the camp was ten or twelve miles from town, and we arrived in ample time to set up our tents. This year I brought along my own pup tent, which was pitched along with several other such shelters at one end of the company street, but most of the boys lived in rather large wall tents, as had been the case during the previous year.

Again John Gooden was the cook, and again we scrounged flat rocks from a nearby stream, and constructed a parapet on each side of the trench in which the fire was to be built. And bridging the two walls of rocks were the large flat pieces of sheet iron, to duplicate the stove that John had used during the previous camp. Then John built a fire, preparatory to cooking supper. In short order the fire was blazing merrily, and then the fun began. The rocks evidently were impregnated with water; soon the water in the rocks became converted to steam, and the rocks began to explode. The cooking area became a little battlefield, with rocks loudly exploding and rock fragments flying every which way like shrapnel. We all beat a hasty retreat, and stood at a respectful distance until the cannonade had ceased; then we had a cold supper. The next day the stove was rebuilt—I don't remember how—and John was able to prepare the meals safely, and according to his own designs.

We had a grand time for two weeks, hiking through the narrow woods and doing the things that Scouts did in those days. As an illustration of the wild country in which we camped I should explain that the camp, situated in a pleasant grove of trees, was bounded on one side by corn fields and on the other by a branch-line railway, which separated the camp from the little stream in which we did our swimming. So we had to cross the tracks to get to the old swimming hole, but that wasn't especially dangerous, since trains were few and far between. I remember that the local passenger train came past about four o'clock each afternoon, a little 4-4-0 engine pulling a couple of coaches, the forward one of which was half baggage car and half smoking car, the rear coach being wholly occupied by seats intended for ladies and children and nonsmoking males. This little train, which today would be dearly beloved by railroad buffs, chugged along right behind my pup tent. It was part of the local scene.

The following year, the summer of 1920, we went by train to our scout camp, forty miles or more from town. On the appointed day we all gathered at the Wabash station on the west side of town, where a coach was parked on a siding right in front of the station. It was our coach, ours alone, and we all felt exhilarated and indeed privileged to have this railway coach reserved for our exclusive use. We climbed aboard, to wait in noisy confusion for the morning train to come along. After a while it appeared over the western horizon, and came steaming down past our coach to the junction of the siding; then it backed up and we were hitched on. In our private coach we rode to camp, or rather to a little town some five miles from our campsite, yelling and carrying on, and very probably driving the scoutmasters almost to distraction. It was a heady experience having our own railroad car, with no strange grown-ups present to inhibit our good spirits.

For some reason, known only to the Muses, I had some months earlier decided to become a bugler, and in line with this strange ambition my parents had given me a brass bugle for a Christmas present. During the winter and spring I had practiced on this instrument, so that by the time the scout camp came along I was moderately proficient, and knew all of the calls. Consequently I performed as one of the two buglers at camp. Bill Gaugh was the other bugler, and I know that he viewed my efforts on the horn with considerable disdain. Bill had been taking trumpet lessons for some years, so he truly was proficient on the bugle. Consequently I think he would have much preferred being the sole bugler, and not having me assaulting the welkin with my amateurish efforts.

Nevertheless I bugled, taking turns with Bill; and sometimes we bugled together. Again I had a pup tent, but this year I shared it with Paul Diss. So it was that every morning I would have to scramble around and get myself up and dressed in time to blow the first bugle calls, which may have been something of a nuisance to Paul, but he put up with it cheerfully.

The Boy Scout camps got me out into the countryside each summer of their existence, but they did not truly satisfy my desire for a more intimate and less formalized life close to nature. Perhaps in 1918 when I went to the first camp I was too young to venture on an independent camping trip. But by the next summer I had grown considerably, both physically and mentally, and an interest in the natural world had come alive. Moreover I had struck up a close personal relationship with the two Green brothers, Harold and Eldon, and was guided to some degree in my natural history interests by their father, who was one of the scoutmasters. Above all I had become a disciple of the nature writer Ernest Thompson Seton, as will be told.

The far end of our living room, that is the end away from the front door and the stair landing, was devoted to bookshelves, and this was one of my favorite haunts. The collection of books was eclectic, including various novels of late Victorian aspect, the *Personal Memoirs of U. S. Grant* (I wondered why anyone would want these volumes; in later life they became one of my cherished possessions), the writing of Dickens of course, and a series of books bound in red, entitled the *John L. Stoddard Lectures*, or something to that effect. As I understand the matter, Mr. Stoddard had traveled around the world, taking pictures and making notes, after which he traveled around a lecture circuit, telling his rapt audiences all about strange lands far beyond the ken of his listeners. Then, he published the lectures, complete with illustrations.

I used to pore over those volumes, time and time again, comfortably seated in an old-fashioned Morris chair at that end of the living room. In these days of television, and with world-wide travel available to millions of people, it all seems incredibly primitive and naive, but for me as a child it was a gateway to the world beyond the limits of midwestern America. The world of Stoddard is today a lost world; glossy pages with pictures of horse-drawn vehicles and street cars, gentlemen in black suits and ladies in long, black skirts, and over all an air of serenity now long vanished. I remember that I always liked to look at the volume which included his visit to the Grand Canyon, with a picture or two of a very early and primitive Flagstaff, Arizona. Little did I realize in those days, almost three-quarters of a century ago, that one day I would be living in Flagstaff.

Then one day I discovered a magical book at the end of the living room. It had been on the shelves for some years, a book that had belonged to my brother Phil, but a book to which for some reason I had paid little if any attention. On the afternoon when I opened it immediately I entered into a bright and shining land of woods and streams and all of the beautiful plants and the fascinating animals that inhabit such an environment. The book was *Two Little Savages* by Ernest Thompson Seton.

I had previously read other Seton books and had enjoyed them immensely, but to me none of them had the enchantment that I found in the pages of *Two Little Savages*. It became my bible as Seton became to me a demi-god, and before I was through with it, several years later, it was literally worn to shreds. I read it and reread it, to live vicariously the life that was experienced by its protagonists—Yan and Sam, the two little savages, and a third chum, Guy. These boys spent part of a summer on a Canadian farm, where they camped in the woods that bordered the cultivated fields, and learned about the natural world around them. Seton made the environment in which the boys found themselves a New World Arcadia—a place to be hungered after. In a two-line preface Seton stated, "Because I have known the torment of thirst I would dig a well where others may drink." I drank often and deeply.

Two Little Savages is essentially a book of woodcraft in narrative form, and Seton told his story well. He was also an accomplished artist with much knowledge and experience in depicting plants and animals, so the book was profusely illustrated, particularly with crisp pen-and-ink drawings on the wide margins of the pages. Those little sketches, hundreds of them, were prized (at least by me) almost as much as the text. As I read the book over and over I dreamed of sunny days exploring woodlands, to become knowledgeable about the life of the forest. (Years later I had the pleasure of meeting Seton on several occasions when he came to the American Museum of Natural History in New York, where I worked, and once I visited him at his "College of Indian Wisdom" outside of Santa Fe, New Mexico.)

Those dreams had their first fruition in the summer of 1919 when I went on a little camping trip with Harold Green and Paul Diss. This was our own adventure, quite apart from the Boy Scout camp that was coming up later in the summer, and as such it was particularly dear to our hearts. We were to be the little savages, modeling so far as we could our activities on Seton's book. We planned for this expedition into the woods to take place on the farm of Harold's uncle and aunt, a few miles to the southwest of Maryville. One part of the farm was traversed by a small stream known as White Cloud Creek (named, I think, after an Indian of some prominence who had once lived in this region) and it was to these riparian wilds, extending perhaps fifty yards or so on each side of the creek, that we directed our eager steps.

So on a sunny summer morning we packed a little homemade wagon that belonged to Harold with food and utensils and some blankets, and on top of all a canvas A-tent with poles and ridgepole that belonged to me, and off we went along a dusty country road to the Mutz farm. It was only four or five miles, so by midmorning we had reached our destination and had set up camp. I think we probably stopped at the Mutz house to take on drinking water; we certainly had no intention of drinking the muddy water that flowed sluggishly along the creek. Our tent was pitched on a bit of high ground next to a little tributary that flowed into White Cloud, and in the bed of this small stream we drove four stakes on which we built a rickety platform—this to hold a box containing a cake that my mother had baked for us, hopefully to soften just a bit our rugged life in the woods. Putting the cake box on that contraption in the creek was a good precaution; it kept the ants at bay.

Such was the beginning of our week in the woods. Camping out in northwestern Missouri was not quite as romantic as depicted by Seton in his book. The days were hot and humid; the nights were only slightly less hot, and still humid; mosquitoes abounded as did other insects; there were tiny mites known as chiggers in the grass, and their attacks were even worse than those of the mosquitoes. They burrowed into the skin under belts and other tight bits of clothing to produce welts that itched almost beyond bearing. There was poison ivy. But we survived.

On the second night at our camp there came a rip-roaring thunderstorm of the kind that makes life exciting in the Middle West. We were awakened, of course, and in the midst of spectacular and terrifying flashes of lightning and a downpour of colossal strength we rushed to the stream to rescue our cake. (Little did we know that all our parents were pacing the floors of their respective bedrooms, plagued by wild imaginings as to what was happening to us.) The storm subsided and we went back to sleep, but alas, in the morning when we looked into our cake box the remains of the cake were covered with hordes of big, black ants.

Our attempt to be little savages, Seton style, sadly came to a somewhat ignoble end. On Sunday of our camping week, Harold's younger brother, Eldon, and a friend came out to visit us. All went well for part of the day, but then we got into a quarrel over something quite inconsequential, as boys will do, with the result that Harold packed up and marched home with his brother and the friend, and Paul and I were left out there alone. That night we cried ourselves to sleep. And the next morning we too packed up and went home. It was a tempest in a teapot; as soon as we all got together again we were fast friends, as usual.

Then, one day, as Harold and I were walking together along a shady street, he pulled out of a pocket a little book and passed it over to me to look at. One glance, and another new world was to me thereby revealed. For it was a pocket bird guide, the likes of which I had never seen—a book of about three by six inches with a brown leatherette cover, and on each of its two hundred pages a color plate (not very good by modern standards) of a bird, accompanied by its name, a short description, a few words purportedly describing its song, some remarks about its nest, and finally a brief note as to its range. "Bird Guide—Land Birds East of the Rockies from Parrots to Bluebirds—by Chester A. Reed." That was on the title page.

Never, or perhaps hardly ever, have I so wanted a book as I wanted that small volume; I saw it as an *Open Sesame* to the panorama of bird life that surrounded me, and of which I was all too ignorant. I yearned for the book, and I talked to my parents about it, time and again. Of course the outcome of all this was quite predictable; when Christmas came around the book was there among my gifts as I so sincerely hoped it would be, and on the flyleaf were inscribed the words "Merry Christmas from Papa and Mama"—neatly printed in my father's hand.

I was never destined to be an ornithologist, but for several years that book was my constant companion, at home and more particularly on my boyish rambles in the woodlands and fields of northwestern Missouri. Those rambles were perhaps my first attempts at natural history in the field. As such they were tentative, unstructured, and unsupervised, yet even so I began to learn things about the world of nature, as exemplified by bird life. In this I was certainly not alone—the long road toward a career in the natural sciences has had its beginning for many with the field observations of birds. Birds are numerous and varied and easy to observe, their colors and songs make them attractive, and their behavior patterns provide much of interest to the observer; it is therefore not surprising that bird watching has been so frequently a first step in the scientific career of more than a few students of life on the earth. So it was with me.

There was adventure and excitement in becoming acquainted with a new bird—"new" at least to me, even though more often than not it was a perfectly common species. I still remember the thrill of my first positive identification of a dickcissel, perched on a tall sunflower in the middle of a hot, dusty field. Here was something in the nature of discovery, such as many years later I was to experience when suddenly, before my eyes, a new fossil was uncovered in its rocky matrix.

There was mystery, too, because some of the birds that I was trying to track down were very secretive. I still remember the haunting call of the black-billed cuckoo, the "rain-crow" as it was commonly called in the Middle West because of its guttural call—a sort of "cow-cow-cow"—that seemed to come when the sky was dark and a storm was imminent. Time and again I tried to track down the cuckoo, while time and again it eluded me by slipping unobtrusively through the undergrowth.

I was experiencing in a rudimentary way, although I did not realize it at the time, some of the satisfactions of science; mystery, discovery, identification, the solving of a puzzle, and the feelings of achievement that come from such activities. Yet it should be added that my attempts in natural history, as exemplified by bird watching, were pitifully naive. I did identify the birds being pursued, but with that my efforts ended. I had no concept of species or of zoological nomenclature; in fact when I first acquired the precious field guide that became so much of my life I found myself completely puzzled by the italicized words beneath the common name of any particular bird in which I was interested. Why, underneath the word "Cardinal" on page 113 of Mr. Reed's book were the two words "*Cardinalis*

cardinalis"? It didn't make sense to me, so I went to the Latin teacher at what was then the normal school, for assistance. But he couldn't help me, either, and for some reason it never occurred to me to take the obvious step—to ask for help from the biology professor. In truth, my knowledge of the world and especially the world of nature was so unorganized that such an evident solution to my problem did not then seem at all clear. I simply did not make a connection between Mr. Leeson, sitting in a laboratory filled with bottles of preserved specimens and tables on which were rows of microscopes, and living, vibrant, colorful birds.

I cannot refrain from making the comparison between myself, fumbling my unguided way into the field of nature, and someone such as Teddy Roosevelt, the boy naturalist, who at the age of ten was making sophisticated drawings of birds and mammals, with their scientific names properly indicated.

My efforts along the fringes of ornithology were at times made by myself, especially on little excursions around our home or in nearby fields and woodland plots, for truth to tell our situation was sufficiently rural so that bird life was everywhere abundant. Longer hikes, sometimes of day-long duration, were taken in company with the Green boys or with other companions. It was all very informal and generally rather spontaneous.

Then the Green family moved eastwardly across the state to Hannibal, the town made internationally famous by the writings of Mark Twain. For a time I felt a bit lonely, but of course there were other companions with whom I could share my interests, among them Marvin Westfall, who has been mentioned as living on Sixth Street, a couple of blocks distant from our Seventh Street house.

I had known Marve casually for some time, but my close friendship with him did not develop until one day, when walking along Sixth Street, I saw a crude wigwam on a vacant lot next to his home. My interest aroused, I poked my head into the door of the shelter to find Marve sitting there cross-legged in an attitude that I assume must be genuinely Indian. We fell to talking, and it soon turned out that Marve, like me, was a devotee of Ernest Thompson Seton and Seton's brand of woodcraft. So it wasn't long before Marve and I were hiking into the limited woodlands of our countryside to learn a bit of natural history according to our own methods.

Old ties were renewed when in the early summer of 1921, the summer after the adventure along White Cloud Creek with Harold Green and Paul Diss, Mr. Green, a pharmacist, came to town on a business trip and invited Paul and me to visit the Green family in Hannibal. We were both thrilled by the prospect—and we waited impatiently for the slow days to pass until it was time for our departure.

We went by train, on a local Wabash train from Maryville to Moberly—

a trip that occupied most of the day, where we changed to a faster and more sophisticated train that during the early hours of the evening whisked us on to Hannibal. We arrived there about ten o'clock in the evening to begin our great adventure.

The ostensible reason for our trip to Hannibal was to participate in a small Boy Scout camp on Salt Creek, a tributary to the Mississippi River. A few days after our arrival we moved out to the campsite where all of us, perhaps a couple of dozen boys, set up pup tents under the supervision of a long-suffering scoutmaster, a young man of undoubted dedication. Even here, where the great Mississippi flowed only a few miles away, the attempt at life in the wilds was limited, for there was a cornfield within a hundred yards of our camp. Nevertheless there were daily activities to keep us occupied, so that the time sped past and soon the day arrived when we all went back into Hannibal.

Then there began a couple of weeks when the two Green boys and Paul and I, along with a couple of other Hannibal boys, arranged our daily activities, and it was then that I became acquainted with the great river. The acquaintance actually began on our first day in Hannibal, before we went on the scout camp. On the morning of that day we were in Mr. Green's drug store when suddenly there was a cry of "Steamboat's coming" and out we dashed to the levee, a few blocks away. It was truly an unrehearsed enactment of the days four score years earlier when Sam Clemens lived in Hannibal. Out there on the river came a stern-wheel steamer, the black smoke pouring from her funnels. A long bridge extended forward from the foredeck, where a group of black deckhands sat around talking, or occasionally indulging in some horseplay.

The steamer, the *Belle of Calhoun,* eased up to the sloping brick levee, and down came the bridge (it was really too long and too wide to call a gangplank) to connect the ship with dry land. Then the procession began, a two-way procession of deckhands carrying cargo from the boat to a warehouse by the levee, and from the warehouse to the boat. Each man carried one object, be it a crate weighing a hundred pounds or a little box six inches square. (At least that is the way it seemed to me; I suppose they did team up on very large pieces of cargo.) While this went on I sat with my friends on some barrels on the levee and watched the proceedings. There were other spectators, too, including some people on the upper deck of the steamboat.

Finally the loads were transferred, off and on, the paddlewheel began to churn in reverse, throwing up a spray of chocolate-brown water, and the *Belle of Calhoun* backed out into midstream. Then the paddlewheel was put into forward rotation, and down the river went the steamboat, with the deckhands lounging on the foredeck and drinking water out of a pail that at the end of a rope had been dipped into the muddy river.

It was a link with the past that long since had disappeared. Today there are contrived excursions by steamboat on the Mississippi, but nothing like the real thing that I had been privileged to witness. It makes me feel as if I am quite ancient (which is the case) and it makes me feel at one with the parton saint of Missouri literature.

And there were other ties with Mark Twain. One day the Green boys took Paul and me to "Mark Twain's Cave," a vast limestone cavern on the edge of town, the locale of some of Tom Sawyer's adventures. A visit to the cave in those days was something of an *ad hoc* adventure; we brought our own candles, we got permission from the owner, and then were left to our own devices. Thus we explored some of the galleries of this famous cave, and in the end we came out into daylight by the same portal through which we had entered. Today, if I am not mistaken, the cave is electrically lighted and there are formal tours of its interior.

That was but one of our adventures. We crossed the river on the railroad bridge (walking, of course) to swim in clear bayous on the Illinois side. And always we explored.

The biggest excitements of our days in Hannibal were the hours spent in looking for Indian artifacts. In this activity we were joined by a boy named Eichelberger (I forget his first name, but I do know that in later years he became an authority on the archeology of the region) and we tramped through plowed fields looking for arrowheads and scrapers, probably at sites where there had been ancient encampments. Here I was instructed as to basic details of artifact types, which opened new vistas before my eyes. Heretofore I had been peering into trees and bushes to watch the goings-on of unsuspecting birds; now I was introduced to life of the past, to be encountered and interpreted by objects found in the ground. We spent quite a few days at this, wandering along the bluffs of the river, stopping now and then to pick wild blackberries, and enjoying an environment that to me was new and exotic.

The time came to go home and so I went, but the lure of archeology, dimly practiced, was with me. I did hope that I might find some artifacts in northwestern Missouri, but at that I was never successful, which was just as well. Very probably I didn't really know where to look. I did, however, continue nature walks with Marve Westfall, if so they might be called. They were not very purposeful but they did get us into the out-of-doors, and that was beneficial exercise. I suppose that if I could have had some adult supervision the nature walks would have had more point to them, but Mr. Green, the scoutmaster who had given me some elementary acquaintance with the outdoor world, was now across the state in Hannibal, and most of the other men in our community who went into those sparse woodlands of our region carried guns with them. I was never interested in hunting, even though many of my peers went out after rabbits and squirrels. Moreover, I was very much against collecting bird's eggs, although that was a practice (albeit illegal) followed by a few boys in our town. Nor did I try my hand at fishing, in part because I had no taste for the kinds of fish—mainly catfish—that inhabited the muddy streams of that part of Missouri, and in part because I found the type of fishing suitable for such game very boring. Sitting on a muddy bank hour after hour watching a little float on the end of a line attached to a long bamboo pole was not my idea of fun.

I tried botanizing, but my efforts along this line were half-hearted at best. I had a little flower guide—a companion piece to the bird guide that was so constantly in my hand—but I found the flowers to be confusing and in a way overwhelming. There were so many of them. It may be that if I had been given some elementary training in the use of botanical keys my attempts to learn something about the plant world would have been more productive; here again I failed because of a lack of any supervision.

The problem of supervision for children and especially for high-school-age juveniles is a tricky one. It seems to me, as an observer, that sometimes there is too much supervision of the coming generation—at least in some quarters. Children are almost denied the joys of being children; they are supposed to be achieving something all of the time. Or in the opposite direction they run wild. I did not have enough supervision, yet I did not run wild, either. I did not know at the time that anything was lacking in my life, but if I could have had a little more direction of my woodland walks certainly my young life would have been enriched.

It so happened that about this time I discovered something different during my excursions into the countryside: fossils. Here were objects in the ground much older than the flint artifacts, and objects of such varied form as to intrigue the mind. These fossils were found in some black shale banks, especially along a little watercourse known as Florida Creek, and they represented the remains of invertebrate animals of Pennsylvanian age, something more than three hundred million years old, that had inhabited the bottom of a seaway occupying what is now the middle of the North American continent. There were shells of brachiopods, and corals, and other fossils typical of those ancient years when great deposits of coal were being formed throughout the world. Since these fossils were so very different from other natural history objects then within my ken I was led, I cannot say inspired, to try to find out something about them in books. The books at hand were of the most elementary sort and of such undistinguished kind that I do not remember anything about them. At any rate I was able to identify after a fashion the fossils I found along Florida Creek. These were my first efforts in paleontology and I developed some not very serious interest in collecting the fossils, to add to the motley array of things that I was accumulating at our house. The fossils I collected touched no sparks of paleontological ambition or even interest within my soul. These objects were not destined to lead me into a life of paleontology; the inspiration for my career was to come later, as will be told. For the present the fossils of Florida Creek were only part, and a small part at that, of a teenager's wildly diverse interests.

The study upstairs has been mentioned. Ostensibly it was my father's room, and he did hold possession of it by virtue of a large desk, especially made for him by a local carpenter and presented to him by my mother on one of his birthdays. But one corner of the room became my "museum." My maternal grandfather shipped to me, from his home in Holton, Kansas, a glass case provided with movable shelves, and here I stored and displayed my treasures. I don't know why my father put up with my idiosyncrasies; my museum took up space that otherwise would have been devoted to bookcases.

At any rate, there it was, with about as varied a collection of objects as may be imagined. There were some arrowheads of course. There was a truly magnificent trilobite (I don't know just how I obtained it) as well as various Carboniferous fossils. Civil War buttons were there. And a couple of birds' nests were included. I recall also an old Mexican spur that my brother Herschel brought to me from Texas. Other things, equally valueless, have escaped my memory.

But that museum was my treasure. I wonder if it was in any way definitive in determining my future, a future of more than sixty years (as of 1988) spent in museums. Probably not, because as will be told it was only during my college years that I became interested in paleontology and thus became involved in museum work. Nevertheless it was perhaps an indication of my interest in collecting things and trying to make something out of them.

VI

New Directions

*I*t was during the summer of 1922, after my junior year in high school, that I learned to drive a car. My father had purchased a Dodge touring car, as such automobiles were then known—a five-passenger vehicle with leather seats and a cloth top. Most of the cars of that era were "open," that is, they were equipped with fabric tops supported by a sort of folding frame so that the top could be collapsed and lowered into a folded arrangement behind the back seat. People liked to drive with the wind in their hair, and since speeds were slow according to modern standards this mode of transportation was indeed pleasant. With the top up in its usual position there was still plenty of breeze surging around the heads of the vehicle's occupants, and of course when it rained there was every chance of getting wet. Consequently when the sky darkened and the clouds lowered there was a frantic rush to haul out the "side curtains" which were stowed somewhere within the "tonneau" (a term now extinct, but once used to denote "the rounded rear body of a motor-car"—Oxford English Dictionary) and get them in place before the rain struck. It was all very primitive but we did not think so.

My driving lessons were quite informal, under the tutelage of my brother Philip, and in the course of a week or so I was ready to take the car on expeditions of varying length. In those days traffic in northwestern Missouri was sparse; there were undulating brick pavements in our town, and beyond the town limits the roads were all dirt, rough and dusty in dry weather, deeply muddy and often impassable when it rained. I might add that a driver's license was not then required, at least not in our part of the country.

Our restricted family, my parents and myself—my two brothers having left the family fold to lead their own independent lives—planned to drive to the Rocky Mountains for a vacation that summer. I would do the bulk of the driving. Preparations were made; the necessary luggage was assembled and much of it was packed on the left running board of the car (running boards were universal automotive features), held in place by a sort of an attached expanding steel gate expressly manufactured for this purpose, and covered with a piece of canvas to protect it against the rain, and lashed in place. Finally we were ready, and off we went, bowling along at the standard speed of twenty to twenty-five miles an hour with a cloud of dust in our wake. If that seems like a stately pace, one must realize that on those roads, with the high-pressure tires we had (seventy-five pounds per square inch) there was not much incentive to drive much faster. Even so we had three blow-outs, and this on a trip of about six hundred miles.

Never will I forget my first glimpse of the Rocky Mountains—the Colorado Front Range looming ahead of us like a great mirage and thrusting its snowy peaks into the blue sky, so that I could not be sure whether it was mountains or clouds that glimmered on the western horizon. To some of the early explorers of the West the Rockies were known as the Shining Mountains, and so they became to me—shining mountains of incredible beauty and mystery. I lost my heart to the Rockies.

We spent a couple of weeks in the mountains, in a valley known as Moraine Park not far from Estes Park. Here was real adventure for a boy who heretofore had known only the flat lands and the rolling hills of the Middle West. I went on hikes by myself and with other people, ventured above timberline, and visited mountain lakes that reflected the images of jagged summits in their crystal waters. I was especially invigorated by the clean, thin mountain air—a marvelous antidote to the heavy, humid atmosphere of the Missouri Valley. It was perhaps my remembrances of the high mountain air that, as much as anything, influenced me to such a degree as to draw me back to the Rockies in the years ahead. For me it was magic.

There was in those days a rustic hotel in Moraine Park, known quite simply as Moraine Lodge, where we stayed during our mountain vacation. (Years ago it was taken over by the National Park Service.) Some of the people at the lodge occupied rooms in the main structure, some of them camped out after a fashion in tents having board floors, as we did, and a few guests lived in separate cabins. Among these privileged folks was an elderly couple, Mr. and Mrs. Thomas Watson, who for quite a few years had been

The Colbert family, 1909

My birthplace, Clarinda, Iowa

Posing with Buster

The young naturalist

Noonday stop at a cow camp, 1924

On St. Louis Pass, Colorado, July 4, 1927

Edwin Hinckley Barbour

William King Gregory

Henry Fairfield Osborn

July 8, 1933

Margaret with my parents, 1934

Our family, 1953: (back) *David, George, Philip;* (front) *Charles, Daniel*

The home in Leonia, New Jersey

At the Rhode Island farm

With George Simpson in Nebraska, 1941

Excavating the skeleton of Hyaenodon, *1941*

In the Permian of Texas, 1943

With Charles Bogert in Florida, 1944

With Al Romer in Texas, 1943

The hotel in Scenic, South Dakota, 1941

With Ray Cowles, photographing a lizard in Florida, 1944

A load of boxed fossils, Arizona, 1946

Our largest alligator, Florida, 1944

*The mastodon bones fished out of the Calasahootchie
River, Florida, 1944*

spending their summer here. Mr. Watson was none other than the man who had helped Alexander Graham Bell invent the telephone; he was the technician who built the equipment that Bell designed. It was he who became historically famous as the first person to hear a sentence spoken over the telephone—those immortal words being a call from Bell in one room of the house where they were conducting their experiments to Watson in an adjoining room, for assistance with the apparatus. Watson said, in an address years later, that it was on a March day when "I heard a complete and intelligible sentence. It made such an impression upon me that I wrote that first sentence in a book I have always preserved. The occasion had not been arranged and rehearsed as I suspect the sending of the first message over the Morse telegraph had been years before, for instead of that noble first telegraphic message—'What hath God wrought?' the first message of the telephone was; 'Mr. Watson, please come here, I want you.'"

Mr. Watson was a friendly gentleman, and he was nice enough to entertain me in his little cabin with stories of his early work on the telephone. One day he presented me with a little booklet entitled "The Birth and Babyhood of the Telephone," this being a printed version of the talk, quoted above, that he had delivered at the Third Annual Convention of the Telephone Pioneers of America, in 1913. On the title page of the booklet he wrote the following inscription:

> Thomas A. Watson
> Estes Park Colo.
> Aug 29th 1922
> Get ready. The opportunity
> is sure to come.

I still have this little reminder of one of the great technical advances of modern times, and needless to say it is much treasured among my possessions.

Mr. Watson liked to read to people (I recently learned that during his middle years he was something of an actor) and I remember him reading short stories to some of us who gathered at his place in the evening.

Such visits were, however, interludes in my days of outdoor activities—hikes on the mountain slopes and through the flower-carpeted mountain parks, where I encountered deer and looked with fascination upon beaver dams and the ponds behind them. Our stay in Moraine Park was all too short and I was very reluctant to have to go home.

But go home we did, and all through my senior year of high school I dreamed of the mountains and had visions of mountain meadows nestling in the embrace of great, rocky peaks. The next summer, after I had graduated from high school, we had another vacation trip, this time with friends to the limitless, wooded Canadian shield north of Lake Superior. It was an interesting experience for me; paddling a canoe across a lake near the International Boundary, where granite cliffs and headlands were covered with endless conifer forests, was something new in my life. But it was not the mountains. I still wanted to go back to a place where I could enjoy alpine vistas.

On the way home from our North Woods vacation we stopped in Chicago for a few days to visit family friends, and during this time I made visits to the Art Institute and to the Field Museum, the latter recently installed in its vast new Grecian temple on the Lake Front after its quarter-century occupation of the "Field-Columbian" building out near the University of Chicago, the building that had served as the Palace of Fine Arts during the Chicago World's Fair of 1893. (Incidentally I had visited the old Field-Columbian Museum with my father, some seven or eight years earlier, when we spent a summer in Chicago.) I liked the Art Institute, but it was the Field Museum that truly fired my imagination. I walked through its great halls where I saw wonders of natural history, seemingly without end, and I thought to myself that it would be more than marvelous if one could work in a place such as this. It was the first glimmering within my consciousness that perhaps the museum world was an environment within which I might spend my future life, yet it seemed so unattainable to me that I dismissed these early longings as being for me beyond the limits of reality. How could I ever hope to enter such a world?

Those weeks before and after our trip north to Minnesota and Ontario, with the memorable visit to the Field Museum in Chicago, had been the summer of my discontent. I had reached the stage of life when no longer did I wish to have hours for play or for sight-seeing, even in my beloved mountains. I wanted to be engaged in some sort of productive work, and since I felt that museums were not to be seriously considered in my plans for the future, I directed my thoughts toward forestry. Forestry had been much in my mind ever since our trip to Colorado during the previous summer. What could be finer, I thought, than to work in the forests and particularly to help in the preservation of those forests, for I had developed a serious interest in conservation.

Forestry became an ambition, but for the moment a rather distant goal. As for museums, they were as I have said merely a dream, a dream with undefined limits because I really had no idea of what I might do, even if I got into a museum. Paleontology, which was to be my life work, and paleontology as practiced within a museum, which was to be my life environment, were as yet beyond my wildest imaginings—this in spite of my brief explorations for fossils along Florida Creek in northwestern Missouri. In fact, I may not have realized at the time that many museums were centers for the study of fossils.

Therefore forestry loomed large in my visions of the future. I had written to some schools of forestry for information about their courses of study, but since no such schools were within what at the time seemed a reasonable distance from my home, and since my ideas concerning forestry were still a bit vague, I settled on beginning my college career at the institution where my father served on the faculty. The Normal had by now progressed to the status of a teachers college, and although any thoughts of becoming a teacher were completely outside the concepts I had of a future career, I did see an opportunity to enroll in standard liberal arts courses. I could live at home, the tuition at the college for state residents was incredibly inexpensive even by the standards of those days, and I could get some reasonably good instruction.

In fact, looking back from the long perspective of more than six decades, I know that I received some excellent instruction. The faculty members at the college were not famed for their research accomplishments, but some of them were first-rate teachers at the undergraduate level. Classes were small and so there was a close relationship between teachers and students; there was an osmosis of learning from the front of the classroom back through the twenty or thirty scholars sitting at their desks, without the intervention of teaching or laboratory assistants. As a result of my three years at the college in Maryville, where I received most of my undergraduate education, compared with the undergraduate studies at the University of Nebraska, where I completed work for my bachelor's degree, I am of the strong opinion that a small liberal arts college is the ideal place at which to obtain an undergraduate education. The large university has facilities not to be found at the small college, but the college has, generally speaking, a faculty interested in students, and a friendly atmosphere which can be truly inspiring to a student struggling to master the facts and philosophies of higher learning.

I fondly remember, after all of these years, some of the teachers who led me into and through those fields of knowledge that have made modern man the sapient being that he is. Anna Painter, teacher of English, was one. It may be recalled that I was fortunate in high school in having Miss Laura Hawkins for my English teacher, because she had a way of making this subject come alive for us, so that many if not all of her pupils looked forward to their reading assignments. It was the same with Miss Painter, although of course at a higher level. I did have other English teachers, but she was the one always to be remembered: a tall, angular Quaker lady with a nice sense of humor, a love of the language, and a gift for seeing the true meaning of what was on the printed page, and for understanding and appreciating the many nuances of fine writing. At this late date I recall little about the details of her teaching; I only remember that what she said, and the guidance she gave us, instilled in me an everlasting affinity for good literature. For example I will never forget her reading to us one day the Song at the end of Shakespeare's *Love's Labour's Lost*, the third stanza of which begins with the familiar words "When icicles hang by the wall," thereby introducing the first of sixteen lines which describe as fully and as sensitively as might be wished the rigors of winter. This small incident remains in my memory because it, together with other things she pointed out to us, made me a confirmed Shakespeare enthusiast. Today I read the Shakespeare plays I like, and that is about twenty of them, over and over again, and I never tire of such reading. Always there is something new, always I marvel at his genius.

Moreover it gives me pleasure to read biographies of Shakespeare and the background studies that tell us what we know about the writing of his plays. Shakespeare, like Mozart, was a true craftsman. He had a job to do and he did it, and that was that. They were both jolly men who savored life to the fullest; not for them was the business of sitting in a garret and suffering the pangs of creativity. For them creativity flowed from the brain down the arm to the hand and on to paper.

Another teacher at the college in Maryville who lives in my memory and who had a great deal of influence upon me was Merton Wilson, professor of chemistry. I don't think I ever had an instructor who could present an abstruse subject so clearly and in such an interesting fashion as did Mr. Wilson. In fact, he made chemistry so appealing to me that I wound up with almost enough credits in this subject for an undergraduate major. Mr. Wilson became a very good friend, and he followed my progress with interest for many years after I had left Missouri.

Still another teacher of note was Joseph Hake, professor of physics. He, too, could make a difficult subject understandable and interesting by reason of the clarity of his teaching. He wasn't easy—one had to work and work hard to satisfy him, so that I found his physics course the toughest undergraduate subject with which I ever struggled. But the end result was worth the struggle. Studies under Professors Hake and Wilson introduced me to the intellectual rigors of science and prepared me in outlook for the very different sciences within which I eventually was to make my career.

So I continued with my education in liberal arts, but always with forestry in the back of my mind. This prompted me during my freshman year at college to make applications to several national forests for summer work; I felt that I needed to get some practical experience of some kind. All of the replies to my letters were negative, except for one, which came from John

V. Leighou, supervisor of the Arapaho National Forest in Colorado. His letter, which for a time had me walking around about three inches above the ground, said that if I so wished I could come to his forest for the summer to work on trails. At last, it seemed to me, I was to have an opportunity to do the kind of work I had been dreaming about, in the mountains where I longed to be.

As the academic year drew near its close I kept waiting for a second letter from Mr. Leighou, telling me when and where to report—something that he had promised in his initial letter. It didn't come, and it didn't come, and as the days wore on I became increasingly concerned—almost desperate. Finally I gathered courage and wrote to Leighou, and this brought an immediate reply; he admitted that the matter of my summer employment had slipped his mind (as well it might since he had other much more important things to think about). Anyway, he told me to come on out to Hot Sulphur Springs, on the west slope of the Continental Divide, west of Denver, where I was to report to John Glendenning, the district forest ranger.

So one day not long afterwards I found myself on the old Moffat Line train, painfully inching its way up to the pass at Corona—indeed so painfully that once or twice it had to back down the grade it had been trying to surmount and try again. But finally we achieved the top, and then it was a long, coasting ride down into Middle Park, which I could see time and again as the train rounded the many hairpin curves during its descent, spread out like a toy miniature landscape far below. At last late in the afternoon, the train arrived at Hot Sulphur Springs, where I disembarked and made my way to the Riverside Hotel nearby, then the only lodging place in town.

The next morning I went to the Forest Service Office on the second floor of the bank building, where I learned that Glendenning was out of town and would not be back for two or three days. Thus I had a chance to become acquainted with Hot Sulphur Springs, at that time a sad little town, its main street flanked by a few business establishments that periodically throughout each day would be shaken by window-rattling, dust-laden winds. For a greenhorn from the lush fields of the Missouri Valley it seemed a daunting and discouraging prospect.

In time Glendenning appeared and as soon as we met he looked me over with a critical and what seemed a not very encouraging eye. I had a feeling that perhaps I was not exactly what he had in mind as a summer assistant—but there I was. So he put me to work for a couple of days, helping him to build a fence to contain his horses. Then we took off into the woods.

For some reason we made our departure after supper, each of us on a horse, with a lead packhorse, and for several hours we rode through the forest, sometimes in deep shadow, sometimes under the light of a full moon.

It was a beautiful and at the same time an eerie experience—certainly a rather unusual way to be introduced to my first summer task.

My first summer task was, almost unbelievably, an attempt to eradicate larkspur in a little valley traversed by Troublesome Creek, out in the center of Middle Park. I suppose some of the cattle people had put pressure on the Forest Service, because cattle graze (by permit) on Forest Service lands and larkspur is poisonous to cattle. I was supposed to put in my days tramping around through the sagebrush with a mattock, and whacking out any larkspur that I happened to see. It was an impossible assignment; I knew it and I'm sure the Forest Service people knew it too, but the money had been appropriated and I was the chosen victim. It was a prospect that I did not look forward to with enthusiasm.

It took Glendenning and me another day of riding after that first night in the forest to reach my camping place on Troublesome Creek. We arrived at our destination late in the afternoon, after a noonday stop at a little log-cabin cow camp that might very well have been the subject for a sketch by Frederick Remington. Our arrival coincided with a rip-snorting mountain thunderstorm, so we hastily unsaddled and unpacked the horses, hauled out the tent, and sat with it draped over our heads until the rain was over. Then we pitched camp. Glendenning spent the night with me, and the next morning he was on his way with the horses, leaving me alone with my thoughts and sufficient food to keep me going for three weeks.

It was a strange beginning; my days were incredibly monotonous, crossing back and forth, up and down the valley, looking for larkspur. And as I have said, I don't think my efforts of larkspur eradication were particularly significant. I did, however, learn what it is like to be alone—completely alone day after day, with never a glimpse of another human being. I suppose this is an experience that is rarely within the ken of twentieth-century people; there are too many inhabitants of our lands today for many folk to get completely away from their fellow beings. I had that experience, not only on Troublesome Creek, but during the following year (quite inadvertently) in Buchanan Canyon, along the west slope of the Continental Divide, as will be told.

I managed to survive, in part by keeping busy at my monotonous work during the day, and in part by enjoying my surroundings in the mornings and evenings. Never shall I forget the beauty of the veery's song in the late afternoon—a crystalline series of descending notes coming from the pine woods on the other side of the little valley. Nor shall I forget the several cougar tracks that I found near my tent when I got up one morning.

Eventually my solitary existence came to an end; Glendenning appeared and took me to a trail camp several miles away, where I was to spend the next month of my summer. It was a big camp for those days, consisting of a hard-nosed trail boss, whom I will call Jackson Phillips, his wife, who served as cook for the outfit, and their little boy, a giant of a man named Harry Douglas, an old Swede, Ben Tandall, and of course myself. There were the horses—everything was done with horses in those times—including two heavy sorrel draft horses, and a string of saddle and pack animals.

We were building new trails in the forest, because trails were important in providing access to remote areas for fire control. The procedure was to "swamp" a swath through the woods about six feet in width, sufficient to accommodate a fully loaded pack horse, after which the stumps left within the cleared swath would be removed, after which the trail itself would be made. The trick for removing stumps was to cut the trees about six feet above the ground (which was tiring business) and then to jerk them out with the heavy team at the end of a long log chain. The chain was fastened to the top of the tall "stump"; thus the leverage was usually adequate to pull the tree out by the roots. The trail was made by plowing a furrow along the middle of the cleared swath and then spreading it into a path by dragging a little steel drag, known as a Martin Ditcher, along its course. Of course the stump pulling, plowing, and dragging was done with the heavy team, which belonged to Phillips.

He was a hard taskmaster, and among other things it was my fate, being the youngest member of the crew, to hold the plow while we made the furrow for the trail. This was strenuous and exciting work, especially when we were on the side of a steep slope. The horses would be positioned, one much higher than the other, where it was difficult for them to keep their footing. Phillips would hold the reins and urge the horses on with loud, blistering shouts, the horses would lunge forward trying to keep their places while they dragged the plow, and I would be at the tail end of the procession, trying to hold the plow more or less upright. Inevitably, about every five or ten feet, the plow would strike a big rock, barely covered by the talus of the slope, to bound high in the air, while I usually bounded head over heels down the slope. Then I would climb back to my place and we would try it all over. It should be mentioned that the plow had specially made steel handles; wooden handles would have been shattered before half a day had run its course.

The final days of my association with this trail crew were spent in a lovely setting beside an alpine lake just at timberline. The sylvan beauty of our campsite was marred to some extent by our horses, who would stand around among our tents and snort and stamp, ring their bells, and make uncouth noises until about three o'clock in the morning. Then off they would go, always over a thousand-foot ridge behind the camp. Of course we had bells on some of the horses and we hobbled some, and one was on a picket rope, yet even so they made their exits, all except the picketed horse, the hobbled horses dashing along at about the speed a man could run, working their hobbled front feet together in a clumsy but efficient gait. At dawn it was the task for one of us to take the remaining horse and go round them up.

Then one night a bear came into camp, the horses panicked, and the picketed horse, belonging to Harry Douglas, fell down and got wound up in the picket rope. The rope cut through one hind leg to the bone, and the poor horse was permanently lamed. After that we forgot about picketing a horse, which made the morning roundup even more difficult than before.

After this work came to an end I was transferred to another trail crew, under the supervision of Ranger John Johnston, working in Arapaho Canyon. It consisted of two other trail stiffs beside myself—Milt Johnson, a young Swede, and John Lind, an old Swede. I finished the summer with them, working at the bottom of a very deep and rough canyon. We had no horses; indeed there was scant pasturage here for the grazing of horses, and we did all our work by hand. We took care of stumps and large boulders with dynamite.

We pitched a tent beside an old moldering trapper's cabin next to the stream—the cabin was too dank to serve us in any way—and from this camp we worked our way up the canyon. It was a confined life; the sun didn't get down into the bottom of the canyon until about ten o'clock in the morning, and it deserted us at about four o'clock in the afternoon. But I enjoyed it, and I enjoyed my companions; particularly I enjoyed the visits of Johnnie Johnston when he came around on inspection trips. Finally the summer came to an end and I went back to Missouri for a second year of college.

There were three more summers of work on the Arapaho forest, all under Johnnie Johnston. He and his wife, Beulah, and their baby boy, Howard, lived in a log ranger station near the western exit of the Moffat Tunnel, then under construction, and their home became for me a haven for recuperation between stints out on the trail. Indeed, the Johnstons became as elder siblings to me, and I enjoyed many pleasant hours in their company. Johnnie was a kindly person who enjoyed life in such a way that the people with him also enjoyed life. He had been raised in Middle Park; he knew the country like the back of his hand and thus he was an excellent leader in planning the work that we had to do.

My second summer in the Forest Service had what seemed an inauspicious beginning. I had written to Johnnie Johnston during the winter asking if I might come to Colorado again and work for him, and he had replied to the effect that there was no work; funds had not been appropriated. But I took a long chance and at the end of the academic year I went out there anyway, hoping almost against hope that something might turn up. So it was that I appeared at the Idlewild Ranger Station quite unannounced, to be greeted by Johnnie with a big smile and encouraging words. It seemed that at the last minute he had received some funds for trail work, and just as I appeared he was wondering how he might get in touch with me to offer some employment.

Plans were quickly made and within a day or so I took off for Arapaho Canyon (where I had finished the last season's work) leading a horse packed with food and equipment and accompanied by a young local boy named Dutch Selak. Dutch, I might add, was of Czech antecedents.

Dutch was a nice boy, but for a young fellow raised in Middle Park he didn't have much practical knowledge about how to take care of himself in the mountains, away from the simple conveniences of a small town. This soon became apparent as we made our way along a mountain trail toward our destination; it was up to me to find the way and to manage our pack horse. All of which was fine, except that I didn't find the way; in crossing a large mountain meadow I missed the trail on the far side—this in spite of a long and persistent search to locate it. Finally I decided that we would strike due west through the woods, for I knew that in so doing we would necessarily come to the rim of Arapaho Canyon.

Then followed several hours of tough going through the trees. It might not have been so bad for the two of us, but maneuvering a loaded pack horse within a primitive woodland where we constantly found our way blocked by tangles of down timber was an exercise in slow frustration. Finally in the late afternoon we came to the edge of the canyon, where we were faced with the problem of getting ourselves and the horse down a couple of thousand feet of precipitous slope. We did it, but in the process the pack slipped off over the horse's head four or five times, and each time we would have to repack him, standing on an impossibly steep slope, with one of us high above the horse, the other far below. Then, just as the shades of night were gathering around us we reached the old camping ground next to the abandoned trapper's cabin, where I had camped with Milt Johnson and John Lind the previous summer.

Later Johnnie came by on an inspection trip, and when he saw what we had done in making that descent into Arapaho Canyon he shook his head wonderingly and asked us how in the hell we ever managed it. I think he concluded that the Lord was on the side of blundering fools.

Dutch was not long with me. He decided that work in the woods was not to his liking, so he made his farewells and took off for the nearest town in the valley. I was then paired with a middle-aged, robust native of the region named Sam Stone. Johnnie had known Sam for many years, indeed ever since he (Johnnie) was a little boy and old Sam was a frequent visitor to Stillwater, the Johnston ranch. So Johnnie hired Sam that summer to work on a trail up Buchanan Canyon, with me serving as Sam's assistant. One of

Sam's virtues was the he knew how to handle explosives. Sam had an old Model T Ford with a Ruxtell axle, a type of conveyance probably unknown to anyone today under the age of about seventy-five years. The Ruxtell axle was a contraption added to a Model T, making the car a sort of primitive jeep. Sam and I would get our supplies in a mountain town, Granby or Grand Lake, take them in his Ford to an old deserted lumber camp at the head of Monarch Lake, and from there proceed by horses up Buchanan Canyon to the site of our work. We used a well-preserved cabin at this place as a sort of staging area, a storehouse in which to keep extra supplies and equipment that we didn't need at the moment. Which was all very well until the day that some cows from a ranch down the canyon got into the cabin while we were working up the canyon. They evidently were able to push the door open, and after getting into the cramped quarters they had invaded, managed to push the door shut—and it stayed shut. The cows were in there for two days, gorging themselves on oats which we had stored there for future use by our horses, and becoming ever more uncomfortable because they needed to be milked. In the meantime the owners were searching high and low for their errant cows; finally having come up the canyon they heard a ruckus inside the cabin and discovered their bloated, milk-laden animals, standing knee-deep in a welter of tipped-over tin cans, a trampled cot, and scattered oats, all liberally plastered with cow manure. Sam and I had a great time cleaning the place up and salvaging our fouled equipment.

One day as we were working far up Buchanan Canyon Johnnie Johnston came along on an inspection trip. The trail we were building skirted a huge rock outcrop, and Johnnie told us to blast off four or five feet of rock with several "mud shots" applied to the surface of the outcrop. (A mud shot is a technique of blasting whereby dynamite is placed against the surface to be blasted and covered with a thick coat of mud; the explosion impacts the rock, to shatter it for a short distance below the point of impact.)

After Johnnie had left, old Sam said to me: "To hell with a mud shot. We can't be bothered."

So Sam found a crack back within the outcrop, and into this he stuffed perhaps sixty sticks of dynamite. The ensuing explosion jarred Buchanan Canyon in a way that it hadn't been shaken since the first days of creation, detached a piece of rock the size of a small house, and sent that large chunk of canyon wall roaring down the side of the mountain, clearing a broad path of destruction through the forest. When Johnnie came back on his next inspection trip he was not amused; in fact, it was about the only time that I ever saw Johnnie really annoyed. But what could he do? He had known Sam ever since he, Johnnie, was a little boy, and thus he saw Sam in a way as an old family retainer, while Sam viewed Johnnie as an upstart young man who shouldn't question his elders.

Sam had his own way of doing things. Once when we were working down at the lower end of the canyon we were getting ready to set off a blast, and nearby there was a sportsman casting for trout in the stream. Did Sam tell the fisherman that we were going to blast? No, he merely informed the stranger to get behind a tree, advice that was ignored since the fisherman quite naturally assumed Sam to be some sort of queer mountain man on the loose. The blast went off; rocks and debris went whistling past the fisherman, who undoubtedly thought the end of the world was at hand. He came out of the water, kicking up spray to right and left, and immediately sat down on the bank to regain his composure.

Then one day Sam went to town and came back bringing in his Ford a generous supply of food, along with a new cot and some other amenities. I thought we were really going to live high, but Sam soon disabused me; these things were for a lady that he was going to fetch from Granby. I thought the worst and Sam disabused me again; this lady was no mountaineering lady of the evening, she was a medium. Sam was going to take her into a very-hard-to-get-at wilderness known as Hell Hole, where there was a lost mine. The mine had been found by a couple of Swedes years ago, the Swedes were long since defunct, but the medium was going to go there and get in touch with their spirits and find the mine for Sam. Then he would be rich.

In fact, if I would join Sam in the venture I would be rich too, not as rich as Sam but rich after a fashion. I excused myself; I was not about to be taken in by any lost mine, of which there are hundreds if not thousands throughout the West.

A couple of days later Sam went back into town, and a day later than that he appeared with the medium, a little old lady who must have been well on toward her eighties if not beyond that geriatric boundary. Poor medium! She was seated uncomfortably on a horse, being led by Sam, who was mounted on his horse. He also had a well-laden pack horse, and among his cargo was a box containing fifty pounds of government dynamite which he had seen fit to appropriate. At the time I was working away by myself on the trail. We exchanged greetings; then Sam and the medium rode off toward Hell Hole. That was the last I ever saw of Sam Stone.

So began my second experience of being completely alone. I had no horses but I had food sufficient for two or three weeks, and I was camped in the middle of a beautiful mountain meadow, replete with alpine flowers and placed within a huge mountainous amphitheater, the ramparts of which rose several thousand feet above my tent. In such a setting I really could not feel sorry for myself. Therefore I went ahead with the trail work, continuing my labors up to timberline and beyond to the pass that marked the divide between the Atlantic and Pacific drainage patterns of North America. Of course I could not do any of the heavy work, especially the blasting, that had been carried on by Sam with my assistance, but I was able to peck away at the trail with shovel and mattock, repairing the damage caused by winter snows and making the path suitable for human boots and horses' hooves.

Interestingly, I kept hearing footfalls of horses coming along the trail, yet the horses never appeared. Johnnie Johnston was due almost any day on an inspection trip; consequently I was expecting him, even to the extent of having hallucinations about horses coming to meet me on the side of the mountain. Then one evening, just before dark, I went down from my tent to the rushing stream for a pail of water, and when I turned around there were Johnnie and Jack Leighou, the forest supervisor, sitting on their horses, grinning at me like a couple of Cheshire cats. I had completely failed to hear the real footfalls of the horses.

Where was old Sam? was their first query. And when I told them what had happened they didn't know whether to be angry at Sam's desertion, and especially at his appropriation of government dynamite, or whether to be amused by the ludicrous unreality of the situation. The latter mood prevailed during much of the ensuing evening as we ate our supper around the campfire, and they made merry jokes about the possibility of my going off on a wacky search for gold. On a more serious note they promptly decided that my continued sojourn in that lovely spot could not be allowed; I would be moved the next morning to Arapaho Canyon to join two trail stiffs there— Clarence Murphy and my companion of the previous summer, Milt Johnson.

The next morning we broke camp and were on our way, and as we came to the mouth of Arapaho Canyon here came Milt Johnson down the trail, headed for the valley of the Colorado River, far beyond us. What was going on? Briefly, Milt was deserting Clarence Murphy because he wanted to work in one of the little mountain towns where he could be near a young lady in whom he was interested. More quips from Johnston and Leighou at my expense about the perils of working on Colorado trails.

We went up the canyon to find Clarence in his camp, all alone and wondering just what he was to do. Our arrival was the happy answer to his dilemma. I would be left with him to spend the rest of the summer on the Arapaho Canyon trail.

Clarence and I almost immediately became good friends, and we spent several interesting weeks working together in the depths of that canyon where the sun was late to reach us and early to leave us. Clarence was a veteran of the First World War (veterans in those days were young men), where he had experienced some harrowing combat during the summer and fall of 1918. For the first time in my life I had an account of the horrors of war from someone who had been there, and it made a deep impression on me.

There isn't much else to say about the rest of the summer, except to add that again I was involved in blasting operations, this time under the supervision of Clarence. He had a big deerhound named Speed, a dog that loved to be with us in the woods but hated dynamite blasts. When we would light the fuse of a charge and go running away, one of us up the trail and one down the trail, Speed would come along with the person of his choice at the moment, and as we stood each behind the protection of a big tree waiting for the explosion, Speed would shiver and whine most piteously. Then came the blast, a rush of air past us, accompanied by a shower of rocks, after which Speed was the happiest dog in that part of the state. He would jump and cavort and bark to tell us in his own way how glad he was that the ordeal was over.

As I went home after that second summer in the Forest Service my thoughts and feelings as to the future were mixed, to say the least. I was beginning to have some doubts as to whether forestry was really the profession I wished to follow. It was a good rough-and-ready way of life, but I was beginning to realize in a vague way that perhaps my tastes were inclined more toward an academic career—perhaps not a cloistered colle-giate life, but something that would involve books combined with a modicum of living in the wilds.

Of course I loved the forest and the living things in the forest. Never will I forget standing under a tree one afternoon, trying to shelter myself from a persistent rain, and watching a pine marten descend from a nearby tree to walk in my direction, never aware of my presence. Again, there is a pleasant memory of sitting on a mossy slope eating a lunch and being intrigued with the overwhelming curiosity displayed by an elegant little weasel that was almost beside itself trying to establish my identity. Back and forth it would scamper just beyond my feet, pausing frequently to peer at me with its head cocked first on one side and then on another. Perhaps it was attracted by the smell of my food; certainly it was of two minds as to just what it should do.

These were familiar things, but the less familiar things were the rocks that surrounded me on every side. I had not as yet enjoyed an opportunity for studying geology, either on my own or under proper instruction. My homeland of northwestern Missouri was a country of farms and fields and small strips of woodlands, as has already been mentioned, and such rocks as might be visible were restricted banks of black shale, sparingly exposed along scattered streams, or an occasional glacial erratic left over from the great ice age. Here there were rocks everywhere; what did they mean?

I was to find out what they meant, and soon, because during the winter following my second Forest Service year I abandoned the idea of forestry in favor of geology and paleontology—of rocks and fossils. This will presently be told; suffice it to say here that the winter of 1925–1926 marked a dividing line in my life, the time of change from a future dimly and uncertainly seen to a future having a degree of clarity and perhaps even certainty. But the change was not to be instantaneous; there was a period of transition, and during that transition I was to spend two more summers in the Arapaho forest, not so much in preparation for my future as a means of continuing summer employment at familiar tasks.

Consequently I went to Colorado again in 1926, to work for Johnnie Johnston, this time spending the summer with a fellow of my own age and general inclinations, Jerry Yetter, a forestry student at what was then the Colorado Agricultural College in Fort Collins. Jerry was already out on the trail when I reported at Idlewild Ranger Station, so with directions as to how to find him I went into the woods, where in due course of time I caught up with him at work with another fellow, a Middle Park local by the name of Chris Young. As companions they had an elegant little buckskin with a black stripe down the middle of its back (it was Jerry's personal saddle horse), another general-purpose bay horse which we called Mizoopy, and a Dalmation dog named Laddie that belonged to Jerry.

For a time the three of us set up camp at the edge of a mountain meadow called Devil's Thumb Park, where we arranged a roof of slender pine saplings and evergreen boughs between two huge boulders, this to serve as our cook shack. From this base we would walk every morning up into the forest on the slopes above us, and every morning at one place where we had to cross a rushing mountain stream on a fallen log Chris would slip off, to land in the icy water waist deep. And every evening on our return to camp Chris would again fall off the log; it seemed to be a sort of daily ceremonial baptism for him.

Chris didn't stay with us very long; he got another job down in the valley more to his liking. So there Jerry and I were, laboring on the trails in a scene of alpine beauty when Johnnie Johnston and Jack Leighou showed up on an inspection trip. Either they brought with them a large work horse, complete with harness, or they made arrangements for us to pick up this horse somewhere—my memory is a bit hazy as to this detail. At any rate we had for a part of our summer the use of this big equine, which we named Charlie. (He probably had a proper name of his own, but we never found that out.)

Charlie was very useful on the trail; we could use him for all sorts of heavy work such as pulling big logs aside or yanking out alders and other underbrush by the roots. Charlie had one idiosyncracy, quite a natural one for a horse, and that was a dislike of the whip. So when he pulled in a half-hearted sort of way one of us would appear in front of him with a little branch from a tree and shout "Charlie!" and he would put his shoulder to the harness in a proper fashion.

(Later that summer I saw an interesting example of Charlie's skill as a logging horse. I was back at Idlewild Ranger Station and had gone over to the Billy Wood sawmill nearby, where Charlie usually worked. There was Charlie down by the sawmill, waiting for some logs to be dragged into the mill, and above him on a little hill a couple of loggers were working on a log deck. They loosened several logs, and two or three of the logs rolled down the hill toward Charlie. I held my breath; I was sure that Charlie was going to be hurt by the big logs rolling toward him. I need not have feared. Charlie heard the logs coming, he turned to face them, and as each log reached him he nimbly leaped over it as it rolled beneath him. It was as nice as a circus performance.)

Of course with these horses, as with other horses that I worked with in the forest, we had the constant problem of nighttime wanderings. Thus our first order of business upon awakening each morning was to stick our heads out of the tent to see if we had any horses. And more than once we had to go out on time-consuming horse hunts, either before breakfast or after having fortified ourselves for such exercise. It is not easy to corner and capture some determined horses in the forest, where there are no fences to contain them.

One of my memories of that summer was the night when Jerry rode into camp (I think he had gone into town for supplies) accompanied by Laddie with a face full of porcupine quills. Laddie was a good mountain dog and he knew enough to avoid porcupines, but this time he had blundered into the porcupine in the dark. Jerry and I spent a couple of hours with the poor dog, one holding him while the other yanked out quills with a pair of pliers. It was a rugged experience for all concerned.

We finished that summer high on the shoulder of James Peak, well above timberline, where the wind whistled around us as, bundled against the cold, we clumsily cleared the trail, and where the horses stood with their heads down and their tails to the howling wind.

Such work continued during my final and fourth summer, when for most of the time I was paired with a student named Barney Dean, from Morningside College in Sioux City, Iowa. That was the year of Lindbergh's epochal flight across the Atlantic Ocean to Paris, and the whole world was agog with wonder at this feat. It will be recalled that Lindbergh flew a plane christened the *Spirit of St. Louis,* so named because the project had been backed by a group of St. Louis business men.

One day as Barney and I were working on the trail there appeared a group of people on horses accompanied by a large packtrain. The party was led by Mr. Knight of St. Louis, one of the men involved with the Lindbergh flight, who was out in the mountains with some friends for a wilderness pack trip. They stopped to chat with us, and I remember visiting for a while with

Mr. Knight as he sat by the side of the trail, enjoying a little rest from the rigors of the saddle.

Late that day the packhorses and mules of the Knight party appeared, making their way down the mountain toward the home ranch. Barney and I tried to head them off, but they galloped past us in fine style, to be followed about twenty minutes later by two irate mounted cowboys. Evidently the horse handlers had to chase the fugitives all the way back to the ranch; the next morning the cowboys appeared again with their charges in tow, the halter of each animal tied to the tail of the beast ahead. The cowboys weren't wasting any time in getting the packtrain back to the marooned vacationers; they stopped for the briefest of talks with us.

For about a month before Barney and I joined forces I worked with an old codger named Pete Mills, and we made our headquarters at Byers Ranger Station, then unoccupied, and for me it holds many pleasant memories. We were there warm and dry and comfortable in the evenings and at night—a welcome change from tents—and above all the place was supplied with lamps so that I could read before turning in after a day in the woods. It was there that I read the first installment of *Jalna* by Mazo de la Roche, in the *Atlantic Monthly*, writing that I found extraordinarily charming. Her description of a summer morning on a Canadian farm has been one of my very pleasant memories for six decades.

And these six decades later I was able to return to Middle Park, thanks to the kindness of Howard Johnston, the little boy that I had seen in Johnnie Johnston's arms, now a man of middle age, who with his wife took my wife and myself there on an October day to see some of the places where I had worked so many years ago. We tried to find Byers Ranger Station, but it was gone. Perhaps we found where it had been, at least we think we did. We went to other haunts of my Forest Service days, most of them changed beyond recognition, for the wild country in which I had worked has now become criss-crossed by paved roads, and everywhere there are resorts and hotels established for the convenience of people interested in winter sports. For me it was a bittersweet pilgrimage.

As I had traveled by train from my home to my work in the Arapaho forest I had often stopped in Lincoln, Nebraska, where my brother Philip, newly married, was living. Phil was an engineer, and had just joined the faculty of the University of Nebraska, to teach civil engineering. It was pleasant and relaxing to visit Phil and his wife, True, and to enjoy the amenities of their home, especially after a summer of labor on forest trails. Morever, it was instructive to visit the university, where I was especially interested in the university museum.

The museum at Lincoln was and is particularly noted for its collection of fossil mammals obtained from Cenozoic sediments, the geologic strata belonging to the Age of Mammals, of the high plains, and these fossils fascinated me. (See the discussion of the Cenozoic and other geologic ages at the end of this chapter.) The skulls and skeletons of ancient horses and camels, rhinoceroses and mastodonts, and carnivores large and small, were to me objects not only of scientific interest because of the insight they provided as to life within the interior of North America many millions of years ago, but also because they were esthetically pleasing. There is a beauty about fossil bones (many if not all such fossils) that transcends their basic quality as the remains of ancient life, a beauty involving the forms of the fossils and the texture of their surfaces. The minerals included in the process of fossilization whereby the bony material is infiltrated and replaced and thereby petrified—that is, turned to stone—often lend color to the fossil that makes it esthetically more interesting to look at than if it had the coloring of the original bone. Of course some fossil bones are white or near-white, as one would expect was originally the case. But many fossil bones may be black or they may show purple or red tints or even other colors, commonly depending on the amount of iron, manganese, and other minerals present during the process of petrification. (In Australia fossils are found in which opal is the replacing mineral, making them indeed objects of great beauty.)

The main reason, however, for my interest in the fossils that I saw in the university museum was their obvious function as records of past life on the earth. Here were the tangible remains of animals that lived in a past incredibly distant from our world, yet showing in spite of their great age all of the minute details, even the microscopic details, that had distinguished them when they were parts of living organisms. There was for me truly a mystique about such objects. Furthermore my thoughts were captivated, even excited, by the knowledge that the fossil bones, so beautifully displayed behind glass, had once been enclosed within rocks—not the rocks that had aroused my curiosity in the mountains, but rocks of a different sort which nonetheless were equally a part of the earth's crust. Here were treasures no less precious in their own way than if they had been nuggets of gold. Such thoughts were very much with me during and after my stopover in Lincoln following my second season of Forest Service work. That was in the early fall of 1925.

It is a common enough experience in the lives of men and women that little things may have great consequences—common enough that there need be no elaboration of the phenomenon at this place. Yet one such little thing looms large in my memory of that time, and the little thing was a letter.

After I got back home that fall the image of the Nebraska museum and its fossils stayed with me, not to go away. As I became immersed in my third year of undergraduate studies the mental pictures of fossils kept impinging upon my consciousness, frequently to drive away thoughts of chemistry or physics or English literature upon which I should have been concentrating my attention. I felt deprived because I had not been offered the opportunity to learn something about geology and paleontology; these subjects were not then available in the college at Maryville. The more I dwelt in my mind upon the mysteries of rocks and fossils, the more I felt dissatisfied with my world as it then existed.

So one day in the early spring of 1926 I sat down as the result of a sudden decision—or perhaps one might call it a whim—and wrote to my brother Phil in Lincoln the letter that I mentioned in a preceding sentence. In this letter I asked Phil if he would be willing to find out what kind of a future there might be in the field of paleontology. It was at best a shot in the dark, a gamble of sorts, and at worst it was a forlorn hope. In whatever light I viewed it I certainly did not expect much to eventuate.

I did not have long to wait. Within a few days I had a reply from Phil; he had gone around to the museum and had talked with Dr. Barbour, the director, who had suggested that I come to Lincoln for an interview. This was more than I had expected and at first I was taken aback. What had been for me something of a fantasy had suddenly become a reality, a situation to be dealt with immediately, with very little time for contemplation and a minimum allotment of time for preparation. Not much in the way of supporting materials were gathered together; about all I can remember were some drawings of modern skeletons that I had made as part of a biology course.

A date was set for my journey, which for some reason coincided with a day that my parents were to be out of town. Never mind, I would manage. The managing involved getting up long before the sun had made its morning appearance, to catch the train that stopped briefly in Maryville on its daily run between St. Louis and Omaha. The night before, I was in a fever of apprehension; could I manage to arise, get a bite, and get to the station at the appointed hour? Just to make sure I asked Marve Westfall to come over and spent the night at our house, which he most obligingly consented to do. Certainly one of us would hear the alarm clock.

My precautionary measures were quite unnecessary, as might have been foretold. Sleep for me was fitful, and I was fully prepared to leap out of bed well before the alarm went off. Marve accompanied me to the station and saw me off, and by the time it was daylight I was well on the way to Omaha, sitting in a chair car watching the rolling hills of Missouri and Iowa slide past the window.

In Omaha I had to change trains, from the Wabash to the Burlington. Then by midmorning or perhaps even earlier I was in Lincoln. Phil met me, and after a lunch downtown he accompanied me to the university where I had my meeting with Dr. Barbour. I don't know what I expected; certainly the meeting was uneventful. Barbour came into an outer office where I was waiting, to usher me to his private sanctum. He was a tall, middle-aged man with gray hair, a sort of imperial beard, pince-nez eyeglasses secured by a chain over one ear from flying to the floor should they pop off the bridge of his nose, and clad in a dark, conservative suit. He was cordiality itself, and conversed easily with me, which was a good thing because I probably did not talk in a very intelligent manner. He looked at my drawings and found them good. And at the end of the interview he suggested that if I should come to the university for the beginning of the fall semester he could give me a student assistantship in the university museum. It was as simple and as informal as that, for those were simple, informal days when student grants-in-aid were rare and tuition fees were minuscule. There were no letters of agreement, nothing was signed; all I had to go on was Dr. Barbour's casual statement made at the end of our conversation together. I went out of his office feeling elated and hoping that he would remember, six months in the future, what he had said.

I spent the evening with my brother and sister-in-law, and a very happy evening it was. After that I bedded down in a guest room to indulge in pleasant dreams, after which, the next day, I returned home.

On the way home from Lincoln, and during the days after I got back from that trip, I gave much thought to what might be ahead for me, which made me become increasingly aware of the step I had taken. Without doubt my life would soon diverge from its previous course to be pointed in a new direction, and as I thought about it I wondered what the details of that direction might be and more particularly *why* I was embarking upon such a course. Why was I so eager to enter a door that opened the way to a possible career and a mode of life filled with uncertainties? Why was I planning to take a first crucial step that would involve me in a course of strange and unknown studies, which in turn offered nothing definite at its end? Why did I wish to become a vertebrate paleontologist?

Above all, it was because of those lovely skulls and skeletons in the Nebraska museum; they had appealed to me as I suppose visions of ivory, apes, and peacocks had filled the thoughts of explorers in ages past. But in my case there was no thought of ownership; I was not (and I never have been) interested in finding fossils for myself. It was what the fossils had to tell us about a world long vanished that caught my imagination. One might say that I came to paleontology by chance; perhaps if I had not visited a museum during a few spare hours my life would have been very different. My conversion to paleontology was largely accidental, and it certainly was sudden.

My own experience paralleled after a fashion the experience of my close friend Alfred S. Romer, one of the great American vertebrate paleontologists, and for many years the doyen of our profession in this country. Al, who never let a good story suffer, liked to tell people that he became a vertebrate paleontologist because he was bitten by a mad dog. What actually happened was that he was bitten by his fox terrier, which was suspected of being rabid, and for this reason he was sent from his home in Connecticut to New York City, for treatments at a branch of the Pasteur Institute. In those days such treatments were painful and protracted, and during the time Al was not being injected and otherwise medically tortured he stayed with some aunts in Brooklyn. And when he was not at either the institute or at his aunts' house, he spent many hours at the American Museum of Natural History, where he was completely excited by the fossils on display. (Al's story of his subsequent training and career in paleontology was, when told by Al, extremely hilarious; one of his charming traits was that although he was serious about his subject he was anything but stuffy about himself.)

Al and I became paleontologists because we were entranced by fossils we saw in museums, and it is probable that other paleontologists chose this field of endeavor for similar reasons. But the motives for becoming a paleontologist have been extraordinarily diverse, and surprisingly enough, as often as not more or less accidental. There is no preordained path that one follows to become a vertebrate paleontologist; there are no cut and dried rules to follow. Some of my colleagues have entered the field because of books they have read, some because of lectures attended in universities and colleges, some because of a childhood fascination with dinosaurs, some because of paleontological field trips in which they have participated, some because of the influence of teachers, either in secondary school or at higher levels, and some for other reasons too various to be described.

Professor William Berryman Scott of Princeton, an outstanding figure in the history of North American vertebrate paleontology, tells how he and his close friend Henry Fairfield Osborn, an equally outstanding figure who during many years made the American Museum of Natural History in New York a world center of vertebrate paleontology, became paleontologists.

Near the end of Junior year [Princeton 1876] there occurred an incident which, though it seemed trivial enough at the time, nevertheless proved to be the pivot on which turned not only all my subsequent career, but that of Harry Osborn as well. He had intended to go into the business of railroads and finance. . . . I had determined to study medicine. . . . We had reached the examination period in June and, one very hot day, had gone down to the canal for a swim. . . . After bathing and dressing, we lay on the canal bank and tried to read Paley, but it was too hot to do real work and we began to talk. I said: "Fellows! I have just been reading in an old *Harper's* an account of a Yale expedition to the Far West in search of fossils; why can't we get up something like that?" I hardly meant my question seriously, but Spier [Francis Spier, who never became a professional paleontologist] and Osborn took to the suggestion at once and, with one voice exclaimed: "We can, let's do it." (*Some Memories of a Paleontologist* [Princeton: Princeton University Press, 1939], page 48.)

Scott and Osborn did, and from that first expedition of theirs they entered upon their paleontological careers to develop in a way that through the years profoundly influenced the growth of vertebrate paleontology not only in North America but also throughout the world.

As contrasted with the experience of Scott and Osborn and Romer and many other paleontologists some of the earlier practitioners of this science became more passively involved with the study of extinct vertebrates. Such as Joseph Leidy, professor of anatomy in the Medical School of the University of Pennsylvania. In the words of W. B. Scott, Leidy was "one of the most remarkable of American men of science in many departments of research, was first in the field and began to publish descriptions of fossils from the Far West in the 'forties of the last century. His reputation became so great, that almost all discoveries of vertebrate fossils in the United States were reported and usually the specimens were sent for description to him." (*Memories*, page 57.) The same was true for Sir Richard Owen, the great English anatomist who was a generation before Leidy, and the same was true for Baron Georges Cuvier, the French anatomist who lived a little earlier than Owen.

But even today, when vertebrate paleontology is a well-established and influential science, the approach to its study and practice is still informal and in a way haphazard. Some of today's paleontologists have come to it by way of geology departments in universities, others by way of biology departments, others by way of medical and veterinary anatomy, and still others by no very formal ways at all. Of course I knew none of this when I was first contemplating the step I had taken, I only knew that I was entering into what for me was an unknown world.

On several preceding pages of this book various geologic time and stratigraphic terms have been employed. At this place an explanation of the geologic time scale will be presented, because there will be frequent references to the divisions of geologic time throughout the remainder of the book.

Our modern concept of geologic time is based upon the study of the rock strata that comprise the crust of the earth. These strata, as measured by radiometric techniques, form a record going back through about four billion years of earth history. Since the strata were deposited consecutively through time it is obvious that the oldest strata are at the bottom of the sequence, the youngest at the top. The larger portion of this four-billion-year record of earth history consists of rocks designated as of *Precambrian* age, such rocks being for the most part devoid of fossils. (Only the youngest of the Precambrian rocks contain traces of ancient life, these consisting of the imprints of soft-bodied organisms.)

An adequate fossil record begins with rocks designated as of *Cambrian* age, appearing about six hundred million years ago. From this point to the present the fossil record is well preserved in various parts of the earth, and it has been divided into large and smaller units, as shown in the table. Remember that the oldest units are at the bottom of the time scale, and that they become progressively younger as one proceeds from the bottom to the top of the sequence. The ages in years of the rock units comprising the geologic column have been determined (rather accurately, we now believe) by radiometric dating, based upon the decay of radioactive elements contained within the rocks.

Perhaps a few words about the origins of these names will be helpful. The names of the eras are based upon Latin words, meaning "ancient life" (Paleozoic), "middle life" (Mesozoic), and "recent life" (Cenozoic). As for the periods, Cambrian comes from *Cambria*, the ancient Latin name of Wales, where rocks of this age were first studied and named. Ordovician and Silurian are based upon the names of two ancient Welsh tribes, the Ordovices and Silures. Devonian comes from Devonshire, England, again as in the case of Cambrian, Ordovician, and Silurian, the region where the rocks were first studied and named. Carboniferous is named for the "coal measures," quite obviously for the abundance of coal deposits in rocks of this age. Mississippian and Pennsylvanian are names based on the regions where early and late Carboniferous rocks were studied in North America. Permian is named for the Province of Perm, in Russia. Triassic is based upon the threefold division of these rocks in central Europe, hence Trias. Jurassic is named after the Jura mountains of Europe. Cretaceous is so named from the chalk cliffs along the English Channel, *creta* being the Latin for chalk. Tertiary and Quaternary are holdover names from an earlier time of geologic studies, when there were only four periods: Primary, Secondary, Tertiary, and Quaternary. The first two terms have been abandoned. Most of the names of the Cenozoic epochs were proposed by Charles Lyell, the great pioneer English paleontologist. He based these names on the proportions of fossil mollusc shells in the sediments. Paleocene means ancient recent; Eocene, dawn of the recent; Oligocene, less recent; Miocene, new recent; Pliocene, more recent; Pleistocene, most recent. These names are universally used, in every language; the geologic time scale is applied world-wide.

ERA	PERIOD	EPOCH	YEARS AGO
Cenozoic	Quaternary	Pleistocene	
	Tertiary	Pliocene Miocene Oligocene Eocene Paleocene	65 million
Mesozoic	Cretaceous	Late Early	
	Jurassic	Late Middle Early	
	Triassic	Late Middle Early	245 million
Paleozoic	Permian	Late Early	
	Carboniferous*	Late Early	
	Devonian	Late Middle Early	
	Silurian	Late Early	
	Ordovician	Late Middle Early	
	Cambrian	Late Middle Early	570 million

Precambrian

*In North America the early and late Carboniferous are called Mississippian and Pennsylvanian, respectively.

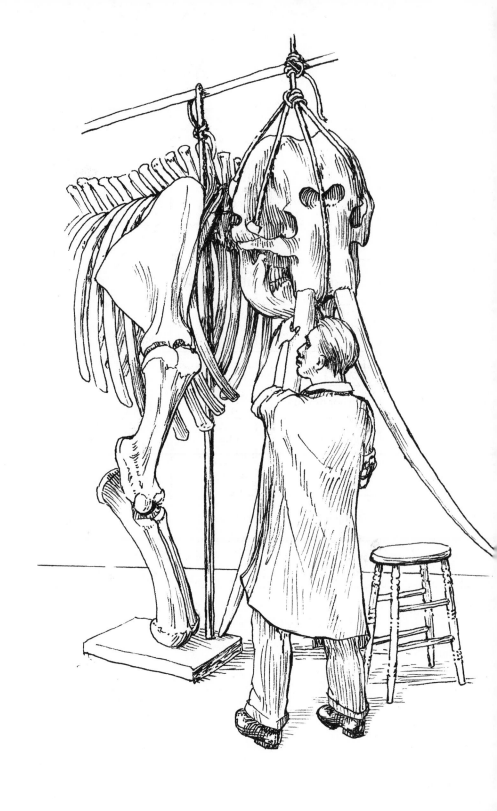

VII

Learning the Craft

*T*he removal from my home in northwestern Missouri to the University of Nebraska, although not very far in terms of distance (a mere one hundred twenty-five miles), was remarkably great insofar as it affected me psychologically. Maryville was a small town, and even though I had been in large cities, Chicago and Denver for example, I had seen them through the eyes of a transient visitor always ready to return to the comfort and security of my home environment. Now I was faced with the reality of going to live away from home, in a city that seemed huge and impersonal to me in spite of the fact that it truly was not a very large city—in those days a prairie metropolis with perhaps something on the order of a hundred thousand inhabitants. Moreover the university also seemed huge and impersonal; it *was* a fairly large university for the times, with a student body of about six thousand. But above all, it seemed threatening, a place where I was an insignificant being, struggling to make my way among thousands of others like me. For the first time in my life I sat in large lecture halls, with the professor far away and seeming oblivious to my existence, with my presence noted by a number on the back of an assigned seat, with an assistant of some kind to check on my attendance, and with other assistants to meet me in a laboratory or to confer with me on a paper I might have written. All in all it was a traumatic and in some ways an unhappy time.

My life was made bearable, however, because of the attention given me by my brother and his wife, and by relationships that I established at the university museum. Otherwise I do not know how I would have survived. At that time the university had no dormitories, so I had to scrounge for a place to live. Phil had belonged to a fraternity when he was in college at the Missouri School of Mines, and so he put the Lincoln branch of his fraternity onto my trail. But the hurly-burly of fraternity life was far removed from the life style that I had in mind, so I made inquiries and tramped the streets until I found quarters in a nice home a dozen blocks or so distant from the university, in the meantime living with my relatives. The result was that within a week or so after having arrived in Lincoln I had become established in reasonable comfort; I had a room to myself and the enjoyment of privacy.

Yet the sense of an ever-present threat loomed all through that first semester for it seemed to me that the university had little interest in whether I was there or not. Perhaps I was unduly sensitive, imagining attitudes on the part of my professors that they truly did not have. I do remember that when I went home for Christmas vacation it was with the greatest foreboding that I faced the prospect of returning to Lincoln to complete the semester. I suppose that my experience was, and still is, the common experience of young, unsophisticated students facing up for the first time to life at a large state university.

By the time the academic year had run its course I had become adjusted to the university and to the city, so that life did not seem nearly so worrisome or frightening as it had seemed when I first entered this new environment. Lincoln was, I discovered, a pleasant city, large enough to have many advantages that I had not enjoyed in my hometown, yet small enough so that one could get around without much effort. Of course the easy way around town was by car, but in those days not many students had cars, as is the case today, so we relied on the public transport system consisting of street cars, commonly designated by the students as "the yellow peril." Many of the cars were little four-wheeled affairs, a bit like the famous Toonerville Trolley, with front and back platforms extending well beyond the front and back wheels. Which tempted students who were feeling especially jolly to crowd onto the back platform and jump up and down in unison, causing the car to jump the track in short order. I don't know quite what was accomplished by this tactic; I suppose it was intended to be fun. Beyond the downtown business district the city consisted largely of one-family homes, each surrounded by a lawn. (Recently, sixty years after my first year in Lincoln, I returned for a visit and was impressed by the expanses of green lawn and the arching trees, shining bright in the afternoon sun.)

Lincoln is the state capital, and when I was there the new State House was being built—not at all like the usual state capitol which is a miniature replica of the building in Washington, but rather a spreading limestone structure with a great tower rising from its center, a tower from the apex of which one could look far across the prairie.

This was the city of General John Pershing, who as a young officer had been in charge of the R.O.T.C. students (Nebraska as a land-grant college was required to maintain a two-year army training course for all male students). I saw Pershing twice; once when he dropped in to the museum, and once, in 1928, when he rode, in a car, in the tenth anniversary parade of Armistice Day. All in all Lincoln was a characteristic middle-western small city, perhaps more town than city, with an atmosphere of general contentment—perhaps too much of such an atmosphere.

The university had its own particular atmosphere, influenced to some extent by a tradition of English letters. This was the place where Willa Cather spent her first years of writing, and it was subsequently the literary cradle of Mari Sandoz. It seemed only natural for me to continue courses in English, the courses I had so enjoyed in high school and at the college in Maryville. So I did, with the result that when it came time for me to graduate, my major was in English, even though I was preparing myself to be a paleontologist.

It seems to me that none of my English professors at Nebraska had quite the feeling for the language that had been so characteristic of Miss Painter, the Quaker lady at the college in Maryville. Still, there was much that I could learn from them. As for other professors, I especially enjoyed studying invertebrate zoology under Dr. Harold Manter, stratigraphy and sedimentation with Dr. A. L. Lugn, and anthropology with Hutton Webster. Manter was a lot of fun; he was a New Englander, and I liked to hear him lecture about the "flat wums" and "round wums." Hutton Webster introduced me to a new world, a world I think every educated person should become acquainted with, a world that affords an understanding of our own culture, an understanding that all too many people do not have. As for Dr. Lugn, I became closely associated with him before my days at Nebraska were over; one summer, as will be told, we were in the field together. He was a short man with reddish hair and the most unusual complexion I have ever seen, for his skin was a sort of purple color. I think it was owing to some medication he had once been forced to take.

Of course I had various friends among the student body at Lincoln. During my first year there I became closely acquainted with a fellow named Harlan Smedley; we were students together in a French course. He was a music major and was devoting his attention to the organ. He held a position as organist in one of the Lincoln churches, and on several occasions I went with him in the evening to a practice session. The organ console was in a loft at the back of the church; it was winter and the church was unheated, but the organ loft was enclosed with a canvas "tent" and a little electric heater inside this enclosure made it reasonably comfortable. There was something a bit eerie to sit there in the tent and to hear the music coming back at us from far down at the front of the church auditorium. I did enjoy it.

The university museum (it was also officially the Nebraska State Museum) was theoretically a museum of natural history, but practically it was a museum of vertebrate paleontology, with some mineralogy thrown in, and with a modicum of biology. As such it reflected its historic development, as is so frequently the case with museums, large and small. Nebraska throughout much of its extent has at the surface large expanses of middle and late Cenozoic sedimentary rocks, and these deposits are notably rich in the fossilized remains of vertebrates, or backboned animals, especially mammals that inhabited the prehistoric interior plains of North America in vast numbers. It is as if Nebraska and adjacent states foretold millions of years ago what the African veldt would be today—with a different fauna, of course. This treasure trove of ancient life had been exploited for many years by Dr. Barbour and of course it was basically because of this collection of fossil mammals that I was at the university.

Dr. Barbour had not forgotten the promise he had made to me, so that as soon as I arrived in Lincoln there was work for me at the museum. Within a few weeks I had become settled there and acquainted with the little coterie of museum people who formed that inner circle where I found refuge. It was not a very large circle.

Dr. Barbour was at the head of the group, a distinguished looking man who might very well have come out of a Wodehouse novel. He had studied under O. C. Marsh at Yale before he came to Nebraska, back the latter years of the nineteenth century, so he had some stories to tell of Marsh, the fabled pioneer of vertebrate paleontology in North America. Marsh's detested rival was Edward Drinker Cope of Philadelphia; and Scott and Osborn, whom we met in the last chapter and who will figure largely in some chapters to come (especially Osborn) were disciples of Cope. Barbour once told me that when he was at Yale, Marsh instructed him to hide all of the specimens that Osborn and Scott, who were scheduled to come to New haven to study fossils in the Peabody Museum, were not supposed to see. So Barbour hid the fossils as instructed. Then, all the time that Scott and Osborn were in the museum, Marsh, who had donned carpet slippers, crept around from corner to corner, hiding behind cases and other vantage points, to spy upon the young followers of Cope.

Incidentally it was my fortune, owing to circumstances and to the time when I began my paleontological career, to have known intimately Barbour, the student of Marsh, as well as Osborn and Scott, the protégés of Cope. Consequently some bits of oral history were passed along to me by protagonists in the early development of North American paleontology. It was my impression from what these men said that nobody really loved Marsh; he was thoroughly self-centered and, to be frank, somewhat unscrupulous. Samuel Wendell Williston, another Marsh student and assistant, was in his middle life one of the great authorities on fossil reptiles. For many years he was a professor at the University of Chicago, where he not only built up a superb collection of Permian reptiles and amphibians, but where he continued studies that he had begun years previously on modern flies. In fact, he was the great authority on North American flies, or Diptera. His daughter, a friend of my wife's and whom I got to know, once told us that her father took to flies when he was working for Marsh— as a sort of anodyne to preserve his sanity. And I remember once having mentioned Marsh to Professor Scott, then an elderly and very dignified man, whereupon Scott turned red in the face and swore sulfurous oaths—this a half-century after his last contacts with Marsh. Scott told me that in his young days Marsh was widely known as "the great dismal swamp."

What about Cope, the Quaker naturalist? He was a man of extraordinary brilliance, one might say a genius, very different from Marsh, who was an industrious plodder. Cope was far from being a saint, but from what I heard I got the impression that he was a man of warmth, and a person with a merry outlook upon life. He was erratic, yet on the whole he was well liked. Soon after the Second World War I was in Philadelphia with my colleague Bobb Schaeffer, and we called on Cope's daughter, Mrs. Collins, then the very elderly widow of a Haverford College professor. We had a pleasant visit with her, but I didn't learn much about her father. We then visited the ancestral Cope home, in Philadelphia, a spacious stone house known as Fairfield, set in extensive grounds with trimmed boxwood hedges lining sidewalks and paths. Here Cope grew up in the midst of a loving family, where he enjoyed the advantages of wealth and culture. We were shown the place by Mrs. Paul Sangree, Cope's grandniece, and at the end of our visit she presented me with a little wooden box, a boy's tool chest, that had belonged to Cope when he was a little boy. It is one of my prized possessions, which I keep upon my desk.

This has been something of a digression and has got ahead of my story, all the result of mentioning Barbour as one of Marsh's students. To get back to Dr. Barbour, he was a kindly soul of distinguished appearance, and as has been mentioned was easily identifiable by an imperial beard and by pince-nez spectacles, secured to his person by a gold chain that terminated in a gold wire loop over one ear. He was not always an easy superior, not because of any harsh administrative habits but rather because he was about as unorganized a person as I have ever known. I don't think he had any plan for the day in his mind when he entered the museum each morning; he seemed to let things develop as the day wore on, suiting his decisions and his actions to the course of events.

During my first year at Nebraska I was required to take the course in general geology since I had not been exposed to that subject. Dr. Barbour was the lecturer for this course, which met the first hour each day in the amphitheater of another building than the museum, where a large class could be accommodated. Every morning he appeared at eight o'clock for that early lecture, and I think he must have indiscriminately grabbed a bunch of lantern slides on his way to class. Consequently our lectures in that course were wonderfully diverse and disconnected and more often than not had little to do with the fundamentals of geology. It was under the tutelage of the teaching assistants that we were exposed to the nitty-gritty facts of the science.

Dr. Barbour was something of a showman as was indicated by some of the museum displays. For instance the old museum was a crowded place with little room for presenting anything of large size. Nevertheless Dr. Barbour had managed to set up the fore limbs, in association with a few vertebrae and their accompanying ribs, of a huge mammoth at the head of the stairs when one ascended from the ground level to the second floor of the building, thereby forming an arch through which one necessarily passed. It was something to see in that old, overflowing building, and of course it helped Barbour to make a point; he could impress upon visitors, especially influential visitors, the need for an adequate and proper museum.

My immediate mentor that first year in Nebraska was Mr. Frederick George Collins, a roly-poly middle-aged little Englishman of considerable erudition and Britannic charm. Mr. Collins had been a business man in Exeter, England, but for many years he had been associated with the museum in that city, with the result that museums were truly his first love. Some years before I arrived in Lincoln his daughter had married a young Lincolnite who was in England as a Rhodes scholar, so when the newly married couple came back to Lincoln to make their home, Mr. Collins and his wife pulled up stakes and followed them. Mr. Collins gravitated to the museum, and soon he was made curator there, to manage the day-to-day functions of supervising collections and overseeing exhibits. Thanks to him I learned many of the basic principles of museum practice.

I was assigned as an assistant to Mr. Collins, and the first task he put me to was an exercise in dustproofing a lot of ancient exhibit cases, made of golden oak. These were upright cases of the type that were widely used in museums during late Victorian times: broad at the base with several sets of drawers for storing specimens, inclined panels of glass on each side at table height beneath which could be exhibited small specimens, and above the sloping glass panels upright glass windows extending to a height of perhaps six or seven feet thereby allowing for the display of larger specimens.

My job every day, when I was not occupied with classes and laboratory sessions, was to attempt the dustproofing of a case by propping up each sloping panel in turn, and applying a border of black, sticky tape along the juncture between the glass and its enclosing frame. It was a fussy and frustrating job; the tape had to be moistened on its gummed side and then applied evenly so that it made a regular, neat border along each edge of the glass panel.

Mr. Collins had found by sad experience that the only effective way to moisten the tape was to *lick* it; using a sponge just did not give it the necessary holding quality. Therefore during the autumn of 1926 I licked what seemed like miles of black tape, somewhat to the temporary detriment of my taste buds. But it wasn't all bad. I was doing over the cases that housed the display of minerals and rocks, so I became acquainted with all sorts of these natural objects.

As time went on during the year, my work with Mr. Collins became more varied and interesting, such as the time when he decided to dispose of some surplus minerals for which there were no records. Dr. Barbour was a regular jackdaw; he could never throw away anything. Thus it was up to Mr. Collins, with my assistance, to dispose of these surplus, museum-wise valueless, specimens without letting Dr. Barbour in on the secret. The solution we devised was to toss the unwanted specimens out of a window of the museum into a rock garden below. After all, such specimens by their nature should enhance the beauty of the rock garden. So we began our exercise, and as luck would have it a passerby thought we were throwing things at him. Consequently he started to bless us out in loud and strident tones, causing us to retreat quickly from the window and to hold our heads in agony, hoping that the rude remarks of the man below us were not wafted through the window of Dr. Barbour's office. Evidently they weren't.

Another occasion was the time when one museum number was found on two different specimens, one a fossil bone, the other a stuffed water bird—I think it was a snipe. Mr. Collins and Phil Orr (of whom more shortly) got into a terrible argument, almost a row, as to how this matter was to be handled. Which specimen should retain the original number, which should receive a new number? How should the catalogue be changed? It was my first experience with the importance of catalogue numbers and it was a lesson noisily and thoroughly imprinted upon my mind.

Phil Orr was a student assistant engaged in the preparation of fossils— the type of work that I really wanted to do, and the type of work that I was to do within a year. But for the present I could only look enviously at Phil working away on fossil bones, as I blunted my appetite for lunch by licking yards of sticky tape. Phil had had previous experience and was well versed in the techniques of fossil preparation, so well versed in fact that at the end of my first academic year he took off for Chicago and a job at the Field Museum. Phil was married, and he and his wife tooted around on and in a motorcycle equipped with a sidecar, a form of transportation rarely seen nowadays. My acquaintance with Phil lasted for only that year (although of course I saw him on various occasions in later years) but during that time he was very kind, and in spare moments taught me many things about fossils.

Particular mention should be made of Professor Frank Schramm, the mainstay of the geology department. He was a no-nonsense sort of teacher who made his students work hard, who at the same time was very fond of the young men under his charge, and especially interested in their future well-being. I say "men" because at that time there were no women in the geology curriculum at Nebraska; it was a rough and tough place strictly for males.

Then there was Marjorie Shanafelt, Dr. Barbour's secretary, an elegant lady who played the harp. A harp stood in the corner of her office, ready to flood the corridor with celestial music during the noon hour or at other odd times.

Then there was Carrie Barbour, Dr. Barbour's sister, an elderly, eccentric lady who performed various tasks for her brother. Much of her work as I recall was tracing drawings of extinct animals from publications to be used as illustrations for a book that Dr. Barbour had in mind. I think that was as far as the book ever got.

Finally I should mention C. Bertrand Schultz, a freshman student when I first went to Lincoln. He was aimed toward paleontology from the beginning; eventually he was to get his advanced degrees, and in due course of time he became director of the Nebraska museum, a post he held for many years.

All of what I have been describing took place in the old museum, a tall, narrow, brick edifice that had been built with the evident plan of being enlarged at some later date. But the addition was never made, so that the building was abruptly truncated on its back side away from the street, and that was the portal through which one entered the museum. In addition to housing the museum, this building was also home for the Department of Geology; consequently there were several professors and classes of students within its precincts. It was a busy and crowded place.

On another part of the campus a new museum–geology–fine-arts building was then under construction, and I was destined to help move some of the museum collections into the new building before the academic year had come to its end. This move began, as I recall, in the late spring and went on through the summer, but I was involved only in the initial phases of the transfer. As things worked out there were no funds for my summer employment, so I returned to Colorado for my last season of work on the Arapaho National Forest.

When I arrived at the university that fall things were settled down after a fashion in the new building, named Morrill Hall in honor of a university trustee who was much interested in paleontology and who had given considerable support to the program of the museum. By now my own position in this program was on a higher level than it had been during the previous year, perhaps by default as much as anything. Phil Orr had by then gone on to the Field Museum, someone was needed to do something about skeletons for exhibits, and the executive finger was pointed at me. Dr. Barbour called me into his office and informed me that I was to put up a skeleton of a little Miocene rhinoceros, *Diceratherium*,* this to be the first fossil skeleton displayed in what were then empty exhibit spaces.

Those empty exhibit spaces in Morrill Hall faced us with a formidable prospect as we entered the new building in the autumn of 1927. The structure was a hybrid affair, designed in part as a museum and in part as a classroom and office building. Around the outside perimeter of the building were the academic rooms, within the interior were the museum spaces, and these museum spaces, instead of being clear, open areas, available for the flexible design of exhibits, either permanent or temporary, were built in, according to a preconceived plan, thus imposing hard strictures upon the people faced with the problem of assembling new exhibits in a new building. Moreover, this building had been planned with the exhibit areas dominating and using up almost all of the museum space; there was little provision for storage space or for workrooms, which are essential to good museum management.

It is instructive to look at Morrill Hall with the benefit of hindsight. I admit that I do not know the history of its conception and execution; when I arrived at the university as an advanced undergraduate the building was already under construction and I viewed it with the admiring eye of an inexperienced and uncritical beholder. I suppose that perhaps Dr. Barbour was a key figure in planning the building, and if so the design was based upon the ideas of a person who was strongly biased in the direction of exhibiting showy specimens. This is quite legitimate up to a certain point; in a place like Nebraska at that time it was important to have spectacular or at least impressive specimens on display in order to develop a sympathetic

---

*Diceratherium is found in the Lower Miocene sediments of western Nebraska. Some paleontologists think that there is another, closely related rhinoceros, *Menoceras*, in these same sediments; other authorities think that the two supposed genera are one, in which case *Diceratherium* is the prior, valid name. In the present context I will opt for *Diceratherium*, partly for the sake of simplicity, partly because that was the name we used back in the twenties.

feeling among the public for the use of tax money to support such an institution. Thus on the main floor of Morrill Hall there were built-in cases, or more properly exhibit areas, on the two sides of the corridors that flanked the classrooms—shallow recesses on the classroom side; long, cavernous recesses, six or eight feet in depth, on the other side of the corridor. All of these display areas had glass fronts, and the ceiling of the corridor between them was arched, thus giving a certain unity to the whole arrangement. As one came into the building from the front entrance there was a large hall—"elephant hall"—again with huge recessed display areas on each side, fronted with great panes of glass. This was for the display of fossil mastodont and elephant skeletons which had been found within the state. All of this made for large exhibition spaces, but as has been said, spaces that were predetermined in arrangement and dimensions.

On the back walls of the large cases lining the corridors, and on the high walls of elephant hall, were frescoes, being executed at the time I was working at the museum by an artist named Elizabeth Dolan. She was truly talented, and of course it was unusual for her to be decorating the walls with frescoes; such work is not often done even today. Her colors were delicate, so that the overall effect was pleasing, making soft backgrounds for the skeletons that were to set up in front of the frescoed walls.

It was within one of the big recessed areas along one of the corridors, the back of which displayed a fresco showing the landscape surrounding the famous fossil quarries in northwestern Nebraska, that I was to mount the skeleton of *Diceratherium*.

It was to be the first of four skeletons with which I became involved during my final two years at the Nebraska museum. *Diceratherium*, unique among rhinoceroses past and present by having two horns arranged side by side on its nose, rather than in the usual fore and aft rhinoceros fashion, was rather small for members of the rhinoceros clan, an animal about three feet in height at the shoulder, having the bulk of a small pony. That little skeleton kept me busy during all of the time I could spare from my academic studies during the first semester of the year. And before I was through with it I came to rue the fact that mammals have to possess so many ribs and so many bones in the feet; they do complicate life for the osteologist setting up a skeleton. In *Diceratherium* there are about one hundred eighty bones in the skeleton, not counting the skull and lower jaws, and of these ninety-three are rib and foot bones. So I spent an inordinate amount of time dealing with bones that comprised half of the skeleton, ribs that were constantly breaking (because the fossil bones were as brittle as glass) and foot bones that had to be set up in their complex articulations. I finally got the skeleton together, with an iron rod through the vertebral column, complexly bent iron supports for the limb bones, and separate rods for the ribs, one along the inner surface of each rib.

The task of applying the rib supports and integrating them into the rest of the armature supporting the skeleton was something to try the patience of Job, but finally I succeeded. The mount wasn't very good, but there it was—one skeleton to represent the riches of Nebraska fossil fields.

Diceratherium was followed by a strange, horselike mammal (from the same strata in western Nebraska that had yielded the rhinoceros) known as *Moropus*, distinguished from its hoofed relatives by having on each foot three toes, each terminating in a large claw. (When fossil chalicotheres, of which *Moropus* was one, were first discovered in France, Baron Georges Cuvier, the great paleontologist, could not believe that the skull, which was horselike, and the large claws found in the same deposit, might possibly have belonged to the same animal. It was only after an articulated skeleton was found that this improbable association was proven.) Evidently *Moropus* and its chalicothere relatives, all cousins of horses and rhinoceroses, made their living by digging in the ground for roots and tubers on which they fed.

Moropus was a big animal, with a skeleton that stood about six feet high at the shoulder, and to begin my work on it a sort of Rube Goldberg scaffolding of wood was constructed on which to arrange the bones of the skeleton. One day smoke began to issue from the door of a heat tunnel that opened into the fossil laboratory of Morrill Hall, to creep and swirl insidiously toward *Moropus*, serenely standing on its temporary scaffold. In no time at all bells began to ring and soon some burly firemen burst into the laboratory, hauling a hose and brandishing axes. Right past *Moropus* they went, while the poor old fossil swayed back and forth and I held my head in anguish, expecting a loud crash and a floor covered with the fragments of fossil bones. But *Moropus* survived the onslaught, the fire in the heat tunnel was subdued, and life returned to normal

The following semester, in the fall of 1928, *Moropus* was succeeded by a gigantic piglike mammal known as *Dinohyus*, coming as did *Diceratherium* and *Moropus* from the Miocene sediments of western Nebraska. *Dinohyus*, about the size of a large buffalo, was one of the prizes in the Nebraska collection.

And following *Dinohyus* there came a modern African elephant, which was an easy task compared to the work on the fossil skeletons.

I could never have carried to completion this program of setting up four skeletons in two academic years without help, and help came in the person of Henry Reider. Henry had been one of the employees of the trucking company that had been engaged to do the heavy moving of collections from the old museum into the new building, and during this maneuver, which had taken place during the summer of 1927, he was completely captivated by the mystique of fossil bones. Consequently during that autumn when I was struggling with *Diceratherium* he was hounding Dr. Barbour for a job. His efforts were successful, so by the time I had gotten into the *Moropus* project Henry arrived on the scene to lend a hand. It was quite a hand.

Henry turned out to be a regular Sam Weller type; he was not afraid to tackle any job, no matter how strange, and he usually managed to carry through with a buoyant air and flying colors. Moreover Henry had many skills, not the least of which was an ability to work with iron. That was important, because we needed to make iron armatures for the skeletons, and such supports were necessarily very complex, being bent to fit the contours of the vertebrae and limb bones. The fossil laboratory in the new museum building had been equipped with an old-fashioned coal-fired forge, and Henry took charge of that.

So with Henry heating and shaping irons we were able to go ahead as a team and get those skeletons in place—where they are today. Henry was exactly suited to the job of mounting fossil skeletons and he made this his life work, spending the rest of his days at the museum. Needless to say his techniques improved, and he set up numerous skeletons which stand today as monuments to his skill.

Mounting the fossil skeletons was invaluable training for me since it gave me the opportunity to learn one phase of paleontological museum work that is not often available to students of the science. My primary interest, however, was in the scientific side of vertebrate paleontology, something that I was also learning during those Nebraska years.

Here let me interject some remarks about the science that I had chosen for my life work. Vertebrate paleontology (like all branches of paleontology) is a science that deals with natural objects, these being fossils that occur in the earth's crust. Fossils are the remains or indications of past life on the earth and they occur in sedimentary rocks, namely sandstones, shales, and limestones that represent deposition by wind, streams, lakes, and oceans. They may be very common or they may be rare, depending upon circumstances. Whatever the nature of the fossils they should be treated with respect because they are invaluable records of the ancient past.

Consequently the initial procedure in the practice of this science is to excavate the fossils from sites where they have been entombed for thousands and more generally millions of years. Because paleontologists and archeologists dig things out of the ground they are for this reason often confused in the public mind. Some of their methods may be similar, but their purposes are quite different. Paleontologists study ancient life as revealed by the remains or traces of extinct animals and plants—in other words, fossils. Archeologists study ancient man as revealed by his remains and his artifacts.

After the first step of excavation the second step is to prepare the fossils in the laboratory, to which they have been removed. This is necessary to make the fossils available for study; more often than not they must be removed from or exposed within the rocky or sandy matrix containing them, in order that they may be examined thoroughly from every angle. The business of preparation, especially the preparation of many fossil vertebrates, is exceedingly painstaking and time consuming. Indeed, work in the laboratory on a fossil may involve ten, twenty, even fifty times the number of hours spent collecting it in the field.

A very necessary third step is to catalogue the fossils, giving each significant specimen a number and listing that number in a museum catalogue with a record of all pertinent data. A fossil without proper accompanying data is worthless. So it is that in the catalogue there are recorded in detail the locality at which the fossil was found, the geologic horizon or level at which it occurred (a very important notation), who found and collected it, the date, and any other facts that are necessary to make the record as complete as possible.

With the fossil prepared and catalogued, the very important fourth step in the procedure then takes place: identification and study. This may be a very lengthy process indeed. It involves comparison of the fossil with other similar fossils so that its relationships may be firmly established. If the fossil represents a hitherto unknown form or if it is otherwise significant, such identification is followed by a careful study and description of the specimen. This may involve a great deal of time and effort on the part of the paleontologist, but it is crucially important if the fossil is to have a real meaning to the world of science and to the public, now and in years to come.

A fifth step, equally as important as the identification and study of the fossil, is its publication. Only then does it become a truly significant object. In this connection I can do no better than to quote a statement by an outstanding archeologist, Leslie Alcock, concerning the publication of archeological discoveries. His remarks are equally applicable to fossils.

Archaeological excavations are not primarily carried out to enrich the cabinets of collectors, whether public or private, nor for the mere delectation of those who take part in them. Although they are often conducted as though these were their true aims, in fact the purpose of excavating is to acquire knowledge, with the further implication that the knowledge so won should be disseminated. With this in mind, it has been well said that the date of a discovery is the date of its publication. This is true also at a deeper level: it is only when the excavator disciplines his eyes, his hands and his mind to the task of drawing and writing up his finds for publication, and using them as foundations for historical inference, that he himself really knows what he has found, in all its manifold implications and equally manifold limitations. In this sense, the publication *is* the discovery. (*Arthur's Britain*, [New York: Penguin Books, 1980], page 153.)

Any paleontologist worth his or her salt takes a great deal of pleasure in thinking of the discoveries he has made in the field and laboratory, but true satisfaction is in the publications that describe and interpret the fossils. More of this later.

A sixth step is the storage of the fossils so that they constitute a valuable archive for future students. This may not seem like much, but orderly, safe storage of specimens, maintained in such a manner that they are readily available, is one of the most important functions of any museum.

Finally there is a seventh step, desirable but not always necessary. This is the exhibition of the fossils, to be seen by the public and by interested students.

It was this final step at which I was occupied during those last two years in the Nebraska museum, when I set up the four skeletons mentioned above, with the invaluable help of Henry Reider. Perhaps I was going at things backward, for when I started work on *Diceratherium* I had not as yet been out in the field to take part in the first step of paleontological practice, the serious collecting of fossils. Certainly I had not done much preparation—the second step—although I picked up quite a few of the techniques of preparation in the course of mounting the skeletons. As for cataloguing, I never did much of this, either at Nebraska or during my subsequent career. The fourth and fifth steps, of research and publication, were for me to be a few years in the future. Students are generally too busy acquiring knowledge to be able to dish it out.

Of these paleontological steps, the general public is of course familiar with the last—exhibition—and with the next to the last—publication, as they may read books on the subject. People are always fascinated by the field work; collecting fossils is exciting, and perhaps even glamorous. And the average visitor to a museum is invariably interested in watching if possible the preparation of fossils, for here a recognizable object can be seen emerging from the rock. (For example, the Tyrrell Museum of Paleontology in Drumheller, Alberta, is built with a large plate-glass window overlooking the preparation laboratory from one of the exhibition halls. It is a prime attraction.)

The most exacting in many ways of all the paleontological procedures, that of study, and preparation of a manuscript, gets little attention, and is almost unknown to the general public. Yet this is the work in which the paleontologist finds pleasure as well as frustration. There cannot be much glamour or excitement to the viewer who may see a man or a woman occupied at poring over and measuring bones, or peering through a microscope, or leafing through a pile of ponderous publications, or setting words down on paper. Yet this is the work toward which all previous efforts have been directed, and it is the work that in the long run becomes imperishable. Museums may come and go, fossils in spite of all the care in the world may conceivably be lost (as has sometimes happened) or destroyed (again as has happened, especially during the last great war), but the written word is about the most indestructible thing that man has devised. Think of the ruins of Rome, and then think of Caesar's *"Gallic Wars,"* as alive today as when it was written two thousand years ago.

As has been remarked I was about to learn some of the other aspects of vertebrate paleontology even while I was laboring with Henry on the skeletal mounts. One such was the scientific collecting of fossils in the field, a process involving not only the search for fossils, but also the determination of their proper stratigraphic position, and after that the technology of taking them out of the ground. The search for fossils involves a lot of walking and climbing. Determining their stratigraphic position involves doing field geology: studying the succession of strata, observing whether these strata have been disarranged by faulting and folding of the earth's crust, making judgments as to the effects of erosion, and so on. The technology of removing fossils involves the proper manner in which to expose them and protect the exposed parts, and especially the craft, for it truly is a craft, of encasing the fossils or concentrations of fossils within heavy plaster casts, so that they can be taken out of the ground and shipped to the laboratory intact.

I had read about all of these practices and had been given a certain amount of instruction concerning them at the university, but as yet I was to try my hand in the field. This I was most anxious to do. It was during the summer following my second academic year in Lincoln that my initial opportunity to do field work came, and needless to say I looked forward to it with the greatest anticipation.

It was the first of two summers of field work devoted to collecting fossils for the museum. Those two field seasons were quite pointedly intended to "enrich the cabinets" of the institution, because there had been a long hiatus in its collecting program, and this period of stagnation, if so it can be called, needed to be corrected. However ideally one may view the motivations for fossil excavations, as so nicely expressed by Leslie Alcock with regard to archeological diggings, there were at that time pragmatic reasons for going out and quite simply looking for fossils, to be collected from the late Cenozoic sediments of western Nebraska. Perhaps by directing our energies at gathering fossils as the fortunes of exploration might provide, materials would begin to be accumulated that would furnish a base for specially directed field campaigns in future years. And here I wish to emphasize something that will be mentioned, probably more than once, in the pages to follow—namely the role of serendipity in paleontology. One may have the most excellently laid plans for a program of summer field work, with the objectives nicely stipulated, and one may enter the field with such objectives the professed goal of the campaign, yet some sudden and unexpected discovery may change everything at almost a moment's notice, to turn the best of plans upside down. Indeed, the art of fossil collecting is the art of dealing with the unexpected, and a good paleontologist, like a good commander on the battlefield, must be flexible and ready to change plans.

But as we set out in early June of 1928 for that summer of high-plains collecting we had no particular goal before us; we were going to collect whatever we could find, and that was that. "We" included Professor A.L. Lugn of the university and myself, off towards the northwestern part of the state in a Model T Ford belonging to Professor Lugn, loaded with camping and collecting equipment. I was fortunate in being able to begin my field experience with the advantage of tutelage in stratigraphy and sedimentation from Lugn; it provided me with some much-needed geological background for my efforts at collecting fossils, as well as affording me an enhanced appreciation of what I was seeing in the field. Geological and paleontological field experience must be acquired by practice and more practice, and proper guidance from an experienced mentor helps the tyro to see and understand many things that otherwise would have been missed. It is a case of developing a discerning eye and an analytical mind.

It should be added that although our plans for the summer campaign were just a bit hazy at the outset, we did collect good materials, some of which I was able subsequently to study, describe, and publish, thereby filling in some of those intermediate steps of paleontological practice between collecting and exhibiting. One small example: on a hot afternoon as I was walking along the bottom of a little canyon (perhaps it would more accurately be called a gully) I saw an object embedded in the bank just ahead of me and at about eye level. I went over, and with the greatest of ease plucked a complete fossil jaw from its ancient resting place, the jaw of a "bear-dog" in perfect condition. Usually fossils don't come with so little effort.

It was an excellent specimen, needing no special treatment to make it available for study, but it was more then that, for eventually it proved to be a new species of its kind, which I named *Hemicyon nebrascensis*, one small bit of evidence in the evolutionary record of the carnivorous mammals, when the bears were developing from their doglike ancestors towards becoming, some millions of years later, the large, powerful, omnivorous predators that we call bears. For me it was an early experience at participating in a significant manner—collecting, studying, describing—at making a contribution to our knowledge of evolution. It was not a large contribution, nor was it especially important, yet there it was as something positive I had done, certainly for my own satisfaction, but more notably as an addition to the published fossil record, for the use of paleontologists in future years. I was beginning to feel some of the compensations for my devotion to the strange profession of paleontology.

When I found that jaw of *Hemicyon* Dr. Lugn and I were working in loose concert with Morris Skinner and James Quinn, two young fellows who were then collecting for the Frick Laboratory of the American Museum of Natural History in New York. Already in my young career as a paleontologist the name of the American Museum carried with it a magic aura. To paleontologists interested in the study of backboned animals the American Museum was then the foremost place in the world housing such fossils, and I think it is fair to say that this is still the case. In those days the American Museum, Osborn, Matthew, Granger, Gregory, (slightly later) Simpson, Brown, were to me magic names, representing paleontological colossi. I sometimes wondered if I would ever meet or get to know them. (I should add that in 1927 Matthew had left New York for Berkeley, yet because of his long career at the American Museum I inevitably thought of him in connection with that institution.) In short, the American Museum was to me a holy place, and I use these words advisedly.

Well, here were Skinner and Quinn, associated with the American Museum (although they had as yet never been there) and consequently having a rather special status in my scheme of things. They were unusual young men, in fact they were unusual throughout many years of paleontological practice and accomplishment. To summarize briefly, they had discovered some skeletons of mastodonts on the Quinn farm near Ainsworth, Nebraska, when they were young lads, and these fossils they sold to the Frick Laboratory and to the Denver Museum. They were then promptly hired by the Frick Laboratory to continue collecting in Nebraska, which they did. Eventually they became noted paleontologists, Morris Skinner spending his professional life with the American Museum, James Quinn becoming associated with the Field Museum in Chicago and subsequently with the University of Arkansas, where he was professor of paleontology. A few years ago Jim Quinn tragically fell to his death while exploring for fossils with Skinner in Nebraska.

In those days of the late twenties Skinner and Quinn were still a couple of uninhibited farm boys, just getting their start. Since they were working in north central Nebraska representing the Frick Laboratory, and since we were there too representing the state museum, there was no reason for us to be jealous of each other. The field was big enough to accommodate our two parties and so for a few weeks we camped together and cooperated. Skinner and Quinn already had a couple of years of field experience under their belts, so they were able to teach me a thing or two.

Being in the field with Morris and Jim *was* an experience. Morrris had an old Model T Ford, stripped down, with only a seat and behind the seat a big box to hold supplies; I think he had originally paid the princely sum of fifteen dollars for it. Of course it was light weight, and he could take it almost anywhere, indeed, in places that our modern breed of field paleontologists would probably hesitate to take a jeep. I had some exciting rides with Morris, but perhaps not as exciting as the ride experienced by Harold Cook, a paleontologist of note. Morris was taking Harold to see their mastodon quarry at the bottom of a canyon cut into the high tableland of Nebraska. They were rolling merrily along with Harold talking a blue streak, when suddenly off they went over the edge of the canyon, sailing through the air to land on a talus slope, from which place they slid and drove down to the quarry. It was Morris's usual way to get to the quarry, but he hadn't told *Harold* that. Harold was speechless for about five minutes, and it took him about an hour to regain his composure.

My most exciting experience with Morris and Jim and their bug was the time they tried to ford a steam known as Plum Creek, a venture that stopped even them and their car. There it sat, hub deep in the water, with sand washing down around it by the minute. The predicament called for drastic action, so Morris hiked out to a nearby farm, borrowed a team of horses, and brought them back to pull the car out of the stream. The horses were hitched to the front of the car, Morris sat on the hood, holding the reins, and Jim took his place in the driver's seat. Morris urged the horses forward; they gave a lunge and promptly turned the car upside down, pinning Jim beneath it in three feet of water. With lightninglike speed Morris jumped into the water and dragged Jim out, waterlogged but unhurt. I had been standing on the bank, ready to take a picture of the car being pulled to dry land; instead I unexpectedly got a picture of the car going over, and then I made a dash into the creek. It was all over before I had taken three long jumps toward the scene of action.

That is all there was to it. They hitched the horses at a different angle, pulled the car into its upright position, pulled it out of the water, and in about a half-hour it was ready to go again.

The favorite Skinner-Quinn sport was for each of them to select strategic spots on opposite sides of a little canyon and then to shoot at each other with rifles. The idea was to keep the other fellow pinned down. I had the unenviable experience one day of crouching behind a big rock with Morris and listening to the rifle bullets whistle past, to bury themselves in the talus behind us. Morris suddenly took off his cap and placed it on the end of his collecting pick and held it out beyond the shelter of the rock, where it was immediately drilled by a shot from Jim. Morris thought that was a great joke; for a greenhorn from the Missouri Valley it seemed to me a strange sort of amusement.

Those were their salad days. As has been said, they became respected paleontologists and they made many important contributions to the science.

After our stint with Skinner and Quinn, Dr. Lugn and I went west to Valentine, Nebraska, in the region of which we spent the rest of the summer. We worked in the sand-hill country, to the south and west of Valentine, especially in the canyon of the Snake River. This was the country so vividly described by Mari Sandoz in her book *Old Jules,* the story of her father, who was one of the settlers of the region in the latter years of the nineteenth century.

The sand hills were like arrested ocean waves, long rolling slopes, up and down, covered with prairie grass. And crossing the sand hills in a car was akin to setting out to sea in a little boat; it was a voyage across an undulating surface where everything seemed the same. I recall that from a camp we had established we drove to a little fossil quarry that we had developed, and we never went back and forth the same way. Sometimes we had to cruise around a bit before we got our bearings to find out where we were going.

Perhaps to some the sand hills might be monotonous, but to me they had a unique beauty. Always the grass was waving in long ripples across the sloping hills, and within the tall grass were flowery gardens. In the late afternoons and the evening there were the clouds and the sunsets—clouds piled immeasurably high into the dome of the sky, and sunsets of spectacular beauty. These were sights to gladden the tired eye after a hot day collecting fossils, down in the confines of Snake River canyon.

We had a good collecting season out there in the sand hills, particularly because we found in the canyon a deposit of *Merycodus* bones, *Merycodus* being a tiny little antelope about the size of a large jackrabbit. At the end of the summer we took the bones back to Lincoln, and that next winter I wrote a letter to Dr. Matthew in California, describing a skull I had collected and making a small point about the attachment of the horn to the skull. In return I had a gracious letter from him.

We finished up that field season by making a trip to Agate, Nebraska, the locale of a famous fossil quarry (which is now a national monument), and there we met for the first time Harold Cook (already mentioned), whose father, Captain James Cook, a famous scout and pioneer, had homesteaded and developed the ranch on which the Agate quarry is located. It was a propitious meeting: we had a long talk with Harold, during the course of which various problems having to do with the geological history of western Nebraska were explored.

Of course I could not know it at the time, but that first visit to Agate was a foreshadowing of things to come. Just ten years later I spent a summer at Agate, where with a field crew a large fossiliferous block was excavated from the quarry. At that time I saw quite a lot of Harold Cook and his charming wife, Margaret, and became acquainted with Captain Cook as well as with his eccentric brother, "Uncle Jack." Agate was quite a little community in those days, a lovely oasis of huge trees through which ran the cool headwaters of the Niobrara River—all in stark contrast to the sun-drenched plains and badlands beyond, stretching to the horizon in every direction.

The following summer I was again in the field in this same part of western Nebraska, this time with Paul McGrew as my assistant. Paul was then a rosy-cheeked undergraduate, and this was his first real contact with vertebrate paleontology. He had entered the university with thoughts of following a career in art, but as chance would have it he volunteered for this expedition. From this point on Paul was "hooked" on vertebrate paleontology. He, too, became an outstanding paleontologist, and for many years was a professor at the University of Wyoming.

We spent most of that summer's field season back in the sand hills, with Valentine as our headquarters. Our camp was comparatively luxurious, a nice wooden cabin resting on top of an underground water tank, with the windmill that supplied the water right there next to the cabin. This was a facility for the convenience of cowboys working for the owner of a large ranch, Mr. P. H. Young; he suggested that we stay there while we collected fossils on his ranch, an arrangement that we accepted with grateful appreciation.

It was essentially a repetition of the previous summer; we gathered more fossils of late Cenozoic age—camels and horses and carnivorous mammals—to add to the collection back in Lincoln.

During my final year at the University of Nebraska I had begun to think about seeking wider horizons. I had my bachelor's degree and was doing a limited amount of graduate work, but I felt that I needed to go elsewhere to continue graduate studies. No lack of appreciation for the benefits I had received or the things I had learned at Lincoln is here implied; I was simply feeling a need that is well recognized by educators—the need to have the experience of more than one university during the pursuit of graduate education. Indeed, it is a well-established fact that those who spend all of their time at one university run the risk of becoming ingrown. It is desirable to change bases, to find out how people are thinking in other places.

Therefore during that last spring at Nebraska I decided to apply for admission and student aid at another university. In order not to have all of my eggs in one basket I sent applications to three places: the University of California at Berkeley, Yale University, and Columbia University. In due course I got a letter from Dr. W. D. Matthew at Berkeley, regretfully informing me that there was no opening there; the places were all filled. (It's-a-small-world department. Four years after having made this application to Berkeley, Dr. Matthew's daughter Margaret and I were married. More of that later.) Then I got a letter from Yale, also informing me that there was no place for me there. Finally I got a letter from Columbia, telling me that if I would promise *not* to accept an offer from another university, they at Columbia would "consider" me for a University Fellowship.

That seemed a bit indefinite to me, so I got an appointment with the dean of the Graduate School at Nebraska, to ask his opinion about this. He felt very certain that the Columbia letter was tantamount to my being accepted and given a University Fellowship—and eventually so it proved to be. Consequently I sent a letter right off to New York, promising that I would not accept a scholarship or fellowship at any other university. Then—the day after I mailed my letter to Columbia—I received a second letter from Yale, informing me that the university had reconsidered, and had awarded me a Sterling Fellowship.

Here was a pretty pickle! I had made my promise to Columbia, but as yet had no definite agreement from that university, while I had a solid award of a fellowship from Yale. There was nothing to do but to write to Yale, to decline the Sterling Fellowship, and then wait anxiously for news from Columbia. There were some uneasy days, but finally confirmation came from Columbia; I was a University Fellow.

Once again the course of my life was determined by a letter. If that second letter from Yale had arrived before I made my promise to Columbia I very probably would have accepted the Sterling Fellowship. My entire scientific career would have been quite different from what it was; in fact I cannot guess how it might have developed. What is of paramount importance is that I probably would not have become intimately acquainted with Margaret Matthew, and I shudder to think of it.

VIII

New York

Riding on the train from Chicago to New York was an exciting adventure—I had never been so far east before—but it was more than that: it was an entrance into a new and a much enlarged phase of my life. Just as my timid, hundred-mile journey from our family home in Missouri to Lincoln, Nebraska, three years earlier, had been a trip accompanied by a certain dread of what lay before me, so this new two-thousand-mile trip was also a venture marked by a feeling of apprehension, a feeling of uncertainty that was perhaps inevitable for one taking such a giant new step into an unknown future. And yet this feeling, raising clouds of doubt as it did, was more than balanced by the feeling of excitement, the exhilarating lift of my entrance into the great city.

The circumstances that had led me toward Columbia University were in the end most fortunate, for Columbia offered to a budding vertebrate paleontologist two attractions that were to be found at no other university. One was the American Museum of Natural History, in which were housed the greatest collections of fossil vertebrates to be found anywhere in the world, collections that thanks to a longstanding arrangement between the university and museum were available to graduate students. The other was Professor William King Gregory, a man of profound erudition, whose knowledge of the vertebrates, *all* of the vertebrates, was unexcelled.

It was a dream come true for me to be able to study under Dr. Gregory, and then, just as I was contemplating this marvelous prospect, in those heady days in Lincoln, after having been informed of my University Fellowship, I saw an item in *Science* (the weekly journal of the American Association for the Advancement of Science) to the effect that Dr. Gregory, along with his colleague Harry Raven, was going to Africa to study gorillas, and would be gone until the end of the year. Thus when I arrived in New York there was no Dr. Gregory present to direct my studies. I would have to make the best of it for a semester.

To get back to the train, and my arrival in the big city, I came in on the Pennsylvania Railroad. Before entering the tunnel into the city the train in those days stopped in the Jersey meadows at "Manhattan Transfer," and in my ignorance I thought that this was where I had to get off. So I did, and then I discovered that I was doing things the hard way, for I eventually wound up in lower Manhattan and had to take an unnecessarily long subway ride up to Broadway and One Hundred Sixteenth Street. I finally made it—it was late afternoon—and came above ground for my first real look at Manhattan and Columbia University. That episode had a long-lasting effect on me in one way, because during the underground journey uptown my sense of direction became dislocated, with the result that when I emerged from the One Hundred Sixteenth Street station I was disoriented by 180 degrees. North was south and south was north, and it was that way for the rest of my life in New York, in other words for forty years.

At any rate I made my way to a dormitory office and was assigned a room in Livingston Hall, which was to be my home for the coming academic year. I must say that my first view of the room was a bit disheartening: it was a bare cubicle furnished with a very heavy oak table and a chair in Mission style, a Spartan bed, and that was about all. It did have the virtue of looking out over South Field, making it nicer than the rooms across the corridor which fronted on the noise of Amsterdam Avenue. Of course I soon became acclimated to my new home, the austerity of which was softened a bit by some window curtains that my mother made and sent to me.

After getting settled I went to the Department of Geology in Schermerhorn Hall, where I was received by Professor Charles Berkey, the chairman of the department. Among other things I was assigned there a desk, complete with accompanying chair and bookcase, one of the prerogatives of geology students, and that was something new to me. It made me feel just a bit important. During the following week or so I became acquainted with the other geology students, all of whom had desks and chairs, and I began to realize that I was very much one of the crowd, with a long and arduous program ahead of me. Columbia at that time had one of the great geology departments in the world, and naturally the level of scholarship among the graduate students was high. There was plenty of competition to keep me on my toes.

Within a day or two after registering at Columbia I went downtown to the American Museum of Natural History to check in there. Of course Professor Gregory was not present—he was off in Africa—but his secretary, Mrs. Meadowcroft, had been expecting me and made me very welcome and saw that I was introduced to some of the people in that end of the building. Within a short period of time that end of the building became a familiar home, much more so than the desk and chair in Schermerhorn Hall, because it was at the museum with its fossils where my interests were centered. And it was at the museum, on the fifth floor in the southeast corner of the huge complex of buildings, where I developed close and lasting friendships.

The American Museum, as it is known to those in the museum profession, was founded in 1869 by a group of forward-looking leaders in New York City, chief among them being Theodore Roosevelt Sr., the father of the twenty-sixth president of the United States. In the six decades since its founding (I am now speaking of the year 1929) it had grown into the largest natural history museum in the world, larger than the natural history division of the Smithsonian Institution, larger than the natural history division of the venerable British Museum, and in the thirty-eight years since 1891 it had become a world center for vertebrate paleontology, this owing to the leadership of Henry Fairfield Osborn.

Osborn, briefly mentioned in a preceding chapter of this narrative, having become established on the faculty of Princeton University following his graduate studies abroad in company with his close friend William Berryman Scott, was called in 1891 to New York to found a department of vertebrate paleontology at the American Museum, and at the same time to be the first dean of the Graduate Faculty at Columbia University. It was an assignment that he approached with great enthusiasm, and one that he carried out with vigor and imagination.

It may be recalled that on a previous page Scott was quoted as saying that Osborn "had intended to go into the business of railroads and finance." It may be added here that Osborn's father was the president of the Illinois Central Railroad and thus not surprisingly was a very wealthy man. He built a large mansion in the form of a castle on the east bank of the Hudson River, opposite West Point, and here Osborn grew up, the privileged child of wealth. Thus Osborn came to the American Museum with the viewpoint of one accustomed to giving commands and expecting them to be obeyed. He was the right person at that time to found and build up an outstanding department of vertebrate paleontology as he did, for although he was in many ways tyrannical and opinionated, he nonetheless was a person of vision, and he had large ideas. He had access to sources of power and money whereby he was able to bring to fruition the visions that were in his mind.

At the museum he gathered around him a superb staff of young paleontologists, including W. D. Matthew, who has been previously mentioned, Jacob Wortman, who had been Cope's assistant, Oliver Perry Hay, O. A. Peterson, James W. Gidley, Walter Granger, Barnum Brown, and others. With these men the museum had from the start an established paleontological staff, able to develop an active program of field collecting and laboratory research.

But Osborn did more than this. In his capacity as professor and dean at Columbia, he instituted a course of graduate studies in paleontology, these to be centered at the museum where the students would have the benefit of large collections for study. It was a case of Mahomet going to the mountain; Columbia did not attempt to maintain collections, for such would be a wasteful duplication of effort. Therefore the graduate courses and graduate research studies in vertebrate paleontology were carried on at the museum, about two miles downtown from the university. Indeed, graduate students of vertebrate paleontology, after having completed their basic graduate courses, spent virtually all of their time at the museum rather than at the university.

Here Osborn trained a distinguished group of paleontologists, including Matthew, one of his first students. Incidentally another of Osborn's students was Clive Forster-Cooper, subsequently Sir Clive, director of the British Museum (Natural History). But it is William King Gregory, Osborn's student and eventually his successor at Columbia University, with whom I am especially concerned at this place.

As I have mentioned, Gregory was an authority on all of the vertebrates, a distinction rarely achieved by students of the backboned animals. For most it is enough to be an expert on some particular group of vertebrates—on reptiles for example, or in an even more limited way on some division within the reptiles. Dr. Gregory was widely acclaimed for his knowledge of fishes, his authoritative eminence in this branch of vertebrate studies being such that for many years he was chairman of the Department of Fishes at the museum. His massive work on fish skulls was and is much respected and used by ichthyologists. At the same time he did much work on the evolution of the amphibians and reptiles, with particular emphasis on the mammallike reptiles that lived during the Permian and Triassic periods more than two hundred million years ago, some of which were the direct ancestors of the mammals. In the years between the two great wars Gregory, D. M. S. Watson of the University of London, Robert Broom of South Africa, and Alfred Romer of Harvard and Charles Camp of Berkeley, both students of Gregory, produced many monographs and lesser works on the mammallike reptiles, thereby making that time, seen in hindsight as a sort of lull during the turbulent political history of the twentieth century, a golden age of research on these important fossils.

Gregory's contributions to our knowledge of birds were by comparison somewhat limited, but his studies of mammals were extraordinarily comprehensive and significant. His doctoral dissertation, *The Orders of Mammals*, was a detailed review of all of the mammals and their relationships. Although he made in-depth studies of various mammalian groups, perhaps his most significant contributions in this field were his many papers on the evolution of the Primates, including the origin and evolution of man. This is a sensitive field, both among scientists and to the general public, so that Dr. Gregory was involved in many controversies concerning man's place in nature. Here he eventually reached conclusions very much at odds with those held by Professor Osborn—which attracted a considerable amount of public attention. Yet through it all Osborn and Gregory remained close friends, a relationship that held until the day of Osborn's death.

It was mentioned that Dr. Gregory was chairman of the Department of Fishes at the museum; he was also chairman of the Department of Comparative Anatomy, a department within the institution that was created especially for him. It reflected the breadth of his interests, and for many years he and his close colleague Harry Raven carried on research that ranged through the wide extent of vertebrate anatomy and relationships. Dr. Gregory, who was not a field paleontologist or zoologist, was in a way a modern-day successor to Cuvier, the great French comparative anatomist who lived during the dangerous years of the French Revolution and after, and who is very widely regarded as the father of vertebrate paleontology. Because of his status as chairman of two departments Dr. Gregory was not exactly a formal member of the Department of Vertebrate Paleontology at the museum, yet he worked closely with and within that department, so that its members considered him as one of their number.

Is it to be wondered, then, that when I was actually within the walls of the museum, I looked forward with some awe and trepidation at the prospect of studying fossil vertebrates under the direction of Dr. Gregory? At the moment I could only wonder what my life would be like, once he returned from Africa, an event scheduled to coincide with the beginning of the second semester of my first academic year at Columbia. I need not have worried; my first meeting with him was not in the least terrifying, and within a few days I came to know him as a gentle and delightful mentor to lead one through the five-hundred-million-year-long intracacies of vertebrate evolution.

Before going on to say something about the Department of Vertebrate Paleontology, which was to be my scientific home for forty years, first as a graduate student with privileges there, subsequently as a regular member of the department, I will add a few more words about the Department of Comparative Anatomy. It was housed on the fifth floor, at the southeast corner of the museum, in a series of rooms that overlooked Central Park. Here Dr. Gregory had a tiny little office (out of which came many large and stimulating ideas) and next to it was another identically tiny office inhabited by Harry Raven, who already has been mentioned. Outside of these offices, and guarding them with her life, was the secretary, Mrs. Meadowcroft. And in the back of a large adjacent room, which served primarily as the Columbia University graduate classroom, sat Helen Ziska, the departmental illustrator.

Harry Raven, a quiet, unassuming man of wide experience, worked closely with Gregory on a varied spectrum of anatomical research. He had the kind of a life that would have made an exciting book, but Harry, being the person he was, never chose to write an account of his experiences. In brief, he was a zoological field man of the highest accomplishments who had worked in many places but especially in the tropical parts of the world. When he came back from Africa with Dr. Gregory (Harry had been the leader of the expedition) during my first year in New York, he brought with him a baby chimpanzee, a little orphan that he had found in the jungle. He named this little ape Meshie, and took her to his home on Long Island, where she lived as a member of the family for several years. She grew up with the Raven children, playing with them and riding her tricycle up and down the front sidewalk with the young Ravens and the other neighborhood kids. For the first year or so Meshie was precocious as compared to the little human beings who were her companions, but then the children caught up and surpassed her, and from about that point the paths of the chimpanzee and her human contemporaries became increasingly divergent. Eventually, when Meshie approached maturity, she had to be placed in a zoological garden—the Brookfield Zoo in Chicago—for she was becoming a bit too strenuous to be living in a house.

But during those first years of her anthropoid childhood it was a lot of fun to have her around. Harry would occasionally bring her to the museum in his car, along with her tricycle, much to the enjoyment of the staff. He would take her to the staff restaurant for lunch, where she would sit at the table with a napkin around her neck and eat with a fork and a spoon most daintily, except that now and then a hind foot would appear above the edge of the table, to assist her at dinner.

Harry had much experience in Africa. He also had worked extensively in the South Pacific, in Indonesia and in Australia and New Zealand. In fact, it was in Australia that he had met the young lady who was to become his wife: Yvonne Raven was very much a part of the museum family, a very popular and active member of the organization known as staff wives.

It was my pleasure to listen to Harry tell about the various faunae of exotic places where he had been—particularly about the vertebrates. Indeed, I learned much about reptilian and mammalian behavior from numerous conversations with Harry, carefully observed accounts that would provide me in years to come with a background of understanding upon which to base conclusions concerning the fossils in which I was interested. Furthermore, it was my privilege to dissect certain animals under his direction; he was an accomplished anatomist. (One year he had a leave of absence from the museum to teach anatomy at the Johns Hopkins Medical School.) His *chef d'oeuvre* was a handsome monograph on the anatomy of the gorilla, published some years after his death.

As has been mentioned, Gregory and Raven were guarded by Mrs. Meadowcroft, who sat at her typewriter just outside and between the doors of their offices. She was a middle-aged, gray-haired lady, almost always dressed in flowing garments, and she seemed to have the cares of the world on her head. It was the usual thing to hear her give vent to a long, drawn-out sigh, as she sat at her desk or as she walked along a corridor on some errand. Yet withal she was not a sad person; it was just her way.

Helen Ziska was a middle-aged German lady who spent her days making anatomical drawings for Gregory and Raven. She was a jolly sort, rather short and plump, who talked with a strong German accent.

At the very southeastern corner of the museum building, on the fifth floor, and then extending to the middle part of the Seventy-seventh Street facade, were the quarters of the Department of Vertebrate Paleontology, conveniently near the Department of Comparative Anatomy, and vice versa. The round tower at the corner of the building was occupied by Professor Osborn, while a large room facing Central Park West, adjacent to the tower, was also a part of Osborn's domain. A corresponding room of large size, and facing Seventy-seventh Street, was occupied by the Osborn Library, founded and partially supported by "the Professor" (also known to us as HFO or Uncle Hank), and housing a most excellent collection of scientific literature dealing with fossil vertebrates. This was one of the most pleasant rooms in the museum; its two large, south-facing windows looked out over Central Park and commanded a stunning view of midtown Manhattan. The room was of dignified proportions, with a high ceiling and a balcony all around three sides. Beneath the balcony and upstairs along those sides were glass-fronted cases holding the treasured books and monographs for which the library was so widely known and respected within the profession. These cases, as well as other furniture within the room, were of deep-red cherry wood, which added to the quiet dignity of the place. There were some long, heavily built tables with green baize covers and comfortable chairs for the accomodation of readers and researchers, while on one side of the room was the ample desk that had once served as the work center in Philadelphia for Edward Drinker Cope.

The library was presided over by Janet Lucas, who had her own desk in a corner of the room by one of the big windows. Miss Lucas, a middle-aged lady when I first entered the museum's paleontological precincts, was the daughter of Dr. Frederick Lucas, a former director of the museum and a man famous in the annals of museum practice and history. Miss Lucas, who had almost literally grown up within the museum walls, was a treasure-trove of American Museum folklore. I regret that she never put down on paper some of the tales about the place when it was smaller and less formal than is the case today.

Miss Lucas occupied her desk in the library until the day she retired, when her place was taken over by Rachel Nichols (the departmental cataloguer), who for many years continued her task of maintaining the catalogue of specimens while serving as Osborn librarian.

Connecting Osborn's tower room with the Osborn Library was a sort of secret passage (one had to swing back a hinged bookcase to enter it and thereby reach Osborn's office from the library), this giving the Professor a means of escape or entrance when he didn't want to walk past his secretaries. It was usually called by Osborn the "er-passage"—a term of some certain embarrassment to him because just off of the er-passage was a little toilet reserved for his exclusive use. The rest of us, not being restricted by Osbornian Victorian delicacies, adopted the term with considerable glee and used it unreservedly, but of course without telling the Professor about our unauthorized adoption of his word.

One other aspect of the Osborn Library should be mentioned. There was a niche in the outer wall between the two big windows, and in this recess Osborn had a marble bust of himself installed. The piece of sculpture had been newly put in place when I first began my association with the museum, and at that time it was not to be easily seen because of the strong light coming in at the windows on each side of the niche. So what did Uncle Hank do but have a bright little spotlight clamped to the rail of the balcony above and to one side of the niche, with the spot directed on the Osbornian visage. That was a typical Osborn gesture.

Perhaps from the foregoing description the Osborn Library is to be pictured as a somewhat old-fashioned room—and it was. But it had charm, and it was a quiet, delightful place in which to spend studious hours. Moreover, it was an elegant room in which to have functions: departmental parties, seminars, and other gatherings. Today, alas, this space no longer functions as it once did. The Osborn Library is now housed on the tenth floor of the Frick wing of vertebrate paleontology in a room that is probably more efficiently utilized but certainly not as delightful to the eye as the old Osborn Library.

Beyond the Osborn Library along the Seventy-seventh Street front of the building were the office-laboratories of the several curators of vertebrate paleontology, while across the corridor in this wing of the building was the preparation laboratory, where fossils were cleaned and prepared and where skeletons were set up for exhibition by the members of the preparation staff.

Lining both sides of this corridor were cases for the storage of fossil mammals. The fossil fishes and reptiles were stored elsewhere, in part within the basement, where huge steel racks held giant dinosaur bones, in part on the sixth floor.

Such were the surroundings where I spent my professional years, and where my paleontological superiors and colleagues lived their scientific lives.

When I arrived in New York the influence of Dr. Matthew was still strongly felt in the Department of Vertebrate Paleontology, although he had by that time been gone for two years, his place having been taken by George Gaylord Simpson, a young man destined to be one of the giants of evolutionary paleontology. Professor Osborn, although long past the age of official retirement, was still very much in command, while Walter Granger and Barnum Brown, by now well advanced into middle age, were active veterans with long years of experience behind them.

For me Walter Granger, curator of fossil mammals, was a very special person. He was a large, friendly man, with a hearty laugh and a deep insight into the nature of people. In a sense he soon became a sort of surrogate father to me, my close friend and advisor until the day of his death more than a decade later, the result of an unexpected heart attack that cut him down when we were in the field on a fossil collecting expedition. (More of that later.) On many an occasion I went to Walter Granger with my problems as well as with my hopes and aspirations. His ready ear and sympathetic advice were of inestimable value to me in those early days when I was wrestling with the shape of my future.

Granger and Matthew had been the closest of friends during the almost four decades that Matthew was at the museum, and through Granger I felt that I got to know Matthew to a certain degree. This acquaintance with Matthew was augmented slightly during my first summer in New York, when he came back to the museum to continue research that had necessarily been interrupted when he accepted a position at the University of California at Berkeley, where he founded the only separate department of paleontology at an American university. (In other institutions paleontology was and is generally taught in a department of geology, occasionally in a department of biology, even more occasionally in a department of anatomy.) During two short months of that summer of 1930 I enjoyed a speaking acquaintance with Matthew, but my contacts with him were limited because he was very busy with his research projects and consequently was for the most part quietly immured with his fossils, out of sight from the rest of us for hours at a time. Also, unbeknownst to me, and I think to most of the people in the department, he was living through the last one hundred days of his life; he died in September following an unsuccessful operation that removed a damaged kidney.

George Simpson, mentioned above, was a slight, sandy-haired man of unprepossessing appearance, about three years older than I. He had had a brilliant career as a graduate student at Yale, after which he had studied at the British Museum as a postdoctoral fellow, and from there he had come to the museum to succeed Matthew. We became colleagues, a relationship that lasted for many years, during which we shared many duties and experiences. Yet in spite of the closeness of our ages I always felt something of a gulf between Simpson and myself; there was never the easy relationship that existed between Granger and me, in spite of the fact that Granger was some thirty years my senior. I think this was owing to the simple fact that Simpson *was* a genius; it was difficult for him to come down in a wholehearted way to the level at which the rest of us operated.

The level at which Dr. Simpson operated was, scientifically speaking, up in the stratosphere. His mind worked in a way that can only be a mystery to most of us; he saw problems and he promptly saw their solutions in a manner that could only inspire awe. Ideas flowed from his brain in a constant stream, and he put them down on paper with incredible ease. I can never forget my oft-seen view of Simpson sitting at his desk, writing his manuscripts with a fountain pen, and in the end with seldom a correction or an emendation of what he had written. In this respect I think a comparison may be made with Shakespeare. One of the poet's contemporaries said that "his mind and hand went together; and what he thought, he uttered with that easiness, that we scarce received from him a blot in his papers." Simpson evidently had a clear understanding of what he intended to write before he put pen to paper, so for him it was largely a matter of transcribing what was in his mind.

His output of scientific papers and monographs, and of books, was quite phenomenal, particularly when one considers the amount of research that goes into the composition of such works. It is not quite the same as writing essays. Furthermore, it must be remembered that not all of Simpson's time was devoted to research in the laboratory and to writing; he was an active field paleontologist who spent several months of each year out in the badlands, collecting the fossils that formed the raw data for his studies.

In short, his accomplishments were prodigious. I felt more than once that I spent my time floundering, while he accomplished his studies and wrote his manuscripts with the greatest of ease. But I never felt truly envious of George Simpson, because almost from the outset I realized that he was a phenomenon and was quite beyond the range of ordinary abilities. As Stephen Jay Gould once wrote to me of Simpson: "I will never figure it out but he was a colossus, and that will endure until the return of Nemesis."

Barnum Brown was another member of the DVP (Department of Vertebrate Paleontology) family, but always a rather distant member. Brown when I knew him as a middle-aged man, always neatly dressed, always distinguished by pince-nez spectacles, and by a domed head almost as bald as a billiard ball (he did have a little fringe of gray hair), was something of a lone wolf. He always had several projects under way, of which he told us little, and he was commonly in and out of his office according to a mysterious schedule that was all his own. He was well known to the public because the main interest of his life was dinosaurs, and dinosaurs have been and still are inordinately popular among people of all ages. Indeed, Brown was a fabulously successful collector of dinosaurs; the hall at the American Museum containing many superb skeletons of Cretaceous dinosaurs is primarily a monument to his successful field expeditions. Unfortunately Brown was not strongly oriented toward research, so that there were not many papers from his pen describing the dinosaurs and other reptiles that he had collected. When Matthew was at the museum he wrote quite a few papers with Brown as a coauthor, and in this way some of Brown's dinosaurs were described. Also, Osborn was always interested in dinosaurs (among his many interests) so that he published some definitive contributions on these interesting reptiles. On the whole, however, Brown's talents were directed toward getting the dinosaurs out of the field and into the museum, and in this capacity he performed an invaluable role as a member of the museum family.

To this roster of the paleontological research staff of the DVP can be added the name of Charles Craig Mook, who like Barnum Brown was concerned with fossil reptiles. But whereas Brown's overriding interest was in dinosaurs, Mook was dedicated to the study of crocodiles. For many years Mook had been research assistant to Professor Osborn, a task that soon was to be passed on to me, as will be told, but when I came to the museum he was spending much of his time on the faculty of New York University, with certain spare hours spent at the museum. I think that Dr. Mook's interest in fossil vertebrates was to a large degree tangential; within a couple of years after I first knew him he became chairman of the Department of Geology at Brooklyn College, and that was where his interests were largely centered for the rest of his life. He was at the time a young middle-aged man, strongly built, dark-haired and bespectacled. Mook, of Dutch descent, lived in Rahway, New Jersey, in an old colonial home, and it seemed to me that he spent quite a lot of energy in traveling back and forth to his widely separated jobs. In spite of the fact that he was at the museum only part of the time we became closely associated in various ways. He was a good friend.

Finally, a pivotal member of the research staff was Rachel Husband Nichols, the cataloguer. She was an especially close friend, who became intimately associated with my wife, Margaret, and myself, soon after we were married, for she married John Nichols, who was the brother of Ira Nichols, who was the husband of Margaret's sister, Elizabeth. Is that completely confusing? Rachel came to the American Museum from Los Angeles, where she had worked in the Los Angeles County Museum, previous to which she had been at the University of Kansas, having migrated there from her home in Oregon. She became a confirmed New Yorker during all of the years she was at the museum, very much interested in and frequently involved in many of the goings on about town.

These were the research scientists with whom I was to be associated in the years to come, and who, needless to say, were to have a great deal of influence on me and particularly on my way of thinking. They were a distinguished group, and so far as my advancement and peace of mind were concerned, a group of friendly and amiable people. It was a good atmosphere for a newcomer to grow up in.

After the war, when I had become well established within the department, our membership—now diminished by the passing of Osborn and Granger—was augmented by the arrival of Bobb Schaeffer, just released from the army, to take charge of our fossil fish collection. Bobb had been a student under Dr. Gregory during the thirties, and at that time I had become well acquainted with him. From the time of his postwar connection with the department until my retirement, a quarter of a century later, we enjoyed a very close scientific and personal relationship of the most friendly nature. We had many good adventures together, in the city and in the field.

I wish to mention, also, Malcolm McKenna and Richard Tedford, my good friends now for many years, who came in to the department during my later years at the American Museum, both to preside over the fossil mammals.

The research staff of the DVP, enumerated above, was only a part of the department, because there was necessarily a support staff of considerable size. There was Janet Lucas, already mentioned, Rolfe Norton Lord, departmental secretary, and three long-suffering ladies who worked under Professor Osborn: Mabel Rice Percy, a sort of editorial assistant, Ruth Tyler, a secretary-editor (who later became editor of the museum's scientific publications), and Florence Milligan, another secretary who also did some editorial work. Then there were the scientific artists, John and Louise Germann, Mildred Clemens, and subsequently Alastair Brown, who illustrated fossils for the scientific publications. Finally there was the preparation staff in the laboratory across the hall from the offices. Here were Albert Thomson, universally known as Bill, head of the lab and an expert preparator of fragile specimens, Charles Lang, who spent most of his time setting up fossil skeletons for exhibit, Jerry Walsh, an ex-Irishman, Otto Falkenbach, an expert in making casts, and Peter Kaisen, George Olsen, and Carl Sorensen, all originally from Denmark.

It was a large department, and sooner or later I was involved in various capacities with all of these people. It would be tedious at this point to remark at length about each individual in this list of names, but I will add a few words about certain of them with whom I was particularly closely associated, and more will be said about the others as occasions require.

The two Germanns, husband and wife, were young folks when I first arrived at the museum, and like Rachel were only a few years older than I was. Within a year after I became associated with the museum staff, Margaret Matthew, the younger daughter of W. D. Matthew, came to the museum also to serve as an artist in the department. So Margaret, Rachel, the Germanns, and I became very firm friends, making up our own little group with common interests within and outside of the museum. We had many good times together.

As for the men in the preparation laboratory, my closest ties were with Bill Thomson, particularly reinforced by a summer we spent together in the White River badlands of South Dakota. Bill had come to the museum when he was still a young lad, and through the years he worked closely with Matthew and Granger. In fact one might say that the three of them developed their scientific skills side by side through the years, so that together they made a paleontological team noteworthy within the profession. Bill and Walter Granger were key figures in the American Museum Central Asiatic Expeditions that made so many outstanding paleontological discoveries in Mongolia during the twenties. Even though there was a great disparity between us in age, I nonetheless had a feeling of close companionship with Bill, as I did with Walter Granger.

I worked quite a lot with Charlie Lang, too, especially on projects that involved the mounting of fossil skeletons for the exhibition halls. As for the other men in the paleontological laboratory, my associations were pleasant, but not so intimate as they were with Bill and, to a lesser extent, Charlie. The ladies who worked with Professor Osborn will be considered in the next chapter.

A memorable member of our group who joined the department some years after my coming to New York was Louis Monaco. Mrs. Lord, mentioned above, had died, so Louis came in as departmental secretary, a position that he occupied for many years. It was a bit unusual to have a male secretary, at least in those days, and Louis was an unusual person in many ways. He was a bit on the volatile side, and so for him life was a succession of crises, large and small. Moreover he soon became very much involved in the fortunes of the department so that he always had something to worry about. With such a personality he was a faithful and conscientious worker.

One of his principal loves was ocean fishing. He belonged to a fishing club, it was called the Varuna Boat Club, located on Sheepshead Bay out on the south shore of Long Island, just off Rockaway Inlet, and every weekend he would sail into oceanic waters, along with some of his boat club friends, to spend long hours in pursuit of various fishes. It was an enthralling hobby for him and a nice one for us, because as often as not he would appear at the department on Monday morning with an armload of fresh fish—fresher than could be obtained in any market—for us to take home. And along with the fish he usually had some stories about his adventures out on the deep. One of his adventures, I recall, was being almost run down by the Queen Mary in a fog.

He was an inveterate storyteller, and he had a store of jokes, some proper and others quite improper, that made him famous among vertebrate paleontologists near and far. He was certainly remembered by paleontologists around the world.

One of the people ensconced in our corner of the museum was Childs Frick. Mr. Frick was the son of Henry Clay Frick, the industrialist who had been a partner of Andrew Carnegie, and consequently Mr. Frick was a man of great wealth. He was an aloof person, perhaps like his father in being what one writer described as a "withdrawn, gelid individual." But whereas Mr. Frick, senior, was devoted to the accumulation of paintings, now to be seen in the Frick Museum, once the Frick mansion, on Fifth Avenue, Mr. Childs Frick was devoted to the accumulation of fossils, specifically fossil mammals of middle and late Cenozoic age. With the sponsorship of Professor Osborn Mr. Frick established his own laboratory of paleontology at the museum, where his employees prepared and catalogued the incredible collections of fossils that the Frick field parties were sending in from various parts of western North America, and even from some foreign localities. (The reader may recall my mention of Morris Skinner and James Quinn, who were collecting fossils for the Frick laboratory in Nebraska, where I became acquainted with them.) In the end the Frick collection was permanently housed in the museum, where in a ten-story wing provided by funds alloted from the Frick will the Department of Vertebrate Paleontology now finds its home.

These members of my paleontological family played important roles in my education during the first two years of my life in New York. The formal graduate studies uptown at Columbia were the necessary basic ingredients of my education, but the relationships that were established with the professionals farther downtown at the museum, and what I learned from these people, were the invaluable leavening agents that added immeasurably to my advancement toward the career on which I had set my mind.

This rather lengthy digression about the people in the two departments at the museum where I made my scientific home has necessarily taken us a bit ahead of the story, but I feel that it has been needed at this place in order to introduce some of the personalities that were to play large parts in my life during the time that I became established as one among the museum group, and for many years thereafter.

In my first year at the museum I knew all of these folks as peers far above my level, for I was then a green and inexperienced graduate student, learning my way about the place. Because during my first semester I had to make do without benefit of instruction from Dr. Gregory, who as we have seen was off in Africa with Harry Raven on the trail of gorillas, I was able in the months before his return to study fossil reptiles under the direction of Dr. Mook. For most of the time, however, I was engaged in graduate course work at Columbia. Consequently during my first year in New York there was a considerable amount of shuttling back and forth between Central Park West at Seventy-seventh Street and Broadway at One Hundred Sixteenth Street.

At the upper or north end of this personal ligation between the museum and Columbia University was Schermerhorn Hall, as it was in the old days before the pressure of numbers and the exigency of so-called progress resulted in its interior transformation, after the war, into a very uninspiring academic structure. Back then, as one entered the big double doors, there was a magnificent sweep of staircase ascending from the ground to the second floor, an architectural *tour de force* that was a delight to the eye. And at the bottom of this staircase was the skeleton of an Irish Elk, so called, excavated from the peat bogs of the Emerald Isle and particularly notable because of its immense, spreading antlers. Here I wrestled with the thorny facts and theories of geology and paleontology under the tutelage of a group of excellent professors.

Dr. Berkey, the chairman of the department, was a slight, wiry man with iron-gray hair and a drooping mustache, a kindly man who was truly interested in the students under his supervision. He lived across the Hudson River in Palisades, New Jersey, and one Sunday each month he and his wife entertained all of the students in the department at his home. These "third Sundays," as they were called, were pleasant occasions where we enjoyed the privilege of relaxing in a suburban atmosphere—removed for a few hours from the noise and bustle of the city. Dr. Berkey was a structural geologist who had played an important role in establishing the location of reservoirs, aqueducts, and other engineering projects for New York City. Indeed, he was involved as well in other great developments, such as Boulder Dam. So he had many interesting tales to tell about the necessary facilities that make possible the existence of a great city—taken for granted by most metropolitan inhabitants.

Douglas Johnson, a noted student of geomorphology, or land forms, was the second man in the department. He was perhaps more of a theorist than was Berkey; certainly he enjoyed an international reputation in his field. He was a tall, very formal person: the kind of professor that was always a bit aloof. A. K. Lobeck, also in geomorphology, was in a way the antithesis of Johnson: an outgoing man who lectured with enthusiasm (as contrasted with Johnson's quiet manner), and whose remarks were given emphasis by the bobbing up and down of a very small, narrow, wisp of a black beard beneath his lower lip, making a sort of exclamation point underneath his clipped mustache. Lobeck had an enviable facility for sketching land forms, so that it was a pleasure to be with him in the field and watch him delineate the scene before him, bringing out with just the right amount of clarity the geologic features that made the landscape what it was. He made excellent illustrations for his scientific papers and books.

Jesse James Galloway was the professor of stratigraphy, a tall, slender man with sharp features and thinning brown hair. Galloway lived up to his name in a way by being something of an academic outlaw, not infrequently terrifying the students who sat in his classes. But he hammered the facts of stratigraphy into our heads in a way that was to be remembered. I will always recall the day, just before my qualifying examination, when he stopped in the middle of his lecture, fixed me with a steely eye, and said: "Mr. Colbert, who was Alexander von Humboldt?" Needless to say he caught me by surprise, but I was ready for him and gave a brief rundown on Humboldt and his accomplishments. After which Professor Galloway gave a grunt (of surprise? of satisfaction?) and went right on where he had left off in his lecture.

Marshall Kay was one of the young members of the faculty, and for one semester he lectured in stratigraphy when Galloway was on a sabbatical leave. Actually Marshall's appointment was at Barnard College, across Broadway from Columbia; subsequently he became a member of the Columbia faculty and devoted his life to the department and the university. He was only two or three years older than I was, and in time we became not only close colleagues, but also neighbors. The Kays lived just down the hill from us in Leonia, New Jersey, where my wife and I settled after the birth of our first son. Eventually Marshall and I collaborated on a large book entitled *Stratigraphy and Life History*, intended for graduate students.

Roy Jed Colony was the professor of petrology, and I struggled through a course in optical petrology under his guidance. This was an evening course that ran from seven until nine, and for me it was in many ways sheer torture. I was tired, I wanted to rest, but I had to sit on a high stool looking down the barrel of a petrographic microscope at thin slides of rocks, which were lovely as seen under polarized light. Colony's lectures helped me get through the long evening sessions. He had a facility in speaking that delighted me; he would embark upon a long sentence which included parenthetical remarks within parenthetical remarks, but at the end he always wound up his locution neatly and definitively. It was a pleasure to listen to such elegant discourse. He was a tiny man, perhaps hardly more than five feet in height, rather chubby, with a round face and a short nose that carried on its bridge a pair of gleaming spectacles.

I learned mineralogy from Paul Kerr, a heavy-set man who knew his subject from a to izzard, but who was no great shakes at lecturing. Never mind, we got a thorough grounding in the subject under his watchful eye.

I could go on, but perhaps this gives some idea of the men under whom I pursued my graduate studies. In one respect I was disappointed and frustrated with my graduate education at Columbia; I wanted ever so much to go up to the College of Physicians and Surgeons, at One Hundred Sixty-eighth Street, and take a full course in human anatomy, but such a thing was unheard of for a paleontology student. I suppose I would have cluttered the medical scene, a student with no thoughts of healing, but I have always felt the deficiency of not having that particular background for my paleontological studies. At least I did get to do some dissecting under the direction of Harry Raven, as has been mentioned.

My life at Columbia was enriched by the daily companionship of my fellow students in the department. They formed a select and a very closely knit group. Needless to say, we spent many hours together outside classrooms and laboratories, but after we individually completed our graduate studies and theses we scattered and for the most part lost track of each other. I have maintained rather tenuous contacts with one of my close student friends, Stewart Sharpe, now retired from long service as a government geologist in Washington.

One advantage in pursuing a student career in New York was the opportunity to follow noncurricular activities offered by the big city. The choice was large and varied, but for me the principal attraction was the theater. In those days one could get a balcony seat for less than a dollar, sometimes a little more, so I became something of an habitué of the Times Square area. From the dormitory I occupied during my first Columbia year, or from International House, which was my home for a couple of years after that, it was a short walk to the subway at One Hundred Sixteenth Street, and a twenty-minute ride from there to Forty-second Street. So I had many pleasant evenings at plays and musicals, sometimes alone, sometimes with fellow students. I saw actors who have since become legends, and I heard music that has since become legendary; I didn't quite realize at the time the privilege I was enjoying when I went to the several Gershwin shows that were on the boards during my first years in New York.

Thus my academic year went by in New York, a busy year devoted to classes, laboratories, studies, conversations, shows, and even such things as trips to the Yankee Stadium or the Polo Grounds. Even though I was far removed from family I did not feel alone; there were more than enough tasks and activities to occupy my mind.

In contrast to the academic year, just completed, my first summer in New York was a lonely time. I stayed on at Livingston Hall for a couple of months, but most of my friends had departed for the summer, the geologists among them to do summer field work. I was working at the museum on weekdays, as will be told on a subsequent page, but my evenings and for the most part my weekends were times of solitary existence. A few of the weekends were enlivened by little geologic trips over to New Jersey or out to Long Island in company with Stewart Sharpe, who lived near Columbia with his parents, and who had a car available. Those escapes from the city were remembered events; I still have a delightful mental picture of our driving along a Long Island wooded road on a perfect June morning, with dappled sunshine on the asphalt and waving grasses at each side, among which were the bright colors of wild flowers, with the refreshing air as a tonic, with a feeling that the earth was young and in every way beautiful and that I was at the threshold of an exciting life. But it was a rare and short interlude in the long, hot summer.

Of course I could read, which I did voluminously, and I could study, which I did sporadically. And I could go to the theater as I had been doing all winter, but the summer theater fare was restricted and the houses, without air conditioning in those days, were stifling hot. An alternative was to go to the cinema, where I could enjoy the comfort of air conditioning, at that time something of an innovation. Or I could go for walks, exploring some of the streets of Manhattan, and especially enjoying the urban rusticity of Central Park or Riverside Park, where the sylvan planning of Frederick Law Olmstead delighted the eye, and where, among other things, I could find here and there a glaciated rock outcrop, its polished surface and the long grooves plowed into the hard schist telling a tale of ten thousand years ago, when an immense continental glacier, the fourth and last of the great Ice Age glaciers, moved down from the Canadian shield to cover vast areas of North America.

That was all very fine, but it isn't much fun to do such things by oneself. So I felt my isolation in a great city where I was surrounded by people; it was the loneliest feeling of all. In fact those summer days in New York were for me lonelier than the weeks I spent completely by myself in the Rocky Mountains, as narrated on a previous page. There I was working and surviving, and although I was isolated from other human beings I felt the companionship of the serrated peaks that rose behind my little tent and of the bright mountain meadow that out in front made a flowery carpet, stretching down to the stream.

Early in August of that first year my solitary evenings and weekends were terminated; I boarded a train for a trip to my home in Missouri and a visit to the University of Nebraska. All this was made possible because Professor Osborn, with whom I was then working, decided that he wanted me to study and measure all of the fossil elephant teeth in the Nebraska Museum—a considerable task. The visit with my parents at the old boyhood home was most welcome; there were still very strong ties with the place where I had grown up. After that, the trip to Lincoln and my two or three weeks of work there made an enjoyable interlude before I was scheduled to return to New York. The elephant teeth at the Nebraska Museum made quite a show after I had them all out of their storage cases and lined up, row upon row, on tables in one of the laboratories. (Fortunately classes had not convened, so I had space to spread out.)

This little trip to the Midwest freshened my spirits and prepared me psychologically for my second year of graduate studies at Columbia. As I entered into this year there were two particular changes in my life. One, perhaps relatively inconsequential but nonetheless important as it affected my creature comforts, was a change of domicile. I shifted from the dormitory to International House on Riverside Drive, where I had a nice room with a magnificent view down the Hudson River. Just in front of my window was the little park between International House and Riverside Church, while to the right was the square bulk of Grant's Tomb. North of Grant's Tomb, in another park, not visible from my window but clearly to be seen if one walked from the front of International House to its southwestern corner, was the Claremont Inn, a picturesque reminder of early nineteenth-century America. At the time of which I am speaking it was a "tony" restaurant, long since converted from its status as a large, comfortable dwelling, once inhabited, if I am not mistaken, for some time by one of the Bonapartes. It was pleasant to see the inn at night, with its bright lights and its colorful awnings—a sparkling gem set at the top of sloping lawns. Of course it represented a world different from the one in which students of limited means lived, yet for me and perhaps for other students at International House it was an elegant and architecturally pleasing sight. Some years later it fell into disrepair, and when no funds were made available for its restoration, it was torn down, which was a decided loss to the city. The park in front of International House had at its southeast corner one of the finest glaciated surfaces to be seen in Manhattan. The exposure was not large but it was choice—a fine polished surface with striations, just at ground level. In line with the policy of supposedly upgrading the city parks this rock surface was covered with dirt and sown to grass. I was dismayed, and complained to Professor Berkey about such desecration of an excellent display of ancient Manhattan natural history. He agreed with me and threw up his hands in a gesture of futility. I suppose it is still covered, and still guarded by a nearby statue of General Butterfield, one of the minor commanders in the Union army.

I lived for a couple of years at International House, an experience for which I will always be grateful. It was truly a cosmopolitan place, where one could become acquainted with students from all over the world—and that is what I did. During that time I found myself on the student council (I forget its precise name) of International House, one result being the experience of attending a dinner for our governing board presided over by John D. Rockefeller Jr. and his wife, Abby. They were enthusiastic patrons of the house; indeed it had been founded largely with their support. At the dinner I had the pleasure of sitting across the table from John D. the third, a tall, angular young man of about my age. We had a pleasant time talking about this and that.

There was an auditorium at International House, the locale for many worthwhile programs and the podium for many interesting guest speakers. I remember that one of the speakers was the famous Indian poet Rabindranath Tagore. To descend from the sublime to the ridiculous, I can admit that on one occasion I took part in a sort of play, and a very corny affair it was. I suppose this affair gave some of the foreign students an insight into the nature of young Americans. Reciprocally foreign students would put on programs for our benefit, always interesting and on those occasions when they dressed in native costumes esthetically pleasing.

The other change, and this was a most important one for me, involved none other than Henry Fairfield Osborn, the founder as already mentioned of the Department of Vertebrate Paleontology, and at the time of which I am writing also president of the museum's Board of Trustees. In short, I became his research assistant—but more of that later.

My second year at Columbia was leading inevitably to that dreaded ordeal, the qualifying examination, the test determining whether or not a graduate student was ready and fit to proceed with the research for his doctorate and to write and defend his dissertation, or whether he would fall by the educational wayside. The examination in geology at Columbia in those days was a three-hour oral affair, the candidate being grilled by the entire geology faculty as well as by chosen faculty members in other disciplines. A circumstance making the examination especially uncomfortable was the fact that it was open; the graduate students in the department were allowed to attend and they did, all of them. So the candidate faced the double psychological hurdle of facing his professors near at hand, while in the background sat an audience made up of his peers watching him sweat it out. The students usually attended not so much because of their interests in the fortunes of the candidates as to learn what kind of questions were asked, and how they were asked, all in anticipation of their own forthcoming ordeals.

So it was that in the late spring of 1931 my days for a month or so were lived with this sword of Damocles suspended over my head. Finally the dreaded day arrived. The examination was set for the afternoon, so I spent the morning sitting on a bench in Riverside Park, looking at the broad sweep of the Hudson and trying not to think too much about what was ahead. At the appointed hour I entered the examination room, seated myself at the head of a long table around which were gathered the professors, and back of which sat all of my companions. I smiled at them weakly.

The examination proceeded through the long hours and I passed, to be complimented by Professor Berkey and cheered by my fellow students.

The summer of 1931 was to be for me far different from that lonely summer of the previous year. For one thing, it was full of activities and plans, because as will be related on a following page Professor Osborn decided to go to England to attend the British Association for the Advancement of Science meetings as well as to continue studies of fossil elephants, and he decided that I was to be there too. So there were preparations to be made, because in those days when overseas travel was by ship such journeys were not so casually undertaken as is the case in this modern age of flight. And for another thing, Margaret Matthew came into my life.

Actually she had come into my life very briefly during the previous summer, although in such a way that neither of us was really aware of anything portending our futures. One day during that first lonesome summer in New York I was up on a stepladder in the long, Seventy-seventh Street fifth-floor corridor of the American Museum, trying to rearrange some fossil elephant teeth in the storage cases that lined the corridor, when I saw two ladies come out of the office where Dr. Matthew was studying, and walk down the hall toward me. I knew by inference that they were Mrs. Matthew and her daughter Margaret, although I had not been introduced to them. They walked past me on their way to the elevator, with little heed of what

I was doing, while I managed to give them a passing glance. It was my first glimpse of two people who would be very important to me in years to come. (I learned, some years later, that Margaret had given more attention to me than I realized at the time, for she told me that she took something beyond an incidental glance at me standing on the ladder and fussing with a drawer full of fossils. She remembered that I was wearing a light-colored coat or laboratory smock, and she even remembered in some detail what I looked like on that summer afternoon, so long ago.)

In the spring of 1931 Margaret graduated from the California College of Arts and Crafts, and with the credentials of this training as well as her demonstrated ability as an artist to recommend her, she applied for a position as a staff artist at the American Museum, where she knew that there were occasional openings for scientific illustrators.

The Department of Vertebrate Paleontology needed another staff artist to draw fossils, so she was accepted for this work; consequently at the beginning of the summer she appeared on the scene, after a tiring cross-country bus trip. It wasn't long before Margaret and I were seeing quite a bit of each other, particularly since among other things she was designated to make illustrations of Siwalik fossils that I was studying.

Just as we were getting nicely acquainted I went off to England for six months or so, but after I returned our friendship continued and matured, so that eventually and probably inevitably we fell in love and became engaged. That came later; in the summer of 1931 our association together was just beginning. That was more than half a century ago; the partnership then beginning was cemented by our wedding in 1933, and has continued to this day.

Here I wish to say something about the background of she who through a time span now approaching six decades has been the "partner of my labors." Margaret Matthew was born into an unusual family. Her father was a paleontologist of international reputation as was her paternal grandfather, George F. Matthew, a Canadian, descended from Loyalists who had sailed from New York in 1783, to make their livings in the wild forests of what became New Brunswick. Life was hard for the Matthew family and it is interesting to see that all of the children of George F. Matthew, except two, came south to follow their careers in the United States. In passing it might be remarked that all of these Matthews were, except for Margaret's father, musical folks, not professionally except for Margaret's Aunt Bess, but in a fun-loving, amateur manner. Indeed, the Matthews were a closely knit family, who enjoyed life in its many dimensions.

Margaret's mother, Kate Lee, was the daughter of an ex-officer in the Confederate army. She was one of eight children (as can also be said of W. D. Matthew) and they too were members of a closely knit family group. Kate

Lee lost her sight when she was a little girl, but after eight years or so of blindness she could see again. Forever after she appreciated the beauties of the world around her to a degree not reached by people who have been fully sighted throughout their lives. She became an expert seamstress, and for some time before her marriage she taught this craft at the Pratt Institute in Brooklyn. Her sister, "Aunty Em," was an accomplished artist, who with her husband ran a firm called the Decorative Designers, devoted to book covers and illustrations. In middle age Aunty Em was given the manuscript of a mystery story for the designing of a book cover, and after reading it she said to herself, "Heck, I can write a better story than that!" Which she did. In the end she wrote more than sixty mystery novels, and for most of them she designed her own book jackets.

So Margaret grew up among people who did things, although it must be said that none of them made much money at their occupations. And she grew up having considerable knowledge as to what paleontologists did and how they lived. Consequently when she decided to face life along with me she knew what she was getting in to.

IX

Osborn and His Elephants

*N*ow to go back a year or so. One day in the spring of 1930 Dr. Mook walked in to my assigned space within one of the office-storerooms at the museum, sat down in a nearby chair, and said: "How would you like to be Professor Osborn's research assistant?" Or words to that effect. I was a bit stunned and a bit pleased as well. Stunned, because Dr. Mook, who had been Osborn's assistant for many years, had given me some inklings of the problems of working under the great man. (He now wanted to get out from under.) Pleased, because I needed something to do during the coming academic year. My University Fellowship was a one-year appointment and was not renewable because the university wished to spread these appointments around. There were only so many such fellowships; I, for example, had been the only University Fellow in the geology department. I had been worrying about how I might continue at Columbia, and this seemed to be the solution to my problem. I agreed, and thereby entered into an association with Osborn that lasted for five years—until the day of his death in November, 1935.

My formal introduction to Professor Osborn took place when Dr. Mook brought him in one day to the Osborn Library. We shook hands and he welcomed me to his service with some remarks as to how he had once been a disciple of Cope, and now I could be his disciple.

Professor Osborn was a complex person. When I knew him and worked with him he was near the end of a very distinguished life and career, and he was quite aware of his distinction. To many people he seemed to be arrogant, which he was. But he had to be seen in context.

He had grown up in a wealthy family during the days of the robber barons—not that his family were robber barons, but his father had been president of the Illinois Central Railroad and therefore a man of importance in the business world. As a student at Princeton Osborn was intending to enter the world of railroads until that June day of 1876, mentioned on a preceding page, when he and Scott and Spier suddenly decided to go west and hunt fossils. Osborn must be given credit for sticking to the decision; with his family money he did not have to devote his life to paleontology; he could have had a very pleasant life as a dilettante, quite free of the stress, devoted application, and criticism that are part of a scientific career. Yet he entered wholeheartedly into the uncertain world of paleontology, going on field trips, studying fossils, and writing prolifically. Moreover he became an administrator, both at the museum and at Columbia, and when I knew him he was still running the museum in a very active way. Although his position was that of president of the Board of Trustees, in practice he was essentially the director with the titular director acting more or less under his supervision.

As might be imagined he had a strong personality and the external appearance to go along with it. He was a large man with a somewhat overwhelming physical presence. His face was distinguished by a rather prominent, almost bulbous nose, and he had a clipped mustache. He had a full head of thick hair. He was always well dressed in a rather formal manner, clad in dark clothes of rich material, and as I recall he often had on a vest with white piping along its borders. Osborn was nothing if not dignified; I could never imagine him behaving in a frivolous manner. In short, he was an epitome of a Victorian-Edwardian gentleman belonging to what in those days was considered as the "upper crust."

The mention of nose and clothes brings to mind a couple of vignettes disclosing Osborn in not quite such regal circumstances. Professor Scott once told me that back in 1877, when he and Osborn and Francis Spier were out in the Bridger Basin of Wyoming the Osbornian nose suffered inordinately from the western sun, becoming as a result prominently red and very noticeable to every passerby. Whereupon an old mountain man accosted the young Osborn, then a slender youth with no mustache, and said: "Young feller, either you had better pull in your nose or pull out the brim of your hat."

As for clothes, one hot day Osborn felt that the temperature and the humidity in his office at the museum were a little too much to be borne with patience. So he took off his coat, he took off his vest, and he let down his suspenders—much to the horror of Miss Percy, who was always at his side. Then as five o'clock drew near Osborn donned his vest and coat, but forgot all about his suspenders. In this state he strode out of his office and down the corridor, his head in the air and the suspenders flapping beneath the lower border of his jacket. It was a sight to delight one and all, but alas! John Germann who was then a young apprentice in the department ran down the hall, flagged the Professor, and told him about the situation. Osborn ducked into the nearest storeroom, corrected his clothes, and then proceeded along the hall and out of the building with his usual royal splendor.

Professor Osborn's movements were ponderous in a sort of elephantine way; if sitting at his desk, for example, he would majestically turn his whole body to confront a visitor, rather than turning his head. And everything he did was on a big scale—including his handwriting. I have a collection of memos from him, written in large letters with the broadest of broad-pointed pens. Walter Meister, when I knew him one of the upper members of the museum administration but in his younger years an employee low on the administrative ladder, once told me that one day during his early years in the institution he was standing by Osborn as the Professor was engaged in signing some letters. As the first letter was passed over to Walter, with its large resplendent signature, Walter picked up a blotter for an obvious purpose, whereupon the Professor held up a warning hand and said: "Walter, never blot the signature of a great man." Uncle Hank was serious; he was *not* joking.

His large, flourishing signature was but one manifestation of his preoccupation with bigness; a more widely evident aspect of this trait was his love of big projects. He was devoted to and justly proud of the immense museum of which so much growth and development had taken place under his guiding hand. He liked big exhibition halls and big animals to go in them, such as dinosaurs and titanotheres (huge rhinoceroslike beasts that lived during the early part of Cenozoic time), and mastodonts and elephants. Indeed, when I joined his forces his massive two-volume monograph on the titanotheres had just been published by the United State Geological Survey, and he was working on an equally or even more massive two-volume monograph of the proboscideans—the mastodonts and elephants.

The Osbornian method of accomplishing these ambitious projects and writing the huge monographs was to have at hand a group of assistants to do the donkey work. My position within the group was that of research assistant, as has been mentioned. It was to be my task to study and measure the specimens that HFO was interested in, and to furnish him reports on which he could base his written descriptions and conclusions. It was the slot that Dr. Mook was vacating, the position that had been variously held, before Mook, by Dr. Matthew and by Dr. Gregory. I must say that I was following some illustrious predecessors.

Miss Mable Rice Percy was an editorial assistant who spent her days putting together and collating Osborn's manuscripts and proofs. It was an exercise unique, I should think, in the annals of scientific research and publication, because Osborn worked in a way that was all his own. In those days the museum had its own printing plant in the basement of the building, and Osborn would send down manuscripts to be set up in galley proof. There was one printer, Nick Caggana, who worked full time for Osborn; he was the only person who could make sense out of what HFO did to his proofs. Osborn would liberally mark up a galley proof in his large, bold hand, in red ink, and then Nick would patiently reset the proof. Another galley, another task of resetting, and this went on through several editions. Then, when the galleys had been corrected, and corrected again and again, they would be set into pages, along with the illustrations that had been prepared. Believe it or not, the whole process was repeated over, and over, and over, with pages being set and reset any number of times. In fact, I know that some pages went through seventeen sets of proofs. In those ancient days all this was done with metal type, one result of which was that there were tons of type on racks in the print shop.

Miss Percy was involved in all of this rigmarole. She was a tiny, little, elderly lady who worshipped the Professor. All day long she skittered about the department, into his office and out, over to the library, always checking and rechecking and worrying, and never questioning HFO's requests, no matter how outrageous and time-consuming they were. Sometimes, in idle moments, I could not help speculating about the names of Osborn and Percy. Could it be that centuries ago, perhaps before the days of Richard II, the ancestors of Miss Percy looked down from their exalted seats in Northumberland to watch the lowly Osborns, toiling on the land?

Miss Ruth Tyler was another editor or perhaps one should say editor-cum-writer, who among other things put the Professor's written words into proper form. (Ruth was a fine grammarian and following her stint with Osborn she became the editor of the museum's scientific publications, a position that she occupied with distinction and efficiency for many years.) She was a vigorous, no-nonsense type of person who viewed some of Osborn's methods with a realistic and skeptical eye. A few years ago she sent me a letter describing one of her experiences with Osborn. It had to do with the first of many trips she had to make to Castle Rock, the Osborn home, which as has been mentioned was literally a sort of a castle high on a hill overlooking the Hudson River opposite West Point. HFO spent his summers there in cool baronial splendor. Not for him the grime and heat of

Manhattan; he ordered his minions, or some of them, to join him up the river for a day at a time.

Wrote Ruth:

"Those trips to Garrison! The first time I was required to go I had to lug the typewriter (full size, not portable) and hoist it on the train from the platform at 125th Street. (I then lived near Columbia.) It was quite a breaking-in. Wasn't he an Experience? He was an education to me, too, for in my naive way I had never known a man so vain and pompous, but I suppose each of us, in our own ways, grew up a little in dealing with him."

There was more to the Garrison trips than is told by Ruth Tyler in her letter to me. It seems that the general practice was for the minion who went to Castle Rock to spend the morning with HFO in his study, after which the Professor would retire to precincts far removed for his noonday meal, while Ruth Tyler or whoever might be involved had lunch brought to a little gazebo, where the sandwich was consumed in lonely splendor. Then at the end of the day there was the train trip back to New York, back to the heat of the city and a late supper.

I, fortunately, never had to go to Garrison.

Still another member of the team was Florence Milligan, who also was engaged in some sort of editorial work. Mention has already been made of the departmental illustrators' corps, the several members of which spent quite a lot of time preparing drawings for the Osborn projects, and the men in the laboratory. Of course these people, illustrators and preparators, did not all work for Osborn all of the time, but they were on call whenever he wanted something done.

After my first meeting with Osborn my marching orders soon appeared—in a letter to Dr. Mook. In part they said:

> I warmly approve of your suggestion of Mr. Colbert's mastering the arrangement of our entire Proboscidean collection, beginning of course with the grinding teeth.
>
> As a most interesting scientific thesis I desire him to specialize on the third superior and inferior grinding teeth
> 1) as to relative mass,
> 2) as to total linear measurement of the rising and falling enamel plates . . .
> 3) as to the total increase in height of the superior and inferior enamel plates during Pleistocene time . . .
> 4) practicability of using this increase as a means of measuring the intervals of Pleistocene time.
> I am confident that we have here a potential time scale. If Mr.

Colbert proves his ability to handle this question well I will make it the subject of a joint investigation with him.

These instructions involved a scientific assault on two problems: evolution and time. The evolutionary problem was concerned with the development of elephants as revealed by the structure of their molar teeth; the time problem had to do with measuring the length of the Pleistocene epoch, the great Ice Age that began in the distant past and ended perhaps ten thousand years ago. (Or perhaps it has not ended; we may very well be living in a warm interval of the Ice Age, a benign climatic interlude between the last great glacial advance when our Paleolithic ancestors hunted woolly mammoths on the frigid steppes of Eurasia and the next glacial invasion from the Arctic which may push southward to bury fields and forests and crush our northern cities.)

So far as elephant evolution is concerned, the exercise in dental measurements that Osborn was proposing for me to make was predicated upon his particular evolutionary concept, which in this case envisaged the elephants as grandly marching through time at a steady pace along an evolutionary path that had its beginnings several million years ago and its end in our modern world. So far as the measurement of Pleistocene time is concerned, Osborn was proposing to use this supposed steady progress of the elephants as a clock on a grand scale. As for this temporal effort, he was floundering at an evanescent and wrong solution. The problem has since been solved by carbon 14 and radiometric methods.

The initial assignment of Osborn's schedule was to be my first paleontological task for the museum, and it occupied much of my time and energy during the lonely summer of 1930 that I have already described. "Mastering the arrangement of our entire Proboscidean collection, beginning of course with the grinding teeth" was a formidable job that involved much climbing up and down a stepladder, pulling out heavy drawers loaded with heavy fossils and pushing them back again, transferring the fossils back and forth between drawers so that like things were together, checking museum numbers and labels and keeping records of what was being done. The grinding teeth of elephants are very large objects, and of course those of fossil elephants are correspondingly large and heavy. Consequently the business of lifting them in and out of drawers was very much like hoisting and juggling large rocks.

The storage cases housing all of these fossil elephant teeth were along one section of the immensely long corridor of the fifth floor of the American Museum, a corridor that in effect stretches between Columbus Avenue and Central Park West, parallel to Seventy-seventh Street. So I spent my days working in a very public place, with people parading up and down the hall through the hours. Of course most of these passersby were museum employees who in short order had a general idea as to what I was up to and thus accepted my peculiar behavior. As for visitors who might have business on the fifth floor, I suppose my activities were perhaps something of a puzzle.

It was during that summer, while I was wrestling with fossil elephant teeth, that I got to meet Dr. Matthew. He had returned to the museum from California to continue his labors on fossil mammal studies that had been under way when he left New York to begin his new life at the University of California at Berkeley. So he was working in an office that opened on to the corridor where I was engaged in my first tasks as requested (more properly as ordered) by Professor Osborn. Dr. Matthew would pass me by and as he passed we would exchange greetings, while on a few occasions he took a few minutes to talk with me. But his time was precious—far more so than any of us realized, because he was living through the last summer of his life. Thus was cut short the scientifically incomplete life of one of our great paleontologists, a scholar of world-wide renown.

I was fortunate in having had the opportunity of talking with him, even though briefly and only occasionally. But I never got to really know him—the man who would have been my father-in-law, had he lived. He has always been a large yet a dim presence to me in my extended family history. Margaret and I often regret the fact that he never lived to see his grandchildren.

Late in the summer, having accomplished the frequently fatiguing task of arranging fossil elephant teeth in their proper places within the storage cases, I had to face up to the "scientific thesis" as indicated by Osborn in his letter of instructions, particularly to items 2 and 3 on his list. These had to do, if one cares to refer back to his letter as quoted on page 163, with the "total linear measurement of the rising and falling enamel plates" and with the "total increase in height of . . . enamel plates during Pleistocene time." Perhaps this is so much proboscidean gibberish to many readers; consequently a few words of explanation will be attempted at this place.

Elephants, fossil and recent, are highly evolved mammals with extraordinarily specialized teeth. Of course we are all familiar with their huge tusks, these being enlarged, second upper incisors, but except for mahouts, people who work in zoos and circuses, and curious zoologists and paleontologists, the remarkable grinding teeth of these giant mammals are but little known. There are just six such teeth on each side, above and below, three milk molars and three "permanent" molars, for a total of twenty-four teeth. But these teeth are very large, so that there is only one, or at the most two teeth erupted and functional on each side, above and below, at any one time. The teeth erupt serially; thus the first milk molar is displaced as it wears down by the second milk molar, which pushes *forward* from its point of origin within the bone, this tooth in turn being displaced by a forwardly erupting third milk molar, and so on through the three molars. The third and last molar comes into place when the elephant reaches maturity. (It should be said that the teeth being pushed forward by the eruption of their successors gradually disintegrate and fall from the front of the jaws.)

Each tooth is composed of tall plates, arranged one behind the other, and enclosed in a heavy mass of dental cement. The plates are composed in each case of two vertical bands of enamel, enclosing and separated from each other by a layer of dentine. When the grinding face of the tooth is worn down, its surface consists of transverse alternating enamel and dentine bands, each pair of enamel bands with enclosed dentine separated fore and aft from the next pair by an interval of cement. Of course the enamel is harder than the dentine and cement so the enamel bands stand up on the grinding face of the molar as hard ridges. These, taken together, form efficient mills for the reduction of bark and roots and leaves and grass to a pulpy mass that can be swallowed and digested.

In a modern Asiatic elephant the first milk molar will have four plates, the second eight plates, the third twelve plates, while the first molar also has twelve plates, the second sixteen plates, and the third twenty to twenty-four plates.

Osborn proposed that we measure the enamel length in the third molars of various fossil elephants. This meant measuring the length of enamel for each plate in the tooth, up and back down. But in a third molar showing partial wear, it was necessary to try to calculate the amount of enamel that had been worn away in those plates that were not entire. If the back plates of such a molar were still unworn (wear on an elephant molar proceeds from front to back) it was possible to make reasonable estimates as to the probable pristine heights of the more anterior, worn plates. Needless to say there was a good deal of estimating going on during the study of such teeth.

A large Pleistocene or Ice Age mammoth might have as many as thirty plates in the third molar, and when the total length of enamel of such a tooth was added up it could be truly impressive—on the order of thirty or forty feet. This *was* something big, and Professor Osborn loved it.

Such great enamel lengths are found only in the mammoths that lived during late Pleistocene times, the kind of mammoths that were depicted by our paleolithic ancestors in the caves of Europe. But the earlier fossil elephants had smaller and less-tall teeth, so their total enamel lengths were shorter. With this in mind Osborn conceived the idea that Pleistocene time could be measured by the enamel lengths of elephant third molars—so many thousands of years per inch, let us say. It was an interesting concept but perhaps a bit too simple. How do we know that elephant molars evolved at a steady rate through Pleistocene time? And what about individual variations in size? These arguments did not loom large in Professor Osborn's thinking.

There is a little more to the story on the purely technical side. Osborn decided to have a lot of the fossil teeth cut longitudinally, down the midline, and then have the cut surfaces polished. Since the teeth were usually mineralized the polished surfaces revealed sections of true beauty—enamel and dentine plates of differing colors embedded in cement of still another color.

Perhaps all of this will give some idea of the nature of my work during the autumn, winter, and spring of 1930–1931. By dint of much measuring and no little bit of calculating and estimating I accumulated some impressive figures on Pleistocene elephant enamel lengths, much to the delight of HFO.

Here we come to the end of Osborn's letter of instructions, in which he said he would make this study the subject of a joint investigation with me. He had his mind made up that we would present a paper at the spring meeting of the American Philosophical Society in Philadelphia. For this we needed some charts. But would Professor Osborn have lantern slides made? Not in the least. He wanted full-size charts; if the enamel length of a fossil molar tooth was thirty feet, he wanted a chart thirty feet long. Consequently in the vernal months of 1931 I supervised some of the museum artists in making a series of such charts, all in color.

The day came for the meeting at the American Philosophical Society; it was a Saturday and we met by prearrangement at the society's building, a lovely old colonial structure next to Independence Hall. I had gone down from New York to Philadelphia by train, taking the rolled-up elephant enamel charts with me; the Professor came down from Castle Rock in his limousine, driven by a uniformed chauffeur. At the philosophical society we joined forces and proceeded to the meeting room, where a small but select audience was present to listen to what the Professor and other participants in the meeting had to say. Among those attending was Professor William J. Sinclair of Princeton, an outspoken paleontologist who was somewhat familiar with what HFO had been doing and who had a not very high opinion of Osborn's ideas and procedures. So before the meeting came to order, Sinclair cornered Osborn at one end of the room and gave Professor a rather vehement critique of the whole elephant enamel business, which didn't faze the Professor the least bit; perhaps he had enjoyed a very good breakfast that morning. At any rate he listened to Sinclair and smiled sweetly without saying much in rebuttal.

The time came for Osborn's presentation, and he arose to deliver it. Then he said: "Mr. Colbert, would you please take one end of the elephant

enamel chart and unroll it while you, Professor Sinclair, hold the other end."
There was nothing Dr. Sinclair could do; he manfully held his end of the
chart while I unrolled it to its full thirty feet, and the Professor talked on. All
the time the Professor was talking I could hear Sinclair at the other end of
the long roll of paper grumbling away—a sort of obbligato to the main
theme. In this way the talk was delivered, and whether it meant much to the
people attending the meeting, I do not know.

I do know that at the end of the session we came out of the beautiful old
building to climb into the Professor's limousine. His biography of Edward
Drinker Cope, his paleontological mentor and hero, had just been pub-
lished, and he wanted to deliver a copy to the Academy of Natural Science,
the institution with which Cope had been connected back in the nineteenth
century. So he instructed the chauffeur to drive us to the Academy. On the
way he told his driver to go the wrong way down a one-way street—an order
to which the chauffeur objected, but HFO would have no back talk. Down
the street we went and inevitably met up with a member of the Philadelphia
Police Force, who wanted to know what we thought we were doing. The
Professor stuck his head out of the window and tried to impress on the officer
who he was—to no avail. We didn't get a ticket, but we did turn around and
ignominiously we went back in the right direction, the Professor all the time
telling me what uncouth people policemen could be.

At length we reached the Academy, to find that it now being late
afternoon of a Saturday the building was closed. This put a crimp in the
Professor's plans; he had intended to present the Cope biography to the
Academy powers that be with all proper ceremony. Instead he had to give it
to a doorman with instructions to pass it along.

By this time he was just a bit disgruntled; officious policemen and closed
museums had taken some of the brightness out of his afternoon. He pointed
toward the Broad Street station of the Pennsylvania Railroad, which was not
far away, and gave me instructions as to how to get there and go home. Then
he boarded his limousine, gave a command to the chauffeur, and the car
disappeared through the dusk on its way to Garrison-on-the-Hudson.

For someone working with Osborn there were bound to be memorable
incidents; it was part of one's association with an historic and a strong-
minded person. One's relationships with Osborn depended to a large degree
on just how one reacted to his imperious and sometimes bullying demands.
With his own equals he certainly was mild mannered and obliging; I never
saw him trying to impose his will on Professor Scott. Of course Scott and
Osborn had been college students together, they had studied together in
Europe, and after that they were for some years colleagues on the Princeton
faculty. Indeed, I got the impression that Scott was the senior member of the

partnership; their friendship was almost invariably expressed as being that of Scott and Osborn, not the other way around.

But for those who worked with Osborn during the long years in New York, it was a matter of the elder man and his younger colleague, or perhaps teacher and student. Osborn was Matthew's professor and he was Gregory's professor; both of these great scientists did their graduate work under Osborn's tutelage. And of course I was a student working under Gregory. There was a difference in age, rank, and experience that could be felt. Yet for all of us, if I may be so presumptious as to place myself in the same category as Matthew and Gregory, there was the necessity to express our own opinions, and often to oppose Osborn in a very definite way. He did not like opposition.

As time went by, from the final years of the nineteenth century through the first three decades of the twentieth century Matthew found his collaboration with Osborn becoming increasingly burdensome. Dr. Matthew was not a man to mince words, and on many occasions he had great differences of viewpoints and opinions with Osborn, which he expressed in no uncertain terms. Indeed, their differences became so profound that in one especially serious matter—the great monographic study of the fossil horses of North America, which had been largely done by Matthew, but to which both of their names were to be affixed—Matthew finally found himself compelled to withdraw his name from the publication. This in spite of the years of work he had devoted to it. Undoubtedly it was a relief to Matthew when he was offered the professorship at the University of California at Berkeley; by this time the intellectual difference with Osborn had become irreconcilable. And this difference was reciprocated by Osborn, who in 1921 wrote to Scott that "I find my conclusions so different from those of Doctor Matthew, for example, that I could not write a joint work with him."

Yet the difference, so deeply felt by Matthew, was never passed on to his family; he did not take his scientific and workplace problems home with him.

As for Gregory, he had more subtle ways of differing with Osborn, for it was Gregory's genius to be able to work with the Professor without raising hackles. Gregory was a gentle man, and although he could maintain his position with firmness and with well-founded reasoning, the logic of which was difficult to dispute, he could at the same time oppose Osborn in such a manner that the Professor would not take offense, even though he disagreed thoroughly with Gregory's position. This was nicely exemplified during the twenties, when both men, very much involved with the evolution of man, came to quite different conclusions as to the evolutionary paths that had been followed during the ascent of human beings to their present position in the organic world. They differed, but it was a friendly difference.

As for me, I was of course very much a junior when my association with Osborn began; after all, there was a difference in our ages of fifty-eight years. From the very beginning I found him demanding, yet I could see that in his own way he was interested in me and in my paleontological progress. He wanted me to get on with my career—that is, as long as I first took care of his wishes. He frequently offered advice as to how I should do this or that, for he felt, I am sure, that I was very much a novice who needed some kindly guidance from a great man (Osborn's evaluation).

We used to have departmental staff meetings in the Osborn Library, where we gathered around a long table covered with green baize, with HFO at one end and with the rest of us disposed along the length of the table on both sides. Rachel Nichols was always designated to keep minutes of our meetings. One time I presented a report on something that the Professor had requested, and he was very much pleased with what I had to say. At the end of the presentation he instructed Rachel to enter in the minutes that "Mr. Colbert presented an excellent report." Then on second thought he said: "Change that to read Mr. Colbert presented a good report; he is not capable of giving an excellent report."

After the meeting everybody was indignant with what HFO had said—except for me. I knew what was in his mind: he felt that I was as yet too inexperienced to do excellent work; maybe at a later date I could rise to such heights. So his statement, which was just a bit tactless, assigned me to my position as a neophyte, with no adverse implications intended. I was not bothered because by that time I had been around him long enough to understand something of the workings of his mind.

That experience of mine was somewhat parallel to an experience Dr. Mook had when he was Osborn's assistant. Mook told me about it with considerable amusement—this was some years after the happening—but at the time it didn't seem so funny. The two of them were together when the phone rang, to be answered by Osborn. Evidently Mrs. Osborn was at the other end of the line, for Dr. Mook heard Osborn say, "No dear, there's no one here with me, only an assistant." And then HFO went on to talk over the phone as if he were quite alone. That was the Professor in one of his unfeeling moments, yet he would have been surprised and hurt if someone (Mook could not have done it) had told him that he had acted without regard for the person in his presence.

To get back to my own life with Osborn, I had made up my mind when I started working on his elephants that I would try to say what I meant; I felt that there was no purpose in my being a yes-man if I was to serve as his research assistant. So I did tell him what I saw as I saw things, not always to his liking. He did not like to be disputed; he certainly did not like to have some of his preconceived ideas proven to be in error. Consequently we had some decided and at times some extended differences of opinion. But although he was frequently annoyed with me, he was never really angry. Perhaps the differences in our ages was a factor; he could be genuinely angry (and perhaps a bit apprehensive?) with Dr. Matthew, because he saw Matthew as a very formidable rival. But as for me, there was no possibility of rivalry involved, so he could afford to look upon my frequent caveats with a degree of amused tolerance.

Thus it was with the problem of stratigraphic levels. Osborn's training and background were more zoological than geological, with the result that he had some personally idiosyncratic ideas as to the succession of geological strata and their contained fossils. He was especially anxious to see stratigraphic levels in the various fossil-bearing formations with which we were concerned, and to see the fossils arranged within those various levels according to what he considered as their stages of evolution; in other words he liked a nice orderly picture in which everything was neatly pigeonholed. Alas! Geological phenomena are not always neatly arranged, but rather may be complex and confused. He often did not trust the observations of the people who had worked in the field and had collected the fossils that he was studying, especially if those observations did not coincide with his ideas as to what should and should not be so. That was a point upon which I frequently had arguments with him—generally to no avail whatsoever. Often, after such set-tos he would reprimand me for having adopted a "defeatist" attitude. (In his later years he frequently accused people who did not align themselves with his way of thinking as being defeatist.) Well, I learned how to accept his pronouncements (not too seriously so far as I was concerned) and thus retained my sanity.

While some of my work on the fossil elephants could result in controversies that I never could win (at least in the Osbornian view of things) some of it was of lighter consequence, even amusing. Never to be forgotten was one of my first proboscidean ventures *with* the Professor, rather than by myself at his behest. He had decided that we should measure the skeleton of the American Mastodon, on exhibit at the museum. So one fine day he and I went down to the fourth floor, accompanied by Rachel Nichols, and by one of our technicians carrying a long stepladder. I was armed with a pair of gigantic calipers, a meter stick, and a metric tape.

Professor Osborn sat himself down at a card table (another item I should have mentioned) along with Rachel, while I swarmed over the skeleton, up and down, fore and aft, making the desired measurements, which I would call out to Rachel, which she would put down on paper. As as I called out each measurement Professor Osborn would repeat what I said in a stentorian voice that rang throughout the exhibition hall and rattled the ribs of the mastodon. I think he liked to hear his voice echoing back and forth beneath the high ceiling. I can't remember how assorted museum visitors reacted to the performance; they probably were sufficiently mystified.

We finished our measurements and went to the elevator to return to the fifth floor. As was his wont, HFO watched the pointers above the elevators doors, and when he saw one showing the car near our floor he shouted UP! in a very authoritative tone. It was a command recognized by the elevator operators, so the car would be stopped at the fourth floor whether it was going up or down. If it was going down, the people on board enjoyed an extra ride up before resuming their downward journey. I don't remember which way the elevator was going that day when he hailed it; whatever may have been the case we went up to our floor and to our offices.

The hall we had just vacated was perhaps Professor Osborn's favorite, because it housed the various skulls and skeletons of fossil elephants and their kin. Consequently I was down there on more than one occasion with him. One time in the hall we met a tall, robust, bald-headed man accompanied by a child—evidently a grandchild, but I do not remember now whether a boy or a girl. Anyway, this gentleman and the Professor exchanged hearty greetings, and then I was introduced to the stranger, who was none other that Charles Dana Gibson, the famous artist and illustrator, the creator of the "Gibson Girl" who was all the rage back at the turn of the century. We had a nice chat and then the Professor and I went on our way.

Professor Osborn, because of his position and because of his wealth, was friend or acquaintance of the mighty on the political scene and so-called upper crust on the social scene. All of which sometimes stood him in good stead, and sometimes did not. Among other things, he had a plan for what he called the Intermuseum Parkway or something like that—a broad curving mall that was to cross Central Park from the American to the Metropolitan Museum. He hired architects and landscape designers to draw maps and elevations of this ambitious project, which never got very far beyond his office. I am sure that he submitted his plans to the park commissioners and to other officials in the city, but there was little interest in the idea. The park planners quite rightly were not about to allow a great mall to bisect the park, so the Professor was engaged in a losing battle from the very start. Yet he never ceased talking about it.

I remember that when I first knew him he had been appointed to a committee to select a name for the new bridge then under construction across the Hudson River, from upper Manhattan to New Jersey. He told me about their deliberations and how they had decided to name it the George Washington Bridge, and that *was* a successful project, giving him much satisfaction.

He had a way of being pompous with political personalities that sometimes backfired. Fred Smythe, who was bursar at the museum, once went down to City Hall with the Professor, to see Joseph McKee, then president of the borough of Manhattan. When they arrived at the borough president's office, Osborn said to the receptionist: "President Osborn to see Mr. McKee." (Remember, Osborn was then president of the museum Board of Trustees.) He and Fred had to sit and wait a few minutes, after which the young lady came out and much to Fred's delight said: "President McKee will now see Mr. Osborn."

A yearly event for all members of the Department of Vertebrate Paleontology were Professor Osborn's Christmas dinners. They were his outlets for expressing his appreciation for work done in the department during the year that was just drawing to a close. They were sumptuous, and they were segregated, because as has been said Osborn lived in a world of class distinctions, such distinctions being based upon the circumstances of the occasion. As for the Christmas dinner, each year distinctions were not matters of social standing or worldly goods, but rather of position on the scientific ladder, and sex. So there were three separate dinners served simultaneously, one in the Osborn Library, one in the paleontological laboratory, and one in Professor Osborn's outer office.

The dinner in the Osborn Library was the most formal and elegant of the three happenings, and it was attended by members of the departmental scientific staff—except for ladies. During the years that I attended these happenings there was only one lady involved, Rachel Nichols—a bona fide staff member but nonetheless a member of the wrong sex. Poor Rachel had to eat with the rest of the female members of the department, Miss Tyler, Miss Percy, Miss Milligan, and Mrs. Lord, who was at that time the departmental secretary—all of them sequestered, as has been said, in Osborn's outer office. Then there was dinner in the laboratory, attended by the preparators, and undoubtedly the most relaxed of the three gatherings. I never attended either of the other two dinners, but I did hear about them from the participants.

A parenthetical footnote. Years earlier, as I heard from some of the people involved, Professor Osborn entertained the department at his home, Castle Rock. Of course this was an all-day affair, but in the Osbornian manner the dinner at midday was segregated, with the scientific staff invited to dine in style in the Osborn dining room, while the preparators, secretaries, and other lesser folk ate in another room down below somewhere in the castle. When Dr. Matthew saw what was going to happen, he refused to go into the dining room; instead he went downstairs and ate with the other bunch. Of course it made a great impression on the people with whom he dined, and undoubtedly a most adverse impression on Osborn.

I was not independent enough to have taken such an action at the dinners I attended, so I sat quietly with my superiors and watched HFO carve the turkey and listened as he told how he learned to carve fowl—a story repeated each year. Incidentally, the dinners were catered by some fancy restaurant in midtown.

It might be added that in earlier years at the museum some of the Christmas affairs were rather elaborate. There is a program extant of the Christmas luncheon (as it was called) of 1916, given by Osborn "in honor of the Society of Vertebrate Paleontology." I don't know how many attended, but it was evidently sufficiently important so there was a printed program with a picture of the skeleton of *Tyrannosaurus* on the cover, with the menu inside, followed by poems about certain fossils, mostly written by Dr. Matthew.

Such stories could be continued, but perhaps what has here been set down will give some idea of the man with whom I spent five years, on and off, studying fossil elephants. He was an imperious man, pompous and vain, tactless and lacking in sensitivity, yet underneath there was a feeling of kindness for those associated with him. He was in many ways a victim of his time and his environment, a time during his young years of a strongly stratified society, and an environment in those days at the turn of the century when he associated with people of wealth. But the world had changed during the decades since his youth, and he had not become adjusted to many of the changes. All of which made life with Osborn interesting and at times hardly to be believed.

X

A Student in Albion

Up to this point I have been trying to tell a story of my beginnings, of an apprenticeship, especially of becoming initiated into the craft of paleontology. Now the story takes a new direction. Having traversed the long and often rocky road of a formal education and the less formal but perhaps more valuable experience of learning by doing, I had arrived face to face with the necessity of embarking upon my own independent research. This was in part to fulfill the requirements of a thesis or dissertation for the doctorate, but more importantly to enter into the theory and practice of paleontological research, which was to be my life occupation. The thesis was of course the immediate problem for me, but it was not an end in itself; rather it was a beginning, an introduction to things that were to come. It was essentially a test that might indicate whether or not I was ready and truly able to be a participant in the world of scientific endeavor.

There has been and is some scorn directed at the doctoral dissertation; I get the impression that the scorn comes from people unacquainted with the scientific disciplines. Perhaps dissertations in some fields may become mired in futile exercises, but I think that dissertations in the scientific disciplines are on the whole solid pieces of work that make valuable contributions to the body of scientific knowledge. I hoped that my thesis, whatever it might be, would prove to be of some lasting value. (Footnote. Perhaps it was; the final publication resulting from my dissertation studies was awarded the Daniel Giraud Elliot Medal for 1935 by the National Academy of Sciences.)

I had given much thought to a thesis problem during my second year in New York: what could it be? Many budding geologists or paleontologists see their dissertation projects growing out of field studies that they have made as assistants to their professors, or from work they have done in field or laboratory on grant projects. In this day and age graduate students expect almost as a matter of course assistance in the form of grants, but a half-century and more ago things were not so well arranged. I did not bring my field projects to Columbia with me, and even though I had become established at the museum after a fashion, there were no funds just then for field projects of my own. Those were the depression years. Furthermore, Dr. Gregory, my advising professor, was not a field paleontologist; he prosecuted his studies on materials collected by other people.

It looked as if that would be my course of action, so I considered the possibilities. I was much interested in the evolution of the carnivorous mammals, and for some time I toyed with the idea of trying to clarify the evolutionary history of the mustelids—the otters and weasels and their kin. Then I found out that Professor E. Raymond Hall at the University of Kansas was deeply involved with the mustelids, so that was erased from my plans. I thought of some other possibilities as a result of reviewing the literature (I don't recall at this stage what they were) and then a very large subject providentially dropped into my lap.

In the early twenties Barnum Brown had been in India, where he made a large collection of Upper Cenozoic mammals from the Siwalik Hills, fronting the massive Himalaya Range. It had been Dr. Matthew's intention to describe this collection; indeed, he had spent some considerable time in 1926 at the Indian Museum in Calcutta and at the British Museum in London studying Siwalik specimens. His tragic death in 1930 came at a time before he had advanced very far with his Siwalik studies so the museum authorities decided that I might take over the work on the American Museum Siwalik mammals. Which I did.

Shortly before his death the museum had published an introductory paper by Dr. Matthew, entitled "Preliminary Observations upon Siwalik Mammals," based largely on the notes that he had made in Calcutta and in London. This in a way served as an introduction to the work that I was to do. (Readers of Kipling may recall that in his great story "Kim," the young lad, Kim, accompanied by the lama and preceded by Hurree Babu, "crossed the Sewaliks" on their journey into the high mountains.)

The Siwalik Hills are composed of great thicknesses of continental deposits— sandstones, siltstones, conglomerates, great boulder beds—and within this orderly jumble of sediments are consecutive assemblages of fossil mammals extending over a time span of many millions of years. The fossils that make up the successive Siwalik faunas have long been known, having first been collected and described in the midnineteenth century by Sir Hugh Falconer and Sir Proby T. Cautley, and more recently in this century by Dr. Guy Pilgrim, of the Geological Survey of India. Falconer, a medical officer and botanist in the service of the British government in India, and Cautley, an army officer, were real paleontological pioneers. The fossil mammals then being found in the Siwalik Hills looked something like modern mammals of India, but then again they looked a bit different. So Falconer and Cautley made collections of modern Indian mammals for comparative purposes, and eventually Falconer brought out the first descriptions of extinct Siwalik mammals. Pilgrim, a paleontologist who supplemented the seminal studies of Falconer and Cautley, was retired but still active when I first began my work on Siwalik mammals; I got to know him well and to work with him.

With all of this earlier work on Siwalik fossils, why should I become involved? Because the materials collected by Barnum Brown were exceptionally fine, so that they not only supplemented in a grand way the fossils that had been previously studied, but also furnished many new specimens that greatly expanded our concepts of the various associations of extinct mammals from the Siwalik Hills. The strategy for my work on Indian fossils mammals was taking shape.

It turned out that this strategy included Dr. Pilgrim, because some years previously he had been invited to study the Siwalik bovids—the antelopes and their relatives—in the New York collection. It also included Professor Osborn because he had already discussed the Siwalik proboscideans—that is the fossil elephants and their cousins, the mastodonts and stegodonts—in his great Proboscidea monograph, to which I was devoting a part of my time and attention. (The mastodonts have already been mentioned in a casual manner. These were the predecessors of the elephants and from some of them the elephants had their origins. Indeed, many of the mastodonts looked very much like smaller editions of elephants, more stocky in build but nonetheless very elephantine in general appearance. Many of the mastodonts had tusks in the lower jaws as well as in the skull, and their molar teeth were much simpler than those of the elephants. The stegodonts were much more elephantine than the mastodonts; in fact they were fully as large as the true elephants, and they had huge tusks in the skull, and teeth that were advanced beyond mastodont teeth in the direction of elephant teeth. But there is good reason to think that the stegodonts may represent an independent line of evolution, derived, as were the elephants, from mastodont ancestors, and paralleling the elephants in structure. However that may be, the stegodonts were numerous in the Siwalik faunas.)

As for my work on Siwalik fossils, there was ample material for me to pursue a wide-ranging study, even without the antelopes and the proboscideans. So I made my plans accordingly.

It so happened that my plans for the second half of 1931 meshed very nicely with Professor Osborn's plans, which included his going to England to attend the British Association for the Advancement of Science meetings and my going to England to work on the elephant tooth enamel project. This meant work at the British Museum (Natural History) where, among other treasures, was one of the three great Siwalik collections, the other two being in Calcutta and New York. At this date I do not remember how the two projects coincided so nicely; I think that Osborn's plan for me to go to England probably came along after I had settled on the Siwalik study as a thesis topic. Certainly if the Professor had not arranged for me to go to England I would not have had the opportunity to study the Siwalik fossils in London, and my research would have been accordingly restricted. Thus it was arranged that I was to go to England coincident with Osborn's trip, and then I was to be allowed to stay on for some time, not only to study Siwalik and other fossils in London, but also to visit various museums on the continent, to look at their fossil collections.

Needless to say it was for me a great opportunity and a great adventure. An ocean crossing in the twenties or thirties was much more of an undertaking than are the air crossings today. One made elaborate plans ahead of time and one took along more luggage than do airborne travelers of this modern age. Furthermore, the trip across the Atlantic, involving not much less than a week on the fastest liners, and something more than that amount of time on the slower boats, provided an interval of adjustment, a real break in one's usual daily life and the exciting experiences of departure and arrival. All in all, a trip abroad in those days of surface travel was a memorable event in one's life.

Professor Osborn had conceived the bright idea of my going to England on the same ship with him but segregated, with Osborn traveling first class and Colbert going third class, as all well-behaved servants should go. It was his plan for me to come up to the first-class deck each day for conferences with him, a plan that was obviously unrealistic and an indication of the sometimes world of fantasy in which he lived. The steamship company would have been quite willing for HFO to come down into third class to visit me, which I am sure was beyond his thoughts, but somewhat less than agreeable for me to be invading the rarified precincts of first class. You paid for your privileges. I pointed these facts out to the Professor, and I suppose my arguments carried some weight, because he agreed that I would make the crossing on a different (and cheaper) ship. As it turned out, I traveled on the *America*, a nice cabin-class vessel (everybody on board in the same category), and had a pleasant voyage, indeed.

At this place I cannot pass up the chance to tell a tale about Osborn and his shipboard plans, as well as other plans, for people with whom he was traveling. The story involves Dr. Gregory and I pass it on as Gregory told it to me.

In 1934, a couple of years after my trip to England and my work there with Osborn, Professor Gregory was invited to give a series of summer lectures at Cambridge University. Osborn also was going to England that summer; perhaps he was going as a companion to Gregory—I don't know. (I might add that at the time, two or three years after the death of Mrs. Osborn, HFO was feeling lonely and in the need of activities that involved other people.) However that may be, they both booked passage on one of the great liners, Osborn to travel sumptuously in a first-class cabin, Gregory to travel somewhat less sumptuously in the most modest of first-class cabins available. (Knowing Dr. Gregory, I strongly suspect that if he had been traveling alone he would have been in second class, where the cabins were cheaper and traveling companions more interesting.)

The day of departure came, Osborn and Gregory were on deck, and at about the time the liner passed the Statue of Liberty Dr. Gregory went down to his cabin for something. To his consternation he found that an overhead pipe in the cabin had sprung a leak so that water was running down and beginning to soak the bed and carpet. He rushed to call the attendant, who in turn rushed to call the engineer, who in turn rushed up from below to survey the damage.

The engineer, after having stopped the flow of water, immediately informed Dr. Gregory that the pipe could not be repaired during the voyage; it would be necessary for the occupant to move out. So the purser was consulted, and soon came up with the information that no other cabins were available. "However," he said brightly, "the Prince of Wales Suite is not occupied so we will have to put you in there." And that was why Dr. Gregory lived in regal splendor during the entire transatlantic crossing. He took great pleasure in entertaining the Professor every afternoon at teatime, while HFO, coming up to the P. of W. Suite from his by comparison cramped cabin, for once had to be on the receiving end of largesse, graciously granted.

The two arrived in London, where they spent a few days before going on to Cambridge, and immediately the Professor decided that Dr. Gregory must needs be properly dressed for his appearances before the scholars of the university. So he hauled Dr. Gregory to his (Osborn's) tailor in Bond Street, and instructed the establishment to fit Gregory out with a morning outfit, consisting of a cutaway coat and striated trousers, plus the other accoutrements that should go with such a combination. Needless to say it cost poor Dr. Gregory a pretty penny.

Then came the day of the first lecture, and Dr. Gregory appeared correctly dressed for the occasion. Alas! It was summertime and everyone in the audience was dressed accordingly—the gentlemen with no jackets, shirt collars open, no neckties, baggy pants or shorts, loafers on the feet, the ladies in the most informal of clothes. That occasion was the one and only appearance of Dr. Gregory's morning outfit. He brought it back to New York, and hung it in a closet as a costly memento of his lectures at Cambridge University.

But there is more to the tale. On the last morning of the return voyage Dr. Gregory was in his quarters (this time a modest stateroom) trying to get his bags packed. The ship was docking and Dr. Gregory felt the pressure of the situation. Who should appear at the door of his cabin but HFO, to demand that Dr. Gregory accompany him to the lounge, where a group of reporters were waiting to interview the great man. Gregory tried to demur, but Uncle Hank would have none of it; he insisted that Dr. Gregory be present for the interview. So they both went into the lounge, to be established on a sofa, with the reporters grouped in front of them. Questions were put to HFO, and he answered at length, while every now and then Dr. Gregory would try to rise, in order to rush back to his cabin, but each time he tried to make his departure Osborn would reach out, grab his arm or his coattail, and pull him back down on the sofa. Poor Dr. Gregory, feeling desperate, finally made his escape, ran to his cabin, and hurriedly finished his packing as best he could.

And when he got out to the gangplank, there was Professor Osborn at the other end, imperiously gesturing to Dr. Gregory to come along, and be quick about it. So ended a memorable (for Gregory) journey.

The time came for us to get our passports. I went down to the passport office, in lower Manhattan in those days, and made my application in the usual way. As for the Professor, he wrote a personal letter to the secretary of state to ask for his passport. He soon received a short reply from the State Department, instructing him to go through the usual channels. He did just that, although I suppose he felt that it was something of a come-down to have to abide by such plebeian procedures. I should mention here that Osborn, sailing on the mighty first-class liner to which he had originally assigned me, was instead accompanied by Dr. Gregory.

The day of my departure was a time of high excitement for me. I had purchased a sort of portable steamer trunk, considerably larger than a suitcase and considerably smaller than an ordinary trunk, and lugging this piece of impedimenta from International House, where I was then living, out to the street, I got a cab to the pier, which was in Hoboken. Soon after I had become established in my little cabin, a crowd from the museum department appeared to see me off—Walter Granger, Rachel Nichols, John and Louise Germann, and Margaret Matthew. We had a jolly party; they had brought a big basket filled with goodies and foolish little gifts, and they had a lot of fun watching me open my presents. It was fun for me, too.

Finally, the "all ashore" call came, and they left me with a feeling of loneliness on my part as I began my great adventure. It was a morning departure, leaving at eleven. I stood at the rail as the ship slowly steamed down the Hudson, through the Narrows and out to sea. Within a few hours the ship was riding the long Atlantic swell and I was beginning to feel less than first rate. This was when the basket brought on board by my well-wishers came to the rescue. Within it were several nice bunches of white grapes; they appealed to me mightily. So that afternoon and evening I had occasional snacks of grapes, which sufficed. By morning I had my sea legs and was able to enjoy the rest of the trip.

And I did enjoy it. There was magic for me in my first trip abroad that has never been quite equaled by any of my subsequent foreign journeys. I was young, the world was bright, and my horizons encompassed wonderful visions of things to come. The unknown experiences ahead of me stirred the pulse.

All of which inspired me to keep a rather full diary of my trip, something I have never since achieved. For I must confess that my subsequent diaries (as distinguished from my geological-paleontological field books) have been to my regret on the laconic side. With such a diary available I take the liberty of inserting excerpts from it throughout the remainder of this account of my visit to England and to the Continent during those days now so far in the past. Perhaps these snippets as they occur will give some idea of the impressions gained of foreign lands, as seen by one who had come of age in the midtwenties.

Thus I note that on board the *America*, "I met [on the second day] at dinner my table companions, Dr. Lorwin, a professor of social sciences from Washington, D.C., Dr. Mario Vidoli, an Italian sanitary engineer returning from a year of study at Harvard, and Mr. C. A. Oldham, an English manufacturing engineer. A very nice lot, to say the least." I should add that I did not go to dinner on the first day at sea; that was when I survived by staying in my cabin and munching grapes. But on that second day, having become adjusted to the motion of the ship, I was very much awake to what was going on around me. So "a little after four P.M. we passed through masses of sea weed from which there flitted numerous flying fish"—a new and exciting sight to me. And on the next evening "just before going to bed, Dr. Vidoli and I went forward where we could look down into the water, sparkling with myriads of luminous things—probably similar to *Noctiluca*. The lights were of a greenish tint, and had the brilliancy of jewels." For me it was almost an emotional experience to see these aspects of marine life that

I had read about but never encountered at first hand. Chalk this up as an advantage of surface travel over flying.

The shipboard days passed pleasantly, for it was a calm voyage. It was good to have this interval of laziness, to be free of outside pressures. And then on August 20 "I was awakened shortly before five in the morning. Dressing was a hasty affair as was breakfast (this time in company with Oldham). At six we had our passports examined and were all ready to get off. But then they held us for a half hour or so while they transported tons of mail sacks to the lighter.

"Finally we boarded the lighter amidst the tons of mail, and after a short wait our small boat pushed off from the big ship. It was a morning long to be remembered; on the one side were the hills of Devon, green and well-kept in the early morning sunlight, and the harbor with its breakwater, and many white gulls against the dark waves, while to the seaward side was the black and white and red ship, steaming rapidly toward the open sea.

"We had a short wait at Plymouth, during which time I had my final visit with Oldham. Then we went through customs, all in all a very casual affair, for the officer merely looked at my luggage and gave it his O.K. After which I boarded the express for London."

My first day in London was a Saturday, which I employed in looking for lodging convenient to the British Museum (Natural History). I found a place in Redcliffe Gardens, near Earl's Court, and made arrangements to move in on the next day, having in the meantime found a room in a hotel for the night. That next morning I shifted my belongings to the room that was to be my home for the rest of the autumn and into the early winter, and after that I devoted myself to some sightseeing.

Of course Westminster Abbey was on my itinerary, and there I found the tombs of Charles Darwin and Charles Lyell, the great geologist who was Darwin's inspiration when Darwin, as a very young man, spent five epochal years on the *Beagle* voyage. I liked the inscription on Lyell's tomb, so I copied it.

Charles Lyell, Baronet, F.R.S. Author of 'The Principles of Geology.' Born at Kinnordy in Forfarshire, November 14, 1797. Died in London, February 22, 1875. Throughout a long and laborious life he sought the means of deciphering the Earth's history in the patient investigation of the present order of Nature. Enlarging the boundaries of knowledge and leaving on scientific thought an enduring influence. 'O Lord how great are thy works and thy thoughts are very deep.'

The next day I made my appearance at the museum, where I met the "keeper" (as the principal curator of a department is designated in the British

Museum) Dr. W. D. Lang. He arranged for some work space that I was to occupy and then turned me over to Dr. W. D. Swinton, assistant keeper. Thus began a friendship that has lasted through the years—years that eventually saw the westward migration of Bill Swinton from London to Toronto, where he served until his retirement as director of the Royal Ontario Museum.

The British Museum, one of the oldest museums in the world, had its origins during the latter part of the seventeenth century in the person of Sir Hans Sloane, a physician endowed with a very large bump of curiosity and an extraordinary zeal for collecting things. During his long life (1660–1753) he amassed an enormous and very miscellaneous collection of natural history objects: gems, Egyptian mummies, Roman and other antiquities, coins, pictures, and a library of some fifty thousand volumes. In his will he offered this collection to the king for the benefit of the British people, and that was the beginning of the museum. For more than a century the museum was located in Bloomsbury where Sloane had spent most of his life, but by the middle of the nineteenth century the Bloomsbury quarters were becoming inordinately crowded. In 1881 the Natural History division of the British Museum was moved to a new building designed by Alfred Waterhouse and located in South Kensington. This museum, universally known to Londoners as the Natural History Museum is none the less the British Museum (Natural History) and is known to the profession as the British Museum. Never mind the building in Bloomsbury; that is the art and archaeology section of the British Museum.

It was here at the British Museum in South Kensington that I was to spend most of the next six months of my life and to establish friendships and emotions that have been with me for much more than a half century. It's a wonderful old place, the South Kensington building, a structure of inspired Victorian gothic with a many-colored terra cotta facade. When I worked there the first time the building appeared to be dull—and it was. But in recent years it has been cleaned; the colors now gleam in their original pristine palette, while all along the front are the sculptured forms of animals and plants, fossil and recent, as executed under the direction of Sir Richard Owen, the first "superintendent" of the institution, as he was then called.

I was just getting used to my surroundings in the museum—I had been there only a couple of days—when "in the middle of the morning one of the doormen came down [I was in the basement] to inform me that Professor Osborn and Dr. Gregory had arrived. I did not see them until lunch time, when, as I was having lunch with Swinton, they arrived in the lunch room. There was a general exchange of greetings followed by a recital of HFO's troubles. It seems he had been rather indisposed for two or three days—he blamed it on the water.

"The afternoon was spent listening to HFO explain the wonders of the elephant enamel system to Dr. Swinton.

"To *His Majesty's Theatre* in the evening, where I saw J. B. Priestley's 'Good Companions'—a most entertaining play." I might add that one of the principal actors in the play was a young man named John Gielgud, and little did I realize at the time that I was witnessing the early stages of a long and distinguished acting career.

When I look over my diary I am constantly amazed at the way in which I got around, and the things I did. I must have been brimming over with energy in those days; it makes me tired now just to read about how I labored at the museum all day, went to plays and pictures in the evenings, made trips hither and yon on my free days. For example on my first Saturday after beginning at the museum I worked all morning studying Siwalik fossils. Then lunch with Swinton. Then we talked of going to a football match, but finally gave it up because Swinton decided that since this was the first game of the season there would be tremendous crowds and it would not be very pleasant. So I decided to see some things. First I went to the Temple Courts. After that along the Embankment to St. Paul's, where I heard a part of the afternoon service. Then to Threadneedle Street, and after that up the Monument (to the great fire of 1666) "where I obtained a splendid view of the city, especially of the Tower and Tower Bridge. After that to Piccadilly, where I dined, saw a movie and then went to my lodging." And on the following day I devoted myself to the London Zoological Society in Regent's Park.

There were things other than fossils to occupy my time in London. Nevertheless the fossils were always there, demanding attention, so on the Monday morning after my pleasant day at the zoo, I was back at the museum studying the bony remains of animals, many of which were the predecessors or even the ancestors of the beasts I had seen in Regent's Park. The first entry in my diary for that day is amusing—at least as viewed from this distance in time.

"The day was spent at the Museum. Most of the time was spent with HFO, consequently little was accomplished. I did manage to get in some work on Siwalik pigs." "Little was accomplished." How true this was of so many of the hours that I spent with Professor Osborn—hours devoted to rehashing problems that already had been worked over to the point of exhaustion, hours spent in futile arguments, hours in which it seemed to me we were running, like the Red Queen, and staying in the same place. As for example: "The morning was spent with HFO, mainly in trying to distinguish the differences (if any) between *Stegodon bombifrons*, *S. genesa* and *S. insignis*. There followed one of our discussions (might I say arguments?) concerning individual variation, in which as always I held up the end for much variation, while he advocated little. The afternoon was spent in finishing my study of Siwalik pigs. I didn't get as far as I had intended for Dr. Swinton and Mr. Sealy [Harold Sealy, Swinton's assistant] spent an hour or so chewing the fat with me. Then I went with Swinton to have tea. Nevertheless the time passed quite pleasantly—and are not friendships to be valued as much as accomplishments? In the evening to the *Theatre Royal* to see 'Marry at Leisure,' a clever and laughable comedy." (I simply could not stay away from the theater.)

As for Siwalik pigs, already mentioned twice, they did fascinate me. They were various and there were among them lines of evolutionary development to intrigue the observer; would that some of them had not become extinct! At this stage of my scientific life I became remarkably interested in the evolution of pigs—pigs of the wild sort, not their modern barnyard variants. That led to an interest in peccaries, which are the New World cousins of the Old World pigs. In fact I devoted many hours to the peccaries with the prospect of eventually doing a monograph upon them. The result was a large thick pile of pages on peccary relationships and their probable evolution through time, and that was the end of it. I suppose this example of unfinished work is not unusual; certainly one reads of authors who have unfinished books in their files. I don't quite know why the peccary monograph got stalled; very probably because I became interested in other projects that were of more importance to me. Yet I still have a great deal of affection for pigs and peccaries—among the more successful and intelligent of the mammals. They deserve to have their story told in a proper and serious manner.

The alternation of Siwalik studies with work on elephants was the usual pattern of my days at the British Museum, and sometimes it seemed as if the elephants dominated my life. Then, on the fourth of September, thanks to Professor Osborn, my prospects for the days and weeks ahead became clarified, much to my satisfaction. From the diary:

"The day was spent on fossil elephants. For several days I've been wondering what would become of my studies of Siwalik fossils, for I haven't had a chance at them lately. At lunch with Dr. Swinton and Professor Osborn (Dr. Gregory being out of town) HFO suggested that after my continental trip I might return to London for an extended stay. That struck me just right, so now I am planning to continue in London until December or thereabouts. I had intended to attend a play but I was unable, several days previously, to get the tickets for what I wanted to see at the price I wanted to pay. But I have secured a ticket to see Jack Buchanan in 'Stand Up and Sing' for next Tuesday, and I'm looking forward to that. Oh yes. An invitation from Sherborn to his house on Thursday next."

In those days the British Museum was full of characters, as I suppose is still the case, and one of the outstanding personalities at that time was C. Davies Sherborn, known to one and all as Squire. Squire was a man of immense erudition, a classical scholar who spent his lifetime compiling the *Index animalium*, a monumental bibliography of animals. When I knew him he was an elderly bachelor with a long beard and an outwardly prickly manner. An invitation to his house was a command, so I looked forward to the following Thursday with some anticipation and a bit of trepidation.

I had dinner that evening with Dr. Gregory, after which we took off for Squire's—in Shepherd's Bush as I recall. We got there by various methods, mostly by bus and by foot and when we arrived we found a number of people from the museum already present—all male. With Squire it would hardly be otherwise. At first we sat around in a circle in the parlor of his flat and talked about this and that, but soon things became more informal so that there were several discussions going on at once. Squire had all sorts of things to whet one's curiosity, and he spent a part of the evening showing us various objects of antiquity, particularly ancient coins. As we were leaving, Squire put in my hand an ancient Roman coin. That was Squire; bluff and superficially crusty, but a man sufficiently sensitive to do a very nice thing for a young tyro like myself.

Professor Osborn wanted me to visit the Piltdown site, where the famous Piltdown remains had been found. At that time they were considered as the genuine relics of a very ancient but anatomically strange human being, and thus the subject of continuing controversy. (Only within recent years was the Piltdown puzzle solved. We now know that the bones were fakes, a broken human cranium buried with a chimpanzee jaw—all of the remains skillfully treated to seem like true fossils.) Osborn also wanted me to become conversant with the Pliocene and the Pleistocene or Ice Age deposits of East Anglia, where in the Pliocene Red Crag, so called, there had been found flint objects which were claimed by a local amateur archeologist, Mr. Reid Moir, to have been made by human hands. If so they would have been much older than any other known human artifacts. I consult the diary to see what was done in preparation for these field studies.

"In the morning I went down to Longacre, to Stanton's, to get some Geological Survey publications and maps, and I found myself in a narrow street filled with open air wholesale shops, and beer trucks, and horses. (All of which sounds a bit Dickensian.) After arriving in Drury Lane, and seeing that I had gone the wrong way, I retraced my steps and came to my destination. The morning was spent in roaming around this district, not the least interesting part of my adventures being the discovery of peculiar corners and angles. Back to the Museum and after lunch to the Royal School of Mines, where I had a conference with Dr. Boswell [then one of the foremost geologists in England] and Mr. Solomon about the Pleistocene of

East Anglia. Dr. Gregory had brought his things over to my place in the morning, so at the end of the day we walked together, back to Redcliffe Gardens, where we dined. Then we took a walk and had a good long conversation together. Back to our lodging, and I looked at his rowing machine that he had brought along. After which I read for a while and finally fell asleep."

There is more to these entries than meets the eye. For one thing, the reader may wonder why Professor Boswell, a man of great scientific distinction, would spend any time with the likes of me. It was not me, it was Osborn. Boswell knew the purpose of my visit and he wanted to be sure that I had my facts straight so I could pass the information on to the great man. It must be remembered that at the time Osborn was a powerful figure in the paleontological world.

The notation about Dr. Gregory needs some explanation. He was staying with Professor Osborn in Mayfair, the section of London inhabited by the nobility and the rich, and at times he found the atmosphere too cloying for his simple tastes. So when HFO had to leave London for some reason, Dr. Gregory came over and camped in my simple digs. I think he enjoyed the change; it certainly was a great privilege for me.

My briefing on the Pliocene and Pleistocene of East Anglia having been accomplished, there was still the matter of the Piltdown site. HFO decided that we should see the director of the Geological Survey to make arrangements for that. He told me to meet him at nine o'clock the next morning at the Geological Survey offices in Jermyn Street, where the survey was then located.

"Professor Osborn," I said, "it's no use going there at nine. The offices do not open until ten o'clock."

"Nonsense!" said HFO. "Meet me there at nine; they will open for me."

And I couldn't persuade him otherwise. I decided, however, to split the difference, so I showed up about nine-thirty at Jermyn Street, and there was Uncle Hank pacing up and down the sidewalk in front of the survey entrance. I joined him and we paced up and down together, while he remarked to me at some length about the slothful habits of our British cousins—a bit unusual, because Osborn was a confirmed Anglophile.

At ten o'clock we were admitted to the building, and according to my diary "we signed our names in a book, and then went to the library to await the arrival of the Director. The Director, however, didn't show up immediately, and HFO, feeling impatient took himself off in the direction of South Kensington. In the meantime Mr. Edmunds (one of the Survey geologists) had arrived, he having corresponded with HFO previously, and we made arrangements for a field trip to Sussex on Friday. I went up to Mr. Edmunds' office with him, where I put in a good portion of the day in going over galley proof of a new Survey Memoir on East Anglia. Shortly before noon I was called down to meet the Director of the Survey, Sir John Flett, and I had a twenty minute conversation with him." I remember him as being a burly man with hairy ears, and very affable.

Of course I had been going ahead with my Siwalik studies as circumstances permitted, and of course I had been measuring elephant enamel lengths by the kilometer, so it seemed, so that we now had reams of new data to add to the measurements we had brought with us from New York. The meetings of the British Association were coming up in about ten days (perhaps it will be remembered that these meetings were the ostensible reason for our coming to Britain) and naturally HFO decided that he needed new, improved, updated thirty-foot-long charts to present at the meeting where he was to give his talk. What to do? For him the answer was simple. "Go over to the Imperial Institute," he said to me, "and tell the director that I would like to have his drafting staff prepare the new charts."

"But Professor Osborn, I can't do that. You will have to make the request."

"Nonsense," he said, "you can ask in my name."

"No." I insisted, "I am sure it would be much better if you asked him in person."

Finally he grudgingly agreed, and the next day the two of us went over to the Imperial Institute (as it was then called) located just behind the Natural History Museum. Of course we were shown in to the director's office; it could hardly be otherwise, considering Osborn's position and reputation. He made his request of the director, which was immediately granted. Then, out on the steps of the institute, he turned to me and said: "See how easy it was!"

The request was easy, for a man of his eminent position in the scientific world. But what followed was not exactly easy for me, because I had to go over to the institute with my data and supervise the making of the charts, all the time giving instructions to a couple of men who were my elders by a good many years. But everything worked out well in the end, and the charts were ready for the British Association meeting.

The session at which Osborn spoke was an enlarged version of the presentation that had been made in Philadelphia some months earlier. And I think the results were about the same; all present listened politely but there was no discussion of the paper at the close of Osborn's remarks. However one member of the assembly arose to remark that he understood Osborn had studied under Huxley in these very precincts. This pleased HFO very much; he *had* studied under Huxley. Moreover, he was very proud of the fact that one day Darwin had entered the room, and he

(Osborn) had been introduced and had shaken Darwin's hand. Elephant enamel was forgotten, old days were remembered and discussed.

My diary of that day tells more about the meetings. "At the geology section Sir Arthur Keith started the session, and HFO followed him (as described above). Then came Lang (of the British Museum) and one or two others. Then D. M. S. Watson got up and delivered a severe criticism against invertebrate paleontologists and their ideas about recapitulation, which started a row that lasted for the rest of the morning. To the College of Surgeons in the afternoon, where we were shown around by Sir Arthur Keith."

Well do I remember that afternoon. Robert Broom, the brilliant and erratic paleontologist from South Africa was there. Keith and Broom provided a study in contrasts; Keith, tall and dignified and almost aloof, Broom a dark-skinned gnome-like man clad in a dark suit and wearing a shirt with a wing collar as he always did, whether in his office, at a public gathering, or out in the field under the rays of a fierce sun and the temperature above one hundred. Keith and Broom were talking back and forth and arguing about human evolution, all the while passing precious fossil skulls into each other's hands, while the rest of us crowded around to listen and be instructed. I still recall with a certain horrified thrill the instant when between them one of the skulls escaped their mutual handling and dropped to what seemed inevitable destruction on the floor. But Broom with a burst of agility more than admirable for a middle-aged, gray-headed man, dove down with his arm and made a flying catch of the fossil inches above the floor. It was typical of Broom; he seemed always to be bursting with energy—always restless, always moving. He was a man about whom legends accumulate; in later years I got to know him well.

Perhaps some additional words about Dr. Broom can be added at this place. He was a quick, incisive Scotsman, educated as a medical doctor. As a young man he went to Australia, where he became interested in the egg-laying monotremes, and the marsupials, and shortly in the large subject of the origin of mammals. He knew that the mammallike reptiles were abundant in South Africa, so he abandoned Australia, went to South Africa with his wife, and set up a medical practice in a little Karroo town, where he would be close to the fossil fields. Thus he earned his keep ministering to the ills of patients in town and country, and spent all of the time that he could muster in the search for and the study of mammallike reptiles.

Erratic though he might have been, Broom was a brilliant man, and through the years he churned out paper after paper describing mammallike reptiles—illustrating his text with his own drawings. In time his contributions, which received world-wide attention among paleontologists, were duly recognized in South Africa, so that he spent the latter part of his life at the museum in Pretoria. Eventually he became an authority on early manlike apes, or apelike men, in southern Africa—this on top of his prodigious work on the mammallike reptiles.

Broom never properly cleaned a specimen before he studied it. He would describe and draw a skull that was half covered by rock, drawing in the sutures between the skull bones where he saw them and where he thought they ought to be when he didn't see them. And he was usually right. I remember that during my early years at the American Museum a South African paleontologist came over to study our South African collection of mammallike reptiles, a collection that had been made by Broom and sold to the museum. Our visitor that winter spent months in the laboratory painfully chipping away the rock from various skulls, so that he could properly see the shapes of the skull bones and the sutures between them. Lo and behold! Most of the time he found the sutures just as Broom had drawn them in!

Broom also came to the American Museum every now and then, and so I got to know him. He was an outrageous person; one never knew what he would say or what he would do. One thing he did do was to pursue the ladies—to such an extent that our librarians had a rule never to go into the stacks alone with Broom. They accompanied him in pairs. It can fairly be said that life was always interesting when Dr. Broom was around.

After the meetings in London I took a train to Norwich, in East Anglia, where within a couple of days I was to meet HFO, to help him look at the Red Crag deposits (near Ipswich) from which those supposed artifacts were being excavated by the enthusiastic Mr. Moir. In Norwich I spent a day at the Castle Museum, located on a small hill in the middle of the city, and specifically named because a part of the museum building is the old Norman keep, the remnant of one of William the Conqueror's castles. That evening Professor Osborn arrived with his ten-year-old grandson, riding in a chauffeur-driven limousine.

The next morning we drove from Norwich to Ipswich, about forty miles to the south, in East Anglia, and there we met Mr. Moir. We went out to the site, where we found a workman of the type the British used to call a "navvy" industriously digging for flints in the Red Crag. Such was the method; he would dig all day and would spread the results of his digging in rows on some planks; then Mr. Moir would appear and go over the flints, picking out the ones that vaguely looked as if they might have been made by human hands— these were the "rostro-carinate eoliths" on which he based his theory of a Pliocene man once inhabiting East Anglia. The results were predictable; out of several dozen flints a few might appear to be extremely primitive, ill-shapen artifacts. The resemblances, it seemed to me, were quite fortu-

itous; after this visit to the site my belief in rostro-carinate eoliths, made by
Pliocene men, was at the zero level.

But Professor Osborn's belief in them was not shaken; to him they were
very real. I didn't even try to argue with him.

We went back into town and had lunch with Mr. Moir, and then Uncle
Hank and the grandson took off for Cambridge, while I remained in Ipswich.
I happened to put up at the Great White Horse Inn, the same place, it will
be remembered, where Mr. Pickwick inadvertently got into the wrong
bedroom, to have a most embarrassing confrontation with a middle-aged
lady, her hair adorned with "yellow curl-papers." Fortunately I was not
involved in any such unexpected adventures, and so I had a good night's
sleep in a room just down the corridor from a door labeled "Mr. Pickwick's
Room," preparatory to joining a field party of geologists sponsored by the
British Association and out to study the geology of East Anglia.

It was a pleasant excursion from which I learned some of the details of
East Anglian geology. At the end of two days in the field we were back in
Norwich, where in the evening our party was entertained by the local
authorities at the Strangers Club, and where there was much speech-
making, followed by many informal conversations among us.

Norwich had by then become somewhat familiar to me, and it was later
to be very much a locale for my activities. For eventually I returned, to
spend more time at the Castle Museum, and out in the countryside of East
Anglia. That was in early December, when the days were short and gray and
there was frost in the air. My interests revolved around the Pliocene and
Pleistocene mammals of the North Sea coast and the relationships of the
sediments in which those fossils are preserved.

When I returned to Norwich for research in the Castle Museum, there
during breaks in my observations of fossils I wandered through the old
Norman keep, marveling at the massive stone walls, and the deep niches
within those walls where archers could stand and fire their arrows through
narrow, vertical slits at any approaching foe. It was in truth a museum almost
nine hundred years old, within which was housed the contemporary
museum.

Mr. Leney, the director of the museum, had made plans to take me to
Cromer, on the North Sea coast, to see the fossil-bearing beds there,
particularly the so-called Forest Bed, from which the remains of many
Plio-Pleistocene mammals had been found—deer, other hoofed mammals,
elephants, and the like. Also he hoped we might visit a Mr. Barclay and a
Mr. Savin, both of whom had during many years collected such fossils. We
wanted to see their collections.

As luck would have it, the day for which the trip had been planned was rather nice—a break in what had been a succession of dark, rainy days. Once again I go to my diary.

"The morning was crisp and nippy, with a refreshing wind and a wan December sun that would peep out occasionally from behind the clouds. I was all in the mood for the trip to Cromer, and when I arrived at the Museum I found Mr. Leney to be in the same mood. He had his car ready, so we got in and away we went. We had a glorious day along the North Sea coast. In the morning to a couple of places along the cliffs, hoping to see some exposures of the Forest Bed, but everything was covered by land slips that had slid down from the tops of the cliffs.

"So we went to Mr. Barclay's country place near Cromer, to see his collection, and as it was just lunch time he asked us to come in and have our noonday meal with him. It was, I suppose, a typical country house of an English squire—a long, rambling house set in the midst of smooth lawns and well-kept shrubbery. Inside, the place was decidedly Victorian, with blue and white china on every ledge and shelf, and rows of bookcases reaching to the ceiling. A large table in the middle of the big parlor was covered with stacks of appropriate magazines, such as *The Illustrated London News*, *Punch, Country Life*, and so on. There was a glass house, too, filled with flowers.

"Mr. Barclay was the kind of Englishman that Americans think of as being typical of the breed. He was of medium size, had a ruddy face and a clipped moustache. He wore a sort of hunting suit and heavy shoes. And his conversation was punctuated with such words as 'rather' and 'jolly.' He liked a little bush out on the lawn because it had a jolly color.

"His son came in just in time for lunch; he was carrying a gun in the crook of his arm. It turned out that he had been ferreting for rabbits, and the old gentleman was quite interested in the results of the morning's hunt.

"After lunch we went around to old Mr. Savin's place to see his collection of Forest Bed mammals, and it was a large collection."

What I didn't put down in my diary was Mr. Savin's domestic arrangements; they were so different from anything I had ever seen that I must add something here. Mr. Savin was a very old gentleman, rather stooped and frail, and long past the age for going out into the unpredictable English climate to collect fossils. His house was right on the coast, and I can remember how the wind howled past the walls—a wind that came roaring in without obstruction from Scandinavia, across the sea. But Mr. Savin was cozy, because squarely in front of the ample fireplace on one side of his little living room was a large armchair with a high back, and behind and on each side of the chair was a large, three-paneled screen. It was specially made for the purpose—it reached from floor to ceiling and the two side wings extended to the wall on each side of the fireplace. There were three glass windows set in the three panels of the screen, while overhead from the ceiling an electric light with a large green shade was positioned above his chair. It was a room within a room, and when he was established in his chair, with the screen panels completely enclosing him and with a nice brisk fire in front, he was indeed as snug as could be. In fact as I looked out at the bleak winter scene I truly envied him.

The story has gotten a little ahead of itself, because my trip to Norwich and the adjoining countryside took place after I had returned from a swing around the Continent, a trip that has been briefly alluded to on preceding pages. That was a journey to see museums and collections of particular significance to me and it embraced an itinerary that went from London to Brussels, to Paris, to Lyon, to Geneva, to Basel, to Stuttgart, to Munich, to Vienna, to Halle, to Berlin, and then back to London by way of the Hook of Holland and Harwich. It was a trip that lasted about six weeks, during the course of which I made the acquaintance of numerous paleontologists and saw many paleontological collections, as well as the museums in which they were housed. And in spare moments I saw things other than fossils.

It was a trip such as paleontologists the world over make, time and again and much more frequently today than was the case a half-century and more ago. For it has been the practice of paleontologists to travel far and wide—to museums for the purpose of studying collections and making the comparisons that are so crucial to people involved with the grand puzzles of relationships and distributions among animals long since vanished from the earth, and to the field to collect fossils. So my trip to the Continent had a purpose, for which reason it kept me very busy all during the time of my journeying.

Looking back over fifty years and more of travel to all parts of the earth (the journey of 1931 was but the first of my foreign adventures) I must point out that trips I have taken have real meaning for me because all of them were made with a purpose. I don't think I could make long trips as a tourist; it is good to see new things and to satisfy one's curiosity, but to travel merely for the sake of sightseeing is, it seems to me, a superficial and even a boring way in which to get acquainted with the world. One of the nice things about paleontological travels is the opportunity to meet people in various countries and to get acquainted with them, to live with them and to share their cultures, to go out into the country away from cities and the roads between cities, in short to see things more or less as the local inhabitants see things.

I will not try to write about this trip in detail or even in a synoptical manner, but a few of the more interesting happenings (at least to me) along the way will be mentioned. And the first of these was a my trip from London to Brussels, which I made by air. Flying was not common in those days, but there were some primitive airlines connecting the large cities of the world.

On October first I took a bus to Croyden, which in those days was the London airport, and there I boarded "a big Handley-Page, with three motors. There were just two of us as passengers, a priest from Toledo, Ohio, and myself. It was his first air trip as well as my own." I might add that we walked across a cement strip set in a grassy field to board the plane, while our luggage was trundled out in a little two-wheeled handcart that had every appearance of having been put together by a local carpenter. I took a picture of that plane; it shows a long, boxy fuselage set between two enormous wings, above and below. A central motor protruded from the front of the fuselage, while on each side there was a motor suspended, so it seemed, between the upper and lower wings.

"Before we realized it we were roaring into the mists of the morning. England spread beneath us like a great, soft green carpet, touched here and there with warm brown and yellow. The chalk cliffs of Dover were easily recognizable and then we were over the Channel. We seemed to float through blue nothingness, for the water was a greenish blue beneath and the air was blue around us, and sea and sky met in an indistinguishable haze. Now and then we would see a ship, ringed around by white foam, but otherwise seemingly floating in space, just as we were doing. Soon we were over France, a country of checker-board fields and red-tiled roofs. White roads crossed and recrossed. Here and there were villages, each with its church in the center. The trip was all too short; soon we were over Brussels. We glided steeply downward, the wheels touched the ground and we felt once more the pull of the earth."

In all of the cities listed above I went to the museums. I visited with the paleontologists and other museum officials that I met, and I looked at collections. And in odd moments, especially in evening hours, I enjoyed the sights to be seen, and not infrequently attended theaters. One of the high points of this trip was my visit to the University of Tübingen, Germany, an institution that is famous for its collections of fossils. In those days the big man at the university museum was Friedrich Freiherr von Huene, a legendary figure in the field of dinosaurian and other reptilian research.

"I arrived at the University at about ten o'clock and after several inquiries succeeded in finding the office of Dr. von Huene. He welcomed me, literally with open arms." Why should von Huene be so cordial to me, a young, unknown student? Probably because I came from the American Museum and relations between the museum and Tübingen were very close. In fact, Professor Osborn had advanced a considerable sum of money to the Tübingen University Museum to pay for a skeleton and other materials of *Plateosaurus*, a Triassic dinosaur that von Huene excavated in southern Germany.

Continuing. "A tall man, rather slender, with brownish-red wavy hair and a closely trimmed Van Dyke beard, he was a striking figure. While we were having our introductory chat his daughter came into the office and I was introduced to her. She was a buxom young lady of medium height, with a roundish face and brown hair, and most noticeable of all, a pair of pince-nez spectacles with a gold chain running back to her ear. It seemed old fashioned to me. She spoke to me in perfect English, as had Dr. von Huene, and in a way I was surprised and in a way I was not."

The daughter was the second of five von Huene girls, whose names began with vowels arranged in order—thus, Alexandra, Erika, Irma, Olga, and Ursula. Mrs. von Huene was English, and so all the members of the family were bilingual. Dr. von Huene came from an East Prussian family of some distinction; consequently he was very proud of the Freiherr in his name.

Dr. von Huene was a completely dedicated paleontologist, and perhaps one of the most unworldly men I have ever known. (These remarks, it should be said, are based upon subsequent acquaintance with him, the result of several visits in later years to Tübingen.) He was also a deeply religious man, and moreover an austere person. The first time I met him he was only recently returned from a very successful expedition to Rio Grande do Sul, Brazil, where he had made a spectacular collection of Triassic reptiles. He enthusiastically showed them to me and I looked at them with considerable awe, though unaware at the time that thirty years later I would go to Brazil and collect similar fossils from the same region where von Huene had worked.

"While we were in the store room examining the fossils, Frau von Huene appeared and asked me to join them at their noon-day meal. So at noon we walked up the hill to the von Huene house. The sun was warm and the day was delightful. After our meal Dr. von Huene and Erika walked with me to the Anthropological Institute to see the Aurignacian skulls that had recently been found in a cave near Tübingen, and after that we walked around and inspected some of the University buildings. Then we walked around town, first going up to the castle, Dr. von Huene explaining to me that it was placed upon a horst block between two graben valleys. [To say it in less geological terms, the castle was on a high hill which had been raised by faulting, while on the two sides of this hill were the valleys, dropped down by the faulting—the faults on each side of the hill separating it from the deep valleys.] Then we walked through the old part of Tübingen."

As can be seen there was a lot of walking that afternoon. I later learned that von Huene was famous for his walking. In fact, when he was a very old man, far into his eighties, he decided to attend a geological meeting in a city about a hundred miles from Tübingen, and moreover he decided to get there by walking. He did, too, covering perhaps thirty miles each day and sleeping in the woods.

"I had the evening meal with the von Huenes—cold pancakes with apple butter and sugar, and after dinner we chatted and looked at pictures that Dr. von Huene had taken on his expeditions. And Miss von Huene told about the two years she spent in America."

Years later I learned from Margaret, then my wife, that Erika von Huene had visited the Matthew family during her American visit; Margaret remembers it well, she was a young teenager at the time.

I have dwelt at some length on my first meetings with von Huene because in subsequent years my paleontological endeavors were to be closely related to work that von Huene had done. In short, I was eventually to become very much involved in the study of Triassic reptiles, and this was the field in which von Huene spent so many years of his life and produced so many publications of note. So although I did not realize it at the time, I was getting to know at first hand the man whose findings and whose conclusions I would be reviewing— sometimes in agreement, sometimes in disagreement. And in later years it would be my privilege to meet von Huene again and eventually to honor him, when I attended a symposium in Tübingen in 1984, designated as the *Third Symposium on Mesozoic Terrestrial Ecosystems*, and dedicated to Friedrich von Huene.

My trip through Europe continued. After my first visit with the von Huene family I made a pilgrimage to the Holzmaden region, where many fine skeletons of ichthyosaurs, plesiosaurs, fishes, crinoids, and other stunning fossils have been discovered and excavated. Then on to Munich, where among other things I witnessed a parade of Hitler's Brown Shirts. This was before Hitler had come to power, but already he was building up his following in anticipation of events that were to shake the world. When I watched those bully boys marching down the street I did not foresee the sinister forces that they represented, but I know I did not like the brown column.

There was an early autumnal snow in Munich, and when I got to Vienna the weather was raw and cold. One memory of Vienna that stays with me was my visit to the Austrian Geological Survey, or whatever the proper name of that agency might be. It was housed in an old ducal palace, and inside I found various members of the organization huddled around stoves in their offices, cozy and warm. But the collections, I discovered, were stored in a grand ballroom of the old palace, a long baroque hall, the former magnificence of which was compromised by rows of plebeian storage cases, arranged in rows down the center of the room. From the ornate ceiling there were massive crystal chandeliers and along each of the two long walls were empty fireplaces, spaced at about twenty- or thirty-foot intervals. It was bitterly cold in that room, and I wondered what it was like back in the days of Austro-Hungarian hegemony, when this hall was the scene of brilliant social affairs, including, I suppose, much formal dancing. It seemed to me that there must have been a constant parade of flunkeys, bringing in wood or coal to keep the fires blazing at their brightest and warmest.

From Vienna to Berlin, and of course I got to see the big German metropolis before the vast destruction of the Second World War and its subsequent partition by the wall. There I purchased a very early model of a Leica camera which served me well for many years. Then back to Britain arriving at Harwich on November 9.

Back in October I had spent a weekend as a guest of Sir Arthur and Lady Smith Woodward at their home near Hayward's Heath, some thirty miles or so south of the center of London, and about a dozen miles north of Brighton on the Channel. Smith Woodward, who for many years had been a very large figure at the British Museum, was now quietly retired, enjoying his role as the Grand Old Man of British vertebrate paleontology. His retirement, as was widely known in British Museum and paleontological circles, was not a particularly happy affair. He had come to the museum as a very young man and had spent his life there, rising to the position of keeper of the Department of Geology. In this position, which he held for many years, he maintained an autocratic rule over his subordinates and over the functioning of the department; he evidently enjoyed his power and he had visions of becoming the director of the museum, but when the time came another man was made the director and Smith Woodward was quietly retired with a knighthood. He didn't want to be a knight; he wanted to be the director of the museum. So he left the place, never to set foot in it again.

Parenthetically, I have never been able to appreciate this lust for power and position. Yet it is a universal trait, going back to our paleolithic ancestors and even beyond, as we know when we see the fight for dominance expressing itself throughout the animal world. Certainly being the director of a museum is no sinecure; from what I have seen over six decades of museum experience, it is one long, constant pain in the neck. And what does it avail the person who holds such a position? Within a few years he (or she) is forgotten; the people who are truly remembered are the scholars, the experts who seek out the truth and make the truth known through their activities, and especially through the things they write. It is the same in universities. Question: Who was Einstein? A question almost anyone can answer. Question: Who was the president of Princeton University during the years that Einstein was there?

But to get back to Smith Woodward. When he left the British Museum he moved down to Hayward's Heath to become established, with Lady Woodward and their daughter, Margaret, in a very comfortable home, known as Hill Place. And it was to Hill Place that a written invitation, perhaps not so much an invitation as a summons, directed me, with information as to what train I should take.

So on an October morning I took the train, and at Hayward's Heath Miss Margaret Woodward was waiting for me. There was another guest, too, Miss Foster, a minor official of some sort in the government. She was a tall and rather distinguished-looking lady, and seemed youngish in spite of her iron-gray hair. She was a friend of Margaret's; they had spent some vacations together on the Continent.

"At Hill Place we were welcomed by Sir Arthur and Lady Woodward— he a jolly old gentleman with a gray Van Dyke beard, a fringe of gray hair around his bald pate, and twinkling eyes. He wore eye glasses having a long, black ribbon on them, and he walked with a sort of rolling gait. Lady Woodward seemed to be somewhat younger than her scientific spouse. She proved to be a charming though at times a determined woman."

It might be added here that Maude Woodward was the daughter of Harry Govier Seeley, an English paleontologist of note who, among other things, was perhaps the first person to recognize the dichotomous nature of dinosaurian evolution.

The next morning there was "a knock on the door at about eight o'clock, and in walked a singularly pretty maid, bringing tea and biscuits." As a matter of fact I had already gotten out of bed (a card posted above the mantel announced "Breakfast at 8:30" and I thought it was time for me to start moving) so when I heard the knock and saw the door start to open I dived back under covers. I was still the uninstructed American but I was learning, and was beginning to become acquainted with the kind of country life hilariously immortalized on a higher and more snobbish level by P. G. Wodehouse. This was still the early thirties; at the Smith Woodward establishment we performed on schedule (the card above the mantel announced the times of the noonday and evening meals, as well as breakfast) and above all, we dressed for dinner. And although Hill Place was not inhabited by the dotty characters so delightfully described by Wodehouse, there were eccentricities. Among others in that house there was Binky, the family dog, a Sealyham who ruled the roost in no uncertain fashion. Sir Arthur was the dog's most humble servant, and as for me, the miserable canine never did get it through his head that I had a right to be there. I did long to give him a swift kick. Alas!

"The morning sun made the green hills sparkle, which was indeed unusual for this season. So after breakfast I elected to sit on the terrace with Sir Arthur; Lady Woodward was determined that I should accompany the womenfolk to an orphanage of some kind of which she was a trustee. But I wanted to visit with Sir Arthur, so the matter ended with my staying behind while the ladies drove off. Sir Arthur and I had a great talk, and he showed me the proofs of his revision of Zittel's *Palaeontology*, Volume Two, on fishes, amphibians and reptiles.

"The ladies finally returned, and Lady Woodward kept telling me about how much I had missed by not going with them. I wasn't at all regretful as to the extent of my misfortune. After tea I had a little walk with Sir Arthur and Binky, and as we walked along Sir Arthur gave me the details of the Piltdown discovery, to which I listened with extreme interest."

A footnote. Smith Woodward was one of the principals in the Piltdown affair; he was instrumental in the excavation of the site, which ostensibly had been discovered by a local amateur, Charles Dawson, a lawyer, living nearby at Uckfield. Although Smith Woodward had devoted his life up to the Piltdown discovery to the study of fossil fishes, and was the great authority in this branch of paleontology, he enthusiastically became involved in the difficult and often treacherous discipline of human evolution, to which he dedicated the last two decades of his life. Indeed, he selected Hayward's Heath as the locale for his retirement because it was close to Piltdown. It was a mercy that he died before the nature of the Piltdown forgery became known—or at least became suspected. Perhaps we shall never know the full truth as to the affair, but there is reason to think that it may have been perpetrated at least in part as a sort of paleontological prank, that got away to become a monstrous inconsistency in the fossil record of early man.

Then in December Swinton decided that since I was alone in London I should spend Christmas with the Smith Woodwards, so there came another invitation. Consequently I took a cab to Victoria Station in midafternoon of December 24, where I made my way through a tremendous crowd to board my train. This second visit to Hill Place was an extended version of my first visit—it lasted for a good part of a week. All in all I had a pleasant but a quiet time that included an old-fashioned English Christmas dinner, and many walks through the wintry English countryside.

Back in London I busied myself with my final observations on Siwalik fossils (for I had only a couple of weeks remaining before taking the ship to New York) and having a last fling in the theater district, and making a final pilgrimage to Sherborn's flat.

It so happened that earlier, while I was working away at the British Museum and making my winter trip to the North Sea coast, Professor Osborn, back in New York, had decided to make a trip around the world with a friend of his, Dr. Brewer, on a chartered cruise ship, the *Stella Polaris*. Moreover, he decided that he wanted me back in New York for final instructions or consultations or whatever you might call them before he departed. So with characteristic Osbornian assumption he cabled to me in care of Thomas Cook ordering my immediate return to New York. But

Thomas Cook did not have me listed and so I never received his cable, and continued my activities in blissful ignorance of HFO's orders. (Why he didn't cable me at the British Museum, I shall never know.)

In due time I arrived back at the American Museum, where I found a feeling of merriment in our department because of a newspaper story that had appeared on the eve of Osborn's departure on the *Stella Polaris*. The headline read "Cruise Liquor Stock Staggers Customs Men." This was during the prohibition era of American history, and the story was concerned with the immense amount of bottled alcohol on the ship when it docked in New York. Continuing, the newspaper account tells how the customs officials who went on board to inspect the ship and who were used to seeing large amounts of bottled alcoholic drinks, were "a bit staggered by the 'tween deck stores. The customs men estimated that each passenger may drink about 275 bottles of wine, twenty-five quarts of spirits and as much beer as he can manage in the hundred days" (of the cruise). Finally, "Among the passengers . . . is Professor Henry Fairfield Osborn, President of the American Museum of Natural History."

Uncle Hank took a set of the Encyclopaedia Britannica along with him on the cruise, and he had indicated that he hoped to give shipboard lectures to the assorted passengers. Some of us had mental pictures of HFO trying to improve the intellectual level of a group of besotted individuals lolling around in drunken stupors.

As for me, the Professor had left behind a letter, outlining things that he wished me to do during his absence. With the work as requested by HFO together with my Siwalik project, there was more than enough to keep me busy. The notes that I had made in Britain and on the Continent afforded the background for me to tackle the Siwalik mammals in earnest, which I did. The work was made significantly pleasant for me by reason of the fact that the museum had assigned Margaret Matthew to do the illustrations of the Siwalik fossils. We worked together and became ever more attached to each other.

The spring of 1932 progressed into the summer and Professor Osborn returned from his cruise, refreshed and well supplied with tales of his experiences, including an account of the dancing girls of Bali whose performance he had viewed with much appreciation. Also, with the beginning of summer, Dr. Guy Pilgrim appeared from England, to study some of the fossils at the American Museum. Since we were both involved with Indian fossils, it fell to me to work with him.

Pilgrim was a delightfully fuzzy individual who never seemed quite prepared for what was to happen next. Here was a man who had spent most of his life in India, yet he appeared in New York in heavy English woolens—quite unsuitable for hot and humid Manhattan summers; perhaps he had not been sufficiently briefed as to what to expect. At any rate, he soon discarded coat and vest when working at the museum, and appeared wearing peculiar-looking shirts (at least to our eyes) characterized by stiff dickies in front. He then decided that he didn't want to wear suspenders (braces, to him) fully exposed to view, so he acquired a belt of white webbing to hold up his trousers. Which was all very good, except that the pants were of dark-blue wool, without any loops for the belt. Consequently he fastened the belt tightly around his middle, about three inches below the top of his pants, thereby causing the trouser tops to flare out above the belt like an opening lily. It made quite a sight.

When Pilgrim first arrived he attended the monthly meeting of the Osborn Research Club, a discussion group of staff scientists. These meetings were always rather formal, held in the Osborn Library, with Uncle Hank sitting up front in a large armchair. On this particular occasion HFO, who loved to indulge in the Grand Gesture, got up and gave a speech of welcome to Dr. Pilgrim. At the end of this talk he held out his hand and said, "Dr. Pilgrim, we take great pleasure in welcoming you to the American Museum of Natural History."

Pilgrim had been sitting quietly puffing on a cigar, so he got up to shake hands with HFO, the stub of his cigar still held between the fingers of his right hand. Osborn grasped Pilgrim's hand firmly and got the hot end of the cigar in his palm, whereupon he let out a cry of surprise, jerked his hand away, as did Pilgrim, while the glowing cigar flew through the air to land on the floor. This brought a shout of laughter from the assembled group.

But Professor Osborn rose to the occasion. "You see," he said, "Dr. Pilgrim is burning with enthusiasm."

That summer and fall as I worked on Siwalik mammals and elephants of all kinds Margaret and I became ever more attached to each other. Here was a new relationship in my life, because I had never before been involved romantically with a girl or a young lady. As has previously been mentioned, during my childhood years Esther Roseberry and I had been constant playmates, and of course in school there had been the usual encounters that take place between boys and girls. But in my high school and college years I had not been one of the dating crowd, in part, I suppose, because of a certain shyness on my part, in part because of my interest in outdoor life. The world for me was predominantly a masculine world until Margaret came into my life, and then things changed.

As has been apparent, the theater was one of my favorite interests, and Margaret was not a bit loath in sharing this with me. So in the fall and winter of 1932 and 1933 we haunted Broadway—and that was a time when young folks such as we were could indulge in the theater at little cost. Balcony seats could be had for a dollar, sometimes less, with the result that we frequently looked down on the stage from upper levels. Of course we went to movies, too, and to concerts, and we dined out, and in general spent many hours together with never a thought of fossils.

For a part of this time Margaret was living with friends on Tieman Place, near Claremont Avenue, just down the street from International House where I lived, and that was convenient. Then she moved far uptown to Riverdale, where she had a room in an apartment with some other friends, and that was not so convenient. It didn't last long; we decided that marriage was what we wanted, so plans were made for the summer of 1933.

The announcement of our engagement was greeted with pleasure and congratulations by family and friends, and during the spring of 1933 we spent many busy hours making our arrangements for things to come. Of course we received gifts, and there were memorable occasions. One of these was a shower for Margaret at the home of John and Louise Germann, the staff artists, who lived north of the city in Valhalla. At the time I was completing my Siwalik studies, which among other things included research on the evolutionary history of the giraffes. In line with this Margaret had been making illustrations delineating fossils representative of these interesting mammals. So, unbeknownst to the two of us John Germann had arranged for one of the museum carpenters to construct a large sewing box in the shape of a giraffe, which he and Louise painted with the appropriate spots. Thus on the day of the shower Margaret was surprised by the presentation of this giraffe, festooned with presents, while her friends stood by, applauding vigorously.

Professor Osborn presented us with a tea set that included a fancy teapot, so designed that it could be turned one way for steeping the tea and another way so that the tea leaves would be out of the water, thus preventing the tea from becoming too strong. And with this he penned a letter in his usual large hand, advising us that it was much better to drink tea than coffee. From Dr. Pilgrim we received an exquisite set of six Georgian teaspoons dating back to the early days of the nineteenth century.

We were married on July 8 in Newark, New Jersey, by "Uncle Percy" Olton (actually a cousin), the rector of an Episcopalian church there. Many years before he had married Margaret's mother and father. It was a small and a quiet wedding attended by some family members and friends, but it proved to be effective. As this is written our fifty-fifth anniversary has come and gone, and we are looking forward to more in the future.

After the wedding we took off by car for a honeymoon trip to Canada, where we spent much of our time in the Gaspe´ Peninsula—in those days a rather isolated place. Then we came down into New Brunswick, the domain of the Matthew family, where Margaret had spent many of her childhood summer vacations. It was a thoroughly delightful trip, one that we have remembered with a great deal of sentimental pleasure. It was a nice way to begin our married life.

Footnote. Mention of New Brunswick leads me to say something about an event of Margaret's summer there in 1921. She was then a little girl of ten and one fine day in July she leaped fully clothed into the Kennebecasis River to rescue from drowning a little five-year-old girl named Sally Morton. Margaret says she will always remember the vision of little Sally, floating face down in water as the current carried her along, her hair streaming out beyond her head. Margaret's description makes me think of Shakespeare's Ophelia, who "Fell in the weeping brook. Her clothes spread wide, /And, mermaid-like, a while they bore her up."

Margaret was presented with a medal by the Royal Canadian Humane Association. It is one of our household treasures.

XI

An Asiatic Interlude

We began our married life in a little apartment on Fort Washington Avenue, near the upper end of Manhattan, very conveniently situated by subway to the museum. Our building was located at the edge of a cliff, with its front facing Bennett Park—a little square occupying what had originally been the site of a Revolutionary War bastion that had been ignominiously surrendered to the British and Hessian troops—while the back of the building was high above the valley below. Thus when we went in the front entrance of our building we had to walk up only three flights to our flat, walk along the hall to our living room, and there from our windows enjoy a view to the east and the north encompassing many miles of upper Manhattan, the Bronx, and even the southern fringes of Westchester County. From this eyrie we had a wide view of the passing scene below, including the goings-on at a group of tennis courts immediately below us. In the winter these courts were flooded, and we had the pleasure of watching the skaters go around and around. This ability to look far and wide was much appreciated by both of us, because we weren't the types to tolerate the confinements of brick walls and narrow courtyards, so common in Manhattan.

Living up on the spine of northern Manhattan afforded us many opportunities to get out and away from our building, and even from the city streets. In those days the Cloisters branch of the Metropolitan Museum had not been built, but there was a museum of medieval art on the property of George Grey Barnard, the famous sculptor, just up the street from us. It consisted to a large extent of things that Barnard had brought from Europe over a period of many years, and at that time was under the supervision of the Metropolitan. So in a matter of ten minutes we could walk up there and enjoy it, and enjoy it we did. Of course it was not as large or as well organized as the Cloisters that came later, but it had an intimate quality about it that was most delightful. And beyond was Inwood Park, a great place to stroll and rest. But above all, we liked to walk across the George Washington Bridge, and then hike along the foot of the Palisades on what was then a woodland trail, where we could hear the song of the wood thrush, and where we could even get a sense of being out of the great city, just across the river. Then back to Manhattan on the Dyckman Street ferry, and home. Or we would take the subway to Two Hundred Forty-second Street, from there take a streetcar through Yonkers, and then hike along the Aqueduct for as many miles as we wished to go. The Aqueduct, it should be explained, was a delightful, grassy right-of-way that covered the huge conduit carrying water from the Croton Reservoir to Manhattan. It extended north for many miles beyond the city, traversing the suburbs as it made its way between houses and lawns and woodlands. Of course it was a popular route for people on foot—casual walkers and dedicated hikers alike.

In the other direction was Downtown, just a few stops on the subway beyond the museum, so we continued to patronize the theater as we had in the days before our marriage. There was, in truth, a great deal more to life than fossils.

Soon after we were married Margaret gave up her illustration work at the museum, thereby having more time for herself, especially more time to do her own things artistically speaking. Perhaps it would have been smart if she had kept on with her job, thus to add her minuscule salary to my minuscule salary, but at the time we didn't see it that way. How differently we managed our affairs than is the case with young people today, when both parties to a new marriage so often are almost forced to work, whether that suits their purposes or not. We felt no such pressure, and we managed to live, albeit simply, on a single salary.

Perhaps this decision was influenced to some degree by a feeling of greater security on my part than previously had been the case, because at the beginning of the year of our marriage I had been appointed as a regular museum staff member with the title of assistant curator. Previously I had occupied a somewhat anomalous position; I had been a research assistant to Professor Osborn, but this listing did not give me the status of a regular member of the scientific staff. Now my place within the museum was regularized, and certainly more secure than it was before. There was every reason to think that if my scientific performance was satisfactory this appointment would be a permanent one.

I was not the only museum person to receive a new appointment with the beginning of the new year. Trubee Davison was named as Professor Osborn's successor, to be the president of the Board of Trustees, and Roy Chapman Andrews was made the new museum director, to succeed George Sherwood. I was to become well acquainted with both of these men.

By a coincidence that reinforced my relationships within the museum "family," it so happened that Trubee Davison was the son of Henry Pomeroy Davison, who was a cousin of Margaret's maternal grandmother, Jane Pomeroy Lee. I suppose if this were a work of fiction, which it most decidedly is not, some exceptions might be taken to the various fortuitous associations and relationships that tied me to the American Museum; research assistant to one museum president, son-in-law of one of the shining lights in the whole history of museum scientific endeavor, and now a family relationship, although a distant one, between Margaret and the incoming president of the institution.

As for Roy Andrews, my association with him was established through his close professional association with Walter Granger, who had been second in command on the Central Asiatic Expeditions and who had collected so many of the fossils that I was to be studying. Roy Andrews was widely known to the world at large at the time he became director of the museum, largely because of the publicity attendant upon the accomplishments of the expeditions in Mongolia, and however one might view Roy Andrews, either as a publicity hound or as an able expedition leader, the publicity was well deserved.

Roy came along well before the days of government grants and other forms of tax-supported research, so any kinds of large research projects had to depend upon private funding. That was the area in which Roy was to prove more than adept. His beginnings at the museum were modest—in fact, he made his start by scrubbing museum floors. He then became a member of the Department of Mammals, where he did some research on whales. But Roy's forte was not the protracted and often nitty-gritty labor of research; his love proved to be work in the field. So in the days after the First World War he had the concept of large, comprehensive expeditions to Central Asia, then a scientific *terra incognita*, for the purpose of collecting objects new to the disciplines of natural history. In this he was immeasurably aided by the pronouncements of Professor Osborn, who at the time was heralding Central Asia in no uncertain terms as the ancestral home of early man. Of course anything to do with the beginnings of man was bound to get attention, so with this argument as a talking point Roy was able to raise funds for a series of expeditions to Mongolia, to study the natural history of that region, and mainly to collect fossils. There were five such expeditions in the twenties, and although the efforts to locate ancestral man came to naught, the discoveries of Mesozoic and Cenozoic reptiles and mammals were abundant and often spectacular. The fruits of some of these discoveries were to be objects of some of my research. Consequently I was doing work that was of more than passing interest to Andrews.

My association with Roy Andrews was always pleasant, and at times convivial. Roy was not a deep thinker, but why should he be? He was charged by some as being a publicity seeker, but one must realize that his public-relations efforts did bring much attention and benefit to the museum. Moreover, he wrote some popular books that were inspiring to a whole generation of young folks. I think the only time I said no to Roy in a very definite manner was when he wanted me to collaborate on a book with him, such collaboration consisting of me doing all of the writing and Roy putting his name on the book as senior author. That was a little more than I wished for. At any rate he took my refusal in good spirit and there were no hard feelings.

When Andrews first assumed the post of museum director I was still largely occupied with Siwalik mammals and ancient elephants. Within a couple of years the Siwalik research came to an end, and when it was published I received some very nice complimentary letters, among others from Professor Osborn, from Professor Scott, and from Sir Arthur Smith Woodward, as well as from friends more or less in my own generation, notably Al Romer and George Simpson. And it was this work that launched me into an extended research program concerned with fossil mammals collected in Asia, specifically in Burma and Mongolia. For which reason this period of my life may be called my "Asiatic interlude"—not because of any first-hand acquaintance at the time with that continent, but merely because I became involved with fossils collected there by other people.

One might say that, as in the immediately preceding years, I was still performing the role of what used to be called a closet naturalist, studying collections that had been found and retrieved from the field by other people. It was not exactly to my liking, but that was the way things were in those depression years. No funds were available for me to go out and do my own field work, but in the storage drawers there were Asiatic fossils waiting to be described. I was only too happy for the opportunity to work on them.

There was a collection of Eocene and later mammals from Burma that Barnum Brown (who it will be remembered had made the Siwalik collection) had excavated when he was in that part of the world. The Burmese collection was made under harsh physical conditions, so harsh indeed that Brown almost died from fevers contracted during the course of this expedition, and it was only through the devoted efforts of Mrs. Brown that he survived.

After this trying episode the Browns went to Samos Island in the eastern Mediterranean where they enjoyed an Arcadian sojourn in an insular outpost of ancient Greece, where his health was restored, and where they excavated a large and important collection of late Cenozoic mammals. (Incidentally, it was my pleasure some years after my work on the Burma collection to describe a complete fossil skeleton of an aardvark in the Samos collection, just one example out of many to show how numerous mammals that we think of as being typically African, had Eurasiatic beginnings.)

There was another collection of Burmese fossils that I described in later years—a suite of Pleistocene mammals collected by the geologist Helmut de Terra and the famous Jesuit paleontologist, scholar, and philosopher, Père Teilhard de Chardin.

Above all, however, there was the research I did on fossil mammals collected in Mongolia by the Central Asiatic Expeditions of the American Museum. Since Walter Granger was the paleontologist on these expeditions, it fell to my lot to describe various fossil mammals that he personally had dug out of the ground. Of course he was always readily at hand to advise me on the field relationships of the fossils with which I was working.

Finally I should mention a large collection of Pleistocene mammals, made by Granger during a winter spent in Szechwan Province, China. These very interesting fossils were found in caves and fissures, where for centuries they had been excavated by the Chinese, to be sold in drug stores as "dragon bones"—as a cure for all kinds of illnesses. The immemorial Chinese practice has been to grind the bones into powder, in order to ingest them, suitably mixed in a drink. One can only speculate as to the vast number of fossils, many of them of great scientific importance, that in this manner have gone down Asiatic gullets through the centuries. The Szechwan fossils that Walter Granger brought back to the museum provided for me a fascinating research problem, on which I was eventually assisted by a Dutch paleontologist, Dirk Hooijer. (The Hooijers came to New York after the war, and we became their very close friends. In 1958 we had the pleasure of visiting them in Holland, and accompanying them on a delightful trip through France and the Low Countries.) Much of my work on Asiatic fossil mammals was descriptive, but it was interpretive, too, and the interpretations had to do with the relationships of these mammals with mammalian associations of similar age in other parts of the world. Thus I became much involved with the distributions of mammals of former times, and especially with the patterns of their intercontinental movements.

It seemed to that Asiatic and African mammals exchanged places through the Mediterranean region (remember the aardvark from Samos?) while there were mammalian wanderings back and forth between Asia and North America by way of a Bering land bridge. To me these interchanges seemed reasonable and logical and they affected my thinking about animals and continents in a most decisive way. What I saw were the wanderings of mammals between continents that were positioned for the most part as they are positioned today. At the time I was doing this work, my interpretations of the intercontinental relationships of late Cenozoic mammals, assuredly valid for that frame of geologic history, definitely colored my views as to the relationships of much earlier continents and much earlier animals. Furthermore, I was influenced by my predecessors and my peers, notably by the work of Dr. Matthew and by George Simpson. Matthew had set forth his views on fossil mammals and continents in his great work *Climate and Evolution* published in 1915. In this publication, which had and still has much influence on the students of mammalian paleontology, he outlined the manner in which mammalian faunas might have spread throughout the world from northern hemisphere centers of origin, utilizing the intercontinental connections that exist today. Briefly, there were interchanges between the Old and New Worlds by way of a Bering land bridge, between North and South America by way of an isthmian connection, between Eurasia and Africa through the Mediterranean region, and from Asia to Australia by way of Indonesia—perhaps across lands that are now submerged. Much the same concept was held by Dr. Simpson. Who was I, then in my salad days, to doubt the authority of such scholars, or to question what seemed to be almost incontrovertible geological evidence?

In those days the theory of a mobile earth, then known as the theory of continental drift, now designated as the theory of plate tectonics, was being advocated by some geologists (it had been proposed by Alfred Wegener just before the First World War) but except for a few enthusiasts such as Alex du Toit of South Africa the idea was given little credence by a large majority of geologists and paleontologists, especially those in the northern hemisphere. This was in part owing to the fact that Wegener was ahead of his time; he had the grand idea, but little hard evidence to back it up. (Such evidence was to come after the Second World War.) A problem, especially for people like me, was that we were looking at the evidence of Cenozoic mammals so far as this evidence might have a bearing on continental arrangements, and extending ideas based upon these fossils to the earlier fossils of late Paleozoic and Mesozoic times. Consequently I, like so many of my contemporary paleontological friends, gave the idea of continental drift short shrift. Later I was to change my mind, but that is a story to be told on a subsequent page. For the time with which I am now dealing the relationships of Asiatic fossil mammals to mammals in other parts of the world were very nicely explained by the intercontinental connections that exist today—or have existed in the recent geologic past.

One discordant note was the inconvenient presence of the pouched marsupials in Australia. I wasn't working on these animals, so I accepted the postulate then current—that they had reached Australia from Eurasia through Indonesia, from a possible ultimate center of origin in the New World. Such a concept would require the presence of marsupials in Asia, on their way down from a Bering crossing, but no fossil marsupials had been found in Mongolia or China. Never mind, we thought that this lack of evidence was a result of the accidents of preservation, which is a nice example of the dangers of basing ideas on negative evidence. It should be added here that within recent years early fossil marsupials have been found in Antarctica, these being very closely related to marsupials of essentially the same geological age in South America. So it now seems evident that the marsupials of Australia ultimately came from South America, Antarctica being the bridge that connected the two areas when they were parts of a great Gondwana supercontinent. But a half-century ago all such relationships were in the realm of the unknown.

In those long vanished days of my early paleontological career I frequently discussed with some of my museum colleagues the various problems having to do with the evolution and distribution of Asiatic mammals through time. By the same token they would talk to me about some of their research problems. We had many things to talk about so inevitably and quite naturally we decided to get together with brown-bag lunches and have our spontaneous noon-time symposia around a table as we munched our sandwiches and drank our coffee and tea. Larger after-lunch meetings of the museum research staff members who were inclined to attend were held daily in the "coffee room," a museum custom of long standing that will be described in a subsequent paragraph, and of course we frequently participated. But there were times when we wished to have our own restricted sessions where we could concentrate on the questions that were currently of particular interest to us. These questions centered to a large extent on evolutionary and distributional problems.

We would get together in a little room somewhere on the fifth floor of the museum; Charles Bogert, my herpetological colleague, Frank Beach, a student of animal behavior, Miles Conrad, ichthyologist, Willis Gertsch, who devoted his life to spiders, and Ernst Mayr, the brilliant ornithologist who was to become one of the great students of evolution in the years ahead. At that stage we were all young and enthusiastic and certainly not mellowed by the passage of time and the increment of experience, so we pitched into our round-table meetings with considerable verve and even with some heated exchanges.

I remember how Frank Beach used to take me apart, and how can I ever forget Ernst Mayr looking down his nose at me and saying in imperious tones, "Don't be naive!" Ernst was ever a man of strong opinions, and he usually could back them up with good, solid evidence. Chuck Bogert, too, had very definite ideas about matters, and he expressed himself forcefully and with more than a little bit of color.

Indeed, it was hard for Chuck to talk without interspersing his discussion with pungent expressions. I remember one day at our little round table Chuck started to tell us a story.

"When I was a little bastard," said Chuck, "some old son-of-a-bitch up in the mountains cut his foot with an axe."

Whereupon we all burst out in laughter, while Chuck stared at us with an air of complete mystification. What was so funny? He was merely talking in his usual manner.

His usual manner of speech included a lexicon of terms that was all his own. "Lily-dipper" was a despicable person, usually the driver of another car, while someone Chuck really disliked was an "S.O.B. summa cum laude with palm fronds." And so on. It reminds me of Mark Twain's story of a countryman in Connecticut: "as goodhearted a young fellow as ever was" whose conversation "poured out with the most fluent facility, as from an inexhaustible crater, and all ablaze from beginning to end with crimson lava jets of desolating and utterly unconscious profanity!" So it was with Chuck; he became a legend.

There was an amusing little incident connected with my studies of Asiatic fossils. Among the materials to which I was devoting my attention were skulls and teeth and other bones of fossil rhinoceroses, some of them apparently on the line of development that culminated in the modern rhinoceroses of Asia, notably the great Indian rhinoceros and the closely related but smaller Sondaican rhinoceros, the former today inhabiting a restricted range in the tropical swamplands of India, the latter (which is extremely rare) confined to swamp environments in Java. Of course I did what was logical, which was to go down the long corridor from my office-laboratory to the Department of Mammalogy to look at some of the rhinoceroses there and make comparisons. I was especially interested in skulls of the Indian rhinoceros, of which there was a considerable series.

But one of the skulls looked different from the others; it was smaller than the typical Indian rhinoceros skulls, and certain features of its bony structure and its dentition differed from the rest of the skulls in the series. The more I looked at it the more I became convinced that it was a skull of *Rhinoceros sondaicus*—a very rare specimen indeed. It had been collected back in the nineteenth century by Maximilian, prince of Wied-Neuwied, and how it had ever ended up at the American Museum is something of a mystery to me. I suppose it was part of an old collection that the museum had purchased.

To digress a bit, the story of Prince Maximilian is a saga in its own right.

He was a younger son in a noble family, and because of this was barred from the privilege of sitting on a throne. Therefore he had to do something else to occupy his time, so instead of living the life of a wastrel as was a common course among younger sons of nobility, he chose the career of a naturalist— and this was back in the days when being a naturalist, especially a field naturalist, could lead to a life of high adventure. Maximilian made expeditions to various parts of the world, and in 1833–1834 he ascended the Missouri River to its headwaters in what is now Montana, collecting animals and plants and studying the Indians who at that time had barely been exposed to contact with people of European origins. A long, hard winter was spent living in a Mandam village near the present site of Bismark, North Dakota. Maximilian had two companions on this exciting adventure, an assistant named David Dreidoppel, and a superb artist named Karl Bodmer. Bodmer executed an incomparable series of paintings, often done under trying conditions, which show the scenery along the Missouri River, and particularly includes striking portraits of Indians. This rare record of the high plains in their pristine days is now securely housed at the Internorth Art Foundation in Omaha, Nebraska.

To get back to the story, the point of my tale is that shortly before I found the skull of the Sondaican rhinoceros in the American Museum, a museum expedition had been sent to the East Indies with considerable fanfare for the purpose of collecting just such an animal, and had failed even to see a rhino, much less collect one. All the time the museum had a skull in its collection—one of three specimens in North American museums, the other two being at the Smithsonian and at Harvard.

My discovery up in the storeroom eventually leaked out, and the newspapers in New York had a lot of fun recounting how I had found an animal in the attic that the museum had spent much time, effort, and money trying to find in the jungle—without success. Harold Anthony, the head of the mammal department, was not entirely pleased with the publicity.

Perhaps this little happening caused some annoyance to Anthony but it was a minor windfall for me; in 1942 I published a paper on *Rhinoceros sondaicus* in which I attempted to show how it might be fitted into the evolutionary history of the genus *Rhinoceros*.

Research on large problems or even problems of moderate size can lead into unexpected byways, and that can be fun. One such unexpected diversion for me was another result of my studies of Asiatic fossil mammals. Among the Siwalik mammals that I described was a large Pleistocene giraffe known as *Sivatherium*. It was a bulky, oxlike animal, much larger than an ox, with legs of normal size, a short neck, and a large skull crowned with most unusual horns or antlers. (Not all of the giraffes were long-legged and long-necked.) The horns of *Sivatherium* consisted of large, palmatelike structures situated on the back of the skull, and in front of them a pair of short, simple pointed horns, just above the eyes. In other words, *Sivatherium* was a four-horned beast, unlike anything that lives on earth today.

One day I received a letter from Dr. Leslie Spier, an archaeologist, including a photograph of a bronze rein ring from a chariot that had been excavated at the ancient Mesopotamian city of Kish, an old Middle East metropolis that has been dated at about 3500 B.C. This rein ring had been described as representing a stag, but interestingly enough, it showed an animal with palmate horns or antlers on the back of the head, and in addition *two small, pointed horns above the eyes.* Furthermore, there appeared to be a halter fastened to the nose.

Could this have been a representation of *Sivatherium?* Is it possible that the ancient inhabitants of Kish had domesticated *Sivatherium*, leading it around by a rope attached to the head? Perhaps the statuette was a fanciful representation, but on the other hand perhaps it did represent *Sivatherium.* Those two little pointed horns above the eyes are hard to explain as figments of the imagination.

I decided to be bold, so I published a paper suggesting that the people of Kish may have been acquainted with *Sivatherium*—which means that this extinct giraffe became extinct quite recently in the history of mammalian evolution. That publication was fifty years ago, in 1936, but it the meantime I have not changed my mind. "Was the extinct giraffe (*Sivatherium*) known to the early Sumerians?"—such was the title of my paper. Perhaps so.

Another side effect of my Asiatic studies was destined to have an interesting, and perhaps an important, paleontological impact. When working on the Burmese fossils, I found one day in the collection a fragment of a small lower jaw containing the roots of a canine and a small premolar tooth, and behind the latter two nicely preserved third and fourth premolars as well as a molar. The teeth were low-crowned and they had every appearance of belonging to a primate of some sort. Of special interest was the fact that the lower jaw was very deep, and obviously would have been rather short if all of it had been present. Moreover this jaw, one of the many Eocene fossils in the Burmese collection, was very old for a primate, if such it might be. It seemed to me that because of the form and development of the teeth and because of the deep, short jaw, this fossil might very well be an early forerunner of the anthropoid apes, and I said so, remarking that the fossil "shows striking resemblances to many of the most advanced primates, such as *Dryopithecus, Proconsul, Simia* and *Gorilla.*" I named it *Amphipithecus*, the Greek *amphi* meaning "about" or "around," the Greek *pithecus* meaning "ape." In other words, an animal about like an ape.

Amphipithecus remained more or less buried in the literature for the better part of half a century without attracting much attention, although there was some discussion of it, with certain paleontologists thinking as I did that it represented an early anthropoid and others thinking that it was more like a lemur. Then in 1978 another jaw fragment containing two molar teeth was discovered in the Eocene beds of Burma, and this new specimen supplemented the original type in a remarkable manner. One might say that the resemblances between the two specimens are almost uncanny, because the new specimen can be fitted behind the first fossil so that together the two pieces constitute a harmonius half of a lower jaw. The authors who in 1985 described the new fossil—Russel Ciochon, Don Savage (a long-time friend of mine), Thaw Tint, and Ba Maw—concluded that *Amphipithecus*, together with another early primate fossil from Burma, *Pondaungia*, raises "the possibility that the origin of the Anthropoidea could have been in southern Asia." Needless to say this was more than a little bit pleasing to me; it is good to know that my only effort in primate paleontology culminated in a truly significant result.

It should not be forgotten that during these years of research on Asiatic fossils I was still continuing with studies of fossil elephants for Professor Osborn. Then on a November morning in 1935 Professor Osborn quietly died, sitting in a chair at his Castle Rock home. Thus ended a distinguished career. There was a solemn memorial service at Saint Bartholomew's in New York.

Naturally my life was affected by Osborn's death, in part because the gigantic second volume of the monograph on fossil elephants was left unfinished. It was up to those of us who remained to bring the work to a conclusion, and we did that. It was finally published in 1942.

Although my association with Osborn had ended I was left with many memories of this unusual, protean man. And my feelings for him were mixed. To reiterate what I have previously written, he was certainly a man of vision and of action, yet his greatness in these respects was flawed by his overweening self-conceit. He was arrogant and difficult, yet underneath these unpleasant traits there was a feeling of kindness and sympathy for those around him. He was class-conscious and something of a snob, yet these feelings on his part were largely the result of the social environment in which he grew up and in which he spent his adult years. Above all, he was totally dedicated to his science and to the great museum that owes so much of its greatness to his efforts.

In later years I had some very pleasant contacts with his son Fairfield, who for a time was the president of the New York Zoological Society, familiar to most New Yorkers as the Bronx Zoo.

During those years of the early thirties, when I was so busily engaged with Asiatic fossil mammals, I became acquainted with, and worked with, Père Teilhard de Chardin, who it will be recalled from a preceding paragraph was involved with Helmut de Terra in making a collection of Pleistocene mammals in Burma. Of course Teilhard is now famous as a philosopher, but I knew him as a paleontologist and that is how I think of him. He was indeed a very fine paleontologist—one of a select body of Jesuits who have made many contributions to the science. Teilhard was a seminarian during the early years of this century and was ordained as a priest shortly before the First World War. He served in the war, and afterwards he pursued graduate studies in Paris. In March, 1922, he successfully defended his thesis on Eocene mammals of France and was granted his doctorate in paleontology. At that time Professor E. Haug, a French paleontologist, noted: "He is certainly marked out for a fine future in science. The board of examiners had no hesitation in conferring on him the title of doctor, with distinction."

Almost immediately he was sent by the museum in Paris to China to participate in a French paleontological mission, and this determined much of the direction of his career. In the late twenties he participated in some of the work of the Central Asiatic Expeditions of the American Museum of Natural History, at which time he became a close friend of Walter Granger. His interest in and involvement with fossil mammals of China continued throughout much of his life, so that whenever he was in New York, which was frequently, he spent part of his time at the museum.

He was a charming person who viewed the passing scene with a perceptive eye. He once wrote of himself: "I am a pilgrim of the future on the way back from a journey made entirely in the past."

In addition to the labors attendant upon completing the Osborn elephant volume, I was involved in the midthirties with editing two works by Dr. Matthew. These were in effect labors of love, because the work on these volumes gave me a feeling of some intimacy with the father-in-law I never really knew. One of the volumes was a new edition of his famous *Climate and Evolution*, originally published by the New York Academy of Sciences in 1915. The new edition was also published by the academy, in 1939, and I had the privilege and pleasure of writing a foreword for it, as well as making annotations throughout the text—made necessary because of new information that had come to light during the almost quarter of a century that had elapsed since the original publication.

A much larger task was my editorial work on his massive monograph describing the fossil mammals from the Paleocene sediments of the San Juan Basin of New Mexico. Although Walter Granger, Dr. Gregory, and I were listed as the editorial board of this work, and although George Simpson read Matthew's manuscript with a trained, critical eye, it was my task to supervise much of the editorial work, the details of which were carried out by Florence Milligan, who has been mentioned as one of Professor Osborn's editors. Dr.

Matthew's unfinished manuscript represented years of field work and research on the primitive mammals found in the San Juan Basin, and even though it was well along toward completion at the time of his death, there were still many loose ends to be tied up. As we said in our preface to the volume, a "great deal of work had to be done in filling in references, in preparing many additional illustrations called for in the text, and in editing." We successfully completed our task, and the volume was published in 1937 by the American Philosophical Society—a large format work of 510 pages, with 64 plates.

At about this time, specifically in 1936, the Academy of Natural Sciences in Philadelphia, the oldest if not the largest natural history museum in North America, decided to try to revive a program in paleontology. This was logical, because the Academy was the locale for some of the pioneer paleontological work in this country. Joseph Leidy carried on there some of his early research on fossil mammals from the Western Territories, and the Academy benefited from its association with Edward Drinker Cope, for three decades after the Civil War. Indeed, the Academy was fully expecting to receive the Cope Collection at the time of his death in 1897, but Professor Osborn prevailed upon J. P. Morgan to purchase the collection for the American Museum, much to the chagrin and annoyance of the folks in Philadelphia. (One of the first tasks performed by Dr. Matthew at the beginning of his museum career was to go to Philadelphia where he catalogued and packed the Cope Collection for shipment to New York.)

So with such an historical incentive the Academy decided to initiate a new program in paleontology, a science that had been moribund there since the end of the nineteenth century. Accordingly I was approached to help out on this, but before I got seriously involved the Academy staged in early 1937 a big event to initiate the new program, namely an international symposium on early man. People were brought in from all over the world, and among others Teilhard was there. It was a great success so far as getting the Academy's name before the public, but I'm afraid it did not bring in much solid financial support, which was really needed.

However that may be, the program for reviving paleontology did get under way and I became an active participant in the effort. So did Benjamin Franklin Howell of Princeton University; it was his task to oversee the development of new research activity in invertebrate paleontology, just as it was my task to do the same for vertebrate paleontology. That is how every Monday Benny and I made our way from Princeton and New York to Philadelphia, to spend the day in supervising and planning. And the Academy added some members to its staff, to carry on during the rest of each week.

Incidentally the circumstances of Benny Howell and me being brought together for the Academy program was one more instance of our living in a small world. When Margaret was a young girl and used to go with her family to New Brunswick up in the Maritimes for the summer, she met and became acquainted with the Howell family, also there for the summer. Professor Howell was collecting and studying fossils in that part of the world, and naturally he became an admirer of Margaret's grandfather, George Frederic Matthew, already mentioned as one of the pioneer students of Acadian paleontology and geology. Benjamin Franklin Howell Jr., who was about Margaret's age, became one of her young acquaintances in those years. Indeed, there was a certain amount of visiting between the Matthew and Howell families.

Footnote: Some years ago an Indian arrowhead was found in the Princeton collection, having been given to Professor Howell by Margaret's grandfather, who had found it in St. John, New Brunswick, in 1919. Don Baird, curator of the Princeton collection, had it mounted in a silver setting by George Frost, a mutual silversmith friend, and presented it to Margaret, to be worn as a locket. It takes its place alongside her lifesaving medal as one of our family treasures.

The work at the Academy was something of a godsend, financially speaking, especially so since our first baby was expected. My salary at the American Museum was still minuscule, and the museum was a bit apologetic about that, but times were hard. Therefore Walter Granger felt it was only fair to allow me a day away each week, with no reduction of my New York salary, to supplement my income. Consequently each Monday was my Academy day, and those days are still vividly remembered.

On Monday mornings I was up at an early hour in order to get to Penn Station so that I could catch the eight o'clock train to Philadelphia. The ride put me into the Broad Street station of Philadelphia at nine-forty, and from there I walked along the parkway to the Academy, which took about ten minutes of my time.

What did I do? In the first place a renovation of the museum space was being planned, so I spent a part of my time planning for storage facilities and for the systematic arrangement of the collections. (Among other things I designed steel storage cases, which were manufactured by a firm in Philadelphia.) In addition, a new paleontological exhibition hall was being planned, and so I had a hand in that. All of this planning and consultation and supervision involved working with Benny Howell, and especially with Edgar B. Howard, curator at the Academy, and with Charles Miegs Biddle Cadwalader, the director. (With a name like that you may be sure that Mr. Cadwalader came from one of the old, old Philadelphia families.)

Edgar Howard was one of my treasured friends at the Academy, a man perhaps fifteen years my senior, who by reason of his position and influence was instrumental in the rebirth of paleontology at the institution. He had spent his early years in New Orleans, but as a young man he came to Philadelphia, where he enjoyed the company of the more affluent members of the Philadelphia community. In those days, before the First World War, it was the thing for certain young Philadelphians to join a troop of horsemen belonging to the National Guard, or something like that. It was a lot of fun until the time, in 1916, when the troop was suddenly called to Mexico, to be a part of the so-called punitive expedition, headed by General Pershing, that was supposed to chase and capture Pancho Villa. Edgar had a lot of interesting stories about their futile pursuit of the famous Mexican "bandit"—perhaps one of the last times in American history when the horse cavalry was used on a large scale.

Then we were in the Great War and Edgar went to France, where during a charge on German positions he was knocked down by a bullet that creased his helmet. That gave him a splitting headache for a while, but otherwise there were no ill effects. Back home after the war he eventually became interested in geology, paleontology, and archeology, and proceeded to go through graduate training at the University of Pennsylvania for his doctorate. He then became involved in research on early man found with ancient mammals in North America. One of his discoveries was that of a mammoth skeleton, with a bone spearpoint embedded in its foot. *Of course* he was very much interested in the development of a paleontological program at the Academy.

Edgar, Benny Howell, and I used to have some great times trying to formulate our plans for the development of the department. Benny was one of the most indefatigable nonstop talkers I have ever come up against, so on many an occasion Edgar and I had a frustrating time trying to get our words in edgewise. It was all in good spirits—one couldn't really get angry with Benny, who was a cheerful soul—but at times it did give us the willies, as the saying goes.

But there was more to my Philadelphia visits than planning facilities for fossils and exhibits and arguing with Professor Howell. After I had been in the program for a couple of years, Bryn Mawr College decided that it would be nice to have a course on vertebrate evolution. The result was that for several years I spent my Monday mornings at Bryn Mawr, lecturing on fossil vertebrates, and my afternoons at the Academy dividing my time between Academy affairs, which by now had settled down a bit, and supervising the Bryn Mawr girls, who had come into town for an afternoon of laboratory exercises with fossils. It was strenuous, but I enjoyed this new experience; the Bryn Mawr students were certainly first class, and eager to learn.

At the end of each Monday I had to reverse my direction in order to catch the five o'clock train to New York. Then the subway and the bus home for a late supper and a weary trip right into bed. All of this continued until and through the academic year of Pearl Harbor, after which the whole program came to an end. It was not revived after the war.

To go back a few years, Asiatic fossils and the Philadelphia program and other crowded events of those midthirties years were exciting enough, but the big happening in the lives of Margaret and myself was the birth of our first son, George, on February 9, 1937. It was an overwhelming happening for us, as is generally the case for all young folks who experience the arrival of their first-born, and needless to say from that time on our life was never again to be as it had been in those first years of our marriage.

When George arrived we were still living up on Fort Washington Avenue, just a few blocks north of the Columbia-Presbyterian Medical Center, where he entered the world. It was a memorable day, two weeks later—that was the period of confinement in those times—when during a snowstorm we took him home in a taxi, to begin a life that no longer was ours alone. And throughout that short ride from the hospital to our apartment he looked at us, as wise as a little owl. Things went well enough and we were learning how to take care of our new charge—in a bumbling sort of way, it is true. Then winter gave way to spring, and we opened the windows to enjoy the fresh, vernal air. But our enjoyment was short-lived, because construction was beginning on a new apartment building down below us at the foot of our cliff, and smoke and soot came filtering in to pepper the covers of George's crib with black spots. That decided us; we must get away from the city, although we wanted to get away in any case because we were feeling confined more than ever by walls and stairways, and by the difficulties of enjoying the open air.

So I began a campaign of looking for living quarters across the river. I went here and I went there, and I will never forget the afternoon when I returned from one prospecting trip, all fired up with enthusiasm, to be met at the door of our apartment by Margaret and George (in her arms) both crying for all they were worth. Poor Margaret! George had begun to cry that afternoon as little babies will, and she could not get him to stop. It went on and on, until she was beside herself and thoroughly discouraged. Such are the trials that beset young parents.

Finally we decided on Leonia, New Jersey, a little town just beyond the west end of the George Washington Bridge. Some of our Columbia friends had moved there, and naturally they persuaded us to come along. Leonia was originally known as The English Neighbourhood, which it was—a little English settlement surrounded by Dutch colonists. So it remained until sometime late in the last century, when certain misguided souls decided to change the name to Leonia, a name the origins of which have been subject to much speculation. As may be apparent from these remarks, it is an old town; in fact it was settled back in the middle of the seventeenth century, not long after a struggling village was being established on the point of Manhattan Island. There are still a few beautiful, old Dutch houses standing in Leonia. It was for many years, before the opening of the George Washington Bridge, a popular backwater locale for New York artists and faculty folk from Columbia, because it was fairly easy to reach by way of the One Hundred Twenty-fifth Street Ferry and a street-car line that ran from the Jersey end of the ferry to various towns along the Hackensack River and Overpeck Creek. Of course the opening of the bridge changed everything, so that the northern part of New Jersey has become in effect one vast suburb. Leonia, however, retained its small-town character; indeed, it didn't have much room in which to grow. So for us it was an appealing place.

We settled in a comfortable old house with a fairly extensive backyard and a barn behind that, which we rented for the incredible sum of fifty dollars a month (money went a long ways in the thirties) and there we stayed for a couple of years. Then Dr. Gregory arranged to go to New Zealand during the spring semester of 1938, and he asked me to teach his graduate course in vertebrate paleontology at Columbia—which I did. This brought in enough extra income to raise heady thoughts of owning our own home, so we started to look around. We found a house up in the hilly part of town, in fact on the back slope of the Palisades, and *there* we stayed for thirty years. It was a plain, square house, anything but elegant, but a practical kind of dwelling that suited our needs pretty well. There was a sloping backyard, the whole area was wooded, and off to the west we enjoyed a grand panorama of the Northern Valley of New Jersey, with the Watchungs rising as long wooded ridges on the far horizon.

We moved into the house just in time for the arrival of David, our second son, on July 19, 1939. It was the year of the World's Fair out in Flushing Meadows on Long Island, and I can remember sitting with Margaret in the Presbyterian Hospital on the night of July 18, waiting for David, and looking out of the window where, across the great city, I could see the lights of the fair and the white needle of the Trylon, as it was called, punctuating the dark sky. David didn't arrive, so finally I went home, and as soon as I got there a call from the hospital came to inform me that he had been born—or rather that *it* had been born, because the lady on the other end of the line cheerfully informed me that she wasn't allowed to tell me the sex of our new baby over the telephone. So I had to spend a night in ignorance—a state of affairs that I remedied early the next morning when I rushed into the hospital.

Philip arrived a year later, on July 16, 1940. That time I was on hand in the waiting room (in those philistine days fathers were not allowed to be present during the delivery) sitting it out on a hot afternoon in company with a neighbor of ours, Mr. Crist. As we chatted together the doctor who was in charge of both our wives came into the room looking very embarrassed, to inform Crist that he was the father of twins. Dr. Damon was embarrassed because he had failed to detect the presence of twins during his prenatal examinations; Mr. Crist was jarred because he wasn't expecting such largesse. It was almost like a scene from a stage comedy; Crist put his hand to his forehead and staggered back a step with a loud cry of surprise. But he soon gained his equanimity.

It was in the Leonia house that our boys grew up; George, who was a little two-year-old when we moved in, David and Philip, Dan born March 28, 1944, and finally Charles born on February 26, 1946. That house was the only home our boys knew until they were grown, and had left to live their own independent lives. Yet from what we have seen of them in the years that have passed since their childhood days, none of them seems to have any particular nostalgic feelings for the old house, or for the town for that matter. The New Jersey home evidently does not occupy the magic place in their minds that is held for me by my boyhood home in Missouri, or for Margaret by her girlhood home at Hastings-on-Hudson, up the river from New York City. I wonder if it is because for them life was less rural than it had been for the two of us; perhaps the influence of the city extended out to them. Or perhaps it is merely a difference in time, the difference between the simpler days of the First World War and the years after, as contrasted with the two decades following the Second War.

Yet even with all of the settlement that was going on around us in northern New Jersey, it seemed to Margaret and to me that Leonia was more small town than suburbia. Its confines were sufficiently limited so that we could walk to almost any place in town. The boys always walked or biked to school and to their various activities; for us there was none of the business of shuttling kids back and forth that occupies so many hours of the week for today's parents.

Our house was after a fashion near to historic ground, because we were only two blocks away from Fort Lee Road, and it was down Fort Lee Road that George Washington and the tatterdemalion remnants of his army retreated to the west after the British forces had captured Fort Washington, in upper Manhattan, and Fort Lee, across the river. It was the low point of the Revolutionary War.

What does this account of family and of Leonia, New Jersey, have to do with Asiatic fossil mammals, with which the earlier part of this chapter was concerned? Nothing, except that it tells something of my other life—the life that after all occupied considerably more than half of each working day, not to mention all of weekend and vacation days. In earlier and simpler times when most people did not venture far from home there was a blending of working life and home life that unified the existence of the individual. The nineteenth-century farmer spent practically all of his time within sight of his home, and even the city dweller more often than not was engaged in a trade or an occupation that was carried on, if not under his domestic roof, at least not very far away. But today there is an overwhelming dichotomy in the lives of people who work—a working life, be it professional or manual, and a home life generally considerably removed from the workplace. Thus a personal narrative that does not give proper attention to both sides of living presents a picture that is less than complete.

So while I was spending part of my time with Asiatic fossils in New York, I was also spending an even greater part of my time with my family—first at Washington Heights in Manhattan and then across the river in New Jersey. And although the work with fossils determined my professional growth, it was life with my family that made me, I hope, a well-rounded person.

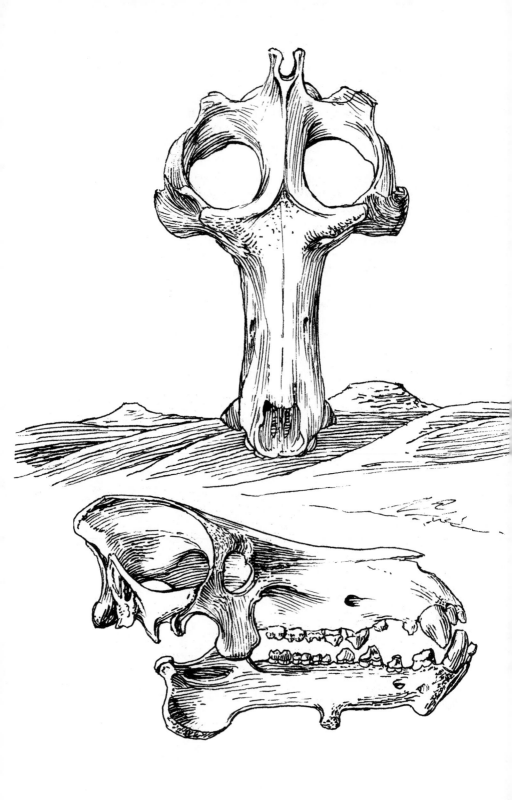

XII

High Plains and Badlands

I had my introduction to paleontological field work, specifically the kind of field work done by vertebrate paleontologists, back in the summer of 1928 and 1929, when I was still at the University of Nebraska—as has already been described. And then my opportunities for work in the field—for the search that reveals fossils as their first traces are encountered in eroding cliffs and banks, for the chance to study in detail and at first hand the relations of fossils *in situ* to their enclosing sediments, for the experience of collecting the fossils on which one is to do research—came to an end. I became through force of circumstances and against my will the sort of closet naturalist that I have already described, studying the fossils collected by other people. This was my situation for nine years, much of which time was devoted to Asiatic fossils, when I was not working on elephants.

Then, thanks to the connection with the Academy of Natural Sciences in Philadelphia, my long absence from the field was broken by reason of a decision by the Academy to send an expedition to Agate, Nebraska, for the purpose of collecting a block of Lower Miocene mammals—the expedition to be under my supervision. Naturally I looked forward to this opportunity with much anticipation, especially since I felt that it would be a chance for me to renew my field experience—an important consideration if I hoped to have a balanced paleontological career.

To be sequestered in the laboratory, no matter how pleasant the environment may be, no matter how many excellent fossils may be at hand, is to be denied a crucial phase of paleontological practice, because as mentioned above there is no substitute for field observations, for the firsthand experience of relating fossils to the stratigraphic succession of the rocks in which they occur. That is why collecting fossils is more than digging them out of the ground. There is a matter of *appreciation* for the fossils that comes only from field experience, a lack of which shows up in the writings of persons who do not have paleontological field experience, and if I may be explicit, especially among some biologists who choose to write about fossils as a part of their evolutionary theorizing. Indeed it is at times maddening for a dyed-in-the-wool paleontologist to read the cavalier statements that may be made by some of these people among whom there is no appreciation for the real significance of fossils. This concerns particularly the ignorance of such people concerning stratigraphic relationships, their failure to realize the significance of the fossil record. These lacunae may show up as pitiful misconceptions, for example when people pontificate, as they sometimes do, about how fossils are superfluous for evolutionary studies because fossils lack the soft parts and therefore are "incomplete." This in face of the fact that fossils present the incontrovertible record of evolutionary change through time.

I had experienced that attitude in a different and with certainly a less uninformed background during my dealings with Professor Osborn. As I have recounted on a previous page, he had a view of field relationships that was often not quite realistic; I don't think he ever truly appreciated how complicated geology can be when one is out there in the cactus and sagebrush trying to make some sense out of the cliffs, the folds, and the faults that bedevil the observer. I remember that once, after one of our discussions (less euphemistically one of our arguments), concerning the succession of fossil-bearing strata, I received from him a memo written in his large, bold hand (he liked to follow up verbal debates with written rebuttals) in which he said: "Exactly the same point of view was taken by Dr. Matthew when I requested him to make with Granger a faunal life zone survey of the Bridger. He assured me it would be impossible! H.F.O."

In a recent appreciation of Dr. Matthew, written by Ronald Rainger, there is the following statement.

Matthew, unlike Osborn and most other students of fossil vertebrates who had a background in biology, was first and foremost a geologist . . . Even after he began to concentrate on vertebrate paleontology in 1894–95, Matthew more so than the great majority of his colleagues, emphasized the importance of geological and stratigraphical problems . . . It was from his vantage point of a geologist doing paleontology that Matthew first reworked and refined previous studies of mammalian classification and phylogeny. ("Just before Simpson: William Diller Matthew's Understanding of Evolution," *Proceedings of the American Philosophical Society,* volume 130:4 [1986], page 459.)

The complete paleontologist is the person who has a good background and appreciation of both biology and geology, who blends the two disciplines in order to arrive at as full an understanding of fossils as possible—their significance as the remains of once living animals and their significance as the record of evolutionary changes as preserved in the rocks.

Perhaps this rather lengthy digression will throw some light on the reasoning behind my wish to get back into field work. It was not a desire to have a good time out in the countryside; there were very serious reasons why I felt that such a move was desirable. And there were good reasons why I would rather have stayed at home with my family. Which brings up the subject of paleontologists, their field work, and their families.

One of the real problems of being a paleontologist is, and has long been, the imposed necessity of going out into the field, often to leave the family behind. The problem is not so acute today as it formerly was; travel is not so arduous today as in earlier years, and it is frequently possible for the family to participate in the paleontologist's summer field program, as once was not the case. Even with little children in the house, it is quite feasible now to load the family into the car and make a summer camping trip a part of the field expedition. That is, of course, if the work is being done within a reasonable distance from home. Far-flung expeditions, especially to foreign lands, are something else again.

In the summer of 1938 we were only recently established in our first New Jersey home, and our first-born, George, was less than a year and a half of age. It was not easy to face the reality of having to leave Margaret and George, even for a part of the summer, which happened to be the case. My projected expedition was to last about two months, but the two months seemed just then to be a long period of separation.

It wasn't easy for Margaret, either, but since she was the daughter and the granddaughter of paleontologists she knew very much at first hand what summers, the times of field trips, might be like for us. Her early childhood memories retained clear images of her father disappearing at the beginning of summer to carry on his field studies and collecting activities in the badlands of the West, and she knew from family history and associations that this was a common pattern in paleontological households. It was something to be accepted, as was the departure of mariners when they went to sea, but it was not easy to accept, even for Margaret with her background. Perhaps something might be said about the Matthew family background.

From their home at Hastings-on-Hudson the Matthew family usually boarded a coastal steamer for a voyage to St. John, New Brunswick, where Dr. Matthew had his roots. There they spent the vacation months on the shores of the Kennebacasis River, near St. John. These sojourns in a countryside that was rural in an old-fashioned nineteenth-century way, were pleasant, always-to-be-remembered family holidays that did much to ease the feelings of separation while Dr. Matthew was out in the western badlands collecting fossils. Usually at the close of the field season Dr. Matthew joined the family in New Brunswick, before they all returned to Hastings for the school year. But Dr. Matthew's separations from his family were not especially long as compared with what some of his predecessors experienced.

Here I am reminded of the experiences of John Bell Hatcher, a noted paleontologist whose career spanned the latter part of the nineteenth century and the early years of the present century. He was the leader of several expeditions to Patagonia, where he made unexcelled collections of fossil mammals for Princeton University. His account of these trips not only makes fascinating reading, but also leads to a realization of how domestically punishing they were. Hatcher had to make a long voyage by sea from New York to Argentina, in those days a matter of several weeks, and once there he had to endure long and time-consuming journeys inland by horse and wagon—all of which added up to being away from his family for more than a year at a time. It is poignant to read Hatcher's story of how he would be without any mail from home for months at a time, because in those days inland Patagonia was a wild and woolly place, quite out of touch with the world. On one of his expeditions he learned only months after the event that his little boy had died. Could we tolerate such things today, even with the most ardent dedication to paleontology?

To get back to the story of my expedition to Agate on behalf of the Philadelphia Academy, my father was visiting us early that summer; he would be with Margaret for a short while after I left. On the afternoon that I departed (I was to take an evening train out of Penn Station) he walked with me to the bus stop in Leonia, as I wheeled my luggage in our baby carriage. When the bus came I was able to hoist my impedimenta on board, and then in New York I managed to haul my luggage onto the subway for the trip to the station. Those were still hard times, and I had no thoughts of taking a cab from far uptown to Thirty-fourth Street.

When my train reached Philadelphia on its way to Chicago I was joined by Edgar Howard, by Mr. Malcolm Lloyd, a very pleasant elderly gentleman who was financing the effort in part and was going along for the experience of participating in a fossil dig, and by Ned Page, a lad in his late teens out for a summer of adventure. I remember that the celebration of the seventy-fifth anniversary of the Battle of Gettysburg had just taken place, and on the Union Pacific train out of Chicago were several veterans of the battle, going back home. Each old warrior—the youngest of them could hardly have been less than ninety years of age—was accompanied by a traveling companion, provided by the government. Indeed the federal authorities had staged an encampment of veterans at Gettysburg and had gathered together all of the survivors of that greatest of battles on the North American continent able to make the trip; it was a final tribute to the boys in blue and the boys in gray. And as I looked at the old, old men sitting in the Pullman cars I sensed very strongly the long years of history that were traveling west that evening. When these men had risked their all on those hot July days three-quarters of a century ago, the land to which we were going was still open prairie across which there rode bands of Dakota warriors. And for me it was in a way a small journey back through time—to the days a decade earlier when I had searched the small canyons and breaks of northern Nebraska for fossil mammals.

We left the train at Scottsbluff, Nebraska, so named from the high, sandy bluffs that rise out of the prairie, a feature that once provided a landmark visible many miles distant, toward which the swaying prairie schooners made their way on westward journeys. There we outfitted ourselves for the final leg of the expedition—among other things by renting a small truck that we could use for our operations. And there, if I remember correctly, we picked up another member for our party, John House, a local boy who was recruited to be our camp cook.

The way to Agate in those days was a dirt road, going north from Mitchell across the sun-drenched high plains to our destination. The green oasis of Agate was a welcome sight, after the hot drive across the prairie.

Agate, in the very northwestern corner of the state of Nebraska, is one of the famous fossil localities in North America. There, rising above the rolling grasslands, are two hills, or more properly one might call them buttes, and in those two hills is a stratum of sandstone almost solidly filled with the bones of Lower Miocene mammals—*Diceratherium*, the small rhinoceros with laterally paired horns; the strange horselike chalicothere, *Moropus*, with claws on its feet; and the gigantic piglike *Dinohyus*. It may be recalled that these were the animals, skeletons of which I had set up in the museum in Lincoln some ten years previously. Also there were tiny little camels so small that they have been compared in size with gazelles, heavy clumsy "bear-dogs," rodents among which one possessed a pair of horns on the nose and made large, corkscrew-shaped burrows, and various other mammals as well, all constituting a faunal assemblage that roamed the plains when they were at a much lower elevation than is now the case, and enjoyed a year-round mild climate.

Today these hills are set aside as a national monument, created to preserve for posterity the remarkable concentration of fossil bones at this place, but when we went there the hills were a part of the Cook Ranch, and it was at the Cook Ranch that we were to spend the summer. It would be easy enough to go on from here to the experiences of our summer campaign, but in good conscience I cannot do this; the Cook Ranch calls for a digression in this story of my 1938 summer.

Captain James H. Cook was one of the remarkable personalities in the history of western North America. He grew up in Michigan, but as a young lad he drifted west to Texas, where he became a cowboy—one of the original, genuine cowboys, not the synthetic kind that infest some western small towns and rodeos today—and soon he made a name for himself. He was a hunter and a trapper in Wyoming, and after that he participated in the Apache war and the Geronimo campaign in the Southwest. Yet although he served as a scout for the United States Cavalry he was at heart a staunch friend of the Indian. Later, when he lived in Nebraska he became a close friend of the Sioux Indians, particularly of the great chief Red Cloud, and he learned to speak the Dakota language fluently. Bands of Dakota Indians came to his ranch every summer for visits.

In 1887 he purchased land on the upper reaches of the Niobrara River and established his homestead. He planted trees and for the first few years of his residence at the ranch he faithfully went around each evening with a wagon loaded with water barrels, to water the struggling saplings. His efforts paid off, so that years later the Cook Ranch became truly a green oasis in the stark prairie, a cool, shady refuge where it was my privilege to spend many a restful afternoon and evening.

The Agate Springs Fossil Quarries were discovered by James H. Cook and his bride one day in 1887 as they were riding across the hills near the Niobrara River. The story is best told in his words.

Riding one day along the picturesque buttes which skirt the beautiful valley of the Niobrara, we came to two high conical hills about three miles from the ranch house. From the tops of these hills there was an unobstructed view of the country for miles up and down the valley. Dismounting and leaving the reins of our bridles trailing on the ground—which meant to our well-trained ponies that they were to remain near the place where we had left them—we climbed the steep side of one of the hills. About halfway to the summit we noticed many fragments of bones scattered about on the ground. I at once concluded that at some period, perhaps years back, an Indian brave had been laid to his last long rest under one of the shelving rocks near the summit of the hill, and that, as was the custom among some tribes of Indians at one time, a number of his ponies had been killed near his body. Happening to notice a peculiar glitter on one of the bone fragments, I picked it up, and I then discovered that it was a beautifully petrified piece of the shaft of some creature's leg bone. The marrow cavity was filled with tiny calcite crystals, enough of which were exposed to cause the glitter which had attracted my attention. Upon our return to the ranch we carried with us what was doubtless the first fossil material ever secured from what are now known to men of science as the Agate Springs Fossil Quarries. (*Fifty Years on the Old Frontier* [Norman, Oklahoma: University of Oklahoma Press, 1957], page 234. The original edition was published in 1923 by the Yale University Press.)

This is an excerpt from a book written by a well-read, literate man—a fascinating firsthand account, honestly told and without any of the star-spangled embroidery that unfortunately characterizes so much of western literature. Captain Cook was truly a "man with perspective," as stated by the distinguished Texas writer J. Frank Dobie, so much so that Cook made the Agate Springs Fossil Quarries freely available to all reputable museums and universities, as did his son Harold in later years. Consequently fossil mammals from Agate are to be seen in numerous North American museums.

In 1938 Captain Cook was living quietly at the Agate Springs ranch, and there I became acquainted with him. He was a small, almost a delicate man, and very quiet. It was difficult sometimes to realize that in his younger years he had lived a life of high adventure, such as forms the subject of the most exciting tales imaginable, having to do with ranching on the unfenced lands of the Southwest and the high plains, of hunting and trapping in the Rockies, of the final Indian campaigns, and of many years spent with the Indians as a champion of their cause.

Captain Cook's brother, "Uncle Jack," a very crusty old bachelor, lived in a little house on the ranch. Agate was a post office, and Uncle Jack was the postmaster, serving the ranchers for miles around. He was as voluble and as cantankerous as Captain Cook was quiet, so he made life interesting at the ranch on numerous occasions.

Captain Cook's son Harold, about eighteen years my senior, was a professional paleontologist, which is not to be wondered at. As a boy he was fascinated by the fossils at the two hills on the ranch, and of course he had a great deal of contact with the paleontologists who came to the ranch to collect fossils. He attended the University of Nebraska, where he studied under my erstwhile boss Dr. Barbour, and then he went to Columbia

University for graduate studies. He took courses under Dr. Gregory, was a close friend of Osborn, and was particularly influenced by Dr. Matthew. Indeed, Matthew and Harold Cook worked together on some joint research problems. Unfortunately, at least from my point of view, Harold was deflected from paleontology to become a petroleum geologist, yet he always maintained a lively interest in fossil vertebrates, especially mammals.

Harold had married Dr. Barbour's daughter and from this union there were four very lively daughters, whom I knew as young girls when I was a student at Nebraska. Then Harold and his wife drifted apart and he remarried, his second wife, Margaret, being an accomplished pianist and a lovely lady in every sense of the word. Harold and Margaret became my understanding and valued friends during that summer of 1938, and their friendship lasted for many years that followed.

Harold was at the ranch when we arrived, and he immediately went with us to our campsite, a little cabin a couple of miles from the ranch house and located at the foot of a long slope leading to the larger of the two fossil-bearing hills—a hill long known as Carnegie Hill because it was first worked extensively by the Carnegie Museum of Pittsburgh. The other, somewhat smaller hill, first explored by the University of Nebraska, is quite logically known as University Hill.

The cabin, built by the Cooks expressly for the use of visiting paleontologists, was enclosed by a fence to keep the range cattle at a distance, and next to it was a well. The water table was not far down, so we enjoyed an abundance of cool water during our stay at Agate. Underneath the cabin lived a family of skunks, and although we often heard them scrabbling around down there, we seldom saw them. They came out at night; we left them alone and they avoided us.

Here I cannot resist the temptation to digress with the story of Jepsen and the skunk—famous in the annals of North American vertebrate paleontology. The late Professor Glen Jepsen, long a student of Cenozoic mammals, was working at Agate one summer back in the twenties, when he was a graduate student at Princeton. And he, with his colleagues, was staying in that same cabin where we had established ourselves in 1938. Moreover there was a family of skunks living beneath the cabin, probably progenitors several generations removed from the skunks who were our underground neighbors.

Jeppy was young and enthusiastic; he decided that he needed a skunk skeleton for a study specimen, and so one evening he set a steel trap near the cabin, the chain of the trap being anchored to a long pole. Sure enough the next day he had a skunk with one foot held tight in the trap. Jep wanted an unblemished skeleton, so how was he to dispatch the skunk? He did not have the means for a lethal injection, so the only method he could think of was to drown the skunk. Therefore he got a big tub, placed it beyond the fence that surrounded the cabin, and laboriously carried out water from the pump, pail by pail, until the tub was full.

Then he gingerly picked up one end of the pole and carried it out to the tub with Mr. Skunk dangling from the far end—so far without creating any kind of a smelly disturbance. Jep lowered the skunk into the tub but the water was not deep enough to immerse the poor creature. Consequently up came the skunk's head, and there was every prospect that this situation could continue indefinitely. There was only one thing to do—at least Jep thought so—which was to push the skunk's head beneath the water and hold it there. Jeppy crept up to the tub, grabbed the skunk by the neck and pushed his head under, whereupon the tail end of the animal came to the surface, and Jeppy got a full blast right in the face and on his chest.

Jep immediately forgot about the skunk; he took a running leap over the fence, grabbed the handle of the pump and started jumping up and down and hollering "Water! Water! Soap!" at the top of his lungs. By this time all of the other members of the field crew were rolling on the ground, convulsed with laughter, but finally someone regained enough control to man the pump handle while Jeppy, stripped to the skin, abundantly lathered and soaked himself. All the while he was yelling and dancing around because the water, straight out of the ground, was almost icy cold.

Just at that moment who should come around the corner of the cabin but Harold Cook's four daughters, at that time girls in their teens and even younger. Jep, horrified at his exposure in front of these innocent damsels, made a flying leap for the door of the cabin, but his trajectory was too high and he caught his head against the lintel with a resounding whack, and this caused him to stagger back and collapse on the ground in full view of one and all.

So goes the official version of the story, the version that I heard Bryan Patterson of the Field Museum recount one evening at a party, while Jep, sitting next to Bryan, kept shaking his head in protest. But at the end of the story Al Romer declared that this *was* the official version, and all present voted in favor, in spite of Jep's protestations.

(I think the only real departure from verisimilitude was the part about Jep banging his head on the doorframe; otherwise the tale stands as told. Whatever happened to the skunk has not been revealed.)

The cabin was not very big; certainly it could not accomodate our crew, so we pitched tents inside the enclosing fence except for John House, who bunked in the cabin. Fortunately there was an old-fashioned ice refrigerator in the cabin, so on the first weekend when we drove to Mitchell for groceries and other supplies we established a routine that was followed all summer. We would do our shopping on Saturday afternoon, having dinner in town, and as often as not go to a movie. Then, the last thing before leaving town we would get a two-hundred-pound chunk of ice, and take it back to camp with us through the cool of the evening. In camp we dug a pit, lined it with sawdust, and stashed the ice there, securely covered with sawdust and a piece of canvas as protection against the daytime sun. Every day John would chip off as much ice as he needed for the icebox, and thus we enjoyed fresh milk and butter, meat, vegetables, and other nutritious food.

We also quickly established our daily routine. John would get up and prepare the breakfast while the rest of us were crawling out of our sleeping bags and getting dressed. Then off to Carnegie Hill for a morning of digging, back to the cabin for lunch, off again for the afternoon, and back again for dinner and the evening.

The evenings were memorable, because as a general thing we would sit outside after our meal and watch the tremendous clouds pile up above the prairie, as only clouds can do in a land of big sky, to be limned by the setting sun with a spectacular display of flashing colors. It so happened that an oil well was being drilled across the valley, a mile or so away, and during our evening reveries we would hear a faint, rhythmic throbbing from the machinery—a small background noise that went on so constantly day and night that we were hardly aware of it. Moreover, since the drilling was a twenty-four-hour operation, the well rig would be spangled with lights at night giving a sort of Christmas-tree effect out there on the wide expanse of the rolling prairie hills.

Every afternoon the superintendent in charge of the drilling would fly over us, to land his plane near the well for an inspection of the project. Then, just as we were finishing our evening meal, or shortly after, he would leave the well and fly straight at our cabin, clearing the roof by a mere twenty or thirty feet. It was his way of saluting us at the day's end.

Our work at Carnegie Hill began by digging into the side of the slope at a place suggested by Harold, to uncover the bone layer. We dug back far enough so that soon we had excavated a sort of cavern or shelter in the hillside, the floor of which was covered by a jumble of fossil bones. Of course we treated the bones with preservative white shellac as they were exposed to view.

Why should the fossil bones at the Agate quarry have been in such a jumble, which according to the dictionary is a "confused mixture"? When attempting to analyze the reason for fossils being in the rocks as they are, this is a question not always easy to answer. Today there is a whole subdiscipline of paleontology, known as taphonomy, devoted to the interpretation of natural burials, and this combined with the geological subdisciplines of sedimentology and stratigraphy seeks to explain as best as possible the reasons for accumulations of bones such as are seen at Agate.

From these studies it would appear that the bones at Agate were deposited rather rapidly in ephemeral stream channels carrying sands mixed with some volcanic ash. The stream channels, being sporadic in nature, indicate that they developed in a semiarid climate, in what must have been an open plains environment. The bones, being predominantly the remains of various hoofed mammals, certainly indicate that the Lower Miocene mammals of what is now western Nebraska were living on a broad plain, perhaps not unlike the plains of today, but at a lower elevation above sea level. (The Rocky Mountain uplift was raising the landscapes of western North America toward the elevations typical of present times, but as yet the mountains and the plains bordering the mountains were at modest heights as compared with the mountains and plains with which we are familiar.)

Furthermore the disarticulated state of most of the large mammals in the bone bed at Agate and the abraded condition of many of the bones indicate that there was a time lag after the death of these animals and before their burial, during which carcasses decayed and were scavenged by predatory animals. Yet the predominant feature of the Agate deposit was and is the incredible concentration of the bones, piled one upon the other so that many parts of the deposit can be characterized as solid masses of bones, with no blank spaces between them. One can only imagine the forces of stream action directed in such a way that carcasses, either whole or partial, as well as almost countless isolated bones, were washed together to be buried in such a vast natural graveyard. That was our digging ground.

Sitting there day after day, scratching down through the sandstone to uncover the jackstraw jumble of bones and teeth and skulls and jaws, was an exercise in tedium interspersed with periods of high excitement. The excitement came when a new bone began to be revealed—its subtle shape becoming apparent as the overlying matrix was scraped away, a matrix that had enveloped the bone through twenty million years of oblivion. Such excitement as a fossil is uncovered is universal; I have never seen anyone, even the most casual bystander, who has not been enthralled by the sight of a fossil gradually taking shape during the process of excavation. So it is not to be wondered at that John House, although ostensibly our cook, spent many hours in the quarry, enthusiastically scratching and digging in the quarry floor.

There is much more to the technique of fossil excavation than exposing the bones as we were doing. That part of our task was only the preliminary phase of what was to be a long and at times a frustrating operation. We were bringing the bones to light so that we might establish the dimensions of our project; we wished to know what we had, but beyond that we needed to know how far to go and how we were to draw the boundaries that would enclose the association of fossils we proposed to take out of the ground.

We were planning to follow well-established paleontological techniques by removing these bones without disturbing their relations to each other; in short it was our predetermined intention to take them out just as they were, enclosed in a solid block of sandstone. Therefore, after exposing the bones on the quarry floor, and treating them so that they would not fracture or crumble, we had to determine what the limits of the block were to be. This was where the problem of boundaries came in; how were we to decide where to define the edges of the block? It was not an easy decision, because the bones formed an uninterrupted mass extending into the hill. Consequently we needed to plot the edges of the block so that there would be a minimum amount of damage to the fossils along those edges. This was done in part by cutting down from the bone level in areas where bones were sparse or missing, and in part, sad as it may seem, by having to cut through some bones. But we did keep the cutting of bones to a minimum. In this way, with many difficult and at times painful decisions being made as to the location of the block's edges, we finally managed to trench around the block so that it stood isolated from the bone layer of which it had been a part.

We then covered the bones on the top of the block with Japanese rice paper, pasted down on them with shellac to make a reasonably tough coating that protected the bones, as well as separating them from the overlying jacket that was to cover the block. Then the jacket was applied, formed by strips of burlap soaked in plaster of paris. It was a process quite analagous to the procedure followed by a physician in putting a cast on a broken limb, but on a grand scale. Thus in the end we had a big block perhaps eight feet or so in length by six feet in width, perhaps bigger (I don't recall now the dimensions), encased on the top and sides by a heavy plaster cast, so that it would be immobilized and could be moved with impunity.

But the block was still part of the rock beneath it. The problem now was to try to make undercuts so that the plastered block could be removed from the resting place where it had remained for so many millions of years. Here was a problem that at times we thought would defeat us, so that on many of our days in the quarry we worked hour after hour with a deadening feeling of despair hanging over us. The undercutting of ordinary plastered blocks usually involves the business of whacking away beneath such blocks with picks, which at best is hard, uncomfortable work. More often than not it is necessary for one to lie on one's side and pick away at the rock—a method of work that does not involve very efficient blows from the instrument being used. But the Agate block was of huge size; we could pick around the edges, but how to work far in underneath the block with any degree of efficiency (and safety) caused us many hours of argument and experimentation.

We tried some large saws; they quickly became blunted and useless. My friend Paul McGrew, who had worked at Agate, sketched for me a scenario whereby we could use a long piece of barbed wire, pulled back and forth by a suffering bone digger at each end of the wire. We tried that; it was a complete failure. In no time the barbs were jerked from the wire and we held in our hands a useless, smooth metal strand. All of which left us as far from a solution to our problem as ever.

We finally adopted a method of our own. With picks and with long rock chisels which could be hammered, we cut a series of parallel tunnels beneath the block, leaving it supported on several pedestals between the tunnels. And through these tunnels we shoved heavy timbers which were then clamped to corresponding timbers on the top of the block with very heavy wires, tightened by turnbuckles. After that, by main strength and awkwardness we cut down the dimensions of the supporting pedestals as much as possible. We also plastered beneath the block as best we could (applying burlap bandages dipped in plaster to the under side of a block and fighting gravity with every move is a particularly frustrating exercise). At last, with much sweat and tears and bad language we had the block in such a condition that we thought it could be moved.

At this juncture we made contact with a contractor in Scottsbluff, and arranged for him to get the block out of the quarry and to the railroad station. Within a few days he appeared, driving a heavy truck on which was mounted a powerful winch. The truck was backed into position. Large steel cables were wrapped around the block and hitched to the winch. Then the machinery was set in motion while we stood aside with our fingers crossed, and prayed. The cables became taut, the winch growled, suddenly there was a cracking jolt, and the block was broken free from its pedestals. It was then pulled up onto the truck for its journey to Scottsbluff, and from there to Philadelphia.

Looking back on this adventure I can see that I was born thirty years too soon. Today there are circular rock saws, mounted on long arms, with which the enterprising paleontologist can cut out blocks with relative ease and equanimity.

That summer at Agate now fades into historic perspective, perhaps because it represents the beginning of the end of a long chapter in the paleontological story at Agate. The quarries at the two hills were first worked in 1891 and 1892, and from that time until after our labors of 1938 they were the paleontological hunting grounds for many museums and universities. As mentioned, the quarries have now been made a national monument as part of the national parks system, and there are plans to use the old ranch house as a visitor center. So a new chapter is well under way at Agate, which is proper and as it should be; the quarries constitute a national treasure and quite rightly are being preserved for future generations. Perhaps there will not be much more removal of blocks to museums; rather it is intended that the quarries will be developed as *in situ* exhibits, with facilities, it is to be hoped, for carrying on research at Agate.

Incidentally a permanent facility there was a dream long held by Dr. Matthew. He envisioned a laboratory at Agate where preparation and even study could be devoted to fossils collected not only at Agate but more widely at fossil localities throughout the region. His dream never was realized (he had thought of it as being a joint effort by a consortium of museums) but today and in the future perhaps it may come to pass in some modified form under the auspices of the National Park Service.

Three years after Agate I was again preparing to go into the field—this time as a member of an American Museum party to collect fossil mammals of Oligocene age in the White River badlands of South Dakota. The summers of 1939 and 1940 had found me staying close to home because in July of each of those years our next two boys were born—David in 1939 and Philip in 1940. All of that was excitement enough. But in 1941 the opportunity to work in the White River badlands developed, and as in 1938 Margaret patiently watched me depart while she stayed at home with the three children. (She did get a reward of sorts later on in the summer; her stepfather and mother had driven from California to New Jersey for a visit, and on their way back west they brought her to South Dakota where we all had a grand reunion. The children, I should add, were being taken care of by some very kind friends.)

Our purpose in going to the White River country was to build up the American Museum collection of Oligocene mammals which had become somewhat depleted through the years by reasons of exchanges with other institutions. So it was planned for me to go out there with Albert Thomson, the head of the American Museum fossil laboratory, to make a representative collection, subsequently to be joined by Walter Granger.

Again we went went by train—from New York to Chicago and from there to Rapid City, South Dakota. In Rapid City Albert (as has been mentioned, known to his intimates as Bill) and I prepared for the summer's campaign. We picked up a car that had been stored in Rapid City, a sort of panel-body truck, and drove southeast to Scenic, a rather sad little settlement in the heart of the badlands. Scenic existed because at one time it was a little shopping place for the surrounding countryside and a center from which to ship cattle on the railroad that ran through town. But then came the automobile; the ranchers went to Rapid City to do their shopping, and cattle were transported by trucks. So Scenic was slowly dying when we were there, the town consisting of a little run-down hotel of sorts, a restaurant, a grocery store, the inevitable bar, and a few houses. It was to be our headquarters for two very hot months.

We were scheduled to stay in the hotel, but after the first night I found our room too hot and too infested for comfort, so for the rest of the summer I abandoned Bill and slept out in the truck. How Bill managed to put up with our quarters I don't know; as for me I have pleasant memories of cool nights in the back of the truck, generally punctuated as I was falling asleep by the sound of the train coming through on its way to Rapid City.

It is interesting how one finds pleasant people even in the bleakest of places. In Scenic we soon became close friends of a young couple who ran the one store in town—Claude and Celia Barry—and the Catholic priest, Father Balfe. The Barrys extended to us many kindnesses, and Father Balfe was a welcome evening visitor with whom we had innumerable interesting talks. He was a progressive-minded young middle-aged man, out of favor with his bishop, so he had been relegated to this wind-swept little parish out in the badlands.

The White River badlands of South Dakota are in effect the quintessential badlands, the *mauvaises terres* of the French explorers who roamed our western wildernesses in the early years of the nineteenth century, the strangely sculptured region encountered by the mountain men as they wandered far and wide while working their way up the wide Missouri in search of furs. Indeed, these badlands are so universally recognized as what badlands ought to look like that they are now contained and protected within a national park by the park service—located along the edge of the Pine Ridge Sioux Indian Reservation.

Fossils were found in these badlands by mountain men working for the American Fur Company, and were first described by Dr. Hiram Prout of St. Louis and by Dr. Joseph Leidy, the pioneer paleontologist at the Philadelphia Academy of Natural Sciences. Prout described a fragment of a titanothere jaw, titanotheres being huge rhinoceroslike mammals, while Leidy described a little camel jaw which he named *Poebrotherium*.

Such discoveries were destined to arouse the interest of curious people, so from that time on through the remainder of the century the White River badlands were explored by many parties of early travelers and scientists. The list of universities and museums and government agencies that sent field parties into the White River badlands is long and comprehensive, and the list of men who collected and studied White River fossils embraces many famous names: Thaddeus Culbertson, Ferdinand Vandiveer Hayden, Othniel Charles Marsh, John Bell Hatcher, William Berryman Scott, and others. Indeed the list could be continued to include numerous paleontologists who have worked throughout the decades of this century, some still active in this field.

There are two reasons why so many institutions and so many people have gone into the White River badlands to search for fossils; first the fossils themselves are numerous and well-preserved, and second, erosion is rapid.

Consequently there is a never-ending supply of fossil mammals coming to light—every year and after every big rainstorm.

That was why we were there: to gather some of the fossil treasures that had been exposed by erosion during the past year or two or three. We had a permit from the federal government for our work (the region by then had been acquired by the park service) and we were prepared to work under government regulations, which stipulated among other things that the fossils we found were to be reported and were to be safely housed at the American Museum of Natural History.

Fossil hunters may be divided into four groups: the professionals, the enlightened amateurs, the dealers, and the hobbyists. The professionals are the paleontologists who work for universities and museums; they collect fossils for their institutions for the purposes of research and education, and almost to a man or woman they have no desire to own fossils as personal property. The enlightened amateurs are people who are profoundly interested in fossils; they collect fossils for themselves or frequently for institutions and they have a lively appreciation of the worth of fossils as scientific objects. The dealers are people who collect fossils to make money; they sell their finds to other people interested in fossils—to people who like to have nice objects to place on the mantel, sometimes even to museums. The hobbyists are people who collect fossils as objects to own, just as one collects postage stamps or other curious things; they may or may not appreciate the meaning of fossils.

It is important that fossils, when collected, go to proper homes. Many common fossils may quite appropriately be held in private hands, but important and rare fossils should be in public institutions where they are carefully cared for and preserved as the basic data upon which we can build our interpretations of past life.

In a region such as the White River badlands, where fossils are abundant and erosion is rapid, there have in the past been far more fossils washed into oblivion than have been collected. Even today, when paleontological collecting is carried on assiduously, there are still many fossils lost because of erosion. So, as mentioned, our campaign that summer was a project directed in part toward saving good fossils from the inevitable forces of erosion. This was illustrated by a personal experience.

One day Bill Thomson and I had spent the morning prospecting in the badlands as we usually did. It was our practice to separate ourselves, a quarter of a mile or so apart, in order to cover the ground as thoroughly as possible. This meant that we trudged across flat areas between badland hills, always looking for signs of bones eroding from the sediments, or following the bases of the hills for telltale signs, or even climbing up and down the slopes in the prosecution of our search. For me it had been a rather barren morning—lots of fossil scrap, the remnants of bones or even skeletons that had gone to pieces under the inexorable forces of rain and wind, but nothing worth serious attention. Just before we were to get together for a lunch of sandwiches, eaten in the scanty shade provided by our parked truck, I climbed up to the top of a little badland peak, mainly to get the benefit of whatever breezes might be blowing in order to cool off a bit. And as I stood there I looked down to see a skeleton exposed below me on the slope of the hill. With an exultant whoop I careened down the side of the hill to see what it was, and I could hardly believe my eyes: it was a beautifully articulated skeleton of a large Oligocene carnivorous mammal known as *Hyaenodon*—a rare fossil treasure.

If I had missed that fossil it would have rested there beneath the hot sun, to be disintegrated by the next violent rainstorm, an event that might have occurred within a week or perhaps within a month or two. At any rate, the skeleton probably would not have been there the following year. We got to it just at the right time, not too early in which case it probably would not have been sufficiently exposed to be visible, and not too late in which case it would have been eroded away. Today this specimen is on exhibit in New York, a testimonial to the good fortune of being there at the right time.

With a succession of such adventures, generally less dramatic, we spent our summer building up a collection of Oligocene mammals from the White River beds. Experiences varied, but the procedures followed similar lines: locating the fossils by exploring the terrain, exposing such specimens as were to be collected, and hardening the fossil bone with thin shellac as it was exposed (fossil hunters today enjoy the use of modern sophisticated hardening or preservative agents—shellac has become very old fashioned), covering the exposed fossil with a bandage of burlap dipped in plaster of paris, and strengthening the plastered specimen with wooden splints—as has already been explained in the account of our work at Agate. Of course the important data concerning each fossil—what it was, its geographic position, its stratigraphic level, and other pertinent facts—were recorded in a field note book. As a final touch each fossil was given a field number, the number duly recorded in the field book. Such were the steps taken in the field, and these constituted one aspect of research, just as surely so as is the more stereotyped image of research—the image of someone clad in a white coat and busy in a laboratory.

One of the many joys of research in the field, whatever form it may take, is the simple fact of being out of doors. Frequently there are discomforts enough—the sun may be hot, the wind may be cold—yet one has a feeling of being in harmony with the natural world, which for a geologist or a paleontologist or a biologist is what it is all about. And the alert naturalist if he is worth his salt has his eyes and ears attuned to more than his own specialty when he is out doing field research. That was what made Darwin such a superb student of the world in which he found himself and it comes out in *The Voyage of the Beagle*, his account of the five-year journey of a naturalist to oceanic islands and through the jungles and pampas of South America.

There were unexpected happenings in the White River badlands. One that I shall never forget was the day that I attracted the attention of a little herd of wild horses—a stallion and his coterie of mares and colts. Evidently they were feeling well fed, so for an hour or two they followed me across the badland flats and along the edges of badland hills, always keeping at a little distance so they could turn and gallop away should I make a move in their direction. But I made no such move, and they kept with me, never realizing in their equine brains that I just might find the bones of their distant ancestors, delicate three-toed horses about the size of small sheep.

One of my vivid recollections of the badlands is of "turtle basin," a badland flat, perhaps an acre or two in extent, the surface of which was dotted with the shells of fossil turtles. Each shell, about the size of a good-sized pumpkin, rested upon a little pedestal of rock, an arrangement owing to the fact that the fossil shell was hard and served as a cap protecting the sediments beneath it while the sediments around it were worn away by the wind and the rain. It was quite a sight; I suppose the turtles have long since vanished. (We did collect a few shells, but there were too many for us to have devoted a large segment of our summer in gathering a large collection.)

One day who should appear in Scenic but Harold and Margaret Cook. It was a happy reunion, and was celebrated by their going out into the field with us for the day. It so happened that Walter Granger was due to join us that evening; he was coming on the train that in those days ran between Chicago and Rapid City. So we prepared a welcome: we made a lei out of onions and when the train stopped ever so briefly in Scenic it was met by our little delegation—the Cooks, the Barrys, Father Balfe, and the bone hunters—singing a welcome song, accompanied by Margaret on the guitar. And as Granger stepped from the train the onion lei was draped around his neck while he was greeted with shouts of welcome. We could see puzzled passengers peering out of the windows of the train, trying to fathom what was going on in the gathering dusk.

That little reunion in Scenic was the last gathering for some old paleontological companions—Walter Granger, Albert Thomson and Harold Cook—and I wonder what thoughts and memories they might have had. I have already mentioned the close association between Granger and W. D. Matthew that had extended through a span of forty years. There was a similar close relationship between Granger and Thomson; they started their careers together back in the nineties with Dr. Matthew and Osborn. Harold Cook, although a bit younger than Granger and Thomson, had enjoyed a very close working relationship with them that dated back to the early years of the present century. So here they were, talking and laughing together as they had in years long gone by, and here I was thoroughly enjoying their banter and their anecdotes. It was an evening that for me was never to be forgotten.

Walter Granger was with us for a week or two and then I went off to join a field conference of the Society of Vertebrate Paleontology which was being held that year in western Nebraska, while Granger and Bill Thomson went to Agate for some rest and recreation with the Cooks while I was away.

After the field conference, which ended at the University in Lincoln, Nebraska, and where I had a nice reunion with Margaret, who was on her way back from her family visit in California to join our children in New Jersey, I went west again for the continuation of our field work. I was to meet Bill and Walter Granger in Lusk, Wyoming, but when I got to Lusk I was greeted by Bill and Harold Cook. I knew the moment I saw them that something was wrong. That previous night Walter Granger had quietly died in his hotel room there—of a heart attack. He was sixty-eight years old.

It was an overwhelming shock to me. Never before had anyone so close to me been taken by death; it was almost as if I had lost my father. Indeed, Walter Granger had been a fatherly advisor to me during those dozen years that I had worked with him at the American Museum. That day Harold drove Thomson and me around the Wyoming countryside, mainly to try to alleviate the pain we felt, and then Bill and I went back to Scenic to pack our gear and get ready for the trip to New York. All thought of continuing the field season had vanished from our plans.

We were met at Pennsylvania Station by a group of friends and relatives, including Margaret, who for me was a most welcome sight, and Roy Chapman Andrews, director of the museum. It was a sad end to the summer and for some time I found it difficult to adjust to the new situation. My comfort was with my family; our three boys had progressed amazingly during my summer's absence, as children will do.

Then on Sunday, December 7, we heard the fateful news on the radio that the Japanese had bombed Pearl Harbor. Life was destined to be different for everybody from that day on, and of course we were affected in various ways. For me, a new paleontological career was just over the horizon, although as yet I did not know it. Soon I was to say farewell to fossil mammals; the summer in White River badlands had been in effect my final large experience in this branch of paleontological research.

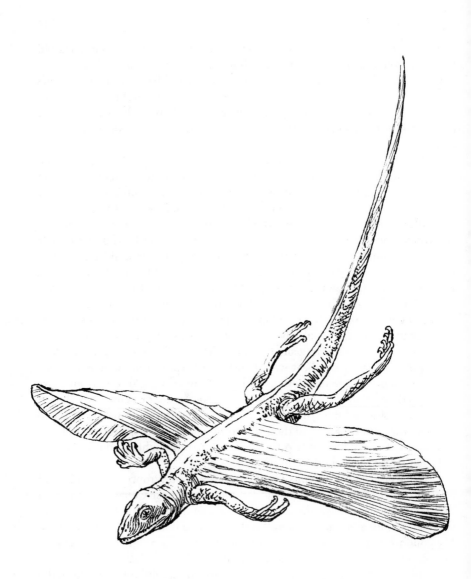

XIII

Introduction to
the Mesozoic

Those weeks and months after Pearl Harbor made a confusing and frustrating time for all Americans, a time before we were organized, a time when we watched with dismay while events went against us in the Pacific and when the crescendo of horrors continued with unabated fury in Europe. It was a time, of course, when there were things other than fossils to think about.

Just what was going to happen to me was very uncertain. Earlier, I think it was in 1940, I had registered for the draft as was then required of all men in my age bracket, but with three small children at home I was not in 1942 a high-priority candidate for the services. Even so I was twice requested during our early war years to volunteer as an officer for overseas service, which I did. One call was from the army, asking me to let them know how much experience I had had in desert regions, so I went downtown somewhere in Manhattan and talked with an officer about my fossil-hunting background—such as it was. Evidently it did not suffice, because I had not been in the deserts they had in mind. The other was from the navy; they were looking for somebody to trap mammals on South Sea islands that might be vectors (the mammals that is) of tropical diseases. This would have been a new departure for me, but I think I might have carried it out. The question of my serving soon became academic, because a well-qualified mammalogist was found who could carry out the work. In the end I served for the duration as an air-raid warden in our little town of Leonia, New Jersey. It was an exercise in unncessary caution—but then at the time we never knew but what German planes might come over some dark night.

Things happened at the museum, too, some related to the war, others not. So far as the war was concerned, we evacuated our type fossils (along with crucial materials from other departments) to a far suburban location in New Jersey, while at the museum in Manhattan we organized fire stations and fire drills. And of course various members of the museum staff went off to war, including George Simpson, who spent several years on very active duty in North Africa and elsewhere.

All of this took place within a year of Walter Granger's death, and then in 1942 Barnum Brown was retired, having passed the statutory age limit. Consequently I was left pretty much alone with the fossil vertebrates, so far as the research staff was concerned. This was not, however, the end of changes taking place, because during this same year I was placed in charge of the fossil amphibians and reptiles, to succeed Brown. This was done on the premise that Simpson eventually would return to resume direction of research on fossil mammals. Of course it was a big change for me—a person who had spent his time up to this point doing research on fossil mammals. But it was not unprecedented in the light of the way institutions operate, and it shifted me into a field that had long been of great interest to me, but hitherto closed territory at the museum so far as I was concerned.

These changes and many more, representing the development of new policies by the trustees, were initiated by Albert E. Parr, the new director of the museum, brought from the Peabody Museum at Yale to succeed Roy Andrews. Bert Parr was an innovative administrator and to many people a controversial figure. He had thought much about museums—what should be their purposes and how they should be used—and he put his ideas into practice with energetic dispatch, at times in the process upsetting some sacred applecarts. Of course the people who were affected by his decisions reacted variously in a gamut that ranged from appreciative approval to vociferous outrage. I think that on the whole the members of the museum staff approved of Bert's actions, although quite naturally some did not. He certainly wafted a breath of fresh air into what had become a deadened atmosphere, among other things by insisting that museum staff salaries, which had been pitifully low, should be comparable to the salaries of university faculty members and support staff in the New York area. He also instituted an integrated salary scale based upon training, ability, and performance, and he created a staff committee for hiring and promotions, whereby prospective staff members to be added to the roster of the museum staff and established staff members up for promotion would be judged by their peers. In addition he put new life into the Council of the Scientific Staff, composed of the heads of the scientific departments, by the initiation of a practice by which he would not attend council meetings unless invited. He wanted the council to be independent. Furthermore, he had innovative ideas about the organization of research and the development of exhibition halls. All of this was in decided contrast to the patchwork pattern of museum practices that previously had prevailed at the institution.

One aspect of Bert Parr's administration that I liked was his willingness to listen to criticism. He obviously did not wish to be surrounded by yes-men. I can remember many an occasion when I differed with him, sometimes to the point of having real whiz-bang arguments, and I know that he respected such opposition so long as it was honest and well founded.

Personally Bert Parr was an attractive figure—a solidly built man with regular features and a shock of thick hair. He was a Norwegian by birth and education, and although he was most fluent in the use of the English language, and although he wrote well, he never quite mastered the English "J." So he would talk about the "mayor" problems that faced us, or the noise caused by the flight of "yet" planes over the city.

The museum had a long tradition that still exists—the "coffee room" where staff members would meet for a half-hour of conversation after lunch. Bert liked to attend these sessions, and nothing pleased him more than to get into a rip-snorting argument about some phase of natural history—the course of evolution, or the geographic distribution of life, or a score of other topics that concern people of our profession. And sometimes when the arguments became heated and protracted, it was hard to cut things off and go back to an afternoon of work. For, it should be added, Bert was a student of oceanic fishes, and he fully understood and appreciated the problems with which research scientists were wrestling. It should be said, also, that although he was administering the largest natural history museum in the world, he carried on his program of research; he was more than an administrator. Furthermore, he was available to those who wished to see him on museum business; one didn't have to wait a week for an appointment.

As can be guessed, the moves that led to Barnum Brown's retirement and my appointment as curator of fossil amphibians and reptiles were the result of Parr's taking over the directorship of the museum. But there were some complications. Bert Parr was a zoologist by training, and he never quite appreciated the difference between the study of extinct and modern animals. He saw no reason why the study of fossil mammals should be separated from that of recent mammals, of fossils reptiles from recent reptiles, and so on. After all, did not the fossils and their modern successors and descendants represent a long continuum of life? Logically yes, practically something else again.

Consequently one of his first acts as director was to abolish the Department of Vertebrate Paleontology, which was a long-established gem in the museum crown, and to assign the various disciplines within the old department to the departments concerned with modern animals. It was all done on paper; the fossil mammals remained physically where they had always been, while the same was true for the fossil reptiles, and so on, all separated by considerable distances within the huge museum building from their modern counterparts. And of course the laboratory of vertebrate paleontology, where fossils were cleaned and prepared, remained in its large and well-equipped quarters. The same was the case for the fossil storerooms; after all, one does not blithely move a large storeroom filled with steel racks holding tons of dinosaur bones.

Simpson and I opposed this reorganization with all of our power, but for the time being Parr prevailed. Among other things this shuffling of titles and responsibilities had the effect of putting Simpson (my senior in age and very much so in accomplishment) as one of the troops within a department administered by a man much his inferior as a scientist, and of placing me as head of a department thereby superseding a close friend, Charles Bogert, one of my contemporaries. It was galling to Simpson and embarrassing to me, and eventually it proved to be unwieldy, as we all knew it would be. Fortunately for me Chuck Bogert accepted the situation with good grace, and we worked together harmoniously for the duration of this unrealistic arrangement. But in the meantime Simpson went off to war feeling very angry and disgruntled. (After the war the Department of Vertebrate Paleontology was reconstituted, with George Simpson as its chairman. It should be said for Parr that he was willing to admit his error; he and Simpson became good friends for a long postwar interval, although eventually a rift between them developed, never to be healed. Chuck Bogert and I were always on good terms with Parr, in spite of the administrative musical chairs to which we were subjected.)

Perhaps I should add at this place a bit of my institutional philosophy. It was never my feeling, and it is still not, that being the head of a department or a division or whatever may be involved is the zenith of human accomplishment. Somebody has to run the show and that's the way it is, but running the show can be a chore and a burden. In our culture there seems to be the accepted view that the ultimate reward in an organization is the top management job, for which reason many a good research scientist, a person doing truly original work, is saddled with routine desk work which he may or may not do well, but which is almost certainly bound to limit and perhaps even prevent his carrying on the imaginative and elegant research for which he is trained and at which he is skilled. I made up my mind not to get caught in this trap; therefore although I was assigned administrative posts during my tenure at the American Museum, I tried as best I could not to let the work of management get in the way of research.

Some years after I became a department head, when I was dean of the Council of the Scientific Staff, I tried to put this philosophy into practice in a very definite manner. It was the policy of the museum that every staff member should have at least one half of his or her time for research—free from routine duties, correspondence, public relations jobs, and the like. So I proposed to our council that we arrange a schedule, applicable to the entire museum, whereby all staff members would devote either a full morning or a full afternoon to research, the half-day so reserved to be decided by a vote participated in by the entire staff. During this reserved time we were not to call each other on the phone, and outside calls were to be postponed so far as possible. Moreover, the administration was not to bother us with demands for our time. The idea was debated back and forth and voted on, but people being what they are, it never succeeded in practice. I might have foreseen that.

Some people in museum or academic positions will get ahead with their research come hell or high water; others will let the niggling details of institutional life get in the way of their proper interests. So it proved to be; the dedicated researchers went ahead with their studies, some of the others were perpetually sidetracked by the exigencies of the moment.

To get back to my shift from research on fossil mammals to studies of fossil reptiles, it was a change of major proportions in the direction of my life, but one that I welcomed. I had long been interested in the so-called lower vertebrates, and now I had the opportunity to work on them. My work on mammals at the American Museum, although most fascinating, had been restricted on the one hand by reason of Simpson's preemption of the field of early mammals in which he was a scholar of profound accomplishment and world-wide recognition, and on the other by the activities of the Frick Laboratories, which preempted on a hitherto unimagined scale the field of later Cenozoic mammals. That was why I had been engaged on Asiatic mammals, of which collections were presently available but where the opportunities at our museum for branching out into new Asiatic fields in the future did not seem to be necessarily promising.

In making the shift from mammals to reptiles I was following a pragmatic and perhaps an opportunistic course of action, but that is often seen in the careers of paleontologists. Indeed, the whole course of a paleontological life is based to a large degree upon opportunism—on what one may find in the field and on how one uses the resources of the laboratory. The laboratory (speaking in an inclusive sense) and the institution in which it is located can be a large determining factor in the shaping of a career. Paleontologists are almost exclusively institutional people, so that the location and the resources of the institution determine in a most positive manner the direction of research careers.

Some paleontologists, it is true, have made their careers by choosing a subject at the beginning of their work and sticking with it through the years. But it seems to me that this approach to paleontology can be restrictive. On the other hand one may be too profuse and wind up by dabbling in too many problems, thereby being superficial and not accomplishing anything in depth. There can be extremes in the study of paleontology, as in any aspect of life; the solution, it seems to me, is to try to maintain a balanced approach to the field.

As for me, I had no qualms about shifting the center of my efforts from mammals to reptiles, or about doing so because I saw opportunities for interesting and significant research by making the change. I was fortunate in having received my graduate training under the guiding hand of William King Gregory, as has been mentioned a respected authority of world-wide acclaim in the study of *all* vertebrates; consequently I had gained from him a broad view of the backboned animals.

In 1943, some months after I had become involved with my newly oriented work at the museum, the assistant director, Wayne Faunce, called me into his office to ask about a field car that was in storage in Glen Rose, Texas, full of equipment. It had been left there by R. T. Bird, Barnum Brown's very accomplished field assistant, in expectation of being used again. But R. T. was now in war work, and there the car rested, eating up storage charges. I did some quick thinking and suggested that perhaps I could go to Texas, pick it up, and drive it back to New York—an idea of which he approved wholeheartedly. Then I wrote to Al Romer at Harvard.

Al was one of the great vertebrate paleontologists of the world, and a noted authority on Permian amphibians and reptiles. I suggested to Al that he join me, that we pick up the truck, that we drive back with it, stopping on the way to examine the Permian Red Beds of Texas, which were on our route. This would give us an opportunity to do some field reconnaissance at a time when travel restrictions were very severe. (I should say the allotment board allowed us just enough gasoline to get the truck home.)

Al was delighted with the idea, and so was I, because it would give me an opportunity not only to look at the Texas Permian with Al, who was the preeminent authority on this subject, but also to have long conversations with him about future research on fossil reptiles. My thoughts were on Triassic and later reptiles, but an acquaintance with the Permian, to be established in the field under Al's critical eye, would give me a pertinent and most desirable background for the studies that I had in mind. Al and I shared the common experience of having been students of Dr. Gregory, although he had preceded me by about a decade. Moreover, Al was one of several Gregory students who had become great authorities on fossil and recent amphibians and reptiles—the others: notably Charles Camp at the University of California at Berkeley, G. K. Noble, who for many years was chairman of the Department of Herpetology at the American Museum, and K. P. Schmidt, who held a similar post at the Field Museum in Chicago.

Al had many interesting stories to tell about the salad days of this unusual quartet (including himself)—interesting tales not only because of the subjects involved but also because Al was not one to let a good story suffer in the telling. Indeed, Al kept me constantly amused during that field trip to Texas. One of his charms was that he never became impressed by his own eminence; one would think, to hear him tell it, that his career was based upon a series of accidents, in which his own abilities played a very minor role. He *only* managed to be a professor at the University of Chicago, and after that at Harvard, to be elected to the National Academy of Sciences (the supreme honor for an American scientist), to be president of the American Association for the Advancement of Science, to receive honors from scientific societies and universities in this country and abroad, as attested by his eight medals given for outstanding scientific achievement and four honorary degrees, and to be internationally recognized during his lifetime as one of the foremost vertebrate paleontologists in the world. Accidents forsooth!

The reader may recall Al's story, outlined on a previous page, of how he became a vertebrate paleontologist because he was bitten by a mad dog. To recapitulate, when he was a young boy he was bitten by the family dog suspected of being rabid, he went to the Pasteur Institute in New York (Al went there, not the dog), and between treatments at the institute he visited the American Museum of National History where he fell in love with the fossil skeletons. And that started him on the road toward a paleontological career.

Such was one version. Another version, perhaps to be taken more seriously, concerns his undergraduate days at Amherst College. There he was pursuing a double major in history and German literature, but he had to take a course to fulfill a science requirement. So he opted for a course in evolution, recommended to him by fellow students as "interesting and not too tough," taught in part by Frederick Brewster Loomis, one of the active vertebrate paleontologists in America at that time. That course reintro-

duced him to some of the old fossil friends that he had seen in New York
while undergoing the Pasteur treatments, and he decided to forget history
and German literature, to go for fossil vertebrates.

Just then the First World War came along, and Al spent a couple of
years in France, where among other things he wound up as an innocent
young lieutenant assigned to supervise a couple of hundred nubile French
mademoiselles who were repairing airplane wings (in those days covered
with fabric), and residing in a camp of their own, surrounded by a high, wire
fence. Al could keep the eager American soldiers stationed nearby *out* of the
ladies' camp, but he couldn't keep the ladies, being free French citizens,
inside their camp, especially after hours. Needless to say, that made an
hilarious tale.

Then, back from the war, he went to Columbia, to study under Dr.
Gregory. He received his doctorate in due course of time, and took his first
job—teaching in the medical school at Bellevue Hospital in New York. In
the midst of this academic year, which was especially strenuous, his big
opportunity came and was seized, according to Romer, in the usual
accidental Romerian manner. Let us have it in his own words.

They started feeding me some sort of capsules (for tension). They
probably told me what they were, but I didn't pay any
attention. . . . Well, along came the anatomists' meetings that
spring, in April. They were out at the University of Chicago, and I
went out. God, I was getting sleepy. I tend to go to sleep when peo-
ple read papers at me, but here, even during ones I was really
interested in, I just couldn't stay awake. I was just dopey. Well, they
were looking for a vertebrate paleontologist and heard I was in town.
So I was invited over to lunch by the chairman of the appropriate
department. I was very sleepy, and he started the proposition—could
I come up for a quarter, give a course or two—(yawn) I wasn't sure—
he went on, could I come out and give a few lectures—(yawn) I
wasn't too sure about that either. If I had been awake, I would have
jumped at this, but dopey as I was, I didn't jump. Well this blasé
attitude apparently was pretty good, because I no sooner got back to
New York than I got a letter offering me an assistant professorship,
which is one up from instructor. . . . Well, I was sleepier than
ever, so I wrote back "Well, I don't know, this time of year is pretty
late for my boss to get a successor for me, and so forth. Hoping you
are the same." And sent it off. Well, a few days later I came to. I had
gone to sleep in the middle of the morning with my eye on a micro-
scope barrel. I went down and saw the medicine man and said,
"Look here, either I've got sleeping sickness, or else it's whatever

dope I'm taking." He said "You damn fool, don't you know what you're taking?" "No." "Chloretone." And the idea was, as you know it's a nice anesthetic. They thought it might put my large intestine to sleep. Instead, it was putting *me* to sleep, and so they took me off it and I woke up, at which point arrived a telegram offering me an associate professorship. I thought, gee, this has worked out pretty well, I've made two jumps now. Could I play it still further and jump from instructor to full professor? I finally decided not, and signed on the dotted line. So chloretone did it. I don't know if it would work for other people or not. (*Anatomical Record*, volume 189 [1977], pages 314–324.)

To get back to the Texas trip, we made plans and in due course of time (it was autumn) we met in Dallas, arriving there together by train, which was the usual thing in those days. Along with Al came Henry Seton, a proper Bostonian of middle age who had been studying paleontology under Al. At the Dallas station we first of all had to take some time for a search to locate Al's luggage, since he had mislaid his baggage checks. The baggage man kindly allowed us back in the storeroom, where we went up and down aisles between steel storage racks until finally we located the missing bags. Then we took a bus from Dallas to Glen Rose, where we found the museum truck safe and sound, loaded to the gunwales with collecting and camping equipment, and resting on four very flat tires.

We had expected that the tires would be no good, so we had procured a government order for new tires, and this we showed to the local garage man, much to his amusement. "It's a nice piece of paper," said he, "but do you think I am going to find any tires? Anyway, I'm going to Dallas on Wednesday, and I'll try."

Then on Wednesday afternoon the garage man appeared with a set of shiny new tires, all ready to put on our truck. It was a mere fluke that he found them in Dallas, for they were an odd size and hardly to be expected in those war years, when shortages of all goods prevailed. The next day he put them on the truck and we were ready for business. The truck was a rattley-bang old piece of automotive equipment, but for the remainder of our trip in that car, people would gather around wherever we stopped, to admire our tires.

We went to the various localities where Al had collected fossils in previous years, to study the sediments and pick up any odd bones we might find. We did find some things, including a tolerable skull of the Permian reptile *Dimetrodon*—the queer reptile with a huge sail on its back, and as I had hoped, there were many conversations with Al about reptilian anatomy and evolution.

Those conversations with Al, more often than not filling in the evenings after a satisfying meal, in turn after an autumnal day in the Permian Red Beds of Texas, were particularly important parts of my introduction to the Mesozoic. Since Al was a superb anatomist especially devoted to the reptiles of Upper Paleozoic and Mesozoic sediments, he had much to say about the relationships of these ancient and often very queer-looking fossils, specifically as revealed by the nature of their skull bones. Here I was, at the beginning of my transition from a mammalian paleontologist, when my attention had been notably engaged with the intracacies of tooth patterns, to a reptilian paleontologist, facing a new set of circumstances where teeth were of lesser importance and where the jigsaw-puzzle-like patterns of skulls bones (so often fused in the mammals) would be of prime consideration, and here I was, enjoying perceptive introductory remarks to my new field of endeavor from the man who at that time was without doubt the first authority in the world on this subject. It was, one might say, the icing on the cake of our Texas trip.

But conversations with Al were by no means limited to the arcane subject of the reptile skull. Al was separated from me by a time gap (approximately nine years) of the same magnitude that divided me from my brother Phil, and thus I felt when I was with Al rather like a younger sibling, seeing him with the same eyes and listening to him with the same ears which in earlier times had learned about a world just a small step removed above and beyond the world of my own intimate experiences. Al had a repertoire of songs not unlike those that Phil had sung when he was home from college, songs such as:

> Let's all go right down to Mary Ann's
> And tickle a tune upon the pianola!
> There's always something nice,
> It's always on the ice
> You never have to ask her for a drink of Cola-Cola.

(Do modern young folks know what a pianola is, or was? It was a prime source of entertainment before the days of hi-fi records, radio, and TV. Indeed, Scott hauled a pianola to the Antarctic on his 1910 expedition, and it graced the expedition hut at Cape Evans.)

Al's store of comic songs and stories was seemingly unlimited, and he was always ready to oblige any audience, large or small. There was the occasion when Al was scheduled to give a lecture at one of our major universities, and as might be expected the auditorium was packed. But no one had a key to the projection booth, and Al *did* need the slides for his lecture. So while a search party was sent out to locate a key, an expedition that occupied the better part of an hour, Al kept the audience enthralled and happy by singing songs, telling stories, and in general putting on an act that might be designated as first-class vaudeville theater.

Once, when Al was an overnight guest at our house, Charles Bogert and his wife, Martha (or Micky, as she preferred to be called), arrived to have dinner with us. Al was really in good form at dinner, telling us among other things about his first fossil expedition to the West, when he joined Paul Miller, the fossil preparator at the University of Chicago (where Al had just received his appointment; see his account on a previous page), at Harrison, Nebraska. On his way to Harrison his old Model T Ford balked in the Ozarks because there was water in the gas, he went to a farmhouse for help, got chased over a fence by the dog, sat on his watch and smashed it, spent the last morning before Harrison arguing with himself as to whether he should spend his final fifty cents for coffee and a doughnut or for enough gas to get him to his destination, and once in Harrison set the town on fire. This last needs a little explanation. It seems that Al and Paul Miller were allowed to sleep in an old store in Harrison, a small western hamlet full of wooden buildings. On the first morning after breakfast Al went out to the outhouse, sat down and lit his pipe and threw the match down the other hole. But the place had not been used for years, it was very dry, and the first thing Al knew he began to feel very warm. The first thing Paul saw was Al leaping out of the outhouse, pursued by flames, and it took the two of them, armed with shovels, a good deal of violent effort to throw enough dirt on the spreading flames to avert a catastrophe. At our dinner party, by the end of this tale Micky Bogert was so overcome that she had to lie down on the floor to recover some semblance of poise.

Al's inhibitions were not of the sort to restrain him. I remember the time when he came to New York, and I took him down the corridor at the museum to see George Simpson. Simpson had just been installed in a new office of (for a museum curator) sophisticated elegance, with a deep carpet on the floor, a shining big desk, curtains on the windows, and so on. The sight dazzled Al, so much so that he immediately went down on his knees and salaamed before Simpson, who was a little taken aback by such behavior. All of which caused me to chide Al for not behaving as a Harvard professor should behave, but Al claimed he was right in the groove, so far as Harvard professors are concerned.

My remembrances of Al Romer are all pleasant. His was a blithe spirit, untrammeled by the conventions of office or of society, and that very much suited my way of looking at things. We had a lot of fun together.

In looking over my field book, more than forty years later, I see that we went to twenty-one Permian localities during the course of our Texas trip, and *that*, so far as I was concerned, made the venture highly satisfactory—scientifically speaking.

The ostensible purpose of our trip was to get the truck and its contained cargo back to New York, so after poking around in the Texas Red Beds for a couple of weeks we started back on the long trek to the East. (Henry had left us before we began our homeward journey; he found the cold autumnal nights of Texas not quite to his liking.)

It was a long and tiring trip; the springs of our truck—Geraldine we called it—had become flat and lifeless during the two or three years that it had rested in the Glen Rose storage garage, weighted down with a heavy load of equipment. Consequently we bumped along at very moderate speeds over rough and winding roads, and consequently we both arrived at our respective homes with very sore backs. Indeed, we were bothered for several years afterwards with bad backs (for some time I had to wear a brace), all as a result of that trip in Geraldine. I should add that the journey home, tiring as it proved to be, was enlivened for me by Al's railroad talk. After high school he had worked for a year as a railroad clerk, and had become very interested in the railroads of North America. So as we chugged our way eastward, he would go into a long digression at every railroad crossing, telling me the course of that particular line, its history, and its present fortunes. All of which helped to ease the tedium of the ride. Perhaps the adventure was not worth its physical cost, but I never heard Al express any regrets about it. As for me, it was one of the most delightful paleontological trips that ever I have taken.

Al Romer and I went to Texas during October and November of 1943, and once I was again settled in our New Jersey domicile and at the museum in New York, I mentally prepared myself for a long sojourn at home and in the office without any further journeys. The war raged and people on the home front were largely confined within their immediate surroundings. Yet in 1944 I was destined to take another trip involving especially interesting experiences.

One day that year I was reading a paper recently published by Raymond B. Cowles, of the University of California at Los Angeles (the man under whom Chuck Bogert, my associate at the American Museum, had received his graduate training), in which he (Cowles) maintained that the extinction of the dinosaurs may have been brought about by a world-wide increase in temperatures in late Cretaceous time. Now this was contrary to the widely held view of paleontologists that the disappearance of the dinosaurs might have been caused in part by the onset of relatively cool world-wide temperatures near the end of the Cretaceous period. I therefore took it upon myself to write to Professor Cowles about this, and we exchanged letters back and forth for some time arguing our viewpoints.

Ray had for many years been involved in the study of temperature tolerances in reptiles, and he was impressed by the fact that these animals, which are "cold-blooded" or ectothermic animals, having no internal mechanism for maintaining a constant body temperature and therefore deriving their body temperature from the environment in which they live, are very sensitive to high temperatures. We often think of reptiles as lovers of the sun, and this may be true up to a point. In the morning, after a cool night, reptiles may come out into the sun to bask, thereby raising their body temperatures to an optimum level, but from that point on the sun can be their enemy. Prolonged exposure to the sun can raise the core body temperature to a fatal level; therefore after basking and obtaining the temperature they like, reptiles commonly retreat into shady places or into the water to enjoy their newly established comfort. Ray, however, was interested in more than body temperature and individual survival; it was his thesis that the raising of world temperatures at the end of Cretaceous times may have adversely affected the reproductive cells of the dinosaurs in a manner that ultimately brought about their extinction.

I was still doubtful, so I suggested to Ray and to Charles Bogert that we get together and experiment with some alligators (the crocodilians being the living reptiles closest in their relationships to the dinosaurs) and they agreed. Those were the days long before modern theories of dinosaurian extinction; they were also the days long before modern arguments about hot-blooded and cold-blooded dinosaurs. Admittedly our thinking along these lines was remarkably restricted compared with the ideas that today are being bruited about, but then we were living in the pioneer days of dinosaur ecology theory.

Plans were made, and a Florida trip was projected for August and September of 1944.

In the meantime Margaret and I had been overjoyed by the birth of our fourth son, Daniel, an event occurring on March 28 of that year. The evening before, Margaret realized that he was on his way, so our good neighbors Tom and Grace Ierardi hauled us across the George Washington Bridge, once again to the Columbia-Presbyterian Medical Center. Grace felt that it was time for a girl, so she had a warm blanket to wrap around Margaret, with a large pink ribbon pinned to it; it was no use, Danny most definitely was not a girl. His appearance within our family made our days at home very busy ones indeed, yet Margaret, being the person she was, agreed to our Florida adventure. She certainly knew how to cope.

Ray came east in August to stay with the Bogerts, and he visited us in our home. Margaret and I immediately became entranced and delighted with him; for me it was the beginning of a long and close friendship that to this day remains a shining memory. Ray was a most unusual person, an original and sometimes an unorthodox thinker, a zoologist with a rich and varied background that provided him with a depth of scientific experience. He had been born and raised in southern Africa, in Natal, in the days when one still traveled by ox-cart, and the years of his boyhood had given him an intimate acquaintance with the wildlife of Africa before the days of tourist safaris and managed game parks. Moreover he had grown up among the Zulus, so he spoke the language fluently. I used to like to get him to talk in Zulu, a click language, and he would cheerfully oblige.

Of course there was a special relationship between Ray and Chuck, that of teacher and student, but one in which there was much for the teacher to learn from his former protégé. Chuck had amassed a truly encyclopedic knowledge of North American reptiles, so Ray was frequently asking Chuck for enlightenment concerning the definitive features of various species, their ranges, habits, and the like, while I lingered on the sidelines trying to soak up as much information as I could.

For the purposes of our project we were fortunate in that the American Museum sponsored the Archbold Biological Field Station in the center of the Florida peninsula, about twenty miles from Sebring. It was a reserve at the time of more than a thousand acres (it has now grown to some six thousand acres) which had been purchased by Richard Archbold, a friend of the museum, and was maintained by him as a locale for biological field studies. Dick, a bachelor, lived at the station, where he made life interesting in various ways.

We took the train to Sebring, where we were met by some of the station staff, waiting to drive us to our destination.

I don't know what I had expected; from Chuck Bogert's description of the station (he had been there on previous occasions) I was prepared to see a rather primitive set-up. Perhaps I got this impression from Chuck because of the somewhat diffident manner in which he told me about the place. Anyway, I was bowled over when we drove along a beautiful drive through the grounds on our way to the center of the station, where Dick greeted us most cordially and introduced us to the facilities. The laboratories and our quarters were in a modern, solidly built building, where we enjoyed all imaginable comforts, including excellent meals prepared by the culinary department of the station staff.

Dick Archbold suffered from narcolepsy, which means that he would suddenly go to sleep at odd times during the day. Often enough at dinner his head would drop forward while he was in the midst of a sentence, and then for a minute or two he would be quite asleep, suddenly to wake up and continue the interrupted sentence. It was harmless enough at dinner, but this physiological manifestation caused problems at other times, especially at those times when Dick decided to drive a car. He did like to drive. There was an elderly Englishman at the station, Mr. Walters—an old family retainer in the Archbold household—and he made it a point to jump into the seat by the driver whenever Dick decided to take the wheel of the car. Mr. Walters would grab the wheel if Dick went to sleep; in addition he kept up a lively flow of conversation while Dick was driving. Since we had occasion to go in the car with Dick on several trips, life at such times took on exciting if not terrifying aspects. Yet Dick had no intention of frightening us; he was, as has been said, a kind and thoughtful person.

Our purpose was to test temperature tolerances in alligators, and for this we obtained a series of these reptiles, ranging in size from babies only recently hatched, to rather large individuals. It would have been nice if we might have had a really big alligator, but how we might have handled it is something to think about. As it so happened, a moderately large male alligator wandered into the station one night, and we welcomed him enthusiastically—if not with open arms. He fulfilled our need for an alligator of considerable size, so we promoted him to the head of the class, occupying an unchallenged position as the top sergeant in our graded series of alligators.

The alligators were kept in a series of outdoor pens; the big male was isolated in a large enclosure with a pool in the middle of it, where he was monarch of his domain. Sometimes at night we would walk over to his cage for a check, and the first thing we would see were his two ruby-red glowing eyes reflected in the light of our electric torches. Then we would hear a series of loud hisses and immediately after there would be a furious charge as he hit the fence with all of his strength. All of which was exciting, but it raised the problem on the first night of such an occurrence as to how we were to capture him for our experiments.

The next morning we went into the enclosure, Chuck carrying a long bamboo pole with a rope noose at its end. The idea was to slip the noose over the saurian's neck, pull the rope tight, and thus secure the alligator for our purposes. Chuck carefully extended the pole with its noose while our subject glared balefully at us, but as soon as the noose went around his neck all hell broke loose—as the saying goes. The alligator grabbed the pole with his powerful jaws and started whirling over and over in the water, splashing spray high in the air. In a trice the bamboo pole was reduced to splinters, although Chuck manfully held on to his end of it. Ray and I in the meantime retreated to positions somewhat removed, all the while cheering Chuck for his noble effort. Well— *that* technique was ruled out.

We finally developed a strategy that proved to be successful. First we would entice the alligator out of the pool onto dry land. Then one of us would approach him from the front to get and hold his attention, a second member of the team would grab his tail and hold on for dear life, while the third member would jump on his back and push his head down on the ground. Then the front man, who had been occupying the attention of the saurian, would rush forward with a short piece of rope, which all the time he had been holding, and tie the reptile's jaws shut. After that he was our prisoner, to do what we would with him; he might struggle, but those fearful jaws were secured. It should be explained that the alligators and their allies have tremendously powerful muscles for closing their jaws, but only two weak muscles, the *depressor mandibulae,* for opening the jaws.

It should be added that the other alligators in our series, being smaller, were comparatively easy to handle.

We subjected those poor alligators to all sorts of indignities; we put them out in the Florida sun, we exposed them to sunlight in "dinosaur poses" by tying them to frames made for the purpose so that some of them stood on their hind legs with their bodies at an angle to the ground, thus simulating the stance of the large carnivorous dinosaurs; we put them in constant-temperature chambers; we put them in tanks of water and then ran hot water in so that the water in the tanks gradually became warmer, and we noted the sequence in which they left the tanks; we put them in tanks and added ice, to see their reaction to cold water; and all through these exercises we took their temperatures at stated intervals by thrusting specially made thermometers into their cloacal openings—which in mammals would be called their rectums.

The results of our experiments showed that the larger alligators heated up and cooled off more slowly than the smaller ones, the rates of their temperature gains and losses being directly proportional to their body masses. Also we found out that their preferred body temperatures, as established by their freely chosen behavior patterns, were only a few degrees below lethal temperatures. Lethal temperature for an alligator is 38 degrees centigrade or 100 degrees Fahrenheit—this we knew—and the preferred temperature we found to be about 34 degrees centigrade. At this temperature level they were vigorous and active—for a reptile.

Perhaps we did not learn much about temperatures and the extinction of dinosaurs, but we did have something to think about. If our largest alligator took a certain amount of time to raise its body temperature a degree when in the sunlight, and another certain amount of time to lose a degree of body temperature in the shade, how might this bear upon temperatures and behavior in dinosaurs? Would it not be possible that in the giant dinosaurs incomparably larger than our largest alligator, the increment and the loss of body heat would be so slow that these animals, although technically "cold-blooded," might have had the essential attribute of a "warm-blooded" animal—that is a more or less constant body temperature—without having to pay the price of warm-bloodedness in terms of the amount of food consumed? We set forth this possibility in the paper we published, and that was long before the dinosaurian "warm-blooded–cold-blooded" debate had erupted. Perhaps our work was of some significance; it was certainly gratifying to see it referred to recently as a "seminal contribution."

This work, coming a year after my Texas trip with Al Romer, was in effect a continuation of my initiation into the world of ancient reptiles. Working with the alligators as we did afforded us, I felt, some insight into the way that dinosaurs might have behaved. It is sometimes fashionable these days to picture dinosaurs in mammalian terms, and very probably these ancient reptiles were often active in a sort of mammalian fashion. But they were reptiles, and it seems to me that close observation of crocodilian behavior gives us valid clues as to dinosaurian activity. Our Florida alligators did not hesitate to get up on all four legs and walk or run about, and we found from our sometimes painful encounters with them that they could be very quick indeed. (In this connection, it is interesting to note that recently the distinguished herpetologist Carl Gans published photographs of *galloping* crocodiles in Australia. Also it should be noted that recent field observations have shown other advanced traits in the crocodilians—strong maternal behavior for example.) In short, the dinosaurs did not necessarily have to be "warm-blooded" in order to behave in a warm-blooded fashion.

Not all of our activities in Florida were devoted to temperature tolerances in alligators. One fine day the lot of us, including Dick Archbold, traveled for some miles along the Calasahootchie River in a motor boat, in part to look at the very late Pleistocene or sub-Recent fossils that were to be found along the banks of this waterway. In the afternoon as we were motoring along we saw something sticking up out of the water, so several of us doffed our clothing and went in to see what the object might be. Imagine our surprise, when we yanked and tugged at it until it came loose from the river bottom, to find ourselves in possession of a large leg bone (the ulna) of a mastodon. This inspired us to more underwater probing, with the result that we dredged up several big mastodon bones—the remains of a proboscidean, a cousin of the elephants, that had roamed across Florida perhaps as recently as eight or ten thousand years ago. This little adventure provided a nice interlude in our alligator work.

The Florida experience was scientifically rewarding, and it gave the three of us many pleasant reminiscences in the years to come. We ended the summer by returning to our respective bases, but my contacts with Ray Cowles were to continue through the years. Of course I saw Chuck Bogert all of the time during our daily activities at the museum. Some months after Florida and the alligators, he served as godfather to our little Danny.

The war was rising to its climax during that winter of 1944 and the following spring, with the result that scientific research was necessarily very restricted. For those of us in paleontology this meant particularly that field studies were almost impossible, because field studies depended upon the use of cars, and one had to have very compelling reasons to obtain the necessary gasoline for anything beyond "essential" driving.

In the spring of 1945 I received an invitation to teach the summer course in paleontology at the University of California at Berkeley, while at the same time Chuck Bogert got an invitation to teach at the University of California at Los Angeles. We made our plans, proposing to drive across country in Chuck's car and arranging our route so that he could drop me off in Berkeley and then go on to Los Angeles. We made an application for fuel to the rationing board, and although they considered our request valid they very parsimoniously allotted gas coupons that would allow us just enough fuel to get there. For that we were thankful. As things turned out it *was* a tight squeeze, and we made it only by coasting down long hills as we went west. But all in all it was a very pleasant trip. There was little traffic on the highways, and the law required us to drive at no more than thirty-five miles an hour (which indeed we were forced to do in order to get there on our gasoline allotment) so we loafed across the land with ample time to see the sights. Not long before we departed on our journey the war in Europe came to an end, and that had the effect of easing travel restrictions later on in the summer.

My summer in Berkeley was to be spent with Margaret's mother and her stepfather, Dr. Ralph Minor, a retired professor of physics at the university. It proved to be a most pleasant time. The Minor house (the house in which Margaret had lived with her family for four years while she attended art school in Oakland) was just up the hill from the North Gate of the campus, which made it very convenient for me. Every afternoon, right after lunch I taught the class, but beyond that my days were free for me to follow my own inclinations.

Those inclinations involved the study of fossils, especially the fossils of Triassic reptiles in the university collections. I had earlier described some phytosaur materials from Pennsylvania, and so I turned part of my attention to phytosaurs at the Museum of Paleontology, the phytosaurs being thecodont reptiles that lived in late Triassic times, during the interval when the first dinosaurs were becoming established on the earth. The early dinosaurs were small reptiles, generally only a few feet in length (although there were a few moderate giants), so the phytosaurs, which were large crocodilelike reptiles, truly ruled the continents in many parts of the earth. Even though the phytosaurs were similar in appearance to crocodiles, so similar indeed that the resemblances are uncanny, they were not crocodilian ancestors. Rather, they were descended from earlier Triassic thecodonts, as were the crocodiles, but whereas the crocodilians persisted to become very successful reptiles, outlasting the dinosaurs and living on into our modern world, the phytosaurs became extinct at the close of Triassic time. Why one line should succeed and the other not is one of those puzzling problems of paleontology. The close resemblances of the two groups of reptiles constitute a prime example of evolutionary parallelism, a phenomenon whereby two or more lines of development branch from a common ancestor to follow similar but separate evolutionary paths.

As I studied the phytosaurs in Berkeley I was impressed by the number of specimens that had been collected at Ghost Ranch, New Mexico. I duly noted the fact, little realizing that Ghost Ranch was to play a very large role in my life in years to come.

The phytosaurs of Ghost Ranch and elsewhere were one part of a general research program that had been developing in my thinking during the past year or so—a program devoted to the amphibians and reptiles, but more specifically as I have suggested to the reptiles that had lived during Triassic times. This plan had its beginnings to some degree during my Texas trip with Al Romer, when frequently we talked about research on fossil reptiles, and increasingly it took form as time passed by. It seemed to me that for the student of vertebrate evolution the land-living animals that had inhabited the Triassic scene are of particular significance. This is because so far as amphibians and reptiles are concerned the Triassic was truly a time of transition, a time when the old lines of evolutionary development as characterized by such animals as the labyrinthodont amphibians, the primitive cotylosaurian reptiles, and the progressive mammallike reptiles— some of which were direct ancestors of the first Triassic mammals—were giving way to the new evolutionary lines as embodied in the first anurans or frogs and the varied thecodont reptiles, some of these in turn ancestral to the dinosaurs, the flying reptiles, and the crocodiles. These latter were the animals destined to rule the continents for the duration of the Mesozoic, a time span of almost two hundred million years.

During that summer in Berkeley I also shared my thoughts with Charles Camp, one of Romer's fellow students already mentioned on a previous page. He was one of my close friends and a respected advisor, who had devoted much time to reptiles of Triassic age. After finishing his degree under Dr. Gregory, Camp had gone to Berkeley, where among other things he became very much involved with Triassic phytosaurs. In the years immediately after the First World War, a conflict in which both he and Romer had served, he spent many summer months working in the Petrified Forest of Arizona, where he made a collection of phytosaurs that he subsequently described in a large and handsome monograph. Also he and his colleagues worked at Ghost Ranch; they had collected the phytosaurs I saw at Berkeley.

It might be added that there were close family connections between our family and the Camp family. In 1927 Margaret's father, after a long career at the American Museum, retired from that institution to accept a position as chairman of a newly organized Department of Paleontology at Berkeley. There he worked closely with Camp and his colleagues. And Margaret, a young student at the California College of Arts and Crafts in Oakland, had frequently spent her spare hours taking care of the Camp children. So Charles Camp was interested in my future plans in a more than casual manner.

While I was still in Berkeley the atomic bombs were dropped on Japan, thus bringing to a close the Second World War. Soon after that, my teaching assignment completed, I took the train to Arizona, where I met Charles and his wife, Jessie, who had already driven there. (As I have remarked, gasoline restrictions had become less restrictive.) There we spent some time in the field together, going over possibilities, and I made plans to come out the next summer to start my campaign of Triassic field work. When I parted company with the Camps in Gallup, New Mexico, they to drive back to Berkeley, I to take the train home, I had some reasonably definite ideas as to what I hoped to do in the next few years.

The phytosaurs that I had studied in Berkeley, and then this little trip through the Triassic of Arizona with Charles and Jessie Camp, did much to influence my immediate, detailed plans for research, just as a couple of years earlier my conversations with Al Romer in Texas had helped me to shape my larger, comprehensive plans. Furthermore, the trip with the Camps enabled me to get acquainted with them in a more intimate manner than had been possible through my casual contacts with them while I was teaching during the summer at the university.

Margaret, as just mentioned, had known the Camps since her art school days in California; I first met them during the summer of 1935, when they came to New York on the first leg of a year-long trip they were making to South Africa. In those days they were of course traveling by ship, and one day we, along with various friends, went down to the waterfront to see them off. Among the people gathered to wish them a good voyage was Archie Roosevelt, the son of Teddy, and evidently one of Charles's acquaintances. We had a jolly time, the jollity being enhanced especially by the offhand remarks made by Jessie, a truly original character.

Charles was a rather elegant person, tall and well-built, with a rugged countenance and with a shock of thick hair that with a little encouragement might have stood up like the crest of a blue jay. Indeed, Charles was a sort of blue jay in human form, a man of often quick, impulsive movement, and quick, impulsive decisions. I remember the story about Camp when he was a graduate student at Columbia and was going through the cafeteria line one day at one of the student dining halls. He had some disagreement with the fellow behind the steam table, whereupon Charles vaulted over the counter, gave his adversary a clip on the side of the head, and vaulted back to continue his progress down the line. He was not a violent person, merely a young man of decided action. Of course when I knew him he had mellowed, yet even so he had definite opinions about the world around him.

All of the Camp children, as well as their parents, were frequently doing things along unconventional lines, so the Camp household was a lively place. Margaret once happened to visit the household before there was a house; there was merely a plot of land on a hillside in Orinda, on the eastern flank of the Berkeley hills. A little trail wound up the hillside; dug into the hill there was set a wood stove, while at each turning of the trail was a bed. At one side, enclosed by the framing for the house, was a little shack, containing a bathroom and a telephone; in this fashion the Camps were living, gypsy fashion, waiting for the house to be built around them. It was a nice plan, since all of this was in the California summer dry season, except that when Margaret was there a light drizzle was soaking the open-air beds. That didn't especially bother the Camps; they were delightfully cavalier about their life style and about the consequences of how they managed their affairs.

When I was there the house was in place and a very nice house it was. I spent a weekend with the Camps, and I will always remember sitting out in front of their house and watching the fog from San Francisco roll over the tops of the Berkeley hills, to dissipate in long, sinuous streamers as it encountered the dry air of the inner valley.

I feel that I was fortunate in having known both Al Romer and Charles Camp. Both had preceded me by about eight or nine years as students of Dr. Gregory, so we had a common bond between us in that respect. They were both outstanding paleontologists, and from both of them I learned much about the fossils in which I was interested. Both were delightful persons, original and lively, and of course very different—each from the other. The days spent with Romer and with Camp were memorable days.

Footnote. Charles Camp, a man of varied interests, lived two professional lives. He was a noted authority on fossil reptiles, especially, as we have seen, those of Triassic age. But in addition he became a respected student of western history, and in his later years he contributed many important papers devoted to the early exploration and settlement of California and the West.

The thoughts that I had shared with Charles Camp during that summer in Berkeley, and the phytosaur specimens that I had studied in the University of California collections, strengthened my resolve to devote my energies, at least for the foreseeable future, to the fascinating problems of

Triassic life. At first I envisaged a program that would include the collecting of and research on Triassic amphibians and reptiles from the southwestern United States, supplemented by work on fossils found along the Atlantic seaboard "close to home." Time was to see my efforts expand into a world-wide effort, as will be told later.

It should be explained at this place that my plans, although including field explorations and studies as their base, embraced far more than the search for fossils. I was thinking in terms of a research program, and research involves many activities—paleontologically speaking (as has been outlined in Chapter VII), the search for fossils, the interpretation of their field relationships, the technical preparation of specimens in the laboratory, the comparative study of the fossils (a long and exacting exercise), the description and illustration of the specimens, and finally, and of particular importance, published descriptions of the research. This last item needs particular emphasis and explanation, because as Professor Alcock, quoted on page 125 above, has so succinctly stated, "the date of a discovery is the date of its publication." In short, research is useless until it has been published, thereby making its results available to the world.

And the scientific publications from a particular pen eventually determine the worth of a scientist. He or she may do many worthwhile things, but the truly important contributions are their publications, and above all their research papers. These, needless to say, are of many kinds and of varying significance. There are the outright descriptive papers that form the nitty-gritty base for the science—in the case of paleontology descriptions of fossils and of associations of fossils, and their relationships to the sediments in which they occur. Such papers do not necessarily make for interesting reading, indeed they often may be most pedestrian in nature. But they are necessary; without them we would lack the factual bases upon which to build our scientific structures. Then there are the interpretive papers which attempt to give wider meanings to the fossils—to their biological and geological relationships. And there are the theoretical works that launch themselves into empyrean heights, sometimes with good reason, sometimes with no reason at all. All such contributions are needed to make the science viable, and the well-tempered paleontologist more often than not is the author of contributions in all of these several categories.

Yet in spite of the appeal of interpretive papers and the glamor of theoretical contributions, the old-fashioned, unfashionable, basic, factual papers are the ones that live. In this respect I am reminded of the great American paleontologist Edward Drinker Cope, whose genius shone like a beacon during the latter half of the nineteenth century. He published voluminously and he had many original interpretations and theories, but today the value of his work is in the descriptions he published of fossil vertebrates of all kinds. His more theoretical papers are almost all resting ignored in the ashcans of discarded scientific ideas. Such will probably be the fate of many paleontological ideas that now are attracting so much attention, not only among paleontologists, but in certain cases among the general public as well. (One need only mention the present-day furor over the extinction of the dinosaurs.)

This is not to say that interpretive and theoretical papers should not be written; they are extraordinarily useful in stirring up arguments, indeed in stirring up tempers, and making people think about the inherent problems of paleontology and geology. But they should be accepted for what they are, and in judging them in a certain scientific perspective should be maintained.

My remarks may be those of an old man, but it seems to me that there is perhaps less freedom of expression in scientific papers than there used to be, which I think is a side effect of what is now called peer review. In the good old days a paleontologist wrote a scientific paper expressing his ideas about the fossils under his purview, and provided it was in reasonably good shape it was edited for grammar and consistency and was published. Undoubtedly there were some bad papers as a result, but they were expressions of individual efforts and views.

Today it is the practice for every scientific paper to be "judged" by the author's peers, which is good and bad. Certainly some howling errors are prevented from seeing the light of day, and frequently and quite rightly the author is asked to look more fully into certain aspects of his subject. But there is an obvious effect of scientific homogenization apparent. I often wonder what might have happened if Robert Broom, the brilliant and eccentric South African paleontologist, had been subjected to the kind of criticism that is now embodied in peer reviews. The fireworks would have lit up the sky all around the Cape of Good Hope.

And as a matter of fantasy, I wonder what would have happened if Shakespeare had been subjected to peer review. Act V of *Macbeth:* "To-morrow, and to-morrow, and to-morrow/Creeps in this petty pace from day to day . . ." Forsooth, Master Will, does one need so many to-morrows and days? Would not one of each suffice?

This has been a considerable digression, but I hope it points up the fact that for research scientists (in the present instance a paleontologist), the publication of his or her studies in proper scientific journals is the very breath of life. How such papers are published matters very much to the scientific author. More general papers and books are fine; they give the paleontologist an opportunity to indulge in speculation and to let off steam in all sorts of ways. But the basic scientific contributions are the things that count; they survive through the decades as gifts to posterity.

Such being the case, the paleontologist writes his research papers with the greatest of preparation and care. They are not dashed off; they require long and detailed examinations and comparisons of fossils, protracted searches through the literature and the study of papers published throughout the world in various languages, as often as not trips to other museums than the one in which the author resides to study and compare pertinent collections, the preparation of illustrations by photography and by an artist or two or three (few paleontologists have the artistic ability to execute their own drawings), and as often as not protracted correspondence and discussions with colleagues concerning the problem at hand. Thus a ten-page scientific paper may represent untold hours of work, not only by the author but also by people who may be working with him.

To give a feeling of some reality to the above remarks I propose to give an actual example of a paleontological study, a study of the usual bread-and-butter kind, and what went into it. For this purpose I use a study of my own, made a number of years ago, mainly because I quite naturally have a first-hand, intimate knowledge of it.

In 1960 three high school boys, Alfred Siefker, Joseph Geiler, and Michael Bandrowski, found a piece of Upper Triassic shale containing a fossil while exploring in an old quarry in North Bergen, New Jersey. The Granton Quarry, as it is known, is located across the Hudson River from Manhattan, about three miles in an air-line northwest of the American Museum of Natural History, thus being perhaps the fossil locality closest to the museum. They brought the specimen to the museum for identification, and it naturally fell to my lot to identify the fossil.

In contrast to most specimens brought in for appraisal, this fossil was immediately recognized as something important. The boys quite naturally at first wanted to hold on to the fossil, but eventually they agreed that the specimen should be placed in a scientific institution. So it was catalogued in the American Museum collections, and I undertook the task of studying and describing it.

It was a small and fragile specimen, imbedded in a black shale, and when first found was partially covered by the rock matrix in which it was preserved. Gil Stucker of the museum paleontological preparation laboratory undertook the delicate task of cleaning the specimen, a task made possible in large part by the use of a piece of modern technological equipment—an "Airdent" machine with which the preparator could direct a fine stream of dry air through a minute nozzle at those parts of the fossil needing attention, this airstream being charged with an abrasive. For our purposes powdered dolomite was used. After several months of close work (one of the early stages in the sequence of paleontological discovery work that have been outlined on a previous page) the fossil was ready for study and description.

It was the fossilized skeleton of a little lizard of sorts, about four inches in length from the tip of the skull to the pelvis. Most of the tail and the hind feet were missing, but otherwise the skeleton was complete. The bones were slender and delicate, and what was most remarkable about this fossil was the elongation of the ribs, ten on each side, so that the longest of them, number three and four in the series, considerably exceeded the distance from the tip of the nose to the pelvis. Here was a remarkably early specialization for a reptile of this kind (indeed, this is one of the earliest of lizardlike reptiles), a specialization quite obviously to provide this ancient animal with a "wing." There could be no doubt about the nature of the specialization, because there is a modern lizard known as *Draco*, living in the Orient, in which the ribs are elongated to support a membrance of skin, thus providing the lizard with a "wing" for gliding. In *Draco* only five ribs are elongated to support the wing membrane, and they are not lengthened to anything like the degree that the fossil ribs are elongated. Even so *Draco* can glide for as much as sixty yards between trees; moreover it can control the direction and to a considerable degree the vertical components of its glide. Thus *Draco* launches itself from one tree, glides in a rather flat trajectory toward another tree, and just before arriving swoops *up* to its landing point on the trunk of the tree to which it had directed its flight.

My good friend and colleague Dr. Pamela Robinson, of the University of London, had earlier described a similar gliding lizard from the Upper Triassic sediments of the Bristol Channel in England. Pamela named her little glider *Kuehneosaurus* (it had been found by a paleontologist named Walter Kuehne); I named the new glider *Icarosaurus siefkeri*. Icarus was the son of Daedelus; the two of them according to Greek legend had been imprisoned on the island of Crete from which they wished to escape. So Daedelus manufactured wings, the surface of which were covered with feathers attached by wax to the wing structures. They flew from Crete to the mainland, but Icarus, an adventurous youth, flew too high, the sun melted the wax, his wings disintegrated, and he fell into the sea. *Icarosaurus* was discovered in sediments that once covered the bottom of a large lake in what is now New Jersey, and like Icarus the little reptile had evidently fallen from the sky into a watery resting place. *Saurus* means lizard. *Siefkeri*, as is evident, was named for one of the boys who found the specimen.

An interesting thing about *Icarosaurus* is that the ribs are so arranged as to form a very nice wing, much more efficient than the wing of the modern *Draco*. The first rib is straight, thus forming a leading edge; the ribs that follow are curved to form a camber. Therefore the wing had a convex upper surface and a concave lower surface, which provided the lift needed for efficient gliding.

These facts and many more came out of my study of the fossil. For instance, the skull, a crucial part of the skeleton for understanding the relationships of the fossil, was composed of a jumble of bones piled in disarray. In order to understand the skull I made replicas of the bones in a plastic material and then assembled them until I got a proper-looking skull. Moreover, with the help of Gil Stucker I made a model of *Icarosaurus* and he cast it in fiberglass. Then I took the model to Columbia University where I submitted it to two aeronautical engineers, and together we discussed and analyzed the wings as they had been reconstructed by Gil and myself. The engineers agreed that *Icarosaurus* had a very nice wing indeed. Here we were looking at one of the first vertebrates to attempt aerial locomotion; true enough it did not fly, but it must have been a very efficient glider.

Of course all of the things I have been describing took a lot of time and study, especially comparisons of *Icarosaurus* with *Kuehneosaurus* and *Draco*. But finally, in 1966, I published my first paper on *Icarosaurus*, an American Museum *Novitates* (a scientific series established by Professor Osborn for the publication of preliminary studies and short contributions) of twenty-three pages, entitled "A Gliding Reptile from the Triassic of New Jersey," illustrated with seven photographs made by Chester Tarka, scientific photographer for our department, and three simple line drawings, made by Michael Insinna, departmental illustrator.

But this was only the beginning. My studies were continuing, and among other things I essayed to make a careful dissection of the "wing" of *Draco*. This I did, describing the arrangement of muscles and ligaments that controlled the wings of *Draco*, not only allowing this little lizard to fold the wings neatly over the back when it is climbing around in trees, but also to spread them for gliding when it so desires. In addition I made studies of wing loading in *Draco*, comparing the figures obtained with the figures for wing loading in soaring birds. Advice was obtained from herpetologists and ornithologists during the course of my work on this paper, as well as from the aeronautical engineers at Columbia University. This paper, entitled "Adaptations for Gliding in the Lizard *Draco*," was published in 1967 as an American Museum *Novitates*, twenty pages, with illustrations again by Mike Insinna.

All of this time I was working on a larger contribution, a detailed study of *Icarosaurus* embodying comparisons with *Kuehneosaurus* and *Draco*. Again, or rather concurrently, advice was afforded me by the experts in other fields of study. The final result was an American Museum *Bulletin* of fifty-eight pages, published in 1970, entitled "The Triassic Gliding Reptile *Icarosaurus*," with illustrations by Tarka and Insinna, as well as drawings by Jennifer Perrott.

So in the end this study involved ten years of time, on and off, with advice from six scientific colleagues, with technical preparation that required several months of work, and with artistic help from a scientific photographer and two illustrators. The result was a total of one hundred and one pages of description published in three scientific contributions.

That is the sort of effort upon which the paleontologist bases his or her career and his or her reputation. As can be seen, it is a cooperative effort; nothing could be accomplished without the assistance of many other people. With such work on the part of the principal investigator, advisors, technicians, and artists, the paleontological base for other studies—popular, theoretical, and the like—is created.

It is only fair that the several people involved in the *Icarosaurus* study should be mentioned.

Dr. Pamela Robinson, University of London, who described *Kuehneosaurus*, and who provided advice and illustrations

Dr. Charles M. Bogert, herpetologist at the American Museum of National History

Dr. Walter Bock of Columbia University, ornithologist and anatomist

Dr. Bruno Boley of Columbia University, aeronautical engineer

Dr. Morton B. Friedman of Columbia University, aeronautical engineer

Dr. John R. Hendrickson of the Center for Cultural and Technical Interchange between East and West, Honolulu, Hawaii, who provided photographs and information about *Draco*

Mr. Chester Tarka, staff photographer, Department of Vertebrate Paleontology, American Museum of National History

Mr. Michael Insinna, scientific illustrator, of the above named department

Miss Jennifer Perrott, scientific illustrator, also of the above named department

There is a trend these days for multiple authorship, which may be good or bad. Personally I like to see a paper by one or two or at most three people; then I have an idea of who is saying what. But today multiple authorship may reach ludicrous limits. I recall a lead paper not so long ago, in the journal *Science*, with twenty authors. Out of curiosity I estimated the number of words in the article and discovered that each author (on a shared basis) was responsible for something less than two hundred words. How many good ideas can come from such authorial dilution?

The first year after the war, and of course the first year after my summer in Berkeley when I had enjoyed the sage advice of Charles Camp, I began my pursuit of the Triassic. But again as in 1944, when the birth of Daniel preceded by a few months the scheduling of our Florida project, so in 1946 the birth of our fifth son, Charles, preceded by a few months my plans for a summer of work in the Triassic of the Southwest. (In looking back across the years I marvel at the way in which Margaret put up with my absences when she had small children, sometimes including newly born children, to tend—all my herself. In 1944 there were four boys including a new baby. In 1946 there were to be five boys and again including a new baby.)

Charles was expected late in February, or perhaps early March. On February 26 there was a birthday party up in the Bronx for Bill Thomson, my companion of White River badland days, now retired and living alone. (His wife had died a few years previously.) It was a lonely life for old Bill, and I made it a point to go to the Bronx every now and then for a visit with him in his somewhat cheerless apartment. On that particular evening a group of us at the museum including the Simpsons had arranged to give Bill a nice birthday party, so we foregathered at his place after work. Margaret did not join us; she did not wish to attempt a tiring journey from our New Jersey home to the Bronx. Instead she went out for an evening painting class with some of her artist friends.

I had not been long at Bill's when a telephone call came from a friend who had planned to paint with Margaret that evening, telling me in a very excited voice that she (the friend) was at the Presbyterian Hospital, where she had just delivered Margaret, who in turn was ready to make a delivery on her own account. Needless to say I left the birthday party with all precipitate haste.

By the time I reached the hospital the new baby had arrived, and of course it again was a boy. Margaret was particularly happy because little Charles had come so quickly that Dr. Damon never arrived for the event, which took place on a trolley in the corridor outside the delivery room. It was the first baby she had while she was fully conscious, and for her it was a wonderful event, because in those benighted days the medical profession was going through a phase when it was thought necessary for mothers to be heavily sedated when their babies were born—in a hospital, of course. So Margaret had given birth to four boys without ever being aware of what was going on. Now, at last and only through the force of circumstances, she experienced a natural birth in which she participated with complete awareness. From then until this day she has been put out that she was not allowed to have all of her babies in the time-honored manner that has been the prerogative of mothers since the days of *Pithecanthropus*, and before.

The next morning when I went back to the hospital I found that through a clerical error Margaret and Charles had been assigned to the Harkness Pavilion, instead of to the Sloane wing, where she had spent lying-in with the other babies. All of which made my hair stand on end, because the Harkness Pavilion was the place frequented by such people as Rockefellers and their ilk, and as was the practice at that time, a mother generally spent ten days to two weeks in bed after the birth of a baby. With views of astronomical bills running through my head I went to the office to ask that my wife and baby be transferred to Sloane, but here Dr. Damon intervened. Perhaps he was a bit chagrined by the fact that Charles arrived at the hospital before he did; at any rate he told me that Margaret deserved a break, so he suggested that she stay in Harkness, and he would subtract the difference between the cost of Harkness and Sloane from his bill.

Consequently Margaret had a very quiet vacation at Harkness in a room by herself, where baby Charles was brought in at all too infrequent intervals for her to admire. March, April, and May busily followed in succession, and by the time I was ready to depart for the Southwest Charles was a fully established member of the family.

The previous year, when I had made a quick reconnaissance of paleontological possibilities in company with Charles Camp we had visited the Davis Ranch, near St. Johns, Arizona. There in some exposures of bluish-gray siltstones of the Triassic Chinle Formation, along a little wash, we had found bones in profusion weathering out of the sediments, so that seemed like a promising place for excavations. Also we had visited the Petrified Forest National Monument (as it was then) and talked with some of the National Park Service people about the possibility of paleontological work in the monument during the following season. Thus I had made plans during the winter, reaching an agreement with Mr. Davis to work on his land, and applying for a permit to work in the Petrified Forest.

In June I went to the Davis Ranch, accompanied by George Whitaker and William Fish, two young technicians from our paleontology laboratory at the American Museum. We were equipped with, among other things, a couple of cast-off army jeeps which the museum had obtained from the government as war surplus at a very nominal sum. Mr. Davis gave us the use of a rough but substantial little cabin on the ranch, near our chosen fossil site.

What followed was one of the strange experiences of my paleontological career. Our fossil site, apparently so promising, proved to be almost barren. We probed and we dug and we prospected, yet in spite of the abundance of fossil fragments on the surface we could not find anything of consequence in place in the sediments, the result being that we spent two or three futile weeks at this place with very little to show for our efforts. Obviously what we had encountered was a "lag gravel"—composed of fossils, but fossils that had weathered out through the years and had become concentrated on the surface as a result of the weathering. Perhaps if we had plowed up the whole area to a depth of two or three feet we might have found some worthwhile materials, but such a procedure was impractical.

The paucity of significant fossil bones at the Davis Ranch was not my only frustrating experience that summer; I had another barren exploratory trip, but one with comical overtones. It all began when a barber in St. Johns, this little town being our base of supply for work at the Davis Ranch, told me that he knew of a place some miles out of town where the ground was "covered with bones." This bit of information caused me to prick up my ears, because the area he indicated was in the general vicinity of a locality where, years before, the paleontologists from Berkeley had established a rich Triassic quarry, filled with the bones of a large, tusked mammallike reptile known as *Placerias*. Perhaps we had a lead for another such deposit.

So the three of us, Bill and George and myself, made a date with our friend, whom I will call Jake, to take us out to this locality. He was a middle-aged man who had spent his life in Arizona doing various things. He had spent his earlier years being a cowboy; barbering was an occupation of his later life, when bones and muscles were a bit too brittle and a bit too slack to be pitted against the idiosyncrasies of western horses. But being an old man of the saddle he was very much taken with our jeep, which seemed to him a mechanical counterpart of a horse. (This was the first summer after the war; our ex-army jeep, sturdy but somewhat the worse from hard usage, was still something of an oddity in the civilian world.)

On the appointed day we drove into St. Johns and picked up Jake, and away we went to the place of bones. He was delighted to be riding in the jeep—it was a new and exhilarating experience for him. About twenty miles out of town we left the road at his direction, and made our way through the sand and across bare rock surfaces, all of the time wending a path between the small juniper trees, about twenty feet in height, that covered the landscape. Because of these trees we could not see very far ahead, but old Jake knew where he wanted us to go and kept giving us directions as to what path we should take. (I should add that winding tire tracks wandered off in various directions, the relics of previous excursions into these arid woodlands.) Of course Jake was enjoying himself immensely; for him it was wonderful to be clattering across the terrain at the speed of a horse, without a horse.

Finally we reached our destination, where we saw a little hillside covered with cow bones. "Well," said Jake, "here are your bones." But they weren't the bones I had in mind. Either he did not recognize them as modern cow bones, which seems unlikely, or he misunderstood our purposes and thought that we were after bones of any description. At any rate we were disappointed and he was a bit crestfallen when he saw our disappointment. There was nothing to do but get in the jeep and go back to town.

We got in, but the jeep would not start; like a balky horse it would seem to have decided that enough was enough for one day. What to do? George took the wheel and the rest of us pushed, and by dint of much exertion we finally managed to elicit some half-hearted noises from the motor. Then it took hold, and away went George in the jeep, grinding along like a miniature tank. For some reason the car had decided to run in low gear, four-wheel drive, and that was that. George could not shift it into any other gear.

So he circled around and yelled at us to jump aboard, which we did, and then we were off for a slow, inexorable cross-country ride. We couldn't speed up, and George didn't dare slow down too much for fear of killing the engine. So we drove along, smoothly over bare rock and soft sand, very roughly over the bumpy places.

Then we came to a gate. Bill and I jumped off to open the gate, while George, with old Jake beside him, took off on a circular drive while we got the gate open. It was one of those western gates, a barbed wire affair that was pulled tight to a post by wire loops that encircled the post as well as a matching post that formed the end of the gate. The wire loops were very tight and it took some struggling on our part to slip them off the gatepost and open the gate, and all the while the jeep roared around in a circle among the juniper trees, sending up a great cloud of dust to mark its course. I shall always retain a mental picture of seeing the dust rising above the little trees, and then having the jeep appear with old Jake smiling rather wanly and bumping up and down, and then seeing the jeep disappear again in the trees, the driver and the by now somewhat disillusioned passenger bouncing around in their seats like tenderfoot riders on hard-trotting horses.

After two or three merry-go-round journeys through the trees we got the gate open, the jeep went through, and then the whole process was repeated while we closed the gate. So it went at gate after gate until we finally reached the paved road. Then we ground along into town, where we went into a yard in front of a garage and George drove the car around and around while I talked to the mechanic. He allowed as to how he could fix it, I signaled George, he turned off the ignition, and the jeep came to an abrupt, bone-shaking stop. I think by then old Jake had had enough of jeeps. He went his way and we went ours, which was a trip to the nearest bar for some refreshment while the car was being fixed.

This little adventure points up the fact that paleontologists have to take note of reported discoveries of fossils, yet they must be prepared for disappointments. Nine times out of ten the supposed fossils, described with enthusiasm by the finder, turn out to be duds. Which is why paleontologists prefer to do their own prospecting and to find their own fossils.

The business of jeeps and gates reminds me of an experience suffered by my friend Paul McGrew. He developed a technique of his own for handling western gates when he was alone in a jeep. If there were ruts in the sand on each side of the gate, as was very commonly the case, Paul would put the jeep in extra-low, four-wheel drive, jump off and run ahead of the jeep, open the gate and watch the car go through, its course being maintained by the ruts in which the wheels were confined, close the gate, and then run to catch up with the car and continue on his way. All this was very fine until the day Paul encountered a very difficult gate. He struggled manfully while the jeep menacingly approached, and then at the last moment Paul had to jump aside and watch the jeep take the gate out by the roots. There is more to hunting fossils than climbing along cliffs.

After the Davis Ranch experience we moved on to the Petrified Forest, where for the first time since the work of Charles Camp in the nineteen twenties (if I am not mistaken) a search was made for Triassic amphibians and reptiles. (In the last few years a comprehensive and intense program for the recovery and study of Triassic vertebrates in the Petrified Forest has been prosecuted with the assistance of paleontologists from the University of California at Berkeley and the New Mexico Museum of National History in Albuquerque. But when we worked there in 1946 there had been a long dormant period in the search for fossil vertebrates, during which without much doubt an unknown number of specimens had been destroyed by erosion.)

My interest in the problem of erosion within the Chinle Formation of the Southwest was stimulated by the work we did that summer in the Petrified Forest. Therefore, on the occasion of some subsequent geological studies in the park (the status of Petrified Forest within the National Park System had been upgraded) I decided to see if some measurements of erosion might be made. One particular happening inspired me to make this attempt. During that first summer of work we located one day an excellent fossil of a large amphibian in the Petrified Forest. The discovery was made at about four o'clock in the afternoon, which was too late to try to collect the specimen, so I suggested to my companions that we return the next morning for the fossil. We went to bed with visions of a very pleasant day ahead, excavating and preserving an important, and incidentally an esthetically pleasing, specimen. But during the night there was a violent rainstorm—not where we were camped, but at the site of the fossil. The next day when we arrived the fossil had virtually disappeared; all we could find were scattered fragments here and there along the wash where during the night there had been a rushing flow of muddy water. That incident stuck in my mind.

Consequently, in 1951 when I was working out of the Museum of Northern Arizona in Flagstaff as my summer headquarters, I made arrangements for a series of wooden stakes to be made, each stake with a line incised around its four sides, about two inches from its upper end, and with a number incised above this line. Then the stakes were taken to the Petrified

Forest, and driven into the ground at certain intervals on varying slopes. Thus at one location we set a line of stakes from the top to the bottom of a badland hill and beyond onto the outwash surface at the base of the hill. The stakes, it should be said, were driven into the ground until the incised line around the stake was flush with the surface. Stakes were set in other localities in the forest, as well as in the desert north of Flagstaff.

Five years later the stakes were individually examined to check the amount of erosion that had taken place, and then five years after that the stakes were again checked. Sporadic examinations have been made in the years since then. In summary, it would appear that on the badlands slopes in the Petrified Forest and at other similar locations in the Southwest where the Chinle Formation is exposed as desert hills without vegetation, there is probably an average rate of erosion amounting to one or two centimeters a year. Of course on the flats below the hills there is frequently filling, where sediments are washed down and then deposited.

All of which points to the probability that fossils are constantly being exposed and destroyed by erosion (which of course we already knew from crude observations) so that if paleontological reconnaissance is not carried on at regular intervals in such places many fossils are bound to be lost. The work with the stakes was useful largely in that it gave some idea as to rates of erosion in the deserts of the Southwest.

All of that work was done, as has been said, in subsequent years. During that first summer we looked for fossils and in the course of things located a beautiful phytosaur skull, *in situ* in the side of a little badland hill along a wash. So we spent a morning exposing it, and then in the early afternoon we encased it, according to the usual paleontological practice, in a plaster jacket.

At about this point in our work the skies became dark and threatening. It looked like trouble, so we covered our fossil with a canvas tarpaulin, weighted down by rocks, drove our jeep to high ground, and waited for things to happen. Things happened in a spectacular way. There was thunder and lightning crashing around us, and then for about twenty or thirty minutes a rainstorm of the utmost violence, during which the wind came up and ripped the canvas cover away from our fossil. Sitting in our jeep, waiting out the storm, we held our heads in despair. But there was more to come.

Just as the rain slackened off, there was a roar and a wall of water came down the wash, carrying everything before it and completely inundating our beautiful fossil in its cast. "This is the end," so I said to myself. There was nothing to do but to wait until the water had subsided, at which time we waded through the mud back to where our fossil had been. Wonder of wonders—and joy supreme! The flood had neatly undercut our specimen and turned it over. All we had to do was to load it on the jeep, go down the wash and rescue our tarpaulin, and drive back to headquarters.

Our luck was providential, and we had had a dramatic demonstration as to the power of water in the desert. Today that skull is one of the choice specimens on exhibit at the American Museum of Natural History.

The two trips that I made during the war (to Texas in 1943 and Florida in 1944), my summer in California in 1945, and my first Triassic expedition in 1946 posed family problems as has already been mentioned, problems that never assumed serious proportions, thanks to Margaret's ability to handle our family affairs while I was away from home, and thanks particularly to her understanding of a paleontologist's life and her tolerance for the situations created by such absences on the part of her spouse. Even so it was not easy for her.

Then there was "the farm" as a family resource. In 1936, Ira and Betty Nichols, her brother-in-law and elder sister respectively, purchased a piece of land in Rhode Island near the little post office of Exeter, south of Providence. It consisted of some eighty acres of secondary woodland, a reversion from the time a century earlier when it had been a farm, and on it there was an old house dating from the early part of the nineteenth century, as well as a little cottage set in the woods, perhaps two hundred yards distant from the house. The Nichols refurbished the house, which needed some working over, and then on numerous occasions they shared it with us. It had been intended by them as a summer retreat (they lived in Providence when they acquired the place) but it so happened that Ira, a psychiatrist at Butler Hospital, had joined the navy medical corps some time before the United States became involved in the Second World War, from which time the Nichols family lived a very peripatetic life for several years. Thus they did not use the house as much as they had expected to. Even after the war, when they were back home, the house on occasion, as well as the cottage, became available to us for our summer vacations.

Our first sojourn on the farm (it was always called that) was in 1937, when George was a baby, and for some reason the Nichols were not occupying the house during the whole summer. Consequently we lived in it for a month, and it made a welcome retreat from our New York apartment. Then in 1942 Margaret spent the summer there with the three boys who at that time constituted our gaggle of offspring, along with little Tom Nichols, on loan from his parents. I commuted up there from New York when I could, and spent my vacation with the family. We were at the farm, in part or in full force, in the successive summers of 1947, 1948, 1949, 1950, and 1951, as well as in 1954 and 1955, summers during which I was away for various periods of time on my Triassic field expeditions.

So the farm was a great boon to us during the years when the boys were small. Later the whole family went west on several occasions as I continued my Triassic field studies, but in those years when the boys were little the farm loomed large in their summertime experiences, and for Margaret it was a godsend. There she could turn the boys loose, and they kept themselves busy and amused during the summer days with little supervision needed on her part.

I must add that I, too, enjoyed many happy times at the farm. On those summers when I was not out in the field it was a place where I could relax happily with the family, and at times it was a place to return to after a summer's campaign in the Southwest.

At the farm there were hikes in the woods, where one might easily get confused if not lost (even in Rhode Island), and where at one place on a little hill there were giant glacial erratics confined among the trees. How often we used to go blueberrying in the fields that reposed like little grassy islands within the woodlands. Down at a little stream behind the cottage were pools where very small boats might be launched, and when we wished to engage in nautical sports we could all pile into the car and drive a few miles in one direction to Larkins Pond for fresh-water bathing, or in other directions to the many beaches along Narragansett Bay.

And never will Margaret and I forget the sound of the whippoorwills as they called at dusk, or the shine of their bright red eyes in the beam of a flashlight. Those were simple and innocent days at the farm, days that will always live in our memories.

Then, in the summer of 1952, a time when I had no western field work scheduled, we went north to New Brunswick for a vacation in the land of Margaret's ancestors. We were fortunate in being able to rent a little cottage high on a hillside above the wide Kennebecasis River, where we enjoyed the cool air, the blue water of the river (actually it is a deep estuary), the spacious skies with high cumulus clouds piled to the zenith on many a day, and where we could delve into the traditions of Loyalist history. It was during this summer that I took the three oldest boys on a trip around the head of the Bay of Fundy to see the Joggins beds—Carboniferous shales in which are preserved the trunks of very ancient trees. Here is the site where some of the oldest amphibians and reptiles in North America are to be found—but we did not find any fossils.

So passed the years and so lived our family during the war and immediately after, when I was becoming acquainted in an intimate way with the Mesozoic and especially with the Triassic of western North America. They were the years that formed a prelude to my extended Triassic work in field and laboratory, work that was to occupy me through four interesting decades. They were the years that recall for Margaret and for me the time when the boys were small, and when, because the boys were small, we were very, very busy. They were precious years.

XIV

Ghost Ranch

State Highway 96, which makes a forty-mile east-to-west connection between its junction with United States Highway 84 on the east and State Highway 44 on the west in north central New Mexico, traverses a rugged land, economically poor and scenically beautiful. As one travels from the west to east the road traverses a gap in a spectacular hogback formed by the tilted rock strata that bound the eastern rim of the San Juan Basin, and enters a region of colorful horizontal rocks that have been eroded through the millenia of geologic time to form great cliffs, rising above an undulating topography covered in part by pine forests, in part by grassland "parks" in which one sees the small, tin-roofed cabins of Hispanic farmers and ranchers who barely scratch a living out of the land, and in part by plateaulike surfaces that form a sparse rangeland for herds of cattle. To the north, as one proceeds eastwardly from Gallina to Coyote to Youngsville, are the immense cliffs that form the edge of Mesa Prieta, their forested crests rising a thousand feet and more above the highway. And east of Youngsville as one comes out onto the rangeland of the flat plateau there is suddenly revealed far beyond a scene of breathtaking beauty.

There, perhaps fifteen miles beyond to the east, and stretching mile after mile to the north and to the south, is a line of huge cliffs, the colors of which almost defy belief. They are cliffs of red and orange, lemon yellow, maroon, chocolate, and brown colors, their tops crowned with juniper and pine forests, their bases defined by the course of the Chama River, a tributary of the Rio Grande. Geologically these colored cliffs comprise a superb Mesozoic section, ranging from bottom to top of Triassic, Jurassic, and Cretaceous sedimentary rocks; visually, or one might say artistically, one is looking at a Georgia O'Keeffe landscape, for this is the country in which O'Keeffe, certainly a towering figure in twentieth-century American art, spent much of her life, where she produced many of the paintings that made her work unique. Down at the base of those cliffs is Ghost Ranch.

Such was the view that greeted my two companions, George Whitaker and Thomas Ierardi, and myself one morning in the year of 1947. It was our first view of the cliffs that rise above Ghost Ranch, and we stopped our jeep and got out to admire the panorama at some leisure.

Here I was back in the Southwest, to continue the exploration of the Triassic that I had begun the year before, when I worked around St. Johns and in the Petrified Forest of Arizona. This year I had with me George, who had been with me for a part of the previous summer, and my good friend Tom, a professor at City College, New York, a next-door neighbor in New Jersey, and a man of curiosity and varied talents who had signed on as a volunteer bone hunter.

We had assembled in Albuquerque and from there had gone northwest into the eastern part of the San Juan Basin, to spend a week or so with George Simpson and his party. It was my intention to go on to the Petrified Forest, where I had a permit to work for the present summer season, but before going there it was my fervent wish to see Ghost Ranch, the locale where, it may be remembered, so many of the phytosaurs that I had studied in Berkeley, in 1945, had been found.

Since Triassic fossils already had been collected at Ghost Ranch, and at the Petrified Forest for that matter, one may ask why I was back in the Southwest for a second summer to look for fossils. Why does the fossil hunter return time and again to the same areas to continue his field work—is it necessary to keep on searching for more fossils? The answer is yes, on two counts. In the first place there is the ever-present hope of finding something new, eroded into view during the passing months since the last time there. As measurements at Petrified Forest indicated, the annual rate of erosion in the Triassic badlands of the Southwest is significant, so that a yearly check in any particular locality is not time wasted. What we know about fossil faunas—the associations of once contemporaneous animals—is never complete, so there is always the challenge to add to the picture of those gatherings of animals which at any particular time may have been living together. The continued search for fossils is in part a matter of increasing our knowledge of past life.

In the second place there is the problem of refining data at hand concerning the associations and occurrences of fossils already found. We hope that new specimens will supply new information about the nature of the faunas to which they belonged. Moreover continued field work serves to refine the stratigraphic facts pertinent to the occurrences of the fossils, this latter consideration being of prime importance as our knowledge of field relationships becomes ever more sophisticated.

Even though I had repeatedly come across references to Ghost Ranch when I was studying phytosaurs in the collections at Berkeley two years previously, and even though I had talked with some of the Berkeley paleontologists about the fossiliferous beds at Ghost Ranch, I was completely unprepared for that first stupendous view of the Ghost Ranch cliffs. Charles Camp and his associates had been quite matter of fact when we talked about Ghost Ranch; I suppose because our conversations were along paleontological lines it never occurred to them to mention that Ghost Ranch is a place that almost rivals Zion Canyon in the beauty of its setting. It reminds me of the manner in which Chuck Bogert didn't prepare me for my first sight of the Archbold station in Florida, when we went there three years previously.

After a long stop to admire the view we went on, turning to the north when we reached Highway 84, and within a few miles we came to a large gate with a sign on it proclaiming that it was Ghost Ranch. On the sign was a silhouette of a cow's skull, the logo of Ghost Ranch. (I later discovered that this logo had been designed for the ranch by Georgia O'Keeffe.) We drove up a dirt road directly toward the cliffs and toward a green oasis within which nestled several buildings. As we arrived a smiling, slightly built man came out to greet us, and introduced himself as Arthur Pack, the owner of the ranch. It was just before noon, and he most cordially invited us in to lunch, and there we met his wife, Phoebe, their children, Arthur and little Phoebe, and the ranch foreman, Herman Hall, and his wife, "Jimmy." Jimmy was the cook for the ranch.

During the course of a most excellent lunch I suggested to Arthur that we would like to spend a few days poking around in the Triassic beds at Ghost Ranch before we went on to our appointed task at the Petrified Forest. Arthur most cordially made us welcome, and so we made plans. We had to return for a few days to the San Juan Basin, but soon we were back at Ghost Ranch, prepared to look it over. We set up our tents in a shady place at the edge of Arroyo del Yeso, as advised by Arthur, and the day after having established camp we began our prospecting. We thought we would try working along some of the canyons that dissect the areas at the base of the cliffs, there to look for promising Triassic exposures.

On the first morning we found in a canyon a mile or so beyond our camp a very nice phytosaur skull. It was too good to pass up, so we settled down to collect it, a process that occupied a couple of days. After getting it safely encased in a plaster jacket and hauled back to camp, we decided to take just two or three days more for such explorations before going on to Arizona.

Again, on the very first morning of renewed prospecting there was another discovery. This time it was George Whitaker who stumbled onto paleontological pay dirt. We had all separated, as was our usual practice, individually to search the exposures (thus covering more ground than if we had kept together) and shortly before noon George came running across a little arroyo with some bone fragments in his hand. They consisted of a part of a small claw and a few accompanying bone pieces equally small, and as soon as I saw them I recognized them as belonging to *Coelophysis*, a very early dinosaur. Tom and I accompanied George to the spot where he had located the fossils, and there on a long talus slope, such a slope being formed at the base of a cliff from the rock debris derived by weathering from the cliff face, were other bone fragments belonging to the same dinosaur. Here was something quite unexpected that immediately changed my thinking about what direction our summer field program might take. I knew from the literature that *Coelophysis* was known only from some very fragmentary fossils, discovered three-quarters of a century earlier in this part of New Mexico by David Baldwin, who collected for Edward Drinker Cope, and briefly described by Cope. In 1915 Friedrich von Huene had described Cope's fossils in more detail and had illustrated them rather fully in a *Bulletin* of the American Museum of Natural History (the fossils are in the museum collection). At the moment of George's initial discovery such was all that we knew about *Coelophysis*, and now within a few moments of scratching around on that talus slope we had found more materials of the little dinosaur than had previously existed.

What to do? The first thing was to get some lunch, so we went back to camp and fortified ourselves for the afternoon. Then we returned to the spot to continue our probing. We followed the bone fragments up the talus slope, where eventually in a small outcropping of rock free from talus we found the stratum from which the bones had been eroding. We dug into the side of the hill that afternoon, and for the next two days, and the more we dug the more we found. There before us was a bone bed of remarkable abundance, a layer of bones consisting of articulated and partially articulated skeletons— skeletons in which the bones were attached to one another more or less in their natural relationships—all belonging to *Coelophysis*. It was a paleontological treasure beyond one's wildest dreams!

Huene's description of 1915 served to give us some idea as to what *Coelophysis* is like, yet even so the published information about this dinosaur was all too scanty. In Huene's paper there are described and figured some scattered vertebrae, some limb bones, parts of two pelvic girdles, and a few other miscellaneous pieces, all quite fragmentary. No skulls or parts of skulls, no jaws, no teeth. And here, as we made our preliminary digging at Ghost Ranch we were beginning to see specimens that would furnish information of the most detailed nature about *Coelophysis.*

Again that question—what were we to do? We had made a discovery quite obviously of extraordinary importance and significance, a discovery from which we could not walk away. It was evident that if we were to follow the discovery with a proper excavation we were faced with a task that would require all of our time and effort for the summer, and perhaps for summers to come. Yet we had a permit, good for this summer, to work at the Petrified Forest. In those days such permits were not easy to obtain; one had to go through channels all the way up to the secretary of the interior and back down again, and that took time and the attention of a good many people in government circles. What would be my standing in bureaucratic eyes after all of that hullabaloo of getting a permit, if I were to ignore it and the trouble it had caused, to spend the summer at Ghost Ranch? But how could I ignore the little dinosaurs of Ghost Ranch?

I indulged in some soul searching and then made my decision, based on the tried and true paleontological principle that one should "gather ye rosebuds while ye may," and opted for Ghost Ranch. Then I had to explain this to the government people, and make my apologies, which at the time did not make them very happy. In the end, however, things turned out satisfactorily; I think the National Park Service personnel directly involved with the situation understood my dilemma, and I hope that eventually I was forgiven in Washington. Perhaps so, because in 1977 the Department of the Interior designated Ghost Ranch as a national landmark, this largely on the basis of the Ghost Ranch dinosaur quarry, and in no small degree to the unremitting efforts of Dr. Stuart Northrop of the University of New Mexico, who, feeling that such should be the case, translated his feelings into action. As still another result of the Ghost Ranch discovery, some years ago the New Mexico legislature made *Coelophysis* the official state fossil. Then to add to the importance of *Coelophysis* in the affairs of the state, the newly established New Mexico Museum of Natural History adopted a reconstruction of this little dinosaur as its logo, so that by now *Coelophysis* is a widely recognized object in that state. Indeed, the museum had the hardware (doorhandles and such things) of its new building embossed with the silhouette of *Coelophysis.* Moreover, the people of New Mexico have, by and large, learned how to pronounce this rather esoteric name that had been bestowed upon the fossil when Cope first described its remains.

But perhaps we are getting ahead of the story, which at this point concerns the development of the Ghost Ranch dinosaur quarry. Here some explanations are in order.

There is a series of successive cliffs and slopes at Ghost Ranch, one above the other, that form the Mesozoic sequence in this region. At the bottom of this impressive pile of ancient sediments is the Chinle Formation of Triassic age, consisting of brilliant red sandstones and siltstones that have weathered to form the ground surface at Ghost Ranch, this surface in many places consisting of badland hills as much as one hundred and fifty feet in height and generally devoid of vegetation. The Chinle beds are relatively soft, and are constantly being eroded to form in many areas the talus slopes of which one has already been mentioned.

Above the Chinle beds is the Entrada sandstone, a massive formation colored beautiful lemon-yellow and salmon tints that may be several hundred feet in thickness. Since this sandstone is so much harder than the underlying Chinle sediments it stands up as vertical cliffs, these cliffs resulting largely from the undermining of their bases by the weathering of the soft Chinle beds beneath them. This undermining causes segments of the Entrada to spall, or split off, from the cliff faces as huge vertical pillars, which break into tremendous boulders as they crash down on the talus slope at the base of the Entrada cliffs. It should be said that the Entrada Formation is of Jurassic age.

Above the Entrada is a capping of gypsum, which varies from a thin band to a topping of considerable thickness, and as seen from a distance looking very much like frosting on a lemon cake. The gypsum layer, also of Jurassic age, is known as the Todilto Formation, and its presence indicates that it was deposited in shallow, periodically shrinking lakes in an arid climate. Some thirty miles to the west of Ghost Ranch, near the little settlement and post office named Gallina, there is a ridge formed by the Entrada and Todilto tipped at a sharp angle from the horizontal; the western side of this ridge, formed entirely by the Todilto gypsum, here present in some thickness, is of a dazzling white aspect under the New Mexico sun. For which reason the early Spanish settlers named the eminence *Cerro Blanco*. (It was at one end of this ridge, where Chinle beds are found, that David Baldwin discovered some of the original bones of *Coelophysis*, later described by Cope. The other bones comprising Cope's original materials were found, I have reason to think, in the vicinity of Ghost Ranch.)

Following the Todilto gypsum in age and in topographic elevation are the long slopes of the Upper Jurassic Morrison Formation, gray to purplish to a dark chocolate in color. These sediments, many hundreds of feet in thickness, contain the bones of giant dinosaurs, occasionally found in the Ghost Ranch region, occurring in great abundance at Dinosaur National

Monument in Utah. It should be said that the Morrison Formation is very widely exposed throughout the western states.

Finally at the top of the series of alternating cliffs and slopes are the cliffs composed of the brownish Dakota sandstone, of early Cretaceous age. These cliffs, forming the skyline at Ghost Ranch, belong to a rock unit that in some areas is noteworthy for its contained fossil leaves—leaves of such familiar plants as oak and sassafras and willow, all marking the early Cretaceous "explosion" of angiosperms, the broad-leaved, flowering plants that were to so influence the evolution of the Cretaceous dinosaurs.

Such is the setting in which we were to spend that summer of 1947, a setting of grandeur in which cliffs of such colors as constantly to amaze the viewer are predominant.

Now for some details. The hill on the side of which we had found the bones of *Coelophysis* dribbling down a long, smooth slope, is a relatively small erosion remnant rising above the general level of the valley floor, the valley in turn traversed by the small stream already mentioned, Arroyo del Yeso—which might be expressed in English as "gypsum wash." Its name derives from the white boulders and rocks and pebbles of Todilto gypsum that abound in the little valley, fallen down, of course, from the gypsum icing that covers the lemon-layer-cake cliffs of the Entrada Formation. A small, very narrow subsidiary valley separates the quarry hill from an opposite slope of Chinle sediments, thickly covered with Entrada boulders, and leading to the base of a huge Entrada cliff to the east, towering above the quarry. On the other side of the hill is the broader reach of the Arroyo del Yeso valley, covered with sagebrush, and leading on the north and west to more Entrada cliffs, with Chinle slopes at their bases.

All of this geology, composed of sedimentary formations, is almost horizontally disposed; there is a slight regional tilting of the rocks, geologically known as the dip, and amounting to about 5 degrees, from southeast to northwest.

Since the rocks containing the bones of *Coelophysis* extend through the little hill where the quarry was to be developed, and since they extend back from the face of the hill at a slight dip, our first task was to dig into the hill above the level of the bone layer, to develop a quarry "floor." That's where our work really began, because in those innocent times we did all of this task with pick and shovel—a tedious procedure that lasted through many days. (In 1981 and 1982, when the quarry was reopened—more of that later—the work was accomplished quickly and painlessly with a big bulldozer.)

As we swung our picks and shovels in the bright New Mexico sun we were made increasingly aware that the Ghost Ranch quarry was going to be a long and difficult operation. The work was hard enough, but what made our days especially hard was the dubious pleasure of living in tents and especially of having to cook our meals over a little gasoline stove. Camping out is all right for a vacation trip, but as a steady thing, week in and week out, when you are trying to get a job done, the outdoor life begins to pall. Moreover the business of writing up field notes at night, sitting on the edge of a canvas cot with a hot Coleman lamp as a source of illumination, and with the various local insects, attracted by the lamp, blundering into your face or onto the page where you are trying to compose your thoughts, can be at times an exercise in frustration.

Therefore we were more than pleased when shortly after we had established our schedule as a summer-long program, Arthur Pack appeared and said in effect, "You boys can't spend the summer here in tents. Why don't you move into the Johnson house?" So we did.

The Johnson house, as it was then known, was a most spacious abode, built in the Southwest Spanish style by Mr. Johnson of Band-Aid fame. It was intended as his summer retreat, but it was empty and obviously was going to be empty for the foreseeable future. Thus we changed our life style almost instantaneously from one of inconvenience to one of comparative luxury. We had a dwelling where we could enjoy the comfort of a large living room in which there were shelves stocked with books, a modern kitchen, and two bedrooms, each with a full bath. It proved to be the most posh living in all of my experience of fossil collecting.

At about this stage in our operations it became clear that we needed more help, so I called New York to ask if Carl Sorensen, one of the senior and experienced members of our laboratory force, could join us for the summer. He could and he did, arriving within about a week at Lamy, New Mexico, the train stop nearest to our operation. With his help we completed digging back and removing the overburden, and from then on we spent the rest of the summer in a paleontological quarry operation of the type that has been well established through years of experience and practice.

We exposed the quarry floor, as has already been mentioned, being careful to stop about a foot or so above the bone level, until we had established an almost horizontal platform some thirty or forty feet in lateral dimensions and extending about fifteen feet or so into the hillside. Fortunately, since we were high on the side of the hill, there was plenty of room beyond the edge of our quarry in which to dispose of our "tailings." After having established the dimensions of the quarry we then started to dig down to the bone level, and as soon as bones began appearing we uncovered them sufficiently to find out what we had. This latter operation was slow, tedious, and exacting work. The fossil bones were very delicate and when first exposed to the air they would crumble if not immediately treated. So as we uncovered them with small hand picks and brushes we coated them with a protective coat of thin shellac, cut with alcohol. (Today, as mentioned, more advanced and sophisticated preservatives are used.) As the bones were hardened, we further protected them in our usual way with thin layers of Japanese rice paper, shellacked to the bones.

As this work promised to stretch out into days and weeks, we decided to build a solid wooden roof over the quarry, in part to make our task more comfortable and to protect us from the summer sun, but more specifically to protect the bones from the baking effect of the sun and from sudden showers. With the roof in place we continued exposing the bone layer.

Sooner or later the layer of bones had to be divided into a series of blocks for removal from the quarry. Ordinarily in a fossil deposit the delineation of blocks is no great problem, but here we faced some agonizing decisions and practices, because with the bones extending in so unbroken an array, we had somehow to cut through the tangle, to separate the bone layer into the afore-mentioned blocks. This meant that rather than cutting through bones to make channels between the blocks being established, we had to remove bones and skulls that would otherwise lie within the limits of the channels. Which meant, in turn, the devising of these channels in such ways as to involve the least disturbance of bones in place, which meant again the creation of some very tortuous little canyons traversing the bone layer, back and forth, right and left. And by little I mean little, because we cut the channels just as narrow as possible —all of which involved much time, much profanity, and many scraped knuckles. But at last the quarry floor was divided into a series of blocks, each block perhaps five or six feet long, and wide, and a couple of feet thick. Then the several blocks were completely encased in jackets of burlap dipped in plaster of paris.

As the reader is by now aware, the preceding paragraph describes a process essentially the same as what had been carried out at Agate, Nebraska, nine years previously. Any differences were largely in the nature of the fossils—dinosaurs two hundred million years old as contrasted with mammals one-tenth that age.

I remember at this time in our operations that Dr. Simpson and his party came over from the San Juan Basin to visit us. I told him that we had just hauled in fifteen hundred pounds of bagged plaster from the lumber yard in Española, the nearest town, at which he asked plaintively if I did not consider this a bit excessive. As things turned out it was not excessive, for in fact we had to get another load of a thousand pounds of plaster.

The blocks, being plastered, were further strengthened by heavy splints, fashioned from large limbs cut from nearby trees. Then came the tedious work of undercutting each block. After the block was sufficiently encased, top, sides, and bottom, the pedestal or pedestals on which it rested were cut away, preparatory to turning the block over.

A heavy chain hoist, suspended from a strong tripod, was attached to the block, and the block was upended. Here came the moment of truth: would the block hold together as it went over? We were lucky—our blocks went over intact, each one of them. Then it was a matter of putting more bandages on what had been the bottom of the block, to make the block completely strong. It should be added that none of the blocks could have been removed from the quarry without the help of Herman Hall, Arthur Pack's foreman, and his bulldozer. Herman graded a road across the arroyo and up the steep slope to the quarry, after which he dragged the blocks, loaded on heavy wooden sleds, down to the ranch headquarters. At the end of the season there was an impressive array of big blocks spread out on the ground, and I must admit that the sight of these massive plaster-enclosed blocks gave us a feeling of satisfaction; they were the tangible evidence of a summer of accomplishment. All that remained was to contract with a trucker to haul the blocks across country to New York, and this we did. When he arrived at the museum he admitted it was one of the heaviest loads he had ever transported across country; he was glad to be done with it.

From what has been said the reader may have gained an impression that ours was a summer of heavy, unremitting toil. Much of what we did was hard work—true enough—but there were many compensations that made the summer a time of delightful experiences. I have already remarked that the Johnson house in which we were ensconced was a most comfortable and rather atypical residence for bone hunters. Beyond that, there was a swimming pool, where each afternoon, following a hard day in the quarry we could refresh ourselves with a brief and stimulating swim. Then, on numerous occasions we would occupy the half hour or so between our swim and suppertime with a happy hour, enjoyed in company with the Packs. Arthur and Phoebe were most generous and cordial in having us in for liquid refreshments, on which occasions there was much good talk as we watched the slanting sun illuminate the green slopes of Pedernal, the ridged mountain miles away that forms a landmark to be seen across the mesas and canyons of northern New Mexico.

Georgia O'Keeffe liked bones—the skulls and pelvic girdles and vertebrae of horses and cattle and deer form the central motif of many of her paintings—and consequently she was interested in what we were doing. So it was that during this and some following summers I became acquainted with O'Keeffe and spent some pleasant hours at her home, located about a half-mile from the Ghost Ranch headquarters. (She had another home in the little town of Abiquiu, about ten miles from Ghost Ranch, but during the summers she spent much of her time at the ranch.) Georgia O'Keeffe had a reputation of being rather distant, and I suppose she had to be, because she was constantly besieged by people of all descriptions. But she was friendly to me, I think in part because of our mutual interest in bones and in part because I had no intention of talking about art in her presence. Indeed, it was the other way around; she was full of questions about geology, about the colorful rocks that surrounded her, and about specimens that she had picked up during the course of her walks across the countryside.

All that has been described in these last few paragraphs occupied our attention and our energies through about three months of that first Ghost Ranch summer. Yet it must be emphasized that such labors were only the beginning of the story. In the laboratory the plaster bandages had to be removed from the blocks after which many months, even a year or two, of preparation were expended on each block. Then, after the fossils had been sufficiently cleaned they became the subjects of research. Only after they were studied and described did they become truly significant paleontological objects. And that is why decades have been involved on the Ghost Ranch project; the time lag between collecting the specimens and finally describing them has been necessarily and almost unbelievably long.

A second summer was spent at Ghost Ranch by George Whitaker and Carl Sorensen, during which they collected more materials including two beautifully articulated skeletons of adult *Coelophysis*, resting side by side, each containing within its body cavity the bones of young dinosaurs. It would appear that *Coelophysis* indulged in cannibalistic habits, which is not rare among modern reptiles.

Years later, in 1981 and 1982, the Ghost Ranch quarry was reopened by the Carnegie Museum of Pittsburgh, the New Mexico Museum, the Museum of Northern Arizona, and Yale University, all working together, and still more blocks were removed. The harvest of dinosaurs from this one quarry has been, to put it mildly, prodigious. It should be added, too, that many blocks have been exchanged, so that various museums in addition to the institutions that worked the quarry have benefitted from the Ghost Ranch deposit. Particular mention should be made of one large block placed in the museum at Ghost Ranch, where it can be seen in association with the cliffs from which it was excavated.

Such are the bare bones of my relationship with Ghost Ranch, a relationship that had its beginnings with the quarry and through the years has grown into a continuing fellowship. That first summer was a time of friendships being established—with Arthur and Phoebe Pack, to whom I owe an everlasting debt, with the other people at the ranch, and with Georgia O'Keeffe.

In subsequent years I kept going back, at first to do supplementary studies of the geology, and then to become involved in a rather intimate way with doings there. Some years after we had developed the quarry Arthur Pack gave the ranch to the Presbyterian Church for a conference center. In 1961 Jim and Ruth Hall (no relations of the Herman Halls) came to the ranch, Jim as director. Under his guidance Ghost Ranch has grown into an internationally acclaimed conference center, where people gather to consider problems of many sorts, great and small.

It so happened that in 1965 Margaret and I, A. W. Crompton, then director of the Peabody Museum at Yale, his young son and a companion, George Haas of Hebrew University in Israel, and Mario Barbarena of the University of Rio Grande do Sul, Brazil, made a trip together in two cars, to see the Triassic of the Southwest. We called it our "four continents" trip—North America, South America, Africa (Crompton's native heath), and the Middle East. It was a great trip, and we enjoyed it thoroughly.

In the course of things we arrived at Ghost Ranch, where Jim Hall had recently taken over as director. Before our visit was over he had recruited "Fuzz" Crompton and me to come to Ghost Ranch the next summer to conduct a seminar on the paleontology of northern New Mexico. Which we did. From then on the seminar became a biennial event, first with Fuzz and me cooperating, one year with Fuzz alone, and in more recent years, since Margaret and I moved to Flagstaff, with me carrying on, enjoying the help of another paleontological friend.

One friend with whom I have worked in recent years has been David Gillette, who some years ago was appointed as paleontologist at the New Mexico Museum of Natural History, and more recently has moved to Salt Lake, to be state paleontologist of Utah. In the interim David and his wife, Lynnet, have become very much a part of the Ghost Ranch picture—Dave taking charge of the final development of the Ghost Ranch quarry, and both he and Lynnet having much to do with the establishment of the paleontological museum at Ghost Ranch, of which Lynnet is now curator.

The moving force behind the paleontological museum at Ghost Ranch has been Jim Hall, who became a dedicated paleontological enthusiast almost from the moment that Fuzz and I started that first seminar, more than twenty years ago. Furthermore Ruth Hall soon was more than a paleontological enthusiast—in short order the fossils of Ghost Ranch occupied her attention and her activities beyond almost anything else in her life. Day after day, year after year, she was out in the badlands looking for fossils, seeing that fossils were properly protected, and giving talks in the field to people of assorted ages, especially to children, about the Triassic life of New Mexico as preserved by the fossils at the ranch. Her interest and her activities culminated, during the summer that Fuzz was conducting the seminar, with the discovery of a large phytosaur skeleton out on the flats, only a mile or so distant from the ranch buildings.

Then a few years ago when the *Coelophysis* quarry was reopened Jim decided that there should be an exhibit at the ranch of the fossils for which the ranch has become famous. A most excellent museum of anthropology had already been established there, so it was decided to expand the building to include paleontology. A new wing was built—the "Ruth Room" ready to accommodate the phytosaur that had been found as well as other fossils, particularly *Coelophysis*. One large block, previously mentioned, remained from the 1981–1982 reopening of the quarry, and it was destined for the Ruth Room.

It was a huge block, but nothing daunted, David Gillette took charge of its removal, with the help of a small army of volunteers, not to mention heavy equipment at the ranch. The block, which had been partially excavated, was finally completely separated from the quarry wall and properly plastered. Then on a snowy day at the end of 1985 it was hauled down to the museum and with a large derrick was lifted over the walls of the unfinished Ruth Room, to be deposited on the floor, where it will remain until doomsday. It had to be put into place *before* the roof of the building was constructed; because of its size it could never have been taken through the doors of the structure. And now Lynnet is preparing the block for exhibition.

This is just one example of how the Ghost Ranch quarry has impinged upon the lives of many people.

Another example has to do with Margaret. In her case it was not so much the Ghost Ranch quarry as such as the Chinle Formation of the Southwest. First she was asked to paint a mural for the Rainbow Forest Museum at the Petrified Forest National Park, showing life of late Triassic time. Then she was asked to paint an even larger mural for the new New Mexico Museum. Both murals are in place, and both are in effect and to a large degree the results of work at the Petrified Forest and at Ghost Ranch. An appreciation of Margaret's work has recently been expressed by David Gillette.

> In the earlier restorations animal behavior was simple and limited largely to predator-prey encounters. With the Colbert mural we now see *Coelophysis* and the phytosaurs as gregarious animals. Evidence for herding in *Coelophysis* had come from the Ghost Ranch quarry, where these nimble predators are represented by growth series, ranging from hatchlings the size of a chicken to adults the size of a turkey or somewhat larger. The parental care suggested by the phytosaur with its cluster of babies, perhaps hatchlings, was based not on fossils but on observations of living crocodiles exhibiting this behavior. Not only did the artist capture the essence of the age of transition, she also developed a theme of increasing behavioral complexity among the dinosaurs and their contemporaries, a subject that has received considerable attention during the past two decades. (*Di-*

nosaurs Past and Present [Seattle: Natural History Museum of Los
Angeles County in association with the University of Washington
Press, 1987], volume 1, page 148.)

Is it any wonder that Ghost Ranch always will be very much a part of my
life? One remembers the pleasure of bright summer days spent beneath its
towering cliffs, the never-to-be-forgotten views of those cliffs seen against
the backdrop of an incredibly blue sky, or sometimes against the lowering
clouds of an approaching storm, or in the late afternoon when the golden
rays of the westering sun emphasized the colors of the cliffs to a degree that
would challenge belief except for the evidence before one's eyes. Or there
are recollections of the excitement of searching for fossils and finding them,
the feeling of accomplishment in the opening and the developing of the
dinosaur quarry, and the pride in seeing that quarry recognized throughout
the world as one of the important sites from which dinosaurs have been
obtained. Again there are the remembrances of the seminars and of the
warm friendships established through the years. Beyond the Ghost Ranch
scene there are the memories of the always interesting research on the
Ghost Ranch fossils.

Many problems have been raised by the dinosaurian remains recovered
from the Triassic sediments beneath the Ghost Ranch cliffs. Questions have
risen to occupy my mind and the minds of other people since that day in
1947 when first we found the fragile bones of *Coelophysis* scattered on the
slope of a small, seemingly insignificant hill. The questions and the search
for answers to them have given real meaning to all of the paleontological
work that has been accomplished through the years at Ghost Ranch.

One of the most immediate questions—a question that came to mind
even as we began to develop the quarry—is this: why is there such a
concentration of dinosaur bones at the Ghost Ranch quarry? And why do the
remains of the little dinosaur *Coelophysis* predominate so overwhelmingly in
the deposit? There are the bones of other reptiles, notably some phytosaur
skulls and scattered postcranial bones, as well as the bones of other
thecodont reptiles, but they are relatively rare. The quarry is most notably
a *Coelophysis* burial ground, and that is a fact to be pondered. Some sort of
selection evidently prevailed more than two hundred million years ago,
resulting in the remarkable accumulation of *Coelophysis* skeletons and
partial skeletons that makes this quarry unusual, if not unique, in the
world-wide roster of dinosaur graveyards.

I used to think that perhaps we see at Ghost Ranch the result of a
catastrophic volcanic eruption, something on the order of the Mount St.
Helens eruption in the state of Washington, a few years ago. It makes a nice
explanation for the rich accumulation of dinosaur remains, an explanation

that may be compared with the explosion of Vesuvius in 79 A.D. which overwhelmed the Roman citizens of Pompeii and Herculaneum. The sticking point is that this solution for the Ghost Ranch dinosaur graveyard, neat as it may be, probably is not right. A volcanic eruption would have produced a lot of ash, and volcanic ash is frequently preserved in ancient sediments as bentonite, a soft gray or white clay that is very unstable— swelling after rainstorms and then drying into a powder that is easily eroded and blown away. The Chinle Formation, the geologic horizon at Ghost Ranch in which the dinosaur quarry is located, is famous for the great amount of bentonite that it contains. Indeed, bentonite in the Chinle makes life hard for engineers and architects in some parts of the Southwest; highways are difficult to maintain on bentonite surfaces; they are continually breaking down and deteriorating into bumpy, rough, wavy surfaces that make driving a car over them anything but a pleasure. Buildings settle and crack in a most alarming fashion; such has been the fate of the headquarters complex at the Petrified Forest National Park, designed by a very famous architect, and built on a surface that has caused a profusion of cracked walls and uneven floors.

To get back to the Ghost Ranch dinosaur quarry, I thought it was a locale typified by abundant bentonite—at least the siltstones there looked bentonitic to me. But in recent years Hilde Schwartz, who specializes in the study of sediments, has analyzed samples from the Ghost Ranch quarry, and she assures me that there is little if any bentonite present. So much for the idea of a volcanic catastrophe to account for the Ghost Ranch dinosaurs.

How, then, are they to be explained? It would seem that some sort of local catastrophe must be invoked, because the dinosaurs found at Ghost Ranch represent a *population* of animals, large and small, old and young. It seems to Hilde, and I think she must be right, that what we see at Ghost Ranch is the result of mass drowning in a stream, with almost immediate burial following the death of the dinosaurs. The articulated nature of the skeletons, with the bones connected one to another, and the lack of abrasion on the bones, would seem to indicate that these unfortunate reptiles were not washed very far downstream, at least not far enough to cause the bodies to be rolled over and over, and battered and torn apart. Moreover, there is no indication that the bones were chewed and broken, as they would have been if the carcasses had been mangled by scavengers. No—the skeletons and partial skeletons are nicely articulated; the most common breakage in the skeletons is the separation of the tail from the body, at a point perhaps of articular weakness, immediately back of the pelvis.

It is common for the skeletons to be preserved in such a way that the head is drawn back to a position immediately above the back part of the trunk, with the long neck sharply flexed into an elegant backward curve.

Such a position would have been caused by a drying and contraction of the ligaments in the neck; this manner of death pose is quite common among the long-necked dinosaurs.

When the various possibilities are taken into account, it seems to me that the Ghost Ranch dinosaurs very possibly perished while they were attempting to cross a stream in flood. Perhaps they represent a single catastrophic occurrence, perhaps they represent an accumulation of skeletons from various attempted stream crossings through a succession of years. It is hardly possible to be dogmatic as to a choice between these options.

There are some modern analogies on which to base this explanation for the accumulation of the dinosaur remains. In Africa today there are numerous occasions (in recent years dramatically recorded on film) when great herds of wildebeest or gnu plunge into flooding rivers, attempting a crossing, with the sad result that innumerable individuals are drowned and carried downstream to be stranded on sand bars. Such happenings take place during their annual migrations, when these animals are impelled to surge forward no matter what obstacles may be in their path.

A similar happening took place in Canada a few years ago, when a great herd of caribou attempted to cross a swollen river. Some ten thousand of the animals perished; their bloated bodies lined the banks of the river for miles downstream.

Such thoughts bring up another problem—why should there have been so many individuals of *Coelophysis* grouped together? Do we see the remains of a "herd" of these dinosaurs? To put the question differently, *should* we see in this case the remains of a dinosaur "herd"? *Coelophysis* was most obviously a carnivorous dinosaur, and carnivorous animals in the modern world ordinarily do not congregate in herds. However, modern crocodiles and alligators do gather together in considerable numbers on the banks of rivers, where they bask in the sun. But this is not exactly herding as we think of the word, which is defined by the Oxford dictionary as "a company of animals of any kind feeding or traveling together." Would a large group of *Coelophysis* be feeding and traveling together, and if so, on what would they be feeding? It is one thing for herbivorous animals to drift along in large herds, cropping the vegetation as they move across the landscape. But how could *Coelophysis* behave in such a fashion? When it comes to eating, predators, even crocodiles, are individualistic, or at most work as pairs or as small groups of individuals. That is, unless some unusual situation brings them together in large numbers.

Let us turn to the *Travels of William Bartram*, in which there is depicted a pristine Florida, as seen by a pioneer American naturalist in 1773.

How shall I express myself so as to convey an adequate idea of it to the reader, and at the same time avoid raising suspicions of my veracity? Should I say, that the river (in this place) from shore to shore, and perhaps near half a mile above and below me, appeared to be one solid bank of fish, of various kinds, pushing through this narrow pass of St. Juan's into the little lake, on their return down the river, and that the alligators were in such incredible numbers, and so close together from shore to shore, that it would have been easy to have walked across on their heads, had the animals been harmless? (Edited by Mark Van Doren [New York: Dover Publications, 1955], page 118.)

So here we have an account by a truthful observer of carnivorous reptiles in a primitive environment, gathered together in great numbers—not herding, but congregating for a feast.

One other bit of evidence may be cited in connection with the accumulation of dinosaur skeletons at Ghost Ranch. In some localities where dinosaur tracks are preserved, it would appear that these ancient reptiles may have wandered across the land in large numbers. At Rocky Hill, Connecticut, for example, there are thousands of Triassic dinosaur tracks, of the same age as the Ghost Ranch skeletons, showing that early dinosaurs had wandered across a mud flat in random groups. Perhaps I have said enough on this score.

Two adult *Coelophysis* skeletons found side by side in the Ghost Ranch quarry, as already mentioned, contain within their body cavities the bones of the young dinosaurs belonging to this species. This raises two interesting alternative possibilities: are the partial skeletons of the little dinosaurs within the body cavities of the adults those of unborn young, or are they the victims of cannibalism?

To consider first the possibility that these are unborn young, various modern reptiles, particularly certain lizards, do give birth to living offspring. It is not birth in the mammalian sense of the word; rather such reptiles, instead of laying eggs, retain the eggs within the oviduct where the young are hatched, subsequently to emerge into a hostile world. But the crocodilians, the reptiles most closely related to the dinosaurs, do not follow this pattern of reproduction, nor do the birds, which appear upon the basis of recent evidence to be closely related to, if not descended from, theropod dinosaurs, the dinosaurian group to which *Coelophysis* belongs. So on this score the probabilities are against live birth in *Coelophysis*. Furthermore, two other facts militate against this explanation for the dinosaur bones within the body cavities of these *Coelophysis* specimens.

One such fact is the small size of the pelvic opening in *Coelophysis* in which the cloaca and the opening of the oviduct were located. The opening is quite adequate for a reptilian egg of the type and size that might be laid by *Coelophysis*; it seems all too small for the passage of a full-term embryo. The other fact is that the bones in the body cavities are those of good-sized young individuals, not of hatchings. They are simply too large and too well formed to have been embryonic.

Therefore one comes to the inevitable conclusion that adult *Coelophysis* individuals did on occasion devour their young, a behavior pattern that is not very pleasant to contemplate but one that is seen in various modern reptiles, including crocodiles and alligators. *Coelophysis* probably did lay eggs, as did other dinosaurs, although such eggs as yet have not been found.

What kind of a reptile was *Coelophysis*? As a reptile it was specialized; as a dinosaur it was primitive. From the stratigraphgic location of *Coelophysis* within the Chinle Formation, that is to say from the level at which it is found within the vast pile of Mesozoic sediments, we can be quite sure that *Coelophysis* was one of the very earliest of the dinosaurs. So it represents the structural type of reptile from which many later dinosaurs were descended. Yet even though *Coelophysis* occupies a position on the lower branches of the dinosaurian evolutionary tree it is anything but primitive when seen against the backdrop of reptilian history. Indeed, when compared with the reptiles of our modern world *Coelophysis* is truly an advanced member of the great class of reptiles.

It is relatively small, as all of the earliest dinosaurs were small, having a length of six feet or a bit more when fully grown, with at least half of this length represented by a long, sinuous tail. The bones are delicate and hollow, in many ways like the bones of birds, so that the skeleton of *Coelophysis*, although sufficiently strong, was lightly constructed. This means that *Coelophysis* was an agile animal, able to run rapidly across the land, able to make quick movements in pursuit of its prey. The adaptations of *Coelophysis* as a running animal are further indicated by its long, slender, very birdlike hind legs, terminating in three toes, with claws, for all the world like the toes of a large bird. (It should be said that tracks left by *Coelophysis* and other related dinosaurs have all the appearance of bird tracks, so that Edward Hitchcock, who collected and studied the tracks of Upper Triassic dinosaurs, so abundantly preserved in the rocks of the Connecticut Valley, thought that he was seeing the footprints of ancient birds, and he thought this to his dying day. That was in the middle of the nineteenth century. It was only some years later that the remains of *Archaeopteryx*, the oldest known bird, were found in the much younger Jurassic lithographic limestones of central Germany.)

Incidentally this gives emphasis to the view already mentioned and now gaining increasing favor among many paleontologists, that the birds actually are descended from theropod dinosaurs similar to *Coelophysis*. A more conservative theory is that such dinosaurs and the birds were derived from a common ancestor. However you may wish to look at the problem there is no denying the fact that *Coelophysis* is indeed very much like a bird in many of its anatomical characters—notably the hollow bones and the structure of the hind limbs. And in this connection it should be noted that if imprints of feathers had not been found with *Archaeopteryx* that early bird probably would have been classified as a reptile, perhaps as a dinosaur. In fact, one partial *Archaeopteryx* skeleton housed in the Tyler Museum in Holland was for many years catalogued as a reptile; only the perceptive eye of John Ostrom of Yale University (my former student and for many years my paleontological colleague) saw it for what it is, just a few years ago.

At their upper ends, the hind limbs of *Coelophysis* are neatly articulated into a strong pelvis, and this joint between pelvis and limbs is a pivot upon which the body of the dinosaur is balanced, its front part—consisting of the torso, neck, and head—being countered by the long, supple tail.

The fore limbs of *Coelophysis* quite obviously were never used for locomotion; they are relatively small, and terminate in three-fingered hands, the long, grasping fingers supplied with sharp claws. Evidently such hands were used as aids in feeding, in grasping prey.

That *Coelophysis* was a predator is amply indicated by the skull, which, although relatively small, is distinguished by its long jaws in which there are numerous sharp, knifelike teeth—more than twenty of them on each side, above and below. This skull, at the end of a long, sinuous neck, was a very efficient mechanism for reaching out and snapping up small animals of all kinds—little reptiles and amphibians, perhaps even fresh-water fishes, perhaps large insects. It is likely that *Coelophysis* was not in the least selective about what it ate, as long as what it ate was in the form of animal life. There is no reason to think, given the structure of the jaws and teeth, that *Coelophysis* ever partook of plant food.

Such was this early dinosaur, and such was the pattern of its bodily structure, which determined the pattern of its daily activities. And interestingly enough, this pattern of anatomical development and of the mode of life for which it was adapted is duplicated in all general aspects and even down to many small details by a dinosaur found in Rhodesia, described and named by my paleontological friend Mike Raath. *Syntarsus*, he called it, and if ever there were close cousins in the world of dinosaurs, *Coelophysis* and *Syntarsus* are those cousins.

All of which shows that the world of late Triassic time was a world in which the continents were closely related, much more closely joined each to the other than is the case today, providing broad avenues for the movements of active animals from one continental region to another. So it was that *Coelophysis* and *Syntarsus*, undoubtedly descended from a common ancestor, wherever that ancestor might have lived, had established themselves in southern Africa and southwestern North America, as the continents existed then, thousands of miles closer to each other than they are in our modern world. And this introduces another dimension into the study and interpretation of *Coelophysis*, namely the manner in which this little dinosaur and its African cousin, *Syntarsus*, fit into the grand concept of plate tectonics.

The theory of plate tectonics, which has grown out of an earlier idea known as continental drift, visualizes an ancient world of Carboniferous, Permian, and Triassic age in which all of the continents were joined into one great supercontinent known as Pangaea. This supercontinent, even though firmly united into one immense land mass, nonetheless consisted of two lesser supercontinents, determined by their positions on the earth of that distant time. One of these, known as Laurasia, occupied the northern hemisphere and was made up of what are now North America, Europe, and Asia—lacking peninsular India. The other, known as Gondwanaland (or more properly Gondwana, a name that although more correct probably will not supplant the term Gondwanaland, which has become firmly established in the literature by wide usage), occupied the southern hemisphere and consisted of what are now Africa, South America, peninsular India, Antarctica, and Australia. Subsequent to the Permian Period when Pangaea was still intact, the great supercontinent was split apart by rifting, and its segments, the continents as we know them, drifted to their present positions. Plate tectonics is a well-established and profound theory that within the past two decades has revolutionized the earth sciences, to make our view of the world more logical and more unified than it previously had been.

In late Triassic time the world was still the one world of Pangaea, although rifting of the supercontinent was in its initial stages. Even so, the several parts of Pangaea were still sufficiently connected so that in effect the supercontinent retained its basic form, with large corridors between the areas comprising it, so that active, land-living animals could move from one part of the land mass to another. Not only was Pangaea physically one world, but also it was one world climatically—a tropical world in which New Mexico was not very far north of the equator, southern Africa was not very far south of the equator, and both areas were closely connected each to the other. That was the world of *Coelophysis* and *Syntarsus*, when dinosaurs were small and when they shared their common land with many other reptiles, some of which were very much their superiors in size and strength.

Thus when I think back to Ghost Ranch I think not only of the great cliffs and of the fossils at the bases of the cliffs; I think also of New Mexico and Africa, and of a distant mirror of time reflecting from its surface a view of the world when dinosaurs were not as yet the rulers of the land.

XV

Laurasia

*M*y adventures at Ghost Ranch, at the Petrified Forest, and at other places in the Southwest where I worked in the Chinle and related formations provided me with some experience with rocks and fossils of late Triassic age. And the same was true for the Triassic of eastern North America—for the Newark series of rocks as exposed directly across from Manhattan, where it will be remembered the little gliding reptile *Icarosaurus* had been found, as well as for these same rocks in Pennsylvania, the Connecticut Valley, and Nova Scotia (of which more later). But if I were to have more than a provincial view of the Triassic it was important for me, sooner or later, to expand my horizons, to become acquainted with the Triassic of Laurasia—eventually of Gondwanaland. Consequently it was providential for me that the first International Geological Congress to be held after the end of World War II was scheduled for the summer of 1948 in Britain, and I was to be given the opportunity of attending it. Furthermore, the revived International Congress of Zoology was planned for that same summer in France, immediately before the geological congress; thus I could attend both meetings.

The zoological congress was important because it afforded the opportunity of meeting with zoologists from around the world and discussing problems with them and attending lectures by them at which subjects of particular interest to me would be considered—notably problems of animal evolution and distribution. More importantly, the geological congress would offer the opportunity not only for discussions and lectures at the meetings in London, but also for field excursions, where I could become acquainted with British Mesozoic formations, including the Triassic. The meetings in England would not take me to the type Triassic which I knew that eventually I must see, but they would give me some first-hand experience with formations closely related to the type Triassic rocks as exposed in central Europe.

Here let me digress for a few explanations. As briefly mentioned in Chapter VI, the rocks of the various geologic systems, from the Cambrian on, were first studied and described in certain parts of Europe during the early years of the nineteenth century, and these regions constitute the *type* areas for the several groups of rocks being considered. As has been noted, the Triassic System (a rock term) consisting of those rocks deposited during the Triassic Period (a time term) was first delineated from studies made in central Europe, notably in Germany. Here the Triassic rocks can be divided into three sequential parts (hence the name Triassic, from the Greek *trias*, meaning "three"), these being the Lower, Middle, and Upper Triassic, or to use the geological names, the Buntsandstein, Muschelkalk, and Keuper. The divisional names for the main Triassic units are old Germanic descriptive words, adopted into the scientific terminology of geology. Buntsandstein is a contraction of *bunter sandstein*, meaning "mottled sandstone" in reference to the color. The name Bunter alone is often used for this lower division of the European continental Triassic sequence. Muschelkalk, or "mussel chalk," refers to the middle division of the Triassic which in Germany is composed of marine limestones containing seashells, and represents an invasion of the sea across central Europe during middle Triassic time. This middle division of the Triassic is absent in England. Keuper, referring to the Upper Triassic, is an old German miner's name.

To continue the story, I would not be leaving for the meetings in France and England until the middle of July, so early in the summer I saw George Whitaker and Carl Sorensen off for Ghost Ranch, where they were to spend a second season in the dinosaur quarry, carrying on the work of the previous year. I might say that they did this in handsome fashion—that was the summer when they found the two beautifully complete adult *Coelophysis* skeletons, side by side. That discovery was to be a nice surprise for me later in the year, when I returned from my European trip.

Then, before leaving for Europe I went to the farm in Rhode Island with the family, to have an early summer holiday there. Not only were all of the Colberts there, but the Bogert family as well—Chuck and Micky, and their two daughters, Derry and Pat. The Bogerts occupied the little cottage in the woods, while our family lived in the farmhouse. But much of our time was spent together as a sort of expanded communal family, eating together and enjoying all sorts of daytime group activities.

Once again I was to desert Margaret and the family, but this time I could leave with the knowledge that during most of my absence she would be enjoying the summer in the Rhode Island woods, with the Bogerts there as company. Perhaps that was a pleasing prospect for her, but the evening before my departure from the farm was anything but propitious. To begin a day that was somewhat less than joyful, our Phil and Pat Bogert both had a bug of some sort, so they were heaving up at frequent intervals. Of course that made for much extra work.

Then as a farewell celebration we were all going to have a picnic supper out under the trees. Margaret and Micky Bogert labored mightily to get the food prepared and out on the picnic table—at which point the rain came. So we all hurriedly had to retreat into a crowded and hot dining room. Then just as we sat down a man appeared at the door; he was a truckdriver who was delivering a load of furniture that was being sent to the farm by the Nichols family (Margaret's sister and brother-in-law), this being surplus furniture that they wanted to store in the farmhouse. The truckdriver had the cheerful news that his van was stuck in the mud on the dirt road leading to the farmhouse, and he needed some help.

Chuck and I abandoned our plates and went back along the road and through the drizzle to help the driver and his assistant get the truck out of the mire. I can't remember at this late date just what we did; eventually we managed to get the truck free so it could be brought on to the house, where an assortment of chairs, tables, and the like was disgorged from its interior, to be carried and stowed by all of us in available corners of the place. By then the dinner hour was long since past and the food was cold, but we did the best we could with what had been intended as a festive meal.

The next morning it was up and away for me; Chuck kindly drove me down to New York.

There was still some magic in a transatlantic voyage back in 1948, as there had been for me seventeen years earlier. Transatlantic air travel had not as yet been established, so I went across on the first Queen Elizabeth, along with, among others, some of the members of the American Olympic team, who were crossing to attend the first postwar Olympics. Thus in company with the other passengers I had the diversion of watching the fencing team practicing on deck every day, or dodging the peregrinations of the bicycle team, as the cyclists rode around on the gently undulating deck.

I disembarked from the ship at Cherbourg, which at that time showed many signs of the fierce fighting that had enveloped France only three or four years earlier. A boat train to Paris and then a week or so at the meetings in Paris, after which I flew across to London.

There were to be two geological excursions for me, one before the scientific sessions in London, one after. The first excursion of about a week's duration was to follow the Mesozoic along the Channel coast, from Lyme Regis where we saw the Upper Triassic and the Lower Jurassic, to Bournemouth, where we ended the trip in the Cretaceous. The second field trip was more extended; sixteen of us went in a chartered bus from London to the very tip of Scotland, and during the course of more than two weeks visited various localities where fossil vertebrates had been found, ranging in age from Silurian to Triassic. Such geological field conferences are fairly frequent occurrences in the life of a paleontologist and I have been on many an excursion, but the two field trips in England were especially enjoyable, and will always remain as bright spots in my memories of geological-paleontological experiences.

Our first trip was so arranged that we stayed throughout its duration at a hotel in Weymouth—this hotel, as I understand the story, having once been the seaside resort of King George IV. In a courtyard of the hotel, visible from the room that I occupied along with Joe Gregory, my long-time friend and a member then of the Yale faculty, there was a large marble bath which we were told had at one time been used by the king. It was now purely ornamental, but was destined during our stay to be slightly less ornamental than it had been, because early one morning some of us heard the sound of a hammer on stone, and looking out we saw one of the members of our party chipping off a piece of the royal bathtub for a geological specimen. I was very glad to see that the culprit was not an American; indeed he was one of the British members of our group, and he should have known better.

There were about thirty of us, under the leadership of Professor P. C. Sylvester-Bradley, a very pleasant Englishman. As for the rest of us, we comprised an international spectrum, Britain and the United States being the most fully represented, with participants from various European nations, and from such far-off places as India and Venezuela.

Every morning we had an early breakfast at the hotel (Sylvester-Bradley had the devil's own time in persuading the hotel to feed us before the regularly appointed hour of eight o'clock) after which we all picked up box lunches prepared by the establishment, bought ourselves drinks of our own preference to take along (I liked English cider), and then boarded a chartered bus that took us to our point of departure for the day. We would walk along the Channel beaches all day, with the sparkling surf on one side, the wall of Mesozoic cliffs on the other. Fortunately, for the most part we had beautiful weather, and that made our excursion a real holiday adventure. After our day along the coast the bus would pick us up in the evening and take us back to the hotel, where we would appear in the dining room, a scruffy, bespattered crowd, not at all in harmony with the rest of the guests, most of whom were enjoying dinner in formal attire. I think the headwaiter shuddered every time he saw us appear.

Then the next morning we would board our bus and go to the spot where we had finished our hiking the day before, to continue our Channel-side exploration of the Mesozoic in southern England. During this week-long Channel walk I enjoyed, among other things, the companionship of Bill Swinton of the British Museum, the friend I had first become acquainted with back in the days before the war, when I was a paleontological novice studying Siwalik mammals at the museum and measuring elephant teeth for Professor Osborn.

A few small happenings lent some color to our walks along the Channel. In fact, on one day we did not walk, because we were to go to some localities that could be reached only by boat, coming in from the sea. So that day we boarded a navy landing craft, courtesy of H. M. Government, and with an escort of Royal Marines coming along in a motor launch, we ran up on the beach at a little cove where some unsuspecting Britons were quietly sitting in beach chairs and enjoying the tranquility of their seaside haven. The ramp of the landing craft went down, and out swarmed a motley group of people all armed with geologic hammers and carrying haversacks on their backs. I think the poor vacationers thought that the second invasion of Britain had begun. At any rate we walked right past them and started hammering on the cliffs in the background, much to their wonderment and that of the marines as well. In fact, one of the men in uniform asked me at some length what we thought we were doing. I tried to make it clear to him.

On another day as we walked the beach an army officer appeared on the cliffs above us and started hollering and waving his arms frantically. It seems we had walked into a mine field (many of the beaches of England had been mined against a Nazi invasion) that as yet had not been deactivated. We gingerly made our way out of *that* situation, under the direction of the officer. It might be added that in those days there were still many evidences of the war to be seen; we were constantly passing ammunition dumps along the back roads of southern England.

Our second trip, after the meetings in London, was a more intimate affair. There were sixteen of us in a chartered bus and our leader was Professor D.M.S. Watson of the University of London, at that time the doyen of British vertebrate paleontologists. Watson was a stocky individual, very energetic, with a rugged, rather prognathous visage, and with about the most intense brown eyes that I have ever seen. I remember one day as we were walking through the woods Stanley Westoll, an English paleontologist of my generation, leaned over to me and, gesturing toward Watson who was trudging along with his head thrust forward and his arms swinging back and forth, said: "See! The perfect Neanderthal man!" In a way Watson was, but I think he was probably smarter than most Neanderthals, although there is no way of making a comparison. Certainly Professor Watson was a man of great erudition and accomplishment, which he put to use in a discussion. He was apt to say "Nonsense!" to a proposition and then try to ride the proposer down. The point was not to be terrified by Watson—stand up to him and argue back, and one could frequently prevail.

Another member of our group was Erik Stensiö, the leader of Swedish paleontologists. He was a very pleasant person, and I will always remember his frequently repeated phrase when someone had found a nice fossil. "This is very important!" Only Stensiö would sing it, as Swedes do. Another Swedish member of our group was Erik Jarvik, a large, rugged Viking who we all thought should have been wearing a helmet with horns on it. Erik was the strong and silent type; it was said of him that he could be silent in seven languages. Make no mistake, Stensiö and Jarvik were carrying on very sophisticated research on early fossil fishes.

Bernhard Peyer was a delightful Swiss from Zürich, and therefore a German-speaking Swiss. But he was very fluent in English, as well as other languages—so fluent indeed that he liked to compose English limericks. *That* was an accomplishment for someone not having English as a first language. Professor Peyer was a large man; he always reminded me of a big, genial bear. He was myopic, and so the world was always whizzing past him; when he caught up with the passing scene he was usually pleasantly surprised.

Rex Parrington of Cambridge University, one of my special friends, was a member of the party. Joe Gregory again was along and we roomed together; Sam Welles of the University of California also was one of our party. In addition there were Errol White, the fossil fish man from the British Museum, Pierre de Saint-Seine, a Jesuit priest-paleontologist, who had been active in the resistance against the German occupying forces, and another Frenchman, General Perruche. I won't try to list the others; suffice it to say that we had a jolly time together, our group being small enough so that we were all intimately acquainted before the trip was two days along the road.

We visited fossil localities from middle England to the tip of Scotland, and in the process I was able to become acquainted with the Keuper sediments as they are seen in this part of Europe. All in all the field trip afforded me a comprehensive view at first hand of the Mesozoic and earlier fossil-bearing deposits of England. Moreover, I should add, I was able by myself to make some independent studies of Triassic rocks in southern England during a few days of free time before our Channel walk. Yet valuable as were these probings of the English Triassic, I *still* lacked the experience I hoped some day to have—namely that of an intimate acquaintance with the type Triassic of central Europe.

It was to be quite a few years before this wish was realized, indeed not until our boys had grown to the stage of being more or less independent. Then in the early autumn of 1962, on our way back from Africa, and again in 1965, when we made another autumnal trip this time devoted solely to a study of the type Triassic sequence, Margaret and I spent some rewarding weeks in southern Germany and in Switzerland, surrounded by Triassic rocks. Both times we enjoyed the privilege of doing geological and paleontological field studies in areas of picturesque beauty—in the Swabian countryside of Württemberg and along the southern border of Switzerland on the side of a mountain high above Lake Lugano.

Our center of operations in Germany was Tübingen, where Professor von Huene had for so many years made the university museum there a center for the study of Triassic amphibians and reptiles. Once again I enjoyed meeting with von Huene (it may be remembered that I had first met him back in 1931) and I had the pleasure of introducing Margaret to him. He was now an old man but a very spry old man, still capable of outwalking people like us, and even young folks in their prime. As an aside, our son Philip, on his way back from Nepal where he had spent three years in the Peace Corps and had devoted his spare time at mountain climbing in the Himalayas, stopped in Tübingen where he visited Professor von Huene, and where the old gentleman gave Phil a breath-taking workout tramping around the town. Also in Tübingen we renewed acquaintances with some of the von Huene daughters, now middle-aged ladies.

Our principal guides to the Germanic Triassic were Dolph Seilacher, professor of geology at the university, and Frank Westphal, also on the geology staff of the university. There were some very nice autumnal days in the field, where we saw the entire Triassic sequence—Buntsandstein, Muschelkalk and Keuper—and learned the details, of which there are indeed many, that involve the succession of these rocks in the various parts of Württemberg. Often we would stop at a store the first thing in the morning to purchase fresh bread—good German fresh bread just out of the oven—and some cheese and tomatoes and other eatables, to take along for our lunch. Then at noon we would sit in the autumn sun and view the Swabian landscape and munch our bread and cheese and feel in tune with an ancient countryside, where long ago Teutonic warriors had drifted through the dark forests as they watched the Roman legions march past. It was a good way to become acquainted with the Triassic where it first was studied.

Dolph Seilacher and his wife, then and on occasions since then, have been very hospitable, entertaining us and taking us around the geologically interesting parts of Swabia. Indeed, at the time of our last visit to southern Germany, in 1984, we stayed with them and spent some time at their vacation place in the Black Forest. Dolph is very much an international type of person, and today he divides his time between the University of Tübingen and Yale.

As for Switzerland, we were there the guests of Emil Kuhn-Schnyder and his wife at their summer place near Lake Lugano. Kuhn-Schnyder, who succeeded Professor Peyer at Zürich, had a very comfortable house on the side of Monte San Giorgio, above Lake Lugano, and there he and his wife had a "family" of university students who were engaged in a long-term project of excavating a Triassic quarry on the very tip of the mountain. Each morning after an excellent breakfast, shared with a contingent of wasps who came in at the screenless windows, we would walk upward along a trail through the woods to the top of Monte San Giorgio, where we commanded a broad view of the lake beneath us and the southern Alps. And there we saw the students working very systematically, digging out the Triassic shales that were dipping steeply along the mountain slope, and carefully mapping every fossil they found. The fossils were reptiles, mostly of marine habitat, of middle Triassic age. It was certainly a pleasant and picturesque way to quarry fossils.

So much for the Central European Triassic. What I had seen, the notes I had made, and the pictures that I had taken formed a record invaluable to me in my future Triassic explorations. I had a basis of comparison for Triassic rocks and fossils that I had seen and was to see in other parts of the world.

This classic Triassic that I had studied in southern Germany, the Triassic that had been first described by the pioneer geologists and paleontologists of the early and middle nineteenth century, was, as we have seen, composed of brownish-red sandstones and siltstones of the Buntsandstein, gray and white limestones of the Muschelkalk, and quite varied sediments ranging from dark shales to rather bright-red sandstones of the Keuper. In looking back I could see the similarities between the European Bunter and the Moenkopi beds of Arizona, where in both regions one finds the abundant footprints of a thecodont reptile known as *Chirotherium*, and the none too abundant skulls and scattered bones of heavy-headed amphibians known as labyrinthodonts. High up in the Triassic sequence there are in both the Germanic Keuper and the Chinle beds of Arizona (which latter sediments have yielded *Coelophysis*) early dinosaurs of varied sorts, thecodont reptiles among which the phytosaurs are particularly prominent, and the almost gigantic skulls of the last of the labyrinthodont amphibians. The comparisons are close, and in tramping across the exposures in the deep green forests of Germany I sensed relationships with the colorful exposures of the southwestern deserts. Both regions, today so very different in their scenic aspects, reveal by the nature of their rocks and fossils that they were once integral parts of a single, broad tropical land.

Such are the intellectual joys of the geologists and the paleontologists in the field. A hike involves more than a communion with nature, although certainly anybody who ventures away from the strictures of city life is all the poorer if he or she is not constantly alert to the surrounding scene—to the plants and to the animal life always at hand. Yet for the student of earth history there is more; the nature of the topography and the attitude of the rocks are the clues to a dynamic theme extending back through millions of years, while the fossils found in many of the rocks tell of evolving life through the ages. It is a story of vast proportions that gives free rein to a controlled imagination whereby the past is invoked in pictures that reveal an earlier world of wonderful appearance, a world as fascinating to the mind and to the eye as were the fanciful creations of medieval writers.

I have already mentioned the Newark beds of eastern North America; at this place I would like to return from the European Triassic, to which the Triassic of the western states has been compared, and give some attention to the Newark Series, which may be compared to the east with the type Triassic across the ocean and to the west with the Triassic on the other side of the North American continent. In years past the Newark beds loomed large in my life, if for no other reason than that for three decades and more I lived on Newark rocks and explored them at close hand.

For the Manhattanite (as I was during my first eight years at Columbia University and the American Museum) the Palisades of the Hudson River loom as a long barrier on the west side of the broad estuary (which the Hudson is in a proper sense), a barrier stretching some miles north beyond the northern limits of New York City. Today the barrier is not as impressive nor as formidable as once it was, for it has been breached and built upon, in recent years with high-rise buildings that detract from the natural beauty of the great rocky wall. Such developments never should have been allowed.

The Palisades are a great sill, an outpouring of volcanic rock that once was intruded between sediments of Triassic age. Thus there are Triassic sandstones and shales below the Palisades and above them as well, and since the rock structure of northern New Jersey dips sharply to the west from the river, the Palisades sill and the overlying sediments form a steep slope dipping down to the Jersey meadows. It was to this back slope of the Palisades that Margaret and I moved in 1937, not long after our eldest boy, George, was born.

At the time the attraction of Leonia, New Jersey, had nothing to do with it being in Triassic territory; rather we went there because it was a nice little town with a reputation for good schools, and because some of our friends had migrated there from Manhattan. Also it was very convenient for people working at the American Museum or at Columbia University. From those places one went uptown on the subway and then took a bus across the George Washington Bridge to Leonia, only a couple of miles beyond the Jersey end of the bridge. Or one could commute by car. Consequently it was owing to such considerations that we chose Leonia, and the fact that the town stood on Triassic ground was about the last thing in my mind.

Those were the days of my "Asiatic interlude" already alluded to, so that I was not giving much attention to Triassic rocks and fossils. Of course I was familiar with the Triassic geology of New Jersey— anyone who went through the graduate program at Columbia was necessarily well aware of the local geological picture—but for me it was of passing interest. Then within a few years I made my switch from mammalian paleontology to the study of Mesozoic reptiles and amphibians, with the result that the Triassic rocks and fossils of New Jersey became a matter of high priority not only in my thinking but also in some of my outdoor activities.

The Granton quarry, where *Icarosaurus* was later to be found, was only a few miles south of our home. This was a particular point of attraction for paleontologists on the prowl in search of Triassic fossils, and during more than thirty years of residence in Leonia I frequently drove down to Granton, usually in the company of paleontological friends, to poke about in the quarry. It was a huge excavation in which black shales of the Triassic Lockatong Formation were exposed in the quarry face beneath the volcanic rocks of the Palisades sill. These shales had originally accumulated as muds in the bottom of a large lake that covered a considerable part of what is now northern New Jersey during the later stages of Triassic history. The muds were fine-grained, and they nicely covered and preserved many animals that lived in the lake and died, or animals that inadvertently fell into the water, as did *Icarosaurus*, to be entombed and fossilized. So at this paleontological lodestone many of us climbed about and cracked rocks in search of fossil treasures, which we found every now and then. There were fishes and those ubiquitous late Triassic reptiles, phytosaurs (as would be expected in a lake deposit), as well as some strange little reptiles unlike what could be found at other Triassic localities. One of these we have called "the deep-tailed swimmer" because the tail was, as our name implies, very deep and narrow, quite obviously as an adaptation for swimming. The limbs of this little reptile are slender, and the skull—alas, there is no skull. Many fruitless hours were spent in searching for a skull, but none was ever found. So the precise relationships of this reptile remain as yet unknown. Another small reptile, *Tanytrachelos*, excavated and studied in recent years by Paul Olsen, now of Columbia University, was also an aquatic type, generally related to the peculiar bizarre reptile *Tanystrophaeus* found in the Keuper of southern Germany.

The Granton fossils are interesting because they represent a *facies*, an ecological association, different from most of the Triassic faunas with which we are familiar. As for more typical Triassic fossils one may go north from New York to the Connecticut Valley, extending north along the Connecticut River through the middle of Connecticut and Massachusetts. Through the years I made several excursions into this region, mainly to see some of the dinosaur tracks for which the Connecticut Valley is famous.

These footprints, made by a variety of early dinosaurs, first attracted serious attention early in the nineteenth century, at which time they were thought to be trackways made by ancient birds. Subsequently, as the knowledge of Mesozoic vertebrates became more complete, it was realized that these were dinosaur footprints, preserved in the Triassic and Lower Jurassic sediments of the Connecticut Valley, literally by the tens of thousands. Today at Rocky Hill, Connecticut, there is a state park at which such dinosaur footprints can be seen in place. John Ostrom was instrumental in the creation and development of this park—a source of great satisfaction to me.

Connecticut Valley dinosaur tracks brings to mind an experience of a friend of mine. Back in the fifties when I was teaching at Columbia, a young man—Bruce Hungerford—came around one day to ask if he could audit my lectures, a request that I was happy to grant. Bruce was a concert pianist, who, of all things, was almost fanatically interested in fossils, especially the fossils of dinosaurs. So he attended my lectures which were concerned with reptilian evolution, and on weekends he sometimes went up to the Connecticut Valley to look for dinosaur footprints. He took with him an assortment of heavy hammers and rock chisels, against the vehement protests of his musical colleagues who insisted that he would injure his hands. But Bruce could not be deterred, he *would* look for dinosaur footprints, and if he found any likely ones he *would* whack them out of the rock.

One time he happened to find some nice prints just outside the walls of the Connecticut State Prison, so without further ado he began to excavate. Within a very short time some officers appeared, to enquire as to what he thought he was up to. In fact *they* thought he was up to making a tunnel under the prison wall, so they took him into custody and for an hour or two (I don't know just how long it was) he was subjected to some pretty intensive questioning. Finally they decided he was harmless and let him go; in fact as I recall the story, some of them gave him a hand at getting a dinosaur footprint.

Bruce became one of the leading concert pianists of the past two or three decades, giving concerts in this country and Europe. But he never lost his interest in dinosaurs, especially dinosaur footprints. The last time that

Margaret and I saw him was when he gave a concert at Carnegie Hall, which must have been in 1968 or 1969—just before we moved to Flagstaff. A few years later he was killed in a motorcar accident; the car that he, his mother, and his sister and others were riding in, going from Manhattan to his home in Westchester, was struck head-on and all of the occupants of his car died. But we have remembrances of Bruce; he made quite a series of records, and always he would send us his newest release. Frequently we listen to Bruce playing Beethoven or Schubert, and think back to years past.

My contacts with the Triassic of eastern North America extended beyond New Jersey and the Connecticut Valley. I described some Newark reptiles from Pennsylvania, and one year when we were completely revising one of the dinosaur halls at the American Museum I had the pleasure of supervising a remounting of a phytosaur skeleton that had been collected by Margaret's father in a North Carolina coal mine, back in the nineties when Dr. Matthew as a young man was just beginning his career at the museum.

Also, two decades ago, I had a nice little trip to the Newark beds of Nova Scotia, where in company with Bill Take of the Halifax Museum an exploration was made along the Annapolis Valley bordering the Bay of Fundy. It was fossil hunting of a different kind. We walked the beaches at low tide, taking with us tide tables, so that we could begin our retreat to high ground as the famous Bay of Fundy tide came in. Except for the waters of the bay and the forested hills beyond I might have thought I was back in the Southwest, because the sandstones were cross-bedded and of a brilliant red color.

This brings up a question that has occupied my mind on various occasions, and indeed has been a subject of enquiry by many geologists through the years—why are continental Triassic sediments so frequently red? I have many memories of red rocks throughout the world—the wave-cut sandstones along the Bay of Fundy that have just been mentioned, the spectacular red cliffs of the Capitol Reef in Utah, the long sweep of red strata on the eastern flanks of the Wind River range in Wyoming, the Chinle hills and cliffs of Arizona and New Mexico where I have spent so many days and weeks, the Dockum beds of Texas, the Buntsandstein and Keuper of southern Germany, the Maleri beds of India, the Red Beds of the Karroo Desert in southern Africa, and the Santa Maria Formation of southern Brazil, as well as other exposures that might be mentioned. For me, in my quest for Triassic reptiles and amphibians there has been a unifying background of red rocks, whatever continent I might be on.

The continental sediments of Permian age also may be red, as can be seen when one travels west from Ghost Ranch on the road toward Gallina. But the Permian red, it seems to me, is more of a brick-red than is the Triassic red, which latter is perhaps more delicate in its shading. At least that is how I see it—so I think I can distinguish what I call a "Triassic red" color characteristic of the rocks among which I have spent so much time.

It used to be thought that the red color was a sign of former deserts; certainly that was a commonly expressed view when I was a student. But opinion has veered pretty much away from such an interpretation. The clear indication of humid conditions in so many of the red Triassic rocks, such as large trees and ferns and water-loving amphibians and phytosaurs in the Chinle beds of the Petrified Forest and other parts of the Southwest, belie the idea of deserts where these organisms lived. No, the red colors are probably of secondary origin, but satisfactory explanations have yet to be propounded. As for me, this problem of color has been an interesting diversion, but a problem that I have not attempted to solve. It is enough to have to struggle with the fossils themselves.

On two occasions my research for the Triassic took me to Israel, the first time by myself, the second time with Margaret as a companion. Both trips were undertaken with strong encouragement from George Haas of Hebrew University in Jerusalem. This leads me to say something about George Haas (already briefly mentioned) and the class of 1905. George and I were both born in 1905, as was Emil Kuhn-Schnyder, mentioned on a preceding page, and Llewelyn Price, to be introduced on a subsequent page. An interesting fact about the four of us, members of the class of 1905, is that we all were (George and Llew are deceased), or are, especially interested in Triassic reptiles. When one considers the relatively small population of vertebrate paleontologists throughout the world, and the range of research problems to which they might direct their attentions, it seems to me something of a coincidence that four of us involved in one particular line of endeavor should all have been born in the same year. This rather incidental and unimportant fact has been something of a bond between us.

George (actually he should be called Georg, which was his christened, Germanic name, but since he frequently referred to himself as George, and even used this name on some of his published papers, I will here use the English name) was educated at the University of Vienna, and went to Israel in the twenties when that nation was coming into being as a result of treaties and decisions arising from the political alignments brought about by the First World War. In Israel George soon established himself as an authority on the herpetology of the Middle East, as well as on fossil amphibians and reptiles found in that part of the world.

Such were his specialties, but there was much more to George than a concern with the extinct and recent cold-blooded vertebrates of Palestine, for George was in every sense of the word a modern example of a Renaissance man. His interests were wide and his erudition was impressive. He spoke several languages fluently as might be expected, and he had an enviable knowledge of Latin and classic Greek. He had a love of literature, ancient and modern. He was a mine of information about the zoology and botany of Israel, and his knowledge of the archeology and history of the Holy Land was prodigious. Consequently one enjoyed an unexcelled liberal education when traveling in Israel with George—an experience that was much appreciated by Margaret and by me. I will always remember Margaret's plucking wild flowers as we tramped around various parts of Israel and showing them to George, and always he knew in detail what he was looking at. He would recite the scientific name of the specimen, and tell us about its distribution, its relationships, and other pertinent data.

As for prehistory and history, George opened our eyes to the basic facts about a land that is all too misunderstood— about why the ancient Israelites hated the Philistines (because the Philistines were iron-age people, while the Israelites, lacking the knowledge of iron-making, were still confined within a more primitive bronze-age culture), or why the Old Testament is in so many respects a fascinating document (because it is history written by bronze-age people).

George, a bachelor, was a large man, rather heavy and clumsy; he was myopic and wore very thick spectacles. In short, he hardly had the appearance of an heroic figure. But through the 1948 war, when Israel was surrounded by Arab enemies and was fighting for its life, George performed many deeds of derring-do. I remember him telling about riding up the road from Tel Aviv to Jerusalem on top of a truck, with sniper fire directed at him all of the way. (When we were in Israel that winding road, hemmed in by hills and trees and thus a perfect locale along its length for ambushes, was lined on both sides by the rusting carcasses of armored cars and other vehicles that had fallen victims to the war. They had been purposely left there as memorials to a bitter struggle.) And I remember him telling how he smuggled fossils under his coat from the original site of Hebrew University on Mount Scopus (at the time completely surrounded by Arab land) to the university at its relocated site in Jerusalem.

In such a land and with a man such as George as our host is it any wonder that frequently there were things other than fossils to occupy our attention? The natural history, the prehistory and history, and the ubiquity of exciting, even dangerous happenings in this troubled land were always with us.

There was the day when George, Margaret, and I missed a hot little fight along the Jordanian border by about half an hour. Within that interval after we had left the area where we had been pleasantly engaged in looking at some of the wild plants under George's tutelage, a little group tried to infiltrate Israeli territory and were promptly repulsed. We were only too happy to have missed that engagement, which we learned about the next day.

And there was the day down in the Negev when one of the two cars we were using got hopelessly stuck in the sand. We tried to dig it out and we tried to pull it with the other car, which was a jeep, all to no avail. Finally a detachment from the Israeli army, down there in the desert on maneuvers, came along and rescued us. But in the meantime Margaret had wandered a little way down the wadi, and while we were all laboring vainly under the hot sun she found in a bank a couple of beautifully formed leaf-shaped flints of a lovely old-rose color, which she brought back for our examination. "Mousterian," said George without a moment's hesitation as Margaret handed them to him, for the university museum. Her little discovery illustrates one of the fascinating facts about Israel; it reveals the activities of mankind that took place through thousands, even tens of thousands of years. In the days when Neanderthal men lived here it was a crossroads for the wanderings of many peoples, of many cultures. Today, many millenia after the years of the Neanderthals, it is still a crossroads, fiercely contested, and that is why the Israeli army was there honing its skills and its weapons. (In fact, on both of my trips to Israel I got mixed up with the army on maneuvers in the Negev and needless to say I was impressed with what I saw. There was no nonsense about what they were doing.)

Speaking of Neanderthals, there is the pleasant memory of the day when George and Margaret and I, along with Professor and Mrs. Raymond Dart of South Africa (Dart being one of the original scholars involved with *Australopithecus* and other very early men in Africa) as well as with Professor and Mrs. Stekhelis of Hebrew University (he being an archeologist), visited a cave near Ma'agan Mikhael not far from Carmel, where the skeleton of a Neanderthal child had been found. And in this cave there was discovered a hyena skull surrounded by a ring of stones— evidently a burial made by a cult of Neanderthals, perhaps related to the Neanderthal "cave bear cult" of Europe. High on the roof of the cave thousands of bats, disturbed by our presence, squeaked and fluttered their wings to create a background of soft noise, protesting the doings of the beings beneath them.

The cave faced the bright blue waters of the eastern Mediterranean shore; we came out of its dim interior into the strong sunlight and made our way down the slope at the foot of the cliff in which the cave was located, to seek the shade of a banana grove, there to eat our lunches. The banana crop had been harvested, but on the trees there were still a few overlooked fruits, and these we picked to supplement our plebeian fare. They were just right, having ripened to the state of perfection on the trees, so we enjoyed a banana feast of truly patrician quality. Then as we rested Professor Stekhelis gave us a demonstration of how to flake a stone-age implement out of a piece of quartz. He knew what he was doing and in very short order he had produced an artifact that would have served very well as a spearhead or perhaps a small handaxe. His performance demonstrated to us how paleolithic men were never in want of stone tools; they could manufacture their artifacts on the spur of the moment.

After the cave and the banana grove we went to Caesarea, the Roman city that once served as an administrative center for the Roman province of Palestine, being the residence of the Roman procurators. It was of course a fascinating place, but as we viewed the ruins, including a large theater sited so that the audience would have faced the sea behind the stage, we could reflect that the fragment of ancient history at which we were looking was closer to us in years many times over than the remains of the Neanderthal culture at Carmel.

What about the Triassic rocks and fossils that I had come to Israel to see? Certainly I had not forgotten them, but Israel, being a country so very rich in human prehistory and history, and George Haas being the man for all seasons that he was, my search for the Triassic in this corner of the world had been delayed for a time because of all of the wonderful nongeological sights that surrounded us. One cannot visit northern and central Israel and remain indifferent to the works of man through the ages. To see the Triassic it is necessary to go into the southern part of the country, specifically to the arid Negev. That we did, and I will write at this place particularly about my second trip into southern Israel, when Margaret was with me.

As usual George was our companion and guide on this trip, but he was assisted by one of his then outstanding graduate students, Eitan Chernov. Eitan is now a respected member of the faculty at Hebrew University, where he is carrying on and elaborating the researches in zoology that had been directed for so many years by George. At the time of which I write Eitan was a most valued fourth member of our group, for he supplemented the teachings of George in an especially useful manner. Being young and spry he could pursue and catch lizards and other small, active members of the local fauna to show us. Furthermore, there were some aspects of Eitan's store of knowledge that went beyond and in a different direction from the encyclopedic well of information that so characterized George. For example, Margaret and I recall particularly the time we were all at Capernaum, the scene of the loaves and the fishes in the New Testament, and there we were examining with much interest an exquisite mosaic floor (the remains of a former chapel) picturing the fabled story. As we were there two nuns came on the scene, seated themselves at one end of the floor, and began to sing most sweetly. The songs were ancient airs, and Eitan, who among other accomplishments is a musicologist, was able to identify and explain them to us. It was a memorable experience.

Another of George's former students was Eviator Nevo, who often accompanied us on our trips around Israel. Evi was teaching at the technical school in Haifa, but he and his wife, who was a medical doctor at a hospital in Haifa, lived on a small kibbutz some miles out from the city. Evi at the time we were in Israel was doing research on fossil frogs. As an aid to his research the kibbutz had built for him a nice little laboratory, equipped with a microscope and other needed research tools so that he could carry on his studies in the rural quiet of the settlement. Evi, too, supplemented George's explanations of the natural history of Israel. With George, Eitan, and Evi as our guides, there was little of what we saw that remained unexplained.

From Jerusalem we drove south to Beersheba, and then south for about thirty miles to the ancient and deserted city of Shivta, once again to be diverted from the pursuit of fossils by the works of man. Shivta was an early Christian city dating back to about the eighth century A.D., and its ruins remain today in the shape of many walls and streets and above all a very fine church fashioned of limestone. Of course there are no roofs today, but one can sense the nature of the city, and one can only marvel at how such a settlement might have existed in the bleak desert that now surrounds it. Perhaps in those days, when the streets and houses of Shivta were full of people, the desert may not have been so bleak; probably, as various students of archeology have theorized, the inhabitants had sophisticated methods of dry farming. Shivta seemed all too real, yet not real either, a city with fresh-looking walls but no roofs, a city of elegant architecture standing deserted in the desert.

We found ourselves in the church, with a vaulted embayment where once the altar had been, and there we sat down on the ground between the still-standing pillars of the nave. The situation seemed appropriate, so I recited a couple of lines from Shakespeare's *Richard II*.

> For God's sake, let us sit upon the ground
> And tell sad stories of the death of kings.

Which pleased George mightily.

South of Shivta by some twenty miles or so is Makhtesh Ramon as I have it in my field book, or Machtesh Ramon, as it is indicated on the map, a huge depression in the desert. In geological terms Machtesh Ramon is an eroded anticline bounded along its southern edge by a long fault. This means that it is an arched structure with its interior exposed by the inexorable forces of erosion and its southern edge abruptly truncated by a long, straight scarp—the result of vertical earth movements. From Mizpe Ramon on the rim, where we had our first view of the structure, Machtesh Ramon is truly a stupendous sight. The floor of the depression, far below, is a rugged desert terrain of colorful brown, gray, and red badlands, punctuated by black mounds, the remains of past volcanic activity. And down there at the bottom of the depression are Triassic badlands, the oldest of the sediments to be exposed (as is the rule in an anticline) while ranging up from this ancient floor to the rim are bands of successively younger sediments of Jurassic and Cretaceous age. It was to the Triassic that our little expedition was directing its attention. Down a rough, winding road we descended, into a Dantesque world of barren rocks and heat.

The sediments of Machtesh Ramon are primarily of marine origin, including the Triassic beds in the center of the depression. Consequently we were looking for the bones of marine reptiles of that age, and we found them. They were the skeletal remains of placodonts, armored reptiles that in their own way were rather like turtles in form, yet were not in the least related to turtles (a nice example of evolutionary convergence), in which the bones of the skull and the jaws were very strong, and armed with flat, millstonelike teeth, nicely adapted for crushing the hard shells of molluscs. I should add that the placodonts of Machtesh Ramon are closely related to placodonts found in the Muschelkalk limestones of southern Germany—an indication that Middle Triassic seas were widely spread across this part of the world. We put a plaster jacket on one of the specimens and while we were waiting for the plaster to dry Margaret smoothed a gob of discarded plaster and carved on it an inscription—"Here lies a long-placated placodont." She buried her handiwork as a token of our efforts, and two years later it was found by George when he returned to this locality—much to his amusement.

A few more journeys within Israel and my search for the Triassic, with collateral views of other Mesozoic sediments, including an incredible concentration of Cretaceous ammonites (Nautilis-like shells) on an upended rock face in Machtesh Ramon, and a horizontal Cretaceous floor with dinosaur footprints near Jerusalem, had ended.

Years afterward Margaret and I still remember Israel with nostalgic affection. It was our privilege to see this presently torn and unhappy land under the best of auspices, with a man who had a deep understanding of the Middle East, who saw it not only from the viewpoint of an inhabitant who had been subjected to several decades of violent history, but also who as a scholar had a large and a profound appreciation of this complex region, the point of a focus for so many different peoples. And when we think back to Israel our thoughts are concerned particularly with the sunny land we saw, where there are successive records of past life and buried records of human wanderings. We think of our excursions with George and his associates, instructing us as to the paleontological record, the archeological treasures, and the plant and animal life, all of which distinguish the Middle East as a land of unusual significance to the natural historian.

A few years ago George was preparing to go to Switzerland, to deliver a series of academic lectures there. The evening before his departure he was packing for a trip that he was never to make; the next morning his body was found by the bed where a partly filled suitcase remained as a testament to his final hour on earth. Thus one member of our class of 1905 peacefully died, preparing as usual for the scholarly days ahead. It was a great privilege to have known him.

XVI

Gondwana

I must admit that when I went to Britain in 1948, the year after our Ghost Ranch discovery, I was not thinking in terms of Laurasia, while Gondwanaland or Gondwana was indeed very far removed from my thoughts. Those years following the Second World War, like the years before the war, were still within the time frame when continental drift, as we called it, was looked upon with disfavor by most geologists. Earth movements according to long-established geological theory were vertical; there was no place in accepted geological usage for broad horizontal movements of the earth's crust. I had had it drummed into my head by Professor Osborn, by George Simpson, by Professor Walter Bucher of Columbia University (certainly one of the world's leading structural geologists), and by other authorities whose opinions I had good reason to respect, that continental drift was a will-o'-the-wisp idea, that Alfred Wegener who had proposed the concept was a dreamer, and that the few geologists who at the time were disciples of Wegener were sadly deluded people. Perhaps the widely held opinion concerning continental drift was summed up by a president of the American Philosophical Society, who said that Wegener's theory was "utter, damned rot." In such an intellectual climate I hardly felt qualified to dispute the prevailing attitudes—and anyway the whole problem did not much concern me.

Walter Bucher was mentioned in the preceding paragraph, and here I would like to digress briefly to say a little more about him. As indicated, he was without doubt one of the outstanding structural geologists in the world. He was also an engaging person on several counts, for he was a sort of nineteenth-century scholar, wonderfully interested in everything he encountered, from great to trivial. All of which made time spent with Walter Bucher unstructured and unpredictable.

He was a short, rather rotund man, with a round face accentuated by round, gleaming spectacles, and when I knew him he had a shiny bald head circled by a fringe of gray hair. He also possessed a closely clipped gray mustache. He was marvelously dynamic, cheerful, and remarkably absent-minded, and might very well have served as a prototype of the absent-minded professor. The wonders of the world as he saw them, and his thoughts about matters seen and unseen, crowded through his mind in such a constant parade that his attention was being ever diverted from one subject to another. This made him a stimulating and at times a worrisome companion, especially when he was at the wheel of a car, for he was generally more interested in the passing scene than in the road ahead.

Bucher was born in Cincinnati, a strongly Germanic city, and when he was quite young his parents moved to Germany, where he grew up. He experienced his higher education at Heidelberg University; then he returned to this country to spend the remainder of his long and productive life. As might be expected, he spoke with a fairly thick German accent, although he spoke and wrote excellent English. His wife was Germanic Swiss and was his boon companion.

The Buchers were our close neighbors in Leonia, New Jersey, for many years living about a block down the hill from our house. And a block up the hill were Norman and Valerie Newell, our particularly close friends. Norman was and is at the museum—an authority in the field of invertebrate paleontology, which has to do with the study of fossil animals without backbones. So with the Buchers below us and the Newells above us on our New Jersey hillside, we enjoyed relationships that extended beyond the boundaries of our being fellow laborers in the field of earth sciences.

One summer Norman and Valerie were on a paleontologial field expedition out West—I think it was in western Texas—and Walter Bucher came to visit them and their field crew. It was quite an experience for Norman, because each morning the three of them would leave camp bright and early to inspect the area where Norman's field crew was working, and each morning they would arrive at their destination, but not until almost lunchtime. On the way from camp to the collecting area Bucher would have to stop to examine the flowers, or to watch the birds, or to lecture at length on some geological phenomenon seen along the side of the road, with

Norman in the meantime generally being reduced to a state of incoherence. Norman loved Walter, as we all did, but he found that intimate association with this man of insatiable curiosity was trying to the soul. And yet one could not help but value those stimulating hours spent with Bucher.

His feats of absent-mindness were legendary and the tales are legion. The one story that I like, and it was vouched for to me by several people who were involved, had to do with a car pool that had been organized by some Columbia professors living in Leonia. The Columbia car pool was set up so that its various members would take turns driving, and of course it was the duty of the driver each day to pick up the other members of the pool. One day it was Walter Bucher's turn to drive, so he dutifully made the rounds and picked up his fellow passengers. Then he drove to his own house and stopped, much to the puzzlement of the other people in the car, and finally he began to honk the horn. Suddenly, to everybody's amazement, it became evident that Bucher was stopping to pick himself up. Of course when this became apparent the whole crowd roared with laughter, not the least among those enjoying the inadvertent joke being Bucher. He was quite aware of his own idiosyncracies and he was invariably amused by his failings. How could one be out of sorts with such a sweet-tempered person?

Of course Bucher was a man of original ideas, and his ideas did not always coincide with current geological thinking. I remember that he once gave me a long argument as to why Meteor Crater in Arizona is a steam-explosion vent and not an impact crater; this in spite of the evidence as to its meteoric origin. As for plate tectonics and continental drift, he was a member of the opposition. Perhaps he came around to the modern concept toward the end of his life—I don't know. But during the years when I was associated with him he was a firm believer in the fixity of continents, so much so that on one occasion, at a geology department party at Columbia, the students presented him with a large wooden anchor—for holding North America in place. As already mentioned, his stance on the problem of continental relationships was influential to my thinking during the immediate postwar years.

So I went to Europe that summer, and I made trips to other foreign parts during the decade or so following with the thought of learning as much as I could about the Triassic rocks and fossils in their local settings with no particular attention being given to such an esoteric theory (as it seemed to me) of shifting continents. As far as I was concerned, the distributions of Mesozoic reptiles and amphibians could be accounted for by stable continents, connected along the lines that are present today—the trans-Bering crossing between North America and Eurasia, the isthmian link between the two Americas, the Middle East route from Eurasia into Africa, and some sort of a vague crossing from Asia through the East Indies to Australia. Antarctica was completely removed from any of my speculations, as was surely the case for many other paleontologists. Subsequently during the course of years, my thinking went through a 180-degree rotation, as will be told, and my own conversion to plate tectonics, as the theory had evolved by the time I became intimately involved with the problem, was largely a result of my work in Gondwanaland.

Gondwanaland was named by Eduard Suess, an Austrian geologist, in his massive work, *Das Antlitz der Erde*, published in the late nineteenth century and translated into English as *The Face of the Earth* in 1904–1924. (If it seems that the translation was a long time in being completed and published it must be remembered that Suess's publication, with Germanic thoroughness, occupied five volumes.) Suess was impressed by the fact that certain late Paleozoic sediments in central India contained a very character-istic fossil plant, *Glossopteris*, and that sedimentary rocks with *Glossopteris* also were present in Africa and Madagascar. Thus Suess envisaged a former continent embracing peninsular India, Madagascar, and Africa, parts of which foundered beneath the waves of the western Indian Ocean. Subse-quently the idea was expanded to include South America and Australia, with great segments of the hypothetical continent having disappeared into the South Atlantic and the eastern part of the Indian Ocean as well.

In my student days, and indeed for some years after the Second World War, a modified concept of Gondwanaland prevailed with many geologists, who saw Gondwanaland, if they admitted that Gondwanaland had existed, as a series of isthmian links between the several southern continents, or perhaps even a series of archipelagos. There still was widespread reluctance to accept continental drift. Yet ironically enough, so far as my own paleontological evolution is concerned, some of the crucial work that was to establish plate tectonics as an almost undeniable fact was going on at Columbia University under my nose.

In the years immediately after the war Maurice Ewing, one of the shining lights in the world of geophysics, was establishing and developing the Lamont Geological Observatory (later the Lamont-Doherty Geological Observatory) at Columbia University. This was a rather independent research institute contained within the geology department of the univer-sity, with which I was affiliated, but physically located about thirty miles up the Hudson River on a large estate that had belonged to Thomas Lamont, and donated to the university by the Lamont family. Here Ewing and his associates were engaged in various imaginative research projects, among which were geophysical surveys of the oceanic basins. The observatory had a research vessel, the *Vema*, which was used for the surveys, and through several years many transects were made across the oceans, defining profiles of the sea bottom with sophisticated echo-locating equipment.

Among the scientists working with Ewing were Bruce Heezen and Marie Tharp, and to make a long story short, they were engaged in a long-term project of mapping the ocean floors, basing their maps on the data gathered by the *Vema* and other research vessels. As a result of their work a series of intricate and detailed maps of the ocean basins was produced, which showed quite clearly that the ocean floors are quite different in topography from the continents. In essence, Heezen and Tharp showed that the oceanic basins are traversed by long ridges showing a spreading of the crust along these submarine elevations, and that the boundaries of the Pacific Basin in particular are marked by deep trenches where the oceanic crust is being depressed, to dive beneath the edges of the adjacent land masses.

Of course I saw some of these maps in their initial stages, and of course I was much impressed by what I saw—yet I was not completely converted to the idea of drifting continents on the basis of the maps. For truth to tell, some of the collateral evidence that in time would corroborate the map pictures either had not as yet been developed, or was in the initial stages of development. Such was the state of things when I made my first trip to Gondwanaland.

My introduction to Gondwanaland came in 1959, when Margaret and I made our first trip to Brazil. I had been invited by the Conselho Nacional de Pesquisas do Brasil, an official research committee corresponding more or less to the National Research Council of the United States of America, to visit our neighbor to the south in order to work with some of my Brazilian colleagues. To our delight, the invitation included Margaret. My hosts were to be Llewellyn Price (already mentioned as one of the four members of the class of 1905), Carlos de Paula Couto and Fausto Luiz de Souza Cunha, the two latter quite obviously good Brazilians with Portuguese names. But what of Llewellyn? He too was a good Brazilian, but with an international background. Llew was born in southern Brazil of American parents, he spent his younger years in Brazil, but came to the United States for his high school and college education. He had dual citizenship; but after several years under the tutelage of Al Romer at Harvard Llew opted for Brazil—he felt his opportunities were there.

We left New York on the day after New Year's Day, and it was a bitterly cold morning, and boarded a Constellation—that was before the days of jets—for a long flight across the equator. But it was to be a pleasant flight, especially because we were traveling on Varig, the Brazilian airline, which was noted for its hospitality and good service. Good service, indeed! There was a sort of head hostess on the plane, a very nice lady *not* in uniform, who did everything possible to make the passengers comfortable. Also there was a chef on board, and marvelous meals were our lot. All of which was in contrast to the ordeal of flying today in cramped seats, with mediocre food served up in plastic containers.

On the morning after our departure from New York our plane circled into the airport at Rio de Janiero, and as we were coming down for our landing I saw that Margaret was crying, so that for an instant I was alarmed. No problem; she was overcome by the beauty of the scene, so overcome that the tears came to her eyes.

On the ground we were met by Llew and Carlos, and they whisked us to a nice little hotel on the beach at Copacabana, which was to be our home for the next week or so. From that day on we lost our hearts to Brazil. Every morning in that little hotel we had our breakfast on a balcony looking out over the ocean, while the surf pounded Copacabana beach. And every day we had new experiences. Never to be forgotten was the day we went to Alta da Boa Vista with Carlos, where we sat in the shade and watched a waterfall slide down over steep, smooth rocks, where the silhouettes of tree ferns were outlined against the tropical sky and where we saw great colorful butterflies fluttering their erratic courses through the deep green forest.

It is written that one time some guests visiting Darwin's home at Down asked him what was the most memorable scene he had witnessed during the voyage of the *Beagle*. Darwin thought it was a view in Chile. Then, according to his custom he retired early. But in a half hour or so he came downstairs in a dressing gown, and told his guests that he had been thinking about the question, and it was his conclusion that for him the most memorable sight was the tropical forest of Brazil.

We became acquainted with several Brazils. The idyllic Brazil of tropical jungles, such as Alta da Boa Vista so close to Rio, is counterbalanced, one might say, by the twentieth-century Brazil of huge cities and skyscrapers, such as Rio itself or the many other metropolitan areas that typify a country growing too fast for its own good. There are contrasts within the cities as one might expect, with squalid *favelas* (or shantytowns) cheek by jowl with luxurious apartment buildings. This is especially evident in Rio, where the *favelas* straggle up the sides of the steep morros (or hills) that rise as huge igneous cones within the city, so that the people of the *favelas*, living in direst poverty, look right into the windows of the plutocrats in their apartments, and vice versa. Or there are the ornate baroque churches that add historic dignity to the city, while around the corner are held primitive macumba rites practiced by the descendants of African slaves. (One night I was awakened in the hotel at Copacabana by the sound of drums and singing, and when I looked out of the window I saw there on the beach a crowd of people performing some sort of mysterious rite. I found out later that they were putting out offerings of food, to be washed to sea by the waves as tributes to their particular deities. The next morning when I asked the desk clerk about it he denied that any such thing had taken place. He was obviously embarrassed or perhaps ashamed to admit that primitive rites could happen in so sophisticated a city as Rio.)

The plan was for us to go to the southernmost part of Brazil, to the state of Rio Grande do Sul, there to explore the Triassic rocks and collect fossils. Consequently after a week or so at Copacabana, a week during which we had reunions with the Price and Couto families (they had spent some time in New York some years previously, when Llew and Carlos studied at the museum), a week about which I could maunder on for pages as to the beauty and excitement of Rio—which I will not—we flew down to Pôrto Alegre, the capital city of Rio Grande do Sul. I was quite unprepared for Pôrto Alegre; I suppose I had visions of a sleepy little city on the edge of the Pampas. We arrived in a large metropolitan center, a city of skyscrapers, a city perhaps comparable in size with Kansas City. That was to be our point of departure for the interior.

There were a few more days of preparation, and then we left for Santa Maria in a field car, a van provided through the courtesy of Professor Irajá Damiani Pinto, the chairman of the Department of Geology at the University of Rio Grande do Sul in Pôrto Alegre. Our drive was over red dirt roads, with *fazendas* (or ranches) to be seen on either side—the houses and outbuildings of which were topped with red tile roofs, accentuated by the bright light of the Brazilian sun. At the Jacui River, incredibly blue against the dark green forest on each bank, we took a primitive ferry, and on our short ride across the river we had the company of a Brazilian cowboy, a gaucho, clad in baggy pants and a pink shirt, a black, wide-brimmed hat, and the inevitable *faca* (or knife) thrust in his belt. We arrived in Santa Maria late in the afternoon.

Santa Maria is a nice little city set right in the middle of a band of red Triassic rocks that crosses the state of Rio Grande do Sul and then curves down toward Uruguay. There we were to have the pleasure of living in a hotel and of traveling from the comfort of good beds and meals in a dining room to our fossil digs on the edge of town. In fact for the only time in my life I went to dig fossils every morning in a taxi—such transportation necessitated by the fact that Irajá needed the van which he had temporarily lent to us, so that for a week or so we were without a field car. We would hail a cab for the short ride to Quilometre Tres (the name of this little suburb indicates how close it was to the middle of town), work all day in the *sangas* (or gulleys, or ditches, or arroyos, or whatever you want to call them), and then get a ride back into town at the end of the day. At Quilometre Tres, which in those days was a sort of market-garden appendage to Santa Maria, where vegetables were grown to be sold daily in town, Llew arranged for us to have our noonday repasts with a local farmer and his family, the Hübners. Each noon we would sit down to a hearty meal of two or three kinds of meat (the noonday meal is the big meal in southern Brazil), home-grown vegetables and other good things, served at a rough table out of doors under the trees. All in all it was a good way to hunt for and collect fossils.

The Triassic Santa Maria Formation, quite obviously named for the little city, is composed of red—in many localities brilliant red—sandstones and siltstones—once again an example of the continental Triassic red beds in which I had spent so many of my last dozen or so field seasons. In the tropical humid climate of Rio Grande do Sul these Triassic sediments erode rapidly, often rather spectacularly, so that in spite of the abundant vegetation covering lowlands and hills, there are numerous exposures in which to search for fossils. The fossils we were looking for and finding were different from the fossils of Triassic age that I had been accustomed to digging up in the sediments of Laurasia, for in the Santa Maria Formation, especially in the vicinity of the city itself, we were encountering more than anything else the bones and skeletons of rhynchosaurs, these being fossil reptiles characteristic of Gondwanaland, but rare in Laurasia.

The rhynchosaurs were not quite like the reptiles with which I was familiar, those from Santa Maria being large reptiles by Triassic standards, about the size of a good-sized pig, with heavy bodies, strong limbs, and short tails. The skull is truly bizarre; it is rather deep, with the front of the skull and lower jaws narrowed into a sort of beak. The cheek teeth are button-shaped and very numerous. It looks as if these strange reptiles might have dug up roots for sustenance. But what is peculiar to me, as well as to other paleontologists and beyond my understanding, is the fact that instead of having teeth at the front of the head, the premaxillary bones of the skull and the front of the lower jaw are shaped and adapted to serve as big teeth, rather like the teeth of huge rodents. But why should any animal have developed such a queer adaptation—exposing live bone to the vicissitudes of wear and tear and the danger of infection? But there it is, as plain as can be and not to be denied, one of the paleontological puzzles yet to be solved.

Llew, Carlos, Fausto, and I excavated a big rhynchosaur at Quilometre Tres, in an eroded *sanga* right beside the road along which there passed a daily procession of little two-wheeled, horse-drawn carts, and across from a row of little wooden cottages. Needless to say we had a daily audience, and among the spectators were Senhor Perreira, a middle-aged gentleman who lived in one of the little cottages across the road, and evidently was enjoying the pleasures of retirement, because he always appeared clad in a suit of pajamas and loose sandals. He was abiding by the old Brazilian definition for living the good retired life—*"sombre e agua fresca e chinelas largas"*—in humid and muddy working in that *sanga*, and two or three times each day we would cross the road to the Perreira house for refreshments, served by the Senhora, a very pleasant, dignified grandmother who walked with stately tread on her bare feet.

For some reason Senhora Perreira got the idea that Carlos was my son, a misapprehension that caused some merriment when it came to the surface. Carlos, only about four years my junior, was a very handsome man in a dark, Latin way, and he did have an unusually young face. Of course Llew and I, being of the class of 1905, were contemporaries except that Llew was eleven days my junior. Fausto was considerably younger than the rest of us; he was a big, strong Portuguese type of Brazilian, and when the time came for some heavy lifting on our rhynchosaur Fausto was the man for the job. All in all we were an efficient and compatible team.

It was terribly rainy while we were trying to get the rhynchosaur out of the ground, and the afore-mentioned mud was ubiquitous, sticky, and red. Then in the midst of our operations it was time for Margaret to leave; she had to fly back home. So we all went with her to the little airport at Santa Maria, and she felt just a bit miffed because we sat around and worried more about our rhynchosaur getting wet than about her taking off into an ominous, black sky. The plane came, a little commuter type of craft that would make a hop to Pôrto Alegre, and she ran out to it in a pelting rain, partially protected by an umbrella held by an airport employee running along beside her. Off went the plane into the black sky (she made the flight to Pôrto Alegre without incident) and back to our sodden rhynchosaur we made our way. From my field book: "We rode back to town in the Varig taxi, through a very heavy rainstorm. Poor rhynchosaur! What will it look like tomorrow?"

Eventually, after several days of very uncomfortable work we got the fossil plastered, at which point Llew made a deal with a passing cart to haul it to the Hübner farm, where we would pack it (along with other fossils) for shipment.

The rhynchosaurs of Santa Maria were not the only Gondwana fossils that we hunted and collected. There were the mammallike reptiles, notably the dicynodonts which at this locality are large, with heavy skeletons, also with bizarre skulls of rather open construction and in which there are no teeth except for a pair of tusks in the skull of many individuals, probably males. Elsewhere in Rio Grande do Sul we were on the trail of mammallike reptiles having advanced evolutionary characters, in other words the reptiles known as theriodonts that were approaching a mammalian grade in their anatomical structure.

In the foregoing paragraph the mammallike reptiles known as dicynodonts as well as those designated as theriodonts have been mentioned. Perhaps this is an appropriate place to say something about these interesting and important reptiles, some of which were on the evolutionary line that was to culminate in the ancestral mammals.

The mammallike reptiles belong to the reptilian order known as the Therapsida that lived during late Paleozoic and Triassic times. The dicynodonts and the theriodonts constitute two suborders of therapsids, the former characterized by their tusked skulls, as mentioned, the latter by skulls and teeth that show in a progressive manner through time an approach toward the mammalian condition, also as mentioned. In fact, the last of the theriodonts approach the mammals so closely, not only in the morphology of the skull and teeth but also in many aspects of the skeleton, that it becomes a matter of definition, based upon rather esoteric anatomical features, whether these fossils should be regarded as reptiles or mammals. As contrasted with the very mammallike theriodonts the dicynodonts became highly specialized, at an early stage in their evolutionary history, along lines quite divergent from the trend toward the mammals. These queer reptiles were almost from their beginnings fashioned to a single pattern of adaptation that was retained through millions of years of their history until their extinction at the end of Triassic time.

We found theriodonts at a place called Pinheiros, where next to a little country store there was a clump of large araucarian pines looking for all the world as if they were the great logs of the Petrified Forest of Arizona come to life. We were in essence collecting Triassic mammallike reptiles figuratively in the shadow of still-living Triassic trees. Actually, as usual in Brazil, we were working in a *sanga* some little way behind the store, while off to the north we could see the escarpment of the great Serra Geral, the immense volcanic flow that covers a large part of Rio Grande do Sul and Santa Catarina to the north.

Rhynchosaurs and dicynodonts and advanced mammallike theriodonts—these are all typical Gondwana reptiles, and the fossils we were collecting in Brazil have their counterparts in southern Africa. Yet even though such was the case, I still was not thoroughly convinced as to the reality of a southern Gondwana continent. Such reptiles both in Brazil and Africa did not necessarily prove a close physical relationship of the continental areas—at least so I thought at the time. One could bring these reptiles during Triassic time from Africa up through Asia, across the Bering connection, down through North America, across a Panamanian isthmus and into South America with the continents arranged about as they are today. It seems like a tortuous journey, but if such animals had expanded their ranges by a mere half a mile a year, which would have been quite feasible for large, active animals, the journey of some twenty thousand miles or so could have been effected in forty or fifty thousand years, and that would seem instantaneous to a present-day observer looking at the Triassic time scale.

instantaneous to a present-day observer looking at the Triassic time scale. From a practical rather than a theoretical point of view, I was, on this, my first trip to Gondwanaland, becoming acquainted in the field with reptiles that eventually I would find throughout other parts of the southern hemisphere, as well as in the Indian peninsula. Such discoveries and such distributions were, in time, to make me a firm believer in Gondwanaland, as will be told.

For the moment, however, my goal was to learn something about the Triassic land-living vertebrates of South America, so after Rio Grande do Sul I made a brief excursion into Argentina to see fossils in museums, and again in the field. As for museums, I had the opportunity to study collections in Buenos Aires and La Plata, while in the field I ventured to the western boundary of the country, where Triassic sediments containing vertebrates are located at the foot of the Andes.

There my host was Dr. Jose Luis Minoprio, a medical man in Mendoza, who happened to be very much interested in fossils. Life with Minoprio, even for a brief few days, turned out to be interesting in many ways. For one thing he was the very antithesis of the stereotypic languid Latin; rather he was brim full of energy. I arrived in Mendoza, my destination after a flight from Pôrto Alegre to Buenos Aires and from there on to the west, landing at about ten o'clock in the evening. There was Dr. Minoprio and some other Argentine paleontologists at the airport to meet me. I was transported to the Minoprio home to spend the night, and to meet in the morning a most delightful family.

I had little time for idle talk or rest during my visit in Mendoza. On the first day I rode out west of town with Minoprio to his little "country place"—a well-appointed cottage surrounded by roses, from where we would venture into the field. As we drove along through a Mediterranean type of countryside, with extensive vineyards on each side of the road (this is a great wine country), Minoprio assured me that although he probably was not a very good doctor, and almost certainly not much of a paleontologist, he *did* know how to drive a car, and while he was telling me this we were barreling along a narrow dusty road, with chickens and goats frantically trying to get out of our way, and me with my heart in my mouth. (As a matter of fact Minoprio was quite a doctor. He was doing research on Chagas disease, the affliction that I am convinced was probably the principal source of Darwin's ill health during the years after he returned from the *Beagle* voyage. Indeed, Darwin makes mention in his journal of being bitten by the vinchuca bug when he was in Mendoza—this bug, which lives in the cracked walls of old adobe buildings, being the vector for the disease. While I was in Mendoza Minoprio one day hauled me to the hospital, put me in a white gown, and took me around the wards to see the people who were the subjects of his study, and as he explained things to me I stood there and nodded my head just as if I understood what it was all about.)

For several days I trailed around in the Triassic badlands west of Mendoza vainly trying to keep up with Minoprio, and certainly I got a good preliminary introduction to the geology in which I was interested. I might add that some years later Margaret and I were back in Mendoza and western Argentina as members of an international Gondwana conference, and we then were taken into the wilds of this land for a very extensive look at the Triassic sediments. Our leader on that later occasion was Rosendo Pascual, an old friend, and the trip was made more than merry by the presence of Al and Ruth Romer.

But to get back to my first Argentinian experience and my adventures with Dr. Minoprio, I will add just one more experience. At the end of a long day in the field we went back to his home in Mendoza, had our showers, and enjoyed a very late dinner as is the custom in that country. At about ten-thirty, when I was dead tired and ready for bed Minoprio said: "Come on—come on, let's go to a movie!" So we all piled into his car and went to a show beginning at eleven P.M. At about two in the morning I crawled into bed and at seven Minoprio was pounding on my door and shouting, "Come on—come on, let's get going!" So off we went on another field trip.

When I got back to Brazil from my Argentinian trip I was glad to have a day to myself for recuperation. At this time my first visit to Gondwanaland was about over. Back in Pôrto Alegre Carlos was very helpful; more than that, he was instrumental in making arrangements for the fossils that we had collected in Rio Grande do Sul to be shipped back to New York. As I found out later, Carlos had spent about a week of his time cutting through Brazilian red tape so that the fossils could be released; how could I ever express my gratitude to him for such dedicated cooperation?

After Pôrto Alegre I flew back to Rio, where a couple of weeks were spent in studying fossils at the Divisão de Mineralogie e Geologie (the geological survey) where Llew worked, and at the National Museum, where Carlos and Fausto worked. Also some very pleasant evenings were spent with the Price family and others. Then home, and from the plane the New York landscape in March looked dismally bare and bleak after the lush green hills of Brazil.

Footnote. Recently (in 1987) I received the first issue of *Paula-Coutiana*, a new paleontological research journal published by the natural history museum in Pôrto Alegre. It is a fitting and lasting tribute to Carlos, who died in 1982.

In a well-ordered world my trips to Gondwanaland should have been integrated parts of a nicely planned schedule, developed when I was first becoming involved in my pursuit of the Triassic. It was not at all that way—the trips just happened as fortunate circumstances dictated. I went to Brazil as I have told because of an invitation from Brazilians, I next went to Africa, as I will now tell, by reason of a grant I obtained from the National Science Foundation, I went to India and Australia as will be told because of another invitation, this time from Indians, and finally I went to Antarctica because of a little fossil, as also will be told. Fortunately Margaret could be my companion on all of these trips except the one to Antarctica, where attending spouses were not allowed.

The trip to Brazil (the first of two) was in 1959. The visit to Africa (also the first of two) was in 1962. I started this trip by myself with a short visit to Copenhagen, where our son David was living, and then I went on to Israel for the visit that I have already described. I left Israel at eleven in the evening on June 14, flew all night, and arrived in Johannesburg in the afternoon of the next day. There I was met by James Kitching and Ian Brink, of Witwatersrand University, two of the paleontologists with whom I was to be closely associated during the weeks to come.

When I went from Israel to South Africa, I was going from one troubled land to another, both troubled in different ways, but it was not my intent to become involved, even to the extent of mild discussions, in what were then and what are even more so now the insoluble problems that plague both of these countries. I was there on a scientific grant for scientific purposes, and I was working with men of science, all of them people of good will, so I concentrated my attention on the geological and paleontological matters that had brought me to those parts of the world. Of course I kept my eyes and my ears open and I learned much about the passing scene.

An advantage of being a scientist in a foreign land, and this applies particularly to people working in the natural sciences, is that to a considerable degree one becomes a part of the local culture. The geologist-paleontologist, especially, is for much of the time out in the field and away from the cities, and for such a person it is possible to see how life is lived in areas that are removed from the political and at times the very difficult social pressures that loom so large on city streets. Moreover, the scientist is working with colleagues who belong to the culture in which he or she is for the time being immersed, so that the foreign land does not seem so foreign as it does to the casual traveler, or even to the government representative— so often assigned to a foreign post and so often isolated in that post from the little details of life that surround him.

Thus I felt fortunate in my association with George Haas and his Israeli colleagues, and as will be here recounted with the several South African paleontologists with whom I worked. I have already mentioned Kitching and Brink. I must also mention A. W. Crompton (Fuzz, who has already been introduced to the reader), Rosalie Ewer (Griff, as she was known to us), and

Ronald Singer. Perhaps this is the place to say something about all of them, and their families.

James Kitching is one of the most remarkable paleontological field men I have ever known. It was my good fortune to go on a field trip with him the first thing after I arrived in Africa. We went out in the Karroo to look for fossils and we found them—only James found ten fossils for every one I located; I have never seen anyone with so sharp an eye for fossils in the rock. James grew up under the tutelage of Robert Broom, the very distinguished and eccentric South African medical doctor–paleontologist. James's training was eminently practical, aimed at going out into the field to find fossils and bringing them into the laboratory to be prepared. But in his late middle years James went through the academic mill, to earn a well-deserved doctorate and to write scientific papers of inestimable value. He was a man of tireless energy and of sharp perception. I learned a lot from James, and I enjoyed many fruitful days in the field with him. James's wife, Betty, was a good paleontological spouse who cheerfully endured his many absences from home when he was on the trail of Karroo fossils.

On the subject of James's sharp eye for fossils, I like the story about the time he was on a train that was traversing the Karroo, and as it went through a cut James saw out of the window a fossil in the side of the railroad cut. This, in spite of the speed of the train and the split second during which James caught sight of the specimen. He got off at the next town, rented a car, and went back and collected the fossil. If anybody else had been involved I would be inclined to doubt the story, but knowing James I have no doubts at all about it.

Ian Brink was and is a committed Afrikaner, married to an accomplished pianist, Anna, who among other things played with an orchestra that broadcast programs throughout South Africa. The Brinks have two daughters both of whom became harpists; it was and is a musical family. Back in 1962 when the girls were small we enjoyed watching them and listening to them at their home in Emmerentia, a section of Johannesburg, where Margaret and I enjoyed the hospitality of the Brink home. We will always be grateful to Ian for taking the time and making the effort to drive us on a trip of several days' duration through the great Kruger game reserve. It was like a journey back into the Pleistocene, when mammals great and small filled the land and man played a very small role indeed in the ecology of the land. A herd of elephants encountered on a narrow dirt road make an impressive, even a somewhat terrifying sight. Little Olga, the elder Brink girl who was with us on the trip, certainly was frightened by their presence; she had painful memories of a former experience with some all too intimate elephants.

Fuzz Crompton, a big, friendly man, was director of the South African Museum in Capetown when Margaret and I were in South Africa in 1962.

We were in the field with him, of which more later. Here I should mention that not long after that first trip to South Africa Fuzz brought his family to the United States, permanently. He was director of the Peabody Museum at Yale University when he went with us on that "four continents" trip through the Southwest; subsequently he became director of the Museum of Comparative Zoology at Harvard.

Rosalie Ewer was a rare soul and a first-rate zoologist. In 1962 she and her husband, also a zoologist, were at the Rhodes University in Grahamstown. Griff was quite a student of the carnivorous mammals; in fact she wrote an authoritative book on these animals. And in line with her interest she had a pet meerkat (a mongoose) when we knew her in South Africa, a restless little animal that liked to snuggle inside Griff's blouse, and stick its head out now and then for a look at the world. Griff always or almost always wore trousers, she had her hair cut short, and she smoked a pipe, yet she was every inch a lady. When we knew her she had two grown children, but they were away from home; perhaps the meerkat consoled her for their absence. After our visit in South Africa the Ewers moved to Ghana, and later they went to London, where Griff died of cancer. Characteristically, she entered a hospital in London, did not tell her friends about it, and there spent her last days in composure.

Ronald Singer, a broad, burly man, taught anatomy in the medical school in Capetown. His wife, Shirley, was an active member of the Black Sash, the organization of South African women who were protesting government policies. As such she endured many indignities on the street, especially outside of government buildings. The Singers, too, left South Africa with their children, Ronald to become professor of anatomy at the University of Chicago.

There were other South Africans with whom we became well acquainted: Professor and Mrs. Dart—he being the man who first described *Australopithecus*; Edna Plumstead of Witwatersrand University, a paleobotanist who on the basis of her plant studies recognized the validity of Gondwanaland early on; Mike Raath, who described the dinosaur *Syntarsus*, so closely related to my old friend *Coelophysis*. I won't try to extend the list; with these introductions having been made let me get on with the story.

On June 18, three days after my arrival in South Africa, James Kitching and I left for a little trip of paleontological exploration through the Great Karroo, a large semidesert basin, famous in the annals of paleontology because of the great quantities of Permian and Triassic reptiles and amphibians, but particularly mammallike reptiles, that have been collected from its extensive exposures during more than a century of fossil prospecting. It may be remembered that in entering Machtesh Ramon in Israel we dropped into a large desert basin, in that instance a topographic basin formed by the weathering of an anticline of uparched rocks. Therefore in Machtesh Ramon the oldest rocks are in the middle of the basin, topographically down in the very depths of the great structure, and that was where we went to look for Triassic fossils. The Great Karroo is an eroded *structural* basin on a grand scale; thus the oldest rocks are around its rim, while in the middle, as represented by the high Drakensberg volcanic mountains, are the youngest rocks. Consequently we were interested in the more peripheral rocks of this basin, where we intended to look for Permian and Lower Triassic fossils.

At this place it may be in order to explain in a brief manner the nature of the rocks, with their included fossils, that James and I were going to see. The rocks of the Karroo have long been classified into a lower and thus an earlier group known as the Beaufort Series, followed by an upper and later group named the Stormberg Series. In their totality these Karroo rocks add up to many thousands of feet in thickness, but of course at any one place only a part of the total section is to be seen. As has been mentioned, one encounters these rocks from oldest to youngest in traveling from the edge into the interior of the Karroo desert, which, as has also been mentioned, is a structural basin. The rocks, as designated by their old, classic names, occur in the following sequence. (In recent years these rocks, especially the lesser units, have been given more formal names, but I will not burden the reader with the new names, even though scientifically speaking they are the more desirable designations.)

	STORMBERG SERIES	
Lower Jurassic	Drakensberg volcanics Cave Sandstone	
Upper Triassic	Red Beds Molteno Formation	
	BEAUFORT SERIES	
Lower Triassic	Upper Beaufort beds Middle Beaufort beds	*Cynognathus* zone *Lystrosaurus* zone *Daptocephalus* zone
Upper Permian	Lower Beaufort beds	*Cistecephalus* zone *Tapinocephalus* zone

In this table the zones of the Beaufort Series are designated by fossils that are typical for each zone.

Such are the dry stratigraphic facts. They show the sequence of Karroo rocks from bottom to top, but a table such as this fails to give any impression of what the rocks really are like. They are more than names; they are great bands and expanses of sediments, weathered into cliffs and lowlands, to form landscapes of truly incredible beauty; and that beauty, added to the geologic facts revealed by the rocks, is what the geologist and the paleontologist see in the field. For southern Africa is a lovely land, as has been said by many people, including my very good friend Raymond Cowles, in his book *Zulu Journal*.

And now, on this wintery July afternoon, I was back again in Hluhluwe, after an absence of almost thirty years. Back to those old ridges where I once photographed rhinoceros, back in the once dangerous *kwa gube* bush. . . . The land was still beautiful beyond description and beyond the efforts of color photographers who attempt to capture its subtleties. Its charm was the result of a combination of many things, not just of a single feature, such as its legacy of the primitive. There was a feel to this land; and I breathed it in with the fragrance of the earth. ([Berkeley: University of California Press, 1959], page 66.)

For me, as for Ray, the magic of Africa was in many things. Always I will remember the crisp winter mornings in the Karroo, always I will remember the multicolored cliffs where we wandered through sunny hours in search of fossils, and always I will remember the call of the little doves—for me the background music of days spent in the field.

It was an early winter morning when we left Johannesburg, and as we drove southwardly away from the huge city we entered a landscape of brown, winter fields, behind which were long cliffs of continental sandstones and other sedimentary rocks, often capped with volcanic flows, and a little village every few miles. The villages were picturesque in their own way, with almost invariably a central town square, usually with a church in the middle of the square, a small straggling cluster of business establishments, then the houses of the white inhabitants, and beyond an area of dwellings inhabited by the black people—small cottages with few amenities, over which on each frosty morning there would hang a pall of wood smoke from the kitchen fires.

By midafternoon we had reached Harrismith, one of the well-known small cities of South Africa (the scene of some fierce fighting during the Boer War at the turn of the century), and there we found a hotel in which to spend the night. A couple of hours of daylight remained available to us, so after getting settled in the hotel we drove out to the edge of town to poke around in the Triassic dongas (these being the equivalent of the Brazilian *sangas*) to look for fossils. And within an hour or so we found *six* skulls of the Lower Triassic mammallike reptile *Lystrosaurus*. This discovery, treated quite casually by James who was used to such things, engendered within me a fever of excitement. Imagine! Six skulls, or one about every ten minutes or so. It was a sample of paleontological richness that was new in my experience, so of course I was excited. Yet the discovery had a significance for me of which at the time I was unaware, because as was to be proven within the next few years, *Lystrosaurus* was to loom large in my life, and beyond that, in the literature of paleontology and geology. In short, *Lystrosaurus* was to occupy a pivotal position in the concept of plate tectonics. More of this later; as of that June afternoon outside Harrismith my interest in *Lystrosaurus* was stimulated largely by its evident abundance in these Lower Triassic sediments. For this very reason the beds containing *Lystrosaurus* in the Karroo have for many years been known as the "*Lystrosaurus* zone."

Let us digress briefly for a look at *Lystrosaurus*.

Lystrosaurus is a mammallike reptile belonging to a group known as dicynodonts, a name that refers to the two tusks in the skull (*di*, two; *cyno*, dog; *odont*, tooth). And these are the only teeth to be seen in *Lystrosaurus*; otherwise the jaws are edentulous, are rather like the beak of a turtle, and in life were encased in horny sheaths. The eyes were placed high in the skull, as were the nostrils, which probably indicate that this reptile in life was semiaquatic, as is the modern hippopotamus, which has eyes and nostrils so placed so as to be above the water line when the rest of the body is submerged. The skull of *Lystrosaurus*, like the skull of all dicynodonts, is an "open" structure, with a long bony arch extending from below the eye to the back of the skull, this in part as a base for jaw muscles. In many species of *Lystrosaurus*, notably *L. murrayi* (the species we had found near Harrismith), the front of the skull in which the tusks are implanted is almost or even fully at a right angle to the skull table, which gives to this reptile the appearance of having collided head-on with a stone wall. All in all the skull of this dicynodont is a truly bizarre piece of bony anatomy. As for the rest of the skeleton, the body of *Lystrosaurus* is very capacious, as might be expected in an animal living on an herbaceous diet—as almost certainly was the case for *Lystrosaurus* and all of the other dicynodonts; the limbs are stout and rather short, the feet are broad, and the tail is quite short. Such is a picture of this, the most abundant animal in the Lower Triassic sediments of South Africa.

I might add that while I was at the Bernard Price Paleontological Institute of Witwatersrand (or Wits, as it is known locally), the center at that university for paleontological research, I conducted a little census of Lower

Triassic fossils in the collection there. And I found that about eighty-five percent of *all* the fossils were *Lystrosaurus*.

To get back to our journey, the next day we drove on from Harrismith, and along the way we went through the "Golden Gate," a magnificent series of red and orange-yellow sandstone cliffs formed by the Upper Triassic and Lower Jurassic Red Beds and Cave Sandstones of the Karroo stratigraphic sequence. It was my first glimpse of these important fossil-bearing beds, which I was to see in more detail a few weeks later. But except for this glimpse James and I limited ourselves to the Upper Permian and Lower Triassic beds, of which there were more than enough to keep us occupied.

To try to tell of all we saw and of all I learned would be pointless at this place; suffice it to say that my education in the Triassic of Gondwanaland was pleasantly enlarged in detail and in outlook under the experienced guidance of James. We tramped across numerous exposures, and as usual James found fossils right and left, while on rare occasions I would come across something worthwhile. In this succession of daily explorations, searching for fossils and observing the cliffs and weathered surfaces where such fossils were to be found, there were two occasions that stand out in my memory with particular clarity.

On the rainy morning of June 23 we drove from Middleburg, where we had spent the night, to Wellwood, a large farm, almost an estate, belonging to Mr. S. H. Rubidge. There was a reason for our drive, because Mr. Rubidge was a man who for many years had been vitally interested in the fossils that occurred on his land; so interested in fact that he built a little museum building of his own, in which reposed a most interesting collection of Karroo fossils.

Mr. Rubidge's interest in Karroo fossils had its inception with a visit of Robert Broom (whom we have already met) to Wellwood, many years ago. And since Broom was involved the visit had its unusual and unforeseen aspects. To begin the story, Mr. Rubidge had found an interesting Karroo fossil skull on his land, and this strange-looking skull quite naturally raised questions in his mind. So he sent it off to Pretoria, where Broom—then associated with the museum there—was asked to evaluate the specimen. Rubidge expected a letter telling him what it was all about; imagine his surprise when Broom appeared in person on the Rubidge doorstep.

That was a characteristic move on Broom's part; he took action in a very positive and immediate manner, and such action involved a quick, preliminary survey of the ground where the fossil had been found. Broom was convinced that the specimen he had seen betokened additional riches. Mr. Rubidge in turn was flabbergasted, flattered, and honored by this visit from the great Dr. Broom, so he immediately put all of the facilities of Wellwood at Dr. Broom's disposal. The result was that Broom took off into the veldt, accompanied by one of Rubidge's farm hands, who in turn was leading a little horse hitched up to a two-wheeled cart.

As usual Broom was dressed in his formal city attire—a dark suit complete with vest, a white shirt, a stiff collar with turned-down wings framing the knot of a black necktie, and shiny shoes. (Broom never wore anything else in the field; khaki field clothes were not in his lexicon of paleontological procedures.) Shortly this oddly-assorted little field party disappeared from the Rubidge view, so the lord of Wellwood turned his attention to other matters, as will be told.

In the meantime Broom was finding fossils, which he deposited in the little two-wheeled cart. His supposition as to the abundance of fossils on the Rubidge farm proved to be correct. Even though he was thoroughly engrossed in the discoveries that he was making, he was soon aware that the midday sun is very hot in the Karroo, so off came his coat, to be tossed into the cart among the fossils. More fossils, more heat, more clothes to be discarded—not only his vest but eventually his shirt and tie and finally everything including his underwear. Only his shoes remained to protect him against the stony ground across which he and the farm hand and the horse with the cart were wandering.

At last it was time to return to the farmhouse, so Broom climbed up on top of the cart, to sit on a mixed-up load of fossils and clothes, and thus he rode triumphantly back with his spoils beneath him. With his disheveled hair and his rather dark skin abundantly exposed to view he must have looked something like a Neanderthal man returning from a successful hunt.

What Broom didn't know was that Mr. Rubidge had quickly spread the word about his distinguished visitor, with the result that various men and ladies from nearby had assembled on the Wellwood lawn and had spread a festive tea on tables set beneath the trees. Around the corner of the barn and in full view of the properly dressed guests appeared this quite naked man, sitting on top of a jumble of fossils and clothes, looking like a figure out of the distant past. The surprise was complete on both sides. There were shrieks of astonishment and hurried words (what Broom said has not been recorded) and during the flurried excitement the distinguished paleontologist disappeared at high speed toward the barn. Within a few moments he reappeared, properly clothed, and the tea party proceeded in a most decorous manner. One thing can be said without fear of contradiction; however the ladies may have felt, Broom was not in the least embarrassed or disconcerted.

That was the beginning of the Rubidge connection with Broom.

We got there to find a rather imposing farmhouse, with well-tended lawns and gardens, and wandering about the place numbers of large, impressive merino sheep. Out back, at a little distance from the house there

The dinosaur quarry, Ghost Ranch, New Mexico, 1947

Undercutting a block at Ghost Ranch, 1947

Small fossils require a close look, Arizona

Camp in the Arizona desert, 1955

Collecting at Comb Ridge, Arizona, 1955

With Columbia graduate students

A moment of academic relaxation

John Ostrom (left) *and Dale Russell* (right) *with their professor*

Margaret sketching in Lesotho, 1962

Searching for fossils in Lesotho, 1962

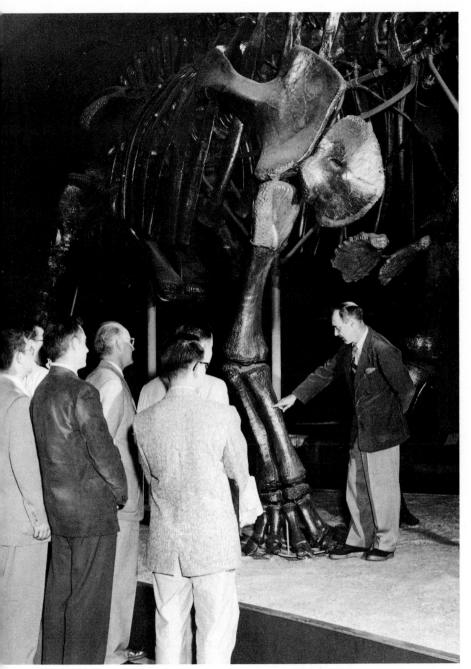

A discussion of dinosaur anatomy

In my office, American Museum of Natural History

A Gond dance, Sironcha, 1964

Margaret and Tapan Roy Chowdhury at the Sironcha dinosaur quarry, 1964

Unearthing large dinosaurs at Sironcha

The ferry, Pranhita River, 1964

At Independence Day garden party, Presidential Palace, New Delhi, 1964

Shivta in the Negev, Israel, 1965

The dedicated fossil collector, Antarctica, 1969

he Antarctic fossil collection, boxed for shipment, 1970

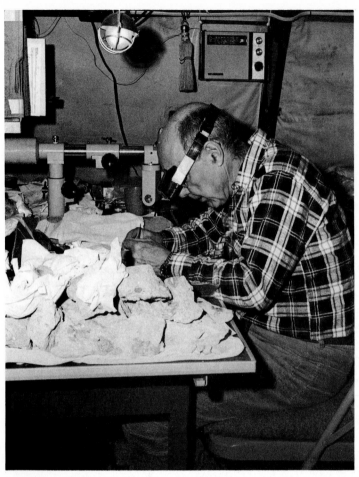

Looking over the day's collection, Antarctica, 1969

*Jack Smith, director, and Granada TV crew, filming
dinosaur tracks in the Arizona desert*

Golden wedding anniversary, Rhode Island, July 8, 1983

was a row of small cottages in which the black farm hands lived. We had tea with the Rubidge family and looked at the fossils, and as we walked about admiring the farm and the surrounding countryside Mr. Rubidge entertained me with a long harangue about how South Africa was misunderstood and put upon by other nations, while I listened and held my peace.

Politics aside, Mr. Rubidge had been a great benefactor of paleontology in South Africa; he had worked with and lent aid to Robert Broom for many years, and subsequently he had been of much help to James. We spent the morning at Wellwood, and then went on to Graaf-Reinet, where James telephoned Mr. Pringle Brodie, a farmer who lived a few miles from town, and arranged for us to stay at his place.

Mr. and Mrs. Brodie were people of English descent, and it was interesting to feel the difference in atmosphere at their place as compared with what we experienced at farms with Afrikaner proprietors. I can only say that everything was more relaxed, or so it seemed to me. We spent several days at the Brodie farm where we enjoyed the warm hospitality of the family. And here we explored the cliffs and flat-topped mesas of Permian age that surrounded the farm, with the result that among other things James found a skull of *Daptocephalus*, a huge dicynodont reptile. We came upon it one afternoon, and after some preliminary digging around the specimen we decided that we would have to return the next day to recover it. It was much too large and heavy for two people to carry back to the house.

So the next morning, according to plans made the evening before, we set off at daylight with Mark Brodie, the grown-up son of the Brodie family, and two farm hands, riding on a tractor that was pulling a two-wheeled cart. Our particular companion on the trip was Bess, the Brodie bitch. She had a very sore paw, damaged by a cut from a sharp rock a day or two previously, but would Bess be left behind? Not at all.

At the locality we got down from the tractor to climb a long slope on which the skull rested, and as we climbed we flushed a small herd of rhebok—small, elegant antelopes—and they bounded up the hill to disappear over its crest. It was a typical African encounter. With the manpower at hand we hauled the fossil skull down the slope, heaved it into the little cart, and got back to the farm for a warm breakfast.

One day as I sat on the porch at the Brodie house I looked out across the land to a flat-topped hill in the distance, a hill of soft-gray siltstones, shales, and sandstones, its flat top being formed by a heavy layer of volcanic rock known as dolerite. Cutting through the side of the hill, like a narrow, almost vertical wall, was a dolerite dyke—the volcanic intrusion that millions of years ago had burned its way upwardly through the sediments to spread out as a horizontal blanket that now formed the top of the hill. I made a sketch and took a picture of what I saw, little realizing at the time that I would within a few years be seeing the same sort of geology in Antarctica, covered with snow.

Our explorations of the Karroo continued, and then on July 1 we drove over the Cape folded belt, the mountains that enclose the Karroo basin on the south, to arrive in Capetown. The next day, in the evening, I went to the airport to meet Margaret, who was arriving on a long flight from Copenhagen, where she had visited our son David, as I had more than a month earlier. From now on we were to share experiences in Africa, and that was a prospect to be viewed with pleasure.

It was amusing, and perhaps symbolic or perhaps not, that during our first night together in Capetown we were awakened by lions roaring. Of course they were lions in the zoo, and we were staying nearby in one of the dormitories at the University of Capetown, where we were being housed as guests attending the annual meeting of the South African Association for the Advancement of Science. I might add that during the same night we were lulled to sleep by a chorus of hundreds, perhaps more properly, thousands of frogs that had come out into the wet grass of the campus lawns. We did enjoy that bell-like music.

After the scientific sessions in Capetown, in which I was much involved, I was off again in search of the Triassic, this time the Upper Triassic, and this time with Margaret as my companion and Fuzz Crompton as our guide. We went into the Great Karroo basin from the south (I had come into it with James Kitching from the north), climbing through the Cape folded belt mountains by way of Toits Cloof Pass—an especially scenic drive—and continuing on to Beaufort West for the night. Then on to Bloemfontein and on to the center of this basin, where, as has been said, we were to find the Upper Triassic sediments exposed around the high volcanic Drakensbergs, the central core of the Karroo Basin.

Straightway we entered Basutoland, now known as Lesotho, an independent little nation surrounded by South Africa. Lesotho has long been a country to itself, owing to the foresight of a perceptive Basuto king or chieftan named Moshesh. Late in the nineteenth century he looked to the southwest and saw the Boer voortrekers approaching, he looked to the north and saw the warlike Zulus descending from that direction, so he asked for British aid. A protectorate was established, which since has become an independent state. But today Lesotho is in a difficult position since it is surrounded by South Africa. Thus the South Africans control passage into and out of Lesotho, which greatly restricts the ability of that state to act as independently as might be wished. Furthermore, a large proportion of Lesotho men go to South Africa to work in the mines, which still further binds the ties between the two nations. However we entered Lesotho with no trouble.

We drove along high mountain roads where we could look down on villages composed of round huts with conical thatched roofs, known as rondavels. And along one such road we met a group of Basuto horsemen, completely muffled in blankets and riding on shaggy ponies. The Basutos are unusual among native Africans, perhaps unique, in that they are horsemen. All the time we were looking for rock exposures where we could see the Upper Triassic Red Beds and Cave Sandstones, and since such exposures are abundant we had ample opportunities to search for fossils.

Here the objects of our paleontological investigations were quite different from the fossils that James and I had seen and collected in the Beaufort beds, for in place of *Lystrosaurus* and related dicynodont reptiles as well as other mammallike reptiles, we were on the trail as well of very advanced mammallike reptiles, so advanced indeed that some of them were on the threshold between reptiles and mammals. Whereas the Beaufort beds are truly dominated by a large and varied assemblage of mammallike reptiles, the Stormberg beds are dominated particularly by early dinosaurs. To state the situation somewhat differently, the dinosaurs that appear so suddenly in the Red Beds and Cave Sandstones represent something new in the history of life—the assumption of dominance on the continents by reptiles that were to rule for the next one hundred fifty million years and more. This rise of the dinosaurs was accompanied by a disappearance of the mammallike reptiles, in part because some of the theriodonts were turning into mammals, in part because others could not compete with the aggressive dinosaurs.

I had seen numerous fossils of South African dinosaurs at Capetown and Johannesburg and Bloemfontein in the museums; now I was to see some of them in the field. One unique and interesting occurrence was at a mission, established years ago by the Paris Evangelical Church, where the original missionary, the Reverend Mr. Ellenberger, had built his home by clearing out a space under a huge overhanging ledge of Cave Sandstone and then building a brick wall to enclose this natural shelter. It was a well-built, cosy habitation, and on the ceiling of one room was a trackway made by a small dinosaur that must have been very similar to *Syntarsus* or *Coelophysis*. So I felt that I was back among old friends.

It was in this general region that Fuzz and I climbed a large slope one day to investigate the Red Beds, while Margaret was in a nice little village at the foot of the slope, visiting with Basuto ladies and getting acquainted with some of their handicrafts. Suddenly a mob of men and boys erupted from the village and came straight at us, brandishing clubs and whooping at the tops of their lungs. I thought for a moment that my last day had come, and Fuzz had the same thoughts (and so did Margaret) but they ran right past us, still yelling and waving clubs, and then we saw that they were chasing a hare. If they caught the poor animal (I never learned how the chase ended) the amount of energy provided by a rabbit stew would have been far exceeded by the amount of energy expended in chasing the rabbit.

We then left Lesotho, but not by far; we went to the Herschel District of South Africa, along the border with Lesotho, and there made ourselves at home at Fort Hook, where according to arrangements that had been concluded by Fuzz we stayed with a nice missionary family, Malcolm and Lorraine Hepburn and their children. The Hepburns ran a trading post at Fort Hook, so it was a center for African tribesmen known as the Tembu. The men, who were farmers and shepherds, were clad in blankets that they fastened over the right shoulder with a clasp; they invariably wore headgear, commonly black hats, and each man had a dassie-skin tobacco pouch suspended around his neck. They always carried stout sticks, or knobkerries, and one day some of them staged a mock stick fight for us that seemed almost too realistic. The women wore colorful blankets, worn over decorated skirts and blouses, and on their heads were handsome turbans. They also wore necklaces and bracelets and metal anklets. Both men and women smoked long-stemmed pipes.

The day we arrived at Fort Hook Fuzz drove into Aliwal North to pick up Griff Ewer, who was going to spend a week or so with us, and that was the beginning of a very interesting time. Margaret and I, and Griff, were bedded down in a couple of rooms at the Hepburn house while Fuzz occupied a rondavel just outside. Every morning the big Hepburn dog would come into our room to tell us it was time to be up and about—and we were up and about, Fuzz, Griff, and I to explore the Upper Triassic rocks, and Margaret, with an African guide and driver, to attend Tembu initiation parties and dances, to learn about their crafts, and to make a collection of Tembu cultural objects for the American Museum. So passed our days, during the course of which Fuzz, Griff, and I found dinosaur bones.

At last it was time for us to return to Capetown; Griff went her way, Fuzz, Margaret, and I drove back along the coastal route, during the course of which trip I saw for the first and only time at Mossel Bay living tunicates, those strange saclike marine animals that are generally thought to be on a line leading to the vertebrates. It was a pleasant trip through a green countryside and as we drove along I had time to reflect upon what I had seen. And what I had seen made Gondwanaland ever more real to me. I had seen a part of Gondwanaland with ties to the west in the presence of Lower Triassic dicynodont and theriodont reptiles, and rhynchosaurs, all of which I had collected in Brazil. Furthermore I had seen a part of Gondwanaland with ties to the north in the presence of Upper Triassic dinosaurs, the likes of which I had collected in North America and studied in Europe. Now, I thought, if only we could find some Triassic reptiles in Antarctica, there could be no doubt in my mind as to the reality of Gondwanaland.

Margaret and I left South Africa for Kenya, where we had a date with Louis Leakey, but just before our departure a telegram came saying that Dr. Leakey was called away—could we postpone our trip and come later? We could not; schedules and tickets had already been arranged and secured. So we went to Kenya anyway, where we were cordially hosted by some of Professor Leakey's colleagues. Among other things we had a memorable trip into the great Rift Valley, which was a place I had long wanted to see.

From Kenya we went to Greece for a little holiday, to see the land where man lived during his "Golden Age." Then to southern Germany for a meeting of the Deutsches Palaeontologische Gesellschaft, including some field trips through the forests of Württemberg to see some of the classic Triassic (a region that I was to explore more at my leisure in a later year), and after that on to Switzerland to see the Triassic in the mountains above Lake Lugano as has already been told.

In Switzerland Margaret had to leave me and go home. I stayed on and then went to England for still another paleontological symposium before I finally flew back to New York. With the termination of this trip I had become acquainted with Triassic rocks and fossils in many crucial areas of Laurasia and Gondwanaland. But there were still three regions that I hoped some day to visit, to complete my Triassic education: peninsular India, Australia, and Antarctica. Would opportunities for such trips ever come my way?

XVII

Gondwana, Continued: The Peninsula

The opportunity to visit India came unexpectedly and sooner than I had ever imagined would be the case, for it was only two years after our African venture that I received an invitation from the Indian Statistical Institute in Calcutta to come to India, accompanied by Margaret, to be the guests of the institute. There was some irony in the situation, because here I was being asked to come to a country I had never visited, but a country certain fossils of which I had described in detail thirty years previously. Those were the Siwalik mammals, discussed on a preceding page, that I had described in a series of papers, culminating in a four-hundred-page monograph, published in the Transactions of the American Philosophical Society in 1935. That monograph had nothing to do with the invitation from the statistical institute; my work on Asiatic mammals was past history. I was going to India because of my interest in Triassic fossils which were considerably more than two hundred million years older than the Siwalik mammals, and occurring in the center of the Indian peninsula, many

351

hundreds of miles south of the Siwalik Hills. As events developed I never did get to the Siwalik exposures, although I would dearly have loved to see the geology of that region bordering the southern base of the immense Himalayan Range, the region where Barnum Brown had collected a great variety of fossil carnivores and rodents, primates and hoofed mammals, and giant proboscideans—the elephants and their kin. I had to forego the romantic hills where Kipling's Kim lived his adventurous young life to spend my time instead in the historic land of the Gonds.

As was told on page 328 of this, my life history, Professor Eduard Suess named a hypothetical ancient continent located largely in the southern hemisphere Gondwanaland, the "land of the Gonds." (Actually Gondwanaland is a somewhat tautological name, because Gondwana means "land of the Gonds." But ever since Suess's creation of the name Gondwanaland in the latter part of the nineteenth century, this designation has become firmly intrenched in the literature of geology and in geologic usage, and will continue to be used, even though many geologists today are trying to get the name Gondwana accepted.)

There was, a good many hundred years ago, a kingdom of the Gonds in central India, and Suess thought that because many of the evidences for his hypothetical continent were to be seen in peninsular India it would be appropriate to name the putative continent after the Gonds. It so happened that our work in India was to take us into Gond country—more of that later.

But to get back to my story, our invitation to India came at the instigation of an old friend, Dr. Pamela Robinson of the University of London, Pamela having at that time been involved for several years in establishing and developing a program of geological-paleontological research at the institute. Pamela, it should be said, had trained several Indian geologists and paleontologists at the University of London, hence her interest in doing everything she could to support the beginnings of the earth sciences at the institution where her students and associates were employed. They were Bimalendu Roychoudhuri, Sohan Lal Jain, and Tapan Roy Chowdhury, the latter two having obtained their doctorates under Pamela's direction.

A few words of explanation are here in order. The Indian Statistical Institute had been founded by Professor Prashanta Mahalanobis, a statistician of world-wide fame, and an outstanding Indian scientist. In spite of its name the institute was a sort of Cal Tech kind of place, because Professor Mahalanobis felt that there should be close ties between statistics and the several scientific disciplines. Consequently he had established some natural history departments within the institute walls, among them being a department of biology and one of geology. The geological department was officially designated as the Geological Studies Unit, and at the time we were there

Bimalendu was the chairman. It should be added that the institute was a sort of quasi-governmental organization; it had its own financing so that it was more or less free of Indian-bureaucracy red tape (which, to tell the truth, is horrendous) yet it had close ties with the government. Professor Mahalanobis was a close personal friend of Jawaharlal Nehru, who in 1964 was the Indian prime minister.

The institute made arrangements for us to fly to India on an Air India plane, and that is how we happened to be at the airport in New York on January 3, 1964, ready to board a flight to India, by way of Europe. (Shades of Brazil! It may be remembered that five years previously we had left for that tropical land on the day after the beginning of the New Year.) We flew to London and from there to Copenhagen where we had a a few days with our son David and his Danish wife, Edith, after which we flew to Frankfurt where we rejoined Air India for our trip to India. We landed in Bombay to change planes, and continued eastwardly, enjoying some excellent views of the Western Ghats and other geological features as we crossed India. Such was our introduction to the land of the Gonds.

It was a misty morning as we reached Calcutta, so we circled several times before coming down, and as we circled we could see again and again the great, sprawling city with the Hooghly River cutting through its midst. At last we were on the ground, to be met by Pamela and Bimalendu, who kindly assisted us through customs. After the formalities we piled into an institute car for a ride that was new in our experience—through smoky, crowded streets with cars of all descriptions, buses, carts pulled by horses and carts pulled by bullocks, rickshaws, and people on foot in hordes. To our unaccustomed eyes it was remarkably picturesque, and above all colorful. Color—that was our first impression of India, and it remained a lasting impression—a land of many hues, especially as seen everywhere in the dress of the people.

We arrived at the institute where flowery leis were draped over our heads and where we met members of the institute staff, among them Tapan, and Pronab Mazamdur, the latter a very skilled technician who worked in the laboratory of the Geological Studies Unit.

Almost immediately we were established in a comfortable apartment within the administrative building of the institute, a building known as Amrapali. Professor Mahalanobis, whom we met that evening after he had arrived from Delhi, also lived in Amrapali with his wife, who at the time of our visit was very ill. Consequently we saw little of Rani Mahalanobis during our stay in Calcutta. (Thirteen years later we were again in Calcutta at which time we became well acquainted with Rani, by then a widow.)

The institute is located on campuslike grounds on Barrackpore Trunk Road, perhaps ten miles from the center of the city. Here the various buildings of the institute are situated among lawns and towering palm trees. In front of Amrapali is a large, square "tank"—actually a pool of considerable dimensions, around the borders of which are trees and colorful flowers. Indeed, the entire campus of the institute is decorated by flowers, some in cultivated flower beds, many in large earthenware pots that are arranged along the walks and in front of the buildings. And around the entire campus is a high wall, punctuated at intervals by gates, there being at each gate a watchman to supervise the comings and goings of people through its portals. Every night, through the night, we would hear the ringing of hourly bells by the gatekeepers, who through twenty-four hours kept their constant vigils. We felt well protected within this enclave, surrounded by the bustling city.

It was nice to feel so protected, because on the day after our arrival Hindu-Muslim riots broke out in Calcutta, to continue for five days. The government proclaimed an exceedingly strict curfew; throughout the city people were confined to their homes and anyone seen on the street was subject to being shot. The riots were far removed from where we were, but every day there were convoys of army trucks, filled with soldiers, roaring up and down Barrackpore Trunk Road just beyond our walls. Yet for us this time of strife was a quiet interval, and since we could roam at will within the protective walls our incarceration was not at all unpleasant. We became acquainted with the people at the institute, and visited the various departments at our pleasure.

Every day we had our meals with Professor Mahalanobis and Pamela Robinson—meals that generally were very protracted affairs because the professor, who loved to talk, not only used mealtimes to instruct us and discuss matters, but also to argue about this and that. Indeed, he usually was so busy talking that it was hard to get him to eat. He had a servant, Bahadur, whose duty it was, under instructions from Rani, to look after the professor, and especially to see that he ate properly. So Bahadur, who stood behind the professor as we ate, was constantly and gently proferring food and trying to get him to pay attention to his plate and eat it clean.

From what has been said it can be seen that Prashanta Mahalanobis was a gentle, unworldly man. He couldn't be bothered with the mundane details of life, and he was very much accustomed to being waited on. In fact, because of his high position in the world of Indian affairs he expected that things would be ordered in his own convenience. I shall never forget the evening that we were to fly with him from Calcutta to New Delhi. We sat in the lounge at Amrapali in pleasant conversation as the time approached for us to go to the airport, but since Prashanta was immersed in one of his long, philosophical disquisitions, airplanes were for the moment about the last things in his thoughts. He did become aware after a while that I was getting nervous; he bade me to be calm and not to worry. At last we all got into an institute car and took off for the airport, by this time much too late to make the plane. But when we arrived at the airport we were waved right onto the airstrip where the plane was waiting for us, and soon we departed, perhaps fifteen or twenty minutes behind schedule.

Prashanta had kept a plane-load of people waiting, but his conscience was clear. There was no intentional arrogance in his action; he merely expected that because he was an important individual other people would defer to his wishes. It was all a part of the hierarchical structure of Indian society. (He tried it once in London and it didn't work. Pamela was pleasantly amused as Prashanta stood at the closed gate and watched his plane take off into the clouds.)

That wild drive out onto the airstrip to board the plane was the beginning of a trip to New Delhi, where we were to meet the prime minister. Despite the great honor, neither Margaret nor I was very enthusiastic about the forthcoming visit, and I think Pamela felt as we did, but Professor Mahalanobis had made very firm arrangements and that was that. On the day of our appointment we spent the morning at the zoological park, and then at five in the afternoon all of us, including Professor Mahalanobis, appeared at the prime minister's residence for tea. We were ushered through long corridors and past many guards to a lounge, where we seated ourselves. Presently Jawaharlal Nehru entered with his daughter Indira Gandhi, destined within a few years to be herself the ruler of India. Nehru looked very tired, as he had reason to be, because it was shortly after the Chinese invasion of Tibet, when India felt her very northern borders to be open to invasion. Furthermore, the prime minister was near the end of a long and a stressful life and was feeling the effect of years gone by.

We talked about Gondwanaland, and I said some words about the encouragement of natural history museums in India, a topic that seemed of particular interest to Mr. Nehru. Also we mentioned that because of the Chinese threat we could not obtain detailed field maps (the sale of such maps had been prohibited, although the same maps were readily obtainable in London), at which the prime minister indicated that the ways of governments are at times wonderfully obtuse. And the professor and the prime minister as old friends had things to say to each other. But by this time Mrs. Gandhi thought that the party had gone on long enough; she frowned and we took the hint and made our departure.

Professor Mahalanobis was indeed an ascetic type of person, tall and thin, and as I have said not much concerned with prosaic details. But he was very determined in what he wanted done, and sometimes he took unusual steps to accomplish his purposes. For instance, when he first founded the statistical institute, he calmly occupied a house that belonged to his wife,

Rani, for institute purposes. Rani was a gracious lady, but she had a will of her own.

Therefore sometime before we arrived in Calcutta, she had arranged for a new house to be built just for herself (Rani had money of her own) and she didn't tell the professor anything about it. Even though she was very ill at the time, the work on the house continued all unknown to Prashanta, and it was completed about the time of our arrival at the institute. So although she could not be there, she arranged from her bed that there would be a grand opening of the new house to which Prashanta and the rest of us would be invited. Consequently one evening we all gathered in the lounge at Amrapali, and from there we walked together several blocks to the new house. When we arrived we saw footprints painted on the walk and the steps leading to the house—these were welcoming signs—and once inside we found the place brightly lighted and decorated for the party. We enjoyed an evening of celebration, with visiting, with exploratory trips into the various rooms of the house, and finally with evening refreshments. Needless to say, Professor Mahalanobis was as much impressed and delighted with the house as the rest of us, but he understood that it was to be Rani's house, and so it was.

He and Rani had no children, but they had a much beloved niece who came to Amrapali frequently for visits. She was an exquisitely beautiful young lady, very animated, and in her always lovely saris was a delight to the eye. I should add that the professor's eminent position did not in the least faze her.

To return from this digression, finally the curfew was lifted (we heard rumors that more than a thousand people had been killed in the rioting, but official figures were never released) and people were again allowed on the streets. But on the first day of freedom the streets had to be clear by five o'clock in the afternoon; loiterers would be subject to arrest. That day we went into the city in an institute car, to do some shopping and to see some sights, but we were careful to make an early departure back to the institute. And as we drove back we saw great white waves of people largely consisting of men clad in white pajamas (loose trousers) and punjabis (flowing waist-coats), the standard Indian dress, hurrying toward their homes. They were traveling on foot, in carts, and by bus, in the latter case filling the buses to suffocation and hanging to the outsides of the vehicles in such numbers that each bus seemed to be composed of masses of outside riders, somehow propelled along by an invisible engine in an invisible conveyance.

On the following day we went back into the city, where the afternoon was spent with Mr. P. P. Satsangi at the Geological Survey, looking at *Lystrosaurus* skulls and skeletons that had been collected in the Lower Triassic Panchet beds along the Damodar River, northwest of Calcutta. This was in preparation for things to come, because we were destined to leave the next day for the Damodar River, to explore the Panchet sediments.

January 17 was the day of our departure; that morning Pamela, Margaret, and I boarded the train that was to take us to Asansol, some one hundred twenty-five miles to the northwest of Calcutta. There we were met by Bimalendu and Satsangi, who had made the trip from Calcutta by Land Rover, and were to take us to our camp some miles distant near the little village of Tiluri. Perhaps this was not the land of Kim's adventures, but it was Kipling country. The station platform at Asansol was a veritable rainbow of colored garments and a polyglot gathering of varied Indian faces. And as we drove through Asansol and on into the country we made our way through streets and roads crowded with people on foot, with people on bicycles, and with people in bullock carts. The sun shone bright and hot and the shadows underneath the trees along the road were black in contrast to the brilliant sunlight.

Our camp was more than a camp, because Bimalendu or somebody with an authoritative voice had arranged for us to bivouac in a rural health center then under construction. So Margaret and I set up camp beds in a nice little building that was destined to be the quarters for a nurse or doctor, Pamela established herself in another similar building, while Bimalendu and Satsangi found space in still another building. Then there were the people of our support staff: Debraj, the cook, a small rather Portuguese-looking person; Ram, a huge man with a fierce mustache; and a couple of lesser helpers. Ram, I should say, was a sort of general factotum who did all sorts of things that needed to be done; he managed things in camp, he brought us tea the first thing every morning, and he went into the field with us, carrying all of our hammers until we needed them. Debraj, Ram, and the others established themselves in still another building of the complex, and that was where we had our meals.

India is a land of many different kinds of peoples, and our camp near Tiluri was not far from a settlement of tribesmen, "aboriginals" as the Indians sometimes call them, known as the Santals. They were people with their distinctive culture, quite different from that of the Hindus or the Moslems, so that they formed a little ethnic island surrounded by the Indian population. Bimalendu arranged for Margaret in company with a driver and a guide to spend several days with the Santals while we looked for fossils. Needless to say it was a fascinating experience for her. The Santal villages (all of us visited one or two of them) were models of cleanliness and order as compared with the usual sloppy, disorderly Indian villages. The houses were neatly whitewashed, the streets and paths were swept free of litter and trash. This impressed but did not inspire imitation from the Indian guide who was with Margaret.

She attended some Santal dances and ceremonies; at one there was a chorus of three Santal maidens neatly clad in colorful saris, with marigolds in their hair. At the end of this ceremony a goat was decapitated and three or four people rushed forward to drink its blood, which was pretty strong stuff for Margaret. Nonetheless she was intensely interested in all that went on and got some excellent pictures of the proceedings.

While she was thus engaged in what might be called ethnological observations the rest of us went into the field to study the geology of the Panchet beds, and to look for fossils. This involved much tramping across the landscape and almost constant encounters with people—for India is a country in which people are everywhere. Of course most of the Indians we met out there in the countryside were simple farmers going about their business or coping with some unscheduled event—such as the morning when we came upon a group of villagers trying to break up a fight between two water buffalo. Their efforts were unavailing, in spite of much shouting and wielding of clubs; the two bovids were engaged in what seemed a fight to the death and it was a terrifying sight. At last, however, one of the cattle, after being knocked off his feet, and subjected to a goring attack, managed to get up and flee, with the other in hot pursuit. That was the last we saw of them.

Such a happening was a diversion but only a short one to our self-appointed task. We were making a transect of the Panchet Formation, studying the rocks in their natural succession and trying to interpret what we saw. We would walk along and at a promising outcrop would call for Ram, who was carrying our geologic hammers in a knapsack, get our respective implements and whack away at the cliff or the bank, examine our hand specimens, and discuss or argue about what we had found. Then back would go the hammers into Ram's knapsack and we would continue our journey. If this procedure, especially the provision of someone to carry our hammers, seems strange to non-Indian eyes, it must be remembered that in India it is most important to provide work as widely as it possible. So Ram was there to carry things for us, and he would have been disturbed, even angered, if we had tried to carry our own hammers.

As we walked across the Panchet exposures we were always hoping for the best of fossils, and so it was propitious that on our second day of such activity I had the good fortune to find a *Lystrosaurus* skull partially exposed in the rock, with good indications of an accompanying skeleton. For me it was quite a thrill; *now* I had found *Lystrosaurus* in India as well as in Africa. Here before us in the field was incontrovertible evidence of a connection, but was it a close connection as would have been the case if this part of India was up against the eastern flank of Africa as postulated according to the tenets of plate tectonics, or was it a more distant connection, if one is to suppose that *Lystrosaurus* got from Africa to India by way of a long journey up through the length of the African continent, across the Middle East, and then back down into the middle of India? As I looked at the skull, with one of its eyes staring up at the heavens, it had too much the appearance of an African fossil, so it seemed to me, to have been widely separated from its southern hemisphere counterpart. Was not this a bit of paleontological evidence that in early Triassic time the Indian peninsula *was* deep within the southern hemisphere?

With such thoughts in my head I joined the rest of our party as we made our way back to camp to get together the materials needed for collecting the fossil. The next morning, as the temple of Tiluri loomed through the early mists, we made our way back to Aswarda Nulla, the place where *Lystrosaurus* awaited us. Getting it out of the ground was a matter of a couple of days of concentrated effort, using the familiar methods that already have been described—digging around the skeleton, preserving it and covering it with a plaster bandage, then turning it over and treating it on the other side.

Of course our activities attracted the attention of numerous Indians who lived in the vicinity, so that throughout the time we were engaged in our task we had a considerable audience of men and boys, always quietly seated at a respectful distance and never getting in our way. (Interestingly, there were never any members of the other sex present to watch our work; perhaps they were too busy with domestic duties to thus fritter away their time.)

On the second day after we got the specimen plastered, we rigged a sling in which to carry it to our Land Rover which was parked a little distance away on the crest of the nulla. A long, strong pole was thrust through the sling, and Ram, a mighty man, took one end of the pole while three of our group took the other end, and in this manner *Lystrosaurus* was carried to the car. That was the end of our adventure in the Lower Triassic Panchet beds. The next day we drove to Asansol and from there took the train back to Calcutta, where we made preparations for another trip, this time to New Delhi.

We were in New Delhi for the Indian Republic Day on January 26. It was an impressive affair, with a tremendous, colorful parade along the broad Rajpath, a parade replete with Indians of all persuasions in their various costumes, with enormous, richly caparisoned elephants, with various units of the Indian army, including the fierce Gurkhas, and at the end a flypast of fighter planes. We sat in a grandstand along the parade route and tried to keep warm as a cold wind, straight from the Himalayas, whipped past and around us. Then in the afternoon we attended a garden party at the presidential palace.

After that a few days of sightseeing—to Agra and the Taj Mahal, an incomparable gem almost beyond description, and later to the ancient, empty city of Fatehpur Sikri, built by Akbar and abandoned after only sixteen years of occupation, largely because of a deficient water supply. Perhaps there is a lesson here.

Our next destination was central India, to see the succession of Triassic sediments along the Pranhita-Godavari river system, and for that we were to take a plane from Delhi to Nagpur. It was an evening flight, and we shared the plane with a large delegation of Russian experts of some sort, the men dressed in rather baggy suits with wide coat lapels, the ladies clad in undistinguished clothes. We all stared at each other during the flight, and at Nagpur we became inextricably mixed, trying to sort out our hotel rooms. At last, and at a very late hour, we got settled in our respective places.

The hotel in Nagpur was not the most modern in its facilities and appointments, so in the morning, for our ablutions, we followed the Indian practice of pouring water over ourselves from brass jugs, the water running across the bathroom floor to a drain in one corner. Our baths were complicated, however, by the fact that the drains of each bathroom flowed into the corresponding bathroom on the floor below, and from there on down, serially. Consequently there were some interesting, even exiting, cascades of water from floor to floor. And when it was all over a servant came into our bathroom, as undoubtedly he did in all of the bathrooms, bearing a large pail of water which he flung (the water, not the pail) with much vigor against the walls and across the floor. We were experiencing the Indian version of the old saying "When in Rome, do as the Romans."

On our first morning in Nagpur we went to the middle of the city for an unexpectedly pleasant visit. It seems that throughout the city center no automobiles are allowed (at least such was the case then) so all traffic was limited to pedestrians and people on bicycles. There was no roar of motors, no fumes, and no frenetic hurrying from one place to another. There was a wonderful sensation of quiet and a lack of speed, and for us this was a brief view of what cities might be, and are not.

In Nagpur we were assembling ourselves and our equipment for a journey into the very heart of Gondwana, into the land of the Gonds in the ancient historical and ethnographical rather than the geological sense of the word. Our party consisted of Pamela, Sohan Jain, Tapan Roy Chowdhury, Pranab, and Debraj, as well as two drivers, and Margaret and myself. Our equipment consisted of two Land Rovers, each pulling a two-wheeled trailer loaded with field and camping equipment as well as food. And our destination, as has been mentioned, was the jungle country along the Godavari-Pranhita rivers, where in spite of a forested landscape we hoped to see Triassic as well as Lower Jurassic sediments. This country, I might add, was marked on an old map I saw some years ago as "unexplored jungle."

The jungle wasn't quite what I expected it to be, for it was not a dense tangle of tropical vegetation; rather it reminded me very much of oak woodlands in the American Midwest. It was fairly open and easy to walk through, yet we knew that this was the home of leopards and tigers, curious cats that might very well have been watching us as we disembarked from our cars at one place to wander in the forest. It was also the home of the Gonds, as we saw on our third day of travel, when we stopped at a little river to look at some Jurassic rocks exposed in the riverbank. Two Gond men were there, and as soon as we got out of our cars they disappeared into the forest as fast as they could run.

I should go back a couple of days in time, however, to say that on the first night after leaving Nagpur we stopped at Chanda, an ancient walled city which is today only partially occupied, and there we made ourselves at home at a government "rest house." (More about rest houses shortly.) Chanda was interesting to us, not only because of its historical aspects but also because a few miles away we would see evidences of Permian glaciation. Therefore on the next morning we drove to the village of Wardha, at the confluence of the Wardha and Penganga rivers, where we took a little boat for a three-kilometer trip up the Penganga River to the site in which we were interested. There we saw the Talchir boulder bed, an exposure containing a varied assortment of large boulders and pebbles as is typical of glacial deposits, while below this boulder bed, along the river we saw a smooth, polished surface, scoured by striations oriented in a northeast-southwest direction, precisely the kind of polished and scoured rock surface that would have resulted from the movement of a glacier. Nearby, as we got down on our hands and knees for a close examination of the striations, there stood a cowherd leaning on a long wand, and beyond him his herd of cattle, drinking from the river. A little way off there was a funeral pyre where some bodies were being cremated.

This locality, with a boulder bed and below it a polished, striated glacial surface, is the only place in India, in fact the only place in the northern hemisphere, where there is such clear evidence of Permian glaciation, dated at more than two hundred fifty million years ago. Yet in South Africa, South America, and Australia there are various places where evidence such as this for Permian glaciation is to be seen. In South Africa there would seem to be a radiation of glacial directions from a center near the Cape; in South America the directions are toward the west and in Australia toward the north. None of these indications of correlated glacial advances make much sense on the continents as they are now placed, but if our modern continents are brought together into a Gondwanaland, with India against the eastern border of Africa, and with South America and Australia to the west and the east of Africa-India, the glacial striae make a very nice pattern, radiating outwardly from a South African center. So what we were looking at on the edge of the Penganga River seemed to be clearly part of an integrated picture showing a Gondwana continent as it had been in Permian times. This of course is physical evidence that precedes in time yet corroborates in content the Lower Triassic paleontological evidence of *Lystrosaurus*, as I had seen it in India and Africa.

With such indications of possible (perhaps probable) past continental relationships in our minds, and set down in our notebooks, we got back into the little boat, went down the river to our waiting cars, and returned to Chanda. The next morning we embarked upon an all-day move to Sironcha, where we were to spend several days at a rest house conveniently located near a dinosaur quarry that was being worked by the institute geologists.

Something was said above about Indian rest houses; perhaps something more may be said at this place. These are places of rest and refreshment for travelers, built and maintained by the government, and they date back many years to the days of the British Raj. Arrangements are made, and if eligible one may stay at a rest house for a nominal fee. The government provides the house and keeps it in order and clean; the traveler brings his or her own bedding and food and is fully responsible for taking care of himself or herself. There is an order of precedence for use of each rest house, posted in a prominent place, and starting at the top with the prime minister it proceeds down through government officials of continuing lesser prominence, on through other dignitaries such as judges and the like, finally winding up with lowly creatures in the form of geologists and biologists. Fortunately for us no one was at the Sironcha Rest House when we arrived, so we had it to ourselves. (If some judge of a high court had been there we would have had to bed ourselves down elsewhere.)

The Sironcha Rest House was an especially nice one, near the river and quite commodius. Thus our party was accomodated, with room to spare. Next to the house was a large palm tree, the home of a noisy contingent of fruit bats, or "flying foxes." These are huge bats with wing spans of about two feet, and very foxlike faces. They do not enjoy the complex echo-location specializations of the insect-eating bats; they do not need such sophisticated built-in devices in their heads because they feed upon fruit which of course is quite stationary. All day long these bats quarreled among themselves in their roost, and then at sundown they departed on their nightly forays. As we watched them against the darkening sky they looked for all the world like the Mesozoic flying reptiles known as pterosaurs, flapping their way across the sunset.

A vision of pterosaurs at Sironcha was appropriate, because as mentioned we were here going to be involved with Jurassic dinosaurs that had lived when pterosaurs filled the skies. Therefore we drove over to the quarry on our first morning at Sironcha, to look at dinosaur bones and to help excavate them. The quarry was a shallow affair in flat ground, and a brush shelter had been built over it to protect the workers from the hot Indian sun. Furthermore, some local people had been hired for the sole purpose of disposing of tailings, so as dirt from the excavation accumulated these folks would scoop it up into shallow baskets and carry it away a hundred feet or so to dump it. In that way it was possible to continue work without being buried under the debris of bone digging.

This excursion upward in time was a diversion from our Triassic program, but not much of a diversion, because we were working in the very earliest beds of Jurassic age, in sediments known as the Kota Formation. Here there were being excavated the bones of a giant dinosaur, a sauropod subsequently set up in Calcutta (the only dinosaur skeleton to be seen in India) and described by Dr. Jain under the name of *Barapasaurus*, and it is significant that this dinosaur was a *giant*. *Barapasaurus* is a nice example of the fact that certain dinosaurs suddenly (in a geological context) became giants, descended from late Triassic dinosaurs of modest size. The road to giantism among these dinosaurs was not a long, slow journey; it was quickly achieved.

We spent several days at the *Barapasaurus* quarry and managed by the usual methods to take out all of the bones that had been exposed at this particular excavation. As the last of the plastered specimens was manhandled into one of our cars we enjoyed the pleasant sensation of something having been accomplished, something tangible in the form of bones for Calcutta. Now we were ready to embark upon the next phase of our field work which would take us back into the Triassic, but before we went on our way there was a very pleasant and a most unusual surprise in the offing.

A Gond village was hidden from us back in the jungle, about fourteen miles from the Sironcha Rest House, and it was our hope to go there and to see a Gond dance. But on our last day of work we realized that by evening we would be too tired for a trip to the Gond village, so one of our camp helpers went there to arrange for the Gonds to come to Sironcha. When he returned to us we thought the plans had been settled, but as evening came on and as the sky grew dark we gave up hope of seeing the Gonds.

Imagine our surprise when the next morning at breakfast about fifty Gonds appeared, having walked through the jungle during the early hours before daybreak. It was a colorful aggregation, the men clad in loose white clothing accentuated by very baggy pants, wearing turbans on their heads, in many cases with a long peacock feather sticking up out of the turban to serve as a waving guidon, and around their waists leather belts to which were attached many little globular bells. The women, too, were different from any women we had seen in India; they were clad in very short tight skirts extending down only about half way to the knees, with red bands around the lower part of each skirt, and each woman wore a short-sleeved blouse or perhaps an abbreviated little shawl, pinned together over the left shoulder. They wore a profusion of beads around their necks, and every woman had a little square mirror below her chin, hanging by a cord around the neck. Each of them had a silver ring through the left side of the nose, and almost all of them wore long red, white, and black streamers of yarn, two on each side suspended from a band around the head. These people were dark-skinned, but it seemed to us that their skin color had a coppery tinge to it, and they had frizzy hair.

The women carried long wands; some of the men carried small clarinetlike instruments while others had little conical-shaped drums suspended from their waists and hanging in front of the bearer so that he could beat his drum with both hands. Two of the men carried a huge drum, perhaps three feet in diameter and four or five feet in length, suspended from a stout pole that they bore on their shoulders. I could see that the drumhead was formed from the skin of a nilgai, a large wild Indian antelope. And from the pole that supported this drum between its two bearers there extended upwardly two widely spaced wands between which was stretched a large woven banner, purple in color, that waved back and forth as the two men swayed their bodies in time to the drum-beats.

The two leaders of the group were prosaically clad in khaki shorts and shirts and each of them carried a big, black umbrella.

They began their dance at about seven in the morning, and it went on for hours. It was intricate, and all during the proceedings the men played their instruments and beat upon their little drums, which properly might be called tabors, these sounds always having a background of deep tones from the big drum. We took many pictures, but how I did wish that we might have had recording equipment at hand! What an opportunity we missed!

At last it was getting late in the morning, and we felt that we had to be on our way. But the Gonds didn't want to let us go; they surrounded our cars, and for a half a mile or so as we slowly drove away from Sironcha, they accompanied us, still playing their little horns and beating the drums and smiling upon us as if we were friends of long standing. It was remarkable experience, and for us a particularly significant one. We were in Gondwana, and we had been with the Gonds! How many geologists can say this?

(Incidentally, the Gonds were as much a fascinating sight for the local Indians as they were for us. Before the morning dance was over several hundred people had congregated around Sironcha Rest House to watch the dancing and to listen to the strange music.)

We now had to get to Bhimaram, a little Indian village on the other side of the Pranhita River, and to cross the river it was necessary for us to take a ferry—of sorts. This vessel consisted of two dugout canoes fastened together by long, transverse timbers, with a platform built on top of the cross-pieces. It was quite a trick getting a Land Rover and a trailer on the ferry, one car and one trailer being the maximum load for a trip. Fortunately the Land Rover had a short wheelbase so it was possible to get it onto the ferry platform by driving it across from the river bank and onto the boat on two planks, which seemed almost not quite strong enough for the weight of the car. But they did hold up, and by very skillful driving the car was inched into place. The trailer was manhandled on behind the car, and then the crossing of the broad river took place, some of the ferrymen rowing with long, heavy oars, one man at the stern poling the craft. I, for one, was relieved when the second crossing was completed, so relieved in fact that I was careless getting off the ferry, slipped, and fell into the river with a loud splash.

Bhimaram is a little village in the jungle, more or less presided over by Raja Reddy. It was Raja Reddy's father who had founded the village in what, as I have mentioned, was indicated on an old map as unexplored jungle. Raja Reddy is a tall, handsome, very dark-skinned Telegu man, very well educated and very much interested in the work of the Geological Studies Unit of the institute. He also is much interested in developing crops and cottage industries that will be of benefit to the people living in and around Bhimaram, so he had at the time, and still has, various agricultural and other projects under way. When we were there in 1964 he had his family with him at Bhimaram; now the children are grown and dispersed.

As we arrived in Bhimaram we saw a neat camp of tents that had been set up at the edge of the village for our geological party, but Margaret and I were whisked right in to Raja Reddy's house, where we, as honored guests, were to stay. It was a commodius, well-appointed dwelling, surrounded by a wall, and furnished in a manner so that no creature comforts were lacking. Among other things Raja Reddy had a large library of books in English and in Telegu, this being the language in Andhra Pradesh. Raja Reddy had a big black dog named Argus; not long before we arrived he had had two dogs, but one night a leopard had leaped over the wall and made away with one of them. (In India leopards are very fond of dogs as staples of their diet; in Africa, as I had learned, they favor not only dogs but also baboons.)

We were at Bhimaram to study the Middle and Upper Triassic beds as exemplified by the sequence from bottom to top of the Yerrapalli, Bhimaram, and Maleri formations. In the Yerrapalli are found mammallike reptiles, especially large tusked dicynodonts, that link this geologic horizon with the sediments in Africa, as well as in South America, that contain similar fossils. The Bhimaram is a sandstone essentially barren of fossils. But the Maleri Formation, of late Triassic age, is of especial interest to a paleontologist from North America, because in it are found fossils closely related to fossils in the Chinle beds of the American Southwest—particularly big solid-skulled amphibians known as metoposaurs, and long-snouted, crocodilelike phytosaurs. In fact, there have been recent indications that perhaps small dinosaurs of the *Coelophysis* type may occur in the Maleri beds. Yet along with such Laurasian type fossils one finds rhynchosaurs in the Maleri sediments, these reptiles, it may be remembered, being especially characteristic of the later Triassic beds of Brazil. They are also found in Africa. So it would seem that by late Triassic time India was a sort of crossroads, where Laurasian land-living vertebrates ventured southwardly to mingle with the usual Gondwana forms.

During our days around Bhimaram we explored particularly the Yerrapali and Maleri exposures, to study the outcrops and to pick up such fossils as we might find. The institute had a quarry in the Yerrapalli where bones of dicynodont reptiles were being excavated in considerable numbers. As for the Maleri beds, I could almost imagine myself back in the Southwest, except that there were no cliffs and canyons, rather little badland exposures in the midst of millet fields. But the sediments, sandstones and siltstones, had the Triassic red color which I had encountered time and again, both in Laurasia and Gondwana.

Some of our wanderings led us into the forest, where on occasions we would see the pug marks of leopards. There were tigers here, too. This is the region where a young British geologist, Peter Robinson, working in collaboration with the institute, was followed by a tiger one day. He had gotten out of his Land Rover to walk down a nulla and look for exposures, while the driver stayed with the car—the usual practice. As Peter disappeared among the trees a tiger emerged from the forest and followed Peter. The driver, sitting in an open field car, was petrified with fear yet there was nothing he could do but sit quietly and hope for the best. The tiger went down the nulla, and for a few moments all was quiet. Then Peter reappeared, coming to the car from another direction. He had made a circle during his little exploratory walk, never aware that he was being followed. Evidently the tiger was curious—that was all.

One night, shortly before our arrival in Bhimaram, Raja Reddy had encountered a tiger as he was driving home through the forest. So on an evening after our arrival, as we were sitting around at the Reddy house enjoying the cool night air, Raja Reddy suddenly said: "Come on! Let's go look for tigers!"

We all piled into his Land Rover, Raja Reddy as the driver, Margaret and I, Jain, Tapan, and a geologist from the institute named Supriya Sen Gupta. It was a hare-brained idea! I'm sure that any self-respecting tiger would have made himself scarce when he heard our car a quarter of a mile away. Anyway we rattled around through the forest, enjoying the cool breezes, and we did see a fox and scare up a sambar deer. But no tigers.

Sooner or later we were bound to get lost, and we did, and we spent a lot of time driving around trying to find out where we were. At last we wound up in a dry rice paddy, and had the devil's own time getting out of *that*, but eventually we made it. It was quite an evening. Such are the goings-on of paleontologists when they aren't looking for fossils.

Sometimes they indulge in silly doings, as for example the day I wrote down some doggerel in my field book, and then read it to our crowd as we had lunch in the field. It amused them—and here it is.

> Let us all pay our homage, each in his own way,
> To the Yerrapalli and the Maleri clay.
> On the Bhimaram sandstone we cast but a glance,
> It carries no fossils—we view it askance,
> Expending our energies, day after day,
> On the Yerrapalli and the Maleri clay.
> The one with tuskéd dicynodonts strange,
> That throughout all Asia and Africa range.
> The other with rhynchocephalians queer,
> Anatomical puzzles through many a year.
> A reptilian harvest our efforts will bring.
> So let us clap hands, join together and sing
> With a derry down, down and a hey nonny hey
> For the Yerrapalli and the Maleri clay.

During our days in Andhra Pradesh, after the explorations around Bhimaram were finished, we went to Hyderabad—this at the invitation of Justice P. Jaganmohan Reddy, a relative of Raja Reddy. Justice Reddy was (and is) a most distinguished-looking, robust man, as well he might be, for at the time we were there he was chief justice of the High Court of Hyderabad. Subsequently he served on the Supreme Court of India.

We had a delightful time at the Reddy house, with Justice and Mrs. Reddy, she being a handsome, poised lady (all of the Reddys were handsome people), and their three almost grown-up children—two young men and a girl. It was a lively family; the younger Reddys were not at all terrified by the distinguished judge, and so it was that around the dinner table there would develop loud, almost acrimonious yet good-natured arguments, with much arm-waving and finger-pointing. Justice Reddy was not always the winner; sometimes the younger generation would make their father back down on some point. All the while Mrs. Reddy quietly held up her end in the debates. We enjoyed all of this most particularly, because the Reddys had so immediately made us feel like members of their family.

Our friendship with all of the Justice Reddys, as we call them, and the

Raja Reddys, has continued through the years, and fortunately we have been able to see them from time to time. This is because the younger generation of Reddys has come to the United States for their higher education, and some of them have remained here. And of course this is a magnet that brings Justice and Mrs. Reddy to our country for visits.

Once again, as I have previously remarked, a great advantage in being a geologist or a paleontologist in a foreign land is that one gets to know the people as friends, not strangers. Today, Margaret and I feel that we have friends all over the world.

There is much more I could write about our Indian adventure, but since to a considerable degree it involves sightseeing trips I will refrain. Suffice it to say that the institute authorities decided we should see things in India, so we visited some of the wonderful places for which this land is famous. We went to Bombay and to the Ellora and Ajanta caves; we went north to Darjeeling and south to Madras, where we were the guests of a fascinating modern Indian lady, Mrs. Swaminathan, who took us to Mahabalipuram. Mrs. Swaminathan always dressed in a flowing white sari, which set off her dark skin to perfection, and she drove a car with skilled abandon. We also went to Benares, where we saw the hordes of religious pilgrims bathing in the holy river, the Ganges.

The few days remaining to us in India, after our various field trips and sightseeing trips, were spent at the institute in Calcutta. There I was able to make some final observations of fossils and to talk things over with my colleagues. There Margaret was able to get some much-needed rest, because on our very last little journey—to Benares—she had picked up a fever and was recuperating from it.

March 22 was our day of departure. Although our invitation from the Indian Statistical Institute was for the express purpose of cooperative research in India, the institute people very kindly agreed that our way home was about as quick by going east as by returning in a westward direction. Therefore we had made arrangements to go home by way of Australia, where I could see one more segment of Gondwanaland. We had seen the Peninsula, now we were to visit the Island.

XVIII

. . . And the Island

We flew from Calcutta to Bangkok, where we stopped for a few days to see some of the sights of this exotic, oriental city, and then we went on to Australia, arriving in Sydney at six in the morning. (It seems to me in this age of air travel that we did then, and we still do, take off and arrive at the most unseemly hours.) In Australia we reentered a familiar world, not so picturesque as India and Thailand, but one to which we could adjust ourselves with the greatest of ease. I might add that although we did not realize it during our stay in India, we did become aware when we got to Australia that we were hungry for meat, so for the first week of our down-under experience we had meat three times a day, including steaks at breakfast.

There were many reasons why I wished to see something of Australia as part of my search for the Triassic in Gondwanaland. I had heard much about it from Harry Raven during my early years at the American Museum, and what he had told me whetted my appetite to see the island continent that zoologically is unique. Australia, although at one time an integral part of Gondwanaland, had been an isolated island for some fifty million years or more—from Eocene times to the present day. So even though it has fossiliferous ties to the other continents all of which once were parts of a supercontinent, it is today very special by reason of the composition of its mammalian fauna.

371

As is well known, and probably needs no particular emphasis here, Australia is a land of monotremes and marsupials, monotremes being the primitive, egg-laying mammals, represented there today by the duck-billed platypus and the spiny echidna, marsupials being the kangaroos, wallabies, koalas, wombats, phalangers (commonly called possums), and the many other pouched mammals that are so characteristic of that land. Also, as is well known to zoologists, but perhaps not fully appreciated by many people, Australia was at the time of Captain Cook's visit in 1770 essentially a continent without placental mammals. There were, of course, bats, because bats are not necessarily confined by oceanic barriers; there were a few rodents, these possibly having been accidentally brought in by the early colonizers of the island, the Aborigines, or perhaps in some cases having arrived there as waifs on floating vegetation; and there was a wild dog, the dingo, quite certainly introduced by early man. Otherwise Australia overwhelmingly belongs to the marsupials, which became adapted in many ways to the ecological niches available to them.

Today it may not be easy for a person in Australia to be aware of the unique Australian mammal fauna, because the English colonizers who first arrived there just two centuries ago have done much to change the look of the land during the years intervening since their early settlement of the continent. All sorts of placental mammals from other parts of the world have been introduced into Australia, so that cattle and sheep and other domestic animals are the animals commonly seen. Some of the introduced mammals have gone wild, a notable example being the oriental buffalo, which now aggressively roams the Outback in large numbers.

I was naturally very much interested in the marsupial (and monotreme) fauna of Australia and the reasons for the pristine domination of the island by animals of this sort. At the time of our visit, there were two explanations for marsupial and monotreme dominance. One, the older theory, was that marsupials—known from Cretaceous fossils in North America and Europe—and monotremes had come into the continent by a route down through Asia and along some kind of an East Indian crossing; the other, favored by the believers in Gondwanaland, was that the marsupials probably had entered Australia from South America by an Antarctic bridge, while the monotremes (which are in a sense modified mammallike reptiles) got there perhaps in a similar manner.

(To jump ahead briefly in this tale, I should say that just a few years ago a marsupial jaw and some upper teeth *were* found in Eocene sediments in Antarctica, these fossils being remarkably close to early Tertiary fossils found in Argentina. That, I think, nails down the Antarctica crossing of marsupials from South America to Australia. It also puts to rest the earlier ideas that marsupials had entered Australia by way of an Asiatic route, an idea that rested in part upon the supposition that since no fossil marsupials are known from Asia, such lack of evidence may have been the results of accidents of preservation or discovery, or both.)

At that time I was not quite convinced about Gondwanaland and an Antarctic route for the marsupials to have entered Australia, but I was nonetheless interested in the marsupials. Moreover, I was especially interested in Mesozoic Australia, which of course was not isolated from the rest of the world during the days of the dinosaurs, no matter what concept of continental relationships one might hold. I certainly was leaning toward Gondwanaland as a reality in geologic history, but for me there were some final steps still to be taken toward a wholehearted belief in the ancient supercontinent. I wanted to see what the evidence in Australia might be.

There were three general regions where I wanted to look around—to see Triassic things, but other things as well. One such area was the eastern coast, the second was Tasmania, the third was Western Australia, and in all of these places I hoped to make some observations that would contribute to my understanding of an ancient world. For this I was to have the advice and help of various paleontological and other friends, notably Dr. Evans, the director, and Harold Fletcher, the curator of paleontology at the Australian Museum in Sydney, Edmund Gill of the Victoria Museum in Melbourne, as well as Jim Warren and Tony Lee of Monash University in that city, Maxwell Banks of the University in Hobart, Tasmania, Jack Woods, director, and Alan Bartholomai, paleontologist, of the Queensland Museum in Brisbane, and David Ride, director, and Duncan Merrilees, paleontologist, of the Western Australian Museum in Perth. Also I was to work in especial close concert with the late John Cosgriff, a fellow American who was in Tasmania on a fellowship. If this seems like a lot of people for me to have been bothering on my own account—such was the case and such is the case in our profession wherever one may be. "They" help us and we help "them," and many a day have I happily devoted to foreign visitors who have wished to see particular geological sites in this country. It is a part of the international aspect of our science, and as I have previously remarked, it has served to establish friendly connections between all of us, the world around.

After a few days in Sydney getting oriented we went to Melbourne, where one of my early objectives was a trip to a locality known as Bacchus Marsh, about fifty miles west of the city, to see a glaciated pavement of Permian age. It will be remembered that I had seen such a pavement along the Penganga River in central India; here in southeastern Australia was a similar polished and scoured rock surface, formed at the same time and by the same glacial system that had ground across rocks that today are on the order of six thousand miles to the northwest of the Australian locality. Today the glacial striae at Bacchus Marsh are oriented in a northerly direction, but if Australia is rotated and brought back to its supposed position in Gondwanaland the striations would have been toward the east. Here was some physical evidence that made sense if viewed within the concept of an ancient supercontinent.

There were other things to do in and around Melbourne, such as going to a wildlife sanctuary with the Gills to have a close look at kangaroos and koalas, and visiting with Jim Warren the private sanctuary near Melbourne maintained by Monash University for research purposes. Margaret and I were amused there by a pet wombat that followed us around, just as if it had been a little dog and not a marsupial.

In Melbourne our path crossed the collective paths of some American friends, Ernest and Judy Lundelius, of the University of Texas, and Bill and Priscilla Turnbull of the Field Museum of Chicago. They were "down under" on research grants, to try to find fossil evidence concerning the early history of Australian marsupials—a daunting task, to say the least. Consequently they were exploring field and forest, searching for localities that might yield some fossils. It was probably inevitable that we would join them on one of their exploratory trips—this to the west of Melbourne in the Grampians, a range of hills rising above the fields of southern Victoria.

It was a pleasant excursion, the Lundelius and Turnbull families, including their children, and ourselves, in two field cars. And while we did not find fossils on that trip we did have a memorable experience, for one day as we were walking through the eucalypt forest we encountered a spiny anteater, or echidna, one of the two types of monotremes living today. (The other, as noted earlier, is the duck-billed platypus.) It was a real thrill for all of us to see a wild echidna, and we spent some little time examining him (or her). We were able to pick the echidna up and get a good close-up look, and to take some photographs, after which we turned the animal loose, whereupon it burrowed into the forest floor at an amazing rate. Almost before we had turned around, ready to resume our walk, the echidna had disappeared below ground.

In this connection I might add that the monotremes are in a sense persistent mammallike reptiles; for us there was a real feeling of being transported back in time as a result of our intimate meeting with this survivor of an ancient age.

One of my prime objectives was to see Triassic beds in Tasmania where Jim Warren had made collections, so after our Melbourne visit we flew to Hobart, where we were met at the airport by John Cosgriff and his wife, Bette. As mentioned, John was in Tasmania on a fellowship (subsequently he was to be established at Wayne State University in Detroit) and he was especially interested in the Triassic amphibians and reptiles of that island. Consequently there was an immediate bond of interest that united us;

furthermore it turned out that both Margaret and Bette Cosgriff had been students at the California College of Arts and Crafts in Oakland, so they had interests in common. The Cosgriffs had their two young sons with them in Hobart.

We were established in Hobart at a hotel on a beach at the end of the bus line, from which headquarters we made various expeditions with the Cosgriffs to see Triassic exposures and other sights. We went to Midway Beach near the city, where we found Triassic bones in some clay deposits enclosed within cross-bedded sandstones—the clay evidently representing old stream beds. And while we had our lunch on the beach Margaret waded out to pluck oysters from nearby rocks and consume their contents raw, just as if she were a Cro-Mognon lady. Another locality near the city was the Knocklofty Quarry, where some years before our visit a Triassic reptile, closely related to the Triassic reptile *Chasmatosaurus*, found in Africa, had been excavated. Here again was Gondwana evidence.

Indeed, we had many enjoyable days in Tasmania, so much so that we truly fell in love with the island, and with the nice city of Hobart as well. And when it came time for us to leave we were loath to go. We had vivid memories of Arcadian days in the Derwent Valley where the apples were ripe on the trees (it was fall in the southern hemisphere) and of a most interesting trip to Port Arthur at the southern tip of Tasmania, where in the bad old days almost two centuries ago convicts were brought from England, to fester in body and mind at what was for them the uttermost end of the earth. It was hard to realize, in this lovely countryside, that at one time men could have imposed such harsh indignities upon their fellow men.

Just before we were to leave Hobart and return to Melbourne, a huge Russian whaler came into Storm Bay, where it anchored about thirty miles or so from the city. Evidently the commander was awaiting instructions from Moscow. The local newspaper, all agog, was much interested in this visitor, so a light plane went out and circled the ship to see what could be seen. What was seen, among other things, was the name of the vessel in Cyrillic letters, which the reporter translated or rather transliterated in a singularly original way. We had been studying Russian, so when Margaret saw the newspaper account she sent them a postcard giving her version of what the name of the vessel really was—for a proper rendering could be made from the garbled translation. The ship was the *Sovietskaya Ukraina*.

Evidently the ship's captain got his orders from Russia at about the same time that we were returning to Melbourne, so when we got there the Russian ship had just arrived and anchored at a pier, where it was opened to visitors. Thousands of Melbournians flocked to see this vessel from a distant and almost forbidden country, while the sailors on shore leave went around the city in tight little groups. We saw them on the streets and in some of the stores, always keeping very close to each other—their psychological protection, I suppose, in a foreign country.

We went north to Queensland, where among other things I saw a nice Cretaceous dinosaur skeleton, recently collected from that area. It was an iguanodont dinosaur, related to that original dinosaur described by Gideon Mantell in England in the third decade of the nineteenth century. Since then, I should add, numerous Triassic dinosaur tracks have been unearthed in Queensland, and studied by one of my colleagues, Tony Thulborn. Moreover a procolophonid reptile skull, very like the little procolophonids found in the *Lystrosaurus* beds of South Africa, also has been collected in Queensland.

To supplement the remarks I have made about the good fortune of paleontologists in having friends in many places throughout the world, I might again add that the person out looking for fossils frequently has the opportunity to see things other than fossils. Therefore, since we were in Brisbane, with the Great Barrier Reef offshore, we made arrangements for a little holiday trip to Heron Island to see that natural wonder. We flew to Gladstone, north of Brisbane, and from there took a sturdy little launch for a trip of several hours to the reef. It was there that for the first time in our lives we were able to make some acquaintance with the zoological variety and the visual wonder of a great coral reef. There is a marine research station on Heron Island, which we frequented, and Margaret enjoyed the experience of exploring the reef with Miss Goh, a student of marine zoology from Kuala Lumpur. It was while they were engaged in this pleasant occupation that several sharks swam in over the edge of the reef to explore in their turn the shallow waters where the two ladies were occupied. One shark came at them, Margaret and Miss Goh stood up in the waist-deep water, determined to sell their lives dearly, but at the last moment the shark, to the unalloyed relief of the ladies, made a sharp 180-degree turn and swam out into the deep water beyond the reef.

Back in Brisbane I bade farewell to Margaret; she was on her way back home, while I was scheduled to venture to the west, into the very northwestern corner of the island continent. One reason for my wish to see that corner of Australia was the usual call of the Triassic, which there had been investigated by John Cosgriff. Indeed, he urged me to do just that. Another was my wish to look into some Cretaceous dinosaur footprints that had been found along the shore at Broome and had been briefly reported in print. I was somewhat dubious as to the published identification that had been assigned to these tracks.

Thus I boarded a plane in Sydney, bound for Perth, which latter city has long enjoyed the distinction of being the most isolated city in the world. To the east of Perth is Adelaide, fifteen hundred miles distant across the great, featureless Nullarbor Plain. To the west are four thousand miles of open ocean before one reaches Madagascar and southern Africa. To the north is Java, fifteen hundred miles distant, and to the south is the South Pole, four thousand miles away. Today, however, Perth does not feel the isolation that it felt in years gone by, because modern communications and the airplane have brought this city within the Australian framework. Today the journey between Adelaide and Perth is a matter of hours, not days.

At Perth I was soon enjoying conversations and the exchange of information with David Ride, whom I had earlier known in England, and Duncan Merrilees, both introduced in an earlier paragraph. The idea agreed to between us in our discussions was for Duncan and me to go to Derby, a little town on the coast something more than a thousand miles to the northeast of Perth, where we could explore the Triassic sediments to the east of the town, and then to Broome, another coastal town about a hundred miles from Derby for the Cretaceous dinosaur tracks. The problem was, how were we to get up there from Perth?

There were two options: to fly or to take a coastal road, this latter involving a journey of several days each way. How could we fly? The earliest passage, according to the MacRobertson-Miller airline, would not be available until the next week, and that would negate our plans, because we wanted to be at Broome on the day of neap tide in order to work on the dinosaur tracks there, these being exposed a little way off shore and generally under water. Of course the journey by car also would get us there too late. What to do?

I was on the point of despair, on the morning of my second day in Perth, when Mr. Bob Vincent, the business officer at the Western Australian Museum, came to our rescue. He heard of our plight, he got in touch with the airline, and almost immediately our problem was solved. I don't know what he said to them, but arrangements were made for us to take a plane that very evening from Perth to Derby. So it was that by noon our plans were set, with the happy result that I enjoyed a pleasant lunch with David and Duncan at a restaurant in a park overlooking Perth. The view of the city was superb, the lunch was excellent, and all seemed right with the world.

That evening Duncan and I turned up at the airport with our luggage. We were checked in, our luggage was weighed, and then *we* were weighed. That seemed to me like a strange procedure; were the weights of passengers so crucial? When we boarded the plane I saw at once why we had been weighed; we were part of the cargo. The plane, an old DC-3, was loaded from floor to ceiling with goods and bags of mail. At the back of the plane were four or perhaps six seats, and two of those we occupied as a species of supercargo, or perhaps more accurately as excess baggage. It was an all-night flight, and we landed at Derby in the early morning, having during the night offloaded part of the cargo at various cattle stations along the way.

We spent several days prospecting the Blina shales of Triassic age, exposed in the Erskine Range to the east of Derby. There we found fossil amphibian bones in a ripple-marked sandstone within the Blina beds, the sediments taken as a whole indicating stream deposits in an ancient delta. And during all of this activity I learned something about field work in the Australian Outback. One of the principal concerns of the explorer in this region is the problem of flies, flies that descend upon one in countless hordes. Our shirts were black with flies that covered us, and our only means for carrying on with some degree of sanity was to adopt the tried and true outback practice of wearing broad-brimmed hats, with a net hanging down from the hat brim to keep the flies off our faces and out of our eyes, ears, and noses. Also it is a common practice in the Outback to suspend corks from threads or strings fastened at close intervals around the edge of the hat brim. Needless to say we kept our sleeves in place down to the wrists and were otherwise covered.

We collected some nice amphibian jaws and other bones in the Blina shales, and made various observations on the Triassic beds as exposed in this part of the world. And in driving back and forth from Derby to our collecting area—a trip of about eighty miles each way—I was intrigued by the queer baobab trees that we saw along the road. One particular giant of a tree had a hollow trunk, and I was told that in former years this tree served as a temporary lockup for petty transgressors of the law.

On the morning of May 25 Duncan and I made the short plane ride from Derby to Broome, arriving at the latter place within an hour after our takeoff. At Broome we were met by Mr. John Tapper, the harbor-master and the man who was to play a crucial role in our attempt to make casts of the dinosaur footprints that were of such interest to us. The casting was to take place on the next day, very late in the afternoon, so there was much for us to do in order to be ready for this exercise in a race against the tide.

It should be explained here that at Broome, on the northwestern coast of Australia, there are the next to greatest tides in the world, the highest tides being of course those of the Bay of Fundy. It all has to do with the configuration of and depth of the ocean bottom in the basin between northwestern Australia and the East Indies; there is an extensive shallow sea floor off the Australian coast so that the tides slop over it like water carried in a shallow pan. Consequently, the dinosaur footprints, which are offshore, are to be seen at low tide, but for most of each month they still remain under water. Only on the day of neap tide does the water retreat to such an extent that the footprints become uncovered, and then for only about forty-five minutes. It was our task to get out there at low tide and make our casts, more properly our molds, if possible.

To accomplish this we had ordered some quick-setting gel from a dental supply house in Perth—the sort of stuff that dentists cram into your mouth when they wish to make molds of teeth that need attention. I think we must have made a serious inroad upon the Perth supply, because whereas a dentist needs only a small amount of such material for any particular occasion, we needed gobs of it—enough to reproduce perhaps a half-dozen dinosaur tracks.

With all of this on our minds, and with some concern for our procedures of the morrow, we checked in that morning at the one hotel in Broome and got our personal effects stowed in our room. The hotel was not at all prepossessing when we viewed it from the road, for it seemed to be largely constructed of corrugated iron, as are so many structures in the Australian Outback. When we got inside we found that it was made in the form of a square "U," with one wing containing the bedrooms, with the wing at right angles to this housing an immense bar, and with the wing on the opposite side of the U devoted to the kitchen and dining room. The space enclosed by the three wings of the hostelry was devoted to a very nice lawn and flower beds, kept fresh and green by a continuous spray from sprinkling devices.

All of which offered promise of a comfortable sojourn, but the amenities hoped for were at the moment clouded by what was going on at the bar. It was full of outback Aussies, having their drinks and shouting and in general making a ruction that might have been heard halfway to Derby. The outback Australians are a rough and ready crowd, in fact of so raffish a cast as to make our western cowboys and lumberjacks look in comparison like the participants in an afternoon tea. I wondered what kind of a night we were to have. I need not have worried; at closing time, and as I remember it closing time was early, the bar turned as quiet as a tomb, so that as things eventuated Duncan and I enjoyed a full night of peaceful slumber. The Australian laws are very strict about the closing of alcoholic refreshment establishments; there is none of the midnight-and-after whooping and hollering that can make the night hideous in America.

While on the subject of Australians I am prompted to say something about an experience with Australians in Africa, a few years after this visit to Broome. It was the year 1970, and I was in South Africa attending the second international Gondwana symposium. As a part of this symposium we had a field trip through the Karroo in a chartered bus, and among the folks participating in this excursion were about a half-dozen Australian geologists and paleontologists. The fact that they were highly trained academic types did not in the least suppress their characteristic Aussie lack of inhibitions.

They were out to look at Gondwana geology, but they were out to have a good time as well.

Since I had been working in the Triassic for many years they immediately dubbed me Red Bed Ned and they thought that was a great sobriquet. Indeed, they took me in as one of theirs and a good time was had by all. But there was an English geologist on the trip, a youngish man of considerable eminence, and the Aussies soon found out that he was inclined to be a bit stuffy. Poor fellow! They made life miserable for him with their pranks; in fact I thought they were a bit too cruel at times.

Certainly their tricks sometimes were apt to be on the crude side. For example, they found an old dried-up sheep carcass out in the veldt, so they rigged it up over the door of the bus with an arrangement of strings, so that they could drop it on the head of any unsuspecting person getting on the bus. They found that procedure immensely entertaining; for the recipient of a suddenly descending sheep carcass the event could be just a bit traumatic.

Still another Australian story, this one told to me years ago by Harry Raven. Back in the early twenties he and Dr. Gregory were in the forests of Queensland, collecting marsupials. The rains came and for two or three days, possibly it was three or four, they were confined to an outback hotel of the kind I have described at Broome. Of course it was an establishment with a few rooms for guests and an enormous bar, in the usual Australian tradition. Not only Gregory and Raven were confined to quarters by the bad weather but also a large contingent of loggers, who were enjoying an enforced vacation.

Naturally they were making the best of the situation in the bar, where noisy arguments went on through long daylight hours. Dr. Gregory, in the meantime, was in his room trying as best he could to write up his field notes. His efforts, however, were periodically interrupted by a deputation from the bar, who came to his room, most respectfully it should be said, to request him to settle some argument that had arisen in the bar. Dr. Gregory would offer his opinion, whereupon the little committee would return to the bar.

Almost immediately Gregory and Raven, in their quarters, would hear a great shout.

"Hooray for the Doc!"

To get back to the story, we had a council of war in the afternoon with Mr. Tapper, as well as with his brother, Mr. Edgar Tapper, and we went out to the beach to plan our campaign. This was something new in my experience; how were we to get the water left in the tracks after the tide went out, out of the tracks? How were we to devise a dam around each footprint, to contain the casting compound so that it would not flow willy-nilly across the rock face? And how were we to do this for a half-dozen tracks, all in the course of little more than half an hour? John Tapper came up with an excellent idea: why not coil a short length of heavy rope around each footprint, to serve as a dam? We welcomed that suggestion with enthusiasm, and accordingly provided ourselves with several lengths of rope from Mr. Tappers's stores.

All the time we were out on the beach I was intrigued by several frigate birds, hovering above some cliffs back of the beach. Evidently there was a constant flow of air against the cliffs, so that the birds could take advantage of this upward current for their own purposes, and their purpose seemed to be to stay in the air at one spot for minutes at a time. So there they were, as if suspended from the heavens by a wire, hardly moving a wing or a tail. It was a fascinating display of aerodynamics. And as we came back into town from our conference on the beach we were greeted by a great flock of white cockatoos, settling onto some vacant land between the widely spaced houses.

The rest of the afternoon and a part of the next morning were spent in constructing some boxes to hold the molds we intended to make. Then on that first evening in Broome at dinner we met Mr. Edgar Truslove, an official of the MacRobertson-Miller airline. It was a most fortunate coincidence, because Mr. Truslove immediately fell in love with our project as we told him about it, and volunteered to help us the next day. Moreover, he would offer invaluable help in getting our molds properly loaded on the plane.

The next afternoon we were all ready for our somewhat experimental and certainly different exercise in the art of fossil casting. The footprints we wished to reproduce were at two places offshore, separated by a hundred yards or so. One site was at Gantheaume Point, the other at Riddell Beach. Late afternoon came and we were poised for action.

First we dashed out to Riddell Beach and began work on the best of a three-footprint trackway there. We coiled the rope around the print, bailed out the track and dried it with towels, mixed the casting gel in a pail and poured it into the track. Then we hustled over to Gantheaume Point and repeated the process on three footprints. Then back to the first print to carefully remove the mold, which of course was flexible, from the track. Then back to Gantheaume Point to extract the three molds there. It all worked out as planned, and we got our molds to high ground and away from the incoming tide just as it started to wash into the dinosaur footprints.

After that we took the molds back to Mr. John Tapper's house and put them into the boxes that we had previously constructed. Then we were ready to return the next day to Perth. We were going this time on a regular passenger plane, and Mr. Truslove, who was accompanying us, supervised in person the loading of our cargo.

Back at the Western Australian Museum the tracks were unpacked; the television people came swarming in to make pictures and get a story about footprints that were made in Australia more than sixty million years ago. And from the molds we had made it was possible to reproduce the tracks just as they existed out in the Cretaceous rocks at Gantheaume Point and Riddell Beach. Thus was completed my adventure in northwestern Australia.

There is a postscript. Three years later Duncan Merrilees and I published a paper in the *Journal of the Royal Society of Western Australia*, in which we described the footprints and concluded that they had been made by a large carnivorous dinosaur, our conclusion being based on the size and shape of the prints and on the fact that at the end of each toe there was the imprint of a large claw. We named the tracks *Megalosauropus broomensis*, meaning "the feet of a megalosaur (a large carnivorous dinosaur) from Broome."

Back to Sydney I went, to spend several days of geologizing in the field with Harold Fletcher of the museum, interspersed with a full Sunday and several evenings reading proof of a book I had written with Marshall Kay of Columbia University. The book, a large, heavy volume, is entitled *Stratigraphy and Life History* and is aimed strictly at graduate students.

So ended my journey of 1964 to India and Australia, a trip during which I learned much about the Mesozoic and most specifically about the Triassic of Gondwanaland. I use the term Gondwanaland advisedly, because by this time I was pretty well convinced that there really *had been* a Gondwanaland.

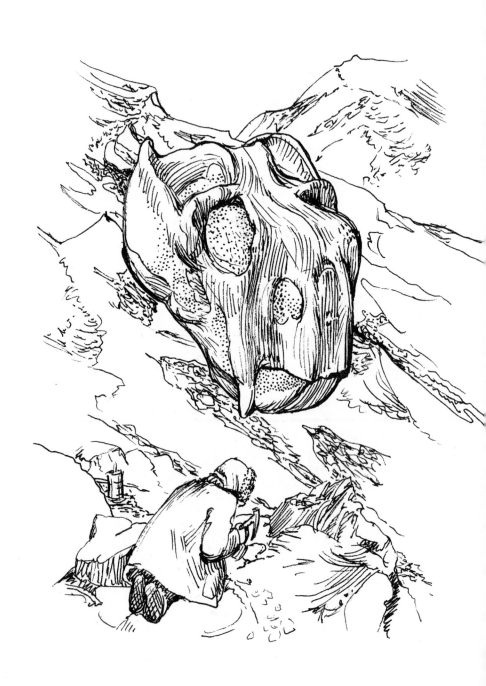

XIX

Antarctica, the Heart of It All

My search for the Triassic in Laurasia and Gondwanaland had its beginnings, of course, soon after the Second World War, when I made my first explorations of Triassic outcrops in the Southwest and when I made that trip to England in 1948, the precursor to many trips to many lands that would take place during the next quarter-century. The earlier of these trips would be made by myself, because our boys were still small and Margaret felt that she had to stay at home with them. Gradually as the boys grew larger she began to take some trips with me, having arranged for her part in such trips to be of relatively short duration and having arranged for someone to stay with the children during her absence. But as time went on her participation in my ventures increased, at those times when we took the whole family with us as we did in 1953 when we spent the summer in Wyoming and in Arizona, and at later times when the boys had become increasingly self-sufficient so that we felt we could safely leave them to their own devices for several weeks or perhaps a couple of months without us.

385

Such were the occasions in 1959 when she went with me to Brazil, in 1964 when we had our trip together to India and Australia, and from then on to the present day. By 1964 our youngest son, Charles, had reached his eighteenth birthday, so by then we had a feeling of independence that allowed us to make plans on our own terms. After the midsixties our lives became oriented around our own present and future affairs, with our five sons (some of whom now had families of their own) living their independent lives. Our years of raising a family (albeit *not* of worrying about our children) had come to an end.

During several of the summers in the nineteen-sixties we had spent some time in Arizona, with the Museum of Northern Arizona in Flagstaff as our headquarters. From this base it was possible to work in Triassic rocks in several directions, and I did just that. As I carried out my field work from the Flagstaff base I got to thinking more and more that this would be a nice place in which to spend my later years, and Margaret was in full agreement with such sentiments. I suppose our feelings became known to some of the people at the Museum of Northern Arizona, so it was no particular surprise when Dr. Edward (Ned) Danson, director of the museum, suggested to me one day when he was in New York on a museum business trip that if Margaret and I wished to settle in Flagstaff, the museum there could accommodate me with a place to work. From then on we lived our lives with this possibility in our minds.

Flagstaff, at the foot of the San Francisco Peaks, these being the massive remnants of an extinct volcano, is a delightful location, the town situated at an elevation of almost seven thousand feet, the peaks rising a mile higher to a maximum elevation of more than twelve thousand feet. The countryside is blanketed with an extensive forest of ponderosa pines; moreover because of the high elevation the landscape in winter is blanketed with a layer of snow that at times may become formidably deep. So much for the stereotype of Arizona as a land of desert and cactus.

Could we move to such a climate? There was one answer to the question—try it out. Therefore, since I had some accumulated vacation available, we decided to spend the winter of 1966–1967 in Flagstaff, where among other things I could work on a book that I had planned to write. The museum had some nice little cottages available for visiting firemen, and one of these was allotted to us. There I wrote my book entitled *Men and Dinosaurs*, which was published in 1968.

That spring of 1967 we returned home, where I was to resume my museum duties, and where we both were to make plans for the coming autumn, an autumn that would involve a trip to Argentina, Brazil, and Uruguay for some Gondwana meetings. As usual life began to get complicated, because late in the summer we got a long-distance call from Bill

Breed, the geologist at the museum in Flagstaff, informing us that there was a two-and-a-half-acre plot of land available in the woods, fronting a county road just to the north of the museum grounds. Margaret immediately got on a plane, flew out to Arizona, and with her heart in her mouth she bought the property. Then off we went to South America for the meetings.

First we went to Argentina where we not only attended meetings but also flew off to Mendoza in western Argentina (where once again I had a reunion with the Minoprio family) and from there went into the field. It was our privilege to penetrate the desert beyond Mendoza and San Juan, where we poked around in Triassic sediments that looked for all the world as if they might have been around Cameron, Arizona, north of Flagstaff.

During the course of these several meetings there was to be an excursion in a chartered bus from southern Brazil to Montevideo, Uruguay, during the course of which we were to visit exposures of Mesozoic rocks in the field. Off we went, a polyglot bus-load of people from all parts of the world, intellectually fired-up for a trip devoted to learning and arguing.

We had assembled in the small Brazilian city of Bagé, not far from the Brazilian-Uruguayan border, ready for our journey, when it developed that there were international complications of some sort. The problem was complex, arcane, and far removed from the world of reality, so there was nothing for us to do but hole up in Bagé hotel rooms for the night while our leaders fought it out with the bureaucrats. The next morning it appeared that things had been straightened out, so we blithely boarded our bus for the trip south. We were scheduled to spend the day between Bagé and the Uruguayan city of Melo—not a very great distance but one in which we would make many stops and spend the hours cracking rocks and talking about what we were finding.

At the border, midway through the morning, our little expedition came to a sudden halt. We were ordered out of the bus, all of our luggage was off-loaded by the side of the road, and then the bus turned around and went back to Bagé. There we were destined to spend the rest of the day, while the Brazilian officials in a little rude hut pored over our passports, after which the Uruguayan officials, in a still smaller and more decrepit hut, not only pored over our passports, but laboriously copied all of the information in each passport—for some reason known only to themselves.

Well, there was nothing to do but make the best of it, so we sat on the grass and visited, and ate and drank what snacks we had with us, while during the afternoon the younger and more vigorous members of our party organized a soccer game (someone had brought a ball along) between the "drifters" and the "nondrifters." I don't remember who won. Eventually, as the sun was sinking toward the western horizon and the shadows were ever lengthening, we finally walked across the border, picked up our documents, identified our luggage, and boarded a new bus that had been brought up for our use.

All thoughts of geologizing over that part of our route had been abandoned. The bus drove straight to Melo, arriving there in the dark, where we hastily registered at a hotel, had a late supper, and fell wearily into our beds. The next day we resumed our trip and managed to squeeze in some geological observations on our way to Montevideo.

That day was made memorable because we were mixed up in a cross-country horse race. The day before, while we were loitering on the north side of the border, we saw numerous beautiful horses being exercised on the south side of the border. It turned out that they were to race across a part of Uruguay the next day—and the next day we kept encountering them, each horse and rider cantering along, followed by a flagged car, the car containing horse-handlers and equipment.

After the meetings in Montevideo we went back to Brazil before returning home. At home we began to think about our newly acquired property, out on the northern edge of Flagstaff. Our son Dan was then a student of architecture at Columbia University, so with our desires at hand he drew up plans for a house. And then, that winter, I took the plans to Flagstaff, where I had conferences with a contractor and a licensed architect, who translated Dan's drawings into properly accredited architectural designs. We made arrangements for work to begin in the fall.

That fall both of us were back in Flagstaff, to see the beginning of our house, after which we went to Mexico with Bill Breed and his wife, Carol (also a geologist), to attend the annual meetings of the Geological Society of America in Mexico City. It sounds like a lot of traveling around, and it was. But we were getting prepared for a new phase of our life, which was to start (as this is written) almost twenty years ago.

As was written in a preceding paragraph life has a way of getting complicated, and I may add that complications seem to arise at remarkably inconvenient times. To go back a few months in time, we were busy in the spring of 1968, making our house plans and getting ready for the builders, when a telephone call reached me in my office at the museum in New York, to inform me that the caller thought he had a fossil bone he had found in Antarctica. If he brought it to New York could I please identify it? Of course I would try. And that is how Antarctica entered my life.

The caller was Ralph Baillie, a student at Ohio State University, who during the previous field season had been exploring with his leader, Dr. Peter Barrett, in the Transantarctic Mountains, about four hundred miles from the South Pole. There in Triassic sediments they had found what they thought looked like a piece of fossil bone. Hence the call. Once again, as had previously happened, mere chance was to have a decisive effect upon my life. Ralph Baille might have called any one of a dozen other paleontologists, but for some reason he chose me.

Ralph was associated with the Institute of Polar Studies at Ohio State—now the Byrd Polar Research Center—an independent research organization affiliated with the university Department of Geology and devoted particularly to the study of polar science, especially geology. Peter Barrett is a New Zealander who was then studying at the polar institute; he since has been well established at Wellington University. Moreover there was and is at the polar institute David Elliot, a transplanted Englishman who for years has directed the work there and who for years has been my very cherished friend. Indeed, Margaret and I have become intimate friends of David and his wife, Ann, and the three Elliot children. That is a story in itself.

To get back to my story of Ralph Baillie and the bone, he appeared a few days after the telephone call, and without delay opened a small parcel to reveal an undoubted fossil bone, resting upon a bed of cotton. Here was something to increase the heartbeat of any paleontologist—the first evidence of an ancient land-living backboned animal from Antarctica! My mind reeled (to use a trite phrase) at the implications of this little fossil, a mere fragment perhaps two inches in length. But it was a diagnostic fragment, because it was the back end of an amphibian jaw, containing the articular surface that had joined the jaw to the skull. Moreover, the outer surface of this fragment was very rough, or rugose, just the kind of bone surface that is so characteristic of what are known as the labyrinthodont amphibians.

For me the identification of this fragmentary fossil was of momentous significance, and I wanted to be doubly sure that I was right. I knew I was, yet nonetheless I wanted a second opinion, so I took the bone with me for a little journey to Princeton University, where my friend Don Baird made his scientific home. Don is one of those paleontologists with a very perceptive eye; he has the faculty for correctly pinning down the most incomplete and discouraging-looking fossil. I knew that if Don agreed with me there was nothing to worry about. Don agreed.

Next, there was the important task of describing the fossil and publishing the description, for until that was accomplished the fossil was scientifically a specimen in limbo. Consequently Peter Barrett and Ralph Baillie as the discoverers, and I as the identifier, brought out a joint paper in the August 2, 1968, issue of *Science*, describing the specimen and giving the particulars of its location and geologic occurrence. This paper attracted more than the usual amount of attention in the scientific community.

I felt that it was important for me that year at Christmas time to attend the annual meeting of the American Association for the Advancement of Science in Dallas, to announce the discovery in person. While I was in

Dallas I met some officials of the National Science Foundation, the governmental agency through which all American Antarctic research is conducted, and I said to them in effect that someone should go back to Antarctica to look for more fossils. Where there was one, there were bound to be more, was the gist of my argument.

"Very well," they said, "why don't you go to look for more fossils?"

"Oh no!" was my reply. "I'm getting ready to retire, and it's not for me at my age to go to Antarctica."

"Don't worry," they said. "You will be taken care of."

That was the beginning of my Antarctic adventure.

I went back home. There was correspondence with David Elliot at the polar institute, and plans were begun for an Antarctic fossil hunt. I was asked to choose some people to go with me as participants in this venture, and I immediately chose my good friend Jim Jensen, of Brigham Young University. Jim is a superb field collector, and I knew that if anybody could insure the success of the project it would be Jim. Jim immediately agreed. I also asked Bill Breed of the Flagstaff Museum and Gil Stucker of the American Museum to join the group. They both enthusiastically agreed, and I thought our field party was all set to go. Alas! There was a hitch in the shape of a medical examination. The National Science Foundation requires all people going to Antarctica to undergo complete medical checkups. Jim and Bill had their examinations and passed. Gil and I spent the day at a naval hospital on Long Island, and whereas I passed, Gil was rejected. It was hard to believe! Gil was bigger and tougher and stronger than I was, and he had a background of outdoor life and fossil collecting under strenuous conditions. But the medicine men didn't like his blood sugar or something like that. Gil demanded a second test, and again he was rejected. It was a great disappointment to both of us. In the end we obtained the services of an Arizona University student, Jon Powell, as the fourth member of our party. All of this took place in the spring.

Summer came, and early in July Margaret and I set out by car for our new home in Flagstaff. We had sold our home in New Jersey, we had taken care of our personal effects in various ways, and such furniture and other household goods that we wished to keep had been sent to Arizona on a moving van. I had not as yet officially retired from the American Museum; the director wanted me to retain my active connection with the institution until after the Antarctic expedition. So I took my annual vacation until time for the trip, after which I would be on terminal leave, thereby continuing my ties with the museum until the following summer. Then I would go on to my pension.

Flagstaff was as lovely as it always is in the summer—pleasant days and cool nights, and dry high-altitude air that is particularly invigorating. As we settled into our new home I could not help feeling a little bit sorry for myself; why was I leaving this place for the bleak rigors of Antarctica? Every day before my departure was a day of appreciation, for the beauty of the land where I was now living—and of regret, for having to leave this land.

At last the fatal day arrived. That was October 20, and as luck would have it, the plane that was to take us to Phoenix could not land in Flagstaff because we were caught in an early, sudden, windy snowstorm. It seemed like an ominous omen. Because of this premature wintery touch Bill Breed and I had to rush around and get a bus, which in turn forced us to catch a later plane for California, where we were due at Travis Air Force Base to begin our long flight to New Zealand and from there to Antarctica, "the Ice."

It *was* a long flight—in an air force Starlifter, and that was a good deal like flying in a barn. In the cavernous interior of the plane were canvas seats all facing toward the rear, and no windows, so we had many hours to while away, wondering where we were. The landings were always interesting because all we could do was to sit and wait for the bump. We made landings in Hawaii and Samoa, and finally we were on the ground in Christchurch, New Zealand—the big staging base for American expeditions to Antarctica.

Our stop in Christchurch was a bit longer than had been planned, because the Antarctic weather was far from cooperative. Every morning before dawn for a week we would have to climb out of our comfortable beds in a Christchurch hotel, gulp down a hasty breakfast, drive out to the airport, don our Antarctic gear (that was a requirement) consisting of thermal underwear, heavy socks, baggy pants, a parka, large ungainly boots, and a warm cap, and then sit and sweat, waiting to get on the plane. And every morning, after we had thus suffered for an hour or two, word would come in that the flight was canceled because of bad Antarctic weather. Then our time was our own for the rest of the day, so after laboriously climbing out of our polar gear and getting into ordinary clothing we were free to do as we wished.

Consequently we had some nice sightseeing trips in and around Christchurch, these largely by courtesy of Allan and Margaret Cookson, newly acquired friends who have now been our very good friends for two decades. Allan was a dentist by profession and a mountaineer by avocation, and he along with several other Christchurch mountain climbers had been hired to go down to the ice with us, to introduce us into the techniques of ice climbing. The Cooksons were a lot of fun, so even though we were delayed day after day from taking off, the days thanks to them passed most pleasantly. One day we drove out to the New Zealand Alps. Other days were spent in the countryside, and in town we enjoyed the beauties of the botanical garden. Christchurch has a remarkably fine garden, and since it was the southern-hemisphere spring, the flowers were out in profusion. As we wandered among flower beds and through groves of trees I again felt sorry for myself; why should I have to leave these paradisiacal surroundings for the huge, grim ice cap? But such thoughts were fleeting. I should add that I was especially interested in our trips to the countryside beyond Christchurch to see the extensive forests of southern beech (*Nothofagus*) covering the steep sides of the mountains. These are the same trees that grow in Tierra Del Fuego, and their presence in these distant parts of the southern hemisphere is regarded by many botanists as an indication of a former Gondwanaland.

On the fifth morning of our enforced vacation we put on our Antarctic gear and then, as before, were told that the flight was scrubbed. We were warned, however, to be back at the airport immediately after lunch, because there was a possibility that the flight would take place that afternoon. Thus for the second time that day we again struggled into our heavy clothing, ready for our flight to the Ice. (I should say at this point that Antarctic clothing was required because it was supposed that if the plane should go down in the polar ocean we would be sufficiently protected against the cold. My own feeling was that if we should go down we would all sink to the bottom like lead weights; I shudder to think what our clothes would have weighed once they were saturated.)

We boarded the Hercules LC-130 for our polar flight. Here I wish to digress briefly to say something about the Hercules. This four-engine propeller plane has revolutionized work in Antarctica. In the old "heroic" days of ships and dog teams anyone exploring in Antarctica had to spend literally about ninety percent of his time just staying alive. Today with the Hercules, equipped for Antarctic landings with huge skis, it is possible to place a group of scientific people at any place on the continent with ample supplies and food. Consequently the modern-day explorer in Antarctica can devote his time to the problems at hand. The interior of the big Hercules looked like the combination of a ferry boat and a moving van. Along the sides of the fuselage were bucket seats, into which the passengers were strapped. The middle of the aircraft was piled high with equipment reaching from floor to ceiling. As in the Starlifter we had no windows to look out of, so it was a case of sitting patiently while the plane droned on to the south. We were about four hours into our journey when all at once we felt the plane banking for a turn. There were some little portholes in the fuselage, and we could see the shafts of sunlight coming through these ports tracking across the inside of the plane as it turned through a 180-degree arc. We were on the way back to Christchurch! The radio from McMurdo Base in Antarctica had informed the pilot that the weather there was bad and that an attempted landing would be dangerous. We had reached the "point of no return" halfway to Antarctica, which meant that if we went on we would have to go all the way. So we turned around.

We arrived in Christchurch late in the evening, wearily got out of our Antarctic gear, wearily backtracked to our hotels, and after a short night wearily arose at four the next morning for another try. This time we made it. We disembarked at Williams Field, the airbase for American Antarctic flights, out on the ice several miles from McMurdo Base, which is built on solid ground. As we emerged from the plane we were slashed by a strong, below-zero wind, and that inspired all of us to huddle into our parkas, red parkas for the scientific people (known as USARPs—United States Antarctic Research Program), green parkas for the navy personnel. Such was to be our dichotomy for the months ahead, a dichotomy further complicated by another subdivision, because the navy officers were separated from their enlisted men, and the USARPs were accorded the temporary status of navy officers, without any ranking.

We got into trucks at the airfield and had a bumpy ride across the ice to McMurdo Base. There I was established in a tiny room with two bunks, in a small wooden hut, a room that I shared with one of the supply people at McMurdo. This introduces another complication in the social situation at McMurdo, for although there was a division between scientists and navy personnel (who were in charge of logistics), there was another division between the navy and the folks who handled the food and the like, these being employees of a private firm, Holmes and Narver, working on a contract. The room I was in was just the length of the bunks, one above the other, with about three feet on one side of the bunks. I had the upper bunk with an allotment of about two feet of headroom. It was cramped, but it was cozy; there were no windows, which made sleeping pleasant, since we were enjoying twenty-four hours of daylight, frequently of strong sunshine, yet since McMurdo Base had an electric plant we had lights; therefore I could retire to my bunk and read for hours during the day. This I did frequently, because it so happened that I was destined to spend about three weeks at McMurdo with my co-workers, again because of bad weather. In Antarctica one bends with the weather.

There was a large dining hall at McMurdo, rather two dining halls, one for officers and USARPs, the other for enlisted men and the Holmes and Narver people. There was a bar, where we could enjoy drinks and movies each evening, and there was a large supply and laboratory building for the geological folks, as well as another one for the biologists. Consequently there were facilities available, so that we could keep busy when not otherwise engaged while we spent our three weeks at McMurdo, waiting to get out to our field camp.

The very first thing we did at McMurdo was to undergo our ice-training course, under the direction of the New Zealanders. Luckily I had Allan Cookson as my teacher, a most fortunate thing for me because I was a remarkably inept pupil. We had to leap into crevasses at the end of a rope and then get hauled out again, we had to cut steps up ice slopes using our ice axes, we had to climb rope ladders up ice cliffs and otherwise perform exercises that were almost too strenuous for me. I was at that time sixty-four years of age which I think made me the oldest of the USARPs, perhaps the oldest of any of the folks at McMurdo. But Allan was very tolerant and put up with my clumsy efforts with good humor. I recall trying to cut my way up an ice cliff with the sweat streaming down into my goggles so that I was half blind—this in spite of the fact that we were warned not to perspire out in the field, because the perspiration would quickly turn to ice and that was not good. Well, what could I do about it?

After the ice course we made some trips to study the geology around McMurdo, and a couple of these little journeys proved to be more exciting than we had bargained for. On the first trip I went with Jim Jensen and Bill Breed, as well as Jim Schopf (now deceased), a paleobotanist, and Jim Collinson, both from Ohio State University, to Allan nunatak (a nunatak being the tip of a mountain sticking up through the glacial ice) about a hundred miles from McMurdo Base. Of course we flew up there in a navy helicopter, and as we neared out destination I could look down and see the snow blowing across the ice in great, gusty waves. We landed, which we should not have done, and were immediately cruelly buffeted; in fact I was knocked down three times during the day by the howling wind. My face was frozen twice, but I was saved from serious injury by Jim Jensen, who noticed my condition and immediately held his hands against my cheeks.

Then in late afternoon we gathered on the ice at the foot of the nunatak, waiting for the helicopter to come and pick us up. It came and circled around us, we jumped up and down and waved, and then the pilot flew away. Evidently he had not seen us, but how he could miss a bunch of red parkas bobbing up and down on the ice was a mystery that we could not explain. Just as we were getting ready to spend the night (a night of daylight) out on the ice we heard him returning. This time he came down and picked us up, and we were all able to enjoy a comfortable night in our beds back at McMurdo.

A second trip to Allan nunatak involved a group of us in two helicopters to look at some Triassic sediments in which we found petrified wood and beds of coal—indications that two hundred fifty million years ago Antarctica was a land of forests and swamps. In one helicopter I was with Jim, Jon Powell, and a South African geologist, Isak Rust. As we were flying back from our day in the field we heard a frantic Mayday signal, telling us of a helicopter crash. So instead of going to the base, our pilot took us to a little research camp in Wright Valley, one of the dry valleys of Antarctica (of which there are several, peculiarly devoid of snow and ice), and there he set us down. At this camp was the pilot of the down helicopter; he was badly burned around the face and neck, but even so he had hiked fourteen miles up the valley from the site of the crash to this camp, where he knew there was a radio. It turned out that the helicopter had lost power, he had landed on the side of a mountain, and as the helicopter slid fifteen hundred feet down the slope it had caught fire. Several people were burned, and two of the men in the helicopter had died.

Our pilot took off with the other pilot, to rescue the injured and get them to McMurdo, and we settled down for a night at the camp with two geologists who were there. They were studying the nearby Meserve Glacier, which flowed from the heights down the side of the valley, to terminate before reaching the valley floor. They kindly supplied us with some extra sleeping bags they had at the camp, and just as I was getting snuggled down and drowsy we heard the clap-clap of a helicopter coming to pick us up. Out I scrambled from my comfortable bed, as did my companions, and we were lined up ready to get on board as soon as the helicopter landed. Pilots do not like to wait.

Three days after this event we boarded a Hercules for the trip to our field camp. It was a magnificent flight up the great Beardmore Glacier, where Scott and his little band had so valiantly struggled and perished, and over the high Transantarctic Mountains toward our camp. This time I was in the pilot's cabin, along with David Elliot, so for us there were extensive views of the terrain over which we were flying. The reason for our exalted places on this flight was one of planning; since we were the co-leaders of the expedition we were scanning the land below, checking maps that we had with us and discussing localities and the possibility of working at some of the places we saw. But for me the incomparable Antarctic scenic effects were flawed somewhat by the remarks that David was making as we flew along, for he would point to a peak of frightening proportions (a peak so high that we were flying opposite rather than above it) and talk enthusiastically about how we could land on this eminence with a helicopter and then climb down a thousand feet to rock layers that might yield some fossils. My view of such a possibility was less than enthusiastic, and fortunately for me we never had to resort to such high alpine tactics. We found our fossils at more reasonable altitudes.

We landed at our camp, located at the edge of an icefield known as Walcott Névé, some thirty-five miles to the east of the Beardmore Glacier, with a stunning view of the Transantarctic Mountain Range, about one-thirty in the afternoon and spent the rest of the afternoon in getting established. The camp consisted of four Jamesway huts, these being portable adaptations of the famous Quonset hut, with folding wooden frames and a heavily insulated fabric covering, and had been set up for us several weeks previously by the navy Seabees, so it was all ready for us to move in. Why such a large and elaborate field camp? It should be explained that months earlier, back in the planning stages, David and his colleagues at the polar institute had decided to make this expedition a multiple effort. Of course Jim Jensen, Bill Breed, Jon Powell, and I would search for fossils as originally planned. But since logistics in Antarctica are so very costly (use of a Hercules plane and helicopters for example) it was decided to enlarge this field campaign to something more than the hunt for ancient reptiles, because the expense of putting a large party into the field would be essentially no greater than that for four bone hunters. Consequently the austral summer was to be devoted to fossil plants, invertebrate fossils, glacial studies, the study of volcanic rocks, meterological observations, and so on.

To accomplish this we had a group of about two dozen scientists, which with the necessary navy support personnel brought the population of our camp up to about forty people. Here I will mention the composition of the group. Of course there were David Elliot and myself and the three other vertebrate paleontologists who already have been accounted for. Then there was William Gealy, stratigrapher, and John Splettstoesser of Ohio State, John at that time being administrator of the polar institute program. There were Jim Collinson, stratigrapher, Henry Brecker doing gravimetric studies, both of Ohio State, Paul Tasch of Wichita State University and his assistant Dietmar Schumacher, who were interested in conchostracans, these being small fresh-water invertebrates. James Schopf of Ohio State and Leon Lambrecht of Belgium and Josef Sekyra of Charles University in Czecho-slovakia were the palebotanists of our group. Isak Rust of South Africa was making general geological studies, while Mike Peterson of Ohio State was studying paleomagnetism. John Gunner was a Precambrian geologist, Don Coates was interested in glacial geology, and the late John Mercer, like David Elliot an Englishman displaced to Ohio State, was working on the problem of geologic ages. Finally there was Roy Cameron and his two assistants, Roger Hanson and George Lacy, working in the field of microbi-ology. No doubt about it, we had a varied group within which there were many ways to look at the Antarctic scene.

Then there were five helicopter pilots and nine mechanics, a cook and his helper, a handyman to do odd jobs around camp, and a medical corpsman who doubled as a radio operator.

A few of the navy people were not the types that we would have chosen to be members of our camp. The cook, for example, was approaching the time for his retirement, and quite frankly he was putting in time with us on the Ice. Perhaps he received special credits for Antarctic duty—I don't know—but whatever the terms of his service might have been, he wasn't exerting himself unduly on our behalf. Our food was all right, but it could have been better, considering the piles of supplies that were piled up high on the side of the hut, excellent food in the outdoor deep freeze of Antarctica. There were ample opportunities for an imaginative cook to have produced some very tasty meals, but he was not especially interested in proving what he might be capable of doing in the culinary line.

Moreover for those of us who were not used to the navy way of doing things (or was it merely the cook's way?) we did get annoyed by the waste of good food that we saw every day. At the end of a meal the leftovers were thrown out; there was no attempt to save food for future use. One day we got into a row with the cook about this—when we saw him throwing away quite a lot of good cooked meat. We let him know in no uncertain terms that we would be very happy to take meat like that with us when we went out on all-day field excursions. He grudgingly gave in to our suggestion.

Then there was the handyman, who was a real pain. There was an unavoidable dichotomy in Antarctica between the navy personnel and the USARPs, as has been pointed out, and on various occasions some of the navy men made pointedly derogatory remarks about those of us on the civilian side of the roster. This was especially true of our handyman.

So one day we took him out in the field with us for an all-day sample of fossil hunting. That took care of *him*; he dragged himself into camp in time for supper, and no more did we hear snide remarks about USARPs.

So there we were (all but the helicopter pilots, who were still to come), with the USARPs occupying one Jamesway hut, the navy people in another, the third hut being a cook house and dining "hall," and the fourth hut, which was a small affair, reserved for the medical corpsman and also serving as the radio shack. The huts were on the whole quite comfortable, for in three of them there was an oil heater, while in the cook-dining hut there was a large oil cookstove. But our comfort was stratified; if one spilled water on the floor it would quickly congeal into ice, at waist level the temperature was that of a well-heated room, while up in the top of the hut, about eight feet above the floor, the temperature was well up in the eighties.

On our first morning in camp David, Jim Schopf, and some others decided to explore a nunatak that we could see on the horizon about five miles away, largely because they had gotten into an argument as to whether the sedimentary rocks which they knew were exposed there were of Permian or Triassic age. I thought I would stay in camp and put some of my things to rights. So David and his fellow adventurers hopped onto motor sleds (our substitutes for the dog teams of former years) and chugged away toward the nunatak. Just before lunch they returned in high excitement—they had found fossil bones! It was as simple as that.

We all had a noisy lunch with much talking and speculating, and then a big crowd of us motored over to the locality with all three of our sleds, each motor sled pulling a light Nansen sled behind it. Sure enough, when we got there we found that the nunatak had on its far side some steep cliffs, with volcanic rocks at the summit and below them Triassic sandstones and siltstones in which there were bones. The cliffs had been named Coalsack Bluff by previous explorers. All of this happened on November 23, 1969. It had been our original intent to go to Graphite Peak, about eighty miles from our camp, by helicopter—the helicopters were to arrive in a day or so—to begin our search in the area where Peter Barrett and Ralph Baillie had found that original fragment of amphibian bone a couple of years previously. Now, it seemed, we would not need to go so far afield, for we had fossils at our back door.

Two days later the three helicopters arrived and it was a beautiful sight to see them coming in, one after the other, to settle down on the ice field in front of our camp. These helicopters had been fitted with auxiliary gas tanks so that they could make the four-hundred-mile flight from McMurdo Base to our camp, and they were accompanied by a Hercules that came along as a sort of "escort ship," to use a navy term. As the helicopters floated down in front of our huts, the Hercules landed at some distance on Walcott Névé, and taxied up to camp. It all looked so smooth, but for one who has been in a Hercules landing on the ice, the experience is anything but smooth. The ice fields and snow fields in Antarctica are carved by the winds into *sastrugi*, which are parallel ridges with furrows between them, the difference between the crests of the ridges and the bottoms of the furrows being something on the order of two feet. The tactic is for the Hercules to land across these ridges, and since the plane is equipped with three skis, each about twelve feet in length, this can be done. But the landing, and likewise the takeoff, is a happening that borders on the traumatic. It feels as if the plane were coming apart; there is a succession of terrible jolts and bumps, and anything loose, including people, if they are so unwise as not to be strapped in, gets thrown about the cabin, willy-nilly. As for me, I was always thankful when we were down and when we were airborne.

The next morning after the arrival of the helicopters, Bill Breed, Jim Jensen, and I were to fly over to Coalsack Bluff on a trial run, to test the feasibility of making some of our trips there by air. We got into a helicopter, and were just ready to lift off when a radio message came in, saying that on board an arriving Hercules were Larry Gould, the dean of Antarctic scientists (he had been second in command on the Byrd expeditions forty years previously), accompanied by Grover Murray, a key figure in the polar research program, and would I please be on hand to greet them. So I got out and stood aside to watch the helicopter take Jim and Bill to Coalsack Bluff. The blades went around faster and faster, the machine rose into the air, and then there was a loud bang, not exactly an explosion but a very loud noise, pieces of metal flew off in different directions, and the helicopter plummeted to the ice with a sickening thud. Fortunately it hadn't gained much altitude, so the crash was not devastating, but it was frightening. I could see the folks inside wrestling with the doors to get them open and I started to run out to the downed craft, but John Splettstoesser, who was standing by my side, grabbed me and shouted, "Don't go! It may catch on fire!" Cheerful thought!

It all happened faster than can be told. Bill and Jim, the pilot and copilot got their doors open and tumbled out and ran away from the machine. Fortunately again, it did not catch fire. But it was a sad wreck. The skids were crumpled, the fuselage was bent and cracked, and the side of the craft was blackened where smoke had poured out.

To assess the damage—it turned out that the drive shaft to the tail rotor had snapped, owing to crystallization of the metal in the extreme Antarctic cold. That did it, so far as our immediate helicopter support was concerned. The shafts from all three craft were taken out and sent to Christchurch for testing and analysis, so that some time went by before two properly tested drive shafts could be sent down from Christchurch and installed. A third shaft was not needed; the downed helicopter was so badly damaged that eventually it was loaded on to a Hercules and flown back out of Antarctica. Whether it was ever put back into service I do not know.

In the meantime we had only two helicopters for the rest of the season, which meant only one helicopter at a time on active duty, because it was policy always to hold one craft in camp for possible emergencies.

To get back to the story, Larry Gould and Grover Murray disembarked from the Hercules to be greeted by the sight of a very much disabled helicopter. At any rate, we had a good visit together before they had to leave—the first real visit I had ever enjoyed with Larry Gould, although I had met him once or twice previously. It was the beginning of many visits and a delightful friendship. Larry, for many years the president of Carlton College in Minnesota (attended by our eldest son, George), had retired to Tucson, Arizona, where he was much cherished by the university. Of course, since Margaret and I have been residents of Arizona for almost twenty years, we get to see Larry and his wife every now and then.

With our helicopter support reduced, we made up our minds to commute back and forth between camp and Coalsack Bluff by motor sled, and that we did for most of the field season. Although as mentioned it had been our original intention to go by helicopter to Graphite Peak as our very first step of the field campaign, discovery of bones at Coalsack Bluff, and after that the wreck of the helicopter, changed all that. Coalsack Bluff was our theater of operation, and we never did get to Graphite Peak. In fact, our original plan was to work at Shackleton Glacier, one hundred fifty miles to the east of our Beardmore camp, during the latter half of the field season, and we never got to that either.

So again in Antarctica, as at Ghost Ranch years previously, my original strategy for a season's work was completely changed by events of the moment. That is what you call tactics, and is applies in geological field work as surely as it does in military operations. Woe to the commander who is inflexible so far as tactics are concerned, as witness Lord Pakenham at the Battle of New Orleans or Burnside at the Battle of Fredericksburg. And I have seen parallel situations (of course on a small scale with no deadly results) in the pursuit of fossils. Overall plans are fine, but it is essential to be ready and willing to adapt the field program to situations as they arise.

Our camp had been sited at Walcott Névé because that was a good place at which to land the big Hercules planes, and with helicopters supposedly available it made a good base for explorations in all directions. Even with our helicopter support reduced we did make a few exploratory trips, and certainly the helicopters were useful to other members of our scientific team, but as for fossils we had enough to do at Coalsack Bluff. Again I may quote the old adage "Gather ye rosebuds while ye may." For our task of gathering paleontological rosebuds the motor sleds fulfilled our purposes very well indeed.

I should say "very well indeed" with some reservations so far as I was concerned. The motor sled took us to a point near the top of the nunatak on the side facing our camp; then we had to walk around to the other side of the nunatak, where it dropped down a long, long way as a steep slope to a little ice-covered lake at the bottom. A part of this slope was covered with ice, while above the ice surface was a large scree covered with loose weathered detritus and scattered rocks. Therefore after leaving the sled there was a choice of putting on crampons (these being spiked contraptions that fasten with straps over one's boots) or of crossing the scree. Bill Breed, being an accomplished climber, generally would put on the crampons, with the aid of which he would cross the icy slope with the greatest ease and casual aplomb. For me any attempt to cross that slope spelled doom and perdition; I could picture myself sliding downward for an immense distance to crash against the ice far below. So I would struggle across the scree, sliding back a step for every step I took forward, eventually to wind up at our fossil site breathless, sweaty, and fatigued before the work of the day had really commenced. Every now and then David Elliot would visit us at our fossil locality, and to my disgust he would bound across the scree, leaping from rock to rock with goatlike agility. In short, my daily battle with the scree left me feeling inferior and exhausted, first in the morning on the way to work and again in the afternoon on the way home. It was a fact of Antarctic life that I had to accept.

We worked at Coalsack Bluff as best we could, but fossil collecting under Antarctic conditions posed some problems. It was not possible to have one's hands exposed for more than a few seconds at a time, so we had to manage our hammers and chisels while wearing big, heavy gloves. It wasn't easy. Furthermore, how was one to plaster specimens with no water available for mixing the plaster? (I had learned a lesson about water in the field during our first day-trip out of McMurdo Base—the day when it was so windy that I repeatedly got knocked over by the breezes. That day, for some reason, less than well considered, I had taken a canteen along. Within a few minutes my canteen was a block of ice.) Jim Jensen, always a man of original ideas, solved the problem with a Primus stove and a supply of beeswax. We would light the stove, melt the wax, and quickly pour it over a specimen wrapped with dry bandages. Immediately the wax hardened, and our specimen was thus immobilized. It must be said that we never tried this method on a large specimen.

The next season, on a paleontological field trip having as its principle collector James Kitching from South Africa, plaster was used by having a little tent at the site and by heating the water. I should mention, speaking of tents, that Jim Jensen had designed and manufactured with the help of his wife a collecting tent which he christened a crab hut. It was a dome-shaped tent, with tubular supports that could be adjusted to different lengths; hence it could be set up on uneven ground. We found it useful at Coalsack Bluff.

Our work at Coalsack Bluff continued day after day, and every day we kept finding fossil bones, which were for the most part the bones of therapsid, or mammallike, reptiles. We found vertebrae and leg bones, which was frustrating to me because those parts of the skeleton behind the skull have remarkable similarities among many kinds of therapsids. Furthermore my difficulties were compounded first by the fact that my acquaintance with the therapsid skeleton was rather limited since I had not studied such fossils in much detail during the course of my researches, and secondly by the circumstance that I didn't have any paleontological literature along for reference. I suppose perhaps I should have brought some books with me to our camp, but at the time it seemed to me that books had a low priority as compared with the food and equipment that were essentials to our work, even to our survival.

That was why during those days of postcranial bones I hoped time and again for a skull or a part of a skull that would afford some truly definitive information as to what we were finding. I suspected we had the reptile *Lystrosaurus*, which as has been told I had already collected in Africa and India, but how could I be sure beyond any doubt? Such were my thoughts on December 4, 1969, as we added another day to the days gone by, searching the exposures on Coalsack Bluff and patiently digging out of those exposures the fossils we encountered. I should add that the rocks at Coalsack

Bluff consisted of sandstones and even some light conglomerates containing rolled pebbles—all denoting the fact that we were looking at ancient stream deposits in which the skeletons of defunct amphibians and reptiles had been tossed, broken apart, and scattered by flowing waters.

As we returned to camp that evening I was still thinking about *Lystrosaurus*, and then, as I was going over the fossils that had been collected during the day I turned my attention to a part of a skull that Jim Jensen had found. But it wasn't much, a piece of the right maxillary bone containing one of the two tusks that are so characteristic of *Lystrosaurus*. A pair of tusks in the skull characterize the dicynodont reptiles, these being the therapsids that are peculiarly specialized in skull anatomy, reflecting adaptations for a very special way of life. So how could I be sure that this maxilla with its little tusk (it was a small specimen) represented *Lystrosaurus* and not some other dicynodont? It was the shape of the bone that gave it away; *Lystrosaurus* has a very deep maxilla, the outer surface of which shows a slight concavity. As is so often the case in paleontology the identification of a specimen is based to a large extent upon a gut feeling—this in addition to familiarity with the kinds of fossils involved. I had that gut feeling—to such a degree that I felt very sure of my identification. So I excitedly told Jim what I had concluded, and he agreed with me.

That evening at our mess I announced Jim's discovery to the rest of the crowd, which elicited shouts of approval and congratulations from one and all. That is, with the exception of Isak Rust, the South African member of the group. Isak was quite calm about it.

"After all," he said, "we have Karroo geology here, why shouldn't we have Karroo fossils?"

His logic was impeccable, and now our discoveries had confirmed his logical statement. Even so we were excited. With the skull fragment solidly pinned down I could now see that many if not most of the bones we had been finding were those of *Lystrosaurus*. This applied especially to a part of an ilium, one of the bones of the pelvis, that had just been unearthed.

It may be recalled that on a previous page of this account I told how when I was in Johannesburg I had made a little survey of fossils from the *Lystrosaurus* zone in South Africa, to discover that about eighty-five percent of all fossils collected from that level belonged to *Lystrosaurus*. Was it possible, I now thought as we talked about the fossils we were finding at Coalsack Bluff, that here we were dealing with a similar situation? Indeed, such was found to be the case, as will be shortly told.

That evening after supper a radio message was received informing us that a Hercules was on the way, and again on board were Larry Gould and Grover Murray, accompanied by Admiral Welch, who was that year in command of the navy personnel in Antarctica. (This time there was something better than a crashed helicopter to mark their visit to our camp.) The big plane landed at about ten-thirty, and as soon as Larry and Grover came into our mess hall I showed them the new skull fragment and explained to them what it all meant. Of course they immediately realized the significance of our find, and were duly impressed. Larry especially so. We went outdoors for some photographs—it should be remembered that the sun was still high in the sky making its daily circular track around the Antarctic sky—and within the hour our visitors had departed. (In a land of twenty-four-hour daylight, daytime and nighttime activities sometimes get out of phase.)

Gould and Murray got back to McMurdo Base, where Larry immediately sent information about our *Lystrosaurus* to the National Science Foundation in Washington. Consequently on December 6, two days after our discovery and identification of undoubted *Lystrosaurus*, a story written by Walter Sullivan appeared on the front page of the *New York Times*. Quoting from the *Times* account: "Dr. Gould said they both (Gould and Murray) considered the find 'not only the most important fossil ever found in Antarctica but one of the truly great fossil finds of all times.'" Well! That did stir things up. Accounts appeared in newspapers and news magazines throughout North America and in Europe and other parts of the world as well.

To go back to the discovery and announcement of *Lystrosaurus* in Antarctica, there was an amusing contretemps at McMurdo Base involving Larry and the press. Of course the newspaper people were anxious to get the story out as soon as possible, but Larry felt, quite rightly, that the announcement should be made by the National Science Foundation. Therefore he insisted that the media folks could not use the radio at McMurdo to get their stories out until after he had filed his report with the National Science Foundation, and that got the wind up among the reporters, especially a newsman from England. There were cries of censorship and the like, but Larry stuck to his guns. In the end no damage was done; the NSF made the announcement and then the media were free to write about the discovery as they wished. Which was what happened, and for any particular paper or other news source the delay incurred amounted to only a few hours, perhaps a day at the most.

The knowledge that now without question we had *Lystrosaurus* at Coalsack Bluff, with the implications of this discovery as it related to *Lystrosaurus* in South Africa, India, and parts of China, spurred us on to search those Triassic exposures as diligently as possible. The result was that we found more fossils but almost all of them were the remains of *Lystrosaurus*, although scattered bones of labyrinthodont amphibians did turn up now and then. Our problem was that we were looking at ancient stream channels, as has been mentioned, within which there had been a sedimentary selection of bones, during the course of which other early Triassic reptiles that so characteristically accompany *Lystrosaurus* in Africa were largely excluded. Perhaps part of this exclusion was owing to the fact that *Lystrosaurus* and the amphibians found with it were water-loving animals; what we needed were sediments of a different provenance, originally fine sands and clays deposited in quiet waters, in which we might expect to find smaller and more delicate bones as well as articulated skeletons. This was to come the next year as shortly will be told.

Perhaps we might have found geological conditions more to our liking at Shackleton Glacier, but as has been mentioned the crash of our helicopter threw a strategic monkeywrench into our schedule, so early in January David Elliot and I agreed to end our season at Coalsack Bluff. Even though we concentrated our efforts at this locality, we did manage to make a few exploratory trips to see what we could see. Thus one day we were lifted by helicopter to Mount Sirius some eight miles from Coalsack, where we spent the day in some futile explorations. And we prospected the bluff, up and down and sideways. In the end we had to be satisfied with the Coalsack Bluff collections, which numbered 437 specimens, and that is not a bad record for a first attempt.

Before we left our Beardmore Camp we had a couple of traditional celebrations, Antarctic style, on Christmas and New Year's Day. Christmas was a self-imposed holiday; we rested in camp and the cook prepared a very special meal for us. New Year's Day likewise was a day off for many in camp, but Bill Breed and I decided to see what we could do. We rode a motor sled out to the Coalsack Bluff site, but about the time we got there the weather looked ominous, so like Napoleon's men in the old folk song we turned around and went back down the hill. Then after lunch the weather looked better, so we got a helicopter ride to the bluff, where we took out a couple of fossils and packed some equipment. Again the weather turned bad, and when our pickup helicopter arrived it had a difficult time landing in the face of an increasing wind. We scrambled on board, and soon were back in camp, where a cookout had been planned as a New Year's celebration.

A fire had been built outside the mess hut, but by the time we had returned to camp the wind was howling and snow was blowing horizontally across the ice field. None of us wanted to be deprived of our New Year's feast, so by turns we would rush out of the hut in little groups, each person carrying a large, juicy steak, grill it as we stood with our backs hunched to the wind, retrieve the steaks, and rush back into the warmth of the hut. It was an ordeal while it lasted, but the steaks were delicious.

Mention of Napoleon in a preceding paragraph reminds me of a little game we had in camp, good-naturedly at the expense of Paul Tasch. Poor old Paul had a regimen where he would go by helicopter to localities at some distance from camp to collect the fossils in which he was interested—the little fresh-water shells known as conchostracans. But unfortunately for him the weather did not cooperate as much as he would have liked, and since one bends with the weather and does not fight it in Antarctica, Paul was forced on numerous occasions to sit idly in camp and bemoan his fate. So we devised a Tasch scale based on Napoleons. One Napoleon was the frustration that little Nappy felt when he lost the Battle of Waterloo, and ten Napoleons equaled one Tasch.

Two days after our New Year's Day cookout, namely on January 3, a Hercules arrived at camp with a delegation from Congress on board. It consisted of five members of the House Committee on Science and Aeronautics, and they were accompanied by some high brass from the National Science Foundation. Of course we had been apprised of this by radio, so when the plane landed we were all there to welcome our visitors. There was a mass march to the mess hut, where the group crowded in to listen to lectures from David Elliot and myself. What we had to tell them seemed satisfactory and I think they decided that we had not wasted the taxpayers' money. There is a picture taken by a navy photographer showing me talking to these dignitaries (looking less than dignified in their Antarctic clothing) with Admiral Welch sitting right up front where for once he was listening and not giving the commands.

Just in case the reader may think that this visit was an unwonted expenditure of money, let it be said that for bookkeeping purposes very little real money was involved. The planes that the congressman rode on were making the trips anyway, so the lawmakers rode along more or less as supercargo.

After the talks we joined the congressmen in the Hercules, for a flight to McMurdo Base. It was the end of our field season and we had made plans to leave camp on this plane. There was the usual rough, rattley-bang take-off and then we circled the Coalsack Bluff site a couple of times while I, from the pilot's cabin, gave a little talk about geology. Then on to McMurdo, landing in time for the evening meal, after which I had a long talk with the chairman of the congressional committee.

Admiral Welch was so favorably impressed by our discoveries—perhaps the news stories and the congressional visit cast our efforts in a significant light—that he arranged for Bill Breed and me to have a flight to the South Pole. Consequently on January 6 we boarded a Hercules at Williams Field for our adventure. The three-hour flight, during the course of which it was inevitable that I should think about Scott and his companions struggling up the Beardmore Glacier week after week, brought us to the pole just in time for lunch. It was a delicious lunch we had, because policy demands that the cook at the polar station is to be absolutely first-rate. Then Bill and I looked around the station, and Bill hung a pahoe feather (a Hopi ceremonial eagle feather denoting good fortune) on the staff of the American flag that is planted at the pole. Around this flag is a circle of national flags, representing all of the countries signatory to the Antarctic treaty. In midafternoon it was time to return, and we were back at McMurdo in time for the evening meal. Such is the course of Antarctic travel in this day and age.

The next day we flew from Antarctica back to Christchurch, along with the congressional delegation. And that was the end of our Antarctic venture.

In due time I was back home in Flagstaff, where I delivered the fossils that we had collected in Antarctica. Margaret had come to California to meet me when I landed on January 14 at the Alameda Naval Air Station, and from nearby Oakland we took a train to Flagstaff, riding in a sleeping car, with the boxes of fossils stowed in the vestibule—this by special arrangement with the Santa Fe officials. It was good to get back and to see the fossils finally at rest in the laboratory at the museum.

My travels were not as yet ended. Margaret and I flew back to New York, where on January 16 I received the American Museum of Natural History Gold Medal for scientific achievement. This was a pleasant way to end the Antarctic trip, and I particularly appreciated the recognition's being given by the institution where I had spent so much of my life. Although I have come to the end of the Antarctic venture, it is not by any means the end of the story.

Arrangements had been made that the collection we found at Coalsack Bluff would be prepared and studied in Flagstaff. Furthermore our work at Coalsack Bluff quite obviously led to another trip the following year, to collect at Shackleton Glacier, the place we never got to during that first year of discovery. I did not go on the expedition to Shackleton Glacier, but as mentioned James Kitching, my old compadre in South Africa, was the principal vertebrate paleontologist. And thanks to James's proverbial eagle eye and the circumstances, a most excellent collection was amassed including many of the reptiles other than *Lystrosaurus* that I had hoped for during the first year. At Shackleton Glacier the types of sediments were present in which were preserved the small fossils and the articulated skeletons that we needed to fill in our picture of the early Triassic fauna of Antarctica.

It became evident that this fauna is essentially identical with the *Lystrosaurus* fauna of South Africa; indeed many of the fossils found in Antarctica are *specifically* identical with African fossils. Thus the details are there, to show that Antarctica and Africa were without doubt part of a single Gondwanaland during early Triassic times.

Bill Breed and I drove in a museum truck to meet James in California, when he returned from Antarctica with the second season's collection. These we took to Flagstaff, to be consolidated with the collection of the previous year. By arrangement all of these fossils were put at my disposal for description, and so it was that during the first decade or so of my retirement, part of my attention was devoted to the description and interpretation of Antarctic fossils. In collaboration with James Kitching and John Cosgriff, and to a large degree by myself, I have to date brought out forty-six published contributions on Antarctic fossils, or involving Antarctic fossils.

This has been the beginning of the study of extinct land-loving vertebrates in the South Polar continent. Since the first two expeditions, there have been subsequent trips—by John Cosgriff, by his colleague Bill Hammer, and by others. But for me there is the satisfaction of having broken the trail in an entirely new paleontological field. Jim Jensen, Bill Breed, Jon Powell, and I did something that will never again be done in the history of science. We opened a *continent*, paleontologically, that in this respect hitherto had been locked.

There are two postscripts to add to the Antarctic story. Postscript number one: our son Phil went to Antarctica on that second paleontological hunt, at Shackleton Glacier. Phil had a background of mountain-climbing experience, in North America, in the Alps, and in the Himalayas, where he had been the first to climb two peaks there. The National Science Foundation liked his expertise as a mountain climber and experience on ice fields, so he went down to the Ice to supervise the climbing and camping activities of field parties. His trip with James Kitching was just the beginning. In the end he made eight trips to Antarctica, wintered-over twice, and on several occasions was in change of field parties.

In recognition of his work in Antarctica a mountain was named after him: Colbert Peak.

Postscript number two: some years after my return from Antarctica the range of nunataks between Coalsack Bluff and Mount Sirius was named after me: the Colbert Hills. Our son Daniel put the finishing touch on that one; he said it sounded to him like a real-estate development.

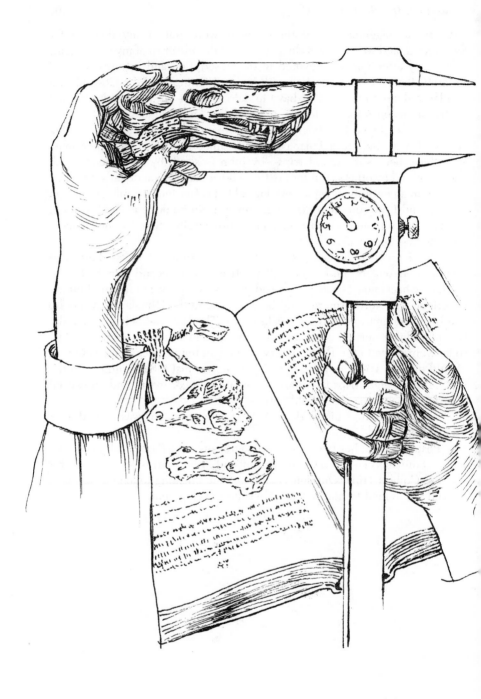

XX

Museum Days

Although my journeys into Laurasia and Gondwanaland, either by myself, or with Margaret as my good companion, loom large in my life story, they occupied only relatively small fractions of my time. A trip to India or Africa or Antarctica might take up two or three months in any particular year, while field work in North America might be even less time-consuming, yet these figures have to be balanced against the much larger stay-at-home segments of each year, which makes it readily apparent that most of my working days were spent within museum walls. This is as it should be; the time spent out in the field gathering data is necessarily much less than the time at a desk or in the laboratory interpreting the data. Indeed, for a vertebrate paleontologist a month in the field often may yield materials that will occupy him for years in the museum—all of which makes the life of the paleontologist seem to be an unending quest.

That is why my life in paleontology was timewise a life spent largely in museums—in the three museums where I have followed my paleontological career for more than sixty years, namely the Nebraska State Museum (three years), the American Museum of Natural History (forty years), and the Museum of Northern Arizona (twenty years). In addition, I have had the privilege of studying in museums throughout the world. Consequently I think I may fairly say that I have had considerable museum experience, at least so far as natural history museums are concerned.

As a result I have through the years developed an appreciation of museums that extends beyond my views of them as places for the pursuit of paleontological knowledge. From the very beginning of my museum career, when I set up skeletons for exhibit in the Nebraska museum, I have been very much interested in the large subject of museology, and this had led me along many byways within the museum world.

It is quite natural for the average museum visitor to think of the museum in the terms of its exhibition halls, which of course are the areas where perhaps ninety-nine percent of all museum visitors have contact with the institution, yet a commonly accepted rule-of-thumb allocation of museum space indicates that no more than forty percent of the floor square-footage should be given over to exhibit halls, corridors, stairways, and other public areas. Therefore for any reputable museum the exhibition halls constitute a minor part of the museum and make only a minor part of the demands on a museum curator's time and energies. (I am speaking of the curators involved in the research and strictly curatorial activities of the museum; the people of the exhibition staff quite obviously spend almost all of their time and energy on the exhibits.) Sometimes the facts just mentioned can lead to curious and perhaps not completely desirable imbalances in the curator's interests and activities. In a large museum, such as the American Museum where I spent so much of my life, there may be curators who devote their entire lives in detailed research along relatively narrow paths of inquiry, with never much thought about the larger aspects of natural history and certainly with no attention given to the development of exhibits. Perhaps this is inevitable; museums are storehouses for objects, and to make those objects meaningful they must be studied in detail. This is the basic research that is at the bottom of everything.

Yet I think it is unfortunate when basic research, as essential as it may be, crowds out all else. Among museum people there are innumerable examples when this is not the case. I have already mentioned Bert Parr, the director of the American Museum, who had time to direct a large institution, to be intimately concerned with exhibits and with educational policies, and yet to carry on his studies of marine fishes. Another outstanding example would be Dillon Ripley, for many years secretary of the Smithsonian Institution and therefore the ultimate director of several huge museums as well as of the National Zoological Park and other institutions that were a part of the Smithsonian. If ever there might seem to be an overwhelming task of administration the Smithsonian is it, yet Ripley was recognized world-wide as an authority in the field of ornithology. So also was Alexander Wetmore (one of my good friends), one of Ripley's predecessors as secretary of the Smithsonian and simultaneously an ornithologist who spent many years in the study of fossil birds.

Other interesting examples of people with two careers, so to speak, might be cited. Vladimir Nabokov, the famous author, spent many of his days studying butterflies at the Harvard Museum of Comparative Zoology. L. M. Klauber, who for many years was the president of a great utility company in California, devoted part of his life to the study of herpetology, with the result that he produced a monumental two-volume monograph on rattlesnakes. A former king of Sweden was an archeologist on the side, and Emperor Hirohito of Japan was during a long life an ardent student of marine life, perhaps not at a museum, but certainly in a well-equipped laboratory of his own, with ready access to museum facilities.

To get back to my own less exalted example, sixty years of life in museums has been for me considerably more than time spent at research. I have had my curating jobs, and perhaps the reader will remember my account in a preceding chapter of how I wrestled with elephant teeth during my early days at the American Museum when I was working with Professor Osborn. It was my good fortune to have spent many years teaching, principally graduate students, and that certainly was a broadening experience. I was involved with exhibits in various ways (more of that later). Then there has been the problem of museology that I have mentioned, the business of museums as broadly encountered, and that occupied quite a bit of my attention during my later years in New York.

To begin with museology (there is no attempt here to stick to a straight chronological pattern), it so happened that in 1953, after we had rehabilitated one of the two dinosaur halls at the American Museum, I thought it would be nice to publish an article telling about some of the innovations that I thought added distinction to the hall. I found, much to my distress, that there was no vehicle for such an article in the United States, so in the end I sent my manuscript to England for possible publication in the *Museums Journal*. My old friend Bill Swinton was an active figure in the British museum world, and he saw to it that the article was published in the British journal. But that got me to thinking—why in the world was there not such a publication in our country, where there are so many museums? The American Association of Museums had a little news bulletin of sorts, the *Museum News*, so modest in format and scope that it offered no possibilities for articles such as the one I had just done.

Therefore I had a talk with Bert Parr about my experience, to learn that this was a problem to which he had given much thought. He agreed that the absence of a good journal for museum affairs was a great deficiency in our land. Some of the other folks at our museum had similar thoughts, so between us and with Bert's blessing we decided to see if we could get something going at the next meeting of the AAM, which as I recall was being held that year in Cincinnati. We attended; I got up and made my pitch for a proper journal to represent the association and to serve as an outlet for ideas, good and bad, by members of the organization. It was clear that the powers that be up on the rostrum were not particularly interested in the proposal; perhaps it entailed too much effort for their consideration. However a committee of three was appointed, of which I was one member, to go into the problem.

A few months later I received a report, drawn up by the other two members and without my knowledge or input, to the effect that a publication such as I had proposed was not feasible. Their action, which I considered just a bit high-handed, got a bit under my skin, so I sent in a dissenting minority report, saying that a publication should be seriously considered. Of course I was outvoted two to one, so the recommendation that no publication be attempted was entered into the proceedings of the association. I then enquired if the officers of the association had any objections to some other organization publishing a journal about museum affairs and was assured that there would be no objections.

That opened the field to us, so with the active leadership of Bert Parr as well as encouragement from Alex White, the president of the Board of Trustees, several of us got together to make plans for a journal of museology. Three of us worked closely together—the late Kay Beneker, Gordon Reekie (now retired), and I—to see what we could do. Actually we were part of a larger group at the museum: Bert Parr, Lester Aronson, Bill Burns, Ruth Norton, John Saunders, Harry Shapiro, and Lothar Witteborg. Those named, along with the three of us, served as the first editorial board. I don't remember all of the details at this late date; I do know that we reviewed publications of a similar nature and that we very positively went into the problem of printing techniques and costs. Among other things I remember a drive we made up to New Haven one day, to talk things over with a printer there, one of several printers we contacted. Gordon and Kay, who between them had excellent esthetic judgments, settled the problems of format, type faces, methods of reproduction of illustrations, and other matters, while I came up with a title for the journal. It was to be called *Curator*. I remember that the president of the museum association got me in a corner and lectured me about what a punk idea it was to try a journal, and especially to call it *Curator*. Nonetheless we went ahead, and in 1958 the first issue came out. *Curator* was a success from the beginning, and today, thirty years later, it is still going strong.

For the first five years I served as editor of *Curator*, and now looking back, I feel a sense (let's face it) of pride in having been a founder of the journal. Ironically, a few years after *Curator* had made its debut, the American Association of Museums upgraded its little news sheet, *Museum News*, into a full-fledged journal, in which there were and are articles in the field of museology, complete with illustrations. Even so, I think *Curator* has the edge in the variety and depth of its contributions.

At this place I would like to quote some of the introductory remarks written by Tom Nicholson, director of the American Museum of Natural History, and for the past eighteen years the editor of *Curator*. I think they point up the contributions to the museum profession that were made by those who were involved in the founding, and who have been involved in three successful decades, of the journal.

With this issue, *Curator* completes its thirtieth year of publication, 120 issues in all—a tribute to Dr. Albert Eide Parr, Director of the Museum in 1958. He sensed a growing need among museologists for greater communication on all aspects of museum work. He intended that this journal fulfill publishing needs outside the scope of scientific and popular publications, that it be a professional journal worthy of the skills and standards of modern museology. He was correct in his analysis.

Founding editor, Dr. Edwin H. Colbert, the Curator and Chairman in the Department of Vertebrate Paleontology, composed an editorial statement for the first issue of Volume 1 in 1958. It is as valid today as it was thirty years ago.

"Museum men and women have things to say and contributions to make to the common fund of museology in all its phases. These by-products of dedication to museum techniques deserve the dignity and the value of a publication that will make them available to colleagues now too scattered and too numerous for informal or easy communication."

The thirty volumes now completed contain substantial research papers, reports on experimentation and innovative museum techniques and historical approaches, historical essays, and practical suggestions for museum management and administration.

Aspects of our journal other than editorial goals have remained remarkably stable as well. The design and graphics have varied hardly at all—a credit to *Curator*'s designer and first layout artist, Gordon R. Reekie. Trim size has varied no more than one-quarter of an inch; bound volumes are still a common size. ("Introduction: Thirty Years of *Curator*," volume 30:4 [1987], pages 263–264.)

Curator was not my only venture at founding a journal, because fifteen years earlier I had, pretty much on my own, developed the *Society of Vertebrate Paleontology News Bulletin* in its present format. The society was founded at Harvard in 1940, and for two or three years George Simpson had brought out, with the aid of our departmental secretary, a mimeographed sheet for distribution to the then small number of members. Then he went off to war, and I decided that perhaps there should be something more than the mimeographed bulletin. Therefore I got together with Brooks Ellis at the museum, and we planned a bulletin that would look like a real bulletin. Brooks at the time was in charge of a large publishing project in the field of micropaleontology, and he had the facilities for doing what I had in mind. So we worked out a journal with a 5½- by 8½-inch format, to be set up by typewriter. I wanted to have a nice cover, so Margaret came to my aid and designed a most attractive cover in the middle of which she created a logo, consisting of four vertebrae of the Permian amphibian *Eryops*, set against a Marsh pick, the field tool that is universally used by vertebrate paleontologists. The publication and the logo both have proved enduring; the *News Bulletin* is now in its forty-fifth year of publication and is distributed world-wide, and Margaret's design was years ago adopted as the official logo of the society.

So far as journals are concerned, I might mention that back in the fifties I served a three-year stint as editor of *Evolution*, the organ of the Society for the Study of Evolution, this being a scientific society of international scope. That was an interesting experience, because I had to deal with contributions on all phases of evolution, not merely paleontology. So I found myself struggling with manuscripts devoted to many aspects of paleontology and biology—invertebrate as well as vertebrate paleontology, invertebrate and vertebrate zoology, entomology, genetics, botany and paleobotany, anthropology, and so on. Fortunately I was able to depend on numerous reviewers to help me with decisions.

Within the American Museum are two great dinosaur halls, assuredly some of the most popular exhibit areas in the immense complex of buildings, even though they are on the fourth floor and must be reached by elevators and stairways. Here are housed the most extensive exhibits of *original* dinosaur skeletons to be seen in the world—resulting from work in the field and laboratory particularly by Osborn, Matthew, Granger, and Barnum Brown. These halls had become rather static by the fifth decade of this century, a situation that was clearly recognized by all of us at the museum, but the depression years had been hard for the institution, as has already been pointed out, and then came the Second World War, when there were things other than museums to think about. After the war, with Bert Parr firmly established in the director's chair, there were some changes in the air, and among the numerous contemplated revisions were plans for renovation of the two halls.

By this time I had become the curator of fossil amphibians and reptiles, so I perforce became very much involved in work on the dinosaur halls. It was a daunting prospect, but one that I looked forward to with much anticipation. My first assignment came when the museum administration decided that the hall containing the huge brontosaur skeleton (and consequently known informally as the brontosaur hall) should be revised. This is a big hall, one hundred fifty feet in length, sixty feet in width, therefore with nine thousand square feet of floor space, and twenty-four feet in height. Such a hall presented many challenges.

As I contemplated the work to be done I harbored some envious thoughts about curators in art museums. A fresh coat of paint, revised lighting, and whacking nails into the walls on which to hang pictures is, as the saying goes, duck soup compared to the labor of putting a big natural-history hall in order. Fortunately I had the advice and help of Kay Beneker, at the time in charge of the exhibits department of the museum.

Some tentative moves had been made in this hall during past years; for example, a start had been made at painting murals above the wall cases in the hall, the space available being something on the order of ten feet in height and more than four hundred accumulated feet in length—a huge area for an artist's brush. I remember that a scaffolding had been put up at one corner of the hall, and some beginnings were attempted on about fifteen feet of mural decoration. The effort was soon abandoned; I think that it became evident there would be years of work involved in the project. I remember, too, that Barnum Brown had thoughts of setting up a skeleton of *Barosaurus*, a sauropod dinosaur equivalent in size to the big brontosaur skeleton already on display. To tell the truth, another sauropod skeleton would have been largely redundant and certainly would have crowded the hall.

Thus when the time came we decided to base the project on the skeletons already at hand. That in good conscience was ambitious enough. Among those skeletons were three notable "free-standing" mounts, meaning skeletons set up so that they could be viewed from all angles, right and left, front and back. These were the big brontosaur already mentioned, properly going by the name of *Apatosaurus*, the weird plated stegosaur, *Stegosaurus*, and the large carnivorous dinosaur, *Allosaurus*. Since the three skeletons had all been collected in the Upper Jurassic Morrison Formation of western North America, we decided that it would be nice to have them grouped on a common base in the center of the hall, and not necessarily aligned fore and aft parallel to the long axis of the hall like box cars in a train shed as then was the case. So with Kay's advice as to what would make an esthetically pleasing arrangement we made our plans.

Fortunately it had been a long-established policy at the museum for large free-standing mounts to be placed upon bases furnished with swiveled wheels, or castors, so the problem of positioning the three skeletons was of no great consequence. We got a gang of men from the maintenance department armed with ropes and pulleys and levers, and in short order the skeletons were placed in the positions that had been determined. Then there was the matter of enclosing the three skeletons, including their original bases, within a single base. This was solved by designing a free-form base to make a large "island" in the middle of the hall.

At this point, however, another problem intruded itself into our dinosaur island. Before the war R. T. Bird had collected in Texas a magnificent Lower Cretaceous trackway consisting of footprints made by a large sauropod dinosaur, of a size similar to our brontosaur skeleton, as well as footprints of a carnivorous dinosaur that must have been very similar to our *Allosaurus*. These prints had been found in a limestone along the Paluxy River near Glen Rose, Texas, and had been excavated by R. T., using a gang of WPA laborers, available in those New Deal days. These footprints were quite spectacular; there was a procession of several front and hind foot impressions, right and left, made by the gigantic sauropod dinosaur, the hind footprints being the size of large washtubs and perhaps a foot in depth. The prints showed the impressions of claw marks, and they even showed the ridges pushed up around the edges of the tracks by the immense weight of the dinosaur. Parallel to this trackway there were the footprints of the giant carnivore—large impressions made by birdlike feet, where at the forward end of the trackway several of the carnivore prints were *within* the prints made by the giant sauropod. It was evident that the carnivore had been following the giant plant-eater; was this not perhaps the record of an ancient hunt across the muddy floor of a lagoon that occurred some eighty million years ago, the traces of which are now preserved in immutable stone? We wanted to have this exciting record on display, incorporated into the dinosaur island.

The trackways rested in boxes, a gigantic jigsaw puzzle of limestone, piled in a courtyard of the museum, and the only feasible way to get them into the dinosaur island as we wished was to have R. T. come back from his retirement home in Florida and take charge. I wrote R. T., he was delighted with the idea, and soon was on hand, to spend several months installing the trackways.

There was another problem. We wanted to put the trackways in the island immediately behind the brontosaur skeleton, as if he had made them—but his tail was in the way. It was not however an insoluble problem. George Whitaker and some of the other men in our laboratory removed the tail of the brontosaur, R. T. installed the tracks, and then our technicians reinstalled the tail, swinging it to one side as if the brontosaur had switched it over that way as he walked along. Then men from the museum shop built up a frame to form the floor of the base and covered it with plaster which was tinted to match the light-gray Glen Rose limestone in which the tracks had been made. All in all it was (and is) a stunning display.

There was one final note. We called in a lighting engineer and he designed lights to be recessed in the ceiling of the hall, so positioned as best to illuminate the dinosaur island.

All of that took care of the middle of the hall, but there were still about four hundred feet of cases along the sides and ends to be filled. This we did with lesser specimens of dinosaurs as well as other reptiles and amphibians that had lived during the earlier years of the Age of Dinosaurs—all of which took much planning and time. Then we had the walls of the hall above the cases painted a deep blue, and the ceiling a lighter blue. That was very fine, except that there still were the immense wall spaces, say some four thousand square feet or more, that needed some kind of attention.

What to do? Bert Parr and I were talking about this one day and Bert came up with the idea of painting white-line drawings of dinosaurs and other reptiles and plants on those deep blue walls, something as if they were drawings on a blackboard. Bert even suggested that we might letter in explanations of the drawings, again something on the order of a blackboard demonstration. So we went to work. A museum artist designed the drawings to scale; these were photographed and made into lantern slides. A projector was then set up and the slides were projected to full size on the walls. After that it was merely a matter of tracing the projected drawings on the walls.

The tracings were made with chalk with the intention of painting over the chalk drawings with white paint, but when the chalk tracings were done they were so appealing—they had a softness that could not be duplicated by paint—that we decided to leave them as they were. After all, they were up high above the cases, where they would not be touched, and chalk will last for a long time. Moreover, these chalk drawings had the virtue of being relatively inexpensive, and flexible in that they could be erased and changed if in time new information made it desirable to do this.

The experiment was a success. The chalk murals were made some thirty-five years ago and are still there. In 1958 I published an article in the first volume of *Curator* entitled "Chalk Murals." The technique has been used elsewhere.

Of course a project of such size as this hall involves some incidents. For example, a painter working on the ceiling walked off the end of his scaffold and crashed through the top of one of the wall cases and landed on the skeleton of a small dinosaur, enclosed therein. Miraculously the man was not hurt—just a few scratches—but the dinosaur skeleton suffered. It took some time to get it back into shape. This was the only bad accident.

I should add that during all of this work on the hall I was kept busy during a part of my time writing labels. Label writing is not easy; the text must not be too long, but it must carry the crucial information. It must be expressed in such terms as to be understood by the visitor, yet the reader should not be written down to.

At the far end of the hall is an alcove, and in this space my colleague Bobb Schaeffer installed an exhibit of fossil fishes while I was busy with the dinosaurs.

At last our task was completed, and late in the spring of 1953 (or was it early summer) the hall was dedicated with proper ceremonies. Then Margaret and I took off with our boys for Wyoming, where we were to divide the summer between that state and later Arizona, for Triassic explorations.

The brontosaur hall occupied the better part of a year of my life, but I did not in the least begrudge the time. It was an exhilarating experience, one to which I shall always look back with pleasure. Moreover it is particularly satisfying to see people coming into that hall, to be engrossed and even overwhelmed by the dinosaurs there.

A few years after the brontosaur hall we again faced up to a task of renovation, this time involving the other big hall which by reason of its domination by the huge Cretaceous carnivore, *Tyrannosaurus rex*, we called the tyrannosaur hall. This hall, in truth a tribute to the lifelong work of Barnum Brown, was quite different from the other hall, and different problems were involved. In the first place, the hall was older than the brontosaur hall, and whereas the hall we had completed depended entirely upon artificial light, the tyrannosaur hall was illuminated by large windows along each side. In dimensions it was quite similar to the brontosaur hall.

Our first decision had to do with lighting. Bert Parr was somewhat in favor of closing off the windows and installing interior lighting, but that would have been frightfully expensive; moreover, Kay Beneker and I liked the daylight in that hall. It made a nice contrast with the brontosaur hall, and moreover the daylight in the tyrannosaur hall exactly suited the bones on display, we thought. They were of a different and lighter color than the older skeletons in the brontosaur hall, and we felt that the daylight brought out to excellent advantage the color and texture of these Cretaceous skeletons. So we kept the windows, and we had the walls painted a light green. Our one disappointment was that we never got fiberglass curtains in the windows, which we wanted, to soften the light.

Again we decided to place the big free mounts on an island, but a different island, more formal than the one in the brontosaur hall. Our new island was to be quite rectangular, and its outer edges were to be formed of a vertical curb, one might say, and beyond that a horizontal step, all covered with black tile. The tile was to be especially made for this purpose. To get ahead a bit in the story, this was all fine, but just as we were ready to have the tile installed the folks in the tile factory went on strike, and this put a kink in that part of our project for several months. We were able, however, to use the time on the other parts of the hall.

To get back to the beginning of the story, we assembled one morning with the crew from the maintenance department once again to shift the big skeletons into the positions they would occupy within the central island. When we arrived in the hall, at about ten o'clock in the morning, there was an art class of about fifty students from Pratt Institute in Brooklyn, making sketches of the big dinosaurs. They were sitting around in little groups and singly, some in chairs, some on the floor, busily looking up at the dinosaurs and down at their sketch pads, doing their individual best to get dinosaur skeletons onto paper. Of course when we appeared and began to shift the skeletons there were anguished cries; we had thrown the traditional monkey wrench into their projects. I felt for them, but there was nothing we could do; we had a dozen or so men at hand, scheduled for this particular job at this particular time, and we had to use them. The poor students had to adapt themselves and their drawings as best they could.

Work on this hall was pretty much a repetition of what we did in the brontosaur hall. We did not attempt any chalk murals; on the walls above the side cases we designed simple texts in large cut-out letters, illustrated with small cut-out paintings, interspersed with the text. Again I was busy with labels, and again, as in the case of the other hall, I gave up much of my time during a year to this hall.

Having said something about museology and the editing of journals, and about the two big exhibition projects, it is pertinent at this place to mention briefly the matter of teaching. As the reader will recall, I originally came to Columbia to study under Professor Gregory, and as a result became inextricably involved with the American Museum, there to spend forty years of my life. Immediately after the war Dr. Gregory was reaching his time of retirement, George Simpson had returned from his war duty, and at this time the authorities at Columbia and at the museum decided that Simpson and I would carry on the teaching that had been begun by Professor Osborn in the nineties and had been carried on by Gregory since 1910. We were to carry on as before, with the graduate students coming down from One Hundred Sixteenth Street to attend graduate courses in the Columbia Room at the museum and for those specializing in vertebrate paleontology to do their theses at the museum under our direction. George was to handle the "higher vertebrates"—the birds and mammals; I was to take on the "lower vertebrates"— the fishes, amphibians, and reptiles.

The first year after the war we made a brave beginning and one that was a bit traumatic for me. Simpson and I decided that we would each sit in on the other's lectures so that our course would be properly integrated. All that was fine, except that the first semester was to be mine, and not only did

Simpson sit in on my lectures, but also Theodosius Dobzhansky, the great geneticist and evolutionist, and Ernst Mayr, the equally great ornithologist and evolutionist. So there I was, trying to get my ideas across to a group of critical graduate students with the mental hazard of Simpson, Mayr, and Dobzhansky sitting in the back row and frowning at me at frequent intervals. It was especially bad when some of the students gave me a hard time.

But the next semester I sat in the back row with Mayr and Dobzhansky, where I was somewhat mollified to see the same students give Simpson a hard time. At any rate we got ourselves shaken down that first year, after which we carried on our cooperative teaching for many years. During those years we had some outstanding students who since have made enviable reputations in their particular fields. And of course we each had some of these students who did their theses under our supervision, much to our pleasure.

Having the discipline and experience of teaching, particularly the teaching of graduate students, as Simpson and I did, was an invaluable part of my life at the American Museum. It was for me a time of learning as well as a time of instruction, for the imparting of knowledge to advanced students is in truth a two-way street. Both professor and student learn and benefit from their mutual interchanges. I was on the Graduate Faculty at Columbia for almost a quarter of a century; then when I retired as Curator Emeritus at the museum I was retired as Professor Emeritus at Columbia, and was presented with an elegant testimonial scroll to that effect.

An article in *Curator*, published a few years ago, contains the following statement:

> Museums are often portrayed as places that attract erudite, eccentric, and arcane personalities. Such people are usually strongly motivated, very opionated, and sometimes a bit self-centered. Thus, as calm as museums seem from the outside, they are usually anything but calm inside. (Charles R. Crumly, "Saving a Legacy," volume 27:3 [1984], page 205.)

How true! And that is what makes museums fun places in which to work. Sometimes the "anything but calm" atmosphere within a museum is the result of internecine quarrels and jealousies, and that is the kind of atmosphere that nobody likes. Fortunately for me, the atmosphere at the American Museum during the years I was there was for the most part lively but friendly. If there was any quarreling or backbiting it was confined to two or a few individuals and did not permeate the place. But there was always something interesting going on, and certainly the museum had its share of what might be called eccentric characters. It was no place for people who wore gray flannel suits, all parted their hair the same way, and behaved in general exactly like one another. All of which reminds me of some of the delightful people, even eccentric people, who lived behind the scenes at the museum.

Certainly Jack Nichols, curator of fishes at the museum, never wore a gray flannel suit. He was a tall, gangling man who surpassed six feet by several inches, who wore a well-wrinkled blue suit and when he went out of doors sported a shapeless hat that must have survived three decades of New York winters, who had wild eyebrows the tips of which rose high against his forehead, and who never managed to get a complete shave on any one day—I suppose it generally took three days for him to manage a full job, so that his cheeks often resembled a half-mowed stubble field. He had two sons fully as tall and gangling as he was, and it was a pleasant sight to see them going down the hall together on those occasions when the sons dropped in for a visit, like three tallships in a channel. Jack was a thoroughly charming person; I used to revel in his conversation.

Dr. Gudger of the fish department was an individualist of another sort. He used to raid wastebaskets for discarded letters, and on the backs of these he would write his manuscripts. It behooved an editor to look at the proper sides of the pages of his manuscripts, otherwise he might be confounded by some piece of inconsequential and forgotten business. Among other things, Dr. Gudger found out one day that I had a nice leather couch in my office-laboratory, and thus for a spell I would return from lunch each day to find him sound asleep in my quarters.

Or there was Harvey Bassler of the herpetology department, who used to come to work about five in the afternoon when all others were going home, to spend the night in his office. He claimed it was very efficient— nobody bothered him, which certainly was true.

A definitely urban touch was added to our place by Dr. Henry Crampton, who worked on invertebrates, and who entered the museum every morning very jauntily attired in an impeccable suit, with a homburg at a certain angle on his head and a cane in his hand. His appearance as a sophisticated man-about-town was augmented by a carefully groomed mustache. Once arrived off came his jacket for a smock and off came the homburg for a beret, which he wore throughout the day indoors, to protect his bald head from drafts and other dangers.

Then there was my very good friend Harry Shapiro of the anthropology department, who kept a cello in his office. Colin Turnbull of the same department had a harpsichord in his office, and these two, with the addition of other musically inclined curators, would enjoy sessions of chamber music during the lunch hour. There was nothing so inspiring, said Harry, as a round of Bach during the interval between morning and afternoon; it made one ready to face the second half of the day with equanimity.

I remember that when I first went to the American Museum there was a highly skilled technician in the anthropology department—Mr. Ichikawa. One time Ichy had a bright idea inspired by the removal of a life-sized figure from one of the ethnological exhibits. He dressed it in ordinary street clothes, placed it face down on the laboratory floor, arranged a large knife so that it protruded from the back of the dummy, sprinkled some ketchup or something that looked like blood on the dummy and on the floor, and then, it being five o'clock, went home. Midnight came, and the night watch entered the laboratory on the usual nocturnal rounds. There, in the beam of the flashlight, was the apparent dead man—whereupon the night patrolman rushed to the phone and called the police. The homicide squad arrived; the detectives were soon disillusioned, and were not amused. Clark Wissler, the head of the department and one of the very distinguished anthropologists of North America, naturally had to call Ichy on the carpet to reprimand him sternly, but I can remember that afterwards Dr. Wissler gleefully told the story, all the while laughing so hard that the tears ran out of his eyes.

The anthropology department at the museum seemed to be a locale for zany happenings, but it was by no means unique. There were offbeat events in our own Department of Vertebrate Paleontology. Such as the time when one of the lab men who liked to recite Coleridge's "Ancient Mariner" was persuaded to give a performance during the noon hour, and just at the instant when the Ancient Mariner shot the albatross someone released a stuffed duck that had been sequestered in the high ceiling of the lab, said duck plummeting down to land at the feet of the narrator. Or the time when I fell victim to one of these plots. It was my birthday, and the fellows in the lab prepared a "cake" by artfully coating an upside-down basin with a very convincing layer of white plaster, realistically showing the marks of the spatula that had supposedly spread the icing, and genuinely decorated with candles. Imagine my disappointment when with my mouth watering I tried to cut the cake.

Or there was the time when Margaret was working at the museum (this was before we were married) and she called me to the studio where she and the other departmental artists worked to ask for some instructions on how to draw a mastodon tooth. As the others looked on she handed the tooth to me, only to drop it just before it reached my hand. It fell to the floor with a resounding crash and shattered into hundreds of fragments, while I almost had heart failure. There was a shout of laughter and then I saw that it had been a plaster tooth, specially prepared for the occasion. (The occasion was April Fool's Day).

The list could be extended, but perhaps this sample gives an idea of how members of the scientific staff sometimes added flavor to the inner sanctum of the institution. All in all they livened up the place and it was harmless enough. They personified the museum, and by their presence and their independent ways made the place an unforgettable and in many ways an interesting and truly delightful environment, envied by visitors. Such are the pleasures of being with, and working with, creative people. And what was true of our museum I found to be true of other museums as well.

The American Museum was in second place so far as idiosyncratic staff is concerned as compared with the British Museum (Natural History) in London, at least when I was there back in the early thirties. Englishmen have always been noted for their independent habits and behavior, as the *New Yorker* magazine demonstrates from time to time with its little "There will always be an England" excerpts. So I found that one had to get used to certain habits and certain practices peculiar to the place. For one thing, it was a building of locked doors; it seemed as if there was a locked door every twenty feet or so, and I was always calling for help to get from A to B. Then there were closed doors—much more so than in the New York museum. The door of each office, at least in those days, had a peephole in its upper panel, covered on the inside by a little round lid. You knocked on the door of the keeper you wanted to see; he came to the door, raised the lid, peeped out, and then if you seemed to be friendly, he welcomed you in. I suppose such physical arrangements even strengthened the individualistic habits of the various museum keepers.

On that first visit of mine of the British Museum I had some fleeting glimpses of Francis Bather, retired, but for many years a pillar of the museum, a great authority on fossil invertebrates and the subject of numerous museum tales. Such as the time when as a young staff member, new to the museum, he decided to leap over a barrier in one of the exhibition halls rather than going around it, this to impress a class of young ladies visiting the museum. Alas! He caught his toe on the barrier as he sailed over and came down flat on his face in front of the young ladies—an event that was witnessed by other museum employees. So his probation, required of all new staff members, was extended for a year.

Another story, related to me by one of the present members of the Department of Geology, tells of Bather in his palmy days coming from his home, ten miles away, to the museum on a bicycle. Every morning, so the story goes, he would butter two slices of bread and put them in a little container along with a raw egg, to be carried via the bicycle to his office. Precisely at one o'clock a museum attendant in a long frock coat would enter Bather's office, put a little pot of water on a burner to heat, pull a large watch from his pocket, drop the egg into the water, and boil it for exactly three minutes. In the meantime Dr. Bather would have unwrapped the two pieces of bread. When the egg was done he would eat it along with one slice of bread. The other slice would be spread with some strawberry jam, kept in a jar in a little cupboard in the office, and that would finish the lunch. By the time the egg was boiled the factotum in the long coat would of course have discreetly disappeared. Such was one routine through the years.

One of my favorite stories about the British Museum was told to me by a trustee of that institution. It seems that staff officers above a certain grade had the pleasure of enjoying carpets in their offices. When the Great Depression came along salaries were cut, and those unfortunate keepers whose salaries went below a certain level lost their carpets; the rugs were unceremoniously yanked out from under their feet.

The stories could go on; this small sampling is presented mainly to emphasize in an anecdotal way the fact that museums have been and generally still are rather unconventional places, inhabited by people of original ideas, having original ways of doing things. May this state of affairs continue into the future, and may museums never become big-brother organizations in which big-business methods impose constraints on the people who, after all, make museums what they are. There have been some trends at certain institutions in this direction in recent years; it is to be hoped that these developments will die a-borning.

(As an example, there is the story about how one of our very large museums decided that it would be a good idea to have some efficiency experts in to observe the manner in which staff members conducted themselves and from that to advise how procedures might be improved and made more efficient. Initially the staff was assembled to listen to a lecture about how one should arrange one's work space for greater productivity. At the end of the lecture it was announced that next week the imported advisors would make the rounds to inspect desks and suggest improvements. What they found when they made their scheduled rounds were desks piled high with esoteric impedimenta, and drawers, which should have held files and papers, filled with whiskey bottles, beer cans, and the like. So the story goes, and I have no reason to doubt it. Whether completely true or not the moral is there: don't push a museum personage too far—you may have cause to regret it.)

So I say three cheers for museums and what they do, and for the people who work in them! The museum person will not get rich, and that's for sure, but he or she will have an interesting life, a life to look back on with great pleasure. This is confirmed in a tangible way by the experiences of the people, including me, who work and who have worked in that massive Romanesque pile on Manhattan Square—between Central Park West and Columbus Avenue, and between Seventy-seventh and Eighty-first streets. There has been a very small turnover in jobs at the museum—a good sign.

People once there have stayed there. Many events during the year bring the museum family together— parties and the like. And every spring there is the annual recognition dinner for employees who have been at the place for twenty-five years and more, and for those employees that have just reached this landmark and are being inducted into the group. It is a jolly reunion and is always well attended; one senses a general feeling of a family get-together. Alas! I am so far away now that I seldom am able to attend, but I am there in spirit, and I feel each year on the day of the twenty-five-year party that there are no regrets on my part for having become a paleontologist, for having gotten into the museum profession, and certainly for having spent four decades of my life at the American Museum of Natural History. This is my panegyric to the old place.

XXI

Dinosaurs in My Life

During more than four decades fate and circumstance have decided that my life should be involved, and very much so, with dinosaurs. I use the words *fate* and *circumstance* advisedly, because back in 1942 when I took over the curatorship of fossil reptiles and amphibians at the American Museum of Natural History dinosaurs did not rank high in my list of personal priorities. As I have already written, my interests were along the line of Triassic research—which might or might not have been concerned with dinosaurs. Yet as I had amply learned from my own experiences, one is not necessarily a master of one's own fate, while the direction of one's interests is as often as not shaped by circumstance.

Perhaps the first circumstance that was to decide the course of my life after 1942 was the presence of the large dinosaur collection and the two dinosaur halls at the American Museum. The gigantic skeletons in those two halls seemed to look down at me whenever I walked through the exhibits, as if to assert their dominance over me and over anything that I might do. The mighty presence of those bones could not be ignored, no matter how much I might think that my interests were elsewhere.

And there was another circumstance—the one that might be called the dinosaur renaissance that seemed to have its beginnings in the years immediately after the Second World War. Dinosaurs had become familiar objects during the latter part of the nineteenth century and the early decades of our present century, this owing in large part to the work of Marsh and Cope in North America, and to the explorations of several museums on our continent, among which the American Museum under the vigorous leadership of Osborn was a leader. Yet it seems to me that in those years paleontologists on the one hand and the public on the other could take dinosaurs as they came, or leave them alone. There was not the world-wide interest in dinosaurs, indeed the fascination often bordering upon infatuation, that is so apparent everywhere today. I seem to have come along at about the time that dinosaurs were beginning to attract renewed attention among old and young, among scientists and lay people, in short almost everybody. It is an interesting phenomenon, not to be easily explained.

I well remember that during my early years in paleontology there was a common tendency for the professionals to look upon the dinosaurs as "gee-whiz" reptiles—nice for displays to impress the public, nice as skeletons to foster public interest in our science, but not of consuming interest to people studying vertebrate evolution, or even reptilian evolution. The dinosaurs, it was thought, constituted a large dead-end branch of evolution; the truly significant reptiles—as maintained by many scholars—were the mammallike reptiles, the reptiles leading to the mammals that were to dominate the past sixty-five million years of life history on the earth. This attitude was held by Dr. Gregory, even though he was about the most catholic of all vertebrate paleontologists; it certainly was the viewpoint of Al Romer, and he passed it on to me during our conversations of the forties and fifties.

Yet at this time there appeared a new, younger group of paleontologists who saw the dinosaurs as ancient reptiles offering a host of interesting problems to be attacked by evolutionists and by students of Mesozoic tetrapod faunas. The dinosaurs as viewed by the postwar paleontologists were *not* dead-end reptiles; rather they were highly successful reptiles that ruled the continents through a time period almost three times as long as the age of mammalian dominance, and in so doing evolved along lines of remarkable variety. For many professional paleontologists the dinosaurs were rather suddenly recognized as reptiles deserving intense and wide-ranging studies, so there was inaugurated a dinosaur renaissance that is still vigorously expanding, to the delight of all who are involved with it. Like many of my colleagues, I was caught up in this renaissance.

Of particular interest to all of us is the way in which the general public also has been caught up in the dinosaur renaissance. Dinosaurs are everywhere; dinosaurs are big business in the literal sense of the word. Like the dinosaur skeletons that looked down upon me in the American Museum halls, dinosaurs in the media and in books galore, as well as in moving pictures, television, and in museum displays, impinge upon the consciousness of citizens large and small throughout the land— throughout the world. Is it any wonder, then, that dinosaurs are of interest to people by the millions?

Even so the wide popularity of dinosaurs today is something at which to wonder. Is it because many of the dinosaurs were giants? Is it because dinosaurs are now extinct? If so, why do not other gigantic, extinct animals generate equal attention? Perhaps the attraction of the dinosaurs is owing, in part, to their esoteric appearances, particularly as they are seen in reconstructions. They are so very different from any animals we know that they carry with them an aura of mystery, a revelation of a world long since vanished and never to be called back. They are the twentieth-century dragons, and although they do not breathe fire, nor do they fly through the air on gigantic wings, their reincarnations as based upon the solid anatomical study of their fossil bones reveal reptiles fully as wondrous as the imaginative creations of medieval man.

Because of the circumstances of dinosaurs at the American Museum and the dinosaur renaissance that was beginning to be recognized, it was my fate one day in the early forties to be called into the office of the assistant director of the museum, Wayne Faunce, to be told that a book about dinosaurs was needed to supplement the museum exhibits. That is how I happened to write my first book—as distinct from scientific papers and monographs. It was called *The Dinosaur Book* and it was published by the museum in 1945, just as the war was coming to its climactic end. It was a small book, but it seemed to fill a need, so much so that it was taken over by McGraw-Hill and issued again a few years later. Moreover it eventually was translated into Spanish and published in Argentina. There are people who still profess to like it, but of course it is now very much out of date. Nonetheless it was a beginning, and since its first appearance I have published a number of books and papers about dinosaurs, with the result that I have become typed as one of the so-called dinosaur authorities.

My dinosaurian scorecard amounts to seven books devoted to dinosaurs, five others in which dinosaurs are given prominent treatment, thirty-two scientific papers and monographs on dinosaurs, others in which dinosaurs are treated in a minor way, and about a dozen popular articles on the subject. A total of fifty-six or a few more contributions having to do with dinosaurs may seem like a lot, but if this number is viewed against a total bibliography of about four hundred works, it can be seen that dinosaurs, even though important in my scientific life, are far from being the primary focus of my paleontological attention. Yet it is probably the cumulative effect of these publications more than anything else that has led some people to regard me as being dedicated to the dinosaurs.

However that may be, my involvement with dinosaurs in a very concrete manner was established with our discovery of the Ghost Ranch quarry in 1947. Perhaps it was a matter of fate; if I had been an ancient Roman I might have thought that the gods had decreed I should go to Ghost Ranch with my companions, there to make the discovery that would profoundly affect the course of my life. But I am not an ancient Roman, and anyway North America and Ghost Ranch and dinosaurs are more removed from ancient Romans than Ultima Thule. Therefore I can only think that it was a combination of circumstances: of my interest in Ghost Ranch as aroused during my days of study in Berkeley in 1945, combined with a decision to do a little exploring at the ranch in 1947, combined in turn with George Whitaker's sharp eye as he scanned a very unprepossessing talus slope, that determined the manner by which I should become directed to research on early dinosaurs, a line of research that has continued through many years of effort.

Finally, my involvement with dinosaurs was determined by the circumstances of the two dinosaur halls at the American Museum being scheduled for revision just as I came along in my new postwar position as curator of fossil reptiles and amphibians. Two years of devotion to those halls, as proved to be the case, involved me in some very extended, three-dimensional dinosaur projects. The dinosaurs became during those years much more than descriptions on printed pages, or pictures of bones, or even the study of disassociated bones. I had to deal with gigantic skeletons (as well as modest skeletons) and to think in terms of their dimensions in space. Among other things it was an exercise in full-scale appreciation.

Therefore, what with being put in charge of the dinosaurs at the American Museum, with the dinosaur renaissance that had its beginnings at about the same time, with experiments on the modern cousins of the dinosaurs (the alligators), with books and other publications, with the Ghost Ranch dinosaurs, and with the work on the two dinosaur halls in New York, I have had some rather intensive first-hand exposure to dinosaurs through the years. Quite naturally this has led me to develop various thoughts and opinions about dinosaurs, which I have expressed in print, on the lecture platform, and in arguments with my colleagues. So I might as well indulge in some retrospective thoughts at this place.

To begin: I have been accused, or perhaps I should say delineated, as being conservative in my views of dinosaurs and of their relationships, of how they lived, and of how they disappeared. So be it; perhaps I am conservative, but I trust that this does not mean I am a stick-in-the-mud in my views about dinosaurs. I have certainly not been inclined to go off the deep end in speculations about dinosaurs—and so much of it is speculation—which is today in fashion and which today brings much attention to the speculator. The speculations about dinosaurs, some with foundations of scientific fact, some wildly imaginative, inspire me to quote from Mark Twain's *Life on the Mississippi*. He is writing about how the great river has shortened itself though the years by making cutoffs in its meandering course. What he has to say is well worth considering by all scientific speculators.

The Mississippi between Cairo and New Orleans was twelve hundred and fifteen miles long one hundred and seventy-six years ago. It was eleven hundred and eighty after the cutoff of 1722. It was one thousand and forty after the American Bend cutoff. It has lost sixty-seven miles since. Consequently its length is only nine hundred and seventy-three miles at present.

Now, if I wanted to be one of those ponderous scientific people, and "let on" what had occurred in the remote past by what had occurred in a given time in the recent past, or what will occur in the far future by what has occurred in late years, what an opportunity is here! Geology never had such a chance, nor such exact data to argue from! Nor "development of species" either! Glacial epochs are great things, but they are vague—vague. Please observe:

In the space of one hundred seventy-six years the Lower Mississippi has shortened itself two hundred and forty-two miles. That is an average of a trifle over one mile and a third per year. Therefore, any calm person, who is not blind or idiotic, can see that in the old Oölitic Silurian Period, just a million years ago next November, the Lower Mississippi River was upwards of one million three hundred thousand miles long, and stuck out over the Gulf of Mexico like a fishing rod. And by the same token any person can see that seven hundred and forty-two years from now the Lower Mississippi will be only a mile and three-quarters long, and Cairo and New Orleans will have joined their streets together, and be plodding comfortably along under a single mayor and a mutual board of aldermen. There is something fascinating about science. One gets such wholesale returns of conjecture out of such a trifling investment of fact. (Chapter 17.)

Let that be an introduction to what follows.

Since nothing having to do with speculation about dinosaurs is as universal and as popular as the problem of extinction, I will right here go to the end of the story and present my thoughts about some of the ideas as to why the dinosaurs, after more than a hundred million years of success, disappeared from the face of the earth some sixty-five million years ago. There are two categories of dinosaur extinction theories—one being that of the extraterrestrial theories, the other the terrestrial theories. Today there is a lot of excitement about the extraterrestrial theories, especially the idea that the demise of the dinosaurs was sudden, and was brought about by a collision of the earth with a large heavenly body—a comet, a meteorite, or an asteroid.

Such a theory assumes that a large object, let us call it a bolide, something on the order of ten kilometers in diameter, struck the earth at the end of the Cretaceous period. This collision supposedly caused a great cloud of dust to encircle the earth, to shut out the sunlight, so that all plant life died because of the lack of light, and this in turn brought to an end the plant-eating dinosaurs, which of course spelled the doom of the carnivorous dinosaurs that ate the plant-eaters. It's a wonderfully simplistic idea, exciting because of its simplicity, and pretty much on a par with Mark Twain's calculations concerning the shortening of the Mississippi River.

This theory is based upon the fact that at certain localities around the earth there is an iridium "spike" (in other words an unusual amount of iridium) in rocks of very late Cretaceous age. Iridium supposedly is rare upon the earth but is relatively abundant in meteorites. Thus the iridium spike indicates the collision of a bolide with the earth, the collision raised the dust, the dust cut off the sunlight, the plants died, the herbivorous dinosaurs were deprived of sustenance, and the carnivorous dinosaurs thus had nothing to eat—so runs the litany, popular with some physicists and viewed with a jaundiced eye by many paleontologists. Physicists who don't know anything worth a tinker's dam about the complexity of life like the idea, because it is orderly, neat, and simple. Such folks like formulae, and if something can't be reduced to a formula it isn't science, so they say. Paleontologists see the earth and its past life as presenting a complex picture to be deciphered, and for them the simple explanation does not suffice.

Furthermore there is a complication having to do with the iridium spike found in some Upper Cretaceous rocks. It has been determined that recent eruptions from Kilauea on the island of Hawaii show a very high iridium content. Therefore how can anyone be sure that the iridium spike in Cretaceous rocks is of extraterrestrial origin? Might it not be owing to the high level of volcanic activity that is recorded in rocks of late Cretaceous age, as is indicated for example by the great Deccan volcanic outpouring in India? Such is the conclusion of Charles Drake of Dartmouth, a personal friend whose judgment I respect, and his colleague, Charles Officer. I suspect that they may be correct. So much for iridium spikes and bolides.

Like most of my paleontological colleagues, I see the extinction of the dinosaurs as being an event of terrestrial proportions. Of course a bolide may have collided with the earth at the end of Cretaceous time, but it would hardly have caused the death of the dinosaurs world-wide, leaving such terrestrial inhabitants as lizards, snakes, crocodiles, turtles, birds, and numerous mammals untouched. No; such a catastrophe as envisioned by the impact theory is all too selective in its effects. And in this connection it is interesting to note that Bill Clemens, a very respected paleontologist, and his colleagues, have found numerous remains of late Cretaceous dinosaurs above the Arctic circle in Alaska, a locale where these reptiles would have annually endured a considerable period of darkness. So much for a dust cloud cutting out all of the light, thereby bringing an end to the dinosaurs.

A new, alternative explanation suggests that the supposed collision killed off most of the marine algae (there is a remarkable dearth of marine algae in rocks of very late Cretaceous age). Marine algae are reputed to be the chief source of dimethyl sulphide, around the nuclei of which water droplets condense to form clouds. Therefore, according to this argument, the collision of the bolide with the earth knocked out the algae, which eventually caused a lack of clouds in the air, which in turn caused a world-wide rise in temperature (because of the absence of the ameliorating effect of a cloud cover), and so the dinosaurs were roasted to death. It gets around the objections raised by Bill Clemens having to do with a lack of sunlight causing the extinction of the dinosaurs, but it goes to the other extreme of too much sunlight without the subtleties of Ray Cowles's idea, expressed so many years ago, that an increase in temperature at the end of the Cretaceous affected the reproductive organs of the dinosaurs. This theory has been cited as "a model of deductive reasoning"; to me it belongs right up there with the other "Mississippi River cutoff" class of theories. So much for the business of roasting the dinosaurs out of existence, while their contemporaries lived happily on through the Cretaceous-Cenozoic transition.

I need not labor the question at greater length at this place. Let those physicists and other people who love the bolide theory live on in their dream world while the paleontologists keep their feet on the ground. I do, however, have one complaint against some of the believers in the sudden death of the dinosaurs by impact, and that is the abuse certain of them heap upon those of us who think that the extinction of the dinosaurs was a complex, terrestrial phenomenon. It's no way to conduct a scientific argument.

So what do I believe?—a question that is often put to me, especially at the end of a lecture. In short, I can only say that I believe the end of the dinosaurs was probably gradual and certainly complicated. I will not attempt to mention all of the earthbound ideas that have been put forward; in my opinion there was probably a combination of several factors, some perhaps quite subtle, that terminated dinosaurian dominance on all of the continents. That is my reply to the question of dinosaurian extinction; I am perfectly agreeable to having other people indulge in the Mississippi River cutoff game.

If the problem of dinosaurian extinction seems mysterious and probably insoluble, the problem at the beginning of their history, namely that of their origin, seems comparatively straightforward. There is little doubt that the dinosaurs, which appeared during the late Triassic time, are the descendants of certain thecodont reptiles, which appeared with the advent of Triassic history. The thecodonts were essentially creatures of the Triassic; having become well established at the opening of Triassic time, they gave rise during the Triassic period to the dinosaurs, and to the crocodiles and the flying reptiles or pterosaurs as well, and then at the end of the period the thecodonts became extinct while their descendants lived on. Here is another problem of extinction: why should the thecodonts have died out? Perhaps because their descendants crowded them out.

And what made the dinosaurs so much more fitted for survival than the thecodonts from which they were derived? Probably to a large degree because of dinosaurian adaptations for locomotion. The dinosaurs were characterized by poses, either on their hind limbs or on all four limbs, whereby the feet were brought in beneath the body, near a midline. This made of them efficient walkers and runners; the force of gravity went down more or less vertically from the body through the limbs to the ground, which was important for the conservation of energy as well as for efficient use of the limbs. Among other things, this posture enabled many of the dinosaurs to become giants, and giant size or even large size is a character contributing to the conservation of energy. Thus the dinosaurs were efficient walkers and very active; we know that from their footprints. They were rather different from the reptiles familiar to us in our modern world.

This brings us to another question, once again in the realm of the Mississippi River cutoff game: were the dinosaurs "cold-blooded" animals like modern reptiles, or were they "warm-blooded" animals like modern birds and mammals? This question has been debated in recent years with almost as much acrimony as have the various extinction theories. We will never know; we can only make conjectures.

It is argued by many that since the dinosaurs were active animals, walking with the feet beneath the body, as shown by trackways, and even in some cases running rapidly, also as shown by footprints, they must have been warm-blooded, or endothermic, with a physiological mechanism for maintaining an internal more-or-less-constant body temperature, rather than being cold-blooded, or ectothermic, deriving their body heat from the environment in which they lived. How else might they have been so successful?

From my work, along with Chuck Bogert and Ray Cowles, on alligators,

I became quite aware that modern ectothermic reptiles, especially large reptiles, can maintain a high level of activity by the behavioral control of their body temperatures. The giant dinosaurs, as I have already pointed out on a previous page, may have enjoyed the benefits of an almost constant body temperature by virtue of their large size. They warmed up slowly and cooled off slowly, and they did not have to take in the huge quantities of food that would have been necessary had they been purely endothermic creatures. This, I think, was a key to their success. But might not some of the small dinosaurs, which we know were very rapid running animals, have been endothermic? Perhaps, yet as Carl Gans's impressive photos of galloping crocodiles have demonstrated, even present-day ectothermic reptiles can behave in a very mammalian fashion. So I think that the question of warm-bloodedness in dinosaurs is a very open question.

This brings up another question, namely the relationship of dinosaurs to birds. Either theropod dinosaurs and birds were descended from a common ancestor, or birds were descended from theropod dinosaurs. John Ostrom has put forward convincing evidence to show that small theropod dinosaurs probably were the direct ancestors of birds. When did the warm-blooded condition of birds become established—in their probable dinosaur ancestors or during the transition from reptile to bird? This is another open question.

The fact that birds may be descended from dinosaurs does not in the least make birds dinosaurs. Yet in a recent classification one author has designated all of the birds as dinosaurs. How silly can one be? Here is a case of allowing logic to run away with the logician into a never-never land of unreality. It is the kind of exercise that so delighted W. S. Gilbert of Gilbert and Sullivan fame (take note especially of such works as *Iolanthe* and *The Pirates of Penzance*).

Perhaps these remarks about dinosaurs will indicate some of my own opinions concerning the ruling reptiles of Mesozoic times. And of course my opinions are for the most part the opinions that have been reached by other people concerned with dinosaurian evolution. I cannot claim to be particularly original in these matters; the field has been intellectually plowed and plowed again by many paleontologists.

This does not imply, however, that the study of dinosaurs is in any way diminished by what has been done in the years past, for it is remarkable how many new dinosaurs are being discovered year in and year out throughout the world; we are far from having a complete knowledge of these ancient reptiles. Needless to say, new discoveries cast new light upon many aspects of dinosaur scholarship, yet it is not only in the discovery of new materials that our knowledge of the dinosaurs is expanding. Students in this field are constantly introducing new ways of looking at the dinosaurs, not only as they see the dinosaurs by themselves, but also as they see them in the way that they (the dinosaurs) are related to other land-living vertebrates. Whatever the methods used it is safe to say that dinosaurs will be studied as assiduously a hundred years from now as is the case today.

As for me, the dinosaurs have loomed large in my life, but as I have pointed out not to the exclusion of other paleontological activities. Furthermore, although I suspect that my paleontological interests, including dinosaurs, will be winding down in the years ahead, there are still many things to occupy my mind and my hands in the time that is left. I propose to say something about this in the next chapter.

XXII

Southwestern Years

Several years before Margaret and I severed our eastern ties to begin a new life in the West, we joined Malcolm and Priscilla McKenna in an informal Russian class conducted by Genya Lux, a fascinating Russian lady who years ago had decided to leave her native country when she discovered that the Soviets were compiling a dossier on her. It was a lot of fun studying under Genya; like so many Russians she was a character cast in an original mold. I never got very far with my Russian (I am one of the world's worst linguists) but Margaret and the McKennas progressed to the point where they could use the language to a certain extent.

So it was that when we were contemplating our move to Arizona Margaret translated a poem by Pushkin, and then she made it into a plaque that for years has adorned the wall of my study at home. On one side of the plaque is the Russian poem, on the other is her translation, which I often read. It has set the tone for our southwestern life, now almost twenty years in the making.

It's time, my dear, it's time! It's peace the heart requires;
The days are flying past, and with each hour expires
A little bit of life. And yet, not knowing whether

439

We swift, perchance, may die, we plan our life together.
This world holds little joy, but peace there is, and scope;
Long have I entertained an enviable hope;
Long I, a weary slave, have contemplated flight
To some far-distant home of work and sheer delight.

The home to which we made our flight is distant, but not so far distant in this day of airplanes and instant communication as was once the case. And it has been a home of delight, even though, as is always the case in an imperfect world where very real things rise up to assert themselves within the most carefully planned schemes for living, there have been problems, just as there were problems in earlier years. Yet all in all we have been lucky, for we have had two decades of work and delight, and I think I can truthfully say of accomplishment as well—Margaret with her artistic endeavors and I with my continued research.

The proof of the pudding is in the eating; Margaret can point to two large murals, various other paintings, and numerous book illustrations completed since we moved to Arizona, and I can point to a series of publications that have appeared at a pace about equal to that achieved before we made our move. Not that such things are necessarily proofs of merit, but I do think they are at least indications of time spent on activities other than just sitting around to watch the world go by.

So here we are, and specifically here I am at the beginning of my seventh decade as a paleontologist, and as is evident from what has been written, still involved with paleontological problems. I am still working with fossils, still writing about them in detail, still writing about the subject of ancient animals in more general terms, and I hope that what I am trying to do I am doing properly, without making too many errors of commission and omission. A problem that faces me these days is how much longer I should carry on such activities.

For there is a time to quit—and it is important to know when to quit—yet quitting is an especially hard problem for folks like myself. Paleontology, especially the kind of paleontology that involves research, is more than a vocation; it is a way of life. One does not simply walk away from a way of life in which one has been totally involved for decades on end; I know this is true from what I know about the history of paleontological careers, past and present. Almost all paleontologists worth their salt have continued to look at fossils, to work with fossils, and more often than not to write about fossils virtually up until their final days of existence. (That is, unless they are bedridden with some terminal illness.) For them there seems no incentive in spending the so-called golden years at play, at the time-filling activities depicted on numerous television screens in the advertisements of retirement homes.

I am trying to think of paleontologists who turned away from their fossils in their later years. One outstanding example was Jacob Wortman, the late-nineteenth-century and turn-of-the-twentieth-century paleontologist, the man who had been Cope's associate and who was at the American Museum of Natural History during those first years of the Department of Vertebrate Paleontology as it was becoming established under Osborn's guiding hand. In 1908, I think it was, Wortman suddenly abandoned the field, went to Brownsville, Texas, and opened a drugstore, where he remained until his death in 1926. I suspect that he had personal reasons for doing this; I suspect that he was troubled by Matthew's rising star. At any rate he became a pharmacist, which was for him relatively simple since he had received a medical education.

There are advantages and dangers for paleontologists to hang on the way they do right to the very end, the advantages being that elderly paleontologists have much to contribute from their accumulated store of knowledge and experience, the dangers being that they may turn into paleontological dodderers, cluttering up the landscape physically and intellectually and making life hard for their colleagues. This latter is a risk that has to be taken, and generally a risk worth the taking. More often than not the emeriti in our profession may partially justify their presence by serving as occasional balance wheels that help to keep some youngsters from flying off at tangents in odd directions.

With the influx of many bright new minds into our profession, when do the oldsters, such as I am, bow out? I remember Al Romer having a long talk with me years ago about how to know when to quit; evidently the subject was much on his mind. Al never quit; he was still a very active paleontologist when his life was unfortunately terminated by an accidental death. Even if he had lived on, I think he would have been busily occupied until the end, for his great mind was ever active. So as has been said, the paleontologist usually remains at work, and fortunately there almost always is room for him to carry on, even though he has relinquished his official duties. Consequently the continuation of a rich and rewarding life in paleontology is possible without stifling the opportunities for young people just beginning their careers.

When does one quit? Never, I suppose. Charles Darwin once said, "When I am obliged to give up observation and experiment I shall die." Death itself ended Darwin's observations and experiments; he was busily at work on April 17, 1882, just two days before he died.

Whether I shall be able to come to such a logical end is for the fates to decide. I do want to continue after a fashion, but to continue at a reduced rate—which is what I am doing at the present time. I spend mornings at my office at the Museum of Northern Arizona, where I have several projects proceeding simultaneously to keep me busy. The afternoons are for resting and doing other things. I hope to maintain this agenda, with the museum work becoming ever less demanding and with time and energy for other activities ever more available.

As for other activities during this time of official retirement, there are many—and they are becoming increasingly more dominant in my life—that do not involve much physical exertion; rather they are times spent in looking back across the years to recall, often with the help of our progeny, the happenings of decades past. They are times also spent in thinking about the present and about the years ahead, especially about the things that remain to be done. For truth to tell my days are so filled, they seem so short, that every evening I am left with many things undone. The same is true for Margaret. We both wish that we might have a day stretcher of some kind, or perhaps an amanuensis, to help us keep up with our self-imposed projects. In the dead of night when sleep so frequently deserts the body and is reluctant to return, then I think about many things and I realize that this is not so good, for I am only compounding my sleeplessness. So I fall back on some of my old remedies—not counting sheep but rather reciting to myself the sequence of the kings of England, or the succession of presidents and vice-presidents, or the generals of the Civil War, or the states and their capitals, or other such trivia. Then if I get back to sleep I can hope to wake up somewhat refreshed. In the morning I can think about that question so often put to people who have been around for a long time: if I had it to do over again would I do it any differently? Probably not. Anyway, as I have already indicated, so many of the things that have decided the course of my life have just happened; they have been things over which I have had little control, and what I have done has been more often than not in response to these events. I suppose this is true for everybody. Certainly I think I have been pretty much a pragmatist and have tried to make the best of situations, often enough when they were not entirely to my liking. And if I had it to do all over again I would hope a few things that have happened had not taken place. Again a trite observation: everybody has this to say.

There are no regrets about having followed the star that led me into paleontology. Perhaps there are other professions that I might have enjoyed just as much, but I have never seen any that I think I would want to exchange for the study of fossils. I will, however, make one secret confession. If I could have been an author of the P. G. Wodehouse stripe, I think that would have been wonderful.

Even though Margaret and I are very busy during these retirement years, we are fortunate in living next to Nature, where the surrounding scene is destined to delight the eye of the beholder. Our house is in a pine wood, on the edge of town, and here we have as neighbors and visitors many birds, including hordes of Stellar jays that swoop up to our feeding station with aerodynamic grace, there to display the elegant crests that so express their emotions, or red-shafted flickers that flash through the green pine boughs like intermittent flames. (Lieutenant Abert, who was in the Southwest before the Civil War as a member of the corps of topographical engineers, never tired of watching the flickers; his field notebooks contain frequent admiring references to these birds.) In the summer red-tailed hawks wheel above us in an incredibly blue sky, while all around violet-green swallows skim past often at arm's length, in their arrow-swift pursuit of insects. Then there are the hummingbirds, seemingly even swifter in their flight than the swallows; they are literally animated bullets. Occasionally there is a golden eagle, and a few miles away we can go to watch bald eagles.

On the ground and in the trees are the Abert squirrels, named after Colonel Abert, the chief of the topographical engineers and the father of Lieutenant Abert. They are handsome squirrels, especially in wintertime, when their fur is thick, their tails are like plumes, and their ears are wonderfully elongated by hairy tassels. The Abert squirrel on the south side of the Grand Canyon and the Kaibab squirrel on the north side are the only tassel-eared squirrels in North America. Now and then we catch a glimpse of a gray fox, one of the most elegant of carnivores. And in the small hours of early morning we often hear the high-pitched, frenzied howling of coyotes, especially if the moon is full. They are very much with us, and it is not uncommon to see them in the daytime. Of course skunks and raccoons and bats are out at night, as is an occasional porcupine. In fact, I am not exactly pleased to see that a porcupine has been working on the limbs of a couple of my pine trees.

On the San Francisco Peaks behind us are deer and elk, wildcats, bears, and perhaps a stray mountain lion now and then. The antlered ruminants are frequently encountered, but the large carnivores are very shy. Nevertheless it is good to know that they are there.

This mountain, already alluded to more than once, is a large extinct volcano, which in Pleistocene time, perhaps a half-million years ago, was probably about sixteen thousand feet in height, but then perhaps it blew its top, much as Mount St. Helens did in Washington in 1980, or perhaps, in accordance with modern theory, it simply collapsed into an empty chamber. So now the peaks, which are high points on the jagged rim of the blown-out or collapsed crater, reach maximum elevations of something more than twelve thousand feet. Even so they rise a mile above our house, the front stoop of which is at 7140 feet. This great peak with its inner basin, the partially enclosed remnant of the former crater, dominates us as it dominates the whole countryside, trapping clouds and thereby initiating the storms of rain and snow that keep our forest green. The peaks form a massive landmark, seen from the Petrified Forest a hundred miles away, and seen from great distances from other directions as well.

It is but one of several hundred volcanic craters (although it is by far the largest) that dot the landscape to the north and east of us. Some of these cones are geologically recent, only a few thousand years old, so that they show almost no weathering on their surfaces, while one of them, Sunset Crater, has been dated by tree-ring technology as having erupted only nine hundred years ago, in fact in the year before the Norman conquest of England.

Today the volcanoes are quiescent, and from out in the grasslands beyond the forest they rise in an almost unreal landscape, like the craters on the moon. I often imagine a scenario in which some peaks of the San Francisco volcanic field might again come to life; would there not then be panic in northern Arizona? This little brainstorm is not as far-fetched as it may sound; remember that Vesuvius was a "dead" volcano, having olive orchards and vineyards within its crater in the years before 79 A.D.., when it blew out its plug and destroyed Pompeii.

The San Franciscos rise a mile above us; the Grand Canyon, just eighty miles to the north, cuts through the Colorado Plateau to a depth of a mile below our elevation. It was here, from the bottom of the canyon to the top of the peaks that C. Hart Merriam, who was active around the turn of the century, established the life zones that have long been standard in biological literature. From the Sonoran Zone as he named it, at the bottom of the canyon, to the Arctic Zone at the top of the peaks, one passes within about fifty miles through transitions of plants and animals that approximate a trip of perhaps three thousand miles from Mexico to Arctic Canada. Of course it is the altitude that makes the difference.

And it is the altitude that lends variety to our lives. In the winter, when people are skiing on the peaks behind our house, we can drive down to Sedona in Oak Creek Canyon, less than thirty miles away, and enjoy warm sunshine and blooming flowers. We look at these differences in the local scene, as well as other aspects of the natural world around us, with appreciative eyes, our senses heightened, I think, by the knowledge that the years ahead are but a fraction of the years behind us. This is a statement of fact clearly recognized, not in the least touched by any feelings of morbidity or sadness. We know that the years to come are there to be lived one at a time, and that is how we intend to live them—one at a time.

Perhaps these remarks give some indication of the environment in which we have been living for almost twenty years. It is a scene far removed from the bustle of New York, the vast halls and the complex behind-the-scenes life at the American Museum, and the home in New Jersey set among deciduous trees and looking westwardly to the volcanic ridges of the Watchungs. Our life of retirement is certainly different from the almost forty years we had together in the great metropolitan milieu, and of course there are things that we miss. But the compensations are such that we do not regret having left the scene where we spent so many years.

At the Museum of Northern Arizona I have been able to continue with my work on Triassic reptiles and amphibians, sitting in a room where I can look out at the snow-covered peaks outlined in dazzling white against a remarkably blue sky—this in place of sitting in a room where I could look out over Central Park at the towering buildings of mid-Manhattan. Both views have been highly esteemed through the years; I am truly thankful that I was never cooped up in one of the very modern buildings to which so many people in our society are condemned, with no external view to rest the eyes, with sealed windows to shut out the air, and with an internal, artificial environment. And at the museum in Arizona I have enjoyed the opportunity not only of working on Triassic fossils inside, but also of going outside and traveling a few miles to Triassic badlands, where there are more fossils to be found.

The museum is a lively place, with various programs going on continually—research programs and public programs. Therefore life is not dull. Moreover, this town across from which we live houses some very special activities suited to the northern Arizona region: three astronomical observatories (because of the pure air), the astrogeology branch of the Geological Survey where the moon and the planets are being mapped and studied, the other activities of the survey, an arboretum where research is being conducted on plants that may be adapted to this high country, Northern Arizona University (one of the three state universities), and an art gallery. Furthermore this is a place of several cultures, the dominant Anglo culture and the somewhat subsidiary Hispanic culture, and the two groups of original people, the Hopi and the Navajo, which with a scattering of other ethnic groups are very much in evidence. Also the archeological evidences of the Indian forebears are abundantly to be seen, all over the Southwest. Consequently we do not feel that we are living in isolation.

With the Grand Canyon to the north, the San Francisco volcanic field between us and the canyon, and with the deserts carved into fossiliferous rock strata surrounding high peaks, this is an area that attracts geologists, paleontologists, and biologists. It has long been famed as a place exciting to anthropologists and archeologists. Therefore interesting people are coming here year in and year out to study the natural history of the region— again a reason for those of us living here not to feel isolated.

Among the visitors to northern Arizona in our years here have been the television folks, who have done stories about the region, or even about what I and my colleagues have been doing. Not only have American producers been with us, but also folks from the BBC and from Granada TV in England, Japanese crews, and others. So I have had the fun of going out with them to make films, then sometimes of seeing the films on the tube. Beyond that, we have become good friends with some of the television folks.

One pleasant experience of some years ago was when Granada television was here, to film some of my work up in the desert north of Flagstaff. Then one day the director, Jack Smith, thought it would be nice to film our so-called backyard, our "garden" as he designated it. So he and the camera man and the sound man and the others spent a pleasant summer day behind our house, making a record of the plants and the mammals and the birds. They enjoyed it ever so much, and so did we. The result was a very nice little story for children entitled "A House in Arizona" that, much to our surprise, was widely broadcast in England and throughout Europe, and was quite popular.

It must not be thought that in these southwestern years we have been totally consumed by our work and with local concerns. The problems of the world impinge upon us, as they do on people through the land, and the outlook is not reassuring. The erosion of our fields, the deterioration of our forests, a Frankenstein technology that bids fair to overwhelm us, and above all an exploding population throughout the world that as Julian Huxley pointed out years ago is already exceeding optimum standards, make one wonder what is ahead. It is difficult for me even to imagine what life will be like a hundred years from now. I can only hope that many of the disturbing, even terrifying, trends that we see today in the environment and in society will be reversed and even stopped. Although I cannot imagine what life will be like a hundred years hence, I can look back to see what life has been like and how it has evolved through the eons of earth history.

There is this to be said about being a paleontologist: one is impressed and even dominated by the long view of life. For that I am grateful. The long view has enabled me to take a retrospective view back though time, to see what the earth and its inhabitants were like, not only thousands but also millions of years ago. The attainment of such a long view has been for me a fascinating exercise in learning that has extended across more than sixty years of my life, and has given far more meaning to my days than the mere earning of a living. Furthermore, my life with Margaret during more than fifty of those sixty years has made my life truly significant; without her there would have been little joy in what I have been able to do. For both of us, the years we spent with our five boys (later with their families) and, now even though they are not nearby, the ties we still maintain and the visits we have, so eagerly looked forward to, are the things that have made and still make our lives enjoyable. That is the way it should be.

Index